W9-CSX-832

History of the American Abolitionist Movement

A Bibliography of Scholarly Articles

Series Editor

John R. McKivigan
Indiana University – Purdue University
Indianapolis

A GARLAND SERIES

Series Contents

Abolitionism and American Law

Edited with introductions by

John R. McKivigan
Indiana University – Purdue University
Indianapolis

GARLAND PUBLISHING, INC.
A MEMBER OF THE TAYLOR & FRANCIS GROUP
New York & London
1999

Library of Congress Cataloging-in-Publication Data

Abolitionism and American law / edited with introductions by John R.
McKivigan.
      p. cm. — (American abolitionist movement : a bibliography
of scholarly articles ; v. 5) a "A Garland series"—Ser. t.p.
Includes bibliographical references.
ISBN 0-8153-3109-6 (alk. paper)
     1. Slavery—Law and legislation—United States—History. 2.
Antislavery movements—United States—History. 3. Abolitionists—
United States—History. I. McKivigan, John R., 1949– II. American
abolitionist movement ; 5.

KF4545.S5 A92 1999
342.73'087—dc21   99-052332

Printed on acid-free, 250-year-life paper
Manufactured in the United States of America

Contents

Series Introduction

The American abolition campaign was the most important reform movement in United States history. It brought thousands of reformers together in a more than three-decade-long battle to end the deeply entrenched institution of slavery and establish racial equality in this country. The American abolition movement was exceptionally diverse: it was religious and secular, moral and political, ethical and legalistic, philosophical and self-interested, Northern and Southern. As dedicated agitators for over thirty years, the abolitionists contributed significantly to forcing the political system to act against slavery and racism.

The still vivid memories of the modern Civil Rights Movement give the abolitionists, the group responsible for first bringing racial issues to public consciousness, a degree of contemporaneousness not often achieved by historical figures. Their advocacy of additional reforms, such as women's rights, pacifism, and temperance, their innovations in propaganda techniques and agitational tactics, and their ultimate resort to violent means to achieve their goals made the early nineteenth-century abolitionists influential role models for all American reformers who came after them.

A Brief History of the American Abolitionist Movement

In colonial era North America, the Society of Friends stood almost alone in the professing that slaveholding was antithetical to Christian piety. The ideological ferment of the Age of Enlightenment followed by the Revolution, however, led some Americans to equate the slaves' right to freedom with the colonists' demand for independence from arbitrary rule. Consequently, Northern states began the gradual emancipation of their slaves. Although the federal government prohibited slavery in the Northwest Territory in 1787 and banned the transatlantic slave trade in 1808, Southern slavery's increasing profitability produced a general reduction of antislavery agitation by the early nineteenth century. What remained of antislavery sentiment became channeled through the African Colonization Society, begun in 1816, to return blacks to their home continent.

The modern American abolition movement emerged in the early 1830s as a byproduct of the upsurge of religious revivalism popularly known as the Second Great Awakening. Revivalistic tenets led abolitionists to regard slavery as the product of personal sin and to demand emancipation as the price of repentance. Abolitionists also recognized that slavery received moral support from racial prejudice, and they lobbied to overturn the nation's many discriminatory practices against blacks.

During the 1830s, the abolitionists attempted to reach and convert a mass audience. Condemning slavery largely on moral grounds, the abolitionists pursued immediate emancipation chiefly through moral suasion tactics applied to slave owners. By means of lecturing agents, petition drives, and a wide variety of printed materials, the American Anti-Slavery Society, founded in 1833, attracted tens of thousands of members. Throughout the 1830s, however, the chief targets of abolitionist efforts — the individual slaveholders and the national religious institutions — rejected antislavery appeals. Instead, opponents attempted to suppress the abolitionist agitation by legal and ecclesiastical enactments and even by mob violence.

One of the most noteworthy features of the early abolitionist campaign was the thousands of women who braved public disapproval to participate. Often veterans of moral reform activities, these women were inspired by a blend of religious principles and republican ideology to call for an immediate end to slavery. Although a few women attended its founding convention in 1833, the American Anti-Slavery Society at first barred women members. Abolitionist women instead formed their own local organizations, which sent representatives to national conventions in 1837, 1838, and 1839, and raised considerable money for the antislavery movement through sponsoring events such as picnics and bazaars.

Another significant element in the new immediate abolitionist movement were African American activists. Some had long records of public opposition to the colonization movement and to the North's pervasive racial discrimination. Fugitive slaves, such as Frederick Douglass and William Wells Brown, provided compelling antislavery testimony. Black abolitionists sometimes encountered patronizing attitudes from their white counterparts and many shifted their labors to self-help and civil rights efforts while a few concentrated on separatist projects such as African emigration.

The widespread rejection of the antislavery program forced abolitionists to reconsider their original moral suasion strategy. Many followed the lead of the Boston abolitionist William Lloyd Garrison and abandoned the churches as hopelessly corrupted by slavery. These "Garrisonians" also adopted pacifistic political practices and counseled Northerners to withhold their sanction from the proslavery Constitution by refusing to vote. The Garrisonians also actively championed women's rights and a program of "universal reform." Many other male abolitionists opposed a public role for female abolitionists — some because of antifeminist principles, and others because they feared a backlash from linking antislavery to an even more unpopular cause. The "woman's issue" became enmeshed with other quarrels among abolitionists regarding tactics in the religious and political spheres. After gaining the right to vote in the AASS's annual meeting in 1839, women provided the Garrisonians with the strength to win control of the society the following year, when their opponents quit to protest the election of a female officer.

Under Garrisonian control, the American Anti-Slavery Society committed itself to nonresistant political practices and advocated the dissolution of the union with slaveholding states. Garrisonians also experimented in dramatic new propaganda techniques to awaken the Northern conscience and prod moderate opponents of slavery into more vigorous action. Women played key roles in the American Anti-Slavery Society after 1840. Maria Weston Chapman of Boston served as one of the society's principal propagandists and oversaw the operation of its main office. Lydia Maria Child edited the Garrisonians' official newspaper for almost two years. Abby Kelley, Lucy Stone, Sojourner Truth, Elizabeth Cady Stanton, and dozens of other women braved insults and threats of physical harms to serve as traveling lecturers and organizers. These public figures became important role models for women seeking to overcome societal barriers to their sex.

Many non-Garrisonian abolitionists regrouped in a new organization, the American and Foreign Anti-Slavery Society. In their lecturing and writing, these abolitionists continued the agitation of religious institutions. They gained valuable allies in the early 1840s in the form of well-organized Methodist, Baptist, and Presbyterian denominational antislavery movements. Their agitation helped foment the sectional schism of the Methodist and Baptist churches in the mid-1840s and the New School Presbyterians in 1857. Even after those divisions, however, abolitionists continued to protest that the Northern church branches still tolerated thousands of Border State slave owners in their fellowship.

The unsatisfactory outcome of these intradenominational efforts did not destroy church-oriented abolitionists' desire to enlist the support of religious bodies; they continued their lobbying of those institutions until the Civil War. Religious abolitionists also attempted to spread their antislavery principles by agitating the fellowship issue inside the nation's network of interdenominational missionary and religious publication societies. When those bodies resisted, the abolitionists created a parallel network of religious benevolent enterprises, such as the American Missionary Association. Despite noteworthy gains inside many denominations during the 1850s, in part influenced by intensifying antislavery sentiment in the political sphere, undiluted abolitionism remained a minority viewpoint in the Northern churches before the Civil War. It is significant that the abolitionists had also made little progress in winning equal treatment for blacks in most Northern religious bodies.

While some non-Garrisonian abolitionists focused on reforming the churches, others shifted their energies to political antislavery reform. Beginning in the mid-1830s, abolitionists petitioned legislatures and interrogated political candidates on slavery-related issues. When no candidate expressed antislavery sentiments, abolitionists often protested by "scattering" their ballots among write-in candidates. When the federal government failed to respond to their petitioning or lobbying, these politically minded abolitionists formed an independent antislavery party.

The new Liberty party was launched in 1840 to pursue emancipation through partisan politics. Although some political abolitionists made efforts to introduce economic considerations into their party's arguments against slavery, the Liberty party platforms in the 1840 and 1844 presidential elections differed little from those of the old antislavery societies. They called for an immediate abolition of slavery wherever constitutionally possible and for the repeal of all racial discriminatory legislation as a moral as well as a political duty.

In the early 1840s, abolitionists were deeply divided about the fledgling Liberty party. Most Garrisonians condemned all political activity, including that of the Liberty party, as an implied endorsement of the legality of slavery. Many non-Garrisonian abolitionists were reluctant to support the Liberty party because of strong allegiance to the Whig party. The Whigs' moralistic rhetoric and occasional support of Sabbatarian practices and prohibition were highly attractive to the same evangelical voters who were most inclined to abolitionism. By bringing a new ethically defined issue into politics, the Liberty party challenged the Whig hold on evangelical voters. The support for the Liberty party presidential candidate James G. Birney — 7,000 votes (0.29 percent) in 1840 and 62,000 (2.31 percent) in 1844 — however, showed that the single issue of slavery was not yet strong enough to turn many voters, evangelical or not, away from the Whigs.

Events in the 1840s fostered a growth of Northern political antislavery sentiment. Public controversy over such issues as the congressional "gag rule" against antislavery petitions, the annexation of Texas as a new slaveholding state, and the disposition of territory won in the Mexican-American War made opposition to the "Slave Power" more respectable in Northern circles. A Liberty party faction led by Salmon P. Chase, Gamaliel Bailey, and Henry B. Stanton advocated electoral cooperation in the 1848 election with groups in the major parties opposed to slavery's extension into the new western states. In a complicated series of intraparty battles, the procoalition forces outmaneuvered all opponents and merged the Liberty party with antiextensionist Whigs and Democrats to create the Free Soil party. Although the new party dropped the Liberty party's support for immediate abolition and black civil rights, it attracted far more voters to its moderate antislavery banner. What the Free Soil party offered in lieu of the Liberty party's high standards was the chance to expand antislavery influence, albeit of a limited nature, in the political system.

Not all Liberty men could accept the compromised antislavery position of the new party. As early as 1845, Birney, William Goodell, and Gerrit Smith had proposed to broaden the Liberty party platform into a program of universal reform. Calling themselves the Liberty League, this faction also advanced the theory that the Constitution did not sanction slavery and that Congress therefore had the power to abolish slavery everywhere in the Union. Although the Liberty League failed to capture control on the Liberty party or to block the Free Soil merger, its members continued to work for their undiluted abolitionist program. Running candidates until the Civil War, first under the old Liberty party name and then the Radical Abolitionist party label, this tiny abolitionist faction attempted to prod the larger antislavery parties to take a stronger position against slavery and racism.

Undeterred by the criticism of either the Garrisonians or the Liberty Leaguers, the moderate political abolitionists gradually built up their electoral strength. The 1848 Free Soil ticket of Martin Van Buren and Charles Francis Adams received 290,000 votes. The passage of the Compromise of 1850, however, temporarily depressed Northern antislavery sentiment and the party received only 156,000 votes in 1852. This trend was reversed with passage in 1854 of the controversial Kansas-Nebraska Act, which repealed the Missouri Compromise bar on slavery in western territories north of 36 30'. The simultaneous rise of nativism in the early 1850s as a political issue weakened traditional party allegiances. No longer able to satisfy either Northern or Southern militants, the Whig party performed poorly in the 1852 election and disintegrated amid the turmoil accompanying the Kanssas-Nebraska Act. At the same time, Free Soilers merged with recent converts to antiextensionsism from the Whigs and Democrats to form the Republican party. The new party attracted a broad range of voters, including many who were more concerned with economic development and freedom from competition with black labor than with ending slavery.

Opposition to events in Kansas, coupled with resistance to the Fugitive Slave Act of 1850, helped produce a new more militant strain of abolitionism. Free blacks joined many younger white abolitionists in blocking the rendition of fugitive slaves from the Northern states. A well-organized "emigration" effort recruited hundred of antislavery settlers for Kansas and armed them so they could forcibly resist the proslavery statehood movement there. Out of the guerrilla skirmishing in "Bleeding Kansas" emerged John Brown. Committed to battling slavery through violent means, Brown received clandestine financial support from antislavery veterans, mainly from the small radical political abolitionist faction. In 1857 and 1858, Brown assembled a small, racially integrated company for an attempt to set up a base in the southern Appalachians to aid slaves to escape. This plan eventually evolved into an unsuccessful attack on the federal arsenal at Harpers Ferry in October 1859 in the forlorn hope of sparking a mass slave insurrection.

The large majority of political abolitionists, eschewed violent tactics, and were content to work with more moderate antislavery Northerners inside the Republican party. Chase, Bailey, and other former Liberty party leaders joined forces with "radical" antislavery defectors from the major parties, such as Joshua Giddings, Charles Sumner, and John P. Hale, to resist efforts by conservative or racist elements in the Republican coalition to shift the party's focus away from moral opposition to slavery's expansion. These efforts were so successful that by 1860 nearly all political abolitionists and even some Garrisonians endorsed the election of Republican Abraham Lincoln as a principled means of battling slavery.

The combined influence of all of these forms of abolitionist agitation helped fan the flames of sectionalism and provoke Southern secession in 1861. The secession of the Southern states led most religious denominations to acknowledge the moral corruption inherent in a slaveholding society. After initial hesitation, most denominations responded to abolitionist entreaties to endorse emancipation. During the Civil War, political abolitionists together with Garrisonians rallied Northern public pressure until President Abraham Lincoln was forced to adopt emancipation as a war goal. In the postwar era, surviving abolitionists continued to lobby the federal government to act to protect the rights of the newly freed African Americans. Ironically, the radical political abolitionists' constitutional interpretation, based on natural rights theory, became the legal justification for much of the Reconstruction era's civil rights legislation. As dedicated agitators for more than thirty years, the abolitionists contributed significantly to moving the political system to act against slavery and racism.

Historical Disputes over American Abolitionism

As relatively few as the abolitionists were in number, they have inspired a great quantity of scholarly study and debate. Historians have hotly disputed the abolitionists' motivation for undertaking their crusade in the 1830s, arguing for the primacy of economic, religious, ideological, or psychological forces. A substantial body of literature, drawing on a wide range of disciplines, has analyzed the personality of the American abolitionists both individually and collectively. In recent years, historians have attempted to rehabilitate the abolitionists from long-standing accusations of mental instability.

Historians also have studied the evolution of abolitionist tactics in the more than three decades of antislavery agitation, but still strongly disagree about their effectiveness. Similar disputes mark scholarly evaluation of the factionalization that occurred in abolitionist ranks in the 1840s and 1850s as a consequence of tactical disagreements. Perhaps the most currently relevant of these disputes concerns the dynamics leading some abolitionists, such as John Brown, to turn to violent means to pursue emancipation.

Another significant area of antislavery studies concerns the interaction of white abolitionists and Northern free blacks. There is an on-going quarrel among scholars over whether racial tensions deeply troubled abolitionist activities. A parallel series of research has demonstrated that gender-role issues likewise generated conflict in the abolitionist ranks.

Questions concerning the abolitionists' relation with more moderate antislavery groups in both the North and South has stimulated an insightful examination of inter-group dynamics inside reform movements. For example, a considerable body of scholarship exists debating the degree to which the nation's churches condemned or condoned the institution of slavery. Another large body of literature concerns the legal disputes occurring over the constitutional standing of slavery and the obligations on the government and private citizens to uphold that institution.

Finally, there is an important body of scholarly work evaluating the abolitionists' impact on the coming of the Civil War, the emancipation of American slaves during that war, the post-war Reconstruction of the nation, and modern race relations. Given the unsettled state of many issues first raised by the abolitionists, scholarly debate on their historical influence continues unabated. As this brief survey indicates, few fields of modern historical scholarship have proven more fruitful or relevant to modern-day concerns than the study of the American abolitionist movement.

Organization of the Series

The five-volume Garland series on the American Abolitionist Movement collects into one reference work the best of twentieth-century scholarship on the history of the antislavery campaign. This series brings together nearly one hundred articles originally published in scores of scholarly journals representing the disciplines of history, law, religious studies, political science, African-American studies, communications, women's studies, literature, American studies, sociology, and psychology. To avoid overlap with other Garland publications, articles dealing primarily with the institution of slavery or black civil rights have been omitted from this series. The American Abolitionist Movement series is organized into five topical volumes:

Volume One: *Abolitionism and American Reform*
Volume Two: *Abolitionism and American Religion*
Volume Three: *Abolitionism and American Politics and Government*
Volume Four: *Abolitionism and Issues of Race and Gender*
Volume Five: *Abolitionism and American Law*

The editor acknowledges the assistance of numerous individuals in putting this series together. Carole Puccino and David Estrin at Garland Publishing kept this project on track and not too far behind schedule. Paul Finkelman drew upon his own considerable knowledge about the history of abolitionism to help the editor conceptualize this series. L. Diane Barnes of West Virginia University introduced the editor to a variety of extremely useful new internet sources, which proved invaluable in locating current scholarship on this topic. The editor's wife, Patricia G. Barnes, served as both muse and sounding board for this project.

Volume Introduction

In their campaign to emancipate the slaves, the abolitionists raised numerous legal and constitutional challenges to that institution. Modern scholars have shown how the nineteenth century legal controversies over abolitionism had a major impact on how the nation today deals with fundamental questions concerning property rights, race relations, criminal extradition, conflicting federal and state jurisdiction, due process for the accused, and interstate comity.

Students of the drafting of the U.S. Constitution have examined the handling of slavery-related issues by the framers. Scholarship represented in this volume demonstrates that compromises over the status of slavery under the proposed Federal Constitution were critical to win the allegiance of several Southern states to the new union. The vagueness of those provisions would produce many subsequent arguments among contemporaries, including the opponents of slavery. Many abolitionists branded the Constitution a proslavery document. A smaller faction, however, utilized natural law arguments to contend that slavery was inherently illegal and that the Constitution could not legitimate it.

Such a natural law position had, in fact, been used as early as the 1780s to win court decisions ruling slavery unconstitutional in Massachusetts. In the Midwest early in the nineteenth century, court rulings based on the same premise also were important in fending off attempts to circumvent the Northwest Ordinance of 1787's ban on slave owning in that territory. In New Jersey, however, the state supreme court in 1845 turned back abolitionist legal efforts to have the state's few remaining slaves liberated on the grounds that human bondage was incompatible with a newly adopted state constitution. As this essay collection shows, legal scholars characterize this defeat of the abolitionists' natural rights views as an indicator of the growing strength of the positivistic understanding of the law that would be frequently employed in defense of slavery down to the Civil War. The infamous Dred Scott decision of 1854 was simply the most dramatic legal ruling illustrating the long-term trend that caused many Northerners to fear that the Supreme Court would some day legalize slavery in the hitherto free states.

The principal legal battleground over slavery revolved around the capture and rendition of fugitive slaves in the Northern states to their Southern owners. Within a decade after ratification of the Constitution, conflicts between authorities in free and slave states forced Congress to pass a law to define the requirements on Northern states and citizens to cooperate in the return of slave runaways. Several authors presented in the volume show that free states responded by passing "personal liberty laws" to extend greater due process protection to the accused than under the federal Fugitive Slave Law of 1793. The New Jersey supreme court even ruled that its state constitution protected all fugitive slaves from rendition. Canadian courts also ruled that existing international laws did not require their officials to return fugitives slaves to U.S. jurisdiction.

Several more articles in the volume examine the legal reaction to Northern resistance to the original fugitive slave law. As part of the sectional compromise of 1850, a more stringent fugitive slave law was passed over opposition of many Northern congressmen. Controversy soon arose over the penalties placed on Northerners who refused to participate in the rendition process and on the extremely few protections accorded the accused in the legal determination of the case. The North responded with a new series of personal liberty laws as well as dramatic instances of violent resistance to the 1850 Fugitive Slave Law's enforcement.

This volume's articles reveal that the abolitionists' impact on United States law and the Constitution did not end with the Civil War. The immediate postwar Reconstruction amendments were both rooted in the radically anti-positivistic, natural rights philosophy long espoused by the radical political abolitionists. Implementing protection for black civil rights, however, proved much more difficult. It took almost a decade of lobbying by African Americans and their aging abolitionist allies to persuade Congress to pass legislation granting federal protection to equal access to public transportation and "places of public amusement." Few efforts were made to enforce this Civil Rights Act of 1875 and the United States Supreme Court declared it unconstitutional in 1883. The "Second Reconstruction" of the 1950s and 1960s, however, witnessed a reaffirmation of the abolitionists' egalitarian principles in American law and public policy.

Further Reading

Campbell, Stanley W. *The Slave-Catchers: Enforcement of the Fugitive Slave Law, 1850–1860* (1968).
Cover, Robert. *Justice Accused: Antislavery and the Judicial Process* (1975).
Curtis, Michael Kent. "The Curious History of Attempts to Suppress Antislavery Speech, Press, and Petitions in 1835–37," *Northwestern University Law Review* (1995).
Cushing, John D. "The Cushing Court and the Abolition of Slavery in Massachusetts: More Notes on the 'Quock Walker Case,'" *American Journal of Legal History* 5 (1961).
Detweiler, Philip F. "Congressional Debate on Slavery and the Declaration of Independence, 1819–1821," *American Historical Review* 63 (1958).
Fehrenbacher, Don E. *The Dred Scott Case: Its Significance in American Law and Politics* (1978).
Ferguson, Robert A. "Story and Transcription in the Trial of John Brown," *Yale Journal of Law and Humanities* 6 (1994).
Finkelman, Paul. *An Imperfect Union: Slavery, Federalism, and Comity* (1981).
———. "Legal Ethics and Fugitive Slaves: The Anthony Burns Case, Judge Loring, and Abolitionist Attorneys," *Cardozo Law Review* 17 (1996).
Gara, Larry. *The Liberty Line: The Legend of the Underground Railroad* (1961).
Hyman, Harold M. *A More Perfect Union: The Impact of the Civil War and Reconstruction on the Constitution* (1973).

Levy, Leonard W. "Sims' Case: The Fugitive Slave Case in Boston in 1851," *Journal of Negro History* 35 (1950).

Morris, Thomas D. *Free Men All: The Personal Liberty Laws of the North, 1780–1861* (1974).

Nelson, William E. "The Impact of the Antislavery Movement upon Styles of Judicial Reasoning in Nineteenth Century America," *Harvard Law Review* 87 (1975).

Nye, Russell B. *Fettered Freedom: Civil Liberties and the Slavery Controversy, 1830–1860* (1949).

Robinson, Donald L. *Slavery in the Structure of American Politics, 1765–1820* (1971).

Roper, Donald M. "In Quest of Judicial Objectivity: The Marshall Court and the Legitimization of Slavery," *Stanford Law Review* 21 (1969).

TenBroeck, Jacobius. *The Antislavery Origins of the Fourteenth Amendment* (1951).

Wiecek, William M. *The Sources of Antislavery Constitutionalism in America, 1760–1865* (1977).

Yanuck, Julius. "The Garner Fugitive Slave Case," *Mississippi Valley Historical Review* 40 (1953).

Zilversmit, Arthur. *The First Emancipation: The Abolition of Slavery in the North* (1967).

The Slavery Provisions of the U.S. Constitution: Means for Emancipation

The Declaration of Independence asserts that all men are created equal and that just governments derive their powers from the consent of the governed. The Federal Constitution not only says nothing explicitly about equality but contains several clauses protecting slaveholders in their enjoyment of property in other men. Chattel slavery denies some men equal rights and the dignity of being ruled by laws to which they have consented, moral possessions proper to human beings, simply as human beings, according to the Declaration. Then are the provisions regarding slaveholding in the United States Constitution consistent with those "self-evident truths" maintained in the Declaration to be the foundations of all just regimes?

The question did not escape the attention of participants in the Constitutional Convention of 1787. At least two of the Framers answered in the negative. On the floor Gouverneur Morris inveighing against the augmentation of Southern representation by counting three-fifths of their slaves protested that slavery was wickedly anomalous in "a government instituted to protect the rights of mankind. . . . " Shortly after the conclusion of the convention Luther Martin fired off an eloquent indictment of what he conceived to be the contradiction created by the slavery provisions between the Declaration and the Constitution. He told the Maryland ratifying convention:

> It was said, that we had just assumed a place among independent nations, in consequence of our opposition to the attempts of Great Britain to *enslave us*; that this opposition was grounded upon the preservation of *those rights* to which God and nature had entitled *us*, not in *particular*, but in *common* with *all the rest of mankind*; that we had *appealed* to the *Supreme Being* for his assistance, as the *God of freedom*, who could not but *approve* our efforts to preserve the *rights* which he had thus *imparted to his creatures*; that now, when we scarcely had risen from our *knees*, from *supplicating* his *aid* and *protection*, in *forming our government* over a *free people*, a government formed pretendedly on the *principles* of *liberty* and for *its preservation*, —in *that* government, to have a provision not only putting it out of *its* power to *restrain* and *prevent* the *slave-trade*, but

1

> *even encouraging that most infamous traffic*, by giving the *states
> power* and *influence* in the *Union, in proportion* as they *cruelly and
> wantonly sport with the rights of their fellow creatures,* ought to be
> considered as a *solemn mockery of,* and *insult to that God,* whose
> protection we had then implored and could not fail to hold us up in
> *detestation,* and render us *contemptible* to every *true friend* of
> liberty in the world.[1] [Emphasis in original]

Martin's indignation was well-founded but could have been extended
back to the Articles of Confederation or, for that matter, to the conduct of the Revolutionary War itself since the Revolution did not
repudiate chattel slavery even as it sought to deliver white Americans
from the political subjugation they charged was *their* enslavement.
Martin surely penetrated to the quick of the irony when he em-
phasized that Americans had based their claims not merely on the
prescriptive rights of British subjects but upon rights they claimed to
possess "in common with all the rest of mankind." Insofar as the
Declaration justifies the colonies' independence on the grounds of a
right to revolution based on the right to be governed by laws to
which one consents, the Declaration would appear to deny that
slavery can be right by nature. During the Revolutionary period
James Otis drew the conclusion that the American arguments for
political liberty required the eventual abolition of slavery.[2]

1. Max Farrand, ed., *The Records of the Federal Convention of 1787* (New Haven: Yale
University Press, 1966, first printing 1911), vol. III, 211. Gouverneur Morris's remark
was made August 8 during debate on the basis of representation, vol. II, 222.
2. Otis called for emancipation in his 1764 pamphlet, *The Rights of the British Colonies
Asserted and Proved.*
  Richard Wells challenged Americans to "reconcile the exercise of SLAVERY with
our *profession of freedom*" [emphasis in original]. *A Few Political Reflections* (1774)
cited in Bernard Bailyn, *Pamphlets of the American Revolution: 1750-1776* (Cambridge, Mass.: Harvard University Press, 1965), vol. I, 145.

> John Allen decried the inconsistency of American libertarians: Blush ye pre-
> tended votaries for freedom! ye trifling patriots! who are making a vain parade
> of being advocates for the liberties of mankind, who are thus making a mockery
> of your profession by trampling on the sacred natural rights and privileges of Af-
> ricans; for while you are fasting, praying, nonimporting, nonexporting, re-
> monstrating, resolving, and pleading for a restoration of your charter rights, you
> at the same time are continuing this lawless, cruel, inhuman, and abominable
> practice of enslaving your fellow creatures...

The Watchman's Alarm to Lord N----h (1774) cited in Bailyn, vol. I. 146.
  And in 1776 Samuel Hopkins reproached his countrymen at length for their "gross,
barefaced, practical inconsistence." *A Dialogue Concerning the Slavery of Africans;
Shewing It To Be the Duty and Interest of the American Colonies to Emancipate All the
African Slaves,* cited in Bailyn, vol. I, 149.

2

Recently Harry V. Jaffa h⌐s renewed Luther Martin's charge that the Constitution stultifies its claims to be a charter for free government by incorporating the slavery provisions. In his essay "The Doughface Dilemma" Jaffa maintains:

> The Constitution of 1787 contained legal guarantees and legal advantages to the institution of chattel slavery—despotism—which were absent from the Articles of Confederation. The intention or purpose of the Constitution, concerning these guarantees and advantages, could not be inferred in any anti-despotic sense, from the language of the Constitution itself.[3]

In another writing Jaffa argues that "The Constitution was perfectly ambiguous with respect to whether it commanded freedom or slavery in the territories,"[4] and, on the basis of observations such as these, he concludes that the Constitution possesses insufficient credentials of its own to establish a republican character but becomes a democratic instrument only insofar as the Declaration is incorporated to resolve its ambiguities in favor of freedom and equality. The understanding of the slavery clauses I propose seeks to mitigate Martin's and Jaffa's charges against the Constitution while agreeing with both men that the principles of the Declaration are the ends which the Constitution ought to promote and the standard by which it ought to be judged. Slavery does indeed appear to be indefensible on the premises of modern republican thought, for the first principle of modern republicanism is the equal title of all men to have respected their natural rights and to be ruled by laws to which they have given their consent. Slavery opposes both the principle of equal rights and its cognate, the requirement of rule by consent.

The question, however, is whether the Framers did not take care to acknowledge this anomaly while also contriving means whereby the anomalous institution might be eradicated and, hence, the two founding documents be brought into a more perfect conformity.

This view of the function of the slavery provisions of the Constitution has found an exponent fully as eloquent as Martin or Jaffa. Lincoln argued in the Cooper Institute Address that the men who devised the Constitution saw in slavery "an evil not to be extended,

3. Harry V. Jaffa, "The Doughface Dilemma or The Invisible Slave in the American Enterprise Institute's Bicentennial" (Claremont, CA: The Claremont Institute for the Study of Statesmanship and Political Philosophy, 1983), 43.
4. Harry V. Jaffa, *How to Think About the American Revolution* (Durham, NC: Carolina Academic Press, 1978), 91.

but to be tolerated and protected only because of and so far as its actual presence among us makes that toleration and protection a necessity."[5] The Constitution did not institute slavery but rather established laws to regulate a condition already existing, and the manifest purpose of the regulations agreed upon in 1787 was to confine slavery to those places where it then existed with the view of setting slavery on a course of eventual extinction.

I consider that Lincoln's position was essentially correct. He may have unwarrantably stretched the evidence upon which his argument chiefly rested, namely, opinions of Framers allegedly hostile to slavery inferred from their actions in Congress subsequent to 1787. And there can be little doubt that the Cooper Institute Address underestimates the extent and the resoluteness of even the early Southerners' determination to hold on to their slaves. But Lincoln's contention can be supported by an analysis of the Constitution pursued on terms somewhat different from the reasoning he himself employs in the Cooper speech. I shall try to supply that analysis by considering the interrelatedness of the several clauses bearing upon slavery in the Constitution.

Given the existence of slaveholding in several of the former colonies in 1787 what constitutional arrangements would best promote liberty and equality? First, a government competent to secure liberty and equality for the eighty-five percent of the population not subject to slavery. In the absence of a strong general government nothing *could* ever be done to alter some of the states' reliance upon slaveholding. Yet in the absence of a strong national government determined to safeguard rights pertaining to men, *precisely as men*, no one would ever move to enact laws to diminish that reliance. Second, a constitution consistent with the equality and consent propositions of the Declaration would need somehow to convey the view that holding property in human beings was repugnant to the essential principles of the regime therein established. Although a constitution consistent with the Declaration might permit slavery to continue for a time under the constraint of some necessity, it could not without denying its principles countenance a *perpetual* toleration of a condition that denies a certain class of men rights deemed to be a parcel of human nature. Third, a constitution that sought to eliminate slavery within a country where it was already long-established would need to

5. Roy P. Basler, ed., *The Collected Works of Abraham Lincoln* (New Brunswick, N.J.: 1953), vol. III 535.

insure the safety of the former slaves once they were emancipated as well as the safety of the former owners. And, if property in slaves was extensive, it would be wise to provide compensation to those who would be required to relinquish their slaves. Proponents of emancipation in slave states would not find it easy to work emancipation through their own legislatures these being largely subject to the influence of slaveholders. Hence, for the sake of initiating legislation for freeing slaves as well as for bearing the expense of compensation and transition to freedom, slaveholding states would have to be drawn into a wider sovereignty, and a sovereignty so designed as to be dominated eventually by nonslaveholding citizens. Fourth, in order to ensure the union of old states under the new and wider sovereignty, that is, to keep the slaveholding states from breaking off while the bonds of union were still tenuous and fragile, it would be necessary to secure these states from premature and irregular acts of emancipation agitated by abolitionists in the nonslaveholding states. Fifth, a constitution seeking to eliminate already established slavery would need to incorporate in its provisions definite powers adequate to the task of eventual emancipation. A constitutional amendment of the sort eventually produced in the post-Civil War Congress could not have won the assent of three-fourths of the states under ordinary circumstances. Hence, by *provisions adequate to the task* we should understand regular processes of legislation requiring nothing like a concurrent majority distributed throughout the states. Moreover, to meet the requirement of gradualism for the sake of domestic tranquility and for the sake of funding compensation by installments, a scheme of emancipation working through ordinary legislative measures and implementing its plan in stages would be preferable to an amendment not likely to be so flexible.

If the criteria just enumerated are indeed the conditions for success in devising a constitution that could bring equality of rights to a slaveholding regime, how well do the provisions of the Federal Constitution accord with these criteria? Creditably well, if not so perfectly as one could wish.

It is estimated that in 1787 the slave population in the three southern states of North Carolina, South Carolina, and Georgia stood at about thirty-five percent.[6] A national authority so deferential to the will of individual states as was the government under the Articles of

6. Donald L. Robinson, *Slavery in the Structure of American Politics 1765-1820* (New York: Harcourt Brace Jovanovich, Inc., 1971), 38-53.

Confederation could not hope to begin the task of setting slavery on a course of eventual extinction. The fate of Jefferson's article indicting the slave trade in the Declaration—struck out at the insistence of representatives from South Carolina—exemplifies the plight of any antislavery legislation under a system in which the states must be treated as merely confederated sovereignties enjoying vetoes over any legislation deemed to encroach on their domestic affairs. The scheme of bicameral representation finally settled upon at the Convention ensures that the minority of slaveholding states shall not be empowered to enforce their views on the rest of their countrymen. The second part of the great compromise on representation also conduces to acting upon slavery with deliberate speed. It is true that the so-called "Federal ratio" (three-fifths of slaves counted toward apportioning Representatives) awards a bonus to slaveholders. But the increment to slaveholding power in Congress came to about five percent and would have diminished if those favoring emancipation had held firm on keeping slavery out of the territories. Even as it was, the increment afforded by the Federal ratio never provided Southerners with a margin sufficient for a majority in the House where the percentage of seats held by Southerners actually declined a little from 1789 to 1820.[7] What the bonus in representation to slaveholders did provide was assurance that any act of emancipation could not be easily won, nor soon. By winning some of what they desired (the Southern delegates in 1787 wanted slaves counted equally with freemen in allotting seats in the House) the Southerners bought time. In the event, Southern congressmen, Senators and Presidents bought the entire game, but not because the Constitution set matters in favor of slaveholders, but because antislavery forces failed to make the most, or indeed to make much at all, of the emancipatory potential of the Constitution. For the purpose of giving the South sufficient weight to ensure that the process of eradicating slavery be responsible and fair, the Federal ratio was about right, whereas that provision did not give slaveholders power sufficient to block a determined majority in the free states.

Besides defining and apportioning governmental powers the Constitution is in some sort a statement of principle declaring what usages and institutions deserve respect. The language of the document conveys a stance towards slavery that can be fairly characterized as a stance against it in principle. Madison was aware of the status of the

7. See Robinson, *Slavery*, 180.

Constitution as a moral pronouncement when he said in the debates on Article 1, Section 9 that "he thought it wrong to admit in the Constitution the idea that there could be property in men."[8] Everyone knows the instances of euphemism and circumlocution resorted to by the Committee on Detail and then the Committee of Style in order to avoid saying *slave*. The one thing evidently agreed upon between the delegates from slaveholding states and their opponents at Philadelphia was the propriety of excising any direct mention of slavery from the clauses that would regulate the institution. Hence whenever grammar requires some reference to the unfortunate subjects of these regulations they are designated under such verbal camouflage as "all other Persons" (Art. 2 Sec. 2, the "Federal ratio"), "such Persons as any of the States now existing shall think proper to admit" (Art. 1 Sec. 9), "Person held to Service or Labour in one State" (Art. 4 Sec. 2). Consequences attach to the Framers' verbal fastidiousness. Disinfecting the document of any direct acknowledgment of slavery imparts to the concessions regarding the census and the return of fugitive slaves a shame-faced character. Those who insisted on keeping the offensive word off the pages of the fundamental law thereby succeeded in making the Constitution blush. Lincoln said that the draftsmen of the Constitution "left this institution [slavery] with many clear marks of disapprobation upon it."[9] Conspicuous omission of the term is one such mark of disapprobation. More substantial for antislavery constitutionalism the avoidance of any explicit acknowledgment of slavery suggests that one cannot look to the supreme law of the land for authorization in owning human beings. Ownership of men will not derive from federal authority. Indeed one clause makes it quite clear that the title to slaves is held only by the authority of state laws. This is the force of the language of Article 4 Sec. 2, "a Person held to service . . . in one State, *under the laws thereof*" [emphasis added]. The original form of the clause had spoken of persons *legally* held to service, but upon objections that the word favored "the idea that slavery was legal in a moral view" the phrase "under the Laws thereof" was substituted coming after the word *State*.[10] Similarly, the

8. Farrand, *Records*, II, 417. Madison's pronouncements in Philadelphia differed, however, from his remarks subsequently to the Virginia ratifying convention where he assured doubting slaveholders that their property was protected against punitive taxation or other means of manumission. See Jonathan Elliot, ed. *The Debates in the Several State Conventions on the Adoption of the Federal Constitution*, 2nd ed. (New York: Burt Franklin, 1888), vol. III, 453 and 621-22.
9. In the debate with Douglas at Alton, Oct. 15, 1858; in Basler, III, 308.
10. Farrand, *Records*, III, 628.

7

clause respecting importation of slaves specifies that the federal government prior to 1808 shall not be authorized to interfere with the importation of such persons as "any of the states now existing shall think proper to admit." It may be going too far to maintain as Justice Curtis did in his dissent from Taney's *Dred Scot* decision, that the Constitution bespeaks a view that slavery violates the natural law and is solely the creation of positive law,[11] but the careful limitation of the legal sanction for slaveholding to the states does make the statement that slavery is the creation of some of the states and not of the general government.

Admittedly the Constitution does not go the length of stating that the United States shall not permit slavery within its boundaries, nor does the temporary limitation upon interdicting importation of slaves give assurance that even that most odious aspect of the traffic in men would certainly cease after the twenty years had expired. Yet something was gained nonetheless in keeping out of the document any statement upholding the idea that one can justly make property of men. If such a statement had found its way into the Constitution, then Taney's contention that slaveholding is a right enjoyed by any American citizen anywhere the flag flies would have been sound interpretation and not, as it was, a perverse imposition upon the Constitution. A statement supporting a right to property in human beings would have meant that nothing other than a constitutional amendment would suffice to remove the blight. If, on the other hand, only state law sustains slaveholding, ordinary legislation at the federal level could, by virtue of the supremacy clause, displace such local laws favoring slavery. More important, there is nothing to give slavery a foothold in the federally administered lands not yet organized into states.

The word chosen to designate the victims of involuntary servitude was *persons*. A person need not be assured of all the privileges and immunities of the *citizens* of any state (Art. 4, Sec. 2). On the other hand, this designation—rather than, say, *slave* or even *inhabitant*— seems to accord a certain dignity that the designee would not enjoy if he were deemed merely property. In the state constitutions it is

---

11. 19 Howard 393 at 791. Curtis was not alone in this view. He referred to the opinion of the U.S. Supreme Court in *Prigg v. Pennsylvania* (1842) and to that of the Supreme Court of Kentucky. Curtis aligned himself with a tradition of jurisprudence going back to the British case of *Somerset v. Stewart* (1772) in which Lord Mansfield held that slavery was contrary to natural law and could legitimately exist in Anglo-American territory only where protected by the positive law.

regularly the person, not the citizen, who is the possessor of rights. The sovereign agents ordaining the Constitution are the *people*, not the *citizens*, of the United States. The Fourth and Fifth Amendments followed the usage of the state constitutions and bills of rights and thus established the legal status of a person in the United States, for the amendment makes *person* (not citizen) the subject of rights of property and liberty. One would think therefore that in the federally-administered territories the slave's rights merely as a person would prevail over the "privileges and immunities" of, say, an emigrating Georgia slaveholder—citizen though the slaveholder might be. Free-soilers in the 1850s based their slogan "freedom national, slavery sectional" precisely on this understanding of the Fifth Amendment. Congress had exclusive authority over the territories, and therefore state laws enforcing slavery could not reach across state lines to affect negroes in territories. At the same time, the Fifth Amendment set limits to congressional encroachment upon rights of liberty and property. The free-soilers completed their case by interpreting due process as what today is termed "substantive due process." That is to say, they held to the view that no regulation which deprived a man of his liberty to dispose of his own labor just on account of his race, no such regulation could accord with due process of law no matter how proper might have been the processes by which that regulation was enacted and enforced.

The Constitution conveys a rhetorical disapprobation of slavery by conspicuous euphemism, dissociates the new government from supporting the principle of slaveholding by defining slavery as the creature of state law, and sets the nation on the course of abolishing the worst part of the slave trade by establishing the national government's authority to end importation. Most decisively, the Constitution also secures arrangements that show fairly clearly how the process of emancipation should proceed. The constitutional instruments required for a deliberate yet inevitable reversal of slaveholding can be discerned in the four provisions that bear directly on slavery.

Each of the sections that appear at first merely concessions to slave owners carries also a stinger that can inflict damage upon those who profit from the peculiar institution. We have seen that the "fugitive slave" provision confines the legality of slaveholding to state law. The concession regarding the apportionment census also holds a promise for antislavery legislation to the extent that congressional policy in the territories should succeed in bringing a preponderance of new free states. Further, Art. 1 Sec. 2 prescribing the ratio in which slaves

9

would be counted for representation is tied to Art. 1 Sec. 9 which states that "No Capitation, or other direct, Tax shall be laid, unless in Proportion to the Census or Enumeration herein before directed to be taken." The debates in convention make it clear that the clause was exacted as part of the price slaveholders would pay for their bonus in representation. The master would be vulnerable to a tax upon every black he owned, although for each slave he would pay only three-fifths of the amount of the tax on his own head. As long as the tax were levied in this proportion non-slaveholders might not be avid to pass a capitation that would cost them something even though it cost the master of numerous slaves much more. Still, the Southern interests feared taxation as a means of curtailing or even abolishing slavery and therefore secured the concession that prior to 1808 no amendment might alter either the census provision or the proportion of taxation provision tied to it (Article 5).

Because the capitation tax is put in double shackles by the requirement of an amendment for its enactment coupled with the extraordinary exclusion from the amendment process prior to 1808, and because, even in the absence of these impediments, Northerners could not be expected to push fervently for such a universal tax, the prospect could not be good of employing capitation as an instrument of emancipation. Yet one must think that Southern fears of abolition through some sort of hostile taxation were well-founded because although the slaveholding interests succeeded in warding off the capitation they did not succeed in protecting themselves against other, indeed other more practicable forms of taxation. In other words, the capitation tax may have been something of an *ignis fatuus,* whereas modes of framing tax legislation more damaging to slavery are still a real potency under the Constitution. Consider George Mason's reply to Madison's assurance, delivered to Virginia ratifyers, that tying direct taxes to the census proportions would protect property in slaves:

> ... gentlemen might think themselves secured by that restriction, in the 4th clause [Art. 1, Sec. 9], that no capitation or other direct tax should be laid but in proportion to the census before directed to be taken; but that when maturely considered, it would be found to be no security whatsoever. It was nothing but a direct assertion, or mere confirmation of the clause which fixed the ratio of taxes and representation. It only meant that the quantum to be raised of each state should be in proportion to their numbers, in the manner therein directed. But the general government was not precluded

from laying the proportion of any particular state on any one species of property they might think proper.

For instance, if five hundred thousand dollars were to be raised, they might lay the whole of the proportion of the Southern states on the blacks, or any one species of property; so that, by laying taxes too heavily on slaves, they might totally annihilate that kind of property.[12]

The key to a responsible emancipation program would appear to be tax legislation not requiring a constitutional amendment. Instead of a capitation Congress might simply lay a tax on the total value of the master's holding in slaves, thereby obliging the master to pay dearly for every slave while he should see an ever diminishing benefit in the suffrage bonus as new (free) states formed from the Western territories. Taxation would also have the effect of undermining Southern unity since it would foment resentment on the part of the plantations whose operation was marginal against those more able to shoulder the levy. An added benefit to regulating slavery by taxing it rather than abolishing it directly would be that the costs of emancipation (including dispersion and relocation of freed blacks) could be partly paid out of these revenues. The prospect would be for encouraging gradual emancipation voluntarily undertaken by masters in response to increasingly onerous taxation.

But of course the condition for a taxing policy that should discriminate against slaveholders was dominance of the Congress by free states.[13] This could be counted upon to occur only if there were some design in the Constitution favoring the formation of new free states, and indeed one may discern such a design. The United States was at this time becoming the disposer of huge tracts of land in the West ceded by the individual states. Part of the work of the Constitutional Convention was to affirm the principle enunciated in the

12. Elliot, *Debates*, III, 457-58

13. In 1797 the Fourth Congress voted in favor of a proposal that would have imposed a tax on Southern landholders computed partly by numbering their slaves. The aim at this time was to raise much needed revenue, not to regulate slavery by taxation, and eventually an indirect tax bill was preferred. But the bill met no resistance on constitutional grounds, and Congress's actions indicate the means it had at its disposal to set taxes on slaves whatever the constraints on "direct" taxes of Art. 1 Sec. 10. On July 14, 1789 President Adams signed into law a bill calling for a tax on slaves and landholdings. Once again the purpose of the tax was revenue and the amount not sufficiently severe to encourage manumissions. See Robinson, *Slavery in the Structure of American Politics*, 257-63.

252 THE POLITICAL SCIENCE REVIEWER

Northwest Ordinances of 1784 and 1787 that the new territories were not to be maintained as colonies but were to be prepared for participation in the Union on the same terms as the original thirteen states. This decision in itself was an important application of the Framers' dedication to a society based upon the acknowledgment of equal rights. Article 4, Sections 3 and 4 incorporate the doctrine of consent and representation affirmed by the Declaration and adhered to in the *second* organic law of the new nation, The Northwest Ordinance of 1787.

In his draft of the Northwest Ordinance of 1784 Jefferson placed the prohibition of slavery immediately after the stipulation that the territorial governments "shall be in republican forms." In fact he did not regard the prohibition of slavery as an ordinary law, but rather deemed it one article of a fundamental "compact" between the people of the new state and the United States (*The Papers of Thomas Jefferson,* Boyd, ed., VI:608). The requirement of republican government for all states would of course find its way into the Constitution as Article 4, Section 4. At law the provision has been inert because judges have held the language lacks determinate content. But one could argue that Jefferson's precedent gives determinate substance to the guarantee of "republican government," at least for the new states. Some antislavery constitutionalists appealed to this section when they contested Congressional acts sanctioning new slaveholding states.[14]

In the same spirit the Constitution deals with the problem of slavery in the territories. First, by virtue of Art. 4, Sec. 3 Congress is given power to "make all needful Rules and Regulations respecting the Territory or other Property belonging to the United States" and to admit new states into the Union. This means that in the process of exercising its authority to regulate territories Congress could regulate slavery or exclude it altogether (as it just had in the Northwest Ordinance of July 1787), and in arranging for admission into the Union of the new states formed in the territories Congress might prohibit slavery as a condition of statehood (as subsequently Congress in some cases did).[15] Second, besides providing these powers adequate to the

14. See William M. Wiecek, *The Sources of Antislavery Constitutionalism in America 1760-1848* (Ithaca: Cornell University Press, 1977), 119-20.
15. From 1798 to 1822 five territorial acts excluded slavery while an equal number permitted the introduction of slaves. The result of these territorial policies was seven states admitted as slaveholding (Tennessee in 1796, Louisiana in 1812, Mississippi in 1817, Alabama in 1819, Missouri in 1821, Arkansas in 1836, and Florida in 1845); five

task of excluding slavery from the territories, the Philadelphia Constitution gives a positive impetus to the project of keeping the territories free. The step is taken in Art. 1, Sec. 9. Joined to the language empowering Congress to interdict the importation of slaves (after 1808) are the words "The Migration . . . of such Persons as any of the states now existing shall think proper to admit. . . . "

The entire provision contains three marks of disapproval to each of which attaches a potential for inflicting damage upon slaveholding. First, the ocean-going traffic is put on notice. Although Congress is not thereby positively enjoined to terminate the African trade, the singling out of this one species of commerce brands the practice with odium, and it was in fact prohibited at the earliest date permitted by the Constitution. When Madison speaks of the intent of the provision in *Federalist* No. 42 he says it should "be considered as a great point gained in favor of humanity, that a period of twenty years may terminate forever, within these States, a traffic which has so long and so loudly upbraided the barbarism of modern policy." That the trade would certainly be halted was treated as a foregone conclusion in the North and not seriously contested in the Southern ratifying conventions. The compromise was only in the suspension of the exercise of the prohibiting power for the twenty years. Moreover, the qualification limiting the application of the term of suspension to "any of the states now existing" meant that slave imports from abroad need not be permitted at any time in any of the territories or the new states. Such importations were in fact prohibited by acts of Congress, prohibited even to those new states where slavery was legal. Thus at least one door was closed to the admission of slaves into new lands.

The other entrance was by way of interstate traffic. For this also a means of prevention is made available. A second power over the spread of slavery accrues to Congress by virtue of the inclusion of "migration" within the same clause that deals with the foreign trade. By withholding Congress from exercising for twenty years an authority to regulate the movement of slaves within the original states the Constitution puts Congress in possession of a power to make such regulations after 1807. It thereby equips the new federal government

---

states came in free (Ohio in 1803, Indiana in 1816, Illinois in 1818, Michigan in 1837, and Iowa in 1846). Illinois at the time of statehood contained an enclave of slaves whose emancipation was fixed for 1825. See Wiecek, *Sources*, 109-10.

with the means of striking much more directly at slaveholding than by terminating importations. The regulations would take the form of commerce restrictions. In the House debates over Missouri a representative from Illinois argued that slavery could be abolished by so fettering the interstate movements of slaves as to prevent the necessary adjustments to the changing slave populations.[16]

More likely to prove enforceable is the third weapon protruding from the sheath of restrictions. The same qualification confining the operation of the provision to "states now existing" operates with respect to migration as with respect to importation, and with the same salutary result. That is, Congress may not for twenty years put clogs upon the traffic in slaves among states existing at the time of ratification, but Congress is left free to interdict movements of slaves from those already existing states into territories or into the new states to be formed from the territories. Note that there is no constitutional sanction for a slaveholder taking his slaves into a territory of the United States. This is consistent with the axiom borne out by the "Fugitive Slave" clause that slavery under the new Constitution is to be solely the creature of the positive law of those states which continued to carry slave codes on their statute books. On the supposition that no new state would enact codes protecting slavery if it had not already in residence slaves to be protected, one might have predicted in 1787 that no new states dedicated to preserving slavery would be added to the Union.[17] Thus, the long-term effect of protecting in-

---

16. See Wiecek, *Sources of Antislavery Constitutionalism*, 118.

17. The full anti-slavery potential of the clauses under consideration can be gathered by noting how the Confederate Constitution recasts the language so as to remove every handle for emancipators. Here are the corresponding clauses regarding slaveholding in territories as incorporated into the Confederate Constitution:

> The Confederate States may acquire new territory; and Congress shall have power to legislate and provide governments for the inhabitants of all territory belonging to the Confederate States, lying without the limits of the several States; and may permit them, at such times and in such manner as it may by law provide, to form States to be admitted into the Confederacy.

> In all such territory, the institution of negro slavery, as it now exists in the Confederate States and Territories shall be recognized and protected by Congress and by the territorial government; and the inhabitants of the several Confederate States and Territories shall have the right to take to such Territory any slaves lawfully held by them in any of the States or Territories of the Confederate States.

The draftsmen of the Confederate Constitution sought to provide for just those rights of emigration into the territories which are *not* secured for slaveholders in the United States Constitution.

terstate slave movement only within the original states would be to encourage the gradual aggregation of new free states and, hence, the eventual development of Congresses that could be expected to employ all the other constitutional weapons harmful to slaveholding.

I have presented Art. 1 Sec. 9 in such a light as to emphasize its efficacy as an instrument for confining slaveholding to the original states. The construction here proposed finds its grounds in syntax and conformity with other sections of the Constitution. Turning to the evidence provided by contemporaneous opinion one encounters uncertainties. The debates in the Convention do make it clear that slavery and *not* immigration as such, was the matter to be regulated by the provision, but the records do not make it clear exactly what the Framers expected to happen in the territories. The state conventions are similarly ambiguous on the subject. James Wilson could assure the Pennsylvania ratifiers that slavery would be confined to areas where it then existed and be permitted nowhere else, yet he does not explain what constitutional mechanism will ensure this development. Southerners cite no constitutional guarantees for extending slavery, but neither do they acknowledge that they are prevented from moving their slaves, or selling them, into the territories. We *can* say that, as evidenced by their agreement to the Northwest Ordinance, Southern congressmen acknowledged Congress's authority to forbid slave movements into the regions north of the Ohio River.

Not until 1819 was there a real joining of the issue in regard to the constitutionality of slave migrations to the territories. The Missouri crisis gave practical urgency to the question while it also marked an important threshold introducing a new constitutional situation. Rufus King brought out the significance of passing beyond the bounds of the original states:

> Slavery cannot exist in Missouri without the consent of Congress; the question therefore may be considered in certain lights as a new one; it being the first instance in which an inquiry respecting slavery, in a case so free from the influence of ancient laws, and usages, and manners of the country, has come before the Senate.[18]

18. *The Substance of Two Speeches On the Missouri Bill Delivered by Mr. King* in Charles R. King, ed., *Life and Correspondence of Rufus King* (New York: G. P. Putnam's Sons, 1894-1900), Appendix IV, 702.

The novelty of Missouri consisted in its being a territory not tied in any way to the laws of any of the original states. In all the earlier cases of a region passing from territorial government to statehood some previously existing state had exercised its authority over the area and, in every case where the territory had passed over into statehood as a slaveholding state, the original governing state had permitted slaveholding while the inhabitants were still living under the temporary territorial government. Hence, it could be argued, for instance, that since property in slaves was permitted by North Carolina in the region that became the Tennessee territory, slaveholding must continue there during the territorial period. This claim on behalf of slaveholders could accommodate to Art. 1 Sec. 9 provided one stretched the meaning of the reservation "states now existing" to include all territorial possessions of the original thirteen states, whether ceded already or not. Apparently some such consideration prompted Congress to treat differently territories ceded by Southern as distinct from Northern free states. But even if one allows that the old laws of the original slaveholding states should extend their influence through the territorial stage of statehood, that allowance would not affect Missouri which had never been under the authority of any state. So Missouri was indeed, as King maintained, a new departure and therefore a decisive test of the nation's will regarding the future of slavery.

King also grasped the principle that would bring the national will into conformity with the purpose that had originally been served by the Constitutional provisions on slavery. In arguing against the idea of extending the "Federal ratio" to a Missouri admitted as a slaveholding state King formulated a sensible guiding rule. The counting of slaves towards representation was a "concession" among the original states and limited thereunto:

> Great, however, as this concession was, it was definite, and its full extent was comprehended. It was a settlement between the original thirteen states. The considerations arising out of their actual condition, their past connection, and the obligation which all felt to promote a reformation in the federal government, were peculiar to the time and to the parties, and are not applicable to the new States which Congress may now be willing to admit into the Union.[19]

19. Chas. King, ed., *Life and Correspondence*, 699.

King correctly perceived that admitting Missouri as a slave state would put the nation on a new footing with respect to slavery. The concessive, and therefore temporary, character of the slaveholding provisions of the Constitution would be obscured. If new states were allowed the same means of protecting property in slaves as the original states had been accorded then the net effect of the Federal ratio and the fugitive slave clauses would no longer be that of securing a gradual and orderly transition to a free society. Instead, those concessions would become powerful weapons for perpetuating and extending slavery. Even if (as proved possible for a time) a line could be drawn northwards of which free soil prevailed, still, the emergence of new slaveholding states south of this line would ensure the perpetuation of slavery perhaps indefinitely into the future. Only by adhering resolutely to the intent of the Framers could this prospect be forestalled. King tried to restore this intent by recalling the original reasons for the concessions to slaveholders and, with those reasons, the limits beyond which no concessions ought to be carried.

We can gather part of the reason who King's efforts failed if we turn to consider what Madison was saying in 1819. King had maintained in his Senate speeches that Congress had authority to prohibit movements of slaves into territories. He referred explicitly to the powers conferred in Art. 1 Sec. 9:

> Since the year 1808 Congress have possessed power to prohibit and have prohibited the further emigration or importation of slaves into any of the old thirteen states, and at all times under the constitution have had power to prohibit such migration or importation into any of the new states or territories of the United States.[20]

Madison complains against what he claims to be the novelty of these doctrines. To Robert Walsh he writes on Nov. 27, 1819:

> The great object of the Convention seemed to be to prohibit the increase [of slave population] by the *importation* of slaves. . . .[21]

Madison now even recollects that the Framers "disclaimed" a power to emancipate slaves. But, on the other hand, he cannot recall their having indicated any "view to control the distribution of [slaves]

20. Chas. King, ed., *Life and Correspondence*, 691.
21. Gaillard Hunt, ed., *The Writings of James Madison* (New York: G. P. Putnam's Sons, 1900-1910), vol. IX, 9.

within the country."[22] In this same letter Madison remarks that Congress has not interdicted slavery in any of the territorial governments it has established. He attempts to explain away the Northwest Ordinance interdiction by observing that it was enacted by the old Congress still under the Articles of Confederation. Yet that enactment was reaffirmed in the first Congress under the Constitution, a Congress in which Madison sat! As for the intent of the slavery prohibition in the Ordinance, Madison assures Walsh that it was only meant to inhibit importations from abroad by excluding one region into which the imported slaves might be sent (this peculiar expedient being required supposedly because Congress did not yet have authority to stop slave importations at the ports of entry). What then was the intent of the clause permitting Congress to regulate migration beyond the boundaries of the original states? Madison now thinks the clause has reference only to immigrants from abroad. One can appreciate how drastically Madison has changed his position by recalling *Federalist* No. 42 in which speaking of precisely the interpretation he now offers Madison had then judged it to have been a "misconstruction" not deserving of an answer.[23]

22. Walter Berns, "The Constitution and the Migration of Slaves," *Yale Law Journal*, LXXVIII (1968), 209, cites two accounts of speeches by Madison that indicate how different was his official position just after ratification of the Constitution. In the First Congress Madison spoke upon a Quaker petition to abolish slavery:

He admitted, that Congress is restricted by the Constitution from taking measures to abolish the slave trade; yet there are a variety of ways by which it could countenance the abolition, and regulations might be made in relation to the introduction of them into the new states to be formed out of the Western Territory. (1 *Annals of Congress*, 1246 [1790])

Berns also cites this reporting of the same speech from 4 Elliot, 408:

He [Mr. Madison] entered into a critical review of the circumstances respecting the adoption of the Constitution; the ideas upon the limitation of the powers of Congress to interfere in the regulation of the commerce in slaves, and showing, that they indeniably were not precluded from interposing in their importation; and generally, to regulate the mode in which every species of business shall be transacted. He adverted to the western country and the cession of Georgia, in which Congress have certainly the power to regulate the subject of slavery....

23. In No. 42 Madison had complained:

Attempts have been made to pervert this clause into an objection against the Constitution, by representing it on the one side as a criminal toleration of an illicit practice, and on another, as calculated to prevent voluntary and beneficial emigrations from Europe to America. I mention these misconstructions, not with a view to give them an answer, for they deserve none; but as specimens of the manner and spirit in which some have thought fit to conduct their opposition to the proposed government. (Jacob Cooke, ed., 282)

I don't think, however, that in 1819 Madison intended to misrepresent the issue to Walsh. When a few months later he writes Monroe he expresses his astonishment over recent arguments ascribing to the Convention the intent of circumscribing slavery by fencing it out of the territories. He asks Monroe to contemplate what would have been the reaction of slaveholding states if they had thought Art. 1 Sec. 9 were designed to prevent their carrying their slaves westward.[24] Although Madison's indignation seems genuine, it is no less difficult to imagine antislavery men accepting tranquilly the notion that all new states should be allowed to come in slave states. But, however that may have been, the clause got into the Constitution and must be explained by reference to some intention more in keeping with the immediate context than Madison's 1820 reversal of his first opinion. As Walter Berns has observed, Madison's own notes on the Convention establish that the preceding debates have reference to slavery, not immigration. The logic of the clause does not point to immigration (why should the immigration laws be reserved to the states but only prior to 1808?). And the tell-tale euphemism *such persons* governs grammatically the entire construction, *migration* as well as *importation.* The balance of evidence favors the conclusion that the clause gives Congress a double weapon suitable for use against internal as well as foreign slave traffic and empowers Congress to exclude both mischiefs from the westward movement of the nation.

It soon became apparent to Americans that the prospects for extirpating slavery in this country could be read in the fate of slavery in the territories. The constitutional status of slaveholding in the Western regions was therefore the question upon which pro and antislavery forces joined issue in the first half of the nineteenth century. The classic rendition of this struggle were, of course, the Lincoln-Douglas debates and the immediate occasion of the debates was Taney's decision in *Dred Scot* which had the effect of committing the federal government to protecting slaveholders in their ownership of slaves wherever they might take them in territory possessed by the United States.

Lincoln sought to reinstate the Missouri Compromise by contending against Taney that the federal government did have the authority to exclude slavery from a territory. Lincoln argued only that Congress was entitled to take such action, not that it was expressly bound by the Constitution to do so. He evidently thought (or at least he refrained

24. See letter of Feb. 10, 1820.

from denying) that Congress might also act within its constitutional authority when permitting slaves to be introduced into some of the territories. Lincoln was certainly right to proclaim that Taney's decision abused the Constitution and set the supreme law of the land against the principles of the Declaration. He could have gone further (perhaps he was prudent not to have gone further) to demonstrate that judged on the basis of Art. 1 Sec. 9 Taney had turned the Constitution inside out. Not only was Congress entitled to keep the territories free of slaves, the design of interconnections among the slavery provisions encourages, if it does not positively prescribe, confinement of slaveholding to the narrowest limits consistent with maintaining the Union.

A consistent federal policy following the model of the Northwest Ordinance and forbidding the migration of slaves to the territories would have revealed the full potency of the constitutional instruments for extirpating slavery. To recapitulate, those instruments are: (1) a power to end the importation of slaves from abroad; (2) a prohibition of slaves from the territories that would predictably lead to Congresses dominated by representatives from free states; (3) powers over commerce, territorial regulation and taxation sufficient in the hands of antislavery Congresses to make slaveholding ever more harassed and expensive while making manumissions ever more attractive and bringing in revenues to help relocate (in Western territories) the number of freed blacks sufficient to assure whites of their safety.

Unhappily the key to setting in motion these instruments is a condition contrary to fact. Early Congresses did not produce a policy of consistently forbidding slaveholding in the territories. Instead Congress permitted slavery to become established in Kentucky, Alabama, Tennessee, and Mississippi having acquiesced to conditions proposed by the southern states who ceded the lands out of which these new states were formed.[25] This compliance to the demands of

25. North Carolina first ceded its western lands without attaching conditions then, having taken alarm, withdrew its cession offering the lands once again (Dec. 22, 1789) on condition that slaveholding should be allowed therein. Virginia and New York in ceding their holdings relinquished "all right, title and claim as well of soil as of jurisdiction." Congress nevertheless agreed to North Carolina's stipulation and thus Jefferson's 1784 proposed prohibition of slavery from all western territories was compromised to extend only to the northern territories. Actually the serpent first entered the garden with the Ordinance of 1787 which although it adopted Jefferson's prohibition confined its operation to regions north of the Ohio River leaving open the question

the Southern states put the Congresses in violation not of the letter but of the spirit of the Constitution. Nonetheless the consequent policy of allowing slaveholding southwards while prohibiting northwards assumed a sort of unofficial status representing an intersectional consensus until it, in turn, was set aside by the still more egregiously unconstitutional fiat of the Taney court. That this national consensus lacked constitutional justification did not prevent it from holding sway over minds justifiably grateful for the intersectional peace it helped to sustain.

The desire of most parties to keep the peace largely accounts for the failure of the federal government to exclude slavery from newly forming states. Other considerations colluded. In the first place, the meaning of the all important clause of Art. 1 Sec. 9 discountenancing territorial slave migration must be discerned by thinking about the related parts of the document. If the Constitution had been made to state flatly *Involuntary servitude shall be confined to those states wherein it is now provided for by law* the spread of slavery would have met with a clearer opposition. As it was, Art. 1 Sec. 9 had to suffer the impositions of the latter-day Madison and Charles Cotesworth Pinckney whose constructions of the provision artfully legitimated the expansion of slaveholding. That this construction contradicts Madison in *Federalist* No. 42, did not prevent its being adopted by Joseph Story in his prestigious *Commentaries on the Constitution of the United States* in 1847. The ferocious slave rebellion in Santo Domingo hardened resistance in the South to any measures that might make Southerners vulnerable to the bloody scenes enacted in the Caribbean. After Santo Domingo many Northerners seemed to feel they could not press antislavery measures against Southerners convinced that the lives of all their dependents were in imminent danger from the numerous slaves in their midst. In March 1798 Albert Gallitin proved an accurate prophet when he pleaded (vainly) during the House debates on establishing a government for the Mississippi territory that this would be the last chance to check slave expansion into the Southwest.

One further element in an explanation why slavery was not set on

---

of the status of slavery in the territories to the south. See the discussion of the western lands and slavery in Arthur Bestor, "State Sovereignty and Slavery: A Reinterpretation of Proslavery Constitutional Doctrine, 1846-1860," *Journal of the Illinois State Historical Society*, vol. 54 (Summer, 1961) 147-62.

the course of gradual extinction chalked forth in the Constitution comes to sight if one reflects upon a remark Walter Berns offers in support of the interpretation of Art. 1 Sec. 9 as a barrier to introducing slaves into United States territories. Berns contends that "no purpose would be served by prohibiting the importation of slaves from abroad if they could, prior to 1808, be imported into South Carolina and then sent on to a new state of territory.[26] Perhaps no honorable purpose would be served by so doing, yet charges were made during the federal Convention against Virginia planters that they aimed to benefit from terminating the foreign trade by supplying to other states and new states slaves from Virginia in the place of further imports from Africa. The idea of a Virginian project to seal off importation from the sea while increasing the state's own traffic in slaves southwards and westwards makes some sense of Madison's reassuring the ratifying convention of the safety of their property in slaves after having argued powerfully against slave importations at Philadelphia. The idea is the more plausible when it is understood that ends more creditable than commercial speculation called for such a plan. Jefferson for a time believed that the South's only hope lay in dispersing its slave population. Exporting blacks to the new lands might bring about the "voluntary" relocation that would enable the Southern plantation owner to let go the ears of his wolf, or at least hold onto one less dangerous.[27] Madison and Jefferson voiced the same opinion, and in almost the same words. In the same correspondence that documents his change of position on the meaning of Art. 1 Sec. 9 we find Madison putting this rhetorical question to Walsh: "Will the aggregate strength, security, tranquility and harmony of the whole nation be advanced or impaired by lessening the proportion of slaves to free people in particular sections of it?" After endorsing this theory of amelioration by dispersion, Madison goes on to make a

26. Berns, "The Constitution and the Migration of Slaves," 219.
27. To John Holmes, Jefferson wrote on April 22, 1820:
> Of one thing I am certain, that as the passage of slaves from one State to another, would not make a slave of a single human being who would not be so without it, so their diffusion over a greater surface would make them individually happier, and proportionally facilitate the accomplishment of their emancipation, by dividing the burden on a greater number of coadjutors."

Andrew A. Lipscomb, ed., *The Writings of Thomas Jefferson* (Washington, D.C.: Thomas Jefferson Memorial Assoc., 1903), vol. XV, 249-50. See also Jefferson's speculations on the Missouri Compromise as a "Tory" plot got up to secure the election of a Federalist President in his letter to the Marquis de La Fayette (Nov. 4, 1823) and correspondence with James Monroe of March 3, 1820.

claim that a nationwide allowance of slaveholding will be necessary to prevent civil war. Indeed he seems to go so far as to suggest that besides enlarging the sphere of republican government and encouraging diversity of interests a third necessary element in a cure for the republican malady of factions is to be found in expanding the reach of slaveholding:

> Parties under some denomination or other must always be expected in a government as free as ours. When the individuals belonging to them are inter-mingled in every part of the whole Country, they strengthen the Union of the whole, while they divide every part. Should a state of parties arise, founded on geographical boundaries and other physical and permanent distinctions which happen to coincide with them, what is to control those great repulsive masses from awful shocks against each other?[28]

The classic defense of popular government worked out in *Federalist No. 10* now takes on this strange refinement: the "republican" remedy for the evils incident to republican government is the unlimited opportunity for owning slaves!

In Madison's view the same means will serve two benign intents: in order to prevent warring factions, permit Virginia and her sister Southern states to disperse their surplus slaves into the territories; in order to improve the conditions of black and white alike, permit Virginia to disperse her slaves into the territories.

It is hard to say to what degree this will-o'-the-wisp of a solution by dispersion contributed to Southern intransigency regarding slavery in the territories. Did this false hope prevent resolute confrontation of hard truths by a Jefferson who in 1784 had drafted policy intended to prevent the introduction of slavery into *all* territories but who, by 1820, was willing to see slavery permitted throughout the new lands he had purchased from France, and did the same mirage distract Madison who, in the Constitutional Convention, was anxious to prevent even the mention of slavery from sullying the new constitution but who, in 1819 was willing to see the reality of chattel slavery extended across the entire nation? Evidently the lure of dispersion served to enervate the statesmanship of the two Virginia presidents whose stature might have been sufficient to have gained a hearing for a call to return to the antislaveholding provisions of the first Northwest Ordinance.

28. Nov. 27, 1819.

However we sort out the causes and whatever the circumstantial justification for permitting the expansion of slavery, it remains true that within thirty years of the ratification of the Constitution slaveholding had been extended into every territory of the United States south of the Mason-Dixon line, including the nation's capital. Nevertheless, this history of constitutional abuse does not demonstrate an inadequacy of the Constitution to secure equal rights for all. Slaveholding procured a longer term of life than the Framers expected because the spirit of the Constitution was not heeded while the provisions meant to contain slaveholding and strangle it were ignored, emasculated, or, as in the case of Art. 1 Sec. 9, positively misconstrued.

We return to the question posed at the outset: Are the provisions regarding slavery in the U. S. Constitution consistent with the principles of liberty and equality set forth in the Declaration of Independence? We ought not forget that in a sense the entire frame of government established by the Constitution is a provision against slavery. The idea of a written higher law, of limitations upon the powers of those who govern, of responsibility to the people, and of separation of executive, legislative, and judicial powers, all answer to the one great theme of rule of law. The essence of the ideal of rule of law is the conception of the act of governing as the product of reason rather than will. The arrangements of the Constitution aim to secure a political life under which no man will be subject to the unrestrained will of another, while every man will be subject to the salutary restraint of uniformly operating laws and regular, deliberative procedures. In the Declaration the equality proposition looks to the foundation of law in man's nature. Human nature can be regarded positively as ordained to rationality or negatively as inclined to prefer its will to any restraint. Men are equal in that their dual nature predominates over every other class feature. Another way of stating this truth is to say that all men stand intermediate between beasts and angels. This moral equality points towards rule of law. Laws uniform in their application and protection and arrived at by consent answer to the dual aspect of human nature. Both the positive aspect of man's nature—his capacity to obey reason—and the negative—his inclination to indulge willfulness—both aspects require that all men be deemed to possess an equal claim to justice or to live under law. Stated negatively, the equality proposition means that it is impossible to identify any class of men as possessed of a natural right to rule. Efforts to certify classes with such a right bring mischief upon everyone including the corruption of the class on behalf of whom the claim is made. Constitutionalism, or rule of law, is the realization of this moral understanding of equality. Viewed negatively as freedom from the arbitrary will of others, rule of law is political liberty. By providing for a political experience in which every man submits his native willfulness to correction by a common rationality the United States Constitution gives form to equality and liberty. That form causes the institution of slavery to reveal fully its anomalous character. Slavery is precisely antithetical to the notion of rule of law, because slavery is a condition which places every restraint on the will of the slave while it places no restraint on the will of the slavemaster. Both master and servant are thus impaired in their political liberty, the slave by being treated as less than a man, the master by being treated as though he were more than a man.

A regime dedicated to the principles of rule of law and moral equality is the best hope for eliminating slavery. Such a regime we might say is bound sooner or later to produce men who perceive slavery to be repugnant to the very essence of the creed that in the first instance produced the national constitution and thereafter was in turn sustained by the habits and convictions daily fostered by those constitutional arrangements. The education in respect for legal restraint inculcated by the Constitution was bound to produce, we might think, a Lincoln who would hold the Union to its proper purpose of freeing slaves, even through the unexpectedly terrific costs in blood that such a purpose required. Lincoln's achievement and the sacrifices endured by those who fought for the Union is an inspiring proof of the capacity of men to prefer fidelity towards a moral idea over the pursuit of lower interests or even at the expense of the most compelling interests of self-preservation. Lincoln's achievement may serve even better than Churchill's to define the utmost attained by Western man since Churchill could muster his people by appealing to the motive of self-preservation whereas Lincoln had to sustain a moral cause in the teeth of that all but decisive motive. Impassioned respect not solely for the ideals of the Declaration but also for a constitutional Union that embodied the ideal set forth in the Declaration appears to have given Lincoln the resolve to carry through that moral cause. The Constitution certainly gave him the necessary instrument in a citizenry habituated to self-government. The Constitution taken as a whole inculcates respect for government by consent and thereby nurtures habits hostile to slavery while its particular provisions are adequate to promote the eradication of slavery in a manner that would preserve at the same time peace, and safety, and the rule of law.

University of Dallas   JOHN ALVIS

The Compromise of 1787

STAUGHTON LYND

Yale University

✤ On July 12, 1787, the Constitutional Convention, meeting in Philadelphia, adopted the three-fifths compromise regarding apportionment of the House of Representatives. On July 13 the Continental Congress, meeting in New York City, adopted the Northwest Ordinance. The three-fifths compromise sanctioned slavery more decidedly than any previous action at a national level.[1] The Ordinance, on the other hand, was in Ulrich Phillips' words "the first and last antislavery achievement by the central government in the period."[2] The Ordinance has become a symbol of the Revolution's liberalism, while the compromise, if not a covenant with death and an agreement with hell, is at least a dramatic instance of its pragmatic conservatism. Why did Congress and Convention act so differently? The answer to this question, could it be found, would surely throw much light upon the troubled relation between the Founding Fathers and the peculiar institution.

Apart from the coincidence of dates, two circumstances make this problem still more intriguing. One is that the Continental

---

[1] This essay takes issue with Professor Max Farrand's belief that the three-fifths compromise was of secondary importance at the Convention, and that the question of the West was separate from the sectional conflict between North and South (Max Farrand, *The Framing of the Constitution of the United States* [New Haven, 1913], 107-11). My reasons for questioning Farrand's approach are presented more fully in Staughton Lynd, "The Abolitionist Critique of the United States Constitution," in Martin Duberman (ed.), *The Antislavery Vanguard* (Princeton, 1965), 209-39.

[2] Ulrich B. Phillips, *American Negro Slavery* (New York and London, 1933), 128.

Congress, at the time it adopted the Ordinance, was controlled by the South. Its temporary president was a Southerner (William Grayson of Virginia); three of the committee of five which drafted the Ordinance were Southerners (Richard Henry Lee and Edward Carrington of Virginia, John Kean of South Carolina); and a Congress with a Southern majority adopted the Ordinance with a single dissenting vote (by a Northerner, Abraham Yates of New York). Why these Southern delegates voted to ban slavery in the Northwest puzzled Nathan Dane of Massachusetts at the time,[3] and has remained a puzzle to historians. Thus B. A. Hinsdale commented that an antislavery clause "had been rejected by Southern men when Mr. Jefferson first brought it forward, and now five of the eight States present are Southern States and eleven of the eighteen men Southern men, and it prevails."[4] Southern sup-

[3] Dane to Rufus King, July 16, 1787, Edmund C. Burnett (ed.), *Letters of the Members of the Continental Congress* (Washington, D. C., 1921-36) (hereafter cited as *LCC*), VIII, 622.

[4] B. A. Hinsdale, *The Old Northwest: The Beginnings Of Our Colonial System* (New York, 1899), 266. John M. Merriam said, similarly, in "The Legislative History of The Ordinance of 1787," *Proceedings of the American Antiquarian Society,* New Series, V (Worcester, 1889), 336: "The most surprising facts in connection with this article are that it hung fire so long when it would seem that its best friends were interested in it; that Dane and King especially were ready on May 10th to vote for an ordinance which omitted it, and that when proposed in Congress as an amendment to a matured plan, it was so readily adopted." Perhaps the fullest set of questions was posed by William F. Poole, *The Ordinance of 1787, And Dr. Manasseh Cutler As An Agent In Its Formation* (Cambridge, Mass., 1876), 19: "Why were three Southern members, all new men, and constituting a majority of the committee, put in charge of an antislavery ordinance for a Northern territory, which had been defeated by the entire vote of the South three years before? If antislavery principles were so popular with Southern members, why did not Mr. Dane insert an antislavery clause in the ordinance which was to have taken its third reading on the 10th of May? As Mr. Johnson of Connecticut was the chairman of that committee, and three out of five of its members were Northern men, why did not the committee make it an antislavery ordinance? Whence did so much light dawn so suddenly upon the mind of Mr. Dane, when associated with a majority of Southern members on another committee? What is the explanation of the entire unanimity of feeling and action on the slavery question, then exhibited for the first and last time, in the whole history of our national legislation?" Poole answered his own questions by saying that Southerners doubtless were thinking of the public revenue the Northwest lands would bring (*ibid.,* 27). Francis S. Philbrick in the monumental introduction to *The Laws Of Illinois Territory 1809-1818* (Springfield, Ill., 1950), clxxxvi, note, stresses that by creating a buffer against British and Indian aggression, the Northwest Territory would promote settlements in the Southwest. No wholly satisfactory explanation has yet been suggested.

port for the Ordinance must puzzle us still more when we set it side-by-side with the determined defense of slavery at the Convention by Deep South delegates such as William Davie of North Carolina and the entire South Carolina group: Pierce Butler, the Pinckneys, and John Rutledge.[5]

A second, less familiar circumstance which thickens the mystery surrounding these events of mid-July is that a number of men were members of both Congress and Convention, and communication between the two bodies was apparently frequent and full. Members of Congress in 1787 who were also named delegates to the Convention were Gorham and King of Massachusetts, Johnson of Connecticut, Blount of North Carolina, Few and Pierce of Georgia, and James Madison of Virginia, who went directly from New York to Philadelphia in early May. A number of men traveled back and forth between the two cities while the Convention was in session. William Pierce returned to New York, where he remained from June 14 to June 18, just after discussion of the rule of representation had begun in Philadelphia, and according to Nathan Dane spoke freely of sectional conflicts at the Convention.[6] Blount and his fellow North Carolinian, Benjamin Hawkins visited Philadelphia from June 19 to July 2, returning to Congress when work on the Northwest Ordinance began. At the same time Pierce again came back from Philadelphia to New York along with his fellow Georgian, Few, like himself a member of both bodies.[7] Others, who, although not members of both groups, very likely carried news from one to the other, included Gouverneur Morris, a Convention delegate who returned to Philadelphia July 2 after a lengthy New York sojourn, and Richard Henry Lee, a member of Congress who took his seat on July 9 after a week in Philadelphia en route.[8] The full text of the Ordinance was, of course, available in Philadelphia

[5] See Davie and C. C. Pinckney on July 12, Butler on July 13, C. C. Pinckney on July 23, C. Pinckney, C. C. Pinckney, and Rutledge on Aug. 22. Max Farrand (ed.), *The Records of the Federal Convention of 1787* (New Haven, 1911) (hereafter cited as *RFC*), I, 593-94, 605; II, 371-73.

[6] Dane to Rufus King, June 19, 1787, *LCC*, VIII, 611.

[7] Wm. Blount to John Gray Blount, June 15, 21, 1787, *ibid.*, VIII, 610, 613; Blount to the Governor of Virginia (Richard Caswell), July 10, 1787, *ibid.*, VIII, 618; Richard Dobbs Spaight to John Gray Blount, July 3, 1787, Alice Barnwell Keith (ed.), *The John Gray Blount Papers* (Raleigh, 1952), I, 315; *RFC*, III, 587, 589.

[8] Lee to Thomas Lee Shippen, *LCC*, VIII, 627, 613, note.

soon after it was passed; however, its essential provisions may have been known to some members of the Convention as early as July 11 or 12.[9]

According to his secretary, Edward Coles, Madison years later suggested that there had been a bargain or compromise between the sections involving both the Ordinance and the Constitution. He said, so Coles stated in the eighteen-fifties:

> Many individuals were members of both bodies, and thus were enabled to know what was passing in each—both sitting with closed doors and in secret sessions. The distracting question of slavery was agitating and retarding the labors of both, and led to conferences and inter-communications of the members, which resulted in a compromise by which the northern or anti-slavery portion of the country agreed to incorporate, into the Ordinance and Constitution, the provision to restore fugitive slaves; and this mutual and concurrent action was the cause of the similarity of the provision contained in both, and had its influence, in creating the great unanimity by which the Ordinance passed, and also in making the Constitution the more acceptable to the slave holders.[10]

Coles, speaking shortly after the passage of the Fugitive Slave Act of 1850, may well have exaggerated the importance of that aspect of the compromise of 1787. But it is difficult to imagine that he misremembered the broad idea that communication and compromise had occurred between Congress and Convention, or that Madison, a member of both bodies, was misinformed.

If other direct testimony exists supporting Madison's account it has not come to my attention. Nevertheless, I believe it is possible to make a tentative reconstruction of Southern motives for accepting the Northwest Ordinance, and of the impact of the Ordinance on the work of the Constitutional Convention.

---

[9] Dane sent a copy of the Northwest Ordinance to King on July 16 (*LCC*, VIII, 621). Madison sent a copy to James Madison on July 28 (*Letters and Other Writings of James Madison* [Philadelphia, 1865], I, 335). According to Poole, 28, note, the Ordinance was first publicly printed in the *Pennsylvania Herald*, July 25, 1787.

[10] Coles' statement begins: "This brings to my recollection what I was told by Mr. Madison, and what I do not remember ever to have seen in print" (Edward Coles, *History of The Ordinance Of 1787* [Philadelphia, 1856], 28-29). A similar theory is presented by Peter Force (*Life Journals and Correspondence of Rev. Manasseh Cutler L.L.D.* [Cincinnati, 1888], II, Appendix D, 419).

I

"The clause respecting slavery was agreed to by the Southern members for the purpose of preventing tobacco and indigo from being made on the N. W. side of the Ohio as well as for sev'l other political reasons." So William Grayson wrote to James Monroe on August 8, 1787.[11] What were the "sev'l other political reasons"? Why did the Southern majority of the Continental Congress unanimously vote for the Northwest Ordinance, despite its antislavery clause?

One answer is as simple as it is surprising: the South expected that the states formed from the Northwest Territory would vote with the South in the sectional conflict then raging in Congress. Late in 1783, when congressional acceptance of Virginia's cession was finally in sight, Thomas Jefferson had written the governor of Virginia: "If a state be first laid off on the [Great] lakes it will add a vote to the Northern scale, if on the Ohio it will add one to the Southern."[12] Jefferson had proposed, and Congress had essentially accepted, a plan to divide the Territory into ten states, some near the lakes and others near the Ohio River. The Ordinance of 1787 provided instead that there be three states running from the river to the lakes, the present Ohio, Indiana, and Illinois. The result was that *both* North and South could hope for their allegiance. Dane of Massachusetts wrote to Rufus King on July 16 that the easternmost state of the three would "no doubt" be settled chiefly from the East, "and there is, I think, full an equal chance of its adopting Eastern politics."[13] A month later he was more confident. Writing again to King on August 12, Dane said:

Much will depend on the directions given to the first settlements in my opinion, and as the Eastern states for the sake of doing away the temporary governments, etc. established in 1784, and for establishing some order in that Country, gave up as much as could be reasonably expected, I think it will be just and proper in them to establish as far as they can

[11] *LCC*, VIII, 631-32.
[12] Jefferson to the Governor of Virginia (Benjamin Harrison), Nov. 11, 1783, *LCC*, VII, 347.
[13] *Ibid.*, VIII, 622.

31

consistently, Eastern politics in it, especially in the state adjoining Pennsylvania.[14]

But the Southern states, too, hoped and expected to dominate the Northwest. On November 3, 1787, the Virginia delegates in Congress wrote to Governor Edmund Randolph:

> Indeed, if it is thought Material to the interest of the Southern States, that their Scale be Strengthened by an accession this quarter, that object will be better secured by the New, than the old plan, because upon the former there may be an early admission of a State [since the states under the new plan would be larger], but upon the latter such an event must be long, or perhaps forever, postponed.[15]

If it was not because they would be slaveholding, it was also not because they were "agrarian" that the South looked forward to the admission of states from the Northwest Territory. Vermont was agrarian, but throughout the seventeen-eighties the South opposed the admission of Vermont because of what Madison called "an habitual jealousy of a predominance of Eastern interest."[16] Clearly the South believed that, unlike Vermont, the Northwest would be settled mainly by Southerners, by an outcropping of the great tide of migrants then flowing over the mountains into Kentucky and Tennessee. Conversely, Rufus King was relying on a predominance of Easterners in the area to produce the "Eastern politics" for which he hoped. Only the event could prove which section's expectations were correct, and so in July 1787 they could join almost unanimously in promoting the Territory's speedy settlement and organization.

What were the other "political reasons" to which Grayson referred? Richard Hildreth, writing in 1849, supposed that the Southern states were "reconciled" to the Ordinance "by the idea, afterward acted upon, of securing the continuation of slavery in the

---

[14] *Ibid.,* VIII, 636. One might say that the Northwest was an eighteenth-century Kansas, in that each section knew its political destiny would be determined by the geographical origins of its settlers.

[15] *Ibid.,* VIII, 672-73.

[16] "Observations Relating To The Influence of Vermont, And The Territorial Claims, On The Politics Of Congress. May 1st, 1782," Henry D. Gilpin (ed.), *The Papers Of James Madison* (Washington, D. C., 1840), I, 123.

32

territory south of the Ohio, under future terms of cession."[17] As we have seen, the South did not need to be reconciled to the Ordinance: it welcomed it in the belief that, even without slaveholding, the Northwest would support the South in national politics. But it is perfectly possible that Hildreth correctly identifies a second motive. For he stresses what many subsequent historians have forgotten, that as late as May 1787 Congress was on the verge of passing an ordinance for the West "the provisions of which extended to the whole western district, both that ceded [the Northwest] and that of which the cession was anticipated [the Southwest]."[18] The ordinance reported on April 26, 1787, was an ordinance "for the government of the western territory."[19] It was read twice but its third and final reading scheduled for May 10 was postponed, and on July 11, "the Committee . . . to whom was referred the report of a committee touching *the temporary government of the western territory* reported an Ordinance for *the government of the territory of the United States North West of the river Ohio*, which was read a first time."[20] [Italics mine.] Thus just at the moment the Convention adopted the three-fifths compromise, Congress for the first time drew an explicit East-West line through the Western territories by legislating for the Northwest alone. What if anything was implied as to the status of slavery south of that line in the region that became the Southwest Territory?

So far as I am aware, at no Southern ratifying convention was any fear expressed that the antislavery portion of the Northwest Ordinance would be applied south of the Ohio River. Southerners presumably knew that North Carolina's cession of the area later called Tennessee read in part: "Provided always, That no regulations made or to be made by Congress shall tend to emancipate slaves, otherwise than shall be directed by the Assembly or legislature of

[17] Richard Hildreth, *The History Of The United States Of America* (New York, 1849), III, 528-29.
[18] *Ibid.*, 527.
[19] *Journals Of The Continental Congress 1774-1789* (Washington, D. C., 1904-37) (hereafter cited as *JCC*), XXXI, 669; XXXII, 242, 281. Actually, the title of the plan as reported on September 19, 1786, and April 26, 1787, was "a plan of a temporary government for such districts, or new states, as shall be laid out by the United States." The print ordered on May 9, when the ordinance was read for a second time, shortened this to the phrase given in the text.
[20] *Ibid.*, XXXII, 313.

such State or States."[21] Other evidence supports the supposition that in legislating against slavery in the Northwest Congress tacitly legislated for it in the Southwest. South Carolinians at the Constitutional Convention were notoriously apprehensive about their slave property, but on August 9, 1787, the South Carolina legislature, undeterred by the Northwest Ordinance, completed the cession of its Western lands.[22] Richard Henry Lee, who in 1784 voted against Jefferson's proposal to ban slavery throughout the West, was mentioned by both Dane and Cutler as a particularly warm supporter of the 1787 Ordinance which banned it only North of the Ohio.

The Northwest Ordinance legislated against slavery in that part of the West where it did not exist and left it alone in the Southwest where it already was. This was generally recognized. "The Western people are already calling out for slaves for their new lands," George Mason told the Constitutional Convention in August.[23] And forty-seven years later Nathan Dane made a revealing statement in a letter to Daniel Webster:

> . . . in the years 1784, '85, '86, and '87, the Eastern members in the Old Congress really thought they were preparing the North-Western Territory principally for New England settlers, and to them the third and sixth articles of compact more especially had reference; therefore, when North Carolina ceded her western territory, and requested this Ordinance to be extended to it, except the *slave* article, that exception had my full assent, because slavery had taken root in it, and it was then probable it would be settled principally by slaveowners.[24]

Thus, while from the standpoint of the North the Ordinance appeared an antislavery triumph, to the South it may have seemed

---

[21] Walter Clark (ed.), *The State Records Of North Carolina* (Goldsboro, No. Carolina, 1905), XXIV, 563. Essentially the same clause was included in the North Carolina cession of December 22, 1789; the act of Congress accepting this first Southwestern cession of April 2, 1790; and the Ordinance for the Southwestern Territory of May 26, 1790 (Clarence E. Carter [ed.], *The Territorial Papers of The United States*, [Washington, D. C., 1936], IV, 7, 16, 18).

[22] Neither the South Carolina cession nor the Georgia cession of February 1, 1788, mentioned slavery (*JCC*, XXXIII, 475-77; XXXIV, 320-26).

[23] *RFC*, II, 370.

[24] Nathan Dane to Daniel Webster, March 26, 1830, in *The Part Taken By Essex County in The Organization And Settlement Of The Northwest Territory* (Salem, Mass., 1889), 40.

the end of the national government's attempt to prohibit slavery South of the Ohio.

A third political reason which may have induced Southern congressmen to support the Northwest Ordinance is suggested by a letter of Benjamin Hawkins of North Carolina. Writing to the governor of North Carolina on July 10, Hawkins said that he and William Blount had returned to Congress from the Convention in the

> hope of being able to procure some aid from the Union towards the protection of our Western Citizens, and of securing and preserving our right to the free and common use of the navigation of the Miss . . . . the latter which is very interesting to the Western citizens of the Southern States . . . has at length, from a variety of circumstances unnecessary as well perhaps as improper to relate been put in a bitter situation than heretofore.[25]

The question of the navigation of the Mississippi was the most serious sectional issue to come before the Continental Congress. It had troubled Congress during the war, when Robert Morris told the French envoy that (in Thomas P. Abernethy's paraphrase) "the strength of the Confederacy lay in the North and that the North should be kept in the ascendancy by curtailing the territory on the Southwest."[26] It took on new intensity in 1786 when John Jay, secretary for foreign affairs, secured congressional approval to sacrifice the right to the navigation in negotiations with Spain. For the South the issue was political as well as economic. Jay obtained his authorization from Congress by seven states to five in a strictly sectional vote; and the South feared, as William Grayson told the Virginia ratifying convention, that "if the Mississippi was yielded to Spain, the migration to the western country would be stopped, and the northern states would, not only retain their inhabitants, but preserve their superiority and influence over that of the southern."[27] The effort of Northern Congressmen to close the Mississippi had the same sectional character

[25] LCC, VIII, 619.
[26] Thomas P. Abernethy, *Western Lands and the American Revolution* (New York, 1937), 203-04, reporting a dispatch by Gérard dated Oct. 20, 1778.
[27] Speech of June 12, 1788, Jonathan Elliot (ed.), *The Debates In The Several State Conventions* (Washington, D. C., 1836), 281.

35

as the attempt by Northern members of Congress and Convention to limit the political representation of new states.

The bitter Mississippi controversy of 1786 became "much entangled" with the problem of evolving a government for the West.[28] On May 10, 1786, a five-man congressional committee with a Southern majority recommended that the number of states to be formed from the Virginia cession be reduced to not less than two nor more than five, but that, as in the plan of 1784, each state should enter the Union when its population was equal to that of the smallest of the original thirteen.[29] This, as the Virginia delegates observed in 1787, was a change which would accelerate the admission of new states. On July 7 Congress unanimously recommended to the states that they revise their acts of cession so that three to five states be formed from the Northwest. But now Northern congressmen began to press to raise the population requirement for admission to one thirteenth of the total population of the original thirteen states at the last census prior to the request for admission.[30] *This* change would have slowed down the admission of the new states. Indeed, had it been applied it would have delayed the admission of Ohio, Indiana, Illinois, Michigan, and Wisconsin an average of thirty-eight years, with Wisconsin excluded from statehood until after 1900.[31] On July 19 a personnel change gave the committee a Northern majority, and on September 19 the committee reported a revised ordinance including both the "Northern" population formula for admission to statehood and a new condition, equally offensive to the South, which provided for admission if "the consent of so many States in Congress is first obtained as may at that time be competent to such admission."[32]

Meantime the North was using its congressional majority to

---

[28] Edmund C. Burnett, *The Continental Congress* (New York, 1941), 653; *ibid.*, 651-53, describes the sequence of events discussed in the following paragraph.

[29] *JCC*, XXX, 251-55; James Monroe to Thomas Jefferson, May 11, 1786, *LCC*, VIII, 359-60.

[30] *JCC*, XXX, 390-94; James Monroe to Thomas Jefferson, July 16, 1786, *LCC*, VIII, 403-04.

[31] George Bancroft, *History Of the Formation Of The Constitution Of The United States Of America* (3rd ed., New York, 1883), II, 104.

[32] *JCC*, XXX, 418 n., 669-73. Philbrick comments, cclxxvi-vii, that this proviso violated the terms of the Virginia cession just as did the clause of the Constitution giving Congress discretionary power over the admission of new states.

change Jay's instructions regarding his negotiations with Spain about Mississippi navigation, which led at least three congressmen seriously to contemplate disunion. And on September 1, 1786, a procedural rule was approved which blocked reconsideration of Jay's instructions unless the same number of states were present (twelve) that had voted them in August.[33]

During the winter Congressman Madison noted that the idea of separate confederacies had for the first time reached the newspapers;[34] and in April, learning that Jay had drawn up a draft treaty with Gardoqui in which the Mississippi navigation was given up, Madison launched a frontal attack. On April 18 he moved that negotiations be transferred to Jefferson in Madrid, a step, he confided to his journal, "which if it should answer no other purpose would at least gain time." In inconclusive debate on the motion on April 23, Gorham (soon to leave for the Convention) stated that he thought the Mississippi *should* be closed to American commerce. On April 25, grasping the nettle, Madison moved to repeal the rule of September 1786. Rufus King (another member of both Congress and Convention) led the opposition which forced a postponement. Nevertheless Madison thought it a victory, writing in his journal:

> It was considered on the whole that the project of shutting the Mississippi was at an end; a point deemed of great importance in reference to the approaching Convention for introducing a change in the federal Government, and to the objection to an increase of its powers foreseen form the jealously [sic] which had been excited by that project.[35]

On May 2 he left for Philadelphia.

The issue of Western government and Mississippi navigation arose once more before Congress lost its quorum in mid-May. On May 9, Congress gave the ordinance for the "western territory"

---

[33] *JCC*, XXX, 323, and XXI, 46-84; *LCC*, VIII, 427-30, 438-42, 449-450. As to disunion, see Theodore Sedgwick to Caleb Strong, Aug. 6, 1786, *ibid.*, VIII, 415-16; James Monroe to the Governor of Virginia (Patrick Henry), Aug. 12, 1786, *ibid.*, VIII, 424-25; Timothy Bloodworth to the Governor of North Carolina (Richard Caswell), Sept. 4, 1786, *ibid.*, VIII, 462. For the rule of Sept. 1. 1786, *JCC*, XXI, 620-21.

[34] "Notes Of Debates In The Continental Congress," entry for Feb. 21, 1787, *JCC*, XXXIII, 724.

[35] *Ibid.*, XXXII, 210, 216-20; XXXIII, 734-39.

its second reading, but also recorded the receipt of a memorial from Samuel Parsons and his associates which led to the postponement of the third reading ordered for May 10. On May 9 Congress received another letter from Jay requesting "express Instructions on the Points in Difference between the United States and the Crown in Spain." On the tenth Pierce and Few of Georgia (both Convention delegates) carried the motion of April 25 repealing the order of September 1786, and on May 11 a committee on new instructions was appointed with a Southern majority.[36]

Therefore, when Congress regained its quorum July 4 the trend of congressional action was favorable to the South with respect to the Mississippi issue, unfavorable in regard to the admission of Western states. Since both strands of policy directly affected Southern prospects for becoming a majority in Congress, the overall position of the South in the Union was very much in doubt.

The first business of the reactivated Congress was to hear a report from the committee on instructions to Jay which affirmed, predictably, that it was an "indispensable obligation to preserve the right of the United States to their territorial bounds and the free Navigation of the Mississippi from its source to the Ocean . . . ."[37] One Northerner at least was not ready to concede defeat. The next day Nathan Dane wrote to Rufus King, now at the Convention in Philadelphia: "What is best for us to do about procuring an attendance of the Eastern States and to renew the subject of the S[panish] Treaty?"[38] But the stand-off achieved by Madison in April was in fact left undisturbed. "The Mississippi is where you left it; i.e. nothing has been done," Grayson wrote to Monroe on August 8. "I . . . think we are safe for the present."[39] The Mississippi question "has been dormant a considerable time," Madison wrote to Washington in October, "and seems likely to remain so."[40] In September 1788 Congress referred the matter to the new government with a declaration of opinion that free navigation

[36] JCC, XXXII, 274-83, 292, note. The members of the committee were Kearny (Delaware), Hawkins (North Carolina), Grayson (Virginia), Few (Georgia), and Pettit (Pennsylvania).
[37] Ibid., XXXII, 299-300.
[38] Dane to King, July 5, 1787, LCC, VIII, 617.
[39] Ibid., VIII, 632-33.
[40] James Madison to George Washington, Oct. 28, 1787, Gaillard Hunt (ed.), The Writings of James Madison (New York, 1900-10), V, 43.

was a clear and essential right and should be supported, thus belatedly confirming the committee report of July 4, 1787.

Dane himself joined in a more substantial concession to Southern views on Western government. The first full draft of the Northwest Ordinance, in Dane's handwriting, included a provision to admit new states when their population reached sixty thousand and completely dropped the stipulation as to the consent of a competent number of states in Congress.[41] Francis Philbrick comments: "There is no evidence on the subject, but the matter was so bitterly contested as to justify suspicion that some understanding preceded Dane's proposal of the new formula."[42]

To sum up this portion of the discussion: The foregoing pages sketch three lines of reasoning which may have led Southerners to support the Northwest Ordinance, despite its antislavery proviso. The Northwest, even without slavery, was expected to support Southern policies in Congress; the Ordinance may have been construed as a tacit endorsement of slavery in the Southwest; and the negotiations that led to the Ordinance appear to have involved an agreement to speed the admission of new states from the Northwest by lowering the population required for admission. Taken together with the continued stalemate on the issue of Mississippi navigation, the Ordinance could well have seemed a Southern victory to the Southern congressional majority.

Two qualifications need emphasis. First, in speaking of "Southerners" or "Southern attitudes" I mean to suggest only that sectional conflict was already so intense that Southern politicians as a group were conscious of defending commonly-recognized sectional interests.[43] There is no intention of obscuring the difference between Grayson and Lee on the issue of slavery, or between Lee and Blount in regard to Southwestern expansion.[44] Second, thus far

[41] The text reads (JCC, XXXII, 342): "and whenever any of the said States shall have sixty thousand free Inhabitants therein, such State shall be admitted by its Delegates into the Congress of the United States, on an equal footing with the original States, in all respects whatever."

[42] Philbrick, cclxxix.

[43] See John R. Alden, *The First South* (Baton Rouge, 1961), *passim.*

[44] A history of these events might be written from the standpoint of land speculation. Lee and his family, as well as Washington, were longtime investors in Ohio Valley lands; uncharacteristically for Southerners, both Lee and Washington opposed immediate opening of Mississippi navigation. Blount was a

I have deliberately ignored Madison's suggestion of cooperation between Congress and Convention, and approached the Northwest Ordinance as the product of sectional compromise within Congress. Whether or not the Ordinance was consciously intended to resolve problems in the Convention, it may have had that effect. We now turn to examine just what those problems were.

II

The coalition which secured the three-fifths compromise at the Convention was not a combination of "large states." It comprised the states of the South aided now by one Northern state, now by another. The key votes were on July 11, when the three-fifths rule was defeated six-four; on July 12, when it was adopted; on July 13, when it was extended to prospective Western states; and on July 14, when by a five-four vote a motion to limit representatives from the West to a number no greater than that from the original thirteen states, was beaten. The sectional pattern is obscured because South Carolina voted agains the three-fifths rule in an effort to have Negroes counted equally with whites. If South Carolina is placed in the "aye" column, one finds Virginia and the states South of it forming a solid South throughout these crucial votes.[45]

---

leading speculator in Southwestern lands and during the summer of 1787 wrote letters to the New York press from an imaginary Westerner demanding the opening of the Mississippi. Grayson held stock in the Indiana Company, as did James Wilson, who defended Westward expansion at the Convention.

[45] On July 11, Massachusetts, Pennsylvania, New Jersey, Maryland, Delaware, South Carolina, voted against the three-fifths ratio, Virginia, North Carolina, Georgia, and Connecticut voted for it. On July 12, Connecticut, Pennsylvania, Maryland, Virginia, North Carolina, and Georgia voted for it, with New Jersey and Delaware opposed, and Massachusetts and South Carolina divided. On July 13, Congress was voted "authority to regulate the number of Representatives" in new states on the basis of the three-fifths ratio by a 9-0 vote with Delaware divided. On July 14, Gerry, seconded by King, moved that "in order to secure the liberties of the States already confederated, the number of Representatives in the 1st. branch of the States which shall hereafter be established, shall never exceed in number, the Representatives from such of the States as shall accede to this confederation." Massachusetts, Connecticut, Delaware, and Maryland voted for this motion, Virginia, North Carolina, South Carolina, Georgia, and New Jersey opposed, with Pennsylvania divided. (RFC, I, 588, 597, 606; II, 3.) It should be noted that New Jersey's delegates to Congress had been instructed to oppose closure of the Mississippi, and voted accordingly in the spring of 1787.

The struggle, as Gouverneur Morris observed, was one "between the two ends of the Union."[46] Madison was still more explicit. On June 29 he stated:

> If there was real danger, I would give the smaller states the defensive weapons.—But there is none from that quarter. The great danger to our general government *is the great southern and northern interests of the continent, being opposed to each other. Look to the votes in congress, and most of them stand divided by the geography of the country, not according to the size of the states.*[47]

The next day Madison reiterated "that the States were divided into different interests not by their difference of size, but by other circumstances; the most material of which resulted partly from climate, but principally from the effects of their having or not having slaves."[48] By July 14 Madison could say that it was "pretty well understood" that the "institution of slavery & its consequences formed the line of discrimination" between the contending groups of states at the Convention.[49]

Early in July delegates' attention turned from the size of their individual states to the size, actual and anticipated, of the sections to which their states belonged. At first Madison's mention of the sectional issue was rather to soften the conflict between large and small states than to bring forward the problems between North and South. But these problems became inescapable when the committee reports of July 5 and 9 brought the Convention to grips with allotment of representation to the West and to the slave. King said in the ensuing discussion that he "was fully convinced that the question concerning a difference of interests did not lie where it had hitherto been discussed, between the great & small States; but between the Southern & Eastern."[50]

The three-fifths rule had been accepted by a nine-two vote on June 11, but it now became once more problematical, because it was connected with Western expansion. For the South, inclusion of slaves in the basis of apportionment for the House and the

[46] Speech of July 13, *RFC*, I, 604. Morris went on to say that in the sectional struggle the Middle States ought to "join their Eastern brethren."
[47] *Ibid.*, I, 476.
[48] *Ibid.*, I, 486.
[49] *Ibid.*, II, 10.
[50] Speech of July 10, *ibid.*, I, 566.

admission of Western states represented equally with the old were alternative means of strengthening its power in Congress. This was because, as Bancroft and Alden have noted, it was generally assumed that the South when strengthened by the West would become the most populous part of the country.[51] Delegate after delegate at the Convention asserted that "the Southern & Western population" would "predominate . . . in a few years," that "N.C. [,] S.C. and Georgia only will in a little time have a majority of people in America," or at least that "the people & strength of America are evidently bearing Southwardly & S. westwdly."[52] Later, at the Virginia ratifying convention, no one questioned that (as Grayson put it) "God and nature have intended . . . that the weight of population should be on this side of the continent."[53] Antifederalists reasoned from this assumption that Virginia should wait until a Southern majority in Congress made it safe to transfer power from the states to the national government. Federalist Wilson Nicholas reasoned from the identical premise to a contrary conclusion. "The influence of New England, and the other northern states is dreaded," Nicholas said,

> there are apprehensions of their combining against us. Not to advert to the improbability and illiberality of this idea it must be supposed, that our population, will in a short period, exceed theirs, as their country is well settled, and we have very extensive, uncultivated tracts. We shall soon out-number them in as great a degree as they do us at this time: therefore this government, which I trust will last to the remotest ages, will be very shortly in our favor.[54]

Nicholas' argument did not convince George Mason. Nicholas showed, stated Mason, "that though the northern states had a most decided majority against us, yet the increase of population among us would in the course of years change it in our favor. A very sound argument indeed, that we should cheerfully burn ourselves to death in hopes of a joyful and happy resurrection!"[55]

[51] Bancroft, II, 87; Alden, 13, 75, 105-06, 131.
[52] The persons quoted are Mason on July 11, Morris and Butler on July 13 (*RFC*, I, 586, 604-05). See also Madison on July 11, 14, 21 (*ibid.*, I, 584-86; II, 9-10, 81).
[53] Speech of June 14, Elliot, III, 343.
[54] Speech of June 6, *ibid.*, III, 121-22.
[55] Speech of June 11, *ibid.*, III, 260-61

The generally accepted premise that the weight of numbers was shifting from North to South gave both sections an interest in discarding the existing arrangement which gave each state one vote in Congress. Writing to Jefferson, Randolph, and Washington before the Convention met, Madison correctly predicted that proportional representation would be "recommended to the Eastern States by the actual superiority of their populousness, and to the Southern by their expected superiority."[56] This was the basis of compromise at the Convention.

It was a compromise excruciatingly difficult to formulate in detail. What was needed, as Mason said on July 11, was a system which accorded the North its present right to predominate but was so framed that when the Southern states grew larger, power would pass to them.[57] But Deep South delegates feared that the North might use even a temporary majority to force emancipation. Thus Butler of South Carolina stated: "The security the Southn. States want is that their negroes may not be taken from them which some gentlemen within or without doors, have a very good mind to do."[58] Northerners, in their turn, feared that the South and West would employ their eventual majority to oppress commerce and thrust America into needless wars. "He must be short sighted indeed," King said,

> who does not foresee that whenever the Southern States shall be more numerous than the Northern, they can & will hold a language that will awe them [the Northern states] into justice. If they threaten to separate now in case injury shall be done them, will their threats be less urgent or effectual, when force shall back their demands?[59]

Ironically, the South expected to dominate the House of Representatives while the North looked for its security to the Senate. Gouverneur Morris asserted on July 13 that he saw "the Southn. Gentlemen will not be satisfied unless they see the way

[56] Madison to Thomas Jefferson, March 19 [18], 1787, Hunt, II, 327; also same to Edmund Randolph, April 8, 1787, and to George Washington, April 16, 1787, ibid., II, 340, 345.

[57] RFC, I, 578, 586. Mason and other Southerners were insisting that a periodic census be mandatory.

[58] Speech of July 13, ibid., I, 594.

[59] Speech of July 12, ibid., I, 595-96.

open to their gaining a majority in the public Councils." This would oblige him "to vote for ye. vicious principle of equality in the 2d. branch in order to provide some defense for the N. States agst. it."[60] Madison, speaking for the South, was equally alarmed at the idea of equal representation in the Senate because of "the perpetuity it would give to the preponderance of the Northn. agst. the Southn." states. "Should a proprtl. representation take place it was true, the N. side would still out-number the other: but not in the same degree, at this time; and every day would tend towards an equilibrium."[61]

This tangle of anxieties was complicated further by the ordinance for government of the West passed by the Continental Congress in 1784. King reminded the Convention on July 6 that Congress had "impoliticly laid it [the west] out into ten States," and covenanted with the settlers to permit any Western state to enter the Union as soon as the number of its inhabitants equalled the population of the smallest of the original thirteen. Since little Delaware had only thirty-five thousand inhabitants, King conclud-ed, a large number of Western states representing very few people might soon be admitted.[62] The Senate could hardly provide a fortress for Northern interests if in the near future it were overwhelmed with twenty new senators from the West.

Thus by early July the conflict of large and small states had been partially transformed into a conflict of North and South. Georgia, the third smallest state in the Union, and South Carolina, smaller than New York or Connecticut, voted as "large" states because they expected to grow and because they expected the section of which they were a part to grow.[63] Massachusetts and Pennsylvania, the

---

[60] *Ibid.*, I, 604.

[61] Speech of July 14, *ibid.*, II, 9-10.

[62] *Ibid.*, I, 541.

[63] In a speech of June 30, Bedford observed that Georgia, South Carolina, and North Carolina behaved as large states, along with Massachusetts and Penn-sylvania, because the Southern states (with the exception of Maryland) expected to grow (RFC, I, 491). On July 2, C. Pinckney referred to Massachusetts, Penn-sylvania, Virginia, North Carolina, South Carolina, and Georgia as "the large States" (*ibid.*, I, 510), they (with the exception of Georgia, which divided) hav-ing just voted against an equality of suffrage in the Senate. Luther Martin, in his *Genuine Information*, stated that Georgia voted as a large state because it had an area larger than Great Britain and thirty times the size of Connecticut, and expected in time a population proportionate to its size (*ibid.*, III, 187).

large Northern states, voted as large states when discussion centered on the balance of power in the existing confederacy; but when Western representation came on the floor, what Bancroft called New England's "ineradicable dread of the coming power of the South-west" tended to draw them toward the "small" state position.[64] Section as well as size was involved in the great Convention crisis which led Franklin to suggest prayer and Washington (as Freeman says) to express despair in a tone he had hardly used since the worst days of the war.[65]

III

What resolved the crisis? Farrand, attempting to account for the change in the tone of the Convention after July 10, was driven to invoke the fact that the weather became cooler.[66] Bancroft, characterizing the passage of the Northwest Ordinance by a Congress racked with sectional strife, concluded that "every man that had a share in it seemed to be led by an invisible hand to do just what was wanted of him."[67] Madison's comment to Coles invites us to search for more adequate explanations by viewing as parts of one whole the events of mid-July in both New York and Philadelphia. Coles' recollection of Madison's memory of events a generation before their conversation[68] can hardly be relied on in detail. What it provides is a fresh point of departure.

The most obvious relationship between the Ordinance and the Constitution is that their fugitive slave clauses are almost identical and their clauses on the sanctity of contracts very

[64] Bancrcoft's dictum (II, 80) was illustrated when on July 5 Gouverneur Morris of Pennsylvania urged the small states to accept proportional representation but also favored "irrevocably" giving the Atlantic states more votes than new states of the West. Madison on the eleventh rightly accused him of adjusting his principles to the "points of the compass." It was Morris' plan of July 5 which two Massachusetts men moved on the fourteenth and for which both Massachusetts and Pennsylvania voted (*RFC*, I, 533-34, 584; II, 3; see also n. 45, above).

[65] Douglas S. Freeman, *George Washington, a Biography* (New York, 1948-57), VI, 100.

[66] ". . . on the night of the twelfth it turned cool" (Farrand, *Framing of the Constitution*, 104).

[67] Bancroft, II, 98.

[68] One assumes that the conversation took place when Coles was Madison's secretary, 1809-15 (E. B. Washburne, *Sketch of Edward Coles, Second Governor of Illinois* [Chicago, 1882], 18-19).

similar.[69] There can be little question that the Convention, which worded these clauses of the Constitution in August, had the Ordinance of July in mind.

There were other ways in which the documents, without duplicating each other, were clearly supplementary. Thus the Ordinance said nothing about retaining the right to the Mississippi navigation, although a clause providing that waterways leading into the Mississippi and St. Lawrence "shall be common highways, and forever free," may have been seen as a precedent.[70] But a requirement that treaties be approved by two-thirds of the Senate was inserted in the Constitution "for the express purpose of preventing a majority of the Senate . . . from giving up the Mississippi."[71] Again, the Constitution was vague about the admission of new states. The Randolph Plan said that admission should be "with the consent of a number of voices in the National legislature less than the whole"; the Committee of Detail reported that the admission of new states should require the consent of two-thirds of the members present in each branch of the legislature; and at the insistence of Gouverneur Morris, Article IV, Section 3 merely stated that "New States may be admitted by Congress into this Union."[72] On the other hand, Article I, Section 2 made it clear that the three-fifths rule for the House would apply to "the several States which may be included within this Union," the agreement voted by the Convention on July 13.[73] Southerners reading this clause in conjunction with the provision of the Ordinance that "whenever any of the said States shall have sixty thousand free Inhabitants therein, such State shall be admitted . . . on an equal footing with the original States, in all respects whatever," might well feel that

[69] Northwest Ordinance, Articles 2 and 6; United States Constitution, Article I, Section 9 and Article IV, Section 3.

[70] A resolution to this effect had been moved by Grayson, seconded by King, and passed by Congress on May 12, 1786 (*JCC*, XXX, 263).

[71] Hugh Williamson to James Madison, June 2, 1788, *LCC*, VIII, 746.

[72] *RFC*, I, 22; II, 188.

[73] Rufus King told the Senate at the time of the Missouri Compromise that the three-fifths rule was merely "a settlement between the original thirteen states," inapplicable to new ones (*ibid.*, III, 430). The Convention resolution of July 13 clearly implies that the "may be included" of Article I, Section 2 was meant to refer to new as well as old states. The Committee of Detail put it: "The members of the House of Representatives shall be chosen . . . by the people of the several States comprehended within this Union" (*ibid.*, II, 178).

they had gained their points about *both* slave representation and the equal representation of new Western states.

All this is consistent with Madison's idea of a connection in the drafting of Ordinance and Constitution. One is, therefore, led to inquire whether consultation between Congress and Convention preceded the drafting of the Northwest Ordinance on July 9-11; whether the nature of the Ordinance was such as to ease the sectional tension then troubling the Convention; and whether the essential features of the Ordinance were reported to members of the Convention in time to influence its voting on July 12-14. Since the answer to all three questions is probably, Yes, I think one can justifiably present the hypothesis that there occurred in July 1787 a sectional compromise involving Congress and Convention, Ordinance and Constitution, essentially similar to those of 1820 and 1850. The business of a hypothesis, I take it, is to present a structure of logic which accounts for the available facts, and is susceptible to proof or disproof. Evidence proving or disproving the hypothesis of a Compromise of 1787 may come to light, or have (unknown to me) already come to light, in any of some dozens of manuscript collections. The hypothesis is brought forward in the hope that such evidence will be forthcoming.

Were there "conferences and inter-communications" (to use the words Coles attributed to Madison) between Congress and Convention in early July? When the Convention adjourned for three days on July 2 to allow a committee of all the states to seek a compromise, four congressmen, three of them members of the Convention, left for New York City. It was this journey of Blount and Hawkins of North Carolina, Pierce and Few of Georgia, that enabled Congress to achieve a quorum for the first time in almost two months.[74] (The accession of the two Southern states also gave the South a majority in Congress.) Richard Henry Lee, who arrived on July 7 and took his seat on July 9, was therefore the fifth prominent Southerner to travel from Philadelphia to New York in less than a week. Hamilton, who left the Convention June 29, was in New York City by July 3.[75] On July 5 Manasseh Cutler arrived

[74] See nn. 6-8 above.

[75] On July 3 Hamilton wrote to George Washington from New York City: "I own to you Sir that I am seriously and deeply distressed at the aspects of the Councils which prevailed when I left Philadelphia" (Harold C. Syrett [ed.], *The Papers of Alexander Hamilton* [New York, 1961-   ], IV, 224).

from Massachusetts. When one recalls that Pierce, on his earlier return from the convention (June 14-18), had spoken freely of "the plans of the Southern, Eastern, or Middle States,"[76] it seems a reasonable conclusion that "conference and inter-communication" occurred.

Was the nature of the Ordinance relevant to the crisis at Philadelphia? If we can assume (as contended earlier) that the prohibition of slavery in the Northwest was not threatening to the South, then the antislavery-fugitive slave clause of the Ordinance may have reassured men like Davie and Butler, just then expressing the first apprehensions about slave property on the floor of the Convention.[77] This was the element in the putative compromise stressed in Coles' recollection. But we have Dane's testimony that the antislavery proviso was added to the Ordinance at the last moment.[78] And Deep South statements of alarm at the Convention continued unabated until the compromise on the slave trade at the end of August.[79]

More significant, surely, were the provisions of the Ordinance concerning the admission of new states. After the Ordinance passed, Dane wrote to King (as already quoted) that "the Eastern states for the sake of doing away the temporary governments, etc. established in 1784, and for establishing some order in that Country, gave up as much as could be reasonably expected." What did the North give up? It gave up its plan to require a large population for admission to statehood, and to make admission depend on the consent of a competent number of states in Congress. The Northwest

[76] See n. 6, above.
[77] See n. 5, above.
[78] Dane to King, July 16, 1787, LCC, VIII, 622. Dane says he omitted an antislavery clause from the draft reported to Congress on July 11 since only Massachusetts of the New England states was present, but that "finding the House favorably disposed" he moved its inclusion, and it was "agreed to without opposition." The draft reported on July 11 did not contain the antislavery clause (JCC, XXXII, 314-20).
[79] Another essay might be written about the compromise of late August. On August 29 Georgia, South Carolina, and North Carolina supported Gouverneur Morris' motion to strike from the Constitution the idea that new states should be admitted on terms of equality with the old (RFC, II, 454). The three Deep South states had just been gratified on the issues of slave importation (which, of course, would add to their political as well as economic strength) and fugitive slaves.

Ordinance even added that "so far as it can be consistent with the general interest of the Confederacy, such admission shall be allowed at an earlier period, and when there may be a less number of free Inhabitants in the State than sixty thousand." Philbrick, the most detailed commentator on the Ordinance, judged this to be so drastic a change in the ordinance almost passed in May that it raised a "suspicion that some understanding" was involved. If the North rather than the South made the major concession in the drafting of the Ordinance, one could make better sense of Grayson's statement to the Virginia ratifying convention that the Ordinance "passed in a lucky moment," leaving Massachusetts "extremely uneasy about it."[80]

But the admission provisions of the Ordinance spoke to the needs of North as well as South. On the one hand, given the Southern assumption that the states of the Northwest (even if non-slaveholding) would strengthen the South in Congress, the provisions for easy and early admission to statehood held out hope to the South of swiftly increasing its forces in the House of Representatives. On the other hand, however, the Ordinance wrote into law what had only been approved in principle the year before: that the Northwest would consist of three to five states rather than of ten. Thus it forestalled the prospect, threatening to the North, of losing control of the Senate. This would explain Dane's statement to King that he thought the population requirement for admission too small, "but, having divided the whole Territory into three States, this number appears to me to be less important."[81]

If (as George Mason put it) what the Convention needed was a plan that recognized the present dominance of the North while providing for eventual transition to a Southern majority, a plan, too, which safeguarded the present minority needs of the South and the future minority needs of the North, the Ordinance supplied a *deus ex machina* uncannily appropriate. The beauty of its admission requirements was that they appeared at the time to promote the South's interests in the House while protecting the North's interests in the Senate. Some necessary ambiguity remained. North as well as South hoped for the political allegiance of at least

---

[80] Speech of June 13, Elliot, III, 331.
[81] Dane to King, July 16, 1787, LCC, VIII, 622.

some of the Northwest states. The clause on slavery could be presented to Southern ratifying conventions as a guarantee of property and to Northern ratifying conventions as a bar to the creation of new slave states.[82] In place of a West vaguely attractive or dangerous, the Ordinance made available a West just sufficiently specific that each section could read in it the fulfillment of its political dreams.

Still, could the essential features of the Ordinance have become known in Philadelphia in time to affect the voting of July 12-14? The answer is, Yes. Whatever the catalyst was at the Convention, it was not yet apparent on July 10, when Washington wrote to Hamilton that matters were if anything worse than at the end of June.[83] That same afternoon, after returning to the appropriate congressional committee a draft of the Ordinance with several amendments, Manasseh Cutler left New York for Philadelphia. Arriving on the twelfth, he spent the evening at the Indian Queen tavern with delegates from the South and Massachusetts—Strong, Gerry, Gorham, Madison, Mason, Martin, Williamson, Rutledge, one of the Pinckneys—together with "Mr. Hamilton of New York," and other, unnamed persons. The morning of the fourteenth he spent with Strong, Martin, Mason, Williamson, Madison, Rutledge, and "Mr. Hamilton, all members of the Convention," before returning to New York City.[84] What better messenger could have been wished than the promoter of the Northwest Ordinance?

Cutler's references make clear that Hamilton was also in Philadelphia. He was not yet there on July 10, Cutler saw him on the twelfth and fourteenth, he did not represent New York at the Convention, and he was back in New York City by the twentieth.[85]

---

[82] Thus James Wilson told the Pennsylvania ratifying convention, December 3, 1787, that "the *new* states which are to be formed, will be under *the control* of congress in this particular; and slaves will never be introduced amongst them" (Elliot, II, 423).

[83] Washington to Hamilton, July 10, 1787, Syrett, IV, 225: "I *almost* despair. . . . I am sorry you went away. I wish you were back." At the end of July 11 the Convention "found itself without having advanced a single step" since July 5 (Farrand, *Framing of the Constitution*, 103).

[84] *Life of Cutler*, II, 242-72.

[85] Washington's letter cited in n. 83 shows that at the time on July 10 when Washington wrote, Hamilton was not in Philadelphia, at least to Washington's knowledge. On July 14 King apologized for referring to New York at the Con-

The purpose of this brief and unofficial visit is unknown. Conceivably, Hamilton left New York late enough to learn the outlines of the Ordinance and arrived in Philadelphia early enough to influence the voting of the twelfth.[86] Hamilton's good friend Gouverneur Morris closed the Convention session of July 11 on a note of intransigence and opened the next morning's session with a proposal to "bridge" the sectional conflict.[87] But at this point one moves from the realm of legitimate speculation to that of uncontrolled fantasy.

If the Northwest Ordinance did in fact influence the compromises of the Constitution, how bitter a pill for its Antifederalist sponsors, Grayson, Lee, and Melancton Smith! And that would not be the only irony. It would mean that the South, backing the Ordinance on the doubly-mistaken assumption that its security lay in the House of Representatives and that the states of the Northwest would give it strength there, had produced a charter of freedom for the Negro; but also, that this charter made possible the Constitution, which gave slavery new sanctions.

Finally, why did Congress and Convention act so differently? The evidence suggests that the motives which moved men in making Ordinance and Constitution were essentially the same. The drafters at Philadelphia were troubled about slavery as were the legislators

---

vention "in the absence of its representatives"; on July 16 Randolph speculated as to how "New York if present" would vote (*RFC*, II, 7, 18; Yates and Lansing, the other New York delegates, left July 10). On July 20 Hamilton wrote a letter to Nathaniel Mitchell from New York City (Syrett, IV, 226).

[86] He might then not only have influenced Massachusetts, Pennsylvania, Maryland, and South Carolina in altering their votes on the three-fifths rule (see n. 45, above), but also have arranged a meeting with Cutler for the twelfth. It does seem odd that at one of the tensest points in the Convention, a quarter of its membership accidentally (as Cutler's journal suggests) happened to be together and willingly idled away an evening with the visitor. See Irving Brant, *James Madison, Father of the Constitution, 1787-1800* (New York, 1950), 98-99, who asks, What brought Madison and Pinckney to the Indian Queen?, and suggests that they may have been preparing large state strategy for a last attempt to block equal suffrage in the Senate. But would they have talked to Cutler about this? My suggestion requires only that *he* talked to *them*.

[87] Morris said on the eleventh that "he could never agree to give such encouragement to the slave trade as would be given by allowing them a representation for their negroes" (*RFC*, I, 588). The next day, while still asserting that "he verily believed the people of Pena. will never agree to a representation of Negros," he proposed that taxation and representation be proportional, with the object, Madison said, "to lessen the eagerness on one side, & the opposition on the other" to the three-fifths rule (*ibid.*, I, 591-93; II, 106 and note).

in New York. But in Congress, Southerners who sought to guarantee slave property and to make possible a stronger Southern voice in Congress saw Northwest settlement, even without slavery, as a means to these ends. At the Convention, sanctions for slavery (the three-fifths clause and the slave trade clause) seemed necessary to bring about the same results: protection against emancipation and a Southern majority in the House. In each case the North made the compromises the South demanded, but in Congress, because of the South's mistaken assumptions about the future of the Northwest, an antislavery clause could be included. The fugitive slave clause adopted unanimously by both bodies shows, if not that there was a sectional compromise between Congress and Convention, at least that the makers of both Ordinance and Constitution were ready to compromise the concept that all men are equal. This was the fundamental compromise of 1787.

Quok Walker, Mumbet, and the Abolition of Slavery in Massachusetts

Arthur Zilversmit*

T HE history of the abolition of slavery in Massachusetts is shrouded in obscurity. The standard textbook story, that slavery was held to be unconstitutional by the Massachusetts courts in the case of Quok Walker, has been seriously questioned in two provocative articles: William O'Brien, S.J., "Did the Jennison Case Outlaw Slavery in Massachusetts?" and John D. Cushing, "The Cushing Court and the Abolition of Slavery in Massachusetts."[1] These articles have raised a series of questions about the nature and the finality of the Walker case and have thereby undermined the traditional interpretation of the abolition of slavery in Massachusetts.

Father O'Brien and Mr. Cushing both point out that there was not a single Quok Walker case, but rather several related legal actions: two civil suits and a criminal case. These cases began in the spring of 1781 when Nathaniel Jennison of Barre discovered that his runaway slave, Quok Walker, was working in the fields of John and Seth Caldwell. When Walker resisted Jennison's command to return to his service, Jennison beat the recalcitrant Negro, brought him home and locked him up for several hours. Walker thereupon successfully sued Jennison for assault and battery—the Worcester Court of Common Pleas ruled that Walker was not a slave and therefore not subject to Jennison's discipline. But Jennison also took his grievances to court. He sued the Caldwells for enticing away his servant and the same court that ruled for the Negro in *Walker* v. *Jennison* awarded damages to the master in the case of *Jennison* v. *Caldwell*. Because these verdicts were apparently contradictory[2] and because

* Mr. Zilversmit is a member of the Department of History, Lake Forest College. He wishes to thank Lake Forest College for a summer faculty research grant which helped in the preparation of these documents for publication.

[1] William O'Brien, S.J., "Did the Jennison Case Outlaw Slavery in Massachusetts?" *William and Mary Quarterly*, 3d Ser., XVII (1960), 219-241; John D. Cushing, "The Cushing Court and the Abolition of Slavery in Massachusetts: More Notes on the 'Quock Walker Case,'" *American Journal of Legal History*, V (1961), 118-144. My account of the Walker-Jennison cases is based on these two articles.

[2] Father O'Brien suggests that the contradictory verdicts might be explained by the fact that Jennison charged the Caldwells with enticing away his *employee* and

the court did not explain the basis for its decision in either case, these cases could not have made a contribution to determining the constitutionality of slavery in Massachusetts. Both decisions, however, were appealed.

The decisions of the Supreme Judicial Court in September 1781 resulted in some clarification. The court dismissed Jennison's appeal (his attorneys had failed to submit the required records); and it overruled the lower court decision to award damages to Jennison in his suit against the Caldwells. The court held in this case (*Caldwell* v. *Jennison*) that Walker was free and that, therefore, the Caldwells had every right to employ him.

Although the Supreme Court's action eliminated the apparent conflict between the two decisions of the lower court, it still left a great deal of ambiguity about the legal status of slavery in Massachusetts. In the appeal the attorneys covered wide ground in their arguments, debating both the scriptural and constitutional aspects of slavery, yet there is no evidence that the jury decided the case on such elevated principles. The members of the jury, not the judges, delivered the decision and the records of the case give no indication of whether the jury decided that Quok Walker was a free man on the basis of a former master's promise of manumission or because slavery was in conflict with the Massachusetts constitution of 1780.

The final case in the series involving Quok Walker and Nathaniel Jennison was a criminal case. In September 1781 Jennison had been indicted for criminal assault for his attack on Walker. Unaccountably, however, the case did not come to trial until April 1783. In this case, the issue of the constitutionality of slavery was clearly raised by one of the five judges who presided at the trial. Chief Justice William Cushing, in his charge to the jury, stated that in his opinion the clause of the constitution which declared all men to be free and equal clearly abolished slavery. Although the decision to convict Jennison was made by the jury and although Cushing was only one of five judges at the trial, it does seem clear that the question of the constitutionality of slavery had been raised during the trial, and there is a presumption that if the 1781 cases had not already established the unconstitutionality of slavery, the 1783 decision did.

Yet, as both Father O'Brien and Mr. Cushing point out, there is almost no contemporary evidence that slavery was abolished by any of the Walker-Jennison cases. Moreover, the significance of the Walker-Jennison cases is obscured by an exchange of letters between Jared Ingersoll and Charles Cushing. In 1798, Jared Ingersoll, an attorney representing the Pennsylvania Society for Promoting the Abolition of Slavery, was at-

---

that therefore Quok Walker's status as a slave was not at issue. When the case was appealed, however, the slavery issue was raised. O'Brien, "Jennison Case," 231-232.

tempting to persuade the Pennsylvania courts that slavery was unconstitutional because it was in violation of the constitution's equal rights clause.[8] He was greatly encouraged, therefore, when he heard from Judge William Cushing and Senator Theodore Sedgwick that the constitutionality of slavery had been the subject of "a solemn decision in Massachusetts." Eager to learn more about a case which must have been similar to the one in which he was engaged, Ingersoll wrote to Charles Cushing, clerk of the Supreme Judicial Court at the time the relevant case was decided.

Cushing's reply was disappointing. He told Ingersoll that "the question has never come directly before our Supreme Court." There had been a case, he recalled, in which a Negro who had run away from his master was beaten by his master in an effort to force him to return. Subsequently, the master was indicted for assault and battery. At the trial, Cushing recalled, "the counsel on Both sides were permitted [to] go into the consideration of slavery for and against as far as their Fancy would lead them . . . [and] some of the Court went largely into the consideration of slavery—and the Jury found the master guilty—but as there was nothing of that committed to writing nothing could be recorded to distinguish this case from any other common assault and Battery."[4] If either the Supreme Court decisions of 1781 or 1783 had in fact constituted "a solemn decision" on the constitutionality of slavery, its effect was limited by the fact that the written records of the case did not touch on the constitutional issue.

II

The ambiguous effects of the Walker-Jennison cases can be explained only by placing them in a wider context of earlier and contemporary litigation on the constitutionality of slavery. In almost every respect the Walker-Jennison cases resemble the "freedom suits" which became increasingly common in the Massachusetts courts in the years before the Revolution. Because Massachusetts slaves had the right to institute civil suits, numbers of them (with the aid of sympathetic attorneys) asked the courts to set them free. In many of these cases the attorneys for the Negroes argued the immorality and unconstitutionality of slavery (under the charter) but, as in the Walker-Jennison cases, the freedom suits usually involved more mundane issues as well—had the Negro been manumitted? Was his mother a slave? As was the case with Quok Walker, it is impossible to determine whether the courts in liberating these slaves re-

[8] See Arthur Zilversmit, *The First Emancipation: The Abolition of Slavery in the North* (Chicago, 1967), 204-205.

[4] The Ingersoll-Cushing exchange is reprinted in O'Brien, "Jennison Case," 221-222; Cushing, "Cushing Court," 135, prints Charles Cushing's letter.

lied on the lofty premises their attorneys raised or whether they only freed Negroes when the master's title was defective in some manner.[5] As in the Walker-Jennison cases, some observers of the pre-war freedom suits assumed that whenever the court decided that the Negro plaintiff was in fact free, the decision had been rendered on the basis of universal principles. Thus John Allen, author of a revolutionary pamphlet, congratulated the referees in a freedom case for having decided that "there was no law of the province to hold a man to serve for life."[6] There is, of course, no evidence that any of the freedom suits established that slavery *per se* was illegal.

III

Since there had been a number of slavery cases before the courts prior to the outbreak of the Revolutionary War, it was to be expected that when the courts re-opened in 1781 they would face similar cases. In May of 1781, Quok Walker instituted the first of the Worcester freedom cases, but a few weeks earlier another series of freedom cases had been instituted in the Court of Common Pleas in Berkshire County, in western Massachusetts. One of these cases involved the most prominent man of the county and in all likelihood was brought to court for the specific purpose of challenging the constitutionality of slavery in Massachusetts.

The Berkshire County freedom cases involved Negroes belonging to Colonel John Ashley of Sheffield. Colonel Ashley was one of the most distinguished and respected citizens of western Massachusetts. A wealthy landowner and merchant, he had represented Berkshire County in the legislature many times since his first term in 1750. Ashley was an officer in the colonial militia. He had been a justice of the peace and had been appointed a judge of the Berkshire Court of Common Pleas when it was first established, serving on the bench until the courts were closed at the beginning of the War for Independence. He was "patriarchal in appearance, of middling size." Known for his prudence and for his careful conduct of his business affairs, he began life "with a reasonable capital, which he increased by industry and good management."[7]

[5] Zilversmit, *First Emancipation*, 103-104; see also L. Kinvin Wroth and Hiller B. Zobel, eds., *Legal Papers of John Adams* (Cambridge, Mass., 1965), II, 48-67.

[6] [John Allen], *The Watchman's Alarm to Lord N . . . . H . . .* (Salem, Mass., 1774), 28n.

[7] Henry W. Taft, "Judicial History of Berkshire," Berkshire Historical Society, *Collections*, I (1892), 104-105; *History of Berkshire County, Massachusetts, With Biographical Sketches of its Prominent Men* (New York, 1885), I, 328, 330; Hamilton Child, comp., *Gazetteer of Berkshire County, Mass. 1725-1885* (Syracuse, 1885), 48, 349-350; Franklin B. Dexter, *Biographical Sketches of the Graduates of Yale College . . .* (New York, 1885-1913) I, 405-406.

The first of Colonel Ashley's freedom cases began in April 1781 when Zach Mullen accused Ashley of assault and abduction, much in the same manner as Quok Walker had accused Nathaniel Jennison. The records of the case are quite sketchy:

Zach Mullen of Sheffield in said County of Berkshire a Negro Man and a Labourer Plaintiff against John Ashley of the same Sheffield Esq. Defendant. In a plea of Trespass for that the said John Ashley at said Sheffield on the twenty fifth day of October last past, with force and Arms, an Assault did make on him the said Zach Mullen, and him the said Zach Mullen did beat, wound and Abuse, take and Imprison there for a long time (to wit) from the said twenty fifth day of October, untill the twenty sixth day of March current, and other outrages on him the said Zach Mullen then and there committed against our Peace and to the Damage of the said Zach Mullen (as he saith) the sum of nine pounds and nineteen shillings. The parties appear and this Case is continued by order of Court to the next term of holding this Court.[8]

When the Court of Common Pleas met in August 1781 the case was postponed again, by agreement between the parties.[9] In February 1782 the case came up once more, as follows: "Zach Mullen Plaintiff against John Ashley Esq. Defendant. In a plea of Trespass etc. see the Records of the last Session of this Court. The said Zach Mullen is three times solemnly called to come into Court, but comes not, and said John Ashley being also called, comes not, but makes Default of appearance here; Wherefore it is considered by the Court, that in this Case neither Plaintiff nor Defendant have any further Day in said Court."[10]

Since neither Zach Mullen nor Colonel Ashley appeared at the February session of the Court of Common Pleas, they must have worked out a satisfactory solution outside the courtroom.[11] The decision to postpone the case in August reflects the fact that the parties to the case were working out an agreement and that this agreement would undoubtedly be influenced by the court's decision in another freedom suit which Colonel Ashley was contesting while the Mullen case was still pending. This was the case of Elizabeth Freeman, affectionately known as Mumbet.

[8] Berkshire Court of Common Pleas, Manuscript Record Book 4A, 24, Superior Court Clerk's Office, Pittsfield, Massachusetts.

[9] *Ibid.*, 53.

[10] *Ibid.*, 237.

[11] Ashley apparently bore no grudge against his former slave; he left Zach Mullen and two other former slaves a legacy in his last will. Codicil to will, dated November 12, 1799, file no. 2195, Berkshire County Court House, Pittsfield, Massachusetts.

In later life, Mumbet was the beloved servant of the Sedgwick family of Stockbridge and her story is celebrated in Berkshire County folklore. She was born in Columbia County, New York, as the property of a Mr. Hogeboom, and became the slave of Colonel Ashley at an early age, probably as a result of Ashley's marriage to Annetje Hogeboom. Among the many stories told of Mumbet is how she shielded her younger sister from the wrath of Mrs. Ashley, intercepting a blow with a heated kitchen shovel wielded by the irate mistress and intended for the younger girl. According to folklore, this cruelty prompted Elizabeth to flee the Ashley household, forcing the colonel to sue for her return. This is unlikely, since the subsequent litigation was instituted by the slave, not the master, and did not involve charges of assault or cruelty. According to Catherine Sedgwick the novelist, Elizabeth was prompted to sue for her freedom after hearing the words of the Declaration of Independence.[12] It is also possible that a group of prominent residents of Berkshire County selected Elizabeth and a Negro man, Brom, who was associated with her in her suit, in order to determine whether or not slavery was constitutional in Massachusetts after the adoption of the new constitution.

Elizabeth Freeman's suit (known as *Brom and Bett* v. *Ashley*) attracted the most talented members of the bar. The defendant was himself a prominent lawyer. The attorneys for the plaintiffs were Theodore Sedgwick and Tapping Reeve. Sedgwick was at the beginning of a brilliant career. He had already served a term in the state legislature and he would go on to serve several more before moving on to the national political scene as United States Senator from Massachusetts. In his later years, Sedgwick served as a justice of the Massachusetts Supreme Court.[18] Tapping Reeve was one of the most influential legal minds of his day. As founder of the famed Litchfield (Connecticut) Law School he trained many of the leading American lawyers of the age.[14] Ashley was represented by David Noble, who later served as a judge of the Court of

[12] Mumbet's story has been told by two of the Sedgwicks: Catherine Sedgwick, "Slavery in New England," *Bentley's Miscellany,* XXXIV (1853), 417-424; and [Theodore Sedgwick], *The Practicability of the Abolition of Slavery: A Lecture Delivered at the Lyceum in Stockbridge, Massachusetts, February, 1831* (New York, 1831), 13-18.

[18] See Richard E. Welch, Jr., *Theodore Sedgwick, Federalist: A Political Portrait* (Middletown, Conn., 1965), 10-11, and *passim.*

[14] Reeve was associated with Sedgwick in another important case before the courts of Berkshire County. See David S. Boardman, "Sketches of the Early Lights of the Litchfield Bar," in Dwight C. Kilbourn, *The Bench and Bar of Litchfield, Connecticut, 1709-1909 . . .* (Litchfield, 1909), 42-44; see George E. Woodbine in *DAB* s.v. "Reeve, Tapping."

Common Pleas, and John Canfield, a leading lawyer of Sharon, Connecticut.[15]

The case began when the attorneys for the Negroes obtained a writ of replevin from the Berkshire County Court of Common Pleas.[16] This writ, an action for the recovery of property, was instituted on the grounds that the Negroes were not the legitimate property of the men who held them. Addressed to the county sheriff, the writ ordered

that justly and without delay you should cause to be replevied, Brom a Negro Man of Sheffield in our said County Labourer, and Bett a Negro Woman of Sheffield aforesaid Spinster; whom John Ashley Esquire and John Ashley Junior Esquire both of Sheffield aforesaid have taken and being so taken detain (as it is said) unless they were taken by our special command, or by the command of our Chief Justice, as for Homicide, or for any other just cause, whereby according to the Usage of this Commonwealth they are not Replevisable, or that you should signify to use the cause, wherefore the said John Ashley and said John Ashley Junior have taken, and so detain their said Brom and Bett.

When the sheriff asked for the release of Brom and Bett, however, Colonel Ashley refused to release them, stating "that the said Brom and Bett were his Servants for Life, thereby claiming a right of servitude in the Persons of the said Brom and Bett."

When, after several attempts,[17] the Ashleys remained firm in their refusal to release Brom and Bett, the stage was set for the issues to come to trial. The court ordered the release of the Negroes, if they could post bonds to guaranty that they would prosecute their case, and told the sheriff to issue a summons to the Ashleys to appear at the next regular session of the Court of Common Pleas on August 21.

When the trial opened, the attorneys for the Ashleys asked for a dismissal and abatement on the grounds that "the said Brom and Bett, are and were at the time of Issuing the original Writ, the legal Negro Servants of the said John Ashley during their Lives, and this the said John is ready to verify, and here of prays the Judgment of this Court, and that the said Suit may be abated." The attorneys for the Negroes replied that the suit should not be abated because Brom and Bett were not "the Negro

[15] Dexter, *Biographical Sketches*, III, 78; II, 736-737.
[16] "A form of action which lies to regain the possession of personal chattels which have been taken from the plaintiff unlawfully," John Bouvier, *Bouvier's Law Dictionary and Concise Encyclopedia*, 8th ed. (Kansas City, Mo., 1914), III, 2890.
[17] The Negroes obtained a pluries writ of replevin on May 28, 1781; the word "pluries" is used when two previous writs have proven ineffective. *Ibid.*, 2612.

Servants or Servants of . . . John Ashley during their lives." After "a full hearing of this Case," it was submitted to the jury, which accepted the claims of the plaintiffs, ruling that "the said Brom and Bett are not and were not at the time of the purchase of the original Writ the legal Negro Servants of him the said John Ashley during life and Assess thirty shillings damages."

The Court "adjudged and determined" in accordance with the jury's verdict that Brom and Bett were free and accepted the jury's recommendation that the Ashleys pay Brom and Bett thirty shillings damages. In addition, the Court assessed the Ashleys the cost of the suit—"five pounds, fourteen shillings, and four pence." Colonel Ashley thereupon served notice that he would appeal this decision at the next session of the Supreme Judicial Court in Berkshire County, and he posted the required appeal bonds.[18]

The Court of Common Pleas held that Brom and Bett were free, but, as in the case of Quok Walker (and the pre-Revolutionary freedom suits), the basis for the court's decision is not given. In one sense, however, the Berkshire County case was less confusing than the Worcester cases—in the case of Brom and Bett there was no promised manumission to cloud the issue. Sedgwick and Reeve do not seem to have argued that there was a defect in Ashley's title to the services of Brom and Bett and therefore the implication is that they argued that under the new constitution no title to a slave could be held valid.[19] Nonetheless, Ashley appealed and a final decision would not be reached until October 1781, when the Supreme Court's circuit would bring it to Berkshire County.

But when the Supreme Court was prepared to hear the case a few weeks after the verdict of the Court of Common Pleas, the case took an unexpected twist, as the record shows:

John Ashley of Sheffield in the County of Berkshire, Esquire Appellant vs. Brom, a negro man and Bett a negro woman, both of Sheffield aforesaid, Appellees, from the Judgment of an Inferior Court of Common pleas, holden at Great Barrington in and for the County of Berkshire on the third Tuesday of August last when and where the Appellees were Plaintiffs, and the Appellant was defendant in a plea of Replevin etc. in the Writ on file, bearing the date the 28th day of May AD. 1781. is at

---

[18] Berkshire Court Record Book 4A, 55-57. The record was published by James M. Rosenthal, "Free Soil in Berkshire County, 1781," *New England Quarterly*, X (1937), 783-785.

[19] Sedgwick's biographer asserts that the case was argued on constitutional grounds. See Richard E. Welch, Jr., "Mumbet and Judge Sedgwick, A Footnote to the Early History of Massachusetts Justice," *Boston Bar Journal*, VIII (1964), 13-14.

large set forth: At which said Inferior Court Judgement was rendered that the said Brom and Bett, are not nor were they, at the time of the purchase of the Original Writ, the legal negro Servants of the said John Ashley, during life, and that the [said] Brom and Bett do recover against the said John Ashley the sum of thirty shillings lawful silver money damages, and the Costs; And now the parties appeared and the Appellant by John Canfield, Esquire his Attorney, confesses Judgment for thirty shillings damage and Cost of suit; It is therefore considered by the Court, that the said Brom and Bett recover against the said John Ashley the sum of thirty shillings lawful money damage and Costs of Suit.[20]

John Ashley had not merely dropped his appeal (as Nathaniel Jennison did in the case of *Walker* v. *Jennison*) but he confessed judgment—that is, he assented to the lower court ruling that Brom and Bett were not slaves. Why did Ashley change his mind about the case between August and October? In all likelihood Ashley accepted the decision of the lower court in October because a few weeks earlier the Supreme Court had ruled in the case of *Caldwell* v. *Jennison* that slavery was unconstitutional in Massachusetts. Since the constitutionality of slavery was probably the only issue in the case of *Brom and Bett* v. *Ashley,* there was no point in pursuing the case after the court had rendered its decision in the Caldwell case. Similarly, Ashley settled his case with Zach Mullen, having agreed to postpone it twice before while waiting for the court to rule on the constitutionality of slavery.

This explanation still leaves several unresolved questions. Why did Charles Cushing make his evasive reply to Jared Ingersoll in 1798? Both Theodore Sedgwick (who had been one of the attorneys in the Berkshire County freedom suit) and William Cushing (who had been Chief Justice at the time the Worcester cases were decided) assured Ingersoll that the constitutionality of slavery had received "a solemn decision," and yet the clerk of the court, brother of the Chief Justice, could not confirm this statement. Yet, Cushing did not deny his brother's claim; he merely asserted that nothing had been put into the record to clearly state that

[20] The records of the case are preserved in the Office of the Clerk of the Supreme Judicial Court for Suffolk County, Suffolk County Courthouse, Boston, Massachusetts. A brief statement of the case is found in "Minute Books of the Superior Court of Judicature, 1789-1794," Box 20, 1. The full record of the case in the Supreme Court is in a manuscript volume, "Supreme Judicial Court, 1781-1782," 96. "Court Files, Suffolk," Vol. 1192, case no. 159966, contains a copy of the pluries writ, with a notation on the reverse that it was delivered June 5, 1781, a record of the pleadings at the trial in the lower court, a copy of the inferior court trial judgment, a statement that Ashley posted bond to guarantee that he would prosecute his appeal, a copy of the verdict of the jury at the first trial, and a statement of costs, totalling £7 10s. 4d.

slavery was unconstitutional. But this was to be expected. The Supreme Court was composed of five judges, each of whom could give an interpretation of the relevant law to the jury, perhaps disagreeing on fundamental points. It was the jury, and not the panel of judges, who delivered the verdict. This was not a system which lent itself to the establishment of clear rulings on difficult points of constitutional interpretation. Moreover, there was as yet no formal system of reporting court decisions, and precedents established during one session of the court might easily be forgotten several years later.[21] But John Ashley's decision to confess judgment a few weeks after the court's ruling in *Caldwell* v. *Jennison* shows that one well-informed lawyer, interested in testing the constitutionality of slavery, was willing to accept the court's ruling as "a solemn decision."

Another question still remains to be answered. If the 1781 decision in *Caldwell* v. *Jennison* established the unconstitutionality of slavery in Massachusetts, why did the Commonwealth revive its criminal case against Jennison in 1783? John D. Cushing's explanation is the most plausible. He argues that Jennison probably failed to prosecute his appeal in the case of *Walker* v. *Jennison* as a result of an agreement whereby all the issues would be presented to the Supreme Court in the single case of *Caldwell* v. *Jennison*. This would avoid the conflicting judgments obtained at the inferior court level. But in June of 1782 Jennison, a poor loser, asked the legislature for permission to re-institute the appeal he had forfeited when his attorneys had not produced the necessary records in September 1781. At the same time the legislature was considering several other petitions on slavery, without taking any definitive action. In this atmosphere of uncertainty, and with Jennison's having broken an agreement not to pursue his appeal in the Walker case, it was thought advisable to clarify the issue once more judicially, and this the court did in *Commonwealth* v. *Jennison*, the case in which Chief Justice Cushing delivered his famous anti-slavery charge to the jury.[22]

It is true, as both Father O'Brien and Mr. Cushing have pointed out, there is surprisingly little contemporary evidence to show that the court's

[21] See "Introduction," Wroth and Zobel, eds., *Adams Legal Papers*, I, xxxviii-lii, for a description of court procedures before the Revolution, procedures which were not changed in the early years of independence. See also Frank W. Grinnell, "The Constitutional History of the Supreme Court of Massachusetts from the Revolution to 1813," *Massachusetts Law Quarterly*, II (1916-17), 474-475. William G. McLoughlin, "The Balkcom Case (1782) and the Pietistic Theory of Separation of Church and State," *Wm. and Mary Qtly.*, 3d Ser., XXIV (1967), 278-279, shows how difficult it was to establish a consistent interpretation of the constitution in the area of religious freedom.
[22] Cushing, "Cushing Court," 130.

decision in *Caldwell* v. *Jennison* ended slavery in Massachusetts. But the action of Colonel John Ashley, in dropping his appeal in *Brom and Bett* v. *Ashley,* would indicate that a month after the court's historic decision at least one master accepted that decision as final and binding. If, as I believe, the case of *Brom and Bett* v. *Ashley* was arranged as a test for the constitutionality of slavery, then the decision of Ashley to confess judgment marked a formal recognition of the abolition of slavery in Massachusetts.[23]

[23] The Supreme Court's decision may also have been instrumental in another case in neighboring Hampshire County. A Negro, Tony, sued Ezra Clapp of Westfield, alleging that Clapp had illegally seized and held him. Tony obtained a writ of replevin and the case was brought before the Hampshire County Court of Common Pleas in August 1781 and postponed. In November 1781, when the case was called, Clapp did not appear, and the court awarded damages and costs to the Negro. It may well be that Clapp, like Ashley, interpreted the decision in *Caldwell* v. *Jennison* as abolishing slavery, and therefore abandoned the case after that decision. See *Tony* v. *Clapp,* Inf. Courts General Sessions, 1771-1781, Record Book 13, 204, 216, Superior Court Clerk's Office, Northampton, Massachusetts.

Was Slavery Unconstitutional Before the Thirteenth Amendment?: Lysander Spooner's Theory of Interpretation

Randy E. Barnett[*]

INTRODUCTION

In 1843, radical abolitionist William Lloyd Garrison called the Constitution of the United States, "a covenant with death and an agreement with hell."[1] Why? Because it sanctioned slavery, one of the greatest crimes that one person can commit against another. Slavery was thought by abolitionists to be a violation of the natural rights of man so fundamental that, as Lincoln once remarked: "If slavery were not wrong, nothing is wrong."[2] Yet the original U.S. Constitution was widely thought to have sanctioned this crime. Even today, many still believe that, until the ratification of the Thirteenth Amendment prohibiting involuntary servitude, slavery previously had been constitutional, and for this reason, the original Constitution was deeply flawed.

But in 1845 one man disagreed with the conventional wisdom. That man insisted that slavery was not only a moral abomination; it was also *unconstitutional*. His name was Lysander Spooner and he defended this position in a book, entitled *The Unconstitutionality of Slavery*.[3] While rejecting his conclusion, Garrison wrote of Spooner's argument: "We admit Mr. Spooner's reasoning to be ingenious— perhaps, as an effort in logic, unanswerable."[4]

Historians of abolitionism know Spooner's name,[5] but lawyers, law professors[6] and their students generally do not. This is a pity. For Lysander Spooner deserves a

---

[*]   Austin B. Fletcher Professor, Boston University School of Law. This Essay is based upon a lecture given at the University of the Pacific, McGeorge School of Law, on March 13, 1997 as part of the Distinguished Speakers Series. It was also presented in faculty workshops at Boston University and the Roger Williams School of Law. © 1997 Randy E. Barnett. Permission to photocopy for classroom use is hereby granted.

1.   *Resolution adopted by the Antislavery Society*, Jan. 27, 1843 ("The compact which exists between the North and the South is a covenant with death and an agreement with hell.").

2.   Letter by Abraham Lincoln to A.G. Hodges, Apr. 4, 1864.

3.   LYSANDER SPOONER, *The Unconstitutionality of Slavery* (1845), *reprinted in* 4 THE COLLECTED WORKS OF LYSANDER SPOONER (Charles Shively ed., 1971) [hereinafter WORKS].

4.   LYSANDER SPOONER, *The Unconstitutionality of Slavery* (1860), 4 WORKS, *supra* note 3 (This quote is taken from an unnumbered page).

5.   *See, e.g.*, ROBERT COVER, JUSTICE ACCUSED: ANTISLAVERY AND THE JUDICIAL PROCESS 154-58 (1975) (discussing Spooner's views on the unconstitutionality of slavery).

6.   A Westlaw search (Lysander +2 Spooner) conducted on March 7, 1997 turned up 37 articles by 32 authors referring to Spooner's writings on a number of subjects, some by law professors and some student notes. Most consist of no more than a sentence or two. Perhaps the most extensive discussion of Spooner's views on interpretation is contained in Hans W. Baade, *"Original Intent" in Historical Perspective: Some Critical Glosses*, 69 TEX. L. REV. 1001, 1046-51 (1991).

place of honor among American lawyers, both for the principles for which he stood against the crowd and for the brilliance with which he defended those principles. In this Essay, though I will be unable to do his analysis complete justice, I want to describe the method of constitutional interpretation that led Spooner to his conclusion about slavery. In many ways, Spooner's interpretive approach has a very modern ring. In important respects, however, his approach is preferable to those commonly used today and worthy of study for this reason alone.

But before I present Spooner's views, I want to tell you something about the life of this remarkable individual.

I. SPOONER'S LIFE AND CAREER[7]

Lysander Spooner was born January 19, 1808, on his father's farm in rural New England near Athol, Massachusetts. Raised as one of nine children, Spooner left home to live in nearby Worcester where, in 1833, he began studying law in the offices of John Davis, a prominent Massachusetts politician who shortly thereafter served as Governor and then Senator. In Davis' absence, Spooner also studied with Charles Allen, a state senator who eventually served as Chief Justice of the Massachusetts Supreme Court.

The rules of the Massachusetts courts in those days required a student to study in a lawyer's office before admission to the bar. College graduates were required to study for three years, while non-graduates were required to do so for five years. Spooner's first act as a lawyer was to challenge what he thought was a rule that discriminated against the poor. After just three years of study, with encouragement from both Davis and Allen (who had graduated from Yale and Harvard respectively), Spooner set up his practice in Worcester in open defiance of the rules. Spooner published a petition in the local newspaper and sent copies of it to each member of the state legislature. He argued that "no one has yet ever dared advocate, in direct terms, so monstrous a principle as that the rich ought to be protected by law from the competition of the poor."[8] In 1836, the legislature abolished the restriction.

Spooner's writing career began at about the same time as his legal one, with essays criticizing Christianity from a deistic perspective.[9] Possibly in part for this reason, his law practice did not flourish and, in 1836, he left Massachusetts to make his fortune in "the West"—meaning in this case, Ohio. There, Spooner vied with other speculators of the time to buy land where future cities would spring up. He

---

7. Except as noted, the biographical information in this section comes from Shively, *Biography, in* 1 WORKS, *supra* note 3, at 15-62. For an intellectual biography focusing more on the evolution of Spooner's views, see James J. Martin, *Lysander Spooner, Dissident Among Dissidents, in* MEN AGAINST THE STATE 167-201 (1970).

8. 1 WORKS, *supra* note 3, at 18.

9. *See* LYSANDER SPOONER, *The Deist's Immortality, and An Essay On Man's Accountability For His Belief* (1834), *reprinted in* 1 WORKS, *supra* note 3; LYSANDER SPOONER, *The Deist's Reply to the Alleged Supernatural Evidences of Christianity* (1836), *reprinted in* 1 WORKS, *supra* note 3.

purchased a tract along the Maumee River for a town called Gilead, which today is named Grand Rapids, Ohio. But Gilead lost out to better connected rivals and a general real estate collapse, so that by 1840, Spooner returned to his father's farm.

After writing about how the banking system should be reformed to avoid the kind of speculative collapse he had experienced,[10] Spooner struck out in an entirely new direction: In 1844, he founded the American Letter Mail Company to contest the U.S. Post Office's monopoly on the delivery of first class mail. Postal rates in those years were notoriously high and several companies arose to challenge the government's monopoly. As he had when he confronted restrictions on entering the Massachusetts bar, Spooner vigorously defended his action with a pamphlet entitled, *The Unconstitutionality of the Laws of Congress Prohibiting Private Mails.*[11] Unfortunately, this time he was up against a more intransigent foe. Although Spooner's mail company was very successful, legal challenges by the government soon exhausted his financial resources and by July, 1844 his business was all but defunct without his ever having the opportunity to fully litigate his constitutional claims.

It was after this dispiriting experience that Spooner returned to Athol and began writing about slavery. With financial assistance from wealthy New York philanthropist and abolitionist Gerrit Smith, Spooner produced the first volume of *The Unconstitutionality of Slavery* in 1845. Spooner's arguments drew criticism to be sure, especially from abolitionist Wendell Phillips,[12] to which in 1847 he responded

---

10. *See* LYSANDER SPOONER, *Constitutional Law, Relative To Credit, Currency, and Banking* (1843), *reprinted in* 5 WORKS, *supra* note 3; LYSANDER SPOONER, *Poverty: Its Illegal Causes, and Legal Cure* (1846), *reprinted in* 5 WORKS, *supra* note 3.

11. *See* LYSANDER SPOONER, *The Unconstitutionality of the Laws of Congress, Prohibiting Private Mails* (1844), *reprinted in* 1 WORKS, *supra* note 3.

12. *See* WENDELL PHILLIPS, REVIEW OF LYSANDER SPOONER'S ESSAY ON THE UNCONSTITUTIONALITY OF SLAVERY (1847) (reprint ed. 1969) [hereinafter PHILLIPS, REVIEW OF SPOONER]. Phillips' essay ran 95 pages and was subsequently republished in 4 MASS. Q. REV. 3 (1851). Phillips' critical reaction to Spooner's essay was predictable insofar as "the chief target of Lysander Spooner's monograph . . . had been Wendell Phillips's tract espousing the contrary thesis of the Constitution as a pro-slavery compact." Baade, *supra* note 6, at 1049 (referring to THE CONSTITUTION: A PRO-SLAVERY COMPACT: OR SELECTIONS FROM THE MADISON PAPERS [Anti-slavery Examiner— No. XI, 1844; 2d ed. 1845] which had been authored by Phillips). Nonetheless, the popularity and influence of Part I of Spooner's book within abolitionist circles, if no other, is evidenced both by the length and obvious care of Phillips' reply, by his reference therein to Spooner's "much-praised essay," (PHILLIPS, REVIEW OF SPOONER, at 69), and by the fact that Phillips published his pamphlet "at his own expense." CARLOS MARTYN, WENDELL PHILLIPS: THE AGITATOR 216 (1890).

in a second, entirely new volume of the book which was appended to the first.[13] The entire work runs nearly 300 pages.

The passion of Spooner's opposition to slavery is evidenced by his conspiratorial efforts to free the captured John Brown. He had met Brown shortly before Brown's ill-fated raid on Harper's Ferry, and afterwards attempted to implement a plan in which radical abolitionists would kidnap the governor of Virginia and hold him hostage for Brown's release. The plan was never acted upon, though Spooner's associates had gone so far as to locate a boat and crew. Spooner also provided legal arguments to aid abolitionists charged with violating the Fugitive Slave Act, and his work on behalf of such defendants led him in 1854 to publish a book, *Trial by Jury*,[14] in which he defended as essential to a free society the jury's role as triers of both fact and law—the position sometimes referred to as "jury nullification."

Until his death in 1887 at the age of 79, Spooner eked out an impoverished existence as a writer, activist, and legal theorist. His writings were extensive, including a lengthy, though never-completed, book defending intellectual property.[15] At a memorial service in his honor the following resolution was passed:

> *Resolved:* That while he fought this good fight and kept the faith, he did not finish his course, for his goal was in the eternities; that, starting in his youth in pursuit of truth, he kept it up through a vigorous manhood, undeterred by poverty, neglect, or scorn, and in his later life relaxed his energies not one jot; that his mental vigor seemed to grow as his physical powers declined; that although, counting his age by years, he was an octogenarian, we chiefly mourn his death, not as that of an old man who has completed his task, but as that of the youngest man among us,—youngest because, after all that he had done, he still had so much service that the best we can do in his memory is to take up his work where he was forced to drop it, carry on with all that

---

13.   Although Spooner and Phillips were locked in debate, given the close timing and multiple publications of their respective essays, the number of revised editions in which additional material was added, and the rarity and imprecision of citation practices in those days, it is not entirely clear at any given point who was responding to which work of the other. Phillips does once mention a "second edition" by Spooner (PHILLIPS, REVIEW OF SPOONER, *supra* note 12, at 53), but the reference to which he refers in Spooner appears in a footnote in Part I (of the 1860 revised edition)—a footnote apparently added in a "second edition" which appeared sometime before Part II was published in 1847. Although James J. Martin says Part II was initially published in 1846 and then attached to Part I in 1847, he consults the 1856 edition of Part II, owing to the fact of "the 1846 edition being especially scarce." MARTIN, *supra* note 3, at 180 n.52. In contrast, on the page facing the reproduction of the 1860 edition, Charles Shively notes that "Part II first appears in 1847, both separately and with Part I." 4 WORKS, *supra* note 3. Moreover, 1847 is its copyright date. Perhaps Martin, not having seen the 1846 edition confused a "second edition" of Part I appearing in 1846 with Part II. Moreover, throughout Phillips' essay, he never refers to any page number in Part II of Spooner's book. In contrast, several arguments in Part II of Spooner's book, indeed entire chapters, are clearly responding to arguments advanced in Phillips' 1847 review. Thus, it appears that Part II of Spooner's work was responding to Phillips review of Part I.

14.   LYSANDER SPOONER, *An Essay on the Trial by Jury* (1852), *reprinted in* 2 WORKS, *supra* note 3.

15.   LYSANDER SPOONER, *The Law of Intellectual Property; or An Essay on the Right of Authors and Inventors to a Perpetual Property in Their Ideas, Vol. I* (1855), *reprinted in* 3 WORKS, *supra* note 3.

we can summon of his energy and indomitable will, and as old age creeps upon us, not lay the harness off, but following his example and Emerson's advice, "obey the voice at eve obeyed at prime."

In the spirit of that resolution let us now consider Lysander Spooner's approach to constitutional interpretation that led him to conclude that slavery was unconstitutional.[16]

II. LEGAL INDETERMINACY AND NEED FOR NATURAL LAW

In setting out his method of constitutional interpretation, Spooner was under no illusions about the determinacy of written texts. Indeed, it was the indeterminacy of written words that Spooner thought gave rise to the need for a theory of interpretation. "The words, in which statutes and constitutions are written," he observed

> are susceptible of so many different meanings,—meanings widely different from, often directly opposite to, each other, in their bearing on men's rights,—that, unless there were some rule of interpretation for determining which of these various meanings are the true ones, there could be no certainty at all as to the meaning of the statutes and constitutions themselves.[17]

As an example of this in the Constitution, he offered the word "free."

> Yet, the word *free* is capable of some ten or twenty different senses. So that, by changing the sense of that single word, some ten or twenty different constitutions would be made out of the same written instrument. But there are, we will suppose, a thousand other words in the constitution, each of which is capable of from two to ten different senses. So that, by changing the sense of only a single word at a time, several thousands of different constitutions would be made.[18]

---

16. In what follows, I include far more and longer quotes from Spooner than is common in a law review article. I do so because, to the extent possible in an essay of this kind, I want the reader to hear Spooner in his own voice.

17. LYSANDER SPOONER, *The Unconstitutionality of Slavery* 137 (rev. ed. 1860), *reprinted in* 4 WORKS, *supra* note 3 [hereinafter SPOONER, *The Unconsistutionality of Slavery*]. Page numbers are to the 1860 "enlarged edition" as reprinted in 4 WORKS, *supra* note 3, which includes both the original version published in 1845, the second part published in 1847, additional appendices, and reviews of earlier editions. This edition, published in Boston, sold for $1.00 in cloth and 75¢ in paper.

18. *Id.* at 138.

Without some way of ascertaining a single meaning, therefore, the whole point of adopting a written statute or constitution would be defeated. "[E]ach written law, in order to be law, must be taken only in some *one* definite and distinct sense; and that definite and distinct sense must be selected from the almost infinite variety of senses which its words are capable of."[19] Spooner then asked, "How is this selection to be made?"[20] For his answer, he turned to natural law.

By natural law Spooner meant a "universal principle of moral obligation, that arises out of the nature of men and their relations to each other, and to other things— and [which] is consequently as unalterable as the nature of men."[21] This he called "the rule, principle, obligation or requirement of natural justice."[22] And the requirement of natural justice "has its origin in the natural rights of individuals, results necessarily from them, keeps them ever in view as its end and purpose, secures their enjoyment, and forbids their violation."[23] Put another way, "this natural law is no other than that rule of natural justice, which results either directly from men's natural rights, or from such acquisitions as they have a *natural* right to make, or from such contracts as they have a *natural* right to enter into."[24]

Years later, Spooner explained his conception of natural law as follows:

The science of mine and thine—the science of justice—is the science of all human rights; of man's rights of person and property; of all his rights to life, liberty, and the pursuit of happiness.

It is the science which alone can tell any man what he can, and cannot, do; what he can, and cannot, have; what he can, and cannot, say, without infringing the rights of any other person.

It is the science of peace; and the only science of peace; since it is the science of which alone can tell us on what conditions mankind can live in peace, or ought to live in peace, with each other.

These conditions are simply these: viz., first that each man shall do, towards every other, all that justice requires him to do; as for example, that he shall pay his debts, that he shall return borrowed or stolen property to its owner, and that he shall make reparation for any injury he may have done to the person or property of another.

The second condition is, that each man shall abstain from doing, to another, anything which justice forbids him to do; as, for example, that he shall abstain from committing theft, robbery, arson, murder, or any other crime against the person or property of another.

---

19. *Id.* at 138-39.
20. *Id.*
21. *Id.* at 5-6.
22. *Id.* at 6.
23. *Id.*
24. *Id.* at 7.

So long as these conditions are fulfilled, men are at peace, and ought to remain at peace, with each other. But when either of these conditions is violated, men are at war. And they must necessarily remain at war until justice is re-established.[25]

The "science of justice," then, was to figure out the preconditions of peace.[26]

Although Spooner wrote in a day when, especially among abolitionists, natural law and natural rights were more familiar than they are today, he did not assume his audience understood these concepts or accepted them. Instead, he explained why an appeal to natural law and natural rights was both inescapable and feasible. Spooner argued that statutes and constitutions must be consistent with natural justice as defined by natural rights because only by so doing would such statutes or constitutions be binding on the citizenry:

Natural justice is either law, or it is not. If it be law, it is always law, and nothing inconsistent with it can ever be made law. If it be not law, then we have no law except that which is prescribed by the reigning power of the state; and all idea of justice being any part of our system of law, any further than it may be specially prescribed, ought to be abandoned; and government ought to acknowledge that its authority rests solely on its power to compel submission, and that there is not necessarily any *moral obligation of obedience* to its mandate.

Putting the matter more succinctly, Spooner wrote: "If legislation be consistent with natural justice, and the natural or intrinsic obligation of the contract of government, it is *obligatory*: if not, not."[27]

For Spooner, then, the choice was a conception of law that was consistent with natural justice, which would then carry with it a duty of obedience, or a conception of law based solely on the successful imposition of power, which there would be no moral duty to obey. "If physical power be the fountain of all law, then law and force are synonymous terms. Or, perhaps, rather, law would be the result of a combination of will and force; of will, united with a physical power sufficient to compel

---

25. Lysander Spooner, *Natural Law; or The Science of Justice* (1882), *reprinted in* 1 Works, *supra* note 3, at 5-6.

26. As might be expected, Spooner thought that "[e]ach individual being secured in the enjoyment of this liberty, must then take the responsibility of his own happiness and well-being. If his necessities require more than his faculties will supply, he must depend upon the voluntary kindness of his fellow-men. . . ." Spooner, *The Unconstitutionality of Slavery, supra* note 17, at 20 n.*. Nevertheless, Spooner maintained that extreme necessity could change a person's obligation if "he be reduced to that extremity where the necessity of self-preservation overrides all abstract rules of conduct, and makes a law for the occasion—an extremity, that would probably never occur but for some antecedent injustice." *Id.*

27. Spooner, *The Unconstitutionality of Slavery, supra* note 17, at 8 n.* (emphasis added).

obedience to it, but not necessary having any moral character whatever."[28] The implications of this definition of law were obvious to Spooner. "On this principle, then—that mere will or power are competent to establish the law that is to govern an act, without reference to the justice or injustice of the act itself, the will and power of any single individual to commit theft, would be sufficient to make the theft lawful, as lawful as is any other act of injustice, which the will and power of communities, or large bodies of men, may be united to accomplish."[29]

But are not the commands of legitimate governments distinguishable from the commands of a thief? Spooner argued that this would only be true on the assumption that a government's legitimacy is not itself a product of mere will or power. "The numbers concerned," he wrote, "do not alter the rule."[30] How then would a government achieve legitimacy? Spooner's answer was the traditional American answer: from the consent of the governed. "[G]overnment can have no powers except as individuals may *rightfully* delegate to it."[31] But once again, Spooner's argument takes on a modern appearance. For he understood as well as any political theorist today the impossibility of gaining unanimous consent.

> Our constitutions purport to be established by "the people," and, *in theory*, "all the people" *consent* to such government as the constitutions authorize. But this consent of "the people" exists only in theory. It has no existence in fact. Government is in reality established by the few; and these few assume the consent of all the rest, without any such consent being actually given.[32]

One might conclude from a lack of actual consent either that the government was illegitimate[33] or that actual consent is not what legitimates government. Or one might contend, as Spooner did in his book on slavery, that the lack of actual consent imposed severe constraints on any government which depended for its legitimacy upon the consent of the governed. Specifically, it limited the government to exercising only those powers to which every honest person could be *presumed* to have consented.[34]

Spooner's answer to the lack of actual assent was, therefore, to employ a presumption based on what today might be called rational choice.

---

28. *Id.* at 12.
29. *Id.* at 12-13.
30. *Id.* at 12.
31. *Id.* at 14.
32. *Id.* at 153; *see id.* at 225 ("The whole matter of the adoption of the constitution is mainly a matter of assumption and theory, rather than of actual fact.").
33. Later in his life Spooner reached this conclusion in what may be his best remembered essay. *See* LYSANDER SPOONER, *No Treason, No. VI: The Constitution of No Authority* (1870), *reprinted in* 1 WORKS, *supra* note 3.
34. SPOONER, *The Unconstitutionality of Slavery, supra* note 17, at 143.

All governments . . . that profess to be founded on the consent of the governed, and yet have authority to violate natural laws, are necessarily frauds. It is not a supposable case, that all or even a very large part, of the governed, can have agreed to them. Justice is evidently the only principle that *everybody* can be presumed to agree to, in the formation of government.[35]

In other words, any government who depends for its legitimacy on the consent of the governed must operate consistent with principles of justice—the conditions of peace—to which everybody presumably could agree.

Moreover, lawmakers must make laws that adhere to natural justice because they have promised to do so, and judges must so construe them: "[E]very instrument, and every man, or body of men, that profess to establish a law, impliedly assert that the law they would establish is reasonable and right. The law, therefore, must, if possible, be construed consistently with that implied assertion."[36]

Finally, because some rights are inalienable, governments cannot claim that the citizenry has consented to their infringement.

[I]n order that the contract of government may be valid and lawful . . . [i]t cannot lawfully authorize government to destroy or take from men their natural rights: for natural rights are inalienable, and can no more be sur- rendered to government—which is but an association of individuals —than to a single individual. They are a necessary attribute of man's nature; and he can no more part with them—to government or anyone else—than with his nature itself.[37]

And this leads Spooner to a particular conception of government's purpose: "But the contract of government may lawfully authorize the adoption of means—not incon- sistent with natural justice—for the better protection of men's natural rights. And this is the legitimate and true object of government."[38]

What of the practicality of basing law on natural justice which, in turn, is based on natural rights? In assessing Spooner's proposal it is important to bear in mind that, while Spooner advocated the non-binding nature of statutes that violate or were *inconsistent* with natural justice, he did not think that abstract principles of justice dictated the precise content of all laws. He allowed, for example, for the necessity of laws to establish much-needed conventions.

---

35. *Id.*
36. *Id.* at 205.
37. *Id.* at 8.
38. *Id.*

This condemnation of written laws must, of course, be understood as applying only to cases where principles and rights are involved, and not as condemning any governmental arrangements, or instrumentalities, that are consistent with natural right, and which must be agreed upon for the purpose of carrying natural law into effect. These things may be varied, as expediency may dictate, so only that they be allowed to infringe no principle of justice. And they must, of course, be written, because they do not exist as fixed principles, or laws in nature.[39]

What he vehemently denied is that natural law was somehow ineffable and unknowable. Because this remains a common objection to natural rights, and as his response to this questions also reveals what he thought to be the content of natural rights, I quote him at length:

The objections made to natural law, on the ground of obscurity, are wholly unfounded. It is true, it must be learned, like any other science, but it is equally true, that it is easily learned. Although as illimitable in its applications as the infinite relations of men to each other, it is, nevertheless, made up of simple elementary principles, of the truth and justice of which every ordinary mind has an almost intuitive perception. *It is the science of justice,*—and almost all men have the same perceptions of what constitutes justice, or of what justice requires, when they understand alike the facts from which their inferences are to be drawn. Men living in contact with each other, and having intercourse together, *cannot avoid* learning natural law, to a very great extent, even if they would. The dealings of men with men, their separate possessions, and their individual wants, are continually forcing upon their minds the questions,—Is this act just? or is it unjust? Is this thing mine? or is it his? And these are questions of natural law; questions, which, in regard to the great mass of cases, are answered alike by the human mind everywhere.[40]

For Spooner, natural law was knowable because, in the abstract, it was limited to the following proposition:

The ultimate truth on this subject is, that man has an inalienable right to so much personal liberty as he will use without invading the rights of others. This liberty is an inherent right of his nature and his faculties. It is an inherent right of his nature and faculties to develope [sic] themselves freely, and without restraint from other natures and faculties, *that have no superior*

---

39. SPOONER, *The Unconstitutionality of Slavery, supra* note 17, at 140 n.*.
40. *Id.* at 140-41 n.†.

prerogatives to his own. And this right has only this limit, viz., that he do not carry the exercise of his own liberty so far as to restrain or infringe the equally free development of the natures and faculties of others. The dividing lines between the equal liberties of each must never be transgressed by either. This principle is the foundation and essence of law and of civil right. And legitimate government is formed by the voluntary association of individuals, for the mutual protection of each of them in the enjoyment of this natural liberty, against those who may be disposed to invade it.[41]

It is a principle so obvious in itself and in most of its applications that children learn it "before they have learned the language by which we describe it"[42]:

Children learn many principles of natural law at a very early age. For example: they learn that when one child has picked up an apple or a flower, it is his, and that his associates may not take it from him against his will. They also learn that if he voluntarily exchange his apple or flower with a playmate, for some other article of desire, he has thereby surrendered his right to it, and must not reclaim it. These are fundamental principles of natural law, which govern most of the greatest interests of individuals and society; yet, children learn them earlier than they learn that three and three are six, or five and five, ten.[43]

Why then is natural law supposed to be so confusing and unknowable? Spooner's answer is surprisingly compelling:

If our governments would but themselves adhere to natural law, there would be little occasion to complain of the ignorance of the people in regard to it. The popular ignorance of law [that is, *just* law] is attributable mainly to the innovations that have been made upon natural law by legislation; whereby our system has become an incongruous mixture of natural and statute law, with no uniform principle pervading it. To learn such a system,—if system it can be called, and if learned it can be,—is a matter of very similar difficulty to what it would take to learn a system of mathematics, which should consist of the mathematics of nature, interspersed with such other mathematics as might be created by legislation, in violation of all the natural principles of numbers and quantities.

But whether the difficulties of learning natural law be greater or less than here represented, they exist in the nature of things and cannot be removed. Legislation, instead of removing, only increases them. This it does

---

41.   *Id.* at 19-20 n.* (emphasis added).
42.   *Id.* at 140-41 n.†.
43.   *Id.*

by innovating upon natural truths and principles, and introducing jargon and contradiction, in the place of order, analogy, consistency, and uniformity.[44]

In this manner, Spooner began his interpretive approach with an affirmation of natural rights that he shared with other abolitionists and with the revolutionary generation that came before him.

III. NATURAL RIGHTS AND CONSTITUTIONAL INTERPRETATION: SPOONER'S ANALYSIS OF SLAVERY

It would seem that the argument against slavery that follows from Spooner's views of natural law and natural rights is obvious and almost trivial. (1) Written laws, including written constitutions, that violate natural justice as defined by natural rights are not to be enforced by judges. (2) Slavery is unjust because it violates the natural rights of the slave. Therefore, (3) slavery is unconstitutional and not to be enforced by judges. Q.E.D. Yet, despite the fact that Spooner would have accepted this syllogism as sufficient to condemn slavery,[45] this was not the principal method of constitutional interpretation he brought to bear on its constitutionality. "I shall not insist," he wrote, "upon the principle . . . that there can be no law contrary to natural right; but shall admit, for the sake of argument, that there may be such laws."[46] His primary interpretive strategy was more interesting.

Spooner argued that the primacy of natural justice meant that the following rule of *statutory* interpretation, enunciated by Chief Justice John Marshall in the 1805 case of *United States v. Fisher*,[47] should be applied to the constitution as well:

Where rights are infringed, where fundamental principles are overthrown, where the general system of laws is departed from, the legislative intention must be expressed with *irresistible clearness*, to induce a court of justice to suppose a design to effect such objects.[48]

---

44. SPOONER, *The Unconstitutionality of Slavery*, *supra* note 17.

45. In Spooner's words, "no rule of civil conduct, that is inconsistent with the natural rights of men, can be rightfully established by government, or consequently be made obligatory as law, either upon the people, or upon judicial tribunals. . . ." *Id.* at 15.

46. *Id.* at 15-16.

47. United States v. Fisher, 6 U.S. [2 Cranch] 358, 390 (1805).

48. SPOONER, *The Unconstitutionality of Slavery*, *supra* note 17, at 18-19 (quoting *United States v. Fisher*) (emphasis added by Spooner). Despite the appeal to Spooner of Marshall's formulation, near the end of his life, Spooner expressed, with his usual feistiness, his loathing for Marshall as a judge:

John Marshall has the reputation of having been the greatest jurist the country has ever had. And he unquestionably would have been a great jurist, if the two fundamental propositions, on which all his legal, political, and constitutional ideas were based had been true.

These two propositions were, first, that government has all power; and, secondly, that the people have no rights.

There two propositions were, with him, cardinal principles, from which, I think, he never departed.

Spooner's rendered this interpretive maxim as follows:

> 1st, that no intention, in violation of natural justice and natural right . . . can be ascribed to the constitution, unless that intention be expressed in terms that are *legally competent* to express such an intention; and 2d, that no terms, except those that are plenary, express, explicit, distinct, unequivocal, *and to which no other meaning can be given,* are *legally competent* to authorize or sanction anything contrary to natural right.[49]

In short, "all language must be construed '*strictly*' in favor of natural right."[50] But, given its rationale, this rule cf construction is not symmetrical.

> The rule of law is materially different as to the terms necessary to legalize and sanction anything contrary to natural right, and those necessary to legalize things that are consistent with natural right. The latter may be sanctioned by natural implication and inference; the former only by inevitable

---

For these reasons, he was the oracle of all the rapacious classes, in whose interest the government was administered. And from them he got all his fame.

LYSANDER SPOONER, *A Letter to Grover Cleveland* 87 (1886), *reprinted in* 1 WORKS, *supra* note 3.

49. SPOONER, *The Unconstitutionality of Slavery, supra* note 17, at 58-59. When he added the second part of the work in 1847, Spooner identified, defended and applied the following fourteen rules of interpretation:

(1) In the interpretation of the Constitution, as of all other laws and contracts, the intention of the instrument must prevail;

(2) The intention of the Constitution must be collected from its words;

(3) We must, if possible, give a word the same meaning appropriate to the subject of the instrument itself;

(4) Where technical words are used, a technical meaning is to be attributed to them;

(5) The sense of every word, that is ambiguous in itself, must, if possible, be determined by reference to the rest of the instrument;

(6) A contract must never, if it be possible to avoid it, be so construed, as that any one of the parties to it, assuming him to understand his rights, and to be of competent mental capacity to make obligatory contracts, may not reasonably be presumed to have consented to it;

(7) Any unjust intention must be expressed with irresistible clearness to induce a court to give a law an unjust meaning;

(8) Where the prevailing principles and provisions of a law are favorable to justice, and general in their nature and terms, no unnecessary exception to them, or to their operation, is to be allowed;

(9) Be guided, in doubtful cased, by the preamble;

(10) One part of the instrument must not be allowed to contradict another, unless the language be so explicit as to make the contradiction inevitable;

(11) The Constitution ought never be construed to violate the law of nations, if any other possible construction exists;

(12) All reasonable doubts must be decided in favor of liberty;

(13) The instrument must be so construed as to give no shelter or effect to fraud;

(14) Never unnecessarily impute to an instrument any intention whatever which it would be unnatural for either reasonable or honest men to entertain.

Id. at 157-205. Spooner's elaboration, defense, and application of these rules are excerpted in Lysander Spooner, *The Unconstitutionality of Slavery,* 28 PAC. L.J. 1015 (1997) [hereinafter McGEORGE EXCERPT].

50. SPOONER, *The Unconstitutionality of Slavery, supra* note 17, at 17-18.

implication, or by language that is full, definite express, explicit, unequivocal, and whose *unavoidable* import is to sanction the *specific wrong* intended.[51]

From this interpretive starting point, we can now see Spooner's basic strategy for finding slavery unconstitutional.

To assert, therefore, that the constitution *intended* to sanction slavery, is, in reality, equivalent to asserting that the *necessary* meaning, the *unavoidable* import of the *words alone* of the constitution, come fully up to the point of a clear, definite, distinct, express, explicit, unequivocal, necessary and peremptory sanction of the specific thing, *human slavery, property in men.* If the *necessary* import of the *words alone* do but fall an iota short of this point, the instrument gives, and, legally speaking, intended to give, no legal sanction to slavery. Now, who can, in good faith, say that the *words alone* of the constitution come up to this point? No one, who knows anything of law, and the meaning of words. Not even the name of the thing, alleged to be sanctioned, is given. The constitution itself contains no designation, description, or necessary admission of the existence of such a thing as slavery, servitude, or the right of property in man. We are obliged to go out of the instrument, and grope among the records of oppression lawlessness and crime—records unmentioned, and of course unsanctioned by the constitution —to *find* the thing, to which it is said that the words of the constitution apply. And when we have found this thing, which the constitution dare not name, we find that the constitution has sanctioned it (if at all) only by enigmatical words, by unnecessary implication and inference, by innuendo and double entendre, and under a name that entirely fails of describing the thing. Everybody must admit that the constitution itself contains no language, from which *alone* any court, that were either strangers to the prior existence of slavery, or that did not assume its prior existence to be legal, could legally decide that the constitution sanctioned it. And this is the true test for determining whether the constitution does, or does not, sanction slavery, viz. whether a court of law, strangers to the prior existence of slavery or not assuming its prior existence to be legal—looking only at the naked language of the instrument—could, consistently with legal rules, judicially determine that it sanctioned slavery. Every lawyer, who deserves that name, knows that the claim for slavery could stand no such test.[52]

---

51. *Id.* at 59.
52. *Id.* at 59-60.

Assuming one accepts the premise that slavery is a natural injustice which violates the natural and inalienable rights of those who are enslaved, Spooner's interpretive strategy gives rise to two obvious questions. First, what about those notorious sections of the Constitution that have long been accepted as sanctioning slavery? Second, what about the evidence of the original intentions of the framers concerning the constitutionality of slavery? Spooner spent the bulk of his nearly three hundred page work addressing these issues—particularly the first one—in detail, and I simply cannot do his analysis complete justice here. Virtually each page of this portion of his book contributes an additional argument, piece of evidence, or refinement of previous arguments. Yet, for you to appreciate his approach to interpretation, I must try to give at least a flavor of his responses.

A. Alleged Textual References to Slavery

There are three passages in the original Constitution that are commonly thought to refer to and constitutionally legitimate slavery. The first is in Article I, Section 2:

> Representatives and direct Taxes shall be apportioned among the several State, which may be included within this Union, according to their respective Numbers, which shall be determined by adding to the whole Number of *free Persons*, including those bound to Service for a Term of Years, and excluding Indians not taxed, three fifths of all *other Persons*.[53]

The term, "other Persons" in this clause is interpreted as referring to slaves. The second passage is also in Article I, but in Section 9:

> The Migration or *Importation of such Persons* as any of the States now existing shall think proper to admit, shall not be prohibited by the Congress prior to the Year one thousand eight hundred and eight, but a Tax or duty may be imposed on such Importation, not exceeding ten dollars for each Person.[54]

The term "Importation of such Persons" in this clause is interpreted as to referring to slaves. The third passage is in Article IV, section 2:

> No *Person held to Service or Labour* in one State, under the Laws thereof, escaping into another, shall, in Consequence of any Law or Regulation therein, be discharged from such Service or Labour, but shall be delivered up on Claim of the Party to whom such Service or Labour may be due.[55]

---

53. U.S. CONST. art. I, § 2 (emphasis added).
54. U.S. CONST. art. I, § 9 (emphasis added).
55. U.S. CONST. art. IV, § 2 (emphasis added).

The term "person held to Service or Labour" in this clause is interpreted as referring to slaves.

One of the striking things about these three passages, when one stops to consider the matter, is that none of them uses the term "slave." As Spooner wrote: "Not even the name of the thing, alleged to be sanctioned, is given."[56] Now we may all think we know the reasons why this word was avoided, but there is one reason that cannot be advanced. The word was not avoided because it was unknown to those who framed and ratified the Constitution or was not in common parlance at the time. Indeed, to the contrary, if one wanted to avoid any ambiguity as to the meaning of these three provisions, and one meant to refer to slaves, then "slave" would be by far the most obvious term to use. Had the framers or ratifiers wished to bind themselves and future generations by their written constitution to sanction slavery, they could have used the word that expressed this intention in no uncertain terms. And yet, for whatever reason, those who wrote and ratified this Constitution chose not to do so. And if by failing to do so, they failed to explicitly ratify and incorporate into the Constitution the natural injustice of slavery, then the reasons for their failure are immaterial. "It is not the intentions men actually had," Spooner contended, "but the intentions they constitutionally expressed, that make up the constitution."[57] Spooner finds one reason for this precept in the indeterminacy of basing legal rules on actual intentions:

> Men's *presumed* intentions were all uniform, all certainly right, and all valid, because they corresponded precisely with what they said by the instrument itself; whereas their actual intentions were almost infinitely various, conflicting with each other, conflicting with what they said by the instrument, and therefore of no legal consequence or validity whatever.[58]

But does this not presuppose the existence of some free-floating "plain-meaning" wholly independent of the intentions of the people who ratified it? Not really. It only presupposes that language comes to have an objective meaning within a particular community that can be discerned independently of individual opinions and usages. Indeed, were language not to have some such meaning, it is not clear how it could serve as a general medium of communication. Moreover, the process of ratification presupposes that the Constitution has meaning independent of individual intentions. As Spooner argued:

> We must admit that the constitution, *of itself, independently of the actual intentions of the people*, expresses some certain fixed, definite, and legal intentions; else the people themselves would express no intentions by

---

56. SPOONER, *The Unconstitutionality of Slavery, supra* note 17, at 59.
57. *Id.* at 226.
58. *Id.*

agreeing to it. The instrument would, in fact, contain nothing that the people *could* agree to. Agreeing to an instrument that had no meaning *of its own*, would only be agreeing to nothing.[59]

How then is the Constitution's meaning to be determined? "[T]he only answer that can be given," Spooner concluded,

> is, that it can be no other than the meaning which its words, interpreted by sound legal rules of interpretation, express. That and that alone is the meaning of the constitution. And whether the people who adopted the constitution really meant the same things which the constitution means, is a matter which they were bound to settle, each individual with himself, before he agreed to the instrument; and it is therefore one with which we have now nothing to do.[60]

By this reasoning if the people ratified a document that failed to clearly authorize slavery and which omits all explicit reference to the practice using the most obvious and well-known term to describe it, we cannot presume that these enigmatic references are to slavery if some other meaning can reasonably be assigned to them.

It is also striking that the terms in two of these three passages refer to persons: *persons* held to service or labor, and the importation of such *persons*. Persons are people and part of "We the People" who presumably assented to the Constitution in order to "establish Justice . . . and secure the Blessings of Liberty"[61] to themselves and their posterity.

> [T]here is no legal ground for denying that the terms " the people of the United States," included the *whole* of the then people of the United States. And if the whole of the people are the parties to it, it must, if possible, be so

---

59. *Id.* at 222; *see id.* at 220 ("[I]f the intentions could be assumed independently of the words, the words would be of no use, and the laws of course would not be written.").

60. *Id.* at 223. Spooner thought that general rules of interpretation were needed to choose among the various meanings of language:

[T]he same words have such various and opposite meanings in common use, that there would be no certainty as to the meaning of the laws themselves, unless there were some *rules* for determining which one of a word's various meanings was to be attached to it, when the word was found in a particular connection. . . . Their office is to determine the legal meaning of a word, or, rather, to *select* the legal meaning of [a] word, out of all the various meanings which the word bears in common use.

Id. at 162. But the rules of interpretation must themselves be selected to enhance the fit between constitutional meaning and justice, for "unless the meaning of words were judged of in this manner, words themselves could not be used in writing laws and contracts, without being liable to be perverted to subserve all manner of injustice. . . ." *Id.* at 163. "[T]he rules are but a transcript of a common principle of morality, to wit, the principle which requires us to attribute good motives and good designs to all the words and actions of our fellow-men, that can reasonably bear such a construction." *Id.* at 164.

61. U.S. CONST. preamble.

construed as to make it such contract as each and every individual might reasonably agree to.[62]

In sum, the Constitution refers in these two clauses to "persons" and in the preamble to "We the People." Nowhere does the Constitution exclude either those persons referred to in these sections or those persons then held as slaves to be excluded from "the People." Persons who are part of the People cannot be presumed to assent to a document that would hold them in bondage. And, short of this, the government of the United States would not rest on the consent of the governed.

Even more fundamentally, creatures who are persons are in possession of certain inalienable natural rights. This much was conceded by those advocates of slavery who were compelled to argue that slaves were not people. Thus, if slaves are not people, and if it is permissible to enslave another only if that other creature is not a person, then these two passages cannot be referring to or sanctioning slavery, since they explicitly refer to "persons" and persons cannot justly be held as slaves.

But Spooner's interpretive methodology requires that the terms in these three passages be given *some* definitive legal meaning. How do we do so? Spooner would require us, if we can, to draw this meaning from the Constitution itself, and failing that from the ordinary meanings these terms have in law or in common usage. What else could these terms be reasonably construed as referencing other than slavery? Although I can relate to you the meanings advocated by Spooner, I cannot recount all the evidence and arguments he provides on behalf of these meanings.[63] Let us take up these passages in order.

1. Distinguishing "Free Persons" from "Other Persons"

First, what does "other persons" as opposed to "free persons" mean in Article I, Section 2? Spooner argues, at length and with considerable authority,[64] that "English law had for centuries used the word 'free' as describing persons possessing citizenship, or some other franchise or peculiar privilege—as distinguished from aliens, and persons not possessed of such franchise or privilege."[65] For instance: "A man was said to be a 'free British subject'—meaning thereby that he was a naturalized or native born citizen of the British government, as distinguished from an alien, or person neither naturalized nor native born."[66]

---

62. SPOONER, *The Unconstitutionality of Slavery, supra* note 17, at 188. I shall consider, below, Spooner's response to the objection that the slave holders cannot be presumed to have agreed to a constitution under which slavery was unconstitutional. *See infra* notes 128-31 and accompanying text.

63. *See generally*, SPOONER, McGEORGE EXCERPT, *supra* note 49.

64. SPOONER, *The Unconstitutionality of Slavery, supra* note 17, at 44-54, 247-55, 265-70.

65. *Id.* at 74.

66. *Id.* at 45.

By this interpretation this clause refers to two classes of persons: free persons and other persons. The class of "free" persons corresponds to what Spooner calls "full citizens," both native born and naturalized, who have not for some reason been dispossessed of their rights of citizenship, perhaps because they are convicted felons, whereas the class of "other persons" corresponds to "partial citizens" or what are commonly called aliens.

> The real distinction between these two classes was, that the first class were *free of the government*—that is, they were *full* members of the State, and could claim the *full* liberty, enjoyment and protection of the laws, *as a matter of right, as being parties to the compact;* while the latter class were not thus free; they could claim hardly anything *as a right*, (perhaps nothing, unless it were the privilege of the writ of *habeas corpus*,) and were only allowed, *as a matter of favor and discretion*, such protection and privileges as the general and State governments should see fit to accord to them.[67]

By this interpretation, taxation and representation are apportioned as follows: each "full citizen" of the United States counts for one; each resident alien or "partial citizen" is counted as two-thirds a full citizen.[68] The reason for the partial taxation and representation of resident aliens, is straight-forward:

> They are protected by our laws, and should pay for that protection. But as they are not allowed the full privileges of citizens, they should not pay an equal tax with the citizens. They contribute to the strength and resources of the government, and therefore they should be represented. But as they are not sufficiently acquainted with our system of government, and as their allegiance is not made sufficiently sure, they are not entitled to an equal voice with the citizens, especially if they are not equally taxed.[69]

But can these two classes be grounded in the Constitution itself? As evidence that this meaning is incorporated in the U.S. Constitution, Spooner looked to the power granted Congress in Article I, Section 8 "To establish an uniform Rule of Naturalization."[70]

> The power of naturalization is, by the constitution, taken from the States, and given exclusively to the United States. The constitution of the United States, therefore, necessarily supposes the existence of aliens—and thus

---

67. *Id.* at 247.
68. Spooner offers a lengthy explanation of why the term "free persons" was preferable to the term "citizen." *See id.* at 251-55.
69. *Id.* at 242-43.
70. U.S. CONST. art. I, § 8, cl. 4.

furnishes the correlative sought for. It furnishes a class both for the word "free," and the words "all other persons," to apply to.[71]

After extensive analysis of both text and general usage, Spooner concludes:

> It is perfectly manifest, from all the evidence given in the preceding pages . . . that the word "free," when used in laws and constitutions, to describe one class of persons, as distinguished from another living under the same laws or constitutions, is not sufficient, *of itself,* to imply slavery as its correlative. The word itself is wholly indefinite, as to the kind of restraint implied as its correlative. And as slavery is the worst, it is necessarily the last, kind of restraint which the law will imply. There must be some other word, or provision, *in the instrument itself,* to warrant such an implication against the other class. But the constitution contains no such other word or provision. It contains nothing but the simple word "free." While, on the other hand, it is full of words and provisions, perfectly explicit, that imply the opposite of slavery.[72]

2. The "Importation of such Persons"

What has Spooner then to say about the meaning of the term "Importation of such Persons" in Article I, Section 9? The argument made by those asserting this to be a reference to slavery is that, because only property can be "imported," any person who is "imported" is a slave. Spooner rejects this definition of "importation." The word "applies correctly to both persons and things. The definition of the verb 'import' is simply 'to bring from a foreign country, or jurisdiction, or from another

---

71. SPOONER, *The Unconstitutionality of Slavery, supra* note 17, at 75. Indeed one authority which Spooner mentions in support of the distinction between "free persons"—meaning—citizens and aliens is Madison's explanation of the Naturalization Clause in Federalist No. 42 in light of the privileges and immunities clause found in the Articles of Confederation. Madison "takes it for granted that the word 'free' was used in that political sense . . . —that is, as distinguishing 'citizens' and the 'inhabitants' or 'people' proper, from aliens and persons not allowed the franchises enjoyed by the 'inhabitants' and 'people' of the States." *Id.* at 53. Spooner was arguing that the word "free persons" meant citizens as distinct from aliens, not because Madison intended this meaning, but because Madison's usage was evidence of this commonly accepted meaning and, therefore, of its legal meaning.

72. *Id.* at 268. In a footnote, Spooner adds the following observation:

> I doubt if a single instance can be found, even in the statutes of the slaveholding States themselves, *in force in* 1789, where the word *free* was used, (as the slave argument claims it was used in the constitution,) to describe either white persons, or the mass of the people *other than slaves,* (that is, the white and free colored,) *as distinguished from the slaves,* unless the statute also contained the word *slave,* or some other evidence, beside the word *free* itself, that that was the sense in which the word *free* was used. If there were no such statute, it proves that, by the usage of legislation, in 1789, even in the slaveholding States themselves, the word *free* was insufficient, *of itself,* to imply slavery as its correlative.

Id. at 268 n.†.

State, into one's own country, jurisdiction or State.'"[73] Spooner's next argument is particularly insightful:

> When we speak of "importing" things, it is true we mentally associate with them the idea of property. But that is simply because *things* are property, and not because the word "import" has any control, in that particular, over the character of the things imported. When we speak of importing "persons," we do not associate with them the idea of property, simply because "persons" are not property.
>
> We speak daily of the "importation of foreigners into the country;" but no one infers therefrom that they are brought in as slaves, but as passengers. . . . A man imports his wife and children—but they are not therefore his slaves, or capable of being owned or sold as his property. A man imports a gang of laborers, to clear lands, cut canals, or construct railroads; but not therefore to be held as slaves."[74]

On the basis of this common usage, Spooner thus reads the term "importation" in this clause to refer to persons coming into the country. Whereas the term "migration" refers to persons going out of the country.[75] "An innocent meaning must be given to the word, if it will bear one. Such is the legal rule."[76]

Spooner offers several other arguments in favor of this interpretation, but one is particularly, though typically, clever. The restriction on the "Importation of Persons" cannot refer to a restriction on Congress' power to refuse to recognize slavery, because Congress' power to naturalize anyone who enters the country is unqualified. Even if it could not *bar* the entry of slaves, by the slavery reading of the clause, it could free every slave thus imported upon arrival. Congress has

> the perfect power to pass laws that shall naturalize every foreigner without distinction, the moment he sets foot on our soil. And they had this power as perfectly prior to 1808, as since. And it is a power entirely inconsistent with the idea that they were bound to admit, and forever after to acknowledge as slaves, all or any who might be attempted to be brought into the country as such.[77]

---

73. *Id.* at 81.
74. *Id.* at 81-82.
75. Spooner might also have offered the following innocent meaning of these terms: "importation" refers to the activity of *one person bringing another* into the country, whereas migration refers to a person who seeks on his or her own behest to enter the country. This would answer those who might think, contrary to Spooner, that the term "migration" refers not only to emigration but to immigration as well. In contrast, notice that the pro-slavery reading of this clause would apply to "migration" as well as "importation," though it is difficult to imagine how chattel slaves can possibly "migrate" or be taxed when they do.
76. *Id.* at 82.
77. *Id.* at 87.

To argue that the power of Congress to naturalize persons held as slaves upon their entry into the county is qualified by the clause barring restrictions on importation is, once again, to assume what is at issue: that "importation of persons" refers to slaves.

3. *"No person held to Service or Labour."*

By now I trust that those of you who are in the "Spoonerian" swing of things can easily generate an "innocent" interpretation of the passage that requires the return of a person held to service or labor in one state who escapes from into another state. Why, of course, "persons held to Service or Labour"[78] refers, not to slaves, but to indentured servants and convicts. It has been estimated that a majority of early immigrants to this country came as indentured servants or convicts.[79] And Northern nonslave states had runaway servant laws akin to the runaway slave laws in slave states.[80]

> Neither "service" nor labor is necessarily slavery; and not being necessarily slavery, the words, cannot, in this case, be strained beyond their necessary meaning, to make them sanction a wrong. . . . An indented apprentice serves and labors for another. He is "held" to do so, under a contract, and for a consideration, that are recognized, by the laws, as legitimate, and consistent with natural right. Yet he is not owned as property. A condemned criminal is "held to labor"—yet he is not owned as property.[81]

Spooner also considers whether the phrase, "No Person held to Service or Labour in one State, *under the Laws thereof*," delegates to states the sole power to declare when someone is or is not held to service, such that, under this provision, Congress and the federal judiciary must defer to state law whenever it defines a persons as being held to service. He answers:

---

78. U.S. CONST. art. IV, § 2.

79. *See* ABBOT EMERSON SMITH, COLONISTS IN BONDAGE: WHITE SERVITUDE AND CONVICT LABOR IN AMERICA, 1607-1776 336 (1947) ("If we exclude the Puritan migrations of the 1630's, it is safe to say that not less than one-half, nor more than two-thirds, of all white immigrants to the colonies were indentured servants or redemptioners or convicts. . . .").

80. ROBERT J. STEINFELD, THE INVENTION OF FREE LABOR: EMPLOYMENT RELATION IN ENGLISH AND AMERICAN LAW AND CULTURE 1350-1870 11 (1991).

> Under colonial, and later state, servant statutes an elaborate set of provisions safeguarded the master's right to the servant's labor during the term of service. These statutes established procedures by which masters could recover runaway servants; subjected runaways to additional servitude, in some cases to multiple additional days of service for each day's absence; and authorized masters to administer corporal punishment to disobedient servants.

Id. at 11. By the way, in Steinfeld's words, "[l]arge numbers of servants continued to be *imported* as late as 1819 . . . . But in 1820, after nearly two centuries, the mass *importation* of indentured servants abruptly came to a halt." *Id.* (emphasis added).

81. SPOONER, *The Unconstitutionality of Slavery, supra* note 17, at 70.

The simple fact, that an act purports to "hold persons to service or labor," clearly cannot, *of itself*, make the act constitutional. If it could, any act, purporting to hold "persons to service or labor," would necessarily be constitutional, without regard to the "persons" so held, or the conditions on which they were held. It would be constitutional, *solely because it purported to hold persons to service or labor.*[82]

Under this theory any person could be made a slave by state law and, by this interpretation of this clause, such "acts of legislatures would be constitutional, *solely because they made slaves of the people.*"[83] Spooner concludes: "Certainly this would be a new test of the constitutionality of laws."[84] To the contrary, any state law purporting to authorize holding a person to service must be assessed to see if it is constitutional and such an assessment would "depend upon a number of contingencies—such as the kind of service or labor required, and the conditions on which it requires. Any service or labor, that is inconsistent with the duties which the constitution requires of the people, is of course not sanctioned by this clause. . . ."[85]

But what of the argument that the framers of the Constitution intended these clauses to refer to slavery, and that the people ratifying the Constitution understood this as well? I turn now to Spooner's analysis of original intent.

B. *The Original Intentions of the Framers and Ratifiers: Wendell Phillips' Critique of Spooner*

Although Spooner persuaded some people that slavery was unconstitutional, including Frederick Douglass,[86] he failed to persuade other abolitionists, such as Garrison, or the judiciary, or posterity. Why were his arguments rejected? The most comprehensive criticism of Spooner was leveled by Wendell Phillips in his *Review of Lysander Spooner's Essay on the Unconstitutionality of Slavery.*[87] Whereas the

---

82. *Id.* at 71.
83. *Id.*
84. *Id.*
85. *Id.* at 72.
86. A speech given by Frederick Douglass in Glasgow, Scotland in March of 1860 concisely tracks most of Spooner's major arguments, cites the same passage from Marshall's opinion in *United States v. Fisher*, and adopts Spooner's interpretive presumption. *See* Frederick Douglass, *The Constitution of the United States: Is it Pro-Slavery or Anti-Slavery?*, *reprinted in* PAUL BREST & SANFORD LEVINSON, PROCESSES OF CONSTITUTIONAL DECISIONMAKING: CASES AND MATERIALS 207 (1992) ("[T]he intentions of those who framed the Constitution, be they good or bad, for slavery or against slavery, are to be respected so far, and so far only, as will find those intentions plainly stated in the Constitution. . . . It was what they said that was adopted by the people, not what they were ashamed or afraid to say, and really omitted to say."). *See also* WILLIAM S. MCFEELY, FREDERICK DOUGLASS 205 (1991) (Douglass' "arguments were those of Lysander Spooner and William Goodell as he had acknowledged at the time of his change of heart about the Constitution in 1851").
87. PHILLIPS, REVIEW OF SPOONER, *supra* note 12. In this volume Phillips pairs Spooner with William Goodell, author of another book arguing that slavery was unconstitutional, though Phillips does not particularly focus on Goodell's arguments. *See* WILLIAM GOODELL, AMERICAN CONSTITUTIONAL LAW AND ITS BEARING UPON

self-educated Spooner slashed at slavery with a broadsword, Phillips, the Harvard-trained student of Joseph Story, assailed Spooner with a rapier. The thrust of Phillips lawyerly and elegantly-written critique was, first, that Spooner had misconstrued or distorted judicial pronouncements as authority for Spooner's interpretive presumption against unjust interpretations. Yet, although Spooner, in his reply to Phillips, supplemented his argument with additional authority, his discussion of the nature of law preceding both Parts I and II clearly shows that his defense of his interpretive principles was normative, rather than based on precedent.

Some of Phillips' polemics against Spooner's theory of interpretation, while persuasive when written, would not ring as true today as they may have sounded at the time. For example, as a *reductio ad absurdum,* he argues that

> if we construe the Constitution according to Mr. Spooner's rules, women are constitutionally eligible to the Presidency and to Congress; nothing but "extraneous and historical evidence" shields us from this result. As Mr. Spooner does not allow of this when it will fix upon a clause any meaning contrary to "natural right," he is bound to hold that woman may now *legally* fill these offices, or to give up his rules. . . .[88]

He then offers capital punishment as another example of something the Supreme Court could prohibit Congress from imposing on pirates pursuant to its Article I, Section 8 powers, should the Court be captured by members of "the Anti-Capital Punishment party."[89] "This would be legitimate on Mr. Spooner's rule, but would it not be absurd?"[90]

There is one other respect in which the passage of time has undermined Phillips' argument. In addition to the three passages considered above, Phillips contends that two additional constitutional provisions are "universally supposed to refer to and recognize Slavery."[91] It would be a useful test of Spooner's theory (and Phillips' critique) for the reader to put down this article and examine the Constitution to find these two provisions. No fair resorting to Madison's Notes to find them. (Those that remember the historical evidence are disqualified.) For Spooner would argue that, like the other three, these two provisions only sanction slavery if they are *assumed* to be about slaves based on recourse to extrinsic evidence.

AMERICAN SLAVERY (1845). Goodell, by the way, relies on the Ninth Amendment (*id.* at 93) and other provisions of the Bill of Rights as embodying a "'spirit' of security to personal rights, and of consequent hostility to slavery." *Id.* at 92.

88. PHILLIPS, REVIEW OF SPOONER, *supra* note 12, at 53-54.

89. *Id.* at 54.

90. *Id.* Regardless of the history, Phillips is clearly on weaker textual ground here since, unlike slavery, the Constitution explicitly refers to capital punishment. *See, e.g.,* U.S. CONST. amend. V ("nor shall any person be twice put in jeopardy of *life* or limb").

91. *Id.* at 26.

Give up? Here is the allegedly "pro-slavery"[92] language: "Congress shall have Power . . . to *suppress Insurrections*."[93] And "The United States shall guarantee to every State in this Union a Republican Form of Government; and shall *protect* each of them against Invasion; and . . . *against domestic Violence*."[94] Now here is Phillips' argument: "The . . . articles relating to insurrection and domestic violence, *perfectly innocent in themselves*—yet being made with the fact directly in view that Slavery exists among us, do deliberately pledge the whole national force against the unhappy slave if he imitate our fathers and resist oppression. . . ."[95] If we adopt the historical approach to interpret the three clauses discussed above, are we not also bound to reject what Phillips concedes to be the "perfectly innocent" interpretation of these clauses in favor of the pro-slavery interpretation? Which interpretation of the text is "strained"?

Phillips also disputed Spooner's claim that slavery had not been expressly authorized in the Constitution with elaborate criticisms of Spooner's textual analysis of the Constitution, colonial charters, statutes, the Declaration of Independence, Articles of Confederation, state constitutions, etc. To be sure, some of Phillips' arguments are persuasive,[96] but Spooner's reply in Part II shows that many miss the mark. For example, to counter Spooner's interpretation of the terms "free persons" and "other persons" in Article I, Section 2, Phillips cites numerous examples of where the word "free" or "freeman" had previously been used in other legal writings as the correlative of slave.[97] In Part II, Spooner argues that, whenever this occurs, it is in juxtaposition, not with the words "other persons" as it is in Article I, Section 2, but with the term "slave" or "negroes."[98] The presence of these words in each of Phillips' examples, Spooner argues, is needed to render the term "free" unambiguous. Standing alone, the words "other persons" is insufficient to do so and, therefore, we are obliged to reject an unjust interpretation of these ambiguous terms in favor of a meaning consistent with justice.

More fundamentally, Phillips hotly rejects Spooner's natural law approach in favor of a strongly majoritarian version of Austinian positivism.[99]

There can be no more self-evident proposition, than that, in every Government, the majority must rule, and their will be *uniformly* obeyed. Now, if the majority enact a wicked law, and the Judge refuses to enforce it,

---

92. *Id.* at 68.

93. U.S. CONST. art. I, § 8 (emphasis added).

94. U.S. CONST. art. IV, § 4 (emphasis added).

95. PHILLIPS, REVIEW OF SPOONER, *supra* note 12, at 26-27 (emphasis added).

96. A comprehensive tally of all the philosophical, textual, and historical issues in dispute and which man got the better of the other in each would be an enormous undertaking that I shall not attempt here.

97. *See* PHILLIPS, REVIEW OF SPOONER, *supra* note 12, at 42-43.

98. *See supra* note 72 and accompanying text.

99. PHILLIPS, REVIEW OF SPOONER, *supra* note 12, at 8 n.* (citing John Austin, *Jurisprudence* (1832)).

which is to yield, the Judge, or the majority? Of course, the first. On any other supposition, Government is impossible.[100]

While this is not the place to examine fully the merits of this claim, in Part II Spooner took issue with the assertion that either legislation or the Constitution itself necessarily reflects the will of the majority:

> Only the male adults are allowed to vote either in the choice of delegates to form constitutions, or in the choice of legislators under the constitutions. These voters comprise not more than *one fifth* of the population. A bare *majority* of these voters,—that is, a little more than *one tenth* of the whole people,—choose the delegates and representatives. And then a *bare majority of these delegates and representatives* (which *majority* were chosen by, and, consequently, represent but little more than *one twentieth* of the whole people,) adopt the constitution, and enact the statutes. Thus the actual makers of constitutions and statutes cannot be said to be the representatives of but little more than *one twentieth* of the people whose rights are affected by their action.[101]

Moreover, in words reminiscent of modern Public Choice theory, Spooner notes that:

> [b]ecause the representative is necessarily chosen for his opinions on one, or at most a few, important topics, when, in fact, he legislates on an hundred, or a thousand others, in regard to many, perhaps most, of which, he differs in opinion from those who actually voted for him. He can, therefore, with certainty, be said to represent nobody but himself.[102]

Thus, for Spooner, the suggestion that representative government constituted rule by the majority was a mere fiction. In light of this, Spooner countered Phillips' objection to the practicality of judicial interpretation that strives to be consistent with natural justice, with a practical objection of his own:

> If the principle is to be acted upon, that the majority have a right to rule arbitrarily, there is no legitimate way of carrying out that principle, but by requiring, either that a majority of the whole people, (or of the voters,) should vote in favor of every separate law, or by requiring the entire

---

100. *Id.* at 10.
101. SPOONER, *The Unconstitutionality of Slavery*, *supra* note 17, at 153. Spooner goes on to observe that, because only a bare majority is required for a quorum, in practice the opinions of only a fortieth of the people need be represented in statutory legislation. *Id.*
102. *Id.* at 154.

unanimity in the representative bodies, who actually represent a majority of the people.[103]

Of course, Spooner denied "that a majority, however large, have any right to rule so as to violate the natural rights of any single individual. It is as unjust for millions if men to murder, ravish, enslave, rob, or otherwise injure a single individual, as it is for another single individual to do it."[104]

Despite the occasional smugness of his tone towards Spooner, Phillips' position was not unmoved by the force of Spooner's arguments. As noted by Hans Baade, whereas in his previous pamphlet Phillips had relied

on the debates of the Philadelphia Convention as reported in Madison's Notes, Phillips now followed Spooner's lead in characterizing the Founding Fathers as mere clerks employed to draft the Constitution. . . .

In a basic shift from the "subjective" originalist position underlying his "Pro-Slavery Compact" tract, Wendell Phillips now argues that the intent of those who had adopted the Constitution had to be ascertained not from convention reports but from contemporaneous expositions.[105]

In defense of this position, Phillips offered many learned authorities and passages from Supreme Court cases, but one stands out: Chief Justice Taney's opinion in *Aldridge v. Williams*[106] decided the same year that Spooner's book was published. In *Williams*, Taney rejects any reliance on "the construction placed upon [the statute in question] by individual members of Congress in the debate which took place on its passage, nor by the motives or reasons assigned by them for supporting or opposing amendments that were offered."[107] While this statement supports Spooner's rejection of Phillips' reliance upon Madison's Notes, Phillips seizes upon Taney's further statement that "we must gather [the] intention [of the majority of

---

103. *Id.* at 154-55 n.*.
104. *Id.*
105. Baade, *supra* note 6, at 1049-50. Phillips now defended reliance on Madison's Notes as "fair and legitimate evidence of the sense in which the Constitution was accepted" by the state conventions. PHILLIPS, REVIEW OF SPOONER, *supra* note 12, at 33.
106. Aldridge v. Williams, 44 U.S. [3 How.] 9 (1845). Phillips also cites for authority, Chief Justice Marshall's opinion in *The Antelope*, 23 U.S. [10 Wheat.] 66 (1815), the case in which Marshall ordered the return to their foreign "owners" of at least some of the slaves captured by pirates who had been apprehended by a United States revenue cutter. The passage by Marshall, which Phillips cites (PHILLIPS, REVIEW OF SPOONER, *supra* note 12, at 23), reads, in part: "That it [the slave trade] is contrary to the law of nature, will scarcely be denied. . . . Whatever might be the answer of the moralist to this question, a jurist must seek its *legal* solution in those principles of action which are sanctioned by the usages, the national acts, and the general assent of the world, of which he considers himself a part." *The Antelope*, 23 U.S. at 66. In contrast, Spooner excoriates Phillips' teacher, Justice Story, for his opinion in Prigg v. Pennsylvania, 41 U.S. [16 Peters] 539 (1842), in which Story rejects all appeals to "uniform rules of interpretation" or "rules of interpretation of a general nature" to reach a pro-slavery outcome on historical grounds. *See* SPOONER, *The Unconstitutionality of Slavery*, *supra* note 17, at 282, Appendix A.
107. *Williams*, 44 U.S. at 24.

both houses] from the language there used, comparing it, when any ambiguity exists, *with the laws on the same subject*, and looking, if necessary, *to the public history of the times in which it was passed.*"[108] That Northern abolitionist Phillips would rely on the authority of Southerner Taney is not merely ironic. If Taney provides authority for an "objective" approach to original intent, Phillips returns the favor by providing Taney the evidence he uses in his most infamous opinion to establish that the intent, and therefore the Constitution itself, is pro-slavery.[109]

For despite Phillips effort to dispute Spooner on Spooner's terms, the principal *theoretical* reason for rejecting Spooner's approach Phillips shared with Chief Justice Taney in his opinion in *Dred Scott v. Stanford*[110]: Spooner's interpretation runs contrary to the intentions of the framers of both the Declaration of Independence and the Constitution. Referring to the Declaration's affirmation "that all men are created equal; that they are endowed by their Creator with certain inalienable rights,"[111] Taney answered:

> The general words above quoted would seem to embrace the whole human family, and if they were used in a similar instrument at this day would be so understood. But it is too clear for dispute, that the enslaved African race were *not intended* to be included, and formed no part of the people who framed and adopted this declaration. . . .[112]

As for the Constitution, Taney interpreted its meaning in light of attitudes towards slaves held by members of the founding generation. "The duty of the court is, to interpret the instrument they have framed, with the best lights we can obtain on the subject, and to administer it as we find it, according to its *true intent* and meaning when it was adopted."[113]

Thus, Taney asserted that "there are two clauses in the Constitution which point directly and specifically to the negro race as a separate class of persons, and show clearly that they were not regarded as a portion of the people or citizens of the Government then formed,"[114] notwithstanding the fact that the word "negro" does not appear in the Constitution. He asserts that "[o]ne of these clauses reserves to each of the thirteen States the right to import slaves until the year 1808, if it thinks proper,"[115] though, in the passage he is discussing, the Constitution refers to "persons" not

---

108. *See* PHILLIPS, REVIEW OF SPOONER, *supra* note 12, at 30 (quoting from Taney's opinion in *Aldridge v. Williams*, 44 U.S. [3 How.] 9 (1845)) (emphasis added).
109. *See* Baade, *supra* note 6, at 1051 (referring to "the embracement of Wendell Phillips's constitutional theory by a Southern-dominated Supreme Court").
110. Dred Scott v. Sandford, 60 U.S. 393 (1857).
111. THE DECLARATION OF INDEPENDENCE para. * (U.S. 1776).
112. *Dred Scott*, 60 U.S. at 410 (emphasis added).
113. *Id.* at 405 (emphasis added).
114. *Id.* at 411.
115. *Id.*

"slaves." He asserts that in "the other provision the States pledge themselves to each other to maintain the right of property of the master, by delivering up to him any slave who may have escaped from his service, and be found within their respective territories,"[116] though in this provision, the Constitution speaks not of slaves, but of "persons held to service." Taney never actually presents any evidence as to the meaning of these clauses, but rather assumes these clauses "directly and specifically"[117] refer to slavery, probably because of the evidence he presents concerning the general attitudes towards and legal treatment of slaves by members of the founding generation.

Though Spooner was seeking the "original meaning"[118] of the Constitution, he did not think this meaning could be grounded on the original intent, either of the Constitution's framers or its ratifiers. One reason I have already mentioned, is his contention that such intentions were hopelessly conflicting and indeterminate.[119] "No two of the members of the convention would probably have agreed in their representations of what the constitution really was. No two of the people would have agreed in their understanding of the constitution when they adopted it."[120] But Spooner also rejected relying on original intentions either of the framers of the constitution or of the ratifiers, even were such intentions determinable. "It is not the intentions men actually had, but the intentions they constitutionally expressed; that make up the constitution."[121]

Spooner's reasons for rejecting the intentions of the Framers as a source of constitutional meaning—reason that are applicable both to Taney and Phillips—sound quite modern:

> The intentions of the framers of the constitution . . . have nothing to do with fixing the legal meaning of the constitution. That convention were not delegated to adopt or establish a constitution; but only to consult, devise and recommend. The instrument, when it came from their hands, was a mere proposal, having no legal force or authority. It finally derived all its validity and obligation, as a frame of government, from its adoption by the people at large.[122]

Spooner rejected any reliance on Madison's then-recently-disclosed notes of the convention (or Elliot's Debates) where these notes reveal an intention that suborns

---

116. *Id.*
117. *Id.*
118. SPOONER, *The Unconstitutionality of Slavery, supra* note 17, at 218 ("It is the original meaning of the constitution itself that we are now seeking for. . . .").
119. *See supra* note 56 and accompanying text.
120. SPOONER, *The Unconstitutionality of Slavery, supra* note 17, at 122.
121. *Id.* at 226.
122. *Id.* at 114.

the written constitution and natural justice.[123] Spooner refers to these as "meagre [sic] snatches of argument, intent or opinion, uttered by a few only of the members; jotted down by one of them, (Mr. Madison,) merely for his own convenience, or from the suggestions of his own mind; and only reported to us fifty years afterwards by a posthumous publication of his papers."[124] He then asks,

> Did Mr. Madison, when he took his oath of office, as President of the United States, swear to support these scraps of debate, which he had filed away among his private papers?—Or did he swear to support that written instrument, which the people of the country had agreed to, and which was known to them, and to all the world, as the constitution of the United States?[125]

Assuming a majority of the convention really had intended to sanction slavery, Spooner rejects any suggestion that this intention would be binding on others. Were this the case:

---

123. *Id.* at 117-18 n.*:
"Elliot's Debates," so often referred to, are, if possible, a more miserable authority than Mr. Madison's notes. He seems to have picked up the most of them from the newspapers of the day, in which they were reported by nobody now probably knows whom. . . . [Spooner then quotes from prefaces to several volumes in which the sources of information are described.] It is from such stuff as this, collected and published thirty-five and forty years after the constitution was adopted—stuff very suitable for constitutional dreams to be made of—that our courts and people now make their constitutional law, in preference to adopting the law of the constitution itself. In this way they manufacture law strong enough to bind three millions of men in slavery.

124. *Id.* at 117.

125. *Id.* For what it is worth, Madison, in response to a representative arguing against the constitutionality of the first national bank, offered the following as guides to interpreting the powers granted to the general government by the Constitution:

[1.] An interpretation that destroys the very characteristic of the Government, cannot be just.

[2.] Were a meaning is clear, the consequences, whatever they may be, are to be admitted; where doubtful, it is fairly triable by its consequences.

[3.] In controverted cases, the meaning of the parties to the instrument, if to be collected by reasonable evidence, is a proper guide.

[4.] Contemporary and concurrent expositions are a reasonable evidence of the meaning of the parties.

[5.] In admitting or rejecting a constructive authority, not only the degree of its incidentality to an express authority is to be regarded, but the degree of its importance also; since on this will depend the probability or improbability of its being left to construction.

1 THE DEBATES AND PROCEEDINGS IN THE CONGRESS OF THE UNITED STATES 1896 (1791). Notice that Madison speaks, perhaps ambiguously, of the *meaning*, not the *intentions*, of the parties to the instrument. Thus, "contemporary and concurrent expositions" may be evidence only of how certain words or terms were commonly used, not whether they were intended to be used in some other manner. But any such meaning must be squared with the overall scheme of government established by other parts of the Constitution. For additional examples of interpretive methods used by the founding generation, see H. Jefferson Powell, *The Original Understanding of Original Intent*, 98 HARV. L. REV. 885 (1985); Baade, *supra* note 6.

Any forty or fifty men, like those who framed the constitution, may now secretly concoct another, that is honest in its terms, and yet in secret conclave confess to each other the criminal objects they intended to accomplish by it, if its honest character should enable them to secure for it the adoption of the people.—But if the people should adopt such a constitution, would they thereby adopt any of the criminal and secret purposes of its authors? Or if the guilty confessions of these conspirators should be revealed fifty years afterwards, would judicial tribunals look to them as giving the government any authority for violating the legal meaning of the words of such constitution, and for so construing them as to subserve the criminal and shameless purposes of its originators?[126]

Most thoughtful modern-day originalists will concede much of this when they are being careful.[127] Instead they assert that it is the intention of the *ratifiers* that provides the basis of a proper interpretation[128] and, as Taney and Phillips argue, everyone in those days knew that the Constitution sanctioned slavery. Spooner rejects the suggestion that there was a consensus among the founding generation that the Constitution *sanctioned* slavery:

If the instrument had contained any tangible sanction of slavery, the people, in some parts of the country certainly, would sooner have had it burned by the hands of the common hangman, than they would have adopted it, and thus sold themselves as pimps to slavery, covered as they were with the scars they had received in fighting the battles of freedom.[129]

Assuming the framers of the Constitution intended to sanction slavery, Spooner offers this as the reason why they chose not to include any explicit reference to slavery. "[T]he members of the convention knew that such was the feeling of a large

---

126. SPOONER, *The Unconstitutionality of Slavery, supra* note 17, at 118.

127. *See, e.g.,* Richard S. Kay, *Adherence to The Original Intentions in Constitutional Adjudication: Three Objections And Responses,* 82 NW. U. L. REV. 226, 247 (1988):

[T]he role of "the People" was played by the special ratifying conventions in the individual states. The drafters at the Philadelphia Convention could claim no such mandate from "the people." Some supporters of the Constitution went so far as to disparage the importance of the Convention, except insofar as it was able to place a proposal before the state conventions.

Id.

128. *See, e.g., id.* ("The inquiry into original intent, therefore, should focus on the intentions of the various ratifying bodies who possessed the constituent authority."); *see also* Richard S. Kay, *"Originalist" Values and Constitutional Interpretation,* 19 HARV. J.L. & PUB. POL'Y 335, 338 (1996) ("The relevant actors were not the actual drafters of the language, but the members of the ratifying conventions that gave it the force of law.").

129. SPOONER, *The Unconstitutionality of Slavery, supra* note 17, at 119.

portion of the people; and for that reason, if for no other, they dared insert in the instrument no legal sanction of slavery."[130]

Construing the Constitution like a contract means that, while the subjective *agreement* of all parties may trump any objective meaning, where there is a subjective *disagreement*, parties are entitled to rely on the objective meaning.[131] So

> [i]f there were a single honest man in the nation, who assented, in good faith, to the honest and legal meaning of the constitution, it would be unjust and unlawful towards him to change the meaning of the instrument so as to sanction slavery, even though every other man in the nation should testify that, in agreeing to the constitution, he intended that slavery should be sanctioned.[132]

But what of Taney's argument that the slaveholders would never have consented to a constitution that did not sanction slavery?[133] Such a hypothetical lack of consent does not move Spooner, because, by this argument slaveholders are presumed to *have* consented to *this* Constitution and yet nevertheless this Constitution did not sanction slavery. "The intentions of all the parties, slaves, slaveholders, and non-slaveholders, throughout the country, must be presumed to have been precisely alike, because, in theory, they all agreed to the same instrument."[134] Moreover, "when communities establish governments for the purpose of maintaining justice and right,

---

130. *Id.*; *see id.* at 201 ("We have abundant evidence that this fraud was intended by some of the *framers* of the constitution. They knew that an instrument legalizing slavery could not gain the assent of the north. They therefore agreed upon an instrument honest in its terms, with the intent of misinterpreting it after it should be adopted. The fraud of the framers, however, does not of itself, implicate the people.").

131. *See* Randy E. Barnett, *The Sound of Silence: Default Rules and Contractual Consent*, 78 VA. L. REV. 821, 858-59 (1992) ("[I]n contract law, we protect a party's reliance on objective appearances, unless it can be shown that the parties shared a common subjective understanding of a term."). *Cf.* E. ALLAN FARNSWORTH, CONTRACTS § 7.9, at p. 511 (2d ed. 1990):

> The court does indeed carry out their intentions in those relatively rare cases in which the parties attached the same meaning to the language in question. But if the parties attached different meanings to that language, the court's task is the more complex one of applying a standard of reasonableness to determine which party's intention is to be carried out at the expense of the other's. And if the parties attached no meaning to that language, its task is to find by a standard of reasonableness a meaning that does not accord with any intention at all.

Id.

132. SPOONER, *The Unconstitutionality of Slavery*, *supra* note 17, at 123.

133. *See, e.g.*, Dred Scott v. Sandford, 60 U.S. 393, 416 (1857): "[I]t cannot be believed that the large slave-holding States regarded [slaves] as included in the word citizens, or would have consented to a Constitution which might compel them to receive them in that character from another State." Of course, none of the *states* ratified the constitution, only the *people* of each state in convention, and therefore Spooner is more careful than Taney when he refers to the consent of slaveholders, rather than "slaveholding states." Moreover, Spooner also notes that slaveholders were themselves a minority among the people of so-called slaveholding states. *See* SPOONER, *The Unconstitutionality of Slavery*, *supra* note 17, at 125.

134. SPOONER, *The Unconstitutionality of Slavery*, *supra* note 17, at 215.

the assent of all the thieves, robbers, pirates, and slaveholders, is as much presumed, as is the assent of the most honest portion of [the] community."[135] Thus, Spooner, concludes:

> There would be just as much reason in saying that it cannot be supposed that thieves, robbers, pirates, or criminals of any kind, would consent to the establishment of governments that should have authority to suppress *their* business, as there is in saying that slaveholders cannot be supposed to consent to a government that should have power to suppress slaveholding.[136]

We may sum up Spooner's analysis of these three clauses as follows: even if we assume that the framers or ratifiers of the Constitution intended to reference slavery in these three passages, when the framers of the Constitution chose to speak euphemistically rather than making their intentions explicit, they simply failed—whether by intention or inadvertence—to effectively incorporate an authorization for slavery into the Constitution. These sections cannot, therefore, prevent other portions of the Constitution[137]—such as that providing for the writ of habeas corpus[138]—from being interpreted to render slavery unconstitutional. Even had everyone in the founding generation "known" that certain clauses were "intended" to sanction slavery,[139] the generally accepted meaning of the language chosen to carry out their intentions fell short of the mark. In this respect, Spooner's version of "original meaning" runs contrary to those modern originalists who base interpretation on original intent.[140] It views the framers as teachers who well-understood the scheme

---

135. *Id.* at 186.

136. *Id.* The passage continues:

If this argument were good for anything, we should have to apply it to the state constitutions, and construe them, if possible, so as to sanction all kinds of crimes which men commit, on the ground that the criminals themselves could not be supposed to have consented to any governments that did not sanction them.

Id.

137. *See id.* at 270-77 (discussing the "power of the general government over slavery").

138. U.S. CONST. art. I, § 9.

139. In this regard, Spooner observed:

Why . . . do not men say distinctly, that the constitution *did* sanction slavery, instead of saying that it *intended* to sanction it? We are not accustomed to use the word *"intention,"* when speaking of the other grants and sanctions of the constitution. We do not say, for example, that the constitution *intended* to authorize congress "to coin money," but that it *did* authorize them to coin it. . . . The reason is obvious. If they were to say unequivocally that it *did* sanction it, they would lay themselves under the necessity of pointing to the *words* that sanction it; and they are aware that the *words alone* of the constitution do not come up to that point.

SPOONER, *The Unconstitutionality of Slavery, supra* note 17, at 57.

140. Richard Kay, for example, distinguishes between "original understanding"—which corresponds to Spooner's "original meaning"—and "original intentions" versions of originalism. Original understanding "differs from the . . . 'original intentions' version by eschewing reliance upon the supposed subjective intentions of the enactors of the Constitution." Kay, *"Originalist" Values and Constitutional Interpretation, supra* note 129, at 337. Kay favors the latter when the two come in conflict:

they adopted, rather than as wardens whose commands must be interpreted consistently with their subjective intentions.[141] Were evidence of history to overrule an innocent interpretation of the text, in Spooner's words, "it would follow that the constitution would, in reality, be *made* by the historians, and not by the people."[142]

Although the founding generation is today often condemned for its refusal to abolish slavery, were Spooner's interpretative method to have been adopted, slaveholders would have been the ones to condemn the framers for their failure of nerve. For they failed to *legally* sanction the crime they could not bring themselves to name.

CONCLUSION: ASSESSING SPOONER'S APPROACH

Lysander Spooner's book, *The Unconstitutionality of Slavery*, represents, perhaps, the most extensive effort to interpret the United States Constitution in light of the natural rights that were expressly recognized in the Declaration of Independence and which provided the background for the written Constitution. Of greatest interest is the sophistication and scope of this approach. Spooner is not content simply to condemn as unenforceable provisions of the Constitution or acts of legislation that he thinks violate natural rights. That part of his analysis consumes a mere twenty pages out of nearly three hundred. In addition, he adopts a presumption in favor of reading the words of a constitution in a light most favorable to justice as defined by natural rights, and then takes on the burden of finding such a meaning. To find a defensible meaning of the words used in the Constitution that is both consistent with legal usage and inconsistent with injustice, Spooner examines other provisions of the Constitution, and how the disputed terms were used in colonial charters,[143] colonial statutes,[144] the Declaration of Independence,[145] state constitutions in 1789,[146] and the Articles of Confederation.[147]

Reading all three hundred pages, one is struck by the herculean nature of Spooner's endeavor—indeed by its similarity to what Ronald Dworkin argues that Hercules, Dworkin's hypothetical judge, ought to do: construct a set of principles of justice that both explain and justify the constitutional text at hand in such a way as to render it consistent with all other texts recognized as authoritative within this legal

---

[L]egitimacy concerns may oblige us to choose a constitutional meaning that was intended by the enactors, even when that meaning was not inferable from an examination of the text, either on its face or in the context of the time of enactment."

Id. at 338. For Spooner, who grounds the legitimacy of the Constitution on the natural rights that persons bring to the compact and on their consent, "legitimacy concerns" cut in the other direction.

141. *See generally* Randy E. Barnett, *The Relevance of Framers' Intent*, 19 HARV. J.L. PUB. POL'Y 403 (1996).

142. SPOONER, *The Unconstitutionality of Slavery*, *supra* note 17, at 284, Appendix A.

143. *See id.* at 21-31.

144. *See id.* at 32-36.

145. *See id.* at 36-39.

146. *See id.* at 39-51.

147. *See id.* at 51-54.

tradition.[148] Where the text and other authoritative materials provide competing meanings, Hercules attempts to make the Constitution, in Dworkin's words, "the best it can be."[149] Here's how Spooner expresses this Dworkinian point (in words that also echo Dworkin's distinction between principle and policy):[150] "When the intentions of statutes and constitutions are not clearly expressed in the instruments themselves, the law always *presumes* them. And it presumes the most *just and beneficial* intentions, which the words of the instruments, taken as a whole, can fairly be made to express, or imply."[151]

Moreover, like Hercules,[152] Spooner views himself as constrained by the very texts and authorities he is attempting to interpret: "Not that, in interpreting written laws, the plain and universal principles of philology are to be *violated*, for the sake of making the laws conform to justice; for that would be equivalent to abolishing all written laws, and abolishing the use of words as a means of describing laws."[153] Spooner allows for, what Dworkin has usefully called "embedded mistakes."[154] An embedded mistake is statute or constitutional provision whose meaning is unjust but which meaning and specific authority cannot be denied. Yet, though such a mistake may still have authority, it does not provide the basis, or what Dworkin refers to as its "gravitational force,"[155] for interpreting by extension other provisions in an unjust manner.

Despite the resemblance between Spooner's and Hercules' interpretive method, Spooner faces a less herculean a task than does Dworkin's Hercules. For Spooner did not have to construct on his own a political theory that did justice to the legal materials he sought to interpret. Instead, he could start with the fundamental assumptions about natural rights and justice that he shared with those who wrote and ratified the Constitution—including many of those who held slaves or defended slavery—and which is reflected in their handiwork here and elsewhere. Thus it

---

148. *See* RONALD DWORKIN, TAKING RIGHTS SERIOUSLY 105-30 (1977); RONALD DWORKIN, LAW'S EMPIRE 239-54 (1986).

149. DWORKIN, LAW'S EMPIRE, *supra* note 149, at 379.
> Judges who accept the interpretive ideal of integrity decide hard cases by trying to find, in some coherent set of principles about people's rights and duties, the best constructive interpretation of the political structure and legal doctrine of their community. They try to make that complex structure and record the best these can be.

Id. at 255.

150. *See* DWORKIN, TAKING RIGHTS SERIOUSLY, *supra* note 149, at 90 ("Arguments of principle are arguments intended to establish an individual right; arguments of policy are arguments intended to establish a collective goal.").

151. SPOONER, *The Unconstitutionality of Slavery, supra* note 17, at 157 (last emphasis added).

152. *See, e.g.,* DWORKIN, LAW'S EMPIRE, *supra* note 149, at 380 ("[Hercules']convictions about justice or wise policy are constrained by his overall interpretive judgment, not only by the text of the statute but also by a variety of considerations of fairness and integrity.").

153. SPOONER, *The Unconstitutionality of Slavery, supra* note 17, at 210.

154. *See* DWORKIN, TAKING RIGHTS SERIOUSLY, *supra* note 149, at 121.

155. *Id.* ("[E]mbedded mistakes are those whose specific authority is fixed so that survives its loss of gravitational force. . . .").

should be no great surprise to find a constitutional meaning that is consistent both with a particular conception of natural rights and with other authoritative texts, when the Constitution and these other texts were all authored by persons who shared the same commitment to natural rights and justice.

Assuming one agreed that Spooner has succeeded in his quest for a reasonable meaning that is consistent with both his and the founding generation's conception of natural justice, there remains the question of whether their conception of justice is correct. Perhaps it is asking too much of a self-educated lawyer from Worcester to provide a complete justification for this then-widely accepted conception of natural rights. Nevertheless, what justification he does offer, while rooted in the classical natural rights tradition, has a surprisingly modern flavor.

The more classical part of Spooner's argument might today be termed prudential: the recognition and respect for a particular set of natural rights are necessary conditions of social peace.[156] Other parts of his argument, particularly his argument for why government has an obligation to respect these prudential norms, resembles the approach known today as "rational choice."[157] Spooner argues that, if government is justified at all,[158] then it can only be on the basis of unanimous consent. But, as unanimous consent was not in fact obtained, then it must be presumed. And the only intention that can be presumed is that to which *all* honest persons would consent. And no honest person would consent to authorize a government to violate the very liberty that government is being instituted to protect.[159] Though Spooner does not maintain it to be impossible for the people to have made a "law" explicitly purporting to alienate a portion of their liberty (as defined by natural rights),[160] it cannot simply be assumed that they have done so in the absence of a clear and unambiguous expression of this intent.

---

156. *See supra* note 25 and accompanying text. For an excellent account of classical natural rights theories, see MICHAEL P. ZUCKERT, NATURAL RIGHTS AND THE NEW REPUBLICANISM (1994).

157. *See, e.g.,* DAVID GAUTHIER, MORALS BY AGREEMENT 9 (1986):

Moral principles are . . . the objects of fully voluntary *ex ante* agreement among rational persons. Such agreement is hypothetical, in supposing a pre-moral context for the adoption of moral rules and practices. But the parties to agreement are real, determinate individuals, distinguished by their capacities, situations, and concerns. . . . As rational persons understanding the structure of their interaction, they recognize a place for mutual constraint, and so for a moral dimension in their affairs.

Id. I do not mean to suggest that the "modern flavor" I attribute to a rational choice approach is not itself rooted in more classical political philosophy. Gauthier considers his approach to be Hobbesian. *See id.* at 10 ("Our theory of morals falls in an unpopular tradition, as the identity of its greatest advocate, Thomas Hobbes, will confirm.").

158. After the Civil War, Spooner came to reject the legitimacy of the Constitution in his famous essay, *No Treason, No. VI: The Constitution of No Authority, supra* note 34. Yet even in his earlier work on slavery, he is careful to argue hypothetically, i.e. *if* the Constitution has authority, then it must be interpreted in the following manner.

159. *Cf.* JOHN LOCKE, TWO TREATISES OF GOVERNMENT II, § 131 (1698) (Mentor ed., 1965), at 398-99. There Locke says that individuals only surrender a portion of their power to enforce their rights to society, "yet it being only with the intention in every one to better preserve himself his Liberty and Property; (For no rational Creature can be supposed to change his condition with an intention to be worse.)." *Id* at 398.

160. However, if the right purported to be alienated was inalienable, any such "law" would not be obligatory or binding in conscience on the citizenry.

Thus, hypothetical consent is asked to do the work that actual consent cannot in justifying the authority exercised in the name of the Constitution,[161] and it does so by presuming a meaning to which all would agree in the absence of clear evidence that would rebut this presumption. Spooner uses much the same approach to justify the method of interpretation he employs:

> But of the reason and authority of all these rules [of interpretation], the reader must necessarily judge for himself; for their authority rests on their reason, and on usage, and not on any statute or constitution enacting them. *And the way for the reader to judge of their soundness is, for him to judge whether they are the rules by which he wishes his own contracts, and the laws on which he himself relies for protection, to be construed.*[162]

Does Spooner's endeavor succeed or is it merely an interesting failure? Since this is a question that can only be answered by assessing all the analysis and evidence Spooner presents, I ask you not to reach your own opinion on the basis of my brief and necessarily incomplete summary, but to read Spooner for yourself.[163] For what it is worth, having read the entire work, my own assessment is that it offers an interpretation of the Constitution that is superior to the rival one presented, for example, by Justice Taney in *Dred Scott*. And, while Wendell Phillips mounted a formidable challenge and exposed some genuine errors of Spooner, for reasons I have given above,[164] I cannot agree with Robert Cover's entirely unsupported claim that Phillips' response "destroyed Spooner's position."[165] Nor can I share David Richards' characterization of Spooner's interpretation of the allegedly pro-slavery provisions of the Constitution, amidst an otherwise favorable treatment, as "textually strained."[166] Bear

---

161. Spooner's later explicit rejection of the authority of the Constitution can be viewed as a rejection of hypothetical consent as a sufficient justification of constitutional legitimacy, although, to my knowledge, he does not discuss this issue, or what motivated his apparent change of heart. *See, e.g.,* LYSANDER SPOONER, *No Treason, No. VI: The Constitution of No Authority, supra* note 34, at 31 ("[T]here exists no such thing as a government created by, or resting upon, any consent, compact, or agreement of 'the people of the United States' with each other. . . .").

162. SPOONER, *The Unconstitutionality of Slavery, supra* note 17, at 222.

163. Of course, you should also read Wendell Phillips' critique of Spooner. Apart from adding balance and showing where Spooner overreached, examining Phillips—after reading Part I of Spooner's book, but before reading Part II—helps explain the presence of some lengthy and seemingly esoteric arguments in Part II, as well as the addition of so much otherwise cumulative evidence and authority.

164. *See supra* Part III.B.

165. COVER, *supra* note 5, at 151 n.*. Cover gives no reasons to support his characterization and fails even to acknowledge Spooner's lengthy response to Phillips in Part II.

166. David A. J. Richards, *Abolitionist Political and Constructional Theory and The Reconstruction Amendments,* 25 LOY. L.A. L. REV. 1187, 1193 (1992):

> The interpretive primacy of political theory was sustained and defended by the most theoretically profound advocate of this position, Lysander Spooner, by denying any weight to the constitutional text or history in conflict with the claims of rights-based political theory. The clauses of the Constitution apparently recognizing state-endorsed slavery were to be interpreted not to recognize slavery on the theory that any interpretation should be accorded the words, no matter how textually strained, that did

in mind that, if Spooner did not succeed, then perhaps *Dred Scott* was rightly decided after all, as were *Prigg* and *The Antelope*.

Instead, I would suggest that, if Spooner failed, it was at a more fundamental level than the specific interpretive issue of whether or not the original Constitution authorized slavery. For if Spooner failed, it was in failing to offer a theory by which the Constitution can be interpreted so as to make laws enacted pursuant to its authority legitimate and therefore binding in conscience on the citizenry. Spooner's later, more radical, writings reflect his own rejection of the Constitution's authority, an authority he had assumed, perhaps *arguendo*, throughout *The Unconstitutionality of Slavery*. Those who wish today to contend that the Constitution has authority to bind the citizenry in conscience should hope that Spooner's interpretive method, if not its specific application to slavery, succeeded.

---

not recognize slavery. . . .
Id. As with Cover, no evidence is educed in support of this claim, though the statement is repeated in David A. J. Richards, *Comparative Revolutionary Constitutionalism: A Research Agenda For Comparative Law*, 26 N.Y.U. J. INT'L L. & POL. 1, 20 (1993). Richards' mischaracterization of Spooner's methodology has given much aid and comfort to Raoul Berger who has quoted it repeatedly in place of dealing directly with Spooner's claims. *See, e.g.,* Raoul Berger, *Constitutional Interpretation and Activist Fantasies*, 82 KY. L.J. 1, 19 (1993/94) (quoting Richards).

Legal Positivism, Abolitionist Litigation, and the New Jersey Slave Case of 1845

Daniel R. Ernst

At 10:00 A.M. on May 21, 1845, 'the tall, straight figure and pale, grave face of the slave's friend, Alvan Stewart', turned toward the justices of the New Jersey Supreme Court as he commenced his opening argument in the companion cases, *State v. Post* and *State v. Van Beuren*. In the ensuing hours, Stewart argued for the immediate abolition of slavery and black apprenticeship in New Jersey. Although Stewart relied upon many authorities, the justices and the attorneys for the defendants believed that his most promising argument was based upon the state constitution of 1844, the first of the state's fundamental laws to declare that 'all men are by nature free and independent'. On the following day, the defense counsel—A.O. Zabriskie, a Hackensack attorney, and Joseph P. Bradley, the future U.S. Supreme Court Justice—spoke with 'much energy and ingenuity' until five o'clock. The reply of the 'Abolition Ajax' lasted until 10:30 and closed with an impassioned appeal to the justices. 'Such was the impressiveness with which the closing appeal of the advocate for freedom was delivered', a newspaperman reported, that none of the large audience wished to 'break the spell his eloquence had cast upon the assembly'. At length, the bench arose, and Chief Justice Joseph Hornblower adjourned the court.[1]

The 'New Jersey Slave Case', as the newspapers of the day called it, was brought by a determined band of abolitionists who sought to win support for emancipation in their state and throughout their country. Although they genuinely hoped to win their case, the abolitionists also brought suit in order

Daniel R. Ernst is a Legal History Fellow at the Institute for Legal Studies of the University of Wisconsin—Madison Law School.

I gratefully acknowledge the assistance of the New Jersey Historical Commission, which supported my research through its Afro-American History Grant-in-Aid Program. I also thank the staffs of the New Jersey Historical Society, the New Jersey State Archives, the New York State Historical Association, and the New York Historical Society for their assistance and permission to quote from materials in their possession. Finally, I thank Stanley N. Katz, Louis P. Masur, and James M. McPherson for their comments on earlier drafts of this paper.

1. Luther Rawson Marsh, ed., *Writings and Speeches of Alvan Stewart on Slavery* (New York, 1860) 26 [hereinafter: March, ed., *Writings of Alvan Stewart*]; Alvan Stewart, *A Legal Argument Before the Supreme Court of the State of New Jersey at this May Term, 1845, at Trenton, for the Deliverance of Four Thousand Persons from Bondage* (New York, 1845) 45, 52 [hereinafter: Stewart, *Legal Argument*]; Newark *Daily Advertiser*, May 22, 1845; New York *Evening Express*, May 24, 1845.

to focus the attention of an indifferent public on their cause. Viewed as one facet of their long campaign to end slavery, the case can tell us much about the New Jersey abolitionists and the racial attitudes of their fellow New Jerseyans.[2]

But *Post* was more than a publicity stunt; it was a lawsuit earnestly argued by talented lawyers and thoughtfully decided by conscientious judges. Like other cases involving slavery, *Post* forced legal actors to reveal their fundamental assumptions about the ultimate source of authority for human law. In eighteenth-century America, those who stopped to think seriously about law found this ultimate authority in the laws of nature and God. Influenced by rational Christianity and moral philosophy, they believed that at some fundamental level positive laws embodied timeless rules and precepts established in nature by a clockmaker God. Unlike later legal thinkers, they would pause and affirm the moral component in Blackstone's famous definition of human law, as 'a rule of civil conduct prescribed by the supreme power in a state, commanding what is right and prohibiting what is wrong'.[3] Unlike later legal thinkers, too, they optimistically assumed that the supreme power of the state would rarely prescribe a moral wrong or violate a moral right.[4]

2. For the outlines of proslavery and antislavery sentiment in antebellum New Jersey, see Theodore Appleby, 'Opinions on Slavery in Burlington County, as Reflected in the New Jersey Mirror, and Burlington County Advertiser, 1830-1861' (M.A. thesis, Rutgers University, 1940) [hereinafter: Appleby, 'Opinions on Slavery']; John Cudd, 'The Unity of Reform: John Grimes and the *New Jersey Freeman*'. *New Jersey History* xcvii (1979) 197-212 [hereinafter: Cudd, 'Unity of Reform']; Philip Curtis Davis, 'The Persistence of Partisan Alignment: Issues, Leaders, and Votes in New Jersey, 1840-1860' (Ph.D. dissertation, Washington University, 1978) 157-203 [hereinafter: Davis, 'Persistence of Partisan Alignment']; Carl E. Hatch, 'Editor David Naar of Trenton: Profile of the Anti-Negro Mind', *New Jersey History* lxxxvi (1968) 70-87; David Armour Hillstrom, 'New Jersey and the Abolition Movement, 1830-1850' (Senior thesis, Princeton University, 1965) [hereinafter: Hillstrom, 'New Jersey and the Abolition Movement']; Francis D. Pingeon, 'Dissenting Attitudes toward the Negro in New Jersey — 1837', *New Jersey History* lxxxix (1971) 197-220; Clement Alexander Price, ed., *Freedom Not Far Distant: A Documentary History of Afro-Americans in New Jersey* (Newark, 1980); Douglas P. Seaton, 'Colonizers and Reluctant Colonists: The New Jersey Colonization Society and the Black Community, 1815-1848', *New Jersey History* xcvi (1978) 7-22; Arthur Zilversmit, 'Liberty and Property: New Jersey and the Abolition of Slavery', *New Jersey History* lxxviii (1970) 215-26 [hereinafter: Zilversmit, 'Liberty and Property'].

3. William Blackstone, *Commentaries on the Laws of England, A Facsimile of the First Edition 1765-1769*, 4 vols. (Chicago, 1979) i, 44; see Robert M. Cover, *Justice Accused: Antislavery and the Judicial Process* (New Haven, 1975) 25-26 [hereinafter: Cover, *Justice Accused*].

4. Morton J. Horwitz, *The Transformation of American Law, 1780-1860* (Cambridge, Mass., 1977) 1-30; Robert W. Gordon, 'Legal Thought and Legal Practice in the Age of American Enterprise, 1870-1920', in Gerald L. Geison, ed., *Professions and Professional Ideologies in America* (Chapel Hill, 1983) 82-97 [hereinafter: Gordon, 'Legal Thought and Legal Practice']; William M. Wiecek, 'Latimer: Lawyers, Abolitionists and the Problem of Unjust Laws', in Lewis Perry and Michael Fellman,

By 1840, such sentiments had become unfashionable, and the 'last of the old race of judges' (like R. Kent Newmyer's Joseph Story) and the practitioners of Federalist jurisprudence (like Stephen Presser's Samuel Chase) were coming to be seen as jurisprudential metaphysicians and partisan elitists.[5] Law was legitimate simply because it was created in a constitutionally ordained fashion, the new legal thinkers held. Lawyers were no longer guardians of the community's moral values; instead, their authority sprung from their superior knowledge of the 'science of the law', which they conceived of in morally neutral, pragmatic terms.[6]

The New Jersey Slave Case illustrates this jurisprudential change. To be sure, the lawyers and judges in the case were moved by concerns that neither they nor we would recognize as legal, such as the immorality of slavery, the social cost of emancipation, and hostility toward radical social movements. Undoubtedly these concerns influenced the decision-making of the justices in the case. Yet, with one exception, all of the legal actors sought to show that their positions were consistent with positivistic rules of legal reasoning. Although arguments from divine or natural law would remain prominent in the popular debate on slavery in the 1840s and 1850s, *Post* reveals that by 1845 such arguments had become unpersuasive in courts of law. To understand this divergence in the forms of popular and legal argument, we must first examine the sentiments of the supporters of the suit, the New Jersey State Anti-Slavery Society.

I

In New Jersey organized abolitionism started slowly and fared poorly. After decades of petitioning and agitation by Quakers in the eighteenth century, New Jersey became the last of the northern states to provide for gradual emancipation. 'An Act for the Gradual Abolition of Slavery' provided that children born to slaves after July 4, 1804 'shall be free' but 'remain servants' until the age of 25 (if male) or 21 (if female). Slaves born before that date remained unfree unless liberated by private manumission.[7]

---

eds., *Antislavery Reconsidered: New Perspectives on the Abolitionists* (Baton Rouge, 1979) 219-25.

5. R. Kent Newmyer, *Supreme Court Justice Joseph Story: Statesman of the Old Republic* (Chapel Hill, 1985) 382-92; Stephen B. Presser and Becky Bair Hurley, 'Saving God's Republic: The Jurisprudence of Samuel Chase', *University of Illinois Law Review* 771-822 (1984); Stephen B. Presser, 'A Tale of Two Judges: Richard Peters, Samuel Chase, and the Broken Promise of Federalist Jurisprudence', 73 *Northwestern University Law Review* 26-111 (1978).

6. See Gordon, 'Legal Thought and Legal Practice', supra note 4 at 82-97; Maxwell Bloomfield, *American Lawyers in a Changing Society, 1776-1876* (Cambridge, Mass., 1976) 136-90.

7. 'Act of Feb. 15, 1804', 1804 N.J. Laws 251. For the history of this legislation, see Arthur Zilversmit, *The First Emancipation: The Abolition of Slavery in the North*

As a result of this act, the slave population dropped from a high of 12,422 in the U.S. Census of 1800 to 674 in the census of 1840, less than 0.2 percent of New Jersey's total population. More than half of these slaves were over fifty-five years old.[8] The slaves were predominantly agricultural workers, and their masters were disproportionately likely to be of Dutch descent.[9]

After winning passage of the act of 1804, New Jersey Quakers directed their efforts to educating free blacks, aiding runaway slaves, and decrying the persistence of an illegal international slave trade.[10] A long hiatus in organized abolitionism in the state ended only in August 1839 with the founding of a New Jersey affiliate of the American Anti-Slavery Society. The eighty-one members who attended the first meeting of the New Jersey State Anti-Slavery Society (NJSASS) announced their intention to attain, 'by all righteous means in our power, the immediate abolition of slavery from our whole land'. While members aimed 'more particularly to the abandonment of this system from our State and the District of Columbia', they also vowed to 'endeavor in the language of Christian warning and persuasion to induce our southern brethren to restore to freedom their imbruted bondmen'.[11]

From its founding the state society had the support of only a tiny fraction of New Jersey's population. None of its members were socially prominent, and few resided outside of the northeastern counties of Bergen, Passaic, Hudson, Essex, and Union.[12] Vilified in the press as 'unreasonable fanatics likely to accomplish no good',[13] the society in 1844 founded its own monthly newspaper, the *New Jersey Freeman*, under the editorship of John

---

(Chicago, 1967) 141-46, 175-76, 184-89, 192-99 [hereinafter: Zilversmit, *First Emancipation*] and Zilversmit, 'Liberty and Property', supra note 2.

8. *Return of the Whole Number of Persons Within the Several Districts of the United States* (Washington, 1801) 34; *Compendium of the Enumeration of the Inhabitants and Statistics of the United States* (Washington, 1841).

9. Peter O. Wacker, 'Patterns and Problems in the Historical Geography of the Afro-American Population of New Jersey, 1726-1860', in Ralph E. Ehrenberg, ed., *Pattern and Process: Research in Historical Geography* (Washington, 1967) 25-72; Steven B. Frakt, 'Patterns of Slave-Holding in Somerset County, N.J.' (Seminar paper, Rutgers University, 1967); Hubert G. Smith, 'Slavery and Attitudes on Slavery, Hunterdon County, N.J.', *Proceedings of the New Jersey Historical Society*, n.s. lviii (1940) 151-69, 240-53. For the work patterns of New Jersey slaves, see Robert Christian Kuser, 'Negro Slavery in New Jersey, 1702-1804' (Senior thesis, Princeton University, 1964) 47-65.

10. Zilversmit, 'Liberty and Property', supra note 2 at 217, 221.

11. New Jersey State Anti-Slavery Society Minutes, August 27, 1839, New Jersey Historical Society [hereinafter: NJSASS Minutes].

12. Hillstrom, 'New Jersey and the Abolition Movement', supra note 2 at 42, 69-70, 72.

13. New Brunswick *Weekly Freedonian*, quoted in Hillstrom, 'New Jersey and the Abolition Movement', supra note 2 at 43-44; see also Theodore Appleby, 'Opinions on Slavery', supra note 2 at 29-30.

Grimes of Boonton. The society often had difficulty in finding a hall for its annual meeting, for, as Grimes complained, 'churches, public halls, school houses, and all such places are in New Jersey with very few exceptions closed against those who feel it a duty to labor for the slave'.[14] Added to such obstacles was the society's chronic shortage of funds, which prevented it from hiring a full-time agent and from adequately supporting the *Freeman*.[15]

Nevertheless, the society continued to meet regularly. When the national organization split over the issue of whether abolitionists should form a political party in 1840, the state society aligned itself with the political abolitionists, albeit after some debate.[16] In August 1840, the society convened as a state convention of the Liberty Party and endorsed the presidential candidacy of James Birney. In the general election Birney received 69 votes, 0.1 percent of New Jersey's total vote. In 1844, a state Liberty Convention again endorsed Birney, who doubled his showing in the general election.[17]

14. *New Jersey Freeman*, June 15, 1844. On the abolitionists' difficulty in obtaining halls, see *New Jersey Freeman*, December 31, 1844. January 31, 1845. On Grimes, see Cudd. 'Unity of Reform'. supra note 2. To understand the national context of anti-abolitionist sentiment in New Jersey, see Leonard L. Richards, *'Gentlemen of Property and Standing': Anti-Abolition Mobs in Jacksonian America* (New York, 1970).

15. *New Jersey Freeman*, 11, February 28, 1845: NJSASS Minutes, supra note 11 at January 17, 1845.

16. The classic account of the division in the national organization is Aileen S. Kraditor, *Means and Ends in American Abolitionism: Garrison and His Critics on Strategy and Tactics, 1834-1850* (New York, 1970). In brief. the conflict pitted the followers of William Lloyd Garrison against abolitionists from New York, who left the American Anti-Slavery Society to form the American and Foreign Anti-Slavery Society. The Garrisonians rejected on moral grounds any political or legal tactic that would implicitly concede the legitimacy of the U.S. Constitution, which they considered a proslavery 'covenant with death, and agreement with hell'. Garrison believed that the broadest aims of abolition—political and civil equality for blacks—could be achieved only by a transformation in the sentiments of the populace. Americans had to be converted to the belief that slavery and race prejudice was a sin. As Kraditor writes, this 'was far too radical—far too subversive of the fundamental arrangements of American society'—to be achieved by governmental mandate.

Political abolitionists, in contrast, thought that the electoral system and the Constitution could be used to end slavery throughout the country. In electoral campaigns they saw a unique opportunity to influence public opinion on a broad scale. Abolitionism could embrace political tactics without abandoning its broadest aims, they believed, because slavery and race prejudice were not yet inextricable components of American society. Thus, they differed from the Garrisonians in their vision of abolitionism as a means of strengthening and preserving an American society that was fundamentally good. See Kraditor. *Means and Ends*, ibid. at 8-9, 165, 200.

17. NJSASS Minutes, supra note 11 at July 20, 1840, August 17, 1840: *New Jersey Freeman*, June 15, 1844. For the New Jersey vote, see *Presidential Elections Since 1789* (Washington, 1975) 67. In 1844, Birney received 131 votes, or 0.2% of the New Jersey total.

During the 1844 campaign Grimes published a ringing endorsement of political action. In seeking immediate abolition, Grimes wrote,

we believe it our duty to make use of *all* honest means, and we do not believe in the possibility of separating moral suasion from political action. The BALLOT BOX is an instrument of great power for good and evil, and we cannot agree to give the enemies of truth the exclusive benefit of it.

Grimes explicitly endorsed the Birney candidacy and asserted in passing, 'slavery exists by *law* and must be abolished by *law*'.[18]

While the state society was articulating its purposes and principles, a wholly unrelated campaign to revise the New Jersey Constitution of 1776 came to fruition. On May 14, 1844, elected delegates (including Chief Justice Joseph Hornblower and his fellow justice, Joseph Fitz Randolph) assembled in a constitutional convention. They worked continuously until July 29, adjourning in time to submit a draft constitution to a popular referendum on August 13.[19] The draft contained the state's first declaration of 'Rights and Privileges'. The first article of the declaration announced:

All men are by nature free and independent, and have certain natural and unalienable rights, among which are those of enjoying and defending life and liberty, acquiring, possessing, and protecting property, and of pursuing and obtaining safety and happiness.[20]

Another provision limited suffrage to white male citizens, making more permanent a ban on black voting first established by statute in 1820.[21]

For the history of the Liberty Party and its close ties to the New York abolitionists, see John R. Hendricks, 'The Liberty Party in New York State, 1838-1848' (Ph.D. dissertation. Fordham University, 1959); Alice Hatcher Henderson, 'The History of the New York State Anti-Slavery Society' (Ph.D. dissertation, University of Michigan, 1963).

18. *New Jersey Freeman*, June 15, 1844. During this period, Alvan Stewart and other prominent political abolitionists participated in the meetings of the state society and the Essex County Auxiliary. NJSASS Minutes, supra note 11 at August 23, 1843 (Lewis Tappan), January 22, 1845 (Alvan Stewart); Essex County Anti-Slavery Society Minute Book, January 10, 1840 (Henry B. Stanton), July 5, 1841 (Lewis Tappan) New Jersey State Historical Society. In addition, when a member proposed that the state society hold an 'Antislavery Camp Meeting', he hoped to 'secure the attendance of a dozen or so of our strongest men: Alvan Stewart, Gerrit Smith, [Joshua] Leavitt, [Henry B.] Stanton, [Rev. John] Pierpont, [Erastus D.] Culver, [Abel] Brown, [Henry H.] Garnet'—all political abolitionists from New York. *New Jersey Freeman*, October 1, 1844; see Gerald Sorin, *The New York Abolitionists: A Case Study of Political Radicalism* (Westport, 1971) 135-36.

19. John E. Bebout, 'Introduction', *Proceedings of the New Jersey State Constitutional Convention of 1844* (Trenton, 1942) lxv [hereinafter: *Proceedings of the Constitutional Convention of 1844*].

20. Ibid. at 614.

21. Blacks (and women) had occasionally voted in New Jersey under the 1776 constitution which enfranchised 'all Inhabitants' meeting certain property and residency requirements. Suffrage was limited to adult white males by the Act of June 1, 1820, 1820 N.J.

As recently as its annual meeting on January 31, 1844, the NJSASS had reaffirmed its 'solemn duty to . . . give the people no rest until the last vestiges of slavery are wiped away and New Jersey becomes in reality what she professes to be—a free state'. Nevertheless, if the free and independent clause lent any support to the abolitionist cause, it was lost on John Grimes. 'In the middle of the nineteenth century we would expect a convention of enlightened freemen in New Jersey to produce a constitution worthy of freemen', he fumed, 'yet the fruits of the late convention are enough to make any liberal soul blush . . . . It is mortifying indeed to think that fifty-eight Jerseymen can spend six weeks in convention and then produce an instrument so behind the age, and it is still more mortifying to find the perfect apathy with which it is received by the people of the state.' In attacking the 'most objectionable item' of the constitution, white male suffrage, Grimes blasted the hypocrisy of the framers: the constitution 'begins by saying "All men are by nature free and independent", carefully leaving out the word "equal", and then declares that "every white male citizen" only shall be allowed to vote'.[22]

Other members of the state society were not so pessimistic. On August 22, the NJSASS resolved that the constitution 'teaches the doctrine of natural and universal liberty' and thus was 'clearly at variance with all the existing laws of this State which favor the maintenance and continuence [sic] of Slavery'. It appointed a committee 'to bring this matter before the proper Courts, that a decision may be obtained, which shall settle the question of the existence of slavery under the new constitution'. The society authorized the committee to mount an immediate appeal for funds and to proceed 'as early as the receipt of funds will warrant'.[23]

Grimes remained skeptical. In reporting the result of the plebescite on the constitution, he merely remarked: 'It is supposed that the constitution will put an end to human chattelship in the State, though it takes from the colored citizens the right of suffrage'.[24] Reporting the resolves of the state society's annual meeting in January 1845, Grimes repeated his attack on the 'odious cutaneous distinctions' of the constitution. He noted that although the constitution struck down 'some of the most important principles of human rights, still in the opinion of many, it emancipates the small remnant of slaves in our state'. Grimes would not say whether emancipation was the 'design of the framers' or 'the result of accident', for this was 'not material for us to decide at present'. He reported that 'nothing has yet been done' in support of the litigation, lamenting that 'the means in

---

Laws 146. See Marion Thompson Wright, 'Negro Suffrage in New Jersey, 1776-1875', *Journal of Negro History* xxxiii (1948) 168-224.

22. NJSASS Minutes, supra note 11 at January 31, 1844; *New Jersey Freeman*, July 25, 1844.

23. *New Jersey Freeman*, August 15, 1844. The members of the five-person committee, which included Grimes, are given in ibid. at September 15, 1844.

24. Ibid. at September 15, 1844.

our hands have been so small as to exceedingly limit the operations of the society in our State'.[25]

But by April 30, Grimes could report that the 'legal existence of slavery under the new constitution in this state is to be argued before the Supreme Court in May'. Although funds were still needed to cover expenses in the case. 'able men are already engaged to argue the cause of liberty'.[26] Apparently Coddrington B. Palmer, a Jersey City lawyer with no other demonstrable connection to the abolitionists, initiated the litigation for the NJSASS.[27] Without any compensation 'except the consciousness of doing good in a good cause', Palmer obtained from Supreme Court Justice James Schureman Nevius a writ of habeas corpus on April 26 and served the writ on John A. Post of Passaic County on May 5. The writ directed Post 'to bring the body of a colored man named William . . . with the cause of his caption and detention' before the supreme court justices in Trenton on May 15. When Post failed to do so, the justices ordered Post to appear before them on May 20 to show why he should not be held in contempt of court for disobeying the writ. At this time Palmer obtained a second writ of habeas corpus. directed to Edward Van Beuren of Bergen County and commanding him 'to bring the body of Mary Tiebout, a colored girl . . . with the cause of her detention' before the justices on May 20.[28]

One week before the scheduled return of these writs, the state society held a quarterly meeting in Newark. A number of the society's 'distinguished friends from New York' were present, including Alvan Stewart, Lewis Tappan. and Henry Garnet. The society considered several resolutions drafted by a business committee that included Stewart and Grimes. The first resolution announced that the society's members considered it their duty 'to bring the question of Slavery and the apprenticeship system growing out of Slavery before the Supreme Court'. The second pledged the members 'to stand by our Counsel and agents in the prosecution' by paying their expenses and providing for the publication of their argument 'for the enlightening [of] the inhabitants of this State and other sections of our country'. It authorized the society's president to raise and spend $150 to meet these obligations. These resolutions, 'having been explained by Mr. Stewart, were adopted

---

25. Ibid., at September 15, 1844, January 31, 1845.

26. Ibid. at April 30, 1845.

27. I have found no reference to Palmer in the minutes of the NJSASS, the minute book of the Essex County auxiliary, the standard collective biographies of New Jersey lawyers, and the local histories for Essex County and Jersey City.

28. *New Jersey Freeman*, July 1, 1845. I have reconstructed the early stages of the litigation from the surviving records for the cases in the New Jersey State Archives: a printed 'State of the Case' prepared for the appeal from the Supreme Court to the Court of Errors and Appeals, the Minutes of the New Jersey Supreme Court, lxxxvi (Feb. 1845-Nov. 1846) 32-33 [hereinafter: Minutes, N.J. Sup. Ct.], and the Docket Book of the New Jersey Supreme Court. i (1842-1850) 203 [hereinafter: Docket Book. N.J. Sup. Ct.].

without debate, and the amount of money subscribed by individuals present'.[29]

Previously the society had articulated two grounds for opposing slavery. First, the society had argued that it was inconsistent with the republican government envisioned by the Declaration of Independence. 'All human beings possess human nature', the society resolved in May 1844, 'and as all rights spring from human nature', all human beings have the same human rights. Moreover, 'as all human beings are equal in *rights*, the *rights* of all are equally entitled to protection'. If a professedly republican government permits slavery, it violates its sacred duty to protect the human rights of its constituents, and becomes 'a despotism unspeakably more vile and detestable than that of the Czars or the Sultans . . . . Such a despotism is our Slaveholding Republic'.[30]

At the same time the state society articulated a second reason for opposing slavery, based on the 'supreme' law of God. 'Whenever man's law comes into conflict with that law, it is utterly void, and should be treated as a nullity.' Thus, 'all constitutions, compacts, and statutory enactments whatsoever are valid and obligatory' only insofar as they embody and apply the grand principles of divine law. Proscribed in the Bible as 'manstealing', an 'impiety toward God', and 'a sin under *all* circumstances', slavery violated divine law and therefore ought to be immediately and unconditionally abandoned.[31]

Now, on the verge of argument in a case ostensibly brought to litigate a provision of the state constitution, the members of the NJSASS endorsed a third ground for opposing slavery: 'We believe the Constitution of the United States, truly interpreted, is an antislavery document in its general principles and tendencies'. They were led to do so by Alvan Stewart. When, in September 1837, Stewart first maintained that the Federal Constitution prohibited slavery, he based his argument on the fifth amendment.[32] Now Stewart invoked the preamble. He first asserted that 'the present constitution is not one that is seen, but one that is felt'. He then asked: 'What is a constitution?' and answered: 'a covenant of one with the whole and the whole with one', 'a covenant for the protection of the weak against the strong and the wicked', 'a fence thrown around the people for the protection of their rights'. Without further elucidation, he leapt to his conclusion: The

---

29. NJSASS Minutes, supra note 11 at May 13, 1845. Grimes reported that the money was pledged 'with a promptness that did honor to the abolitionists present'. *New Jersey Freeman*, June 1, 1845.

30. *New Jersey Freeman*, June 15, 1844.

31. Ibid. at September 15, 1844; NJSASS Minutes, supra note 11 at January 31, 1844, August 23, 1843; *New Jersey Freeman*, June 15, 1844.

32. Stewart's address, delivered before the New-York State Anti-Slavery Society, was originally published in the Utica (N.Y.) *Friend of Man*, October 18, 1837, and is reprinted in Jacobus tenBroek, *Equal Under Law* (New York, 1965) 281-95.

preamble, 'the living expositor of the constitution itself', was 'ample proof' that the Framers intended to abolish slavery.[33]

That the state society adopted the resolution is not surprising: its members admired Stewart, and his argument was consistent with their earlier resolution on the irreconcilability of republican government and slavery. Nevertheless the May 13 meeting shows that although *Post* was the society's case, Stewart would not hesitate to use it as a vehicle for arguing, for the first time before sitting judges, his own theories of antislavery constitutionalism.

II

In the years before he gave up his law practice for antislavery agitation, Alvan Stewart (1790-1849) established a reputation for brilliant and eccentric advocacy in the courts of central New York. 'It was proverbial of Stewart as a lawyer', a close friend and former law partner recalled, 'that he always succeeded in every suit commenced by himself. From 1826 to 1836 I do not remember an exception to this rule; embracing more than one hundred suits.'[34] Foremost in lawyers' remembrances of Stewart's legal exploits was his seriocomic courtroom persona. Stewart was 'of commanding stature', standing over six feet, but loosely made, with large bones and long arms, and he was 'awkward in his movements, and careless in his dress. His very appearance would raise a laugh'. The comic nature of his performance captivated observers who focused on Stewart's deadpan expression, which he wore 'with the most earnest solemnity, while his hearers were surrendering themselves to irrepressible laughter' over one of his ironic comments.[35] Those who most fully appreciated the masterful calculation in Stewart's performance looked more closely, at his eyes. Large and dark, these were 'of great service in his speeches, starting out so full as to command an unusual scope of vision, and as he rolled them around, they seemed to have the capacity of indefinite enlargement'. Then, as he approached the climax of his speech, he shut them together, 'as if to concentrate [their] power and intensity till a rim of fire seemed to burn between the lids. One was always sure to be charmed, if he could get a position between the advocate and the jury, and watched the flames of the orator's eye.'[36]

Stewart coupled this striking appearance with biting wit and crescendoing

---

33. *New Jersey Freeman*, June 1, 1845.

34. G.C. Saxton to Alvan Stewart, Jr., October 23, 1849, Alvan Stewart Papers, New-York Historical Society [hereinafter: 'Saxton to Stewart'].

35. Account of *William Allen v. Seward and Northway*, Alvin Stewart Papers, Folder NM 261.57, New York State Historical Association [hereinafter: 'Allen v. Seward']; *History of Otsego County, New York* (Philadelphia, 1878) 30.

36. Allen v. Seward, supra note 35.

arguments *ad absurdum*. Theodore Dwight Weld recalled Stewart's 'batteries of wit, irony and sarcasm' and his 'power with the *reductio ad absurdum* in argument, in which he had no peer'.[37] Stewart's former law partner concurred: 'No man ever excelled Alvan Stewart in wit', he wrote, 'and this was his great weapon with which he demolished all his adversaries. Advancing step by step with the best figures and quotations from ancient and modern poets and authors . . . , he would hold the court, jury, and whole audience in a war of laughter until he had completely annihilated the defence and position of his adversary.'[38] But when considered apart from 'the manner, the tone, the air, the expression of countenance' with which Stewart delivered them, his arguments were often tiresome and laborious. Although jurors might succumb to the wit of his addresses, a skeptical judge who critically examined their content often found them flawed.[39]

When Stewart discussed the law before religious audiences or in popular forums, he stressed the divine basis for human law, although in disappointingly laconic terms. Stewart maintained that Christianity (as manifested in the Bible) supplied moral principles that all human law should embrace. In an address to a sabbath school society in 1834 he stated: 'We have no wise law, either of statute, common, or constitutional, which is acknowledged by the men of this generation, but the spirit of its principle will fall within some of these holy sayings [preserved in the Bible], so that the good man is constrained to acknowledge Bible wisdom and Bible law the prototype of all human law'. But although Stewart asserted that 'the Religion of Jesus Christ is a part of the Law of the Land', he never discussed what obligation citizens and government officials owed human laws which violated the 'wisdom' and 'law' of the Bible. Human law *ought* to follow divine law, but *must* it to be legally valid?[40]

William M. Wiecek has classed Stewart with other 'radical constitutionalists' who believed that natural or divine law had a 'legally binding force' that limited the power and legislation of government. According to this

37. Quoted in Marshall, ed., *Writings of Alvan Stewart*, supra note 1 at 36.

38. Saxton to Stewart, supra note 34.

39. William Goodell, quoted in Marsh, ed., *Writings of Alvan Stewart*, supra note 1 at 33. One practitioner frankly stated, 'Stewart was not a profound lawyer. He had read considerable law; but it was a sort of desultory reading'. Levi Beardsley, *Reminiscences; Personal and Other Incidents: Early Settlement of Otsego County* (New York, 1852) 168.

    For a case where judges resisted a characteristic argument by Stewart, see *Stewart v. Hawley*, 21 Wendell 552 (N.Y. Sup. Ct. 1839), discussed in Daniel R. Ernst, 'Church-State Issues and the Law, 1607-1870', in *The Church-State Issue in American History: A Bibliographical Guide* (Westport, Conn., forthcoming).

40. Address before the Sabbath School Society, Utica, New York, July 4, 1834, Alvan Stewart Papers, New-York Historical Society. Similarly, Stewart told the American Bible Society in May 1834 that Christianity was 'that power which stands behind the constitution and laws and sets them all in motion'. 'The Bible the Only Preservative of a Republican Form of Government', Alvan Stewart Papers, New-York Historical Society.

'modern' approach, natural law supplied judges with standards which they should use to measure positive law, unlike the traditional approach, which directed judges to consult natural law only in situations not covered by positive law.[41]

Unquestionably, one of Wiecek's radicals, Lysander Spooner, endorsed the 'modern' jurisprudence of natural law in his *Unconstitutionality of Slavery*, which appeared in 1845.[42] As we have seen, the resolutions of the NJSASS also endorsed the supremacy of divine or natural law over positive law. But Stewart himself stopped short of embracing this approach. Without fully appreciating the difficulty of the task, Stewart sought to reconcile his understanding of the divine basis of human law with the new, positivistic notion of the rule of law. He did this by arguing that divine or natural law required jurists to construe positive legal sources in favor of the slave. Higher law supplied a rule of construing human law, not standards which human law must meet to be valid.

The best statement of Stewart's moral rule of constitutional interpretation appeared in a letter to the editor of the *Philanthropist* in April 1842. The social compact upon which the American constitutions were erected never included slaves; therefore, state governments lacked the 'moral jurisdiction over the African' needed to reduce 'the quantum of his political and personal rights below the average of the great community'. For this reason, every constitution and statute 'morally, so far as it bears on the slave, is clearly null and void in the court of conscience, it being made to take rights from him, without his consent, and which natural justice would declare wrong'. The conclusion Stewart drew from the moral nullity of slave law in the court of conscience was not that it was legally void in courts of law. Rather, Stewart concluded that abolitionists should not let positivistic scruples prevent them from putting forward even outlandish constitutional arguments. It was 'craven' and 'morally preposterous' to admit to a construction of such 'piratical legislation' if it supported slaveholders. Abolitionists should put forward arguments based on the war power, the treaty power, and the guarantee clause, for 'who dare affirm or deny that some of these powers may be equal to the abolition of slavery in all the States?'[43]

---

41. Wiecek, *The Sources of Antislavery Constitutionalism in America* (Ithaca, 1977) 249-74 [hereinafter: Wiecek, *Antislavery Constitutionalism*].

42. On Spooner, see ibid. at 257-58; Lewis Perry, *Radical Abolitionism: Anarchy and the Government of God in Antislavery Thought* (Ithaca, 1973) 194-208.

43. Marsh, ed., *Writings of Alvan Stewart*, supra note 1 at 355-58. In assessing Stewart's 'Constitutional Argument on the Subject of Slavery', supra note 32, Robert Cover aptly describes Stewart's reasoning as being 'founded wholly on constitutional text and requires nothing more than a suspension of reason concerning the origin, intent, and past interpretation' of the due process clause. Cover, *Justice Accused*, supra note 3 at 157.

III

The conviction that abolitionists were morally justified in arguing for unlikely interpretations of constitutional provisions, regardless of the intent of their framers, goes far toward explaining the argument Stewart delivered on May 21, 1845.[44] Fairly characterized by the Trenton *State Gazette* as remarkable for 'its powerful though disjointed reasoning, its warm appeals to the best feelings of human nature [and] its ingenious and copious accumulation of terms of abhorrence and contempt of slavery', Stewart's speech repeatedly urged the justices to do 'justice through law' by giving his arguments 'the benefit of every sensible doubt, which may cloud the mind of this Honorable court'.[45]

Stewart relied upon three distinct authorities. The first was the common-law. *Somerset* doctrine, which drew upon the traditional understanding of the place of natural law in the jurisprudence of late eighteenth- and early nineteenth-century Anglo-America. According to this understanding, statutes. the common law, equity, admiralty law, and the law of nations provided courts with rules of decision. Natural law was a residual category, providing only raw principles from which judges might fashion rules of decision when no other system of law applied. Lord Mansfield adopted this view in *Somerset's Case* (1772). Slavery was 'so odious', Mansfield wrote, 'that nothing can be suffered to support it, but positive law'. Because slavery violated natural law, and because none of the other systems of law had established slavery in England, no slaves could be held there.[46] In *Commonwealth v. Aves* (1836), Chief Justice Lemuel Shaw cited *Somerset* in support of his decision to free a six-year-old girl who had visited the state with her mistress.[47]

---

44. The argument was postponed to May 21 when 'professional duties' prevented Zabriskie from appearing on the 20th. On the morning of the 21st, the court denied Bradley's motion for a postponement to the following term, which he had made in order to give the 'grave and important principles' of the case sufficient study. New York *Evening Express*, May 21, 1845; Trenton *State Gazette*, May 21, 1845.

45. Trenton *State Gazette*, May 23, 1845; Stewart, *Legal Argument*, supra note 1 at 13. For a thorough summary of Stewart's argument, see Paul Finkelman, *Slavery in the Courtroom: An Annotated Bibliography of American Cases* (Washington, D.C., 1985) 152-55.

46. Somerset v. Stewart, Lofft 1, 19, 98 Eng. Rep. 499, 540 (K.B. 1772). On the American reception of *Somerset*, see Wiecek, *Antislavery Constitutionalism*, supra note 41 at 20-39; Cover, *Justice Accused*, supra note 3 at 16-18; Paul Finkelman, *An Imperfect Union: Slavery, Federalism, and Comity* (Chapel Hill, 1981) 70-125 [hereinafter: Finkelman, *Imperfect Union*]; A. Leon Higginbotham, Jr., *In the Matter of Color: Race and the American Legal Process: The Colonial Period* (New York, 1978) 313-68.

47. Commonwealth v. Aves, 35 Mass. (18 Pickering) 193 (1836). On *Aves*, see Leonard W. Levy, *The Law of the Commonwealth and Chief Justice Shaw* (Cambridge, Mass., 1957) 59-71; Finkelman, *Imperfect Union*, supra note 46, 103-14.

Stewart urged the court to adopt the reasoning of *Somerset* and *Aves*. Slavery violated natural law ('that great Omnipotent law of God, ever in full force') by violating man's right to life, liberty, and property.[48] 'All the intendments of law and justice are opposed to it, so that . . . it can only exist by force of positive law. The *lex scripta* must be its foundation, and that I think you no longer have.' Slavery had sprung up in New Jersey from 'the barbarous custom of a few inhuman planters' and was of too recent origin to qualify as common law. If the court had any 'well-grounded doubt as to the authority' for the existence of slavery in New Jersey, it should 'give humanity the advantage and put [slavery] to death'.[49]

Stewart's second legal source was the free and independent clause of the Constitution of 1844, which, he claimed, adopted the law of nature 'in the most solemn form as a rule of action'. This adoption gave the law of nature the force of constitutional law. As a result, New Jersey judges could henceforth strike down institutions that violated natural law by applying conventional canons of judicial review. Slavery was 'the exact converse of every proposition contained in the first article' of the 1844 constitution; the court should therefore abolish it in New Jersey.[50]

Stewart's third source was the U.S. Constitution, which, he told the court, was 'an Anti-slavery document, in its general spirit and tendencies'.[51] Stewart made four arguments which ultimately relied on the Constitution. First, he argued that slavery deprived slaves of life, liberty, and property in violation of the due process clause of the fifth amendment. He repeated in substance the reasoning he published in his earlier 'Constitutional Argument on the Subject of Slavery'. The clause required that no person be denied liberty unless 'by due process of law', and this, Stewart asserted, required indictment by a grand jury, conviction by a petit jury, and sentencing by a court of competent jurisdiction.[52]

Second, Stewart argued that slavery deprived New Jersey of 'a Republican form of Government' in violation of the guarantee clause of article IV. 'The exercise of judicial power through the Federal or State judiciaries' was an appropriate way to implement this guarantee; therefore the court should declare New Jersey's slave laws null and void.[53] Third, the institution stripped New Jersey's slaves of the human rights which all constitutions are

---

48. Stewart, *Legal Argument*, supra note 1 at 23. Although Stewart asserted that slavery violated the Ten Commandments, he did not argue that divine law was an independent basis for deciding *Post*. Ibid. at 34. Divine law was only significant to his argument insofar as it defined natural law.

49. Ibid. at 17-19, 27.

50. Ibid. at 23-24.

51. Ibid. at 36.

52. Ibid. at 35. On this earlier argument, see note 32 supra.

53. Ibid. at 37-38.

created to protect. It therefore contravened 'the very idea of a Constitution of the United States', as embodied in the preamble.[54]

Stewart's fourth and most bizarre argument turned upon the Treaty of Ghent and the supremacy clause of article VI. The tenth article of the treaty pledged the best efforts of the United States and Great Britain to end 'the traffic in slaves'. Stewart maintained that this phrase referred not to the international slave trade, but to 'slavery generally in the two countries'. Thus, the treaty, made binding on the states by the supremacy clause, obligated the New Jersey Supreme Court 'to employ all the power it constitutionally may possess by its decision, to fulfill this engagement of the nation'.[55]

Stewart realized that his constitutional arguments were outlandish, and he anticipated the responses of the defendants' counsel. First, he maintained that the intent of the participants in the Federal Convention was irrelevant. Those participants merely reported a draft of the Constitution; they did not adopt one. The true adopters, whose intent *was* relevant, were the people of the individual states gathered in the ratifying conventions. If these 'adopters ever thought of slavery, they did not think to name it, and must have supposed it near its end, and they did not wish to disgrace the nation by the admission that so foul and base a thing ever existed'.[56] Their noble sentiments supported his argument, regardless of the 'secret cabalistic meaning' that some found in Madison's recently published notes on the Convention.[57]

Second, Stewart urged the justices to ignore the policy implications of abolition. When the judges granted the writs of habeas corpus, Stewart recalled, 'it was remarked by one of the members of the court, that this case would require great consideration from its effect on the towns of this State, as it might subject said towns to the maintenance of worn-out, aged and infirm slaves in the shape of paupers'. Although this result was possible, such a policy consideration should not influence how the judges dispensed 'constitutional justice'. He concluded by quoting Lord Mansfield in *Somerset*: 'We have no authority to regulate the conditions on which the law shall operate . . . . We cannot direct the law, the law must direct us.'[58]

---

54. Ibid. at 38-40.

55. Ibid. at 20.

56. Ibid. at 36-37, 42. Similarly, Stewart maintained that, in interpreting the New Jersey constitution, judges should consider the thought of the 'sober-minded, brave, and considerate Jerseyman' who voted for its adoption. Ibid. at 47.

57. Ibid. at 37. Cf. H. Jefferson Powell, 'The Original Understanding of Original Intent', 98 *Harvard Law Review* 885-948 (1985).

58. Thus, Robert Cover erred in minimizing the public policy implications of the justices' decision in *Post*. Cover, *Justice Accused*, supra note 2 at 59. True, the case would not overturn the dominant labor system of the state, but emancipation under the 1804 act had been a very expensive process for New Jersey. At one point the cost of maintaining abandoned children accounted for half of all state expenditures. See Davis, 'Persistence

Stewart spoke until six o'clock, whereupon the court adjourned. On the following morning Abraham Ootout Zabriskie (1807-1873), counsel for the master of the apprentice, addressed the court. No lawyer more fully embodied the power, boldness, and self-confidence of the managerial class that emerged during the industrialization of the antebellum North. Biographical descriptions of Zabriskie repeatedly employed images of force and bulk. 'He was a large and imposing looking man, with dignity of bearing and a good deal of gruffness of manner', recalled one biographer, 'conscious of his strength and confident in his decisions'.[59] A judge remembered 'the weight of his power as a professional antagonist'. 'Everything about Mr. Zabriskie's mind was massive like his body', observed a funeral orator.[60] And this mind and body were devoted to the service of New Jersey's nascent industries. Through his active role as a director or trustee in railroads, banks, life insurance companies and public utilities, he developed a reputation as both 'an able and learned lawyer' and 'a sagacious business man'.[61] Nothing more fittingly testified to his intellectual and physical energy and his organic relationship to the free enterprise economy than the decision of the New Jersey Railroad and Transportation Company to name the state's second coal-burning steam engine the 'A.O. Zabriskie', in honor of its general counsel and director.[62]

Zabriskie began by lumping the abolitionists with other radicals of the day in a sweeping *argumentum absurdum*: 'If we admit with the abolitionists that the first clause of the bill of rights is "repugnant" to slavery', Zabriskie snorted, 'we must also admit with the Fourierites, Anti-Renters, Socialists, Owenites, and Fanny Wright-ists that it is repugnant to the laws giving husbands control of wives, masters of apprentices, parents of children, and landlords of the fruits of the labor of tenants'. Fortunately, the free and independent clause 'was but a mere abstract proposition with the Convention who made and the people who adopted' the 1844 constitution. After reading from the proceedings of the convention, he declared that 'it would be a

---

of Partisan Alignment', supra note 2 at 165-66; Zilversmit, *First Emancipation*, supra note 7 at 195-99; Henry Scofield Cooley, *A Study of Slavery in New Jersey* (Baltimore, 1896) 27. Even after the legislature prohibited the use of state funds for this purpose, the cost of emancipation remained a public issue as tight-fisted townships sued each other to determine responsibility for the support of destitute former slaves. South Brunswick v. East Brunswick, 8 N.J.L. (3 Halsted) 64 (1824); Overseers of the Poor of Perth Amboy v. Overseers of the Poor of Piscataway, 19 N.J.L. (4 Harrison) 173 (1842); Overseers of Morris v. Overseers of Warren, 26 N.J.L. (2 Dutcher) 312 (1857).

59. Edward Quinton Keasbey, *The Courts and Lawyers of New Jersey, 1661-1912* (New York, 1912) ii, 742 [hereinafter: Keasbey, *Courts and Lawyers of New Jersey*].

60. *Obituary Addresses and Proceedings of the Bar on the Occasion of the Death of Abraham O. Zabriskie* (Jersey City, 1874) 5, 67.

61. John Whitehead, *The Judicial and Civil History of New Jersey* (n.p., 1897) ii, 387-88 [hereinafter: Whitehead, *Judicial and Civil History*].

62. Jacob Weart, 'Chancellor Abraham O. Zabriskie', *New Jersey Law Journal* xx (1897) 328.

judicial fraud' upon the people of New Jersey to adopt Stewart's interpretation of the clause. In addition, Zabriskie quoted from statutes and case law regulating black apprenticeship and slavery in New Jersey, concluding that the *Somerset* doctrine was inapplicable and that 'the slaves and apprentices were better off as they are'.[63]

That afternoon a young lawyer, Joseph Philo Bradley (1813-1892), appeared for the slaveholder, John Post. Like Zabriskie, Bradley sympathized with the spirit of free enterprise abroad in America. In an autobiographical sketch he depicted his life as a classic nineteenth-century progress from a boyhood in rural New York to a lucrative law practice and finally a position on the Supreme Court, and he gave thanks that the United States was a country that promoted 'the unimpeded, unrestrained, free development of the *individual man*'.[64] He broke into the legal profession as an associate of the general counsel for one of the principal railroads in the state, the New Jersey Railroad and Transportation Company. In time he would become the general counsel and a director of the 'Joint Companies'—a collection of transportation interests directed by the Camden and Amboy Railroad. The Joint Companies monopolized Bradley's business almost as much as they monopolized freight traffic between Philadelphia and New York, although Bradley still found time to serve as actuary and later as president of two life insurance concerns.[65]

Bradley unequivocally endorsed a positivistic understanding of the law. In a lecture to the students of the University of Pennsylvania Law School he dissented from Blackstone's definition of law, restating it without Blackstone's acknowledgement of the moral basis of law. Law, he maintained, 'is that body of rules which a political society enforces by physical power for the protection of its members, in their persons and property, and the promotion of their happiness. Whatsoever rule of conduct is not enforced by the physical power of society is not law. It may be a rule of morals, or of courtesy, or of honor; but it is not law.'[66] Although some men evidenced the true nobility of their nature by their self-control, 'which restrains,

---

63. New York *Evening Express*, May 23, 1845.

64. The sketch is discussed in Ruth Whiteside, 'Justice Joseph Bradley and the Reconstruction Amendments' (Ph.D. dissertation, Rice University, 1981), 9-11 [hereinafter: Whiteside, 'Bradley and the Reconstruction Amendments'], which contains an excellent account of Bradley's early years and New Jersey law practice. See also Charles Fairman's many articles on Bradley, including 'Mr. Justice Bradley', in Allison Dunham and Philip B. Kurland, eds. *Mr. Justice* (Chicago, 1956) 69-95; 'What Makes a Great Justice? Mr. Justice Bradley and the Supreme Court, 1870-1892', 30 *Boston University Law Review* 49-102 (1950); and 'The Education of a Justice: Justice Bradley and Some of His Colleagues', 1 *Stanford Law Review* 217-55 (1949).

65. On Bradley's railroad business, which one (undoubtedly biased) observer believed made him '*heart, body and soul* Camden and Amboy', see Whiteside, 'Bradley and the Reconstruction Amendments', supra note 64 at 31-34, 57-61, 125.

66. Charles Bradley, ed., *Miscellaneous Writings of the Late Hon. Joseph P. Bradley* (Newark, 1901) 299.

governs and subdues the impulses, appetites, passions and desires', society required some external coercive power to discipline 'brutish men and coarse natures'. Law, the 'concentrated power of the community', performed this role.[67]

In his lecture Bradley encouraged the law students to look beyond their lawbooks. 'The lawyer ought, indeed, to know almost everything, for there is nothing in human affairs that he may not, some time or other, have to do with.' Certainly Bradley followed his own advice: he left hundreds of pages of writings on political, historical, religious, mathematical, and scientific topics. But too much of his learning was sterile erudition showing little appreciation of the human realities underlying these subjects. He loved discipline and diligence for their own sake; he once confessed that he could spend 'days sometimes following up a thing, just for the sake of conquering the difficulty without any benefit or advantage to myself'.[68]

This temperament carried over to his formalistic legal style. Although few Supreme Court justices could match his formidable legal knowledge, he has passed into history as a 'near-great' judge. The great justices established reputations for their statesmanship, for their hatred of injustice, for their incisive understanding of American democracy. Bradley's 'special intellectual distinction was thoroughness'.[69] He approached cases as the logician and mathematician he was, and his 'conclusions were the result of logic—were arrived at by close reasoning'. So rigorous was Bradley's approach that when he was appointed to the Supreme Court, the high priest of formalistic jurisprudence, Thomas M. Cooley, predicted he would become one of the 'profoundest jurists of the English-speaking race'.[70]

Bradley's erudition was evident in his argument in *Post*. In a rhetorical flourish, Stewart had asserted that slavery violated the Ten Commandments;[71] now Bradley responded with an arcane discussion of the practice of slavery in biblical times. In doing so, he never claimed juridical significance for his conclusion that ancient Jewish tribes practiced slavery; instead, he used careful, arid scholarship in an attempt to win back those who, like a correspondent of the Newark *Daily Advertiser*, had been moved by

---

67. Ibid. at 300, 238. See also Bradley's article on 'Law' in *Supplement to Encyclopedia Britannica*, 4 vols. (New York, 1886) iii, 568-73.

68. Quoted by Cortland Parker, 'Justice Joseph P. Bradley', 28 *American Law Review* 508 (1894) [hereinafter: Parker, 'Bradley'].

69. This was the judgment of his close friend and fellow lawyer, Cortland Parker. See ibid. at 489. Bradley was rated 'near-great' in a survey of law school deans and professors of law, history, and political science conducted in 1970. Albert P. Blaustein and Roy M. Mersky, *The First One Hundred Justices: Statistical Studies on the Supreme Court of the United States* (Hamden, Conn., 1978) 32-51. See also Leon Friedman, 'Joseph P. Bradley', in *The Justices of the United States Supreme Court, 1789-1969: Their Lives and Major Decisions*, 5 vols. (New York, 1969) ii, 1181-200.

70. Parker, 'Bradley', supra note 68 at 491; George C. Worth, 'Hon. Joseph P. Bradley: The Passing of a Great Lawgiver', *New Jersey Law Journal* xx (1897) 299.

71. See note 48 supra.

Stewart's 'thrilling sketch of the first manifestations of God's displeasure against Slavery and Slaveholders'.[72]

Bradley similarly sought to dissipate the force of Stewart's oratory by urging the justices to consider the actual conditions of slavery in New Jersey. These bore little resemblance to Stewart's lurid portrayal of the institution. The New Jersey slave was 'nothing more nor less than a servant for life' and protected by state laws regulating the relation between masters and apprentices. Bradley maintained that the slaves lived 'among the farmers, in their families, like their children', where they were 'better off than if they would be free'. All were over forty, and many were too infirm to work. Emancipation would deny them the 'support of the families in which they live', including 'clothing and food and shelter all the days of their life, in sickness and in health'. Bradley stressed that 'he was not in favor of slavery; but it was quite another consideration whether they shall be turned out adrift upon the world'.[73]

Bradley rejected two of Stewart's three legal arguments.[74] First, Bradley disputed Stewart's assertion that no positive law protected slavery in New Jersey, citing 'a great many passages' in the laws of the colony and state. Second, like Zabriskie, he argued that the free and independent clause did not abolish slavery, but he took a more formalistic position than did his fellow counsel on the issue of how to determine the intent of the framers. Bradley saw no need to refer to the proceedings of the convention. He argued that a judge should consult such sources only if the language used in a constitutional text was ambiguous. The judge should first attempt to interpret the text in light of 'the *usus loquendi*—the use or common acceptance of the language'. Consulting this usage, Bradley maintained that the first article was 'a mere political formula' that Americans had used to justify their repudiation of English rule. This was the sole meaning of the first article, which, like the Declaration of Independence, neither referred to nor was ever intended to refer to slavery.[75]

Stewart's reply to the defendants' counsel displayed great oratorical skill but little willingness to engage their legal arguments. He praised Bradley: 'There were a great many good points about the young counsellor—he would like to see him as zealous in arguing a good cause.' On Zabriskie, however, Stewart trained his sarcastic wit. He chided Zabriskie for 'gravely

72. Newark *Daily Advertiser*, May 22, 1845.

73. New York *Evening Express*, May 23, 1845. During his unsuccessful congressional campaign in 1862, Bradley similarly professed to believing slavery a great evil, but he denied that he was an abolitionist. He preferred gradual emancipation and colonization to the immediate abolition of slavery in the South, which, he argued, would be in the interest of neither slave nor master. See Whiteside, 'Bradley and the Reconstruction Amendments', supra note 64 at 90-94.

74. According to the newspaper account of the argument, neither Bradley nor Zabriskie wasted any breath on Stewart's interpretation of the U.S. Constitution.

75. New York *Evening Express*, May 23, 1845.

informing' the court that Coddrington Palmer, the first abolitionist 'seen
alive' in Bergen County, was not tarred and feathered when he served the
writ on Post. Stewart supposed that Zabriskie made this statement 'as a
distinguished compliment to his neighbors in that county, and as the highest
proof that they have ever given of their civilization'. If so, Stewart hoped
that Zabriskie's neighbors would 'never, in an evil hour, fall below this high
water mark of their advancing elevation'.[76]

In addition, Stewart argued that Zabriskie's parade of 'the various
cliques, factions, sects, and reformers of the day' was irrelevant to the case.
He 'had no sympathy with the Fourierites, the Non-resistants, the Owenites,
the Garrisonites, nor any other *ites*',[77] Stewart protested; he was arguing a
'dry law question, which is, whether slavery in the State of New Jersey is
a *legal* and *lawful* institution'. He explained that he sought the abolition of
slavery 'by law and by the Constitution', and he took Zabriskie's comments
as an opportunity to expound upon the Liberty Party platform. Stewart
finally closed around 10:30 P.M. with an eloquent and emotional appeal on
behalf of the slave and the apprentice.[78]

On July 17 the Supreme Court announced its decision. By a 3-1 vote it
upheld slavery and black apprenticeship in New Jersey.[79] No single opinion
commanded the support of a majority of the court. Justice James Schureman
Nevius (1786-1859) wrote an opinion in which Justice John Preston
Carpenter (1804-1876) concurred.[80] Nevius, the second oldest man on the
bench, was not generally considered by the bar 'as having a very accurate
knowledge of the law', and the bar did not 'place the fullest confidence in
his decisions'. He was remembered as being a religious man, 'early trained
in the catechism and indoctrinated in the system of evangelical truth by

76. Ibid. at May 24, 1845; Stewart, *Legal Argument*, supra note 1 at 45.

77. New York *Evening Express*, May 24, 1845.

78. Stewart, *Legal Argument*, supra note 1 at 46-47; New York *Evening Express*, May 24, 1845.

79. One member of the five-judge court, Ira Condict Whitehead (1789-1867), abstained. He had missed the argument of the case, having 'gone to hold Morris [County] Circuit'. Joseph C. Hornblower, *Notes of Arguments Made in the Supreme Court of New Jersey from November Term 1833 to October 1846*, 2 vols., ii, 16, New Jersey State Archives.

79. In the interim, the NJSASS had busied itself with plans to publish and circulate Stewart's argument. At a meeting of the society in Newark on June 26, 'the few friends' who were in attendance took 1,700 copies to disseminate. The society thanked Palmer and Stewart for their efforts, and noted that Stewart had asked the society to reimburse him only for his expenses in arguing the case and printing the argument. *New Jersey Freeman*, July 1, 1845.

80. The reporter noted that Carpenter 'concurred in the result of the opinion delivered by Justice Nevius, and in the general tenor of the reasoning on which it is founded'. State v. Post, 19 N.J.L. (Spencer) 368, 386 (N.J. Sup. Ct. 1845). Carpenter was the son of the owner of a glassworks; 'as a judge of the Supreme Court he was held in high esteem by his associates and by the bar of the State for his ability, learning, and uniform good judgment'. Whitehead, *Judicial and Civil History*, supra note 61 at 15-16.

pious parents', a constant reader of the Bible, and given to the 'habit of family and secret prayer'.[81]

Despite his religious belief, Nevius generally adopted Bradley's formalistic reasoning, giving only a passing nod to the notion that human law should not be repugnant to higher law. Nevius began by professing that although he sincerely respected 'the zeal and human spirit' which Stewart evidenced in his 'pathetic appeals' for the colored race, 'much of the argument seemed rather addressed to the feelings than the legal intelligence of the court'. *Post* did not require Nevius to enter upon 'a disquisition as to [slavery's] origin, its history, its abuse, or the principles upon which it has been attempted to be sustained and justified'. This was so because the court had 'no power to enact a law, nor to set aside a law, even to remedy what we may consider a great private or public wrong or . . . a great political evil; that power belongs to another department of the government. We can only declare what the law is and *whether consistent with the law of God*, and the fundamental or constitutional law of society.'[82] *Post* required the most scrupulous judicial constraint, because a decision against the masters would absolve them from the obligation to support their slaves and throw that obligation on the communities where the masters resided.

Even though Nevius stated that the judiciary had some obligation to measure human institutions against divine law, he strictly limited his opinion to the reasoning Bradley suggested. Initially, he rejected Stewart's invocation of the *Somerset* doctrine, citing charters and statutes to 'prove not only that slavery existed and was tolerated but that it was recognized and treated as a legal institution' from the founding of New Jersey to the present.[83] Nevius then rejected Stewart's argument from the free and independent clause. This clause, interpreted 'according to its natural use and acceptation', merely announced 'that men in their social state are free to adopt their own form of government and enact their own laws'. It did not define the individual rights of men, and it did not interfere with their domestic relations or legal status. 'Had the convention intended to abolish slavery', he reasoned, 'it would have adopted some clear and definite provision to effect it, and not have left so important and grave a question,

---

81. John Whitehead, 'The Supreme Court of New Jersey', *Green Bag* iii (1891), 453 [hereinafter: Whitehead, 'Supreme Court of New Jersey']; Lucius Q.C. Elmer, *The Constitution and Government of the Province and State of New Jersey, with . . . Reminiscences of the Bench and Bar* (Newark, 1872) 347-49 [hereinafter: Elmer, *Reminiscences*].

82. State v. Post, 19 N.J.L. (Spencer) 368, 369, 370, 372 (N.J. Sup. Ct. 1845) (emphasis supplied).

83. Ibid. at 372. See also ibid. at 383 (Randolph, J.) (distinguishes England and Massachusetts from New Jersey, where 'slavery in some form or other has been recognized and provided for, from the settlement of the country to the present moment').

involving such extensive consequences, to depend upon the doubtful construction of an indefinite abstract political proposition'.[84]

The opinion of Justice James Fitz Randolph (1803-1873), followed Zabriskie's argument.[85] He stressed the folly of immediate emancipation in New Jersey, which would thrust 'out the aged and the decrepid [sic] and the helpless infant, from their comfortable homes, to become inmates of a poor house'. Randolph did not hesitate to draw upon his own recollections of the 1844 convention. Anyone who had attended, he asserted, could not forget 'the little interest that was felt generally in the convention respecting the bill of rights, and how large a portion of the members considered it of small importance'. The members of the convention intended generally 'to assert the principles on which men, in a state of nature, enter into government' but never sought to give the first article 'a mandatory character'. After supporting his position by quoting the proceedings of the convention, Randolph concluded that a decision for the petitioners would constitute 'a wanton stretch of judicial power and a fraud upon those, who framed, as well as those, who adopted' the constitution.[86]

Although the official report of *Post* records Chief Justice Hornblower's dissenting vote, it does not print his opinion. Newspaper accounts of the case simply note that Hornblower 'stated his dissent verbally'.[87] Although a written draft of the opinion once existed, it no longer survives among his personal papers.[88] Yet Hornblower's jurisprudential and antislavery writings suggest the reasons for his dissent and for his decision to deliver it orally. Like Supreme Court Justice Joseph Story, Hornblower belonged to 'an old

---

84. Ibid. at 374-75. Nevius's opinion contains only a passing reference to the Federal Constitution. Without mentioning Stewart's arguments or the defense counsels' failure to respond to them, Nevius noted that the express language of the Constitution recognized the relation of master and slave, that no court had ever held slavery unconstitutional, and that, on the contrary, state and federal courts had often held that the Constitution did not affect the institution. Ibid. at 375-76.

85. Randolph's opinions 'were sensible, well reasoned out, and the result of an honest and severely industrious search for every principle involved in the cause'. Whitehead, 'Supreme Court of New Jersey', supra note 81 at 456.

86. State v. Post, 19 N.J.L. (Spencer) 368, 380, 384, 385 (N.J. Sup. Ct. 1845).

87. New York *Evening Express*, July 19, 1845; Trenton *State Gazette*, July 18, 1845; Newark *Daily Advertiser*, July 19, 1845.

88. A draft of a letter among Hornblower's personal papers alludes to his opinion in *Post* and continues:

> I should not like a public annunciation of it, without first reviewing it. It is now more than ten years ago since I wrote it. After the occasion of delivering it passed away, I put it somewhere among my files of finished business papers. If I can find leisure to look it up and think upon reperusal of it it will be of any service to the cause, I may send you a copy, or at least, extracts from it.

Joseph C. Hornblower to Crosby and Nichols, March 24, 1857, Joseph C. Hornblower Papers, Box 10, New Jersey Historical Society [hereinafter cited by box number as Hornblower Papers].

race of judges' whose jurisprudence was increasingly considered archaic in the pragmatic world of mid-nineteenth-century America.

IV

Joseph Coerten Hornblower (1777-1864) had the great good fortune to live to see the popular estimation of his ideas pass from odd and quaint to authentic and antique. A Federalist, Whig. and Republican, Hornblower gave inimitable support to the new antislavery party's claim to vindicate the original intent of the Founding Fathers. The party's leaders shrewdly called upon this wan and feeble witness to testify at the 1856 Republican Convention, where he served as Chairman of New Jersey's delegation, and in the 1860 election, where he was one of Lincoln's electors and president of the electoral college. Here was a man who was older than the flag, who had attended the confederation congress with his father, and who verified, ostensibly from personal knowledge, the Republican history of the Framers' attitudes toward slavery.[89]

Hornblower clearly gloried in his reputation as a relic. In a letter to the 1856 Republican convention he saluted the creation of a party, whose 'very name gives a fresh impetus to the blood (now chilled with the frost of many winters) which first coursed in my veins, when, in the midst of the revolutionary struggle, . . . I was born into the world an American *freeman*, under the banners of liberty. I am rejoiced and thankful that I have been spared to see the day when the friends of human liberty have once more raised the "Republican" standard.'[90] And again, in 1857, he wrote,

I was but a boy, it is true. when the federal constitution was adopted. but the addition of a few years advanced me to an age in life. when I began to enquire for myself and to feel and take an interest in the government and the welfare of my country. The 'peculiar institution' and the obnoxious features in the constitution, growing out of its existence, were even then the subjects of conversation and of anxious forebodings. But they were submitted to in the confident belief that slavery would decrease in the course of a few years, entirely cease to exist, under the genial influence of free principles and a more enlightened policy and a better Christianity. This was the language and hope of the older politicians and patriots of that day. . . . But that hope has long since perished.[91]

---

89. For Hornblower's service to the Republican Party and the legends about his age, see William Nelson, *Joseph Coerten Hornblower* (Cambridge, Mass., 1894) 23-24 [hereinafter: Nelson, *Hornblower*]; Richard S. Field, 'Address on the Life and Character of the Hon. Joseph C. Hornblower', *Proceedings of the New Jersey Historical Society* x (1865-1866) 28 [hereinafter: Field, 'Hornblower']. For the Republican version of the Founding Fathers' expectation for slavery, see Eric Foner, *Free Soil, Free Labor, Free Men: The Ideology of the Republican Party before the Civil War* (New York, 1970) 75-76.

90. The letter, dated February 21, 1856, survives as a clipping from an unidentified newspaper in the Hornblower Papers, Box 2, supra note 88.

91. Hornblower to Crosby and Nichols, March 24, 1857, Hornblower Papers, supra note

In 1845, however, the national political events which would raise the value attached to Hornblower's opinions were still in the future, and to many members of the New Jersey bar he was a tiresome eccentric whose unpredictable decision-making during fourteen years as chief justice had undermined precedent and established canons of interpretation. They took their revenge in their memoirs and Bench and Bar biographies. His chief defect as a judge, wrote a lawyer who practiced before him, was 'his want of that resolute self-will which seems necessary to produce a firm adherence to settled opinions'. At the time of his nomination as chief justice it was said 'that he had every requisite of a good judge but sound judgment'.[92] A good equity lawyer, being 'partial to the principles upon which justice was administered there', Hornblower was too impulsive to be a common-law judge, too easily moved by 'an almost morbidly keen sense of right . . . impelling him to decide according to his sympathies or according to what, in his belief, the law ought to be'.[93] 'His generous impulses sometimes outran his judgment', observed a charitable biographer; a more distant one noted that his opinions 'lacked compactness and precision, were frequently disconnected, and seemed the result of yielding to impulse, and not to logic and argument'.[94]

Hornblower's understanding of the relationship between law and morality, which younger lawyers considered so objectionable, is best revealed in his writing about slavery. As Hornblower's memorialist nervously confided, 'by many, even of his political friends, he was thought to be somewhat radical upon this subject'.[95] An undated letter to a minister who had sent him a sermon on obedience to human laws provides grounds for these suspicions. Hornblower attacked those who, unlike the minister, urged compliance with laws relating to slavery. Their writings, he wrote, 'have done more to revive and inculcate the odious and I had hoped forever exploded doctrine of *absolutism* than if they had at once and unqualifiedly adopted the arguments and the language of *Sir Robert Filmer*, published more than three centuries ago'. Hornblower preferred the counsel of Christopher St. Germain, 'a great and *good lawyer*', who in his *Doctor and Student* 'did not hesitate to maintain the rights of conscience and to exalt the law of God above mere human laws'. Hornblower denied that 'we are bound not only

---

88. In addition, upon taking his chair as president of the electoral college in 1860, Hornblower 'made an affecting and interesting speech—one of the last he ever delivered—in which he referred to his long life, declared himself to be an American Republican, and avowed his conviction that the principles for which he was contending were those of Washington and the early Fathers of the Republic'. Field, 'Hornblower', supra note 89 at 41.

92. Elmer, *Reminiscences*, supra note 81 at 362, 363.

93. Field, 'Hornblower', supra note 89 at 29-30; Nelson, *Hornblower*, supra note 89 at 12.

94. Nelson, *Hornblower*, supra note 89 at 21; Whitehead, 'The Supreme Court of New Jersey', supra note 81 at 423.

95. Field, 'Hornblower', supra note 89 at 40; see also Elmer, *Reminiscences*, supra note 81 at 371.

quietly to submit but actively and personally to engage, in executing the enactments of government and perform the services required by us' if they are contrary to divine law. Rather, we must follow the 'specific, . . . certain, uniform rule of action' established in the Decalogue 'in every possible condition and in all the relations of life'.[96]

And yet, Hornblower did not always possess the courage to stand by his convictions. In *State v. Sheriff of Burlington County* (1836), Hornblower wrote (in dicta) that the Fugitive Slave Law of 1793 was unconstitutional. At the time he agreed that the opinion not be published, 'it being thought best on a conference between my associates and myself not to agitate the public mind on the question'.[97] He found the courage to publicize his convictions in the popular uproar over the passage of the Fugitive Slave Law of 1850. Only after 1850 did he consent to the publication of his opinion;[98] only then did he attack such laws in the pages of the Newark *Daily Advertiser* as '*inhuman, cruel*, and *demoralizing*', and '*eminently unconstitutional* in various respects and impolitic in their provisions'.[99]

This failure of faith may explain Hornblower's strange inconsistencies in the convention which drafted the 1844 constitution—inconsistencies which seem to have persuaded New Jersey's governor not to reappoint him in 1846.[100] The euologists who knew Hornblower best thought he 'was highly gratified at the adoption' of the free and independent clause, which he 'fondly hoped and believed would forever put an end to what still remained of slavery in New Jersey'.[101] Yet the proceedings of the

96. Hornblower to Rev. A.D. Smith (n.d.), Hornblower Papers, Box 2, supra note 88. Internal evidence suggests that Hornblower wrote the letter sometime in 1851 and that the sermon which prompted the letter was Asa Dodge Smith, *Obedience to Human Law: A Discourse Delivered on the Day of Public Thanksgiving, December 12, 1850* (New York, 1851).

97. Hornblower to John C. Ten Eyck (n.d.), Hornblower Papers, Box 10, supra note 88. Salmon P. Chase relied upon a newspaper report of *Sheriff of Burlington* in arguing the *Slave Matilda* case in 1837. Salmon P. Chase to Hornblower, April 3 1851, Hornblower Papers, Box 2, supra note 88; *Speech of Salmon P. Chase, in the Case of the Colored Woman, Matilda* (Cincinnati, 1837) 18.

98. See, for example, New York *Evening Post*, August 1, 1851; John Codman Hurd, *The Law of Freedom and Bondage in the United States*, 2 vols., (New York, 1858-1867) ii, 64-66.

99. Newark *Daily Advertiser*, April 10, 1851.

100. Elmer, *Reminiscences*, supra note 81 at 370, claimed that the governor declined to renominate Hornblower 'on the ground that in the convention of which they were fellow members, he had shown too much disposition to change his opinions'.

101. Nelson, *Hornblower*, supra note 89 at 16-17; Field, 'Hornblower', supra note 89 at 38. I have found no basis for the assertion that Hornblower unsuccessfully attempted 'to obtain the insertion of a clause putting an end to slavery in the State', which appears in *The Biographical Encyclopedia of New Jersey of the Nineteenth Century* (Philadelphia, 1877) 77; see also Marion T. Wright, 'New Jersey Laws and the Negro', *Journal of Negro History* xxviii (1943) 184; and Whiteside, 'Bradley and the Reconstruction Amendments', supra note 64 at 47.

convention suggest that Hornblower had cause to doubt that the clause would achieve this end.

When James Parker introduced the report of the committee that drafted the 'Rights and Privileges' section of the 1844 constitution, he described it merely as 'a compilation of truthful axioms and sound landmarks which would serve as a guide to legislation [and] which speaks [sic] for themselves'. William Ewing, while not objecting to the principles declared in the section, thought it 'entirely unnecessary'. Discussion of the section would take up much time and not 'lead to subjects of legislation'. Consequently, he moved to dispense with consideration of the section. Hornblower agreed that some of the articles in the section were 'no more than mere abstract propositions of self-evident truths, and unnecessary', but others, including the third and fourth articles (on religious freedom), ought to become part of the constitution. In response, Ewing reiterated his position: 'These are only abstract propositions which are improper here, and will only serve to confuse the minds of the members.' If the members were really inclined to discuss the articles, Ewing would 'find very little difficulty in proving that all are not true, as for instance' the free and independent clause of the first article.[102]

Ewing's motion failed, and the convention began to consider each article in turn. The first article was in the following form:

> All men are born equally free and independent, and have certain natural and unalienable rights, among which are those of enjoying and defending life and liberty, acquiring, possessing and protecting property, and of pursuing and obtaining safety and happiness.[103]

Hornblower commenced the discussion of the first article by moving that the word 'equal' be inserted after the word 'certain'. In opposition, several speakers feared that future interpreters of the motion might 'lead to inferences which are not now thought of'. One pointed to the constitution's suffrage provision, which limited the vote to '*white* male citizens'. If the motion carried, he argued, the first article would declare all men equal, while the suffrage provision would not. 'If all men are born equal', he asked, 'when do they lose this equality?' Hornblower's motion failed, and the convention moved on to the next article.[104]

Later, after the convention had completed its consideration of the

---

102. *Proceedings of the Constitutional Convention of 1844*, supra note 19 at 139.

103. Ibid. at 51.

104. Ibid. at 139-40. Weeks later, a committee of revision reported the article in its final form, with the words 'by nature' substituted for 'born equally'. The full convention adopted this version without reported debate. Although the committee had been empowered 'to alter or amend the phraseology, without altering the meaning of the several' sections, Randolph maintained in *Post* that the change revealed the convention's intent to state rights which men possess 'by or in a state of nature' but which might be altered once human governments were established. Ibid. at 422, 583, 589; State v. Post, 19 N.J.L. (Spencer) 368, 380 (N.J. Sup. Ct. 1845).

declaration of rights and privileges, Hornblower offered an additional article. He now maintained that had the question 'whether we should have a bill of rights at all [been] distinctly raised, I should have voted against it . . . . Although I was born in revolutionary times, at the first dawning of my reasoning powers, I imbibed the doctrine that these rights were our own. They are written on our hearts.' But if some rights were to be specified, Hornblower wanted to ensure that unenumerated rights would not be deemed unprotected by a subsequent interpreter of the constitution. He therefore suggested a saving clause 'to the effect that this bill of rights shall not abridge or take away any natural rights which are not here enumerated'. With one amendment, the convention adopted Hornblower's clause.[105]

Hornblower's actions at the constitutional convention provides some basis for surmising the grounds for his dissent in *Post*. In his only surviving reference to the dissent, Hornblower cryptically describes it as stating 'that under the new Constitution of this State (in the formation of which I had a part as a member of the Convention that formed it) slavery had ceased to exist in New Jersey'.[106] Conceivably, Hornblower relied upon the free and independent clause, but to do so he had to overlook the convention's clearly expressed intent in two respects. First, he had to find that the free and independent clause was a judicial rule of decision, and not just an 'abstract proposition'. Second, he had to find egalitarian implications in the clause, even though the convention had specifically rejected his attempt to make them more obvious.

Alternately, Hornblower might have pointed to his saving clause. Regardless of the intent of the convention in framing the free and independent clause, he might have reasoned, the convention left untouched the natural rights 'written on our hearts'. These rights of life, liberty, and property were superior to positive law, and any human institution—such as slavery—which violated those rights should be struck down by a court of law.

In either case, Hornblower's brand of constitutional interpretation was even more radical than Stewart's similarly acontextual interpretation of the U.S. Constitution. If Hornblower relied on the free and independent clause, he could do so only by disregarding the clearly expressed and contrary intent of the framers. If he relied upon his saving clause, he could do so only by embracing the 'modern' jurisprudence of natural law; unlike Stewart, he could invoke no positive law to buttress his argument. Thus, any attempt to justify his decision would have forced Hornblower to reveal the fundamental role of natural law in his jurisprudential thinking. He would have had to reveal himself as being hopelessly out of step with the new, positivistic

---

105. The convention deleted the word 'natural' because, as a speaker noted, the convention had been 'treating of *civil* as well as *natural* rights'. *Proceedings of the Constitutional Convention of 1844*, supra note 19 at 169-71.

106. Hornblower to Crosby and Nichols, March 24, 1857, Hornblower Papers, Box 10, supra note 88.

jurisprudence, and this he lacked the courage or the conviction to do. Nothing in his subsequent antislavery efforts, nothing in his later posing for the Republican Party could change the sad truth that when the time came to stand up and be counted, Joseph Hornblower crouched.

V

The story of the New Jersey Slave Case ends anticlimactically. Outraged by the 'barefaced sophistry' of the judges, the abolitionists resolved to take the case before the Court of Errors and Appeals.[107] But before initiating the appeal, they turned to the state legislature. Meeting in Trenton in January, 1846 shortly before the opening of the legislative session, the abolitionists attacked the outcome in *Post*, which, they claimed, showed that in New Jersey 'pro Slavery pervertions [sic] prevail in place of just interpretations'. The case had shown the society's members that they fought not only for the slaves but also for themselves:

> We had no conception when we began to labor in this cause, that the fetters were already forged for us. [W]e soon found that in calmly consenting [to] Slavery, we had well nigh brought our necks into the yoke. We found that not only the Declaration of Independence was regarded as a Rhetorical flourish, but the Bill of Rights of every state was equally unmeaning and inoperative.

The society's resolve in the face of *Post* is well-captured in Grimes's editorial on the meeting: 'We should spare no effort to get this black stain wiped away. If we fail in all the courts we will go to the legislature and if we fail here we will go back to the people and persevere until truth shall be heard and justice be done'.[108]

Although petitions 'for the immediate abolition of slavery' were introduced in the legislature on the last day of the society's meeting, the measure that became law in April stopped well short of the abolitionists' aims. The act formally abolished slavery in New Jersey but also declared the slaves apprentices for life, 'bound to the service of' their masters until discharged by a duly executed certificate or will. It neither removed the lifelong obligation of New Jersey's slaves to labor for their masters nor affected the status of blacks already serving apprenticeships under the 1804 statute.[109]

Unsatisfied, the abolitionists finally took concrete steps to appeal *Post*, but inadequate fund-raising and organizational difficulties delayed argument

---

107. *New Jersey Freeman*, August 7, 1845. The Court of Errors and Appeals consisted of the chancellor, the supreme court justices, and several 'special' judges, who need not have been lawyers. Its jurisdiction was confined to the review of questions of law in cases initiating in the state's common-law and equity courts. See Keasbey, *Courts and Lawyers of New Jersey*, supra note 59 at i, 420-27.

108. *New Jersey Freeman*, February 11, 1846.

109. Trenton *State Gazette*, January 30, 1846; 'An Act to Abolish Slavery', *(N.J. Stat. Rev.)* 382 (1847).

until 1848.[110] In February, by a 7-1 vote, the Court of Errors and Appeals affirmed the decision of the Supreme Court without issuing written opinions.[111]

The abolitionists struggled on, but the New Jersey Slave Case had ended. In retrospect, the case was an ambiguous incident in the history of the pursuit of moral ends by legal means. As William Wiecek has argued, Stewart's acontextual construction of the Constitution anticipated the expansive interpretation of libertarian guarantees by American judges in the twentieth century.[112] But Stewart's argument is equally notable for its strained attempts to find a basis in positive law for the antislavery cause. When an impassioned abolitionist like Stewart felt compelled to call emancipation a 'dry law question', an epoch had ended in American jurisprudence. A vibrant legal tradition had run to ground, represented only by the strangely reticent chief justice, Joseph Hornblower.

110. On the progress of the appeal, see Docket Book, N.J. Sup. Ct., supra note 28 at i, 203; Minutes, N.J. Sup. Ct., supra note 28 at lxxxvi, 83; Joseph Bradley Papers, Docket Book, 85, New Jersey Historical Society; *New Jersey Freeman*, May 14, 1846, January 7, 1847, February 16, 1847, May 15, 1847, January 26, 1848, February 5, 1848.

111. State v. Post, 21 N.J.L. (1 Zabriskie) 699 (N.J. Ct. Err. & App. 1848). On February 19, the affirmance of *State v. Post* by the Court of Errors was noted in the supreme court's docket. No similar note appears in the entry for *State v. Van Beuren*. The case may have been dismissed as moot, for if Mary Tiebout was nineteen in March 1845, she must have been over twenty-one (and therefore free under the 1804 act) in February 1848. Docket Book, N.J. Sup. Ct., supra note 28 at i, 203.

112. Wiecek, *Antislavery Constitutionalism*, supra note 41 at 274-75.

Slavery and Abolition Before the United States Supreme Court, 1820–1860

WILLIAM M. WIECEK

I NVIDIOUS contemporary opinions of Chief Justice Roger B. Taney have mischievously obstructed our efforts to understand the policy-making role of the antebellum United States Supreme Court. The judgment of the "five slaveholders who compose a majority of the Court," snorted Horace Greeley after the decision in *Dred Scott* v. *Sandford*, "is entitled to just so much moral weight as would be the judgment of a majority of those congregated in any Washington barroom."[1] "The name of Taney is to be hooted down the page of history," hooted Charles Sumner in an often-quoted anti-eulogy. "He administered justice at last wickedly, and degraded the judiciary of the country, and degraded the age."[2] Greeley, Sumner, and others thereby fixed a proslavery image on the late antebellum Court, based almost entirely on the *Dred Scott* case, that endured for half a century.

But in a landmark 1911 essay, Edward S. Corwin defended Taney's *Dred Scott* opinion as grounded in precedent.[3] Charles Warren attacked Taney's Republican critics in his magisterial 1923 history of the Supreme Court.[4] Charles Evans Hughes, Chief Justice of the United States, lent the prestige of his office to the rehabilitation of Taney's reputation in a widely noted 1931 dedicatory address.[5] Finally, in 1937, Felix Frankfurter interred the "five slaveholders and two or three doughfaces" image. He refuted the view of Taney as "the leader of a band of militant 'agrarian,' 'localist,' 'pro-slavery' judges," and scorned the "dramatic conflict between Darkness and Light: [John]

William M. Wiecek is professor of history in the University of Missouri.

[1] New York *Tribune*, March 7, 1857.
[2] *Congressional Globe*, 38 Cong., 2 Sess., 1012 (Feb. 23, 1865).
[3] Edward S. Corwin, "The Dred Scott Decision in the Light of Contemporary Legal Doctrines," *American Historical Review*, XVII (Oct. 1911), 52–69.
[4] Charles Warren, *The Supreme Court in United States History* (3 vols., Boston, 1923), III, 1–51.
[5] Charles Evans Hughes, "Roger Brooke Taney," *American Bar Association Journal*, XVII (Dec. 1931), 785–90.

Marshall, the architect of a nation; Taney, the bigoted provincial and protector of slavery."[6]

Liberated from its advocacy role of condemning or defending Taney, subsequent scholarship has sought an understanding of him, his Court, and the role they played in the slavery controversy. Whether from the warmly sympathetic vantage of the work of Carl Brent Swisher,[7] or the coldly critical view of Arthur Bestor,[8] or through exhaustive surveys of the *Dred Scott* decision itself,[9] scholars have provided an enduring description of the Supreme Court's policy-making role. But modern studies of the United States Supreme Court and its slavery-related cases sometimes share two characteristics that hamper a fuller understanding of the Court: their focus is the *Dred Scott* case, which they view at least implicitly as an aberration.[10] As an alternative, this essay adopts the historian's usual method of working from beginnings forward in time, searching for the Court's unfolding development of attitudes toward cases involving slavery and the abolition movement. Approached in this way, *Dred Scott* does not appear exceptional or anomalous; rather, it emerges as a natural result of judge-made doctrines and tendencies that had been developing for two decades.

The Marshall Court, unlike its successor, always displayed a delicate sense of its own limitations in slavery issues. The individual justices were not indifferent to slavery; quite the contrary. Several members of the Court, as well as Marshall's predecessor, Chief Justice John Jay, played prominent roles in organizations or episodes that figured in the slavery controversy. Before his elevation to the Court, Jay had been an active member of the New-York Society for Promoting the Manumission of Slaves and Protecting Such of Them as Have Been or

[6] Felix Frankfurter, *The Commerce Clause under Marshall, Taney and Waite* (Chapel Hill, 1937), 48. The "five slaveholders and two or three doughfaces" phrase was another Horace Greeley contribution. New York *Tribune*, March 5, 1857.

[7] Carl Brent Swisher, *Roger B. Taney* (New York, 1936); Carl Brent Swisher, "Dred Scott One Hundred Years After," *Journal of Politics*, XIX (May 1957), 167–83; Carl Brent Swisher, "Mr. Chief Justice Taney," Allison Dunham and Philip B. Kurland, eds., *Mr. Justice* (Chicago, 1964), 203–30; *History of the United States Supreme Court of the United States: The Taney Period, 1836–64* (New York, 1974).

[8] Arthur Bestor, "State Sovereignty and Slavery: A Reinterpretation of Proslavery Constitutional Doctrine, 1846–1860," *Journal of the Illinois State Historical Society*, LIV (Summer 1961), 117–80.

[9] Walter Ehrlich, "A History of the Dred Scott Case" (doctoral dissertation, Washington University, St. Louis, 1950); Vincent C. Hopkins, *Dred Scott's Case* (New York, 1951).

[10] Exceptions to the second generalization are Corwin, "Dred Scott Decision in the Light of Contemporary Legal Doctrines"; Bestor, "State Sovereignty and Slavery"; Robert J. Harris, "Chief Justice Taney: Prophet of Reform and Reaction," *Vanderbilt Law Review*, 10 (Feb. 1957), 227–57; Helen Tunnicliff Catterall, "Some Antecedents of the Dred Scott Case," *American Historical Review*, XXX (Oct. 1924), 56–70; and Paul Finkelman, "The Nationalization of Slavery: A Counterfactual Approach to the 1860s," *Louisiana Studies*, XIV (Fall 1975), 213–40.

May be Liberated, one of the earliest precursors of the later antislavery societies. Long after his retirement from the bench, Jay entered the controversy over Missouri's admission as a slave state in 1819–1820 by publishing a public letter supporting the power of Congress under the migration-or-importation clause to restrict the spread of slavery by refusing to admit Missouri.[11]

Chief Justice Marshall, from a different vantage, was as active as his predecessor, but more circumspect, as a member of the American Colonization Society (ACS), an organization dedicated to the voluntary expatriation of former slaves and their settlement in Liberia. Associate Justice Bushrod Washington was also an active colonizationist and served as honorary president of ACS. He embarrassed ACS members having antislavery principles, though, by selling off many of his slaves to the deep South for insubordination and suspected contamination with abolitionist sentiments.[12]

Justice Joseph Story was an exuberant opponent of the international slave trade, and, in a more muted way, of Missouri's admission as a slave state. In the Missouri controversy, Story spoke at a public meeting in Salem, Massachusetts, opposing Missouri's admission.[13] In charges to grand juries at Boston, Providence, Rhode Island, and Portland, Maine, he condemned the slave trade and slavery itself as "repugnant to the natural rights of man and the dictates of justice."[14]

The question of the legitimacy of slavery that Story was alluding to had been raised in Lord Chief Justice Mansfield's opinion in *Somerset* v. *Stewart* (King's Bench, 1772).[15] Mansfield was there reported to have held that a master's power over his slave, including the power to seize, confine, deport, and sell, "must be recognized by the law of the country where it is used. The power of a master over his slave has been extremely different, in different countries. The state of slavery is of such a nature, that it is incapable of being introduced on any reasons, moral or political; but only [by] positive law. . . ." This strong assertion led later lawyers and jurists construing the phrase "the law of the country where it is used" to exalt public-policy considerations of the forum jurisdiction rather than the foreign jurisdiction in conflicts and in-

[11] Henry P. Johnston, ed., *The Correspondence and Public Papers of John Jay* (4 vols., New York, 1890–1893), IV, 430–31; U.S. Constitution, art. I, sec. 9, cl. 1.

[12] P. J. Staudenraus, *The African Colonization Movement, 1816–1865* (New York, 1961), 173.

[13] William W. Story, ed., *The Life and Letters of Joseph Story* (2 vols., Boston, 1851), I, 359–61.

[14] Story, *Life and Letters of Joseph Story*, I, 336; William W. Story, ed., *The Miscellaneous Writings of Joseph Story* (Boston, 1852), 122–47.

[15] *Somerset* v. *Stewart*, 98 English Reports 499 (1772) at 510. See William M. Wiecek, "Somerset: Lord Mansfield and the Legitimacy of Slavery in the Anglo-American World," *University of Chicago Law Review*, 42 (Fall 1974), 86–146.

ternational law cases involving extra-domiciliary slaves. As presiding judge of the United States Circuit Court for Massachusetts in 1822, Story found just such a case on his docket.

United States v. *La Jeune Eugenie* (1822) provided Story with a chance to condemn the international slave trade from the bench, and he eagerly seized it.[16] *La Jeune Eugenie* was an exhaustive and magisterial dissertation on the bases of public international law, which Story saw as threefold: 1) natural law ("the general principles of right and wrong"); 2) "usages" (*i.e.*, custom); and 3) positive law (treaty enactments and municipal law). Redefining the law of nations in the ancient Roman sense of the *jus gentium*, Story held that it included every principle "that may be fairly deduced by correct reasoning from the rights and duties of nations, and the nature of moral obligation." Such principles, he held, were enforceable as ordinary law in American courts.

On the base of natural-law foundations, Story held the slave trade "repugnant to the great principles of Christian duty, the dictates of natural religion, the obligations of good faith and morality, and the eternal maxims of social justice" and as inconsistent with "any system of law that purports to rest on the authority of reason or revelation. And it is sufficient to stamp any trade as interdicted by public law, when it can justly be affirmed, that it is repugnant to the general principles of justice and humanity." *La Jeune Eugenie* was obviously predicated on attitudes toward slavery different from those entertained by a member of the Virginia elite who was himself a slaveholder.

Though opposed to slavery in the abstract, like all Virginians Marshall had an acute sense of the difficulties of abolishing it. He was especially sensitive to the problem of a large free black population, which he thought immiscible with white society; hence his support for colonization.[17] When Marshall had an opportunity to speak to the issues Story had addressed, he rebuked his colleague's antislavery zeal. In *The Antelope* (1825),[18] Marshall made two concessions to the spirit of Story's *La Jeune Eugenie* and Mansfield's *Somerset*: in dicta he condemned the slave trade as contrary to "the law of nature" and adopted by implication the *Somerset* idea that slavery and the slave trade could

[16] *United States* v. *La Jeune Eugenie*, 26 Federal Cases 832 (1822) at 846–48.

[17] See *The Fifteenth Annual Report of the American Society for Colonizing the Free People of Colour of the United States* (Washington, 1832), vi-viii; Robert Kenneth Faulkner, *The Jurisprudence of John Marshall* (Princeton, 1968), 50–51; and Albert J. Beveridge, *The Life of John Marshall: The Building of the Nation, 1815–1835* (Boston, 1919), 473–79.

[18] *The Antelope*, 10 Wheat. 66 (1825) at 122; see John T. Noonan, Jr., *The Antelope: The Ordeal of the Recaptured Africans in the Administrations of James Monroe and John Quincy Adams* (Berkeley, 1977); and Donald M. Roper, "In Quest of Judicial Objectivity: The Marshall Court and the Legitimation of Slavery," *Stanford Law Review*, 21 (Feb. 1969), 532–39.

be established only by positive law, which in *The Antelope* meant municipal law or clearly defined international custom. But by accepting custom as the basis of positive law, Marshall repudiated *La Jeune Eugenie*. The maritime powers had legitimated the slave trade by engaging in it, protecting it by statute, and regulating it by treaty, thus providing the "usages" and municipal law necessary to sustain the trade's legitimacy. Marshall dropped a broad hint to Story that a judge's moral and humanitarian instincts should not influence his judgment on what the law is. Story, unrepentant, in 1842 still considered his *La Jeune Eugenie* opinion to be the definitive word on the illegitimacy of the slave trade,[19] while a Boston abolitionist lawyer, Ellis Gray Loring, dismissed *The Antelope* as mere dicta of no "binding authority."[20]

Two other decisions of the Marshall court helped establish the dominance of Marshall's rather than Story's attitudes. In *Mima Queen* v. *Hepburn* (1813),[21] Marshall refused to bend evidentiary rules to permit hearsay testimony concerning an *inter vivos* promise to free a slave, even though all eyewitnesses to the promise were dead. Marshall lamely explained that "[h]owever the feelings of the individual may be interested on the part of a person claiming freedom," if hearsay rules were relaxed, "no man could feel safe in any property, a claim to which might be supported by proof so easily obtained." *Mima Queen* hampered the work of the abolition societies in protecting the freedom of individual blacks.[22] Sixteen years later, in *Boyce* v. *Anderson* (1829),[23] Marshall relaxed slightly his rigid conception of slaves as property to hold a common carrier responsible for the death of slaves he was carrying by applying rules of liability governing passengers, not inanimate cargo. The wording of this opinion suggests, however, that Marshall was moved not so much by the humanity of the slave-victims as by concern for their shipper-master.

In only one instance did a member of the Marshall Court abandon discretion and accept a head-on confrontation with slavery—and in that instance his position went unsupported by his brethren. Justice William Johnson, a South Carolinian, presided over the circuit that included his native state. In the aftermath of the Denmark Vesey slave insurrection scare of 1822, South Carolina enacted the first of the Negro seamen's

[19] Story, *Life and Letters of Joseph Story*, II, 430–31.
[20] Ellis Gray Loring to John Quincy Adams, Nov. 14, 1839, Loring Family Papers (Schlesinger Library, Radcliffe College).
[21] *Mima Queen* v. *Hepburn*, 7 Cranch 290 (1813) at 295–96.
[22] Duncan J. MacLeod, *Slavery, Race and the American Revolution* (Cambridge, Eng., 1974), 110, 118.
[23] *Boyce* v. *Anderson*, 2 Pet. 150 (1829) at 154–56.

acts, which provided that any free black seaman debarking from a vessel in any port of the state was to be jailed until his ship cleared, with the ship's master liable for the costs of the incarceration. A black seaman not redeemed by his captain could be sold into slavery.[24] British and northern shippers protested the statute. In *Elkison* v. *Deliesseline* (1823), Johnson held the act unconstitutional on the grounds that it interfered with the "paramount and exclusive" power of Congress to regulate interstate and foreign commerce and that it violated the 1815 Anglo-American commercial convention.[25]

Johnson's *Elkison* opinion became the subject of sharp pamphlet and newspaper debate in South Carolina, which only provoked the combative justice to a more firm and heated defense of his opinion. His chance to expand on the commerce-clause reasoning came next year when the case of *Gibbons* v. *Ogden* (1824) came up before the Supreme Court.[26] Though Marshall's opinion held a New York monopoly unconstitutional because of its conflict with federal commerce-regulatory power, Johnson found his chief's reasoning inadequate, and elaborated on federal commerce power in what is a *ne plus ultra* of judicial nationalism. Johnson insisted, as he had in *Elkison*, that federal power was exclusive of state regulatory power, even in the absence of a federal statute. None of this had any effect on Carolinians' attitudes; authorities continued to enforce the Seamen's Act in defiance of Johnson's opinions.

Marshall responded to a challenge on circuit similar to the one Johnson faced in South Carolina in a way that discloses the temperamental differences between the two men. Marshall faced a challenge to a federal statute barring the importation of free blacks into a state that had forbidden their importation by law.[27] He coolly declined to pass on the issue, explaining to Story that "fuel is continually adding to the fire at which the exaltees are about to roast the judicial department . . . a case has been brought before me in which I might have considered [the act's] constitutionality had I chosen to do so, but it was not absolutely necessary, and, as I am not fond of butting against a wall in sport, I escaped on the construction of the act."[28]

[24] Thomas Cooper and David J. McCord, comps., *The Statutes at Large of South Carolina* (9 vols., Columbia, S.C., 1836–1841), VII, 461–62.

[25] *Elkison* v. *Deliesseline*, 8 Federal Cases 493 (1823) at 495.

[26] *Gibbons* v. *Ogden*, 9 Wheat. 1 (1824) at 227–33; for a more extended discussion, see Maurice G. Baxter, *The Steamboat Monopoly: Gibbons v. Ogden, 1824* (New York, 1972), 57–60.

[27] *The Wilson* v. *United States*, 30 Federal Cases 239 (1820); act of Feb. 28, 1803, *U.S. Statutes at Large*, II, 205–06.

[28] John Marshall to Joseph Story, Sept. 26, 1823, Joseph Story Papers (Massachusetts Historical Society, Boston).

After the immediatist antislavery societies had formed (1831–1833) and replaced the old, gradualistic abolition societies, their members determined to challenge slavery's legitimacy before the United States Supreme Court. At the 1837 convention of the New England Anti-Slavery Society, the Reverend Orange Scott, a Methodist minister, predicted that "the Judges of the land" would hold slavery unconstitutional.[29] Next year the business committee of the society suggested that it could "lend them [slaves] our aid in bringing their cause before the [Supreme] court of the United States to ascertain if a man can be held in bondage agreeably to the principles contained in the Declaration of Independence or the Constitution of our country."[30] Abolitionist editor Joshua Leavitt suggested to Salmon P. Chase, then a Cincinnati lawyer who had made a name for himself in antislavery activity, that slavery be challenged in a test case made up for the purpose.[31] But before anything could come of Leavitt's suggestion, abolitionists suddenly found themselves with a dramatic case on their hands that posed complicated political challenges and an exciting opportunity to dramatize slavery questions before the high court.

The cases of the *Amistad* began when a Portuguese slaver brought fifty-two Africans of the Mendi tribe from Guinea to Cuba in 1839, in violation of Spanish laws banning the international trade, and sold them to two Spanish subjects in the Cuban slave mart. The purchasers transported them on a Spanish-flag coasting schooner, the *Amistad*, from Havana to Camaguey province. En route, somewhere in Cuban waters or on the high seas, the captives rose in rebellion, macheted the captain and cook, and commanded the purchasers to steer a course to Africa. They did so by day, but by night set a northerly course in hopes of landing at a friendly port in one of the American slave states. As it turned out, they landed near Long Island, New York, where they were captured by an American coastal survey brig and taken across Long Island Sound to New London, Connecticut.

There a series of complicated legal maneuvers began when the United States Attorney for Connecticut charged the captives with piracy and murder, and had them indicted by a federal grand jury. There was an irony in charging the Africans, rather than the slavers, with piracy, because the captives were *prima facie* free men, illegally enslaved, who

---

[29] *Proceedings of the Fourth New England Anti-Slavery Convention, Held in Boston, . . . 1837* (Boston, 1837), 18.

[30] Quoted in Bayard Tuckerman, *William Jay and the Constitutional Movement for the Abolition of Slavery* (New York, 1894), 86–87.

[31] Joshua Leavitt to Salmon P. Chase, Dec. 6, 1841, Salmon P. Chase Papers (Historical Society of Pennsylvania, Philadelphia).

had acted in self-defense. They had been brought to Cuba in violation not only of Spanish law but of joint conventions delegitimating the international slave trade. They had been in Cuba only a few days, too short a time to acquire slave status under Cuban law, and were being carried from one port to another in Cuba illegally under falsified papers that tried to conceal the facts of their illegal capture.

At the same time the criminal proceedings were begun, the commander of the survey brig brought a libel before the United States District Court sitting in admiralty, claiming salvage of the vessel and its human cargo. The Cuban owners gracelessly intervened in this admiralty proceeding, attaching the captives and denying the right to salvage on the grounds that the Mendi were their property, and that the American sailors, who were in a branch of the public naval service that was a predecessor of the modern Coast Guard and Coast and Geodetic Survey, were merely performing their duty. To round out the series of initial legal actions, abolitionists had the Cuban claimants arrested in New York and committed on a charge of false imprisonment. This last action never came to trial and had only nuisance value.

The executive branch of the federal government did its best to re-enslave the captives and ship them back to Cuba. President Martin Van Buren, up for reelection and courting the South, put the services of the State Department, various federal attorneys, and the navy at the service of the Cubans, hoping to dispose of the case in the federal courts as quickly and antiseptically as possible. He had a warship standing by to whisk the captives off to Havana as soon as the federal courts resolved the proceedings in favor of the claimants, as he confidently expected they would. United States Attorney General Felix Grundy, a Tennessean, gratuitously submitted an opinion supporting the Cubans' legal position, arguing that the blacks were slaves, that American courts had no jurisdiction to try them, and that the president was therefore obliged to turn them over to Cuban authorities.[32]

The first legal action was aborted in the United States Circuit Court by Justice Smith Thompson, who dismissed the criminal proceedings against the blacks because the jurisdiction of American courts did not reach offenses committed on alien-flag vessels on the high seas or in

[32] For a survey of the whole episode, see Samuel Flagg Bemis, *John Quincy Adams and the Union* (New York, 1956), 384–415. Adams forced Martin Van Buren to release documents that disclosed the President's proslavery complicity: these were reprinted as ''Africans Taken in the Amistad,'' Executive Document 188, Series 366, 26 Cong., 1 Sess. (April 15, 1840). Felix Grundy's opinion is published there. Charles G. Haines and Foster Sherwood, *The Role of the Supreme Court in American Government and Politics, 1835–1864* (Berkeley, 1957), 98–110, has much detail on legal aspects of the controversy.

foreign waters.[33] This left the admiralty proceedings in the District Court as the main theater of legal action, and abolitionists channeled their efforts into it. They were not laboring just to vindicate an abstract theory; the illegal international slave trade persisted through the Civil War, and any legal victories that abolitionists could score against it would have some practical application.

The abolitionist lawyers Seth Staples, Theodore Sedgwick, Jr., Roger Sherman Baldwin, and Loring appeared as attorneys for the Mendi, with Loring busily trying to bring John Quincy Adams into the action. Sedgwick, in plotting legal strategy, assumed that *The Antelope* had held that legal rights could be acquired in the international trade and that "it is too late or rather let us hope too early to contend in the courts of the U.S. that there can be no property in Human Beings—in Africans at least—decision after decision settles the matter." Hence he rejected an approach that might have tried to hold the mutineers free on *La Jeune Eugenie*-type reasoning, recommending instead that abolitionists use the case to demonstrate the extent to which American laws were subverted to the support of slavery.[34] But to everyone's surprise, in the District Court proceeding Judge Andrew T. Judson held that the captives were free men under the laws of Spain, and that, in any event, there could be no salvage in them because the state of Connecticut did not recognize the status of slavery. The Circuit Court (Thompson and Judson), affirmed this holding *pro forma* to send it on up to the Supreme Court.

In arguments before the high court, United States Attorney General Henry D. Gilpin (successor to the recently deceased Grundy) maintained that the federal government was obliged to render the Africans to the Cuban claimants because their slave status was attested by the Cuban shipping papers. He insisted that courts could not go behind the face of the document to determine whether it was falsified, as everyone assumed it was—the practice was a notorious way for American consular officials to augment their official income. Baldwin for the Africans based his argument on the postulate that the federal government lacked power to enslave. Since the captives were free at the time they came into New York and Connecticut waters, and since they could not be held as slaves under the laws of those states, the federal government could not force

[33] *The African Captives. Trial of the Prisoners of the Amistad on the Writ of Habeas Corpus, before the Circuit Court of the United States . . .* (New York, 1839).
[34] Theodore Sedgwick, Jr., memorandum of remarks to Lewis Tappan, Oct. 12, 1839, Lewis Tappan Papers (Library of Congress); accord, Loring to Elizur Wright, Feb. 22, 1837, Ellis Gray Loring Papers (Houghton Library, Harvard University.).

them into slavery or deprive them of their natural state of freedom.[35] Adams, whom Loring had finally brought into the case, supplemented Baldwin's lawyer-like effort with a long rhetorical condemnation of the proslavery connivance of the Van Buren administration. He reinforced this with a powerful *argumentum ad verecundiam*, pointing out that as secretary of state he himself had negotiated the 1819 readoption of the Spanish-American treaty of 1795 that formed the basis of the Cubans' claim. The treaty required that "all ships and merchandise, of what nature soever, which shall be rescued out of the hands of any pirates" should be restored. Never, Adams insisted, had he as the American negotiator thought that the term "merchandise" could include men.[36]

Again to everyone's surprise, the Supreme Court, through Justice Story, held against the Cubans on the grounds that there was no valid proof that the captives were slaves.[37] Though Story's failure to adopt the premises of Baldwin's argument was a disappointment to abolitionists, his holding that allegedly falsified consular papers could be impugned for fraud was a valuable practical concession to abolitionist efforts to strike at the slave trade.

Perhaps because their energies were thrown so totally into the *Amistad* effort, abolitionists at first missed the significance of another case then coming up to the Supreme Court that raised tangled questions about the validity of the 1793 Fugitive Slave Act and state personal liberty laws. *Prigg* v. *Pennsylvania* (1842) and other fugitive-slave cases bear out Justice Oliver Wendell Holmes' dictum that "Great cases like hard cases make bad law."[38] Such cases raised intricate questions about the relationship of the nation to the states in the American federal system, and these issues had to be resolved on the basis of fluid and inchoate concepts borrowed from public international law governing the relations of sovereign states among themselves. Fugitive-slave cases required judges to assign responsibilities and rights in the working of American federalism in ways that the framers had chosen to evade; they had political repercussions that courts were ill-equipped to cope with; and they juxtaposed conflicting demands of legality and morality.

Abolitionists before 1840 had annually but unsystematically attacked

[35] Roger Sherman Baldwin, *Argument before the Supreme Court of the United States, in the case of the United States, appellants,* vs. *Cinque, and others, Africans of the Amistad* (New York, 1841).

[36] John Quincy Adams, *Argument of John Quincy Adams, Before the Supreme Court of the United States, in the Case of the United States, Appellants, vs. Cinque and Others, Africans, Captured in the Schooner Amistad, . . . reported in the 10th, 11th and 12th volumes of Wheaton's Reports* (New York, 1841).

[37] *U.S.* v. *The Amistad*, 15 Pet. 518 (1841).

[38] *Northern Securities Co.* v. *United States*, 193 U.S. 197 (1904) at 400.

the constitutionality of the 1793 act, principally on the grounds that it denied the right of jury trial guaranteed in the Sixth and Seventh Amendments and that the federal government under the Tenth Amendment lacked power to legislate on the subject, the fugitive-slave clause imposing nothing more than a restriction on the states. But they had not used litigation as a vehicle for their efforts, and legislative struggles in Massachusetts, Pennsylvania, Ohio, New York, and elsewhere over personal liberty laws diverted their attention from the possibility of bringing up test cases. Abolitionists did, however, carry on the tradition of the old abolition societies in calling on Congress to repeal or amend the 1793 act and in rescuing or providing counsel to individual victims of the act.

Pennsylvania's 1826 personal liberty act was unpopular with slave-catchers and slave-owners because it repealed previous statutory authorization for the right of reception, by which an owner or his agent could seize a slave without formal process; it prohibited state judges from acting solely on a slave-catcher's oath when authorizing seizure; and it made the owner's oath of ownership inadmissible in removal hearings.[39] It had thus been a source of conflict with Maryland from the date of its enactment. The easy passage of fugitive slaves across the Mason-Dixon line annoyed Maryland slave-owners, while the activity of slave-catchers affronted Pennsylvanians. To get an authoritative ruling on the permissible scope of state personal liberty laws, the two states agreed to create a test case, and Pennsylvania took the unusual step of authorizing such litigation by statute.[40] Edward Prigg, a slave-catcher who claimed to be the agent of a Maryland slave-mistress, had procured the seizure of Margaret Morgan, allegedly a slave of his principal, together with her children, including one who was born a year after she had come to Pennsylvania with her husband, a free black. A state justice of the peace had issued a warrant for her arrest, but refused to participate further in removal proceedings under the federal act, a right he enjoyed under the 1826 state statute. Prigg thereupon carried off the woman and her children to Maryland without securing a certificate of removal required by the state law. To make up a test case, Prigg voluntarily returned to Pennsylvania and submitted himself to prosecution for violation of the 1826 act. He was convicted, and his conviction was upheld on appeal in the state courts. He then procured a writ of error

[39] Acts of the General Assembly of the Commonwealth of Pennsylvania (Harrisburg, 1826), 150–55.

[40] Laws of the General Assembly of the Commonwealth of Pennsylvania . . . 1838–39 (Harrisburg, 1839), 218–20.

from the United States Supreme Court, alleging the unconstitutionality of the state law and the infringement of his rights under the federal act.

A symptom suggesting that *Prigg*[41] was one of those hard cases that make bad law is that contemporaries and historians have disagreed on what the case held. Seven justices (all but John Catron and John McKinley) filed opinions. Four things may be said with assurance about this case: there was a majority of the Court; Story wrote the opinion for that majority; that majority agreed on all but three issues canvassed in all the opinions; and there was a significant division on the Court on only one of those three issues.[42] To determine what the Court held, as distinguished from points that had only minority support, it might be useful to distinguish between controverted and non-controverted issues. On the non-controverted issues, the Court was unanimous, with the possible and problematical exception of Justice Henry Baldwin.

Stated baldly, the non-controverted holdings and dicta of Story's opinion are these:

1) The Constitution's fugitive slave clause[43] was a compromise between northern and southern states necessary to the latters' ratification of the Constitution. This is sometimes called the "historical necessity" thesis.[44] As so often happens, the Court's history was bad; no evidence exists that the fugitive clause was a *sine qua non* for southern ratification.

2) The federal Fugitive Slave Act of 1793 was not unconstitutional. This point included two sub-issues on which the justices differed chiefly in emphasis: a) in the abstract, Congress had power to enact some sort of statute under the fugitive slave clause; b) the 1793 act was such a statute.

3) Even without federal statutory provisions, the master of a runaway had a right of recaption that he could exercise in any state. On this point, there was an implicit conflict among the justices as to whether this right was derived, as Story maintained, from the common law, or whether it was derived from the Constitution's fugitive-slave clause.

4) The Pennsylvania act of 1826 was unconstitutional because it conflicted with the masters' rights protected by the federal act.

The justices disagreed among themselves on three issues. The only one that produced a significant division among them was whether the

[41] *Prigg* v. *Pennsylvania*, 16 Pet. 539 (1842).

[42] See Joseph C. Burke, "What Did the Prigg Decision Really Decide?" *Pennsylvania Magazine of History and Biography*, XCIII (Jan. 1969), 73–85, for an alternative analysis of the make-up and holding of the Court. The Reporter of the Court, the able and experienced Richard Peters, labeled Story's opinion as being for the Court. Six of the seven justices writing opinions referred, in one verbal formula or another, to an opinion of the majority of the Court (Henry Baldwin being the exception), and all implied that Story had spoken for the majority.

[43] U.S. Constitution, Art. IV, sec. 2, cl. 3.

[44] The historical necessity thesis was first voiced in a significant judicial opinion by Chief Justice William Tilghman of the Pennsylvania Supreme Court in *Wright* v. *Deacon*, 5 Sergeant & Rawle 62 (1819).

federal act pre-empted all state statutes on the subject of fugitive recaptures. All the justices agreed that no state could enact legislation interfering either with the master's right of recaption or with the federal act; the only real question was whether a state could enact legislation supportive of the federal law. Five justices held that a state could not: Story, John McLean, and James M. Wayne explicitly, and Catron and McKinley, who, because they did not file separate opinions, must be presumed to have endorsed Story's opinion on the point. Three justices, Peter V. Daniel, Taney, and Thompson, explicitly dissented from this position, each claiming that the state governments could (and Taney insisting that they must) enact supportive legislation making recaption of fugitives easier.[45] The view of the dissenters on this point was vindicated in *Moore* v. *Illinois* (1852),[46] which upheld the constitutionality of an Illinois statute prohibiting the harboring of fugitive slaves.

Two other dicta commanded the assent of only one justice apiece; each was a unique view that received no other support. First, McLean claimed that the states could properly enact laws to prohibit the kidnapping of free blacks, so long as such a statute avoided entirely the problem of recapture of fugitives. (How it could possibly do so, he did not bother to explain.) Second, Story asserted that the federal government could not constitutionally oblige state officials (*e.g.*, sheriffs or justices of the peace) to participate in the enforcement of the federal fugitive slave act, and that a state might properly prohibit them, by statute, from so acting.

Story believed that this last point, which commentators often wrongly consider a "holding" of the Court, was a "Triumph of Freedom" because it committed the Supreme Court to "a recognition of the locality of slavery, as the creature of municipal law," *i.e.*, that it incorporated the doctrine of *Somerset*.[47] This, however, sounds like *post hoc* rationalization by Story in response to abolitionist criticism, especially in view of a letter of April 29, 1842, that Story wrote to Senator John Berrien of Georgia, urging Congress to revise the federal fugitive statute by extending the powers of federal commissioners to fugitive cases so as to provide a federal mechanism that would fill the vacuum created by state officials' non-cooperation in enforcement of the

[45] Baldwin did not speak to this point, though, according to James M. Wayne, he would have accepted Story's preemption position if pressed; *Prigg* v. *Pennsylvania*, 16 Pet. 539 (1842) at 637.

[46] *Moore* v. *Illinois*, 14 How. 13 (1852).

[47] Story as quoted by Charles Sumner, who was his protégé and confidant. Sumner to Chase, March 12, 1847, Chase Papers (Library of Congress). Story's son maintained the same position, claiming that this part of Story's opinion left the door open to enactment of further state personal liberty laws along the line of Pennsylvania's. Story, *Life and Letters of Joseph Story*, II, 392–95.

federal act. Story urged that Berrien promote the revision quietly so as not to provoke debate.[48] Moreover, a year and a half later Story delivered an impassioned plea to his students at the Harvard Law School urging them to respect the obligations of the fugitive slave clause.[49]

Whatever Story's real attitude, if he intended his point to be a major concession to antislavery hopes, abolitionists usually missed the hint entirely. They condemned his *Prigg* opinion as "monstrous" and as establishing "the principle of slavery as the law of the whole Union, on the ruins of State sovereignty, habeas corpus, and jury trials."[50] Samuel Ringgold Ward, a black abolitionist, felt himself so discouraged and threatened by the consequences of the opinion that he determined to move to Kingston in Upper Canada.[51]

Before 1845, abolitionists did not find an occasion for a formal, full-dress restatement of their principles in the United States Supreme Court. Representative Joshua Giddings of Ohio began exploring possibilities in Congress in 1845,[52] but a judicial opportunity soon presented itself in a case affecting the rights, not of a fugitive black, but of a white conductor of the Underground Railroad in Ohio. Salmon P. Chase had acquired a nickname in Kentucky and Ohio as "the attorney-general for runaway negroes" because of his frequent representation of fugitives. When a case arose involving the liability of a white man under section 4 of the 1793 statute for harboring or concealing a fugitive slave, Chase seized the chance abolitionists missed in *Prigg* to present a full challenge to the statute before the United States Supreme Court.

For his arguments in *Jones* v. *Van Zandt* (1847), Chase used the infantry of legal argument on technical questions concerning the sufficiency of notice and the meaning of harboring, but wheeled in his artillery to attack the constitutionality of the 1793 act. Because slavery was exclusively a state institution, Congress had no power to "create, continue, or enforce" it. Chase claimed that the Declaration of In-

[48] Story to John M. Berrien, April 29, 1842, John Macpherson Berrien Papers, microfilm roll 1, Southern Historical Collection (Library of the University of North Carolina, Chapel Hill).

[49] Charles Richard Williams, ed., *Diary and Letters of Rutherford Birchard Hayes* (2 vols., Columbus, 1922–1926), I, 131. The future President was then a law student in Story's classes.

[50] Alvan Stewart, "The Act of 1793," Luther Rawson Marsh, ed., *Writings and Speeches of Alvan Stewart on Slavery* (New York, 1860), 387; Cincinnati *Philanthropist*, March 30, 1842. See also "The Duty of Colored Americans," *Emancipator and Free American*, March 31, 1842; "The Constitution and Fugitive Slaves," Cincinnati *Philanthropist*, Dec. 24, 1842; "The Disunion Pledge," Cincinnati *Weekly Herald and Philanthropist*, July 23, 1845.

[51] Samuel R. Ward to Gerrit Smith, April 18, 1842, Gerrit Smith Miller Collection (Syracuse University).

[52] [Joshua R. Giddings] *The Rights of the Free States Subverted; Or, An Enumeration of Some of the Most Prominent Instances in Which the Federal Constitution Has Been Violated by Our National Government, for the Benefit of Slavery* (Washington, 1845).

dependence was "an authentic promulgation of the common law of the Union in respect to the inviolability and inalienability of personal liberty, and inconsistent with the longer continuance of slavery in any of the states." Slavery was contrary to "natural right." Slave laws therefore "must necessarily be local and municipal." When a slave entered a free jurisdiction, his slave status dropped off, not because a positive law freed him, but "because he continues to be a man and leaves behind him the law of force." The Fugitive Slave Act violated the due process, unreasonable-searches-and-seizures, and civil jury trial provisions of the Bill of Rights. The Tenth Amendment reserved to the states, and withdrew from the federal government, the power to regulate fugitive recaptures.[53]

Chase added a novel argument to antislavery constitutionalism when he suggested that there were two sorts of clauses in the federal Constitution: those creating the machinery of government, and those that were articles of compact among the states. The fugitive-slave clause was one of the latter, and as such it carried with it none of the presumptions of congressional power that went along with the former. He concluded by urging the Court to reject the holding of *Prigg* on the constitutionality of the 1793 act.

The Supreme Court, through Justice Levi Woodbury, refused to do this and reaffirmed *Prigg*. Woodbury also chose to meet head-on the claim that courts must refuse to give effect to immoral legislation. He evaded the moral issue by restating a commonplace attitude of contemporary jurists, particularly those of Jacksonian inclinations, that might be called the concept of the "judicial automaton." Woodbury dismissed Chase's argument about "the supposed inexpediency and invalidity of all laws recognizing slavery, or any right of property in man" as "a political question, settled by each state for itself." The fugitive slave clause was "one of [the] sacred compromises . . . which we possess no authority as a judicial body to modify or overrule." Then the judge-as-moral-automaton: "Whatever may be the theoretical opinions . . . as to the expediency of some of those compromises or of the right of property in persons which they recognize," Woodbury asserted, "this court has no alternative, while they exist, but to stand by the constitution and the laws with fidelity to their duties and their oaths. Their path is a straight and narrow one, to go where that constitution and the laws lead, and not to break both, by traveling without or beyond

[53] S. P. Chase, *Reclamation of Fugitives from Service. An Argument for the Defendant Submitted to the Supreme Court of the United States . . . in the Case of Wharton Jones vs. John Vanzandt* (Cincinnati, 1847), 85, 77, 84.

them.''[54] Story, Woodbury's predecessor, shared this attitude. ''. . . I have sworn to support . . . [the United States Constitution],'' Story once wrote, ''and I cannot forget or repudiate my solemn obligations at pleasure. You know full well that I have ever been opposed to slavery. But I take my standard of duty *as a Judge* from the Constitution.''[55]

Abolitionists were disgusted with the *Van Zandt* opinion and its author. Writing of Woodbury's doughface attitude, Chase remarked ''I can well imagine the deep scorn and contempt swelling in the bosoms of the southern judges, as they beheld Levi on his belly crawling through that opinion.''[56] The Supreme Court ''cannot be trusted at all when that great corporate interest [*i.e.*, slavery] is in question,'' he wrote in discouragement to Sumner, ''and all attempts to compromise the matter by getting the court committed on such matters as the locality of slavery [*i.e.*, *Somerset*], in decisions of leading questions in favor of the slaveholders, will be found as unavailing as the efforts of the Philistines with their green with[e]s upon Samson.''[57]

Only certain kinds of slavery cases could come before the United States Supreme Court: those involving the presence of a supposed slave in a state other than that of his domicile. Fugitives comprised one category of such slaves; other kinds raised different constitutional issues. One of the more difficult was that of a slave sent from one state to another for sale.

Abolitionists since the mid-1830s had been urging Congress to abolish the interstate slave trade. This agitation began to penetrate the consciousness of slavery's defenders on the bench and at the bar. In United States Supreme Court decisions of the 1840s can be traced the emergence of a judicial proslavery doctrine that was reactive to the abolitionist effort, but that carried the thinking of a majority of the justices as far in a proslavery direction as abolitionists hoped to bring them in the other. This proslavery tendency was stimulated by the only significant case involving the interstate slave trade ever decided by the United States Supreme Court, *Groves* v. *Slaughter* (1841). The significance of this case for emergent proslavery can best be understood against a background, not of abolitionist efforts, but of divisions on the Court on federal and state power over interstate commerce that did not involve the slave trade.

[54] *Jones* v. *Van Zandt*, 5 How. 215 (1847) at 231.
[55] Story, *Life and Letters of Joseph Story*, II, 431.
[56] Chase to John P. Hale, May 12, 1847, Chase Papers.
[57] *Diary and Correspondence of Salmon P. Chase, Annual Report of the American Historical Association for the Year 1902* (2 vols., Washington, 1902), II, 114.

The landmark commerce-clause opinions of the Marshall Court. *Gibbons* v. *Ogden* (1824), *Brown* v. *Maryland* (1827), and *Willson* v. *Black Bird Creek Marsh Co.* (1829)[58] had not resolved the question whether federal control over interstate commerce was exclusive of state power, or whether the states retained some concurrent power over such commerce. Conservative nationalists like Marshall, Story, and Daniel Webster, fearing what Webster called "irregular & dangerous acts of State Legislation,"[59] hoped to squelch state interference with the national economy and hence leaned toward the federal-exclusivity end of the spectrum. Defenders of state power like Justice Daniel, however, saw the issue as being rather one of preventing federal interference with the control that the states exercised over their institutions and economy, and hence tended to exalt considerations of state police power. This exclusivity-police power dichotomy was skewed, particularly for conservative nationalists, by southern fears that a northern-dominated Congress might meddle with the slave trade via the commerce clause.

These various problems were raised implicitly during Taney's first term in *Mayor of New York* v. *Miln* (1837). A New York statute required masters of incoming vessels to provide a passenger manifest to help the state control the immigration of paupers and other undesirables. Justice Philip Pendleton Barbour, for the majority, upheld the statute on police-power grounds and stated that it did not regulate interstate commerce in a manner that would run afoul of the commerce clause. Story, dissenting, claimed that federal power was exclusive. Justice Thompson concurred with the majority on separate grounds, admitting that the statute was a regulation of commerce, but was permissible as a state power concurrent with that of Congress. These three opinions indicated that the Court was divided on the commerce clause/police power problem, and that a comparable case involving the ingress of free or enslaved blacks would add a slavery overlay to the commerce issue, difficult enough in itself.[60]

This was the doctrinal background of the *Groves* case. The factual background derived from the economy and society of Mississippi in the 1830s. Mississippi in 1832 amended its constitution to prohibit the importation of slaves into the state for sale as merchandise, with an

---

[58] *Gibbons* v. *Ogden*, 9 Wheat. 1 (1824); *Brown* v. *Maryland*, 12 Wheat. 419 (1827); *Willson* v. *Black Bird Creek Marsh Co.*, 2 Pet. 245 (1829).

[59] [J. W. McIntyre, ed.] *The Writings and Speeches of Daniel Webster* (18 vols., Boston, 1903), XVI, 470.

[60] *Mayor of New York* v. *Miln*, 11 Pet. 102 (1837) at 130–43, 156–61, 144–53. However, Justice Wayne, in his Passenger Cases opinion, claimed that Justice Baldwin did not concur in Philip P. Barbour's opinion, and that it lacked a majority of the Court. *Smith* v. *Turner, Norris* v. *Boston*, 7 How. 283 (1849) at 432.

exemption for bona fide settlers who bought slaves out of state. A variety of motives prompted enactment of this clause: suspicion and dislike of slave traders; the importation of suspected insurrectionists; unethical and illegal practices in the business; fear of an excessively numerous slave population; desire to discourage speculation in slaves; hope of stemming the outflow of capital and the rise of indebtedness; and perhaps a desire to keep up the prices of slaves already in the state.[61] But the state legislature did not enact enforcement legislation, and a purchaser defaulted on a note given for purchase of some slaves, alleging the illegality of consideration (*i.e.*, that the sale of slaves was prohibited under the state constitution).

Slaves as objects of commerce in the *Groves* case stood as surrogates for other classes of blacks in the general problem of state control of Negro migration. Potentially affected also were state statutes prohibiting the ingress of free blacks, including the Negro seamen's acts; regulating or protecting runaways; relating to sojourners' slaves or slaves accidentally in a free jurisdiction by mischance, such as shipwreck; and affecting slaves being shipped through one state en route to another. Potentially even state control of white persons, such as that of itinerant abolitionists in the South or of slave-catchers in the North, might be involved.

Like *Prigg* the next year, *Groves* took abolitionists unawares, and they did not contribute to arguments. Henry Clay and Webster, among counsel for the seller, argued that the state constitutional prohibition was void as an infringement on the exclusive power of Congress to regulate the interstate slave trade.[62] This position posed a problem for conservatives like Clay and Webster: comforting though the posture of exclusive federal regulation might be to a nationalist, it was just this power that abolitionists were calling on Congress to exercise in abolition of the slave trade, a position that Clay and Webster did not remotely endorse. This aspect of the case unsettled the proslavery majority of the Court, so that even without abolitionist participation in argument, momentous issues were canvassed in the opinions.

Reflecting the divisions within the Court both on the commerce clause/police power point and on federal versus state control of the interstate slave trade, the Court handed down four opinions.[63] Thompson's

[61] Charles Sackett Sydnor, *Slavery in Mississippi* (New York, 1933), 157–67.

[62] Arguments are at 10 *Law. Ed.* 800 (1841) at 802–18; on Daniel Webster's exclusivist position, see Maurice G. Baxter, *Daniel Webster & the Supreme Court* (Amherst, 1966), 209–13.

[63] *Groves* v. *Slaughter*, 15 Pet. 449 (1841) at 496–503. Smith Thompson delivered the Court's judgment and an opinion for himself and Wayne; Roger B. Taney, John McLean, and Baldwin concurred on differing grounds; John McKinley and Story dissented without opinion; John Catron did not sit because of illness and Barbour had just died.

opinion for the Court avoided all the difficult issues in the case by holding that the constitutional provision was not self-actuating and that it needed state legislation to invalidate the commercial importation of slaves. But McLean, for whatever reason, chose to deliver a semi-abolitionist opinion, arguing that federal commerce power over the interstate slave trade was exclusive, that slaves were persons under the federal Constitution and that ''The character of property is given them by the local [*i.e.*, state] law,'' an oblique endorsement of *Somerset* and some points in the antislavery constitutional argument.

McLean's foray into this touchy area provoked an angry counter-concurrence by Taney, and a characteristically irregular concurrence by Henry Baldwin. Taney adopted the polar opposite of Webster's and McLean's exclusivist position, insisting that state power over the ingress of blacks of whatever condition was exclusive of federal power, whether that power be derived from the commerce clause or any other source. Reading between the lines, one can detect in Taney's opinion the echoes of a past controversy, that over the Negro seamen's acts,[64] as well as a reaction to a contemporary one, the abolitionist demand for abolition of the slave trade.

Henry Baldwin adopted not only Webster's argument that federal power was exclusive, but also another point that Clay had made, namely that it was ''conservative'' in the sense that it could be exercised only to protect, not to destroy, interstate traffic in slaves. He touched on almost every conceivable issue in the constitutional problem of the interstate slave trade: states may not prohibit the trade because of the privileges-and-immunities clause (Baldwin was referring to the privileges of slave-owners, of course, and was voicing the proslavery counterpart to abolitionists' arguments about the rights of blacks under the clause); owners' rights in slaves were protected by the due process clause of the Fifth Amendment; any state law interfering with the passage of a master with his slaves from one jurisdiction to another or with the rights of a master accidentally in the state with his slaves would be void; and slaves were, in the eyes of the law, property, not persons. Henry Baldwin's opinion was a Black Mass of abolitionist constitutionalism.

Taney's determination to annihilate antislavery constitutional ideas was abetted by a quality of his personal leadership of the Court that differentiated his tenure from his predecessor's. Marshall had firmly discouraged dissents and concurrences, in an effort to have the Court

---

[64] In 1832, U.S. Attorney General Taney drafted an opinion, never published, defending the consititutionality of the Negro seamen's acts; excerpted in Swisher, ''Mr. Chief Justice Taney,'' 209–13.

speak with one voice, going so far as to mute his own strong convictions in support of a majority that he did not always support. Taney, by contrast, did not share Marshall's abhorrence of multifarious opinions in one case, and as chief justice was tolerant of multiple-opinion decisions. He himself felt strongly compelled to speak out whenever slavery issues came up, as they did in McLean's *Groves* concurrence, and he never succeeded in restraining his strong inclination to launch into dicta. As a specimen of judicial workmanship, *Dred Scott* epitomized all these undesirable traits of Taney's style, but it was not unprecedented.

In 1844 the Kentucky Court of Appeals was confronted with a fugitive-slave case raising *Somerset* issues. A Kentucky master had permitted several of his slaves to work for wages in Ohio and Indiana. After they returned to Kentucky, the slaves ran off, allegedly with the help of Jacob Strader, the owner of the vessel on which they made their escape, who was then sued by their owner under a Kentucky statute making an abettor of fugitives liable for their value. Strader defended on the grounds that the slaves, having been sent by their master to a free jurisdiction, had thereby been liberated and had not lost their freedom on their return to Kentucky. Hence they were not fugitive slaves, but rather free men exercising their natural right to personal mobility. The Kentucky court ruled this defense insufficient and upheld Strader's liability under the statute.[65]

On appeal to the United States Supreme Court, Taney in 1851 denied that the Supreme Court had jurisdiction, on the grounds that the question of the slaves' status was one to be determined by state law and exclusively by the state courts, and, that the state court's decision on that issue was conclusive on all federal courts.[66] This was unexceptionable contemporary legal doctrine. But Taney was uneasy over the crescendo of abolitionist attacks on slavery, and went on to indulge himself in a tendency he had that was to produce the fatal result of *Dred Scott*: he let fall several gratuitous dicta on issues not before him in an effort to resolve, through judicial means, questions that were metajudicial.

Taney admitted at the outset of his opinion that the question of the slaves' status was "not before us" and that the court had no jurisdiction over it. McLean and Catron, concurring, agreed and chided Taney for nevertheless going into the issue. Taney stated, "Every state has an undoubted right to determine the status, or domestic and social condition,

[65] *Graham v. Strader*, 5 B. Monroe 173 (Ky. 1844).
[66] *Strader v. Graham*, 10 How. 83 (1851) at 93.

of the persons domiciled within its territory''; but then added this fateful qualification: ''except in so far as the powers of the states in this respect are restrained, or duties and obligations imposed on them, by the Constitution of the United States.'' It is difficult to discern precisely what, if anything, Taney meant in this passage. If restricted to the fugitive slave clause, it was a truistic observation. But, as with Taney's other utterances on slavery, it had a mischievous potential, and was vague enough to be applicable to categories of blacks other than fugitives, as, for example, sojourners' slaves.

Taney went further. He explicitly stated that the Northwest Ordinance was defunct, having been superseded by the state constitutions. And he hinted that its ''perpetual'' and inviolable ''compact'' could not restrain the right of the states carved out of its territory from establishing slavery if they chose to do so, because that would put them in an inferior status vis-a-vis other states in the union. This dictum implied that Congress could not constitutionally impose an enforceable condition on the admission of a new state that it abolish slavery. Here Taney seemed to be reversing a statement of Justice Catron in *Permoli* v. *New Orleans* (1845)[67] that Congress could stipulate elements that a territory must present in its constitution when it applies for statehood, and could reject the constitution if those elements were lacking. This proslavery tendency to unsettle what northerners regarded as fundamental constitutional settlements was repeated in the repeal of the Missouri Compromise (1854) and in Taney's assertion of its unconstitutionality in the *Dred Scott* case three years later.

The abolitionist leader, James G. Birney, reacted sharply to these *Strader* dicta. He charged that ''in order to reach our colored people—especially the free portion of them—our Supreme Court are willing to trample down & disregard the constitutional safeguards of all our rights.'' He also pointed out that the holding of *Strader*, read in the light of *Prigg* and the 1850 Fugitive Slave Act, would empower any southern state to enslave any free black found within its borders. This, in turn, would virtually legitimate kidnapping under the easy mechanism of the 1850 act. Free blacks in free states were little better off than slaves in the South in terms of security for their personal liberty. Birney despondently recommended that blacks migrate to Liberia.[68]

[67] *Permoli* v. *First Municipality of New Orleans*, 3 How. 589 (1845) at 609–10.

[68] James Gillespie Birney, *Examination of the decision of the Supreme court of the United States, in the Case of Strader, Gorman and Armstrong vs. Graham delivered at its December term, 1850: concluding with an address to the free colored people, advising them to remove to Liberia* (Cincinnati, 1852); James G. Birney, untitled ms. on violation of habeas corpus (1852), vol. 16, James G. Birney Papers (William L. Clements Library, University of Michigan).

In the 1850s, abolitionists and others began to suspect that the Supreme Court might force slavery into the free states. Two decades earlier, this would have been dismissed as a lurid fantasy of paranoid imaginations, but the *Dred Scott* case and the repeal of the Missouri Compromise unsettled constitutional arrangements in ways that seemed to question the power of the northern states to repel the incursion of slavery.[69] Concurrently, Taney's determination to put down abolitionist constitutional theory intensified. Within the space of two years, he first denied to Congress any power that might be exercised to inhibit the spread of slavery into the territories, and then arrogated to the federal courts powers to override state judicial power to protect state citizens in slavery-related confrontations.

Taney's *Dred Scott* opinion is conventionally read as an essay on the expansion of slavery into the territories, and correctly so.[70] But taken together with Justice Samuel Nelson's concurring opinion, it also seemed to suggest that there were federal or state constitutional inhibitions on the power of the northern states to preserve their free status, to protect their black and white populations within or outside their domicile, and to regulate the status of non-residents within their borders. Nelson resurrected Taney's *Strader* qualification of six years earlier and restated it nearly verbatim, thus reviving fears of its potentially sinister impact on state (not congressional) power. Taney's grudging concession of the power of the states to make citizens of whom they please was offset by his denial that blacks might thereby become ''citizens'' entitled to the privileges and immunities specified in Article IV section 2 of the Constitution and by his insistence that, upon migration, these black free-state citizens would lose their status and acquire whatever status the state they removed to might choose to confer on them. These state-power points were overshadowed by the ensuing part of Taney's opinion limiting congressional power over the territories. But even had Taney never entered into the territories-clause and due-process-clause portions of his opinion, its import would have alarmed northerners already sensitized to slavery's penetration of their jurisdictions.

Abraham Lincoln capitalized on the link between repeal of the Missouri Compromise by the Kansas-Nebraska Act of 1854 and Taney's *Dred Scott* opinion in the Lincoln-Douglas debates of 1858, but he was not

[69] For a reading of *Dred Scott* in this light, and its political repercussions, see Wiecek, ''*Somerset*,'' 138–40; Richard H. Sewell, *Ballots for Freedom: Antislavery Politics in the United States, 1837–1860* (New York, 1976), 299–304; and Paul Finkelman, ''A More Perfect Union? Slavery, Comity, and Federalism, 1787–1861'' (doctoral dissertation, University of Chicago, 1976).
[70] *Dred Scott v. Sandford*, 19 How. 393 (1857).

alone in his perception that the Supreme Court now threatened the free states as well as the territories. Someone as far from Lincoln politically as Ohio's anti-abolitionist Democratic Senator George Pugh argued that if the Taney/Nelson extrapolation of *Strader* were valid for the territories, it was equally valid for the states.[71] The Vermont legislature complained that the privileges-and-immunities clause, read in the light of the *Dred Scott* decision, "would convert every State into a slaveholding State, precisely as it now makes every Territory a slaveholding Territory. . . ."[72] New York Judge Samuel Foot feared that the contracts clause of Article I, section 10 would not only make unconstitutional all the northern state abolition laws, but also restore retroactively the rights of southern owners of fugitive slaves to their runaways and to the children of female fugitives.[73]

Far from allaying such fears, southerners reinforced them by repudiating the *Somerset* decision. Political abolitionists had derived the slogan of "Freedom national, slavery sectional" from Mansfield's language. Southern defenders of slavery after the *Dred Scott* decision developed a mirror image of this doctrine, a set of ideas that might be called "Slavery National." "What is local and municipal is the *abolition* of slavery," maintained the Carolinian J. H. Thornwell in a pro-secession tract. "The States that are now non-slaveholding, have been made so by positive statute. Slavery exists, of course, in every nation in which it is not prohibited."[74] He was echoed by the New York racist John H. Van Evrie, who extolled the *Dred Scott* decision as implying a "universal recognition of 'slavery' as the natural relation of the races [as] the basis of the common law. . . . it followed of necessity that 'freedom' 'free negroism' or legal equality of negroes, was the creature of the lex loci or municipal law."[75] To be fair to Taney, this was reading into his opinion more than could be fairly implied, but *Dred Scott* did suggest a direction in which the thinking of the high court majority was evolving, and had the war not intervened, it was not impossible that such doctrines might find some acceptance in the United States Supreme Court.

Lincoln had warned that a "nice little niche [might be] filled with

[71] *Congressional Globe*, 35 Cong., 2 Sess., 1249–51 (Feb. 23, 1859).

[72] Vermont, House of Representatives, *Report of the Select Committee on Slavery, the Dred Scott Decision, and the Action of the Federal Government Thereon* . . . (Montpelier, 1858), 7.

[73] Samuel A. Foot, *An Examination of the Case of Dred Scott Against Sandford, on Tuesday evening, 28th December, 1858* (New York, 1859), 13–15.

[74] J. H. Thornwell, *The State of the Country. An Article Republished From the Southern Presbyterian Review* (Columbia, S.C., 1861), 13; see also Missouri Senator James Green, *Congressional Globe*, 36 Cong., 1 Sess., appendix 78 (Jan. 11, 1860).

[75] *The Dred Scott Decision. Opinion of Chief Justice Taney, with an Introduction by Dr. J. H. Van Evrie* . . . (New York, 1863), iv.

another Supreme Court decision'' abrogating the power of the free states to exclude slavery.[76] A case soon went on its way up to the Supreme Court that provided the opportunity he foresaw. In *Lemmon* v. *The People* (1860),[77] the New York Court of Appeals had declared free a group of slaves in transit through the state from one slaveholding jurisdiction to another. The New York judges confuted Taney's premises by adapting *Somerset* doctrine: a slave becomes free by coming into the free jurisdiction of New York.

Judge Foot and the Reverend Theodore Parker had earlier warned that the slave-owner's appeal of an adverse decision in *Lemmon* would permit the United States Supreme Court to take the last, fatal step in annihilating the constitutional antislavery position.[78] Foot concluded that the Supreme Court had changed the American Constitution ''so fundamentally, as to nationalize slavery, and turn this nation into a great slaveholding republic.''[79] The Vermont legislature's select committee on slavery complained that ''Power, unlimited, can be found in the constitution and in Congress, to extend, protect and perpetuate, but none to limit, restrain, or prohibit this great national evil. Slavery is made the rule and freedom the exception.''[80] Suiting its response to its sentiments, the Vermont legislature adopted the ''Freedom Act'' of 1858, which, in addition to expanding even more the scope of the state's personal liberty laws, defied Congress and the *Prigg* decision by providing that any slave coming into Vermont, under whatever circumstances, with or without the permission of his master, was free.[81]

The onset of war aborted the whole controversy engendered by *Strader-Dred Scott-Lemmon*, and speculation about what Taney and his associates might have done had war not come must be hypothetical.[82] What Taney did do, however, remains germane. Seeing that the northern states were willing to wage war to preserve the Union, he supported secession, though he chose to stay on as Chief Justice of the United States in order to oppose the Lincoln administration's actions against the southern states and its intrusions on civil liberties in both sections. Angered at northern state court resistance to *Dred Scott*, as exemplified in the expanded

[76] Robert W. Johannsen, ed., *The Lincoln-Douglas Debates of 1858* (New York, 1965), 19.

[77] *Lemmon* v. *People*, 20 N.Y. 562 (Court of Appeals, 1860).

[78] Samuel A. Foot, *Reasons for Joining the Republican party. Reasons of Hon. Samuel A. Foot, Late Judge of the Supreme Court of New York, for accepting Republican nomination* (New York [?], 1855), 4; Theodore Parker, *The Present Aspect of Slavery in America and the Immediate Duty of the North* . . . (Boston, 1858), 20. The case had been pending in New York courts since 1852.

[79] Foot, *Dred Scott*, 19.

[80] Vermont, House of Representatives, *Report*, 13.

[81] *The Acts and Resolves* . . . *of the State of Vermont* . . . *1858* (Bradford, Vt., 1858), 42.

[82] Finkelman, ''The Nationalization of Slavery'' pursues this hypothetical inquiry.

Somerset doctrines of *Lemmon* and the Ohio case of *Anderson* v. *Poindexter* (1857)[83] or in the Maine Supreme Judicial Court's rejection of his dicta,[84] Taney took extraordinary measures. He drafted a supplement to his *Dred Scott* opinion, declaring that its principles extended to all blacks, not just those descended from slave ancestors. The American Revolution "was not designed to subvert the established order of society and social relations, nor to sweep away traditional usages and established opinions." Similarly, in Taney's canon of interpretation, the Declaration of Independence was "intended as a conservative measure, and not as revolutionary"; all blacks of necessity had to be deemed to be excluded from its terms.[85] And in his mournful last years, he composed anticipatory "opinions," perhaps to be used should an appropriate case ever come before him, in which he declared both the Legal Tender Acts and conscription to be unconstitutional, and insisted that all northern states had a constitutional obligation to surrender any black claimed as a slave in a suit instituted by his owner "for the purpose of recovering him as property."[86] Death mercifully relieved him in 1864 from witnessing ratification of the Thirteenth Amendment and its state counterparts.

Arthur Bestor has shown that Taney's proslavery constitutionalism was not inherently hostile to a nationalizing, centralizing growth of federal power.[87] When slavery could best be protected by an expansion of federal authority at the expense of the states, Taney did not hesitate to do so. *Ableman* v. *Booth* (1859), Taney's last official pronouncement on the slavery controversy, demonstrates this.[88] The Wisconsin Supreme Court had impeded the enforceability of the fugitive slave acts by making state habeas corpus available to an abolitionist detained in federal custody for violation of the 1850 act. Taney repelled this challenge in a strongly nationalistic opinion supporting the superiority of federal judicial authority over state process in a confrontation between them.

Before the Civil War, many things had restrained the justices of the Supreme Court from trying to resolve slavery issues beyond the competence of the judiciary: Marshall's sense of the limits on his power, kept lively by the sniping of Thomas Jefferson, Spencer Roane, and other Virginians; a constitutional consensus that held-most matters pertaining

[83] *Anderson* v. *Poindexter*, 6 Ohio State 622 (1857).

[84] "Opinions of the Justices . . . 1857," 44 Maine 505 (1857).

[85] Reprinted in Samuel Tyler, *Memoir of Roger Brooke Taney, LL.D.* (Baltimore, 1872). 578–605, 600.

[86] Swisher, *Roger B. Taney*, 570–72; unpublished draft memorandum [1860?], in "Oddments" file, Roger B. Taney Papers (Library of Congress).

[87] Bestor, "State Sovereignty and Slavery."

[88] *Ableman* v. *Booth*, 21 How. 506 (1859).

to slavery outside the authority of the federal government and exclusively for the states; the restricted nature of cases—only those involving extra-domiciliary slaves—that could come before the federal courts; and, in the early years of the Taney Court, a seeming sense that slavery questions were both explosive and intractable.

By a sad irony, Chief Justice Taney, supported by Justice Woodbury, had himself called into being precisely the legal doctrine needed to deflect such cases from the federal courts. In *Luther* v. *Borden* (1849), Taney declined to resolve the question of which government of Rhode Island was the legitimate one in the months of the Dorr Rebellion (1842) on the grounds that this was a ''political question'' to be resolved by the legislative and executive branches of government, rather than the judiciary.[89] If ever a court needed a sense that issues coming before it presented questions that could not be resolved by judges, it was in the slavery cases of the 1840s and 1850s. Yet Taney and most of his associates, invited by Congress and impelled by their own strongly-held convictions, embraced these issues with a foolhardy bravado, discovered that they had become sorcerer's apprentices, and thereby contributed to the destabilization of the constitutional system that hastened the Civil War. Slavery in some of its aspects was a constitutional problem, but the Supreme Court's disastrous handling of it serves as a caution that not all constitutional issues are susceptible of being resolved by courts. If war is too serious to be entrusted to the military, at times the American constitution is too serious to be relinquished to the judges.

[89] *Luther* v. *Borden*, 7 How. 1 (1849).

THE INDIANA SUPREME COURT
AND THE STRUGGLE AGAINST SLAVERY

SANDRA BOYD WILLIAMS*

James Scott of Clark County, Jesse Holman of Dearborn County and John Johnson of Knox County, took the bench for the first term of the Indiana Supreme Court on May 5, 1817.[1] Only two cases were on motion to the court in the first term, and only three in the second term.[2] By the court's second term, Isaac Blackford had been appointed to the bench to fill the vacancy left by the death of John Johnson.[3]

Indiana had just attained statehood, and its supreme court was quickly confronted with the issue of slavery. From its very first opinions dealing with slavery, the court held that Indiana was a free state that allowed neither slavery nor involuntary servitude.[4] With a few aberrations, the court held the line against slavery through numerous opinions decided before and during the Civil War era. This task was not always easy because Indiana borders Kentucky, at that time, a slaveholding state. This Article examines the historical, political and social context of a few of the court's more significant cases, decided between its inception in 1817 and 1866.

Three years after its inception, the Indiana Supreme Court heard its first slavery case. *Lasselle v. State*[5] examined the Knox Circuit Court's ruling in *Polly (a woman of colour) v. Lasselle* that allowed Lasselle to exercise ownership over Polly.[6] Lasselle had bought Polly's mother from Indians inhabiting the Northwest Territory before it was ceded to the United States. While in Lasselle's custody, Polly filed for a writ of habeas corpus in the trial court seeking her freedom.[7] Polly's attorneys argued that although her mother may have been taken by Indians and sold as a slave, "yet by the laws of nature and nation," neither Polly nor her

---

* Attorney, Locke Reynolds Boyd & Weisell, Indianapolis, Indiana. B.A., 1983, Purdue University; J.D., 1986, University of Wisconsin Law School. Former Staff Attorney for the Indiana Supreme Court. Currently practicing in the Appellate Section of Locke Reynolds Boyd & Weisell.

The author would like to thank Clarence Williams, Locke Reynolds Boyd & Weisell, Julia Orzeske, Donald Kite, Sr., Randall Thompson, Justice Richard Givan, Chief Justice Randall Shepard, and the staff of the Indiana State Library for their support, research assistance and comments during the writing of this paper.

1. 1 LEANDER J. MONKS, COURTS AND LAWYERS OF INDIANA 181 (1916).
2. ISRAEL G. BLAKE, THE HOLMANS OF VERAESTAU 16 (1943).
3. 1 MONKS, *supra* note 1, at 182.
4. State v. Lasselle, 1 Blackf. 60 (Ind. 1820); *In re* Clark, 1 Blackf. 122 (Ind. 1821) (entitled in the reporter as "The Case of Mary Clark, a Woman of Color").
5. 1 Blackf. at 60.
6. *Id.* at 61.
7. Record at 1, Polly (a woman of colour) v. Lasselle (Knox Cir. Ct. 1820) (handwritten) (contained in Indiana Supreme Court case file, State v. Lasselle, July term, 1820, on file with Indiana State Archives, Commission on Public Records, Indianapolis) [hereinafter *Polly (a woman of colour)*].

offspring could be held as slaves.[8] Specifically, Polly's attorneys argued that because Polly was born after the Ordinance of 1787, which prohibited slavery and involuntary servitude in the Northwest Territory,[9] she was entitled to freedom.[10]

The Knox Circuit Court determined that: (1) because Polly's mother was a slave prior to the passage of the Ordinance of 1787 and prior to the Northwest Territory being ceded from Virginia, where slavery was legal, passage of the Ordinance of 1787 did not liberate Polly's mother[11]; and (2) because, in slave states, the master was entitled to the benefit of the slave and the slave's offspring, there is "no reason why it should not be the case here."[12] Therefore, the court held that Polly "was born a slave, [and Lasselle] can hold her as such."[13]

The Indiana Supreme Court reversed the decision of the trial court, freed Polly, and awarded her costs against Lasselle.[14] Relying on the Indiana Constitution of 1816, Judge Scott wrote:

> In the 11th article of that instrument, sec. 7, it is declared, that "There shall be neither slavery nor involuntary servitude in this State, otherwise than for the punishment of crimes, whereof the party shall have been duly convicted." It is evident that by these provisions, the framers of our constitution intended a total and entire prohibition of slavery in this State; and we can conceive of no form of words in which that intention could have been more clearly expressed.[15]

The will of Indiana's people, as expressed in her constitution, was that "slavery can have no existence in the State of Indiana . . . ."[16]

In addition to being the first case decided by the Indiana Supreme Court addressing the issue of slavery, *Lasselle* is notable for a number of other reasons, including the parties and the attorneys involved. Hyacinthe Lasselle was a man of some fame as the principal tavernkeeper in Vincennes, Indiana.[17] Jacob Call, who later became a judge and eventually a congressman, was Lasselle's attorney.[18] Amory Kinney, Moses Tabbs and Col. George McDonald represented Polly.[19]

---

8. *Id.* at 3.

9. Ordinance of 1787, art. 6 (1787), *in* LAWS OF THE NORTHWEST TERRITORY 1788-1802, at 69 (Cincinnati, n.p. 1833) ("There shall be neither slavery nor involuntary servitude in the said territory, otherwise than in the punishment of crimes whereof the party shall have been duly convicted . . . .").

10. *Polly (a woman of colour), supra* note 7, at 3.

11. *Id.* at 4.

12. *Id.* at 5.

13. *Id.* at 6.

14. *Lasselle,* 1 Blackf. at 63.

15. *Id.* at 62. *See also* IND. CONST. of 1816, art. XI, § 7.

16. *Lasselle,* 1 Blackf. at 62.

17. Dorothy Clark, *First Local News Editor Voiced Anti-Slavery View,* TERRE HAUTE TRIB.-STAR, Jan. 16, 1966, at 4.

18. *Id.*

19. *Id.*

Amory Kinney had read law in the office of Samuel Nelson who later became a U.S. Supreme Court Justice.[20] Kinney's law partner and brother-in-law was John Willson Osborn, the owner and editor of Terre Haute's first newspaper.[21] Moses Tabbs was the son-in-law of Charles Carroll, one of the signers of the Declaration of Independence.[22] Col. George McDonald was the mentor and father-in-law of Judge Isaac Blackford.[23]

One year after its decision in *Lasselle*, the Indiana Supreme Court reexamined the issue of slavery, this time disguised as a personal services contract. On November 6, 1821, the supreme court decided the case of "a woman of colour called Mary Clark."[24] Court records reveal that in 1914 Mary had been purchased as a "slave for life" by Benjamin L. Harrison in Kentucky.[25] Harrison brought Mary to Vincennes, Indiana in 1815, and freed her. Contemporaneously with her release from slavery, Mary contracted with Harrison to be his indentured servant for thirty years.[26] On October 24, 1816, Harrison "cancelled, annulled and destroyed" the contract for indenture, thereby liberating Mary.[27] On the same day, however, Mary, "a free woman of colour," bound herself to General W. Johnston, his heirs, executor, administrator and assigns as an indentured servant and house maid for twenty years.[28] On his part, General Johnston agreed to:

> find, provide and allow unto her, during all her aforesaid term of servitude, good and wholesome meat, drink, lodging, washing and apparel both linen and woollen, fit and convenient for such a servant. And upon the expiration of her term of servitude, she serving out her present indenture faithfully, give unto her one suit of new clothes (not to exceed however in value twenty dollars) and also one flax wheel.[29]

Mary's signature was indicated on the contracts with an "X."[30]

Mary filed for a writ of habeas corpus, claiming that General Johnston "without any just or legal claim" held her as a slave.[31] General Johnston argued that he had purchased Mary from Harrison for $350 that Harrison had emancipated Mary and that Mary had indentured herself to Johnston for twenty years.[32] The

---

20. *Id.*
21. *Id.*
22. *Id.*
23. *Id.*
24. *In re* Clark, 1 Blackf. 122 (Ind. 1821).
25. Record at 4, Mary Clark v. General W. Johnston (Knox Cir. Ct. 1821) (handwritten) (contained in Indiana Supreme Court case file, Mary Clark v. G.W. Johnston, Nov. term, 1821, on file with Indiana State Archives, Commission on Public Records, Indianapolis).
26. *Id.*
27. *Id.* at 4-5.
28. *Id.* at 5.
29. *Id.* at 6.
30. *Id.*
31. *Id.* at 1.
32. *Id.* at 3.

circuit court determined that Mary should be returned to General Johnston, her putative master, to serve out the remainder of her indenture.[33] The circuit court also ordered that General Johnston "recover . . . his costs and charges" from Mary.[34]

The Indiana Supreme Court reversed. As it had in *Lasselle*, the court relied on the Indiana Constitution's unequivocal prohibition of slavery and involuntary servitude.[35] After noting that all Indiana citizens (including Mary, a woman of colour) could properly enter into contracts, the supreme court held that contracts for personal service could not be enforced through specific performance.[36] Judge Holman wrote:

> Such a performance, if enforced by law, would produce a state of servitude as degrading and demoralizing in its consequences, as a state of absolute slavery; and if enforced under a government like ours, which acknowledges a personal equality, it would be productive of a state of feeling more discordant and irritating than slavery itself. Consequently, if all other contracts were specifically enforced by law, it would be impolitic to extend the principle to contracts for personal service.[37]

The court found that by petitioning for a writ of habeas corpus, Mary conclusively demonstrated that her servitude was involuntary.[38] Once the fact of involuntary servitude was established, the court merely applied the law. Involuntary servitude was outlawed in Indiana under its constitution.[39] Accordingly, the law could not contradict Mary's declaration to be discharged, and she was freed.[40] Mary was awarded costs of eighteen dollars and seventy-four and one half cents.[41] Apparently, however, Mary never received her costs from Johnston. The return of the writ of execution states that Johnston had no property or real estate to satisfy the judgment.[42]

Just as the attorneys and parties in *Lasselle* were notable, so too were the attorneys in the case *In re Clark*. Mary was represented by Charles Dewey, who,

---

33. *Id.* at 7.
34. *Id.*
35. *In re* Clark, 1 Blackf. at 123 (citing IND. CONST. of 1816, art. XI, § 7).
36. *Id.* at 123-24.
37. *Id.* at 124-25.
38. *Id.* at 123.
39. IND. CONST. of 1816, art. XI, § 7.
40. *In re* Clark, 1 Blackf. at 126.
41. Letter from Henry P. Coburn, Indiana Supreme Court Clerk, to Harrison County Sheriff (Dec. 1, 1821) (contained in Indiana Supreme Court case file, Mary Clark v. G.W. Johnston, Nov. term, 1821, on file with Indiana State Archives, Commission on Public Records, Indianapolis).
42. Note dated Apr. 2, 1822, on reverse side of letter from Henry P. Coburn, Indiana Supreme Court Clerk, to Harrison County Sheriff (Feb. 26, 1822) (contained in Indiana Supreme Court case file, Mary Clark v. G.W. Johnston, Nov. term, 1821, on file with Indiana State Archives, Commission of Public Records, Indianapolis).

fifteen years later, was appointed to the Indiana Supreme Court.[43] Johnston was represented by Jacob Call, the same attorney who had represented Lasselle the previous year.[44] Judge Holman, the author of the supreme court opinion, was considered a moderate abolitionist.[45] When Holman came to Indiana from Kentucky around 1810, he brought his wife's slaves with him and freed them.[46]

In 1825, the Indiana Supreme Court heard the appeal of a capital murder case from the Clark Circuit Court.[47] The appellant, designated as "Jerry (a man of colour)," had been convicted of murdering his master and sentenced to death.[48] Jerry appealed his conviction on the ground that the verdict was contrary to the evidence.[49] In an opinion written by Judge Holman, the supreme court reversed the conviction, noting "strong doubts" regarding whether the testimony supported the verdict, and the case was remanded for a new trial.[50] This decision made a strong statement about the Indiana Supreme Court's commitment to justice for all citizens, black and white.

In 1831, Judges Scott and Holman were replaced on the supreme court by Stephen C. Stevens and John T. McKinney.[51] By this time, the political tide was changing in Indiana. Whereas Indiana legislation in the early 1800s was very much aimed at protecting the rights of persons of color within Indiana, later legislation retreated from this position. For example, in 1839, the Indiana legislature passed a general resolution on the subject of slavery, declaring that "Any interference in the domestic institutions of the slaveholding states of this Union . . . either by congress or the state legislatures, is contrary to the compact by which those states became members of the Union."[52] This marked a significant change in Indiana's slavery policy and probably resulted from the pressures from Indiana's southern border state, Kentucky.[53] In response to Indiana's changed policy, Kentucky adopted a resolution praising its "enlightened, liberal, and patriotic, sister State."[54]

---

43. 1 MONKS, *supra* note 1, at 198, 292.
44. 1 *id.* at 292.
45. BLAKE, *supra* note 2, at 28.
46. *Id.*; 1 MONKS, *supra* note 1, at 186.
47. Jerry v. State, 1 Blackf. 395 (Ind. 1825).
48. *Id.* at 396.
49. *Id.*
50. *Id.* at 398-99.
51. 1 MONKS, *supra* note 1, at 194.
52. Resolution of Jan. 29, 1839, ch. 302, 1838 Ind. Acts 353; *see generally* Emma L. Thornbrough, *Indiana and Fugitive Slave Legislation*, 50 IND. MAG. HIST. 201, 217-218 (1954).
53. Thornbrough, *supra* note 52, at 214-18. During this period, slaves constituted approximately 25% of the population of the South. The 1790 census found 697,642 slaves in the United States, most of them living in the South. By 1860, this population had grown to 3,922,760, all of them in the South. Paul Finkelman, *The Centrality of the Peculiar Institution in American Legal Development*, 68 CHI.-KENT L. REV. 1009, 1032 (1993); U.S. CENSUS BUREAU, NEGRO POPULATION, 1790-1915, at 57 (1918).
54. Resolution of Feb. 23, 1839, 1838 Ky. Acts 390; Thornbrough, *supra* note 52, at 218.

310 INDIANA LAW REVIEW [Vol. 30:305

Along with changing tide in Indiana, the federal statutory and case law became increasingly hostile towards slaves seeking freedom. In 1842, the U.S. Supreme Court decided *Prigg v. Pennsylvania*.[55] Pennsylvania had enacted a law which made it an offense against the state to seize and remove a fugitive slave. This made Pennsylvania a haven for runaway slaves and a stop on the underground railroad. Edward Prigg was indicted under this law for feloniously removing Margaret Morgan, a black woman, from Pennsylvania and taking her to Maryland for the purpose of selling and disposing of her as a slave.[56] Prigg was actually a bounty hunter for a woman who claimed that Morgan was her runaway slave.[57] In an opinion delivered by Justice Story, the Taney Supreme Court struck down the Pennsylvania law as unconstitutional.[58] The *Prigg* Court held that federal legislation dealing with fugitive slaves superseded all state legislation on the same subject and by necessary implication prohibited its enforcement.[59] As one writer put it, *Prigg* determined that southern slaveholders and their agents had a constitutional right to "self-help" to seize fugitive slaves and obtain their return.[60]

Shortly after the U.S. Supreme Court decided *Prigg*, the Indiana Supreme Court heard an appeal from the Elkhart Circuit Court. In *Graves v. State*,[61] Joseph Graves, Elisha Coleman and Hugh Longmore were tried and found guilty of inciting a riot.[62] The riot was sparked when Graves, Coleman and Longmore seized Thomas Blackman, an alleged fugitive slave from Kentucky who Graves claimed to be his property.[63] Bystanders sought to prevent the defendants from forcibly taking Blackman before the magistrate.[64] The trial court's instructions to the jury contained Indiana's procedures for seizing fugitive slaves rather than the procedures contained in the federal law on that subject.[65] (The Indiana procedures were more favorable to the alleged fugitive than the federal procedures.[66]) The jury found in favor of the state, and the court fined the defendants thirty dollars

---

55. 41 U.S. (16 Pet.) 539 (1842).

56. *Id.* at 543.

57. *Id.* at 539; *see also* Graves v. State, 1 Ind. 368, 371 (1849).

58. *Prigg*, 41 U.S. (16 Pet.) at 625-26. Chief Justice Taney dissented from that part of the Court's opinion which held that states could not be compelled to enforce the provisions of the federal law regarding fugitives because this was a function of the federal government. Taney believed that all states had a binding obligation to enforce the federal law. *Id.* at 633 (Taney, C.J., dissenting). Fourteen years later, Chief Justice Taney authored the opinion in *Dred Scott v. Sandford*, 60 U.S. (19 How.) 393 (1856), holding that slaves were property and that slaveholders had constitutionally protected property rights in slaves.

59. *Prigg*, 41 U.S. (16 Pet.) at 617-18, 622.

60. Derrick Bell, *Learning the Three "I's" of America's Slave Heritage*, 68 CHI.-KENT L. REV. 1037, 1046 (1993).

61. 1 Ind. 368 (1849).

62. *Id.*

63. *Id.* at 369.

64. *Id.*

65. *Id.*

66. *See id.* at 369-70.

each.[67] On appeal, the Indiana Supreme Court held that it was bound by the *Prigg* opinion.[68] Consequently, the court held that the trial court should have instructed the jury on federal procedures for seizing fugitive slaves. The case was reversed and remanded for a new trial.[69]

Although *Prigg* was primarily used to benefit slaveholders in retrieving alleged runaway slaves, in at least one instance it was used for the opposite effect. Three years after reversing the convictions of Graves, Coleman and Longmore for inciting a riot while trying to seize an alleged fugitive slave, the Indiana Supreme Court reversed a conviction for aiding a slave to escape. In *Donnell v. State*,[70] Luther Donnell had been convicted in the Decatur Circuit Court of "inducing the escape of" and "secreting" away a "certain woman of color, called Caroline" alleged to be the slave of George Ray of Kentucky.[71] Using the federal preemption analysis of *Prigg*, the Indiana Supreme Court held that the part of the Indiana statute under which Donnell had been convicted was unconstitutional and void because it concerned an issue upon which the U.S. Congress had exclusive jurisdiction.[72]

One of the most offensive laws during this period was the Fugitive Slave Law of 1850,[73] the strictest slaveholder protectionist measure to date. It provided that federal commissioners were to hear fugitive slave cases "in a summary manner" and could issue warrants to turn over the fugitive upon evidence that the accused was a runaway slave.[74] The evidence could be as slight as an affidavit providing the physical description of the runaway.[75] This law expressly prohibited the commissioners from admitting testimony of the alleged fugitive,[76] permitted imprisonment of any person hindering an arrest[77] and provided for the expenditure

---

67.   *Id.* at 368-69; Record at 5, Joseph A. Graves v. State (Elkhart Cir. Ct. 1849) (handwritten) (contained in Indiana Supreme Court case file, Graves v. State, May term, 1849, on file with Indiana State Archives, Commission on Public Records, Indianapolis).

68.   *Graves*, 1 Ind. at 370.

69.   *Id.* at 372.

70.   3 Ind. 480 (1852).

71.   *Id.* at 480-81; Record at 3, Luther A. Donnell v. State (Decatur Cir. Ct. 1852) (handwritten) (contained in Indiana Supreme Court case file, Donnell v. State, Nov. term, 1852, on file with Indiana State Archives, Commission on Public Records, Indianapolis).

72.   *Donnell*, 3 Ind. at 481. *Donnell* was written by Judge Samuel Perkins, who is known primarily for spending his leisure time on the bench preparing an *Indiana Digest* and later *The Indiana Practice* treatise. 1 MONKS, *supra* note 1, at 207.

73.   Fugitive Slave Law of 1850, ch. 60, 9 Stat. 462 (1850) (repealed 1864). The Fugitive Slave Law of 1850 amended the 1793 law. Fugitive Slave Law of 1793, ch. 7, 1 Stat. 302 (1793) (repealed 1864). The 1850 law was adopted in response to the demands of the representatives of the slave states and was part of a series of measures known as the Compromise of 1850. EMMA L. THORNBROUGH, THE NEGRO IN INDIANA BEFORE 1900, at 114-115 (1957).

74.   Fugitive Slave Law of 1850, § 6, 9 Stat. at 463.

75.   *Id.* § 10 at 465.

76.   *Id.* § 6 at 463.

77.   *Id.* § 7 at 464.

of federal funds to recover fugitives.[78]   Officials were paid ten dollars if the accused was determined to be a fugitive, but only five dollars if the accused was not.[79]

Obviously, under this statute, every black person was in danger of being declared a fugitive, taken south, and sold into slavery. Armed with this weapon, many unscrupulous slaveholders and slave catchers literally kidnapped free blacks and sold them into slavery. The Fugitive Slave Law of 1850 provided a strong incentive for blacks to seek refuge in Canada, where they would be beyond the reach of the slave catchers.[80]   As a result of this act, trips increased along the underground railroad, which went through Indiana on the way to Canada.[81]   The act also resulted in Indiana anti-slavery jurisprudence, prompting *Freeman v. Robinson*,[82] which was decided in 1855.

Freeman was a free black man who came to Indianapolis in 1844 and "who through hard work and thrift had acquired some real estate, including a house and garden and a restaurant."[83]   According to the 1850 census, Freeman was the wealthiest black person in Indianapolis, owning property valued at $7000.[84] Pleasant Ellington, a Methodist preacher and a major slaveholder in St. Louis, claimed that Freeman was his runaway slave, "Sam."[85]   He and three other men came to Indianapolis to recapture Freeman who he claimed had run away eighteen years earlier, while Ellington was residing in Kentucky.[86]

Assisted by a Deputy U.S. Marshal, Ellington induced Freeman to go to the commissioner's office by telling him that he was required to give testimony before the justice of the peace.[87]   While in the commissioner's office, Ellington sought to examine Freeman without his clothes on.[88]   Both Ellington's attorney and the Deputy Marshal ordered Freeman to remove his clothing for inspection, but upon his attorneys' advice, Freeman refused.[89]   Ellington then requested that the Deputy Marshal forcibly remove Freeman's clothing, but the Deputy Marshal did not believe he had the authority to do so and therefore refused.[90]   Undaunted, Ellington telegraphed the Marshal himself and demanded that he come to Indianapolis.

---

78.   *Id.* § 9 at 465.
79.   *Id.* § 8 at 464.
80.   THORNBROUGH, *supra* note 73, at 53-54.
81.   *Id.* at 40, 53-54.
82.   7 Ind. 321 (1855). For a detailed account of the historical events associated with the *Freeman* case, see Charles H. Money, *The Fugitive Slave Law in Indiana*, 17 IND. MAG. HIST. 180-97 (1921).
83.   THORNBROUGH, *supra* note 73, at 115.
84.   *Id.* at 142-43 n.39.
85.   *Id.* at 115.
86.   *Id.*; Money, *supra* note 82, at 159, 182-83.
87.   Money, *supra* note 82, at 182.
88.   *Id.* at 183.
89.   *Id.*
90.   *Id.*

When U.S. Marshal John Robinson arrived, he complied with Ellington's request, physically removing Freeman's clothing so that Ellington and his three witnesses could "inspect" Freeman.[91] Having completely examined Freeman, Ellington and his witnesses were ready to testify to all the marks on Freeman's body and swear in court that those marks established Freeman as Ellington's runaway slave, Sam.[92]

Freeman had a reputation, among blacks and whites in Indianapolis, for being a good, honest and industrious man.[93] When newspapers reported the fraudulent manner in which Freeman was induced to appear at the commissioner's office, as well as the violence of Freeman's examination, the public was outraged.[94] Freeman's attorneys went to the Marion Circuit Court and obtained a writ of habeas corpus claiming that Freeman could prove that he was a free man.[95] That court, however, determined that it did not have jurisdiction over the case and Freeman was remanded to the custody of the U.S. Marshal pending the federal commissioner's decision.[96]

Freeman's attorneys then sought bail for their client for the nine weeks he would otherwise have to remain in jail.[97] A note was drawn for $1600 and signed by 100 citizens, including Judge Blackford and well-known attorney Calvin Fletcher.[98] In addition, a bond for $4000 was signed by a number of citizens owning property with a total value of more than half a million dollars to indemnify him.[99] Despite these efforts, the commissioner denied bail and ordered Freeman held in jail.[100] U.S. Marshal Robinson, thereafter, charged Freeman three dollars per day for a guard to watch over him.[101]

To prove Freeman was indeed a free man, his attorneys traveled to his previous home in Georgia to obtain witnesses to testify on his behalf.[102] Several witnesses came.[103] Freeman's attorneys were also able to locate the real "Sam," who had fled to Canada after passage of the Fugitive Slave Law.[104] Freeman's attorneys offered to pay Ellington's expenses to Canada to verify Sam's identity,

---

91. *The Freeman Case*, THE LOCOMOTIVE (Indianapolis), Sept. 24, 1853, at 1.

92. Money, *supra* note 82, at 183.

93. *Id.* at 180-81.

94. THE LOCOMOTIVE (Indianapolis), Aug. 20, 1853, at 2; *id.* Sept. 24, 1853, at 1; *id.*, May 13, 1854, at 3.

95. Money, *supra* note 82, at 186.

96. *Id.*

97. *Id.*

98. *Id.* at 186-87.

99. *Id.* at 187.

100. *Id.*

101. *Id.*

102. *The Freeman Case, supra* note 91, at 1; THE LOCOMOTIVE (Indianapolis), Aug. 20, 1853, at 2.

103. INDIANAPOLIS MORNING, Aug. 26, 1853, at 3; THE LOCOMOTIVE (Indianapolis), Aug. 20, 1853, at 2; *The Freeman Case, supra* note 91, at 1.

104. *The Freeman Case, supra* note 91, at 1.

but Ellington refused.[105] Faced with the mounting evidence, Ellington gave up the fight, and the commissioner dismissed the case.[106] This case had attracted significant attention throughout Indiana, and upon the dismissal of the case, a Fort Wayne newspaper observed that "[i]f Freeman had not had money and friends he must inevitably have been taken off into bondage."[107]

The cost of his freedom exhausted Freeman's savings and caused him great discomfort and humiliation.[108] He brought suit for $10,000 damages against Ellington in Marion Circuit Court.[109] After testimony by the Deputy Marshal who had initially tricked Freeman into going to the commissioner's office, the case was settled in Freeman's favor for $2000 plus costs of the suit. The trial court duly entered the judgment.[110] Unfortunately, Freeman never collected because Ellington sold all his property and left St. Louis.[111]

Freeman v. Robinson,[112] was the appeal of the suit Freeman filed in Marion Circuit Court against U.S. Marshal Robinson for assault and extortion in forcing Freeman to submit to a naked examination and requiring him to pay three dollars per day while in jail. Robinson challenged the jurisdiction of the Marion Circuit Court to hear the case based on the fact that Robinson was a Rush County resident.[113] This challenge relied upon an Indiana statute which provided that a suit must be commenced in the county where the defendant resided.[114] Freeman responded that under another provision of the same statute, if the cause arose against a "public officer" for an act done by him by virtue of his office, suit could be commenced in the county where the cause arose.[115] The trial court ruled in Marshal Robinson's favor, and Freeman appealed.[116]

The Indiana Supreme Court, Judge Gookins writing, affirmed the trial court on the basis of improper venue.[117] The court determined that "public officer" in the statute authorizing suits against public officers in the county where the injury occurred only referred to officers of the state and not officers of the federal government.[118] The supreme court, however, rejected Marshal Robinson's federal preemption argument and determined that because assault and battery and extortion were not part his official duties under the Fugitive Slave Law, Freeman

---

105. *Id.*
106. *Id.*
107. FORT WAYNE SENTINEL, Sept. 8, 1853, at 2.
108. THORNBROUGH, *supra* note 73, at 116.
109. THE LOCOMOTIVE, Sept. 3, 1853, at 2.
110. THE LOCOMOTIVE, May 13, 1854, at 3.
111. Money, *supra* note 82, at 194-95.
112. 7 Ind. 321 (1855).
113. *Id.* at 321-22.
114. 2 IND. REV. STAT. pt. 2, ch. 1, § 33 (1852) (superseded); *Freeman*, 7 Ind. at 323-24.
115. 2 IND. REV. STAT. pt. 2, ch. 1, § 29 (1852) (superseded); *Freeman*, 7 Ind. at 324.
116. *Freeman*, 7 Ind. at 322.
117. *Id.* at 324.
118. *Id.*

could maintain his action for personal injury against the Marshal.[119]

The Freeman case was a hard-fought battle with prominent attorneys on both sides. Freeman was represented by John Ketchum, Lucien Barbour and John Coburn, all of whom were known to be excellent anti-slavery lawyers.[120] In addition, John Coburn was the son of Henry P. Coburn, who was the Indiana Supreme Court Clerk during the time *In re Clark* and *Graves v. State* were decided.[121] Ellington was represented by Jonathan Liston and Thomas Walpole, also noted attorneys of the time.[122] Jonathan Liston and Isaac Blackford represented Robinson.[123] Judge Gookins, who wrote the opinion for the supreme court, had practiced law with Amory Kinney, the attorney for Polly in the *Lasselle* case, and had served a newspaper apprenticeship under John W. Osborn, Amory Kinney's law partner and brother-in-law.[124]

Freeman's ordeal profoundly affected the people of Indiana and demonstrated that under the Fugitive Slave Law of 1850, free blacks were likely to be forced into slavery. John Freeman eventually left Indiana and moved to Canada.[125] Marshal Robinson, who had been a very high ranking political figure before *Freeman*, was never able to recover from the negative publicity he received.[126]

The same year that the Indiana Supreme Court decided *Freeman*, it also decided *Woodward v. State*,[127] an appeal from the Hendricks Circuit Court. Jordan Woodward was a black man who had been indicted for assault and battery with intent to murder a white man.[128] At his trial, Woodward offered the testimony of another black man to show that Woodward had acted in self-defense.[129] The trial court refused to allow the testimony based on an Indiana statute prohibiting blacks from testifying in any case in which any white person was a party in interest.[130]

On appeal, Woodward was represented by John L. Ketchum, one of the attorneys who had represented John Freeman. In his brief, Ketchum argued that the trial court erred in refusing the testimony because the statute did not apply.[131] Although Woodward was black, his attorney argued, the other "party" to the cause

---

119. *Id.* at 322-23.
120. Money, *supra* note 82, at 181.
121. OLIVER H. SMITH, EARLY INDIANA TRIALS AND SKETCHES 367 (Cincinnati, Moore, Wilstach, Keys & Co. 1858).
122. Money, *supra* note 82, at 181.
123. *Freeman*, 7 Ind. at 321.
124. 1 MONKS, *supra* note 1, at 251.
125. Money, *supra* note 82, at 197.
126. *Id.* at 184; *see* John Robinson, *Letter to the Editor*, INDIANAPOLIS DAILY JOURNAL, Dec. 27, 1855, at 2.
127. 6 Ind. 492 (1855).
128. *Id.*
129. *Id.*
130. *Id.*; Act of Feb. 14, 1853, ch. 42, § 1, 1853 Ind. Acts 60, 60 (superseded).
131. Brief for Appellant at 1, Woodward v. State, 6 Ind. 492 (1855) (handwritten) (contained in Indiana Supreme Court case file, Woodward v. State, May term, 1855, on file with Indiana State Archives, Commission on Public Records, Indianapolis).

was the State of Indiana, which was "not a 'white person.'"[132] As Ketchum eloquently asserted in his brief, the state "is rather a lady of changeable complexion—graciously taking the hue she finds in her adversary."[133] The supreme court, in a per curiam opinion agreed, holding that the state was not a person of any particular color, and therefore, the trial court erred in rejecting the witness.[134]

A decade after the *Freeman* case demonstrated to the people of Indiana the harsh effects of the Fugitive Slave Law of 1850, the Indiana Supreme Court issued an important opinion entitled *Smith v. Moody*.[135] In that case, the court tackled article XIII of the Indiana Constitution of 1851. Article XIII prohibited blacks and persons of mixed race from coming into or settling in the state after the adoption of the constitution.[136] It further provided that all contracts made with any black person coming into the state in violation of article XIII were void.[137] In addition, at the first legislative session after the Constitution was adopted, the Indiana legislature passed "an act to enforce the 13th article of the Constitution," making it unlawful for blacks to come into, settle in, or become inhabitants of Indiana.[138]

In *Smith*, the black plaintiff (Smith) sued on a promissory note.[139] The white defendants argued that the contract at issue was void because Smith had come into and settled in Indiana after November 1, 1851, in violation of article XIII.[140] Smith responded that he was a citizen of Ohio, by birth, and, pursuant to the U.S. Constitution, was entitled to all the privileges and immunities of citizens in the several states.[141] The trial court rendered judgment in favor of the defendants.[142]

Smith appealed to the Indiana Supreme Court. In an opinion by Chief Judge Gregory, the court held that article XIII of the Indiana Constitution was void because it was repugnant to the Constitution of the United States.[143] The court also held that free persons of African descent, born within a particular state, and made citizens of that state, are thereby made citizens of the United States and entitled to all the privileges and immunities of citizens in the several states.[144]

The importance of this case is punctuated by the fact that the court previously had upheld application of article XIII in several cases.[145] The fact that an entirely

---

132. *Id.*
133. *Id.*
134. *Woodward*, 6 Ind. at 492.
135. 26 Ind. 299 (1866).
136. IND. CONST. art. XIII, § 1 (repealed 1881).
137. *Id.* § 2 (repealed 1881).
138. 1 IND. REV. STAT. ch. 74, §§ 1-9 (1852) (repealed 1867).
139. *Smith*, 26 Ind. at 299.
140. *Id.*
141. *Id.*
142. *Id.* at 300.
143. *Id.* at 302.
144. *Id.* at 306-07.
145. *See, e.g.*, Barkshire v. State, 7 Ind. 389 (1856).

new court took office on January 1, 1865,[146] may explain the reversal on this issue. From *Lasselle v. State* to *Smith v. Moody*, the Indiana Supreme Court made both bold and subtle statements against slavery and involuntary servitude. It refused to allow its halls to be used as a means for one citizen to exercise ownership over another—whether it be by trickery, force or humiliation. Over time, it withstood the erosive forces of imprudent and impudent legislation. Even though an Indiana favorite son was a party to Mary's "transfer of employment," the Indiana Supreme Court denied these slaveholders sanctuary in their attempts to circumvent anti-slavery legislation by terming it "indentured servitude." Given the political and social climate at the time these decisions were made, the court's position was nothing less than extraordinary.

---

146.   Robert C. Gregory, James S. Frazer, Jehu T. Elliott and Charles A. Ray were all newly elected to the supreme court in 1864. 1 MONKS, *supra* note 1, at 254, 302.

The Kidnapping of John Davis
and the Adoption of the Fugitive Slave Law
of 1793

By PAUL FINKELMAN

IN 1791 GOVERNOR THOMAS MIFFLIN OF PENNSYLVANIA REQUESTED THE extradition of three Virginians who were accused of kidnapping a black named John, or John Davis, and taking him from Pennsylvania to Virginia, where he was enslaved. Governor Beverley Randolph of Virginia ultimately refused to extradite the three men, claiming that John was really a fugitive slave who had escaped into Pennsylvania. Mifflin then turned to President George Washington, who asked Congress to adopt legislation on both interstate extradition and fugitive slave rendition. The result was the adoption, in February 1793, of a four-part statute dealing with both questions, which is commonly known as the Fugitive Slave Law of 1793. This article explores the origins and legislative history of that act.

Late in the Constitutional Convention, Pierce Butler and Charles Pinckney of South Carolina proposed that a fugitive slave clause be added to the article requiring the interstate extradition of fugitives from justice. James Wilson of Pennsylvania objected to the juxtaposition because "this would oblige the Executive of the State to do it, at the public expence." Butler discreetly "withdrew his proposition in order that some particular provision might be made apart from this article." A day later the convention, without debate or formal vote, adopted the fugitive slave provision as a separate article of the draft constitution.[1] Eventually the two clauses emerged as

---

[1] The only other response to Pinckney and Butler's proposal was Roger Sherman's sarcastic observation that he "saw no more propriety in the public seizing and surrendering a slave or servant, than a horse." Max Farrand, ed., *The Records of the Federal Convention of 1787* (4 vols.; New Haven, 1911–1937), II, 443 (quotations in text and note), 453–54. The history of this clause is discussed in Paul Finkelman, "Slavery and the Constitutional Convention: Making a Covenant With Death," in Richard Beeman, Stephen Botein, and Edward C. Carter, II, eds., *Beyond Confederation: Origins of the Constitution and American National Identity* (Chapel Hill and London, 1987), 219–24. See also William M. Wiecek,

---

MR. FINKELMAN is a visiting associate professor at Brooklyn Law School.

THE JOURNAL OF SOUTHERN HISTORY
Vol. LVI, No. 3, August 1990

succeeding paragraphs in Article IV, Section 2 of the Constitution.[2]

The paucity of debate over the fugitive slave clause is remarkable because by the end of August 1787, when the convention adopted the clause, slavery had emerged as one of the major stumbling blocks to a stronger union. While it was morally offensive to a number of northern delegates, some southerners defended slavery with an analysis that anticipated the "positive good" arguments of the antebellum period. Nevertheless, unlike the debates over the slave trade, the three-fifths clause, the taxation of exports, and the regulation of commerce, the proposal for a fugitive slave clause generated no serious opposition.[3] The delegates to the Constitutional Convention may have been simply too exhausted for further strenuous debate. It is more likely, however, that the northern delegates failed to appreciate the legal problems and moral dilemmas that the rendition of fugitive slaves would pose. In 1787 even those northern states that were in the process of gradual abolition, such as Pennsylvania, recognized the need to return runaway slaves to their owners.[4]

Both the fugitives from justice clause and the fugitive slave clause dealt with a similar problem—the return to one state of persons found in another. Implicit in both clauses was an expectation of interstate cooperation. The criminal extradition clause appeared to guarantee a pro forma process between governors. The fugitive slave clause suggested a similar process between a slaveowner and local authorities. The slim records of the Philadelphia Convention indicate that most of the Framers assumed, incorrectly as it turned out, that state and local authorities would cooperate in the extradition of fugitives from justice and the rendition of fugitive slaves.

The subsequent history of the two clauses shows that the Framers miscalculated. The Virginia-Pennsylvania controversy of 1788–1791 quickly put the nation on notice that the interstate cooperation necessary for a smooth implementation of these clauses had failed to materialize. This controversy, over the kidnapping of John Davis, is particularly important because it led to the adoption of the 1793 act dealing

---

"The Witch at the Christening: Slavery and the Constitution's Origins," in Leonard W. Levy and Dennis J. Mahoney, eds., *The Framing and Ratification of the Constitution* (New York and London, 1987), 167–84.

[2] The fugitive slave clause reads: "No person held to Service or Labour in one State, under the Laws thereof, escaping into another, shall, in Consequence of any Law or Regulation therein, be discharged from such Service or Labour, but shall be delivered up on Claim of the Party to whom such Service or Labour may be due."

[3] See Finkelman, "Slavery and the Constitutional Convention," 219–24.

[4] "An Act for the Gradual Abolition of Slavery," Act of March 1, 1780, *Laws of the Commonwealth of Pennsylvania* (4 vols.; Philadelphia, 1810), I, 492–93. Section 9 of this law provided for the return of fugitive slaves. The gradual abolition acts of Rhode Island and Connecticut, both passed in 1784, had similar provisions.

with both fugitives from justice and fugitive slaves.[5]

The Davis case had important implications for the rendition of fugitive slaves because the three fugitives from justice that Pennsylvania sought were charged with kidnapping a free black. The problem of kidnapping free blacks quickly emerged as a mirror image of the problem of fugitive slaves. Just as southern states demanded the right to retrieve runaway slaves, northern states demanded the right to protect their free black residents from being kidnapped and sold into servitude in the South. The rights of personal liberty and the claims of personal property caused sectional strife from 1787 until the Civil War.[6]

The history of the adoption of the 1793 law illustrates the importance of slavery to national politics in the 1790s.[7] This history also demonstrates that in this early period southerners were quick to perceive a threat to slavery and just as quick to organize to protect that institution. Northerners were unwilling to endorse slavery, and the institution disturbed many of them. But in legislative battles from 1791 to 1793 northern senators and congressmen were less willing, or less

[5] "An Act respecting fugitives from justice, and persons escaping from the service of their masters," Act of February 12, 1793, in *The Public Statutes at Large of the United States . . .* , I (1845), 302 (hereinafter cited as Act of 1793). William R. Leslie, "A Study in the Origins of Interstate Rendition: The Big Beaver Creek Murders," *American Historical Review*, LVII (October 1951), 63–76, argues that the 1793 law resulted from a conflict between Pennsylvania and Virginia over the rendition of the four men charged with killing peaceful Delaware Indians. Coincidentally, some of those wanted for the Indian killings were also involved in the kidnapping of the free black John Davis. However, as this article demonstrates, the 1793 law regulating both the extradition of fugitives from justice and the rendition of fugitive slaves was a result of Governor Thomas Mifflin's seeking the return of the three Virginians for kidnapping John Davis, who the Virginians claimed was a fugitive slave. Critical to this analysis is the fact that on August 24, 1791, Governor Mifflin praised Governor Beverley Randolph for his cooperation in seeking the arrest of the men charged with killing the Delaware Indians. Yet this was over a month after Governor Mifflin had written to President George Washington complaining about Virginia's noncompliance in the extradition of the men who kidnapped John Davis. This chronology shows that the connection of this case, and the 1793 law, to the Big Beaver Creek murders is coincidental. Thomas Mifflin, "To the Assembly concerning the State of the Commonwealth," August 24, 1791, in George Edward Read, ed., *Pennsylvania Archives: Fourth Series*, Vol. IV (Harrisburg, 1900), 178–81.

[6] There were numerous well-known antebellum conflicts over the return of both fugitives from justice and fugitive slaves. On fugitive slave rendition see especially Thomas D. Morris, *Free Men All: The Personal Liberty Laws of the North, 1780-1861* (Baltimore, 1974). See also Robert M. Cover, *Justice Accused: Antislavery and the Judicial Process* (New Haven, Conn., and London, 1975). On conflicts over the interstate rendition of fugitives from justice see Paul Finkelman, "States' Rights, North and South in Antebellum America," in Kermit L. Hall and James W. Ely, Jr., eds., *An Uncertain Tradition: Constitutionalism and the History of the South* (Athens, Ga., and London, 1989), 125–58; and Paul Finkelman, "The Protection of Black Rights in Seward's New York," *Civil War History*, XXXIV (September 1988), 211–34.

[7] For a discussion of this problem in the first Congress see Joseph C. Burke, "The Proslavery Argument in the First Congress," *Duquesne Review*, XIV (1969), 3–15, and Howard A. Ohline, "Slavery, Economics, and Congressional Politics, 1790," *Journal of Southern History*, XLVI (August 1980), 335–60. See generally Donald L. Robinson, *Slavery in the Structure of American Politics, 1765-1820* (New York, 1971).

able, to protect free blacks and fugitives seeking refuge in the emerging free states. The northern lawmakers also failed to protect their white constituents who aided fugitive slaves for humanitarian reasons, hired fugitive slaves for purely business reasons, or protected runaways on the assumption that they were actually free people. Furthermore, northerners in Congress appear to have failed to appreciate the dangers that slavehunting posed to both free blacks and antislavery whites. In 1793 northerners in Congress who opposed slavery voted in favor of an extradition law that included provisions for the return of fugitive slaves. They voted this way, no doubt, on the assumption that good faith enforcement of the law would lead to a more harmonious union. This assumption of course proved to be quite wrong. The immediate catalyst for the 1793 law—the conflict between Pennsylvania and Virginia—should have put the northern members of Congress on notice that cooperation and interstate harmony were unlikely when southerners felt their slave property was even slightly endangered.

The conflict between Pennsylvania and Virginia emerged from Pennsylvania's program to end all slavery in that commonwealth and the confusion caused by uncertainty as to the location of state boundaries in the wake of the Revolution.[8] Immediately at issue was the status of John Davis and the three Virginians accused of kidnapping him. The conflict was complicated by Virginia officials' proslavery views, which were already quite evident in the early 1790s.[9] This conflict eventually led to the passage in 1793 of a federal law regulating both the extradition of fugitives from justice and the rendition of fugitive slaves.

John Davis gained his freedom under Pennsylvania's Gradual Emancipation Act of 1780. That law declared that all children born of slaves in Pennsylvania after March 1, 1780, were free at birth, subject to a period of indenture.[10] The law allowed masters to retain any slaves they owned in Pennsylvania on March 1, 1780, provided they registered each slave with a court clerk before November 1, 1780. The registration fee was two dollars per slave, and any slave not

[8] On the controversy over the boundary between Virginia and Pennsylvania see Peter S. Onuf, *The Origins of the Federal Republic: Jurisdictional Controversies in the United States, 1775-1787* (Philadelphia, 1983), 49–66. Uncertainty over these boundaries began in the colonial period.

[9] On the general support for slavery in Virginia in the early national period see Robert McColley, *Slavery and Jeffersonian Virginia* (Urbana, 1964), 182–89.

[10] The indenture period was designed to allow masters time to educate the children of their slaves and to teach them a trade. It also enabled the master to recoup most or all of the cost of raising the children of their slaves. Robert William Fogel and Stanley L. Engerman, "Philanthropy at Bargain Prices: Notes on the Economics of Gradual Emancipation," *Journal of Legal Studies*, III (June 1974), 377–401.

registered by that date immediately became free.[11]

The 1780 law put all slaveowners in Pennsylvania on notice that they needed to register their slaves. It also left some slaveowners in a quandary. Throughout the 1770s the exact location of the Pennsylvania-Virginia border remained uncertain. Inhabitants of what became Westmoreland and Washington counties lived in an area claimed by Pennsylvania under its charter but dominated by Virginia. Some people in the area no doubt actually believed they lived in Virginia. Others certainly expected that in the end they would come under Virginia's jurisdiction. As late as 1783 Virginians living in the area "cherished the hope that a final determination would return them to Virginia." Still others believed that western Pennsylvania would be turned into a separate state, especially after Congress's resolutions of September and October 1780 indicated the national legislature's "intention to form new states in its prospective national domain . . . ."[12] The combination of the political and jurisdictional confusion and the "cherished" hopes of some settlers made many slaveowners in the area unwilling to register their slaves under Pennsylvania law. Registration not only cost money but also implied an acceptance of Pennsylvania's jurisdiction over them, when in fact they still either maintained their allegiance to Virginia or wanted to create their own state.[13]

Slaveowners who did not register their slaves risked losing them if in fact it turned out that they lived in Pennsylvania. Nevertheless, many slaveowners in western Pennsylvania did not register their slaves under the 1780 law, even though on August 31, 1779, commissioners from the two states finally agreed on the exact location of the border and on September 23, 1780, the Pennsylvania legislature adopted a resolution accepting the work of the commissioners. This agreement, however, was not finally ratified by both state legislatures until April 1, 1784.[14]

[11] "An Act for the Gradual Abolition of Slavery," Act of March 1, 1780, *Laws of the Commonwealth of Pennsylvania*, I, 492–93. The drafting and adoption of this act are discussed in Arthur Zilversmit, *The First Emancipation: The Abolition of Slavery in the North* (Chicago and London, 1967), 124–37. The law is put in a larger context in William M. Wiecek, *The Sources of Antislavery Constitutionalism in America, 1760–1848* (Ithaca, N. Y., and London, 1977), and David Brion Davis, *The Problem of Slavery in the Age of Revolution* (Ithaca, N. Y., and London, 1975). See also A. Leon Higginbotham, *In the Matter of Color: Race and the American Legal Process, The Colonial Period* (New York, 1978), 299–310.

[12] Onuf, *Origins of the Federal Republic*, 49–60 (quotations on p. 60).

[13] Acceptance of Pennsylvania's jurisdiction, which registration implied, threatened many land titles in the area, which were based on Virginia claims. Thus in 1780 some slaveowners in the area faced the dilemma that they could only protect their slave property by jeopardizing their land claims.

[14] "Virginia Claims to Land in Western Pennsylvania," in William Henry Egle, ed., *Pennsylvania Archives: Third Series*, Vol. III (Harrisburg, 1894), 485–504. See Onuf, *Origins*

In 1782, two years before final action on this agreement, Pennsylvania provided some relief for slaveowners in the two western counties. The 1782 law allowed slaveowners in the disputed territory until January 1, 1783, to register their slaves, provided they proved that they had owned those slaves, in Pennsylvania, on September 23, 1780.[15] This statute showed Pennsylvania's desire to woo the loyalty of the western settlers. It may also have been a response to Virginia's demand of July 23, 1780, that Pennsylvania respect "the private property and rights of all persons, acquired under, founded on, or recognized by the laws of either" state. In any event, whatever its impetus, most slaveowners in the area probably welcomed Pennsylvania's 1782 law and registered their slaves under it.[16]

One owner who did not take advantage of this law was Mr. Davis, who had moved from Maryland to what he thought was Virginia or what he hoped would become Virginia, but what in fact turned out to be Pennsylvania. In 1782 Davis failed to register his slave John. In 1788 Davis took John to Virginia, where he rented John to Mr. Miller. A group of John's neighbors, allegedly members of the Pennsylvania Abolition Society,[17] found John in Virginia and brought him back to Pennsylvania. Miller, fearful that Davis would hold him liable for the value of the slave, hired three Virginians, Francis McGuire, Baldwin Parsons, and Absolom Wells, to recover John. In May 1788 they went to Pennsylvania, found John, and forcibly brought him back to Virginia. Davis subsequently sold John to a planter who lived along the Potomac River in eastern Virginia. In November 1788 the court of oyer and terminer in Washington County, Pennsylvania, indicted the three Virginians for kidnapping. This precipitated the first interstate conflict over the rendition of fugitives from justice.[18]

Early in 1790 members of the Washington County branch of the Pennsylvania Abolition Society asked the parent society in Philadelphia

of the Federal Republic, 57–59.

[15] "An act to Redress Certain Grievances, Within the Counties of Westmoreland and Washington," Act of April 13, 1782. *Laws of the Commonwealth of Pennsylvania,* I, 496. For a discussion of the judicial construction of this law see Paul Finkelman, *An Imperfect Union: Slavery, Federalism, and Comity* (Chapel Hill, 1981), 60–62.

[16] June 23, 1780, *Journal of the House of Delegates,* 1780 session, 60–61, quoted and cited in Onuf, *Origins of the Federal Republic,* 60–61 and *n*70.

[17] Its formal name was the Pennsylvania Society for Promoting the Abolition of Slavery, the Relief of Free Negroes Unlawfully Held in Bondage, and for Improving the Condition of the African Race.

[18] Wm. Mimachan and Benj. Biggs to the Governor [Beverley Randolph], November 20, 1791, in William R. Palmer and Sherwin McRae, eds., *Calendar of Virginia State Papers . . . ,* Vol. V (Richmond, 1885), 396–98; Mifflin, "To the Assembly Concerning the State of the Commonwealth."

for help in recovering John. The Philadelphia society had little advice, except to suggest that John abscond from his new owner and return to Pennsylvania. The Washington County group found this suggestion dangerous, because if the escape was unsuccessful it would lead to "an aggravated repetition of his past sufferings," and after a failed escape John's new owner "might have hurried him beyond our reach forever." Instead, the Washington County society hired a Virginia attorney named White, a nephew of Congressman Alexander White, to recover John. This tactic proved unsuccessful, and John remained a slave in Virginia.[19]

By this time the three kidnappers, McGuire, Parsons, and Wells, had been under indictment for over two years but remained at large in Virginia. In December 1790 the Washington County society again sought the aid of their more prestigious brethren in Philadelphia, this time to help secure the extradition of the three kidnappers. In May 1791 the Philadelphia society petitioned Governor Thomas Mifflin of Pennsylvania, telling him that "a crime of deeper die" could not be found in the Pennsylvania "criminal code . . . than that of taking off a freeman and carrying off with intent to sell him, and actually selling him as a slave . . . ."[20]

In June, Governor Mifflin sent Virginia's governor, Beverley Randolph, copies of the indictments and a cordial note, requesting the extradition of the three Virginians, "agreeably to the provisions contained in the second section of the fourth article of the constitution of the United States." Mifflin also asked Randolph to "extend your interference on this occasion as far as it may be expedient to restore the negro to his freedom." In this last matter Mifflin relied on Randolph's "regard for justice and humanity."[21]

Instead of responding directly to Mifflin's request, Governor Randolph turned the matter over to James Innes, Virginia's attorney general.[22] Innes objected to the extradition procedure for a variety

[19] Alex. Addison to [the Committee of Correspondence of] the Pennsylvania Society for promoting the Abolition of Slavery, the Relief of Free Negroes unlawfully Held in Bondage, and for the Improvement of the Condition of the African Race [hereinafter to be called the Pennsylvania Abolition Society], December 6, 1790, Committee of Correspondence, Letterbook, Vol. 1, page 72, Papers of the Pennsylvania Abolition Society (Historical Society of Pennsylvania, Philadelphia; hereinafter cited as PAS Papers), microfilm reel 11.

[20] *Ibid.*; Pennsylvania Abolition Society, General Meeting Minutebook, Vol. 1, page 154, minutes of May 30, 1791, PAS Papers, microfilm reel 11; "To Thomas Mifflin, Governor of Pennsylvania: The Memorial of the Pennsylvania Society for Promoting the abolition of slavery . . . , " in *American State Papers: Class X. Miscellaneous*, Vol. I (Washington, 1834), 39.

[21] Governor Thomas Mifflin to Governor Beverley Randolph, June 4, 1791, in *American State Papers: Class X. Miscellaneous*, I, 40.

[22] Beverley Randolph to Innes, June 14, 1791, *Calendar of Virginia State Papers*, V, 326–28. This contrasts with Randolph's willingness, a month earlier, to issue a proclamation for

of technical and procedural reasons. He argued that because the indictments accused the three men of kidnapping "*violently*, and not *feloniously*," the alleged crimes could not be considered felonies but were merely "*other crimes*" under the extradition clause of the Constitution. Innes further argued that the kidnapping of a free black, under Virginia law, amounted only "to a trespass . . . as between the parties" and "but to a breach of the Peace" between the state and the defendants. Having explained how Virginia law treated the kidnapping of free blacks, he then asserted, incorrectly, that the laws of Pennsylvania on this subject were the same as those of Virginia. This led Innes to the bizarre conclusion that in cases involving minor crimes extradition was only possible when there was "an exclusive Jurisdiction in the State making the demand." Innes advised Governor Randolph that if the three kidnappers were tried in Pennsylvania and found guilty of the crime of trespass or breach of the peace "and their personal presence should be necessary for their punishment, it will be then time enough to make a demand of them."[23]

Innes's position was that the alleged kidnappers had committed only a minor offense over which either Virginia or Pennsylvania had jurisdiction. Therefore, Virginia need not extradite the men unless they were actually convicted of the offense. But while arguing for Virginia's jurisdiction over the alleged kidnappers, Innes did not suggest that the state of Virginia was under any obligation to arrest them and bring them to trial. He did, however, make it clear that if Virginia actually prosecuted them, the charge would not be kidnapping or any other felony. Rather, they would be tried for the minor crime of "trespass."

The weakness of these arguments and conclusions must have been apparent, even to Innes. Thus he offered a second set of arguments. Innes conceded that all constitutional "requisites [had] been satisfied" and that Pennsylvania had "an exclusive Jurisdiction over" the crimes. Still he opposed extradition. Innes argued that "every free man in Virginia is entitled to the unmolested enjoyment of his liberty, unless" deprived of it by federal law, the Constitution, or Virginia law. Since the kidnappers had not run afoul of any of these sources of law, Innes believed that Virginia authorities had no legal right to arrest

the arrest of two Virginians for the murder of four Indians in Pennsylvania. Randolph later rescinded the proclamation, and this became the second instance in which Virginia refused to comply with a Pennsylvania extradition requisition. "Proclamation of Governor Beverley Randolph," May 3, 1791, and "In Council," January 3, 1792, both *ibid.*, 298–99, 421–22. The relationship between these two incidents is discussed in Leslie, "A Study in the Origins of Interstate Rendition." See references in note 5 above.

[23] Beverley Randolph to Innes, June 14, 1791, and Innes to Beverley Randolph, undated, in *Calendar of Virginia State Papers*, V, 326–28 (first and second quotations on p. 326; third through sixth quotations on p. 327).

the men. Since they could not be arrested in Virginia, they obviously could not be returned to Pennsylvania.[24]

In July, Governor Randolph sent Mifflin his formal refusal to order the arrest and extradition of the three fugitives from justice along with a copy of Innes's report.[25] Mifflin responded by sending copies of the indictments and his correspondence with Randolph, including the Innes opinion, to President George Washington. Mifflin argued that Innes's analysis of the criminal extradition clause of the Constitution was "inaccurate." He told Washington that the three Virginians were charged with serious offenses, which upon conviction could lead to heavy fines and up to twelve months confinement at hard labor. This was hardly a mere "trespass," as Innes had asserted. Mifflin asked Washington to consider the entire problem and to seek "the interposition of the Federal Legislature" so as to "obviate all doubt and embarrassment upon a constitutional question so delicate and important." Washington forwarded the communications to Secretary of State Thomas Jefferson, who in turn gave them to United States Attorney General Edmund Randolph.[26]

After reviewing all the papers sent by Governor Mifflin, Attorney General Randolph concluded that fault for the conflict lay with both governors. The attorney general thought that Mifflin's extradition requisition was defective in two ways. First, Mifflin had failed to provide an authenticated copy of the laws that the fugitives allegedly had violated. Second, Mifflin had neglected to provide some basis for the conclusion that the three men had actually fled from Pennsylvania into Virginia. Randolph noted that one of the three men, Absolom Wells, was in fact under arrest and in custody in Pennsylvania.[27]

On the other side of the question, Attorney General Randolph had little sympathy for Innes's arguments. Randolph thought it "notorious, that the crime is cognizable in Pennsylvania only." Virginia had no jurisdiction over the issue. The Constitution directed that an offender be tried "in the State where crimes shall have been committed," which in this case was Pennsylvania. Nor did Randolph

---

[24] Innes to Randolph, undated, *ibid.* (quotations on p. 327).

[25] Governor Randolph to Mifflin, June 20, 1791, and July 8, 1791, *ibid.*, 329, 340–41.

[26] Mifflin to President Washington, July 18, 1791; Attorney General Edmund Randolph to Washington, July 20, 1791, both in *American State Papers: Class X. Miscellaneous*, I, 38–39, 41–43 (quotations on p. 39). According to his biographer, Attorney General Randolph was not related to Governor Beverley Randolph. John J. Reardon, *Edmund Randolph: A Biography* (New York and London, 1974), 514.

[27] Edmund Randolph to Washington, July 20, 1791, in *American State Papers: Class X. Miscellaneous*, I, 41–42. A few weeks later, on August 2, Governor Mifflin informed President Washington that Wells was in fact in custody but that the other two men remained at large. Mifflin to President Washington, August 2, 1791, and certification of Edward Burd [Prothonotary of the Pennsylvania Supreme Court], November 10, 1788, *ibid.*, 43.

have any patience for the suggestion that the state of Virginia lacked the authority to arrest the offenders. Indeed, to preserve interstate peace and harmony Randolph considered it the duty of the governor to act. The only alternative was for one state to invade another searching for criminals.[28]

Attorney General Randolph concluded his analysis by noting "that it would have been more precise in the Governor of Pennsylvania" to send his counterpart "an authenticated copy of the law declaring the offence" and "that it was essential that he should transmit sufficient evidence" of the alleged criminals "having fled from . . . justice" in Pennsylvania and into Virginia. Without that evidence the governor of Virginia was correct in not delivering the fugitives. But "with it" Virginia's governor "ought not to refuse."[29]

Randolph then gave Washington some political advice. Randolph noted that Governor Mifflin was "anxious that this matter should be laid before Congress . . . ." Randolph did not think this was advisable "at this stage of the business." He noted that "a single letter has gone from the Governor of Pennsylvania to the Governor of Virginia." Furthermore, although the Virginia governor had refused to comply with the request, this "proceeded from a deficiency of proof . . . ." The attorney general urged Washington to give the Pennsylvania governor time to supply full proof. Only if the governor of Virginia still denied the request should the president intervene. To do so at this point "would establish a precedent" for federal intervention "in every embryo dispute between States . . . ."[30]

Partially following Randolph's advice, Washington sent copies of the attorney general's analysis to both governors. The governors continued to correspond, and Governor Mifflin indicated his willingness to follow Attorney General Randolph's suggestion for a more complete extradition request and, as he reported to the Pennsylvania legislature, "took measures for a scrupulous adherence to the forms which were expected . . . ."[31]

---

[28] *Ibid.*, 42.

[29] *Ibid.*

[30] *Ibid.*, 42–43.

[31] Mifflin to Washington, August 2, 1791, *ibid.*, 43; Mifflin, "To the Assembly concerning the State of the Commonwealth," 180. Randolph's biographer states that Washington fully followed the attorney general's advice and that Mifflin, in turn, accepted Randolph's suggestions. Reardon, *Edmund Randolph*, 202. This is true only to the extent that Washington passed Randolph's suggestions on to the two governors and to the extent that Mifflin continued to negotiate with Governor Randolph. However, Washington clearly ignored Attorney General Randolph's advice about not asking Congress to become involved in the controversy. Washington turned the entire matter over to Congress shortly after the new session opened in October 1791. President Washington to "Gentlemen of the Senate and of the House of Representatives," October 27, 1791, in *American State Papers: Class X. Miscellaneous*, I, 38.

Despite Mifflin's implementation of Attorney General Randolph's suggestions and his conciliatory stance with Governor Randolph, aid from the Virginia executive was not forthcoming. Virginia's governor soon came under pressure from citizens in the western part of the state to refuse to extradite McGuire and Parsons. These petitions accused members of the Pennsylvania Abolition Society of stealing slaves in Virginia and of seizing the slaves of Virginians traveling west. The state legislators from McGuire's county told Governor Randolph that John was in fact a slave who had been "seduced" into Pennsylvania and that when McGuire, Parsons, and Wells heard about this they were "roused by a just indignation against such nefarious practices" and "went out and brought the negro back."[32]

In January 1792 Governor Mifflin reported to the Pennsylvania legislature that Virginia still refused to return the fugitives from justice. Instead, the Virginia governor complained that Pennsylvanians were "seducing and harboring the slaves of the Virginians." Mifflin promised to investigate this question while continuing the correspondence in the hope—a futile hope, as it turned out—that the kidnappers might be returned for trial.[33]

While the governors of Pennsylvania and Virginia sparred inconclusively, President Washington decided to act. On October 27, 1791, Washington sent Congress copies of his correspondence with Governor Mifflin and of Attorney General Randolph's report. On October 31 the House appointed a three-man committee—Theodore Sedgwick and Shearjashub Bourne, both of Massachusetts, and Alexander White of Virginia—"to prepare and bring in a bill or bills, providing the means" for the extradition of fugitives from justice. The committee was also charged with the responsibility of "providing the mode by which" fugitive slaves might be returned to their owners. Thus from the onset extradition and rendition were tied together. On November 15 Sedgwick reported "a bill respecting fugitives from justice and from the service of masters."[34]

Extradition and rendition seem to have been linked for two reasons.

[32] Wm. Mimachan and Benj. Biggs to the Governor, November 20, 1791, in *Calendar of Virginia State Papers*, V, 397 (quotations); see also John Waller and Horatio Hall to the Governor, November 20, 1791, *ibid.*, 402–3.

[33] Thomas Mifflin, "To the Assembly concerning . . . the surrender of fugitives . . . ," January 25, 1792, in *Pennsylvania Archives: Fourth Series*, Vol. IV, 218–21 (quotation on p. 221).

[34] President Washington to "Gentlemen of the Senate and of the House of Representatives," 38; *Journal of the House of Representatives*, IV, 2 Cong., 1 Sess., 15, 17 (first and second quotations), 30 (third quotation) (House debates of October 28, October 31, and November 15, 1791); *Annals of Congress*, 2 Cong., 1 Sess., 18 (Senate debate of October 27, 1791), and 147, 148 (House debate of October 28, 1791).

Most immediately, the controversy between Virginia and Pennsylvania involved both issues. Virginia asserted that John was a runaway slave and thus his return was a vindication of the fugitive slave clause; Pennsylvania, on the other hand, claimed that John Davis had become free under the Pennsylvania Gradual Abolition Act and had then been kidnapped and that those who took him to Virginia should be extradited to face prosecution. From the beginning Congress was forced to face both issues in tandem. A second reason for the linkage of the two issues no doubt stems from their juxtaposition in the Constitution. The Philadelphia Convention had seen them as related problems, and so did Congress. Both dealt with a similar procedural question and with the important constitutional issue of interstate comity. Not surprisingly, Congress simultaneously dealt with both issues.

The proposed House bill treated fugitive slaves and fugitives from justice in much the same way. In the case of a fugitive from justice the governor in one state communicated his request for an extradition to the governor of another state. When seeking a fugitive slave the claimant was required to apply for an arrest warrant to the governor of the state where the fugitive was found. In both cases the governor of the state where the alleged fugitive was hiding would issue warrants "to all sheriffs, their deputies, and other officers" empowered to "execute warrants in criminal prosecutions" in the state, "commanding" them to arrest the fugitive. The fugitive would then be delivered to officers of the state making the claim or, in the case of slaves, to the claimant. The House bill contained no requirement for a hearing or other proceeding before a judge or magistrate. In the case of a fugitive from justice the state authorities making the claim returned the alleged criminal to the state where he was wanted, and he would be tried. In the case of a slave, the claimant simply took the alleged fugitive back to the slave state he or she supposedly came from. Any officer failing to act on either type of warrant or anyone interfering with the rendition process was subject to fines, which were to be "recovered by indictment" in federal courts.[35]

Significantly, the House bill treated the rendition of both fugitives from justice and fugitives slaves as quasi-criminal matters. Thus the bill obligated northern states to pay their officers to hunt fugitive slaves. This is ironic because at the Constitutional Convention a major reason for not tying rendition to extradition in the same clause was northern opposition to the costs imposed on the free states.[36]

[35] U. S. House of Representatives, 2 Cong., 1 Sess., *A Bill respecting Fugitives from Justice and from the Service of Masters*, printed broadside (New-York Historical Society, New York; hereinafter cited as House Bill of 1791). This appears to be the only extant copy of the bill. None is known to exist in the National Archives.

[36] Farrand, ed., *Records of the Federal Convention*, II, 443, 453. For a discussion of this see Finkelman, "Slavery and the Constitutional Convention," 219–24.

Under this bill, both rendition procedures were summary and did not allow the person seized as a fugitive to make any defense before extradition. This procedure raised due process questions for fugitives from justice and much weightier questions of the same sort for blacks claimed as runaway slaves.

The drafters of this bill no doubt assumed that requests for fugitives from justice would be based on probable cause, arrest warrants, or actual indictments. The bill required that the request be "by an instrument in writing, authenticated by the signature of the Governor or other first executive officer and by the seal of such state."[37] Furthermore, the House members must have assumed that once returned, a fugitive from justice would face a trial where he would be afforded an opportunity to prove his innocence.

This procedure contrasts sharply with the provisions for returning fugitive slaves. The bill required that fugitive slaves be seized at the request of the claimant, based on "the depositions of two or more credible persons, that the person so claimed doth owe, under the laws of the state from which he fled, service or labor to the person claiming" the slave. The proposed bill did not say who could witness the depositions or if they had to be taken under oath.[38] This was a far cry from the standards of evidence necessary to obtain an arrest warrant or a grand jury indictment, which presumably a governor would want before he committed his signature to an extradition request. Warrants and indictments were issued only after probable cause had been presented to judges or members of grand juries, all of whom were uninterested third parties. Under the proposed bill alleged fugitive slaves could be seized on the basis of depositions from private claimants with obvious pecuniary interests in the outcome. Even more important, the lawmakers had no reason to expect that alleged fugitive slaves would receive any hearing or trial once they were returned

[37] House Bill of 1791, paragraph one.

[38] *Ibid.*, paragraph two (quotation). Paragraph one of the 1791 bill, which deals with the extradition of fugitives from justice, is explicit about such matters as requiring an extradition requisition "in writing, authenticated by the signature of the Governor" and "by the seal of such state." Similarly, the bill required that the govenor issue a warrant "under his hand and the seal of the same state . . . ." In the description of the "deposition" necessary to arrest a fugitive slave such details are omitted. Thus it is not clear if the drafters of this bill intended to require a sworn deposition, taken before a judge. It seems that if they had meant this they would have spelled out these requirements. The drafters of the bill probably did not intend a deposition in chancery, which is the precursor of the modern interrogatory, in which the witness is questioned under oath by attorneys for either or both sides of the case. It obviously would have been impossible for an alleged fugitive to send an attorney to a southern state to depose a person who might offer evidence against him. Thus the meaning of "deposition" in this bill is unclear. An early treatise on American law (although one written many years after this law was debated) noted that depositions were "not favored by the law." Francis Hilliard, *The Elements of Law* . . . (Boston and New York, 1835), 308.

to a slave state. These procedures invited abuse by kidnappers.

This bill also raised questions about the nature of federalism in the new republic. The bill placed the entire authority for fugitive slave rendition in the hands of governors and sheriffs, and yet if these officers failed to act on a deposition or interfered with rendition, they faced harsh monetary penalties enforced in the federal courts. Slaveowners seeking fugitives were to turn first to state officials for aid. But if they failed to act, slaveowners had recourse to the national government. Most state and local officials would probably have cooperated with the law,[39] but under pressure from the early abolition societies, it is quite possible that some would have either ignored the law or resisted it, thus setting the stage for state-federal conflicts at a time when the national government was weak. The bill, as drafted, may also have been unconstitutional because it required state officials to act. It is not clear if the Congress had the power to require actions by state officials. In 1842, in *Prigg* v. *Pennsylvania*, the United States Supreme Court would in fact rule that Congress could not compel state officials to enforce a federal law.[40]

Whether constitutional or not, the bill never came to a final vote. The bill was introduced on November 15, 1791, read twice, and scheduled for a third reading. Despite this energetic start, the bill was never considered again.[41] Why the House ceased consideration of the issue at this point is uncertain. It may be, as William R. Leslie argued, "that Congress thought it more fitting for the upper chamber to draft bills pertaining to interstate relations since the upper chamber represented states as states." Thus the House may have ceased action on the bill in deference to the Senate.[42] But it is also likely that once congressmen studied the bill they found it was severely flawed since it threatened the federalism of the new nation, the liberty of free northern blacks, and the pocketbooks of northerners who interfered with the rendition of a fugitive. Many fugitive slaves had lived so long in the North that their white neighbors might have defended them on the assumption that they were free. Under this proposed law such action could have resulted in a costly fine.

The following March the Senate appointed George Cabot of

[39] Even in the late antebellum period, when tensions were much greater and opposition to slavery much stronger, probably a majority of northerners complied with the Fugitive Slave Law of 1850. Although I think his thesis of northern support for the 1850 law is overstated, Stanley W. Campbell, *The Slave Catchers: Enforcement of the Fugitive Slave Law, 1850-1860* (Chapel Hill, 1968), vii–viii, does demonstrate that many northerners willingly enforced the law.

[40] House Bill of 1791; *Prigg* v. *Pennsylvania*, 16 Peters (41 U.S.) 539 (1842).

[41] *Journal of the House of Representatives*, IV, 2 Cong., 1 Sess., 30, 32–34 (debates of November 15, 18, 1791).

[42] Leslie, "A Study in the Origins of Interstate Rendition," 73n.

Massachusetts, Roger Sherman of Connecticut, and Ralph Izard of South Carolina "to consider the expediency of . . . a bill respecting fugitives from justice and from the service of masters." This committee had not reported back to the Senate by the time the session ended in May.[43]

On November 22, 1792, at the beginning of the next session of Congress, the Senate appointed a new three-man committee, chaired by Cabot, to consider criminal extradition and fugitive slave rendition. During much of the next two months the Senate considered a number of proposals on this issue that, for the sake of clarity, will be designated Senate Bill 1, Senate Bill 2, Senate Bill 3, and the Final Senate Bill. On December 20 the Cabot committee reported a bill that was debated until December 28, when it was recommitted. This was Senate Bill 1.[44] On January 3, 1793, the Cabot committee, which had been expanded to five members, reported a series of amendments that completely rewrote Senate Bill 1. This amended bill will be designated Senate Bill 2.[45] On January 14 the Senate amended Senate Bill 2 with a series of deletions and additions that resulted in Senate Bill 3.[46] On January 18 the Senate passed a combination of Senate bills 2 and 3 along with amendments made between January 15 and January 17. This will be designated as the Final Senate Bill. The House made only minor changes, which the Senate accepted. President Washington signed the bill on February 12, 1793.

An analysis of the legislative odyssey from Senate Bill 1 to the Final Senate Bill shows the alternatives the Senate considered. The fugitive slave provision of the various bills created great conflict in

[43] *Journal of the Senate*, IV, 2 Cong., 1 Sess., 170 (debate of March 30, 1792); *Annals of Cong.*, 2 Cong., 1 Sess., 115 (quotation).

[44] U. S. Senate, 2 Cong., 2 Sess., "Bill respecting fugitives from Justice and persons escaping from the service of their masters, Dec. 20, 1792," handwritten draft in file Sen. 2A-D1, Bills and Resolutions, 1789–1968, Records of the United States Senate, Record Group 46 (National Archives and Records Service, Washington; hereinafter cited as RG 46). The same file also contains a three-page version of the bill, which was printed by John Fenno, and is hereinafter cited as Senate Bill 1. The Senate Journal does not indicate when this printing was ordered.

[45] U. S. Senate, 2 Cong., 2 Sess., "Amendments Reported by the Committee on the Bill respecting fugitives from justice and persons escaping from the service of their masters," *ibid*. There is no known printed version of this bill, which is hereinafter cited as Senate Bill 2.

[46] U. S. Senate, 2 Cong., 2 Sess., "Amendments reported on the report of the Committee respecting fugitives from Justice and Persons escaping from the service of their masters, January 14, 1793," *ibid*. (hereinafter cited as Senate Bill 3). These amendments, along with the text of Senate Bill 2, were printed by John Fenno as *The Report of the Committee on the Bill Respecting Fugitives from Justice and Persons Escaping from the Service of their Masters, as Proposed and Amended* ([Philadelphia, 1793]). The only printed version of this I have found is marked up with the amendments that were added between January 15 and 17. A handwritten notation on this heavily marked-up printed bill reads: "The Bill passed the Senate, January 18th 1793." This version is found in file Sen. 2A-D1, RG 46, and is hereinafter cited as Printed and Amended Senate Bill 3.

the Senate. The record suggests that the southerners in the Senate generally had the upper hand. With the exception of one clause introduced in Senate Bill 2 and deleted in the Final Senate Bill, all of the bills favored slaveowners at the expense of northern whites, free blacks, and fugitive slaves. The law that emerged from these debates ultimately offered little protection for the North and at the same time satisfied most of the slaveowners in the Congress. From the beginning of the session southerners dominated the committee responsible for drafting the bill. While northerners ultimately succeeded in eliminating some of the most proslavery features of Senate Bill 1 and Senate Bill 2, the Final Bill nevertheless was a southern victory.

This victory began on November 22, 1792, with the appointment of a committee consisting of George Cabot of Massachusetts and two slaveowners, George Read of Delaware and Samuel Johnston of North Carolina. While Cabot chaired the committee, Johnston seems to have been its dominant force. On December 20 Johnston reported Senate Bill 1, and on December 21 the Senate began a second reading of the bill, which consisted of three sections. The first two dealt with fugitives from justice, the last with fugitive slaves. Senate Bill 1 was awkwardly drafted and poorly written. More important, it threatened the emerging balance between the states and the national government.

In many ways Senate Bill 1 posed a direct threat to the power of the states. The bill authorized governors to call on all citizens of a state to help capture a fugitive from justice and provided fines and jail terms for citizens who refused to aid in the capture of fugitives. Senate Bill 1 would also have required state officials to aid in the rendition of fugitive slaves.

The threat Senate Bill 1 posed to the states was minor in comparison to its threat to free blacks, fugitive slaves, and their white supporters. In many ways this bill was more threatening and less fair than the House bill of the previous year. Senate Bill 1 permitted the return of a fugitive slave based on the deposition of one "credible person." As with the House Bill of 1791, there was no requirement that this deposition be sworn before any court or public official. Moreover, a single deposition, even if sworn, established such a low evidentiary threshold that it would have set the stage for the kidnapping of free blacks.

Senate Bill 1 required state and local law enforcement officials to arrest fugitive slaves and turn them over to claimants on the basis of this single deposition. Law enforcement officers who refused to cooperate were subject to fines, and citizens who harbored fugitive slaves or obstructed their return could also be fined. Senate Bill 1 called for a specific sum of money—to be determined by the Congress—to be forfeited to the claimant "for every day the person owing such labour or service shall be harboured or concealed." Beyond that, the claimant retained the right to sue those who helped his slaves. Under Senate Bill 1 such suits could be brought in either the state or the federal courts.[47] Depending on how much the daily penalty turned out to be and how the terms "harboured" and "concealed" were defined, the law might have meant bankruptcy for northerners who simply hired runaway slaves.

Opposition to Senate Bill 1 grew until December 28, when the Senate defeated a motion to postpone all consideration of the question until the next session of Congress. Instead, the Senate returned Senate Bill 1 to an expanded committee that included Roger Sherman of Connecticut and Virginia's John Taylor of Caroline. Southerners, voting as a block, made sure that the committee continued to be dominated by slaveowners.[48]

On January 3 this newly constituted committee presented a series of amendments that effectively created a new bill—Senate Bill 2. These new proposals were read and ordered to "be printed for the use of the Senate." Senate Bill 2 also contained three sections, but only one focused on fugitives from justice; the other two dealt with fugitive slaves.[49]

Senate Bill 2 reflected a compromise between slaveowners seeking to protect their property and northerners seeking to protect the rights of blacks. The bill protected free blacks in three ways: First, Senate Bill 2 required that anyone seized as a fugitive slave be brought before a judge or magistrate before being removed from the state, thereby preventing some kidnappings by requiring a judicial proceeding before removal. Second, Senate Bill 2 made two changes in the evidentiary requirement necessary to remove a fugitive slave. Under the House Bill of 1791 and under Senate Bill 1 either one or two depositions were sufficient to require that a magistrate order the seizure of an alleged fugitive slave. Senate Bill 2 required "proof to the satisfaction" of the judge or magistrate hearing the case. This proof had

---

[47] Senate Bill 1.

[48] *Journal of the Senate*, V, 2 Cong., 2 Sess., 16, 24–26 (debates of November 22, 1792; and December 20, 21, 24, 26, 27, 28, 1792). All members of the committee were chosen by ballot. In the vote to choose the original committee members and the vote to expand the committee, southern senators appear to have been more unified than their northern colleagues about whom they wanted on the committee. Both Johnston of North Carolina and Taylor of Virginia received the most votes in the balloting for the committee spots. This suggests that the southerners in the Senate understood that the issue here was vital to their section's needs. U. S. Senate, 2 Cong., 2 Sess., "Lists of the Yeas and Nays," 2 Cong., 2 Sess., File 2A-J1, RG 46.

[49] *Journal of the Senate*, V, 2 Cong., 2 Sess., 28 (debate of January 3, 1793); Senate Bill 2.

to be sworn, either in the form of "oral testimony or affidavit taken before and certified by a magistrate." Finally, Senate Bill 2 provided that no judge could grant a certificate of removal if the alleged fugitive was "a native of, or hath resided in the state or territory wherein he or she shall be so arrested for a term of _____ years immediately previous to such arrest, and shall moreover show probable cause that he or she is entitled to Freedom." Instead, the claimant and the alleged fugitive were to "be left to contest their rights under the laws of the state where such arrest shall be made." This language established a type of "statute of limitations" on fugitive slave rendition for whatever number of years had been inserted in the blank in the phrase "term of _____ years." This provision created a presumption of freedom for blacks who were born in free states or who had lived in them for many years. This presumption could not be rebutted by deposition, affidavit, or even oral testimony. It could be overturned only through a trial in the state where the alleged fugitive was claimed. This provision protected some free blacks from being kidnapped and would have also prevented the rendition of some fugitives.[50] In parts of New England and Pennsylvania it would have been impossible to win custody of a black under the "laws of the state where" the fugitive was found. Some judges and many jurors would have sided with alleged fugitives.[51] Equally important, this provision helped preserve federalism by giving the states exclusive jurisdiction over the status of blacks who had lived within their territory for a sufficient length of time.[52]

Slaveowners, however, also stood to gain some new benefits from Senate Bill 2. Owners or their agents were empowered to seize fugitive slaves on their own, without first going before a magistrate to obtain a warrant or waiting for a local law enforcement official to act. This right of self-help, which was also in the final version of the law, enabled masters to seize their runaway slaves on their own. Senate Bill 2 required slaveowners to bring the captured fugitive before a magistrate in order to obtain a certificate of removal. However, the revised bill allowed claimants to prove ownership using "oral testimony." Thus a master could seize a slave while in "hot pursuit" without first obtaining depositions or affidavits. The test for removal

---

[50] Senate Bill 2.

[51] Robinson, *Slavery in the Structure of American Politics*, 286.

[52] In general American law (at least until the Dred Scott decision in 1857) gave the states complete autonomy over the status of their residents. Thus this provision would have been consistent with most American law. However, the entire purpose of the fugitive slave provision was to nullify the common law and prevent localities from altering the status of slaves who escaped to their jurisdiction. This provision would have, in effect, nullified at least part of the Constitution's Fugitive Slave Clause.

was "proof to the satisfaction of the judge or magistrate." This open-ended requirement could have worked to the benefit of slaveowners in many cases. Also useful to slaveowners was a provision that allowed the seizure and arrest of a fugitive slave in absence of the claimant. Under Senate Bill 2 local law enforcement officials could be required to arrest a fugitive slave and then to notify the owner of the capture. As with Senate Bill 1, Senate Bill 2 allowed monetary damages against law enforcement officials for noncooperation and provided for fines or imprisonment when private citizens interfered with the rendition of fugitive slaves.[53]

The Senate debated Senate Bill 2 on and off from January 3 until January 13. During this debate the amount of the fine for helping fugitive slaves was fixed at five hundred dollars. However, not much progress was made toward final passage of the bill. Instead, senators raised objections to some parts of the bill and offered various amendments to improve it. South Carolina's Senator Pierce Butler—the man who had first proposed the fugitive slave clause at the Constitutional Convention—unsuccessfully proposed amendments that would have aided masters seeking runaways.[54]

On January 14 another series of amendments was proposed. Senate Bill 3 consists of these amendments combined with what remained from Senate Bill 2. Senate Bill 3 was debated for the next three days. On January 14 and 16 the Senate journal reported that there had been "progress," while on January 15 the journal only noted that there had been "debate." During the three days of debate the Senate accepted a number of these newest amendments.[55]

In the debates over Senate Bill 3 the Senate expanded the definition of what constituted a breach of the law. Senate Bill 2 limited the penalty—which was set at five hundred dollars—to those who might "knowingly and wilfully obstruct" the return of a fugitive slave. Senate Bill 3 changed this language to "knowingly and willingly obstruct." Sometime between January 14 and January 17 the Senate added new language, penalizing anyone who would "obstruct or hinder" a "claimant his Agent or attorney" in "seizing and arresting" an alleged fugitive.[56] This was clearly a last-minute victory for slaveowners. The word "hinder" implied that the penalty might be recovered from someone who did little more than delay a rendition in order to find

---

[53] Senate Bill 2.

[54] Printed and Amended Senate Bill 3; U. S. Senate, 2 Cong., 2 Sess., "Mr. Butlers motion fugitives from Justice &c.," Sen. 2A-B1, RG 46.

[55] Printed and Amended Senate Bill 3. *Journal of the Senate*, V, 2 Cong., 2 Sess., 33–34 (debates of January 14–16, 1793).

[56] *Ibid.* (debates of January 14–17, 1793).

evidence that helped the alleged fugitive. The use of the word suggests that the Senate wanted to create a rendition process that would be quick and streamlined.

This change, which benefited slaveowners, was at least partially offset by the removal of clauses from the proposed bill[57] requiring local law enforcement officials to seize fugitive slaves at the direction of masters or their agents or, in the absence of an owner or agent, to arrest and incarcerate them until their owner arrived. These clauses would have turned northerners into slave catchers, which was intolerable to a society that was gradually dismantling slavery altogether.[58] With these deletions a slaveowner would be required to capture a runaway slave on his own and then bring the slave before a judge or magistrate for a certificate of removal. Removing northern law enforcement officials from the rendition process was seen as a victory for opponents of slavery.

Northerners were no doubt happy to see their role in enforcement removed from the bill, but this change was also a blessing to slaveowners who then were not dependent on northerners for aid in the rendition process. Slaveowners could use this right of self-help to seize their slaves and take them back to the South. Eventually, the U. S. Supreme Court approved this sort of fugitive slave rendition as long as it was done without a breach of the peace.[59] Unscrupulous slave catchers could more easily remove free blacks if the slave catchers did not have to rely on northern cooperation. There is no indication that this concerned members of the House and Senate, even though the bill before Congress originated because of such a problem.

The final debates on Senate Bill 3 led to two other changes beneficial to the South. The Senate deleted a provision mandating that civil suits for damages against those who interfered with the return of fugitive slaves be brought "in any court of the United States." At this time very few federal courts existed, and this provision limited the ability of slaveowners to sue people who harbored or rescued their slaves.[60] The removal of this provision allowed slaveowners to

---

[57] Similar clauses were also in the previous version of the bill, Senate Bill 2.

[58] On the end of slavery in the North see generally Zilversmit, *First Emancipation*. By 1792 New York and New Jersey were the only northern states that had not either abolished slavery outright or adopted gradual emancipation statutes; New York passed its law in 1799 and New Jersey in 1804. *Ibid.*, 175–200.

[59] The Court held this in *Prigg* v. *Pennsylvania*.

[60] Printed and Amended Senate Bill 3. An alternative would have been to create more federal courts and judgeships, but this was not a realistic possibility at the time, and no one in the Senate contemplated this solution. Ultimately slaveowners found northern courts inhospitable to their claims, and they were forced to rely on the federal courts. This is just one of many reasons that southerners eventually found the 1793 law unsatisfactory. Paul Finkelman, "*Prigg* v. *Pennsylvania* and Northern State Courts: Anti-Slavery Use of a Pro-Slavery Decision," *Civil War History*, XXV (March 1979), 5–35.

choose the most convenient forum—federal or state—for suing those who aided their runaway slaves.

The most important victory for slaveowners in the final shaping of the law was the deletion of the clause that denied certificates of removal for alleged fugitives who had lived for a long time or who had been born in the state where they were captured. The deletion of this clause meant that no alleged fugitive could interpose a claim that he or she was born free or had been emancipated and then obtain a trial on his or her substantive right to freedom in the place where he or she lived. In order to remove a black from a free state— even one born in that state—the claimant had only to meet the minimal evidentiary requirements of the law.

There was an eleventh hour attempt to roll back one proslavery change in the bill. On January 17 an unnamed senator proposed that the five-hundred-dollar penalty for those who aided fugitive slaves be deleted "for the purpose of inserting a less sum." The Senate defeated this proposal and in an unrecorded vote passed the entire measure and sent it on to the House.[61]

The House received the Senate bill on Friday, January 18. On January 21 the House gave the bill two readings and ordered that one hundred copies of it be printed. The House scheduled a third reading for January 30, but the bill did not come up until February 4, when in a committee of the whole, the House made a minor change in the wording of the first section, which dealt with fugitives from justice. Andrew Moore of Virginia then proposed a substantial increase in fines for people who helped fugitive slaves. According to the *Pennsylvania Journal*, "this motion occasioned some debate" in the House before it was defeated. The next day the House passed the bill by a vote of forty-eight to seven. Five of the negative votes came from northerners. The two southern opponents, John Francis Mercer of Maryland and Josiah Parker of Virginia, had been active Anti-Federalists during the ratification struggle, and they probably opposed the centralizing tendencies of the bill. Six northerners, some of whom opposed slavery in subsequent congressional debates, failed to vote on the bill.[62] However, a few northerners who actively opposed slavery, such as Elias Boudinot and Jonathan Dayton of New Jersey, voted in favor of the bill, probably because they thought it was an

[61] *Journal of the Senate*, V, 2 Cong., 2 Sess., 35 (February 22, 1793).

[62] *Journal of the House of Representatives*, V, 2 Cong., 2 Sess., 87–88, 104, 105, 106, 113, 116, 121 (debates of January 21, February 4, 5, 8, 9, 14, 1793); *Annals of Cong.*, 2 Cong., 2 Sess., 862 (House debate of January 21, 1793); Philadelphia *Pennsylvania Gazette*, January 30 and February 13, 1793; Philadelphia *Pennsylvania Journal and Weekly Advertiser*, January 30 and February 13, 1793 (quotation); Philadelphia *Gazette of the United States*, February 6, 1793.

adequate compromise between the two sections.[63] The bill was immediately returned to the Senate, which concurred in the House version later that day. The next day, February 8, the speaker of the house and the vice president in the Senate signed the bill and sent it to the president. On February 12 President Washington signed the bill into law.[64]

Because the records of Congress for this period are scant, it is impossible to reconstruct fully the debates. It is clear, however, that the Fugitive Slave Law did not sail smoothly through the Congress. The debates in the Senate were particularly bitter. The deletion of virtually all of Senate Bill 1 and many of the provisions of Senate Bills 2 and 3 indicates the divisions within the Senate. The report in the *Journal of the Senate* that "progress" was made on January 14 and 16 suggests that progress had been slow up to that point.

The last-minute effort in the Senate to lower the penalty for those who aided fugitive slaves also suggests the sectional aspects of the debate. Some northern senators were obviously unhappy with a law that might financially destroy their ethically motivated constituents. Five hundred dollars in 1793 was a substantial sum of money. This northern opposition indicates that even in the 1790s opposition to slavery had some force. The defeat of this amendment, combined with other changes in the law favorable to the South, similarly suggests that the southern senators were far more unified in debate than were their northern counterparts. The southerners, although outnumbered in the Senate, were able to mold the 1793 act to protect their interests. This was similar to what southern politicians had successfully accomplished at the Constitutional Convention in 1787 and also in the First Congress.

The attempt by Congressman Moore to increase the penalties for those who helped fugitive slaves escape suggests that some southerners doubted the bill would be effective in preventing northerners from aiding fugitive slaves. But the failure of his motion should not be seen as a defeat of southern interests. More likely it indicated that most members of the House, including those from the South, did

---

[63] Boudinot and Dayton do not appear to have traded their support for the bill for economic gain or other special interests. Ohline, "Slavery, Economics, and Congressional Politics, 1790," argues that in 1790 some northerners, although significantly *not* Elias Boudinot, failed to support an aggressively antislavery position because it would undermine their desire for southern support for economic legislation, such as assumption of the state war debts. He notes that "some New Englanders did admit privately that the assumption of state debts took precedence over antislavery." *Ibid.*, 350. This was consistent with the position that New Englanders took at the Constitutional Convention, trading their support for the slave trade for South Carolinian support for the commerce clause. See Finkelman, "Slavery and the Constitutional Convention," 217–23.

[64] *Journal of the Senate*, V, 2 Cong., 2 Sess., 47, 48, 51, 53, 57 (February 5, 6, 8, 11, 14, 1793).

not want to prolong debate over a bill that, in one form or another, had been under consideration for over a year. A full debate of Moore's amendment might have undermined the whole bill. Most southerners in the House must have realized that a five-hundred-dollar penalty was high enough, especially since the bill preserved a suit at common law for any other costs or losses associated with someone interfering with the rendition process. This included a suit for the full value of any slaves actually lost.

The law that Washington signed contained four separate sections. The first two dealt with the extradition of fugitives from justice and the last two with the rendition of fugitive slaves. This order of the sections mirrored the form of Article IV, Section 2, of the Constitution.

Sections one and two set out the responsibilities of the governors in criminal extradition cases. A governor seeking a fugitive from justice was required to send to his counterpart a copy of an indictment, "or an affidavit made before a magistrate," charging the alleged fugitive with a crime. These had to be certified by the governor of the state "from whence the person so charged fled." The governor receiving this information was to then arrest the fugitive and notify "the executive authority making such demand" or his appointed agent. If no agent claimed the fugitive within six months, the fugitive was to be released. Anyone rescuing a fugitive from custody would be subject to a fine of up to five hundred dollars and up to a year in prison.[65]

Section one of the law declared that "it shall be the duty of the executive authority" to act on an extradition requisition. The law did not, however, indicate what might happen if a governor failed to act. Following the language of the Constitution, the statute simply set out the mode of procedure for the govenors to follow. In 1861 the Supreme Court would hold that this procedure, while required by the Constitution, could not be imposed on a governor. If a state governor refused to act there was nothing the Supreme Court or any other branch of the federal government could do to compel his cooperation.[66]

Sections three and four of the law, dealing with the rendition of fugitive slaves, failed to vest responsibility for the enforcement of the law in any one person or official. Nor was the requirement of proof precise. Section three outlined a three-stage process for rendition. First, a slaveowner, or the owner's agent, seized a runaway slave. The alleged slave was then brought before any federal judge, state judge, "or before any magistrate of a county, city or town cor-

---

[65] Act of 1793.
[66] Ibid.; Commonwealth of Kentucky v. Dennison, 24 Howard (65 U.S.) 66 (1861).

porate" where the fugitive was seized. The claimant then had to offer "proof to the satisfaction of such judge or magistrate" that the person claimed was a fugitive slave owned by the claimant. This proof could be oral or through an "affidavit taken before, and certified by, a magistrate" of the state from which the alleged slave had fled. Upon satisfactory proof the official hearing the case issued a certificate of removal to the claimant. Under section four of the act, any person interfering with this process could be sued for a five-hundred-dollar penalty by the owner of the alleged slave. In addition, the owner could initiate a separate suit for any "injuries" caused by this interference. Injuries, in this context, might include both loss of the slave, physical damages to the claimant or the slave, or the costs of the rendition.[67]

On the day that George Washington signed the 1793 law the Pennsylvania Abolition Society warned its members of the pending legislation. Society members worried about the use of affidavits sworn before southern judges. They did not trust southerners who sought to capture runaway slaves or to kidnap free blacks. They also feared that northern magistrates would allow renditions based on suspect affidavits. The society's committee of correspondence reported that there was "reason to fear" that the new law would "be productive of mischievous consequences to the poor Negro Slaves appearing to be calculated with very unfavorable intentions towards them . . . ." The society complained that the bill was "artfully framed" with "the word Slave avoided," which meant that only the most vigilant opponents of bondage would be aware of the danger. Society members feared the new law would "strengthen the hands of weak magistrates" who would be used by masters to recover fugitive slaves.[68]

The members of the abolition society must have recognized the irony of this new situation. They had initially written to Governor Mifflin to help secure the extradition of whites accused of kidnapping a free black. Their letter set in motion a chain of events that led to a weak criminal extradition law and a relatively strong fugitive slave law. Under the new law the governor of Virginia could have resisted the demands for the three kidnappers. But under the same law, many fugitive slaves were unable to protect their newly found freedom. Even blacks like John Davis, who had a bona fide claim to freedom, could not protect their liberty under the new law. Ironically,

<hr/>

[67] Act of 1793.

[68] See copy of bill with handwritten notations in Manumissions Box 4B, PAS Papers, microfilm reel 24, p. 184; J[ames] P[emberton] [Chairman of the Committee of Correspondence] to Alex. Addison, February 12, 1793, Committee of Correspondence, Letterbook, 1789–1794, Vol. I, 103–4 (quotation on p. 104), PAS Papers, microfilm reel 11.

the well-intentioned letter of the abolition society and the equally well intentioned letter of Governor Mifflin to President Washington led to this dangerous result. The Pennsylvania abolitionists probably had not expected Mifflin to turn to Washington for help. Nor could the Pennsylvania abolitionists have foreseen that Washington would turn the matter over to Congress. Had they realized that their letter would lead to federal legislation, they might not have written it. After all, they knew from the experience of 1790 that the northern majority in Congress was weak on slavery issues. The adoption of the 1793 law only underscores this.

In 1790 northern congressmen had failed to support antislavery petitions presented by the Pennsylvania Abolition Society. The northerners perhaps had taken this position as part of a quid pro quo for southern support for various economic programs, such as the Bank of the United States and the federal assumption of state revolutionary war debts.[69] However, it seems more likely that they had refused to oppose the interests of the slave states because of what historian William M. Wiecek has called the "federal consensus" on slavery—that the national government not interfere with slavery in the states and that support for slavery was part of the national compact necessary to keep the union together.[70] This analysis helps to explain the debates that led to the Fugitive Slave Law.

In 1792 and 1793 northern congressmen and senators did not seek an economic quid pro quo from the South, as they had in 1790. Assumption of the state debt was already in place, as was the Bank of the United States. Thus the northerners, who dominated both houses of Congress, might have taken a stronger stand on extradition and fugitive slave rendition. That they did not do so suggests that the "federal consensus" was already in place.

In addition to the "federal consensus," three other factors explain the adoption of the 1793 law. First, a majority of northerners were not overly concerned about slavery even though they opposed the institution. Second, the southerners were able, even in the early 1790s, to create a united front to defend their most valuable institution. Finally, those few northerners who did oppose slavery appear to have misunderstood the stakes of the fugitive slave question. They voted for a bill northerners later grew to hate.

Ironically, southerners also came to despise the law of 1793. However harsh it was, southerners continuously demanded even stronger

[69] Ohline, "Slavery, Economics, and Congressional Politics."
[70] Wiecek, *Sources of Antislavery Constitutionalism*, 16 (quotation).

measures.[71] The federal courts were too few to aid them, and after 1842 many northern state courts refused to take jurisdiction in fugitive slave cases.[72]

In the end then, the 1793 law worked poorly. It did not even resolve the issues immediately surrounding its passage: the fugitive Virginians were never returned to Pennsylvania and John Davis remained a slave, his freedom lost forever. In 1850 southerners obtained new and harsher amendments to the 1793 law. These amendments, in a number of ways, resembled the bill drafted by the House in 1791. The 1850 amendments came too late, however, to restore sectional harmony; they only undermined it further.

[71] Marion G. McDougall, *Fugitive Slaves: 1619–1865* (Boston, 1891), lists most of the southern attempts to amend the 1793 law prior to the passage of the Fugitive Slave Law of 1850, which was technically an amendment of the 1793 law.

[72] Finkelman, "*Prigg* v. *Pennsylvania* and Northern State Courts."

PRIGG V. PENNSYLVANIA
AND NORTHERN STATE COURTS:
Anti-Slavery Use of a
Pro-Slavery Decision

Paul Finkelman

ONE YEAR AFTER IT was announced, John Quincy Adams spent most of a day "in transient reading the report" of *Prigg v. Pennsylvania,* "otherwise called the Fugitive Slave Case." He ruefully noted that *Prigg,* consisted of "seven judges, every one of them dissenting from the reasoning of all the rest, and every one of them coming to the same conclusion—the transcendent omnipotence of slavery in these United States, riveted by a clause in the Constitution. . . ." The meaning of the report for Adams, and for most anti-slavery advocates, was clear. The "slave power" had won another victory. This victory was particularly painful because the "opinion of the court" was written by a Massachusetts man and an opponent of slavery. But, Joseph Story, in upholding the Constitution was forced to uphold slavery as well. Thus, when Vice-President Henry Wilson wrote his history of the period he was forced to conclude "this decision of the Supreme Court seemed and was evidently designed to be strongly favorable to the slaveholders. . . ." However, with the advantage of hindsight Wilson could happily add that the decision "became, by legitimate inference and by its practical workings, often a real means of protection and defence" of fugitive slaves.[1] Ultimately, Northern jurists, lawyers, and legislators were able to turn this pro-slavery decision into an anti-slavery tool.

Since 1842 lawyers, judges, politicians, and historians have struggled to understand what the Court actually decided in *Prigg.* This

[1] *Prigg v. Pennsylvania,* 16 Peters (U.S.) 539 (1842); Charles Francis Adams (ed.), *Memoirs of John Quincy Adams* (Philadelphia, 1876) XI, 336; Henry Wilson, *The History of the Rise and Fall of the Slave Power in America* (Boston, 1872), I, 473. The author would like to thank Louis Gerteis, University of Missouri-St. Louis; William Wiecek, University of Missouri-Columbia; and Michael Weinberg, Washington University, for their helpful criticism and suggestions. Portions of this article were presented at the 1978 meeting of the Organization of American Historians.

Civil War History, Vol. XXV, No. 1 Copyright © 1979 by The Kent State University Press
0009-8078/79/2501-0001 $01.55/0

complicated case was critical for a number of reasons: it was the first time the Supreme Court interpreted the Constitution's fugitive slave clause; the decision upheld the constitutionality of the Fugitive Slave Law of 1793, and in so doing gave positive constitutional protection for slavery and the right of a master to recapture a runaway slave; at the same time, the Pennsylvania personal liberty law of 1826, and by extension similar laws in other states, was declared unconstitutional. The decision also allowed states to refuse to enforce the federal law, which in turn led to increased Southern demands for a new fugitive slave law. Because the case dealt with so many issues, there has been much confusion as to what was decided and what was dicta, and what the holding and dicta really meant. This confusion was heightened by the fact that six justices wrote opinions concurring with the general results of the case, one justice dissented, and two justices voted with the majority, but gave no opinion at all.[2]

The facts surrounding the case are also complicated. A Maryland slaveowner named Ashmore allowed two of his old and infirm slaves to live in virtual freedom. This couple raised a daughter named Margaret, who was never claimed as a slave by Ashmore. Margaret ultimately married a free black named Jerry Morgan, and the couple moved to Pennsylvania in 1832. In 1837 Ashmore's niece and heiress hired Edward Prigg to bring Margaret and her children back to Maryland, where Miss Ashmore claimed them as her rightful property. The birthplace of the children further complicated the case. Those born of a slave mother in Maryland were slaves, under Maryland law, but those born in Pennsylvania were free, since under the laws of Pennsylvania, and most other free states, no one born in a free state could be a slave. At least one, and perhaps more, of Margaret Morgan's children was born in Pennsylvania, and were thus free and should not have been considered fugitive slaves. This fact would be conveniently ignored by the United States Supreme Court, even though it underscored the need for personal liberty laws and due process protection for alleged fugitives.[3]

While not complicating the legal aspects of the case, Margaret Morgan's lifelong status—as a slave allowed to live as a free person— certainly added to the moral dilemmas raised by slavery. Morgan was not simply a runaway slave. She was a mother, a wife, and for five years a

---

[2] *Prigg, passim*; see also Joseph C. Burke, "What Did the Prigg Decision Really Decide?", *Pennsylvania Magazine of History and Biography* XCII (1969), 73-85; and William M. Wiecek, *The Sources of Antislavery Constitutionalism in America, 1760-1848* (Ithaca, 1977), for different interpretations of which particular judges supported Story's "opinion of the court" on each aspect of the opinion. It appears that Story did not have a solid majority behind him on every specific issue and that his majority contained different judges on each issue. All questions concerning Story's supporters on the Court may never be satisfactorily answered. What is more important, I think, it that Story's opinion was accepted as the decision or "opinion of the Court" at the time it was delivered and that a majority of the justices supported the fugitive slave law and slavery. In this sense, John Quincy Adams' observations (n. 1) may be the best analysis of the case.

[3] *Prigg*, at 608-10; *The Philanthropist* Mar. 30, 1842.

peaceable resident of York County, Pennsylvania. Her removal to Maryland did more than deprive her of her liberty; it deprived her husband of his wife and the community of a useful neighbor. Had her free-born children remained in Pennsylvania, they would have been deprived of their mother. Under these circumstances many York residents might easily have believed Morgan was actually kidnapped into bondage, and that even if Ashmore had a legitimate legal claim to Morgan, somehow it was a claim that ought not to have been enforced precisely because it had been allowed to remain dormant so many years. Thus, in this case the basic offensiveness of slavery was exaggerated because the person claimed was not a stranger, in flight from her master, but a longtime resident of the community who had lived as a free woman for most of her life.

When Edward Prigg arrived in York County, he applied to Justice of the Peace Thomas Henderson for a warrant to arrest Margaret Morgan as a fugitive slave. This warrant was required by "An Act to Give Effect to the Provisions of the Constitution of the United States Relative to Fugitives From Labor, For the protection of Free People of Color, and to Prevent Kidnapping," passed by the Pennsylvania legislature in 1826.[4] It was this "personal liberty" statute that the Supreme Court would ultimately declare unconstitutional.

After Prigg obtained the warrant, he arrested Morgan and brought her back to Judge Henderson, in compliance with the 1826 law, but Henderson at this point "refused to take further cognisance of said case." Acting on his own, Prigg then took Morgan and her children to Maryland.[5] This violated the 1826 law, which required that anyone wishing to remove fugitive slaves from the state had first to obtain a certificate of removal from a Pennsylvania authority. This was in addition to the certificate of removal required by the federal Fugitive Slave Law of 1793. The proof required under the Pennsylvania law was much stricter than that required under the federal law, and thus put an extra burden on the master wishing to reclaim a runaway. The federal act merely required the claimant prove "to the satisfaction of" a judge or magistrate, either "by oral testimony or affidavit" that the person brought before the court was the claimant's slave. Under the Pennsylvania law, however, an affidavit stating the "claimant's title to the service of such fugitive, and also the name, age, and description of the person of such fugitive" was required. This affidavit had to be "accompanied by the certificate of the authority" of the justice who administered the oath, and had to be signed by a court clerk and "authenticated by the seal of the court of record." The oath of the owner or "other person interested" was expressly prohibited as proof of ownership. In addition, this law required a warrant for arrest, followed by a trial at which the alleged fugitive could testify. The statute

---

[4] *Prigg*, at 543-608; *Pennsylvania Session Laws, 1826*, 150-55.
[5] *Prigg*, at 608-10.

contained numerous other bureaucratic provisions which hindered removal of fugitives and provided for severe penalties for judges or claimants who did not follow the exact letter of the law. It is possible that Judge Henderson refused to take further cognizance of the case because Prigg was unable to fulfill all the requirements of the law.[6]

Because Prigg removed Morgan and her children without a certificate from a state judge, he was indicted for kidnapping, along with his three associates. At first Maryland officials would not agree to his extradition. However, in 1839 the Pennsylvania legislature passed an act which ultimately allowed the case to be tried. This act provided that any of the four defendants could post a thousand dollars bond until a final decision was reached. The defendants and the state would then agree upon a statement of facts, which would be presented to a jury at the court of quarter sessions. A special verdict would be given, solely on the basis of these facts. If the defendants lost, they would have a right to appeal to the Pennsylvania Supreme Court. If they lost there, they would have six months to appeal to the United States Supreme Court and no attempt to carry out any sentence would be made until after its decision. However, if the Pennsylvania Supreme Court found in favor of the defendants there would be no appeal and they would be freed. The express purpose of this law was "so that all questions touching the constitutionality of" the act of 1826 might "be fully and clearly raised" by the special verdict and ultimately determined by the United States Supreme Court. Thus, Prigg was convicted, his conviction upheld by a pro-forma decision of the Pennsylvania Supreme Court, and the case appealed to the United States Supreme Court, all within less than a year.[7] It was left to that court to decide what interstate obligations existed for free and slave states under the fugitive slave clause of the Constitution and the Fugitive Slave Law of 1793.

I

In his "opinion of the Court," Justice Joseph Story reached three conclusions which combined to produce a major pro-slavery decision. First, Story found the Act of 1793 constitutional; second, he declared that state laws interfering with the rendition of fugitive slaves were unconstitutional; third, he discovered that the fugitive slave clause was in part self-executing, and that an owner or agent could compel a fugitive's return under a right of self-help, without relying on any statute or judicial procedure.

Although the least surprising of these holdings, it was by no means inevitable that the Act of 1793 should have been found constitutional.

---

[6] *Prigg*, at 543-608. See also Carl B. Swisher, *Roger B. Taney* (New York, 1936), 421 on Henderson being "fearful" of issuing the certificate.

[7] *Pennsylvania Session Laws, 1839*, 218-220.

The State of Pennsylvania argued that Congress had no power to legislate on the subject because it was not one of the enumerated powers.[8] Since the fugitive slave clause was part of the comity provisions of Article IV, and appears to be directed at the States, rather than Congress, Pennsylvania's argument on Congressional power was at least reasonable, if unsuccessful. In addition to this technical argument, the 1793 act might have been invalidated because it violated other aspects of the Constitution. It denied free blacks and alleged slaves the rights to a jury trial, habeas corpus, double jeopardy protection, and other Bill of Rights protections. Although alleged fugitives were not charged with "crimes," it would not have been unreasonable for the Court to demand that constitutional due process protections be accorded to persons who would be condemned to a lifetime of servitude should they lose their case. Although not the draconian monstrosity Congress would conjure up in 1850, the first fugitive slave law violated the constitutional protections that Americans had always cherished.[9]

Story's finding that exclusive jurisdiction over fugitive slaves lay with the federal government was hardly surprising, given his strong nationalist ideology. Although this position violated the states' rights philosophy of most of the slave states, it nevertheless gave strong support for slavery. First, it voided Northern personal liberty laws, like Pennsylvania's, because they encroached upon the exclusive legislative preserve of Congress. Second, it put the power of the federal government behind the master and the slave system. Finally, it placed those who opposed the rendition of fugitive slaves in the uncomfortable position of having to violate the Constitution, as well as federal laws.

The exclusivity ruling has been the most misunderstood aspect of this decision. Even Chief Justice Taney seems to have exaggerated its scope, although his statements, which will be discussed below, may have been designed for their political effect. Story did not declare, as one historian recently put it, that "the Northern states were not obliged to, indeed could not constitutionally, assist in the return of slaves."[10] On the contrary, Story explicity declared that "state magistrates may, if they choose, exercise that authority" necessary to enforce the law, unless they were "prohibited by state legislation" from doing so. Many Northern judges and state legislatures eventually chose not to enforce the law, but

---

[8] *Prigg*, at 620-22; This strict constructionist argument based on the enumerated powers of Article I, Section 8 was basic to the anti-slavery argument of many political abolitionists. For example, see Salmon P. Chase making the same argument before the U.S. Supreme Court in 1847, in S.P. Chase, *Reclamation of Fugitives From Service* (Cincinnati, 1847), 75.

[9] *U.S. Statutes, 1793*, Chap. 51, "An Act Respecting Fugitives From Justice, And Persons Escaping From the Service of Their Masters"; *Thirty-First Congress, Session I*, Chap. 60, 1850, "An Act To Amend, and Supplementary to the Act Entitled 'An Act Respecting Fugitives . . .' "

[10] R. Kent Newmyer, *The Supreme Court Under Marshall and Taney* (New York, 1968), 125.

this was not demanded by Story. He only recognized that under the federal system the state legislatures could not "be compelled to enforce" a statute passed by Congress. Story also asserted that under the Constitution the states did not "have a right to interfere, and, as it were, by way of complement to the legislation of Congress, to prescribe additional regulations, and what they may deem auxiliary provisions for" the enforcement of the federal law and the Constitutions's fugitive slave clause. But, this was not, as Taney erroneously argued, an injunction against state legislation which might positively aid in the enforcement of the federal law. In the next to last paragraph of his opinion, Story went out of his way to "guard . . . against any possible misconstruction" of the Court's views on what the states could do to aid in the rendition of fugitive slaves.

We entertain no doubt whatsoever, that the states, in virtue of their general police power, possess full jurisdiction to arrest and restrain runaway slaves, and remove them from their borders, and otherwise to secure themselves against their depredations and evil example. . . . The rights of the owners of fugitive slaves are in no just sense interfered with, or regulated by such a course; and in many cases, the operations of this police power, although designed generally for other purposes, for the protection, safety, and peace of the state, may essentially promote and aid the interests of the owners.[11]

Indeed, ten years later, in *Moore v. Illinois*, the Court upheld a statute which accomplished this goal.[12] Story's opinion prohibited only those state statutes designed to "interfere with or to obstruct the just rights of the owner to reclaim his slave. . . ."[13]

By declaring that states could control and arrest fugitive slaves, and that state judges could, and indeed ought to, enforce the Fugitive Slave Law, Story gave important support to slavery. Some Northern judges and legislatures would follow Story's advice and support the rendition of fugitive slaves. Naturally all of the slave states continued to support such an interpretation.

Joseph Story's son, William Wetmore Story, considered the decision a "triumph of freedom" because "it localized slavery, and made it a municipal institution of the States, not recognized by international law, and except so far as the exact terms of the clause relating to fugitive slaves extended, not recognized by the Constitution."[14] This filiopietistic explanation is hardly consistent with the thrust of the opinion, or its results. Among other things, this was the first Supreme Court opinion in which slavery was explicitly recognized as a constitutionally protected institution with special privileges within the Union. Indeed, far from making slavery a purely local institution, Story's decision was a giant

---

[11] *Prigg*, at 622, 615, 614, and 625.

[12] *Moore v. Illinois*, 14 Howard (U.S.) 13 (1852).

[13] *Prigg*, at 625.

[14] William Wetmore Story, *The Life and Letters of Joseph Story* (Boston, 1851) II, 392-93.

step forward in making it a national one. This becomes even more clear when we examine the third finding in his opinion.

Story's conclusion that a master had a personal right to recapture his slave without following any judicial procedure was the most unexpected of all. Under the fugitive slave clause, Story found "a positive and unqualified recognition of the right of the owner in the slave, unaffected by any state law or regulation whatsoever." This led to the conclusion that "the owner must, therefore, have the right to seize and repossess the slave, which the local laws of his own state confer upon him as property; and we all know that this right of seizure and recaption is universally acknowledged in all the slaveholding states." Under the Constitution, Story found "the owner of a slave is clothed with entire authority, in every state in the Union, to seize and recapture his slave." The only qualification to this was that it must be done "without any breach of the peace, or illegal violence." In short, Story found the clause "may be properly said to execute itself, and require no aid from legislation, state or national."[15]

This right of recaption without "aid of legislation"—the self-help rule—was extraordinary for four reasons. First, the constitutional clause stated a fugitive from labor was to "be delivered up on Claim" of the owner. This implies that the framers of the clause foresaw some procedure by which an alleged fugitive could be handed over—delivered up —to the claimant. Second, this interpretation ran counter to the statute of 1793, which Story had declared constitutional "in all its leading provisions." The statute clearly defined a procedure, however minimal, which was to be followed in returning fugitives. By asserting a right of recaption, Story was in effect denying that the federal law was necessary or that the master needed to follow it. Indeed, this aspect of the opinion leads to the bizarre situation of a Supreme Court Justice holding a federal statute constitutional, but telling citizens they need not comply with the requirements of that statute when asserting their federal rights. Third, this interpretation was an open invitation for the kidnapping of free blacks. Finally, Story's self-help rule gave an extraterritorial effect to slavery that no one up to that time had contemplated.[16] These last two results must be examined in some detail, for a true understanding of the impact of *Prigg*, particularly on blacks and abolitionists.

Under Story's reading of the Constitution, a white could seize any black, free or fugitive, as long as there was no noticeable breach of the peace. Without a federal anti-kidnapping statute, a national police force, or a hearing in a free state, free blacks could easily be kidnapped and

---

[15] *Prigg*, at 613.

[16] For a discussion of extraterritoriality and slavery, see Arthur Bestor, "State Sovereignty and Slavery: A Reinterpretation of Proslavery Constitutional Doctrine, 1846-1860," *Journal of the Illinois State Historical Society*, LIV (1961), 117-180.

enslaved in the South.[17] As the black abolitionist Samuel Ringgold Ward sadly noted: "I can see no kind of legal protection for any colored man's liberties. Everything is made as easy as possible for the kidnapper."[18] The *Philanthropist*, published in Cincinnati, the largest Northern city bordering on a slave state, feared the impact of *Prigg* on that city's free black population. The self-help rule was "The most revolting feature of the decision."

Let a slave catcher from Kentucky lay hands on a free colored person in Ohio, and drag him into slavery, and how can he be punished? Congress can do nothing; Ohio is impotent; . . . Not a single legal security has a single citizen of this State, against the acts of violence of the two hundred and fifty thousand slave holders of this republic. . . .[19]

The extraterritorial implications of the decision were even more frightening. Far from localizing slavery, Story's ruling applied slave-state law to the free states. Thus, in the case of Margaret Morgan's child, a free resident of Pennsylvania, born in that state, was seized and made a slave. Under Maryland law, Morgan was a slave and therefore so was her child. Under Pennsylvania law, of course, no one born in that state could be a slave. But, in overturning Prigg's conviction, Story legitimized his action in taking the child to Maryland. Thus, Story's ruling favored slavery at the expense of freedom in cases involving fugitives and the conflict of laws.[20] The very reasoning behind Story's ruling is critical. He noted that "this right of seizure and recaption is universally acknowledged in all the slaveholding states" and therefore it ought to be upheld in federal cases.[21] Under this logic the fugitive slave clause, and perhaps the Constitution as a whole, could be seen, not as a compromise between slavery and freedom, but as compromising of freedom in favor of slavery. The *Philanthropist* noted that this aspect of the decision was "a terrible illustration" of "the utter incompatibility of slavery and liberty." By permitting "one false principle to lie at the basis of society," the

[17] For examples of this, see Solomon Northrup, *Twelve Years a Slave* (Auburn, Buffalo, and Cincinnati, 1853). See also, legal cases discussed below, *In re Belt*, 1 Parker Cr. R. (N.Y.) 169 (1848); *Commonwealth v. Auld*, 4 Pa. L. J. 507 (1850); and *Commonwealth v. Alberti*, 2 Parsons (Pennsylvania) 495 (1851).

[18] Jane H. and William H. Pease, *They Who Would Be Free: Blacks' Search For Freedom, 1831-1861* (New York, 1974), 213, n. 23.

[19] *The Philanthropist*, Mar. 30, 1842.

[20] *The Philanthropist* (Mar. 30, 1842) complained that "every judge seemed to think that the rights of the slaveowner were the only objects of Constitutional protection. No construction favorable to liberty was hinted at." Five years later, Salmon P. Chase suggested to Charles Sumner that "slaveholding aggression" would make any localization of slavery impossible and "all attempts to compromise the matter by getting the [supreme] court committed on such matters as the locality of slavery, in decisions of leading questions in favor of slaveholders, will be found . . . unavailing." Chase to Sumner, Apr. 24, 1847, Sumner Papers, Houghton Library. For a general study of slavery and the conflict of laws, see Paul Finkelman, "A More Perfect Union? Slavery, Comity, and Federalism, 1787-1861," (Ph. D. dissertation, University of Chicago, 1976).

[21] *Prigg*, at 613.

Founding Fathers had "already laid the axe at the root of the tree."[22] As a correspondent to another abolitionist paper glumly concluded, the *Prigg* decision "settled it as the law of the country, that no non-slaveholding state has any right to enact laws securing a jury trial to alleged fugitives from southern slavery, nor to punish those who may choose to kidnap any inhabitant of a free state."[23]

In essence, the right of recaption brought the institutional force of slavery into the North. Abolitionists thought the decision "establishes slavery as the law of the whole Union, on the ruins of state sovereignty, habeas corpus and the jury trial." And they were probably right in this assessment, at least in terms of fugitive slaves and the threat to free blacks. This extraterritoriality, combined with Story's determination that "the national government is clothed with the appropriate authority and function to enforce" the fugitive slave clause, made *Prigg* a major victory for the nascent "slave power." To support the right of recaption, Story quoted Blackstone's *Commentaries* on the common law right to recover one's property, thus implying that there was perhaps a federal common-law protection of slave property written into the Constitution. In reaching his highly nationalistic conclusions about federal power and federal exclusivity, Story implicitly rejected the notion, suggested in some earlier cases, that slavery "was to be penned in the narrowest permissible limits."[24]

A critical underpinning to this nationalistic doctrine was Story's historical argument "that is cannot be doubted that" the fugitive slave clause "constituted a fundamental article, without the adoption of which the Union could not have been formed." He based his assertion upon the recent publication of James Madison's *Notes of . . . the Federal Convention*, but Madison's *Notes* show that of all the clauses relating to slavery, the fugitive slave clause was the least debated and the least important. It was added at the very end of the convention, and it is likely the Constitution would have been accepted without it. Unlike slave importation, the South would not have lost any rights by accepting the Constitution without this clause. Thus, Story supported his opinion, and

---

[22] *The Philanthropist*, Mar. 30, 1842.

[23] Quoted in Pease and Pease, *They Who Would Be Free*, 213.

[24] *The Philanthropist*, Mar. 30, 1842; *Prigg*, at 613-615; Gerald T. Dunne, *Joseph Story and the Rise of the Supreme Court* (New York, 1970), 394. In the same term that *Prigg* was decided Justice Story wrote the decision in *Swift v. Tyson*, 16 Peters (U.S.) 1 (1842), which created a federal common law for commercial and private law. In *Prigg* Story created a federal common law right of recaption. There are interesting parallels between the two cases: both argued for a federal common law; both strongly supported judicial nationalism; and both were attempts to create a uniform law on a difficult interstate conflict-of-laws question and to ease administration of these laws. While Story makes no reference to *Swift* in *Prigg*, it is possible to see similar modes of thinking and judicial goals in the two cases.

remained consistent in his judicial nationalist ideology, by accepting a pro-slavery interpretation of the Constitution's origins.[25]

In his study of slavery and the judicial system, Robert Cover has found Story to be "as close to [a] confirmed" opponent "of slavery as existed on the bench." A recent biographer declares that of Story's "personal detestation" of slavery "there can be no doubt."[26] Both assessments of the Justice's personal views are correct. In fact, they help explain why Story placed his opinion within a framework of judicial nationalism and constitutional necessity. But they also underscore the fact that whatever Story may have believed or felt about slavery did not effect his decision making, at least in this case. Story's own anti-slavery convictions thus seem to confirm the Garrisonian argument that the Constitution was a pro-slavery compact, for only under such a Constitution would an anti-slavery jurist like Story be forced to write a pro-slavery decision.

II

Whether intentional or not, the ultimate logic of Story's strong nationalist position led to a small bit of anti-slavery *dicta*. By entrusting the enforcement of the fugitive slave clause solely to Congress, Story was forced to conclude that the states could not be held responsible for its enforcement. This led him to the further conclusion that although Congress could authorize state judges and officials to enforce the law, Congress could not require them to do so. That would be a violation of federalism and states' rights. Thus, Story found that the constitutional clause "did not point out any state functionaries, or any state action to carry its provisions into effect." The Justice concluded: "The states cannot, therefore, be compelled to enforce them; and it might well be deemed an unconstitutional exercise of power of interpretation, to insist that the states are bound to carry into effect the duties of the national government, nowhere delegated or intrusted to them by the Constitution." Although state magistrates were not constitutionally bound to enforce the law, Story felt that they "may, if they so choose, exercise that authority, unless prohibited by state legislation."[27]

[25] *Prigg*, at 610-12. For Madison's notes see Adrienne Koch (ed.), *Notes of the Debates in the Federal Convention of 1787 Reported by James Madison* (Athens, Ohio, 1966), 545-46, 552. Madison's *Notes* were published in 1840 and were used by all sides in the debates over slavery. The Garrisonians in particular used them to prove that the Constitution was indeed a pro-slavery compact. See Wendell Phillips, *The Constitution: A Pro-Slavery Compact: Selections From the Madison Papers &c.* (New York, n.d.; originally published in New York, 1844). David Ruggles, another Garrisonian, thought "the friends of freedom" should stop "taking issue against Joseph Story, or the Supreme Court, for explaining the true bearing of the law," although he thought it unconstitutional because it denied jury trials. *Liberator*, Feb. 10, 1843.

[26] Robert Cover, *Justice Acused: Antislavery and the Judicial Process* (New Haven, 1975), 171; Dunne, *Joseph Story and the Rise of the Supreme Court*, 396.

[27] *Prigg*, at 625, 615-16, and *passim*; see also, *Liberator*, Feb. 10, 1843. In his letter David

This last statement appeared to some people as an open suggestion to the free-state legislatures that they bar their courts and officials from enforcing the federal act. Some have seen it as Story's anti-slavery contribution to what was otherwise a pro-slavery decision. According to his son, the Justice believed this part of the decision was also a "triumph of freedom" because "it promised practically to nullify the Act of Congress,—it being generally supposed to be impracticable to reclaim fugitive slaves in the free States, except with the aid of State legislation and State authority."[28]

There is no doubt Story opposed slavery, and in his early years on the bench he vigorously criticized it. In 1819, he went so far as to speak out against the admission of Missouri as a slave state.[29] At the time of *Prigg*, however, Story was reluctant to attack the peculiar institution. Perhaps he felt that anti-slavery sentiments would only exacerbate the growing sectional tensions. More likely, however, he believed that the Constitution demanded federal protection for masters seeking their fugitive slaves. As Robert Cover has persuasively argued, Story was tied to notions of positive law and proper judical standards.[30] Thus, it is unlikely he would have attempted anything as radical and devious as trying to undercut his own opinion with one or two pieces of well-placed anti-slavery *dicta*. Rather, the logic of Story's reasoning, and his commitment to nationalism, federalism, and the Constitution, led him to the not inconsistent position that if federal jurisdiction was exclusive, Congress could not force the states to enforce the law. This assumption is supported by an embarrassing section of a letter which Story's son failed to include when compiling the collection of his father's correspondence.[31]

Writing to Senator John Berrien of Georgia shortly after the *Prigg* decision was announced, Story suggested a way to enforce the Fugitive

---

Ruggles also thought *Prigg* "has emancipated and rebuked the people of the [free] States . . . for volunteering their *legal* and *military* support to the odious system of slavery." Some Garrisonians were able to see some utility to *Prigg* because it allowed the free states to disassociate themselves from slavery and because, as stated in n.25 above; it proved their contention that the Constitution was pro-slavery. It would be wrong, however, to assert that Story was a secret Garrisonian. And it would also be wrong to assert that any abolitionists liked the decision, even if it gave philosophical support to them.

[28] Story, *Life and Letters*, II, 393.

[29] *Ibid.*, I, 359-61.

[30] Cover, *Justice Accused*, esp. 240-41. Cover concludes that "our records do not permit even a solid guess" as to whether or not *Prigg* was meant to be an anti-slavery decision in disguise; if this is the case, "then we have a truly extraordinary ameliorist effort." As information below indicates, Story did not intend to sabotage the law with his decision. In language similar to Stewart's, the 1843 *Annual Report* of the Massachusetts Anti-Slavery Society (p. 15) condemned Justice Baldwin's pro-slavery concurrance for "a servility of spirit worth of Scroggs and Jeffries."

[31] Story, *Life and Letters*, II, 404-405. The deleted portion of the letter is printed in full in James McClellan, *Joseph Story and the American Constitution* (Norman, Okla., 1971), 262-63n. See also, n. 32., below.

Slave Law without relying on the states. He thought Congress could pass an innocuous bill, "without creating the slightest sensation in Congress, if the provision were made general," which would allow the federal courts to appoint commissioners "in every county" and thus "meet the practical difficulty now presented by the refusal of State Magistrates" to enforce the law. Revealing that his respect for law enforcement was greater than his anti-slavery sentiments, Story suggested how this could be accomplished:

It might be unwise to provoke debate to insert a Special clause . . . referring to the fugitive Slave Act of 1793. Suppose you add at the end of the first section: '& shall & may exercise all the powers, that any State judge, Magistrate, or Justice of the Peace may exercise under any other Law or Laws of the United States.'

Story's sole reason for writing this letter was "the desire to further a true administration of public Justice."[32] Seven years later Congress would incorporate these ideas into the Fugitive Slave Law of 1850.

Even before the *Prigg* decision was written, anti-slavery advocates realized its importance. As early as 1839 Salmon P. Chase was following the case in the Pennsylvania courts. In January, 1841, over a year before oral arguments, John Quincy Adams made two trips to the Supreme Court "for a printed copy of the record" in *Prigg* and noted in his diary this was "another slavery question case."[33] At the time of oral arguments Adams was defending himself against a censure motion in the House of Representatives. Adams was aided by the abolitionist organizer Theodore Dwight Weld, who, two days after the censure motion was tabled, wrote his wife that oral arguments in the Prigg case had ended. Weld predicted: "The decision will involve the Constitutionality of the laws of Mass., N.Y., and other northern states lately passed granting trial by jury to alleged fugitives. Of course the trial is one of immense importance."[34]

When the decision was finally announced it was widely discussed, generally viewed as a victory for slavery, but not always understood. The conservative New York *Herald* thought it would "have the most salutory effect in repressing the incendiary movements of the abolitionists, and in quieting the just apprehensions entertained at the South."[35] Garrison's *Liberator*, on the other hand, predicted that it would

[32] Story to John McPherson Berrien, Apr. 29, 1842, reprinted in McClellan, *Joseph Story and the American Constitution*, 262-63n; also available in John McPherson Berrien Papers, Southern Historical Collection, University of North Carolina (microfilm roll 1).

[33] Thomas D. Morris, *Free Men All: The Personal Liberty Laws of the North 1780-1861* (Baltimore, 1974), 95; Adams (ed.,) *Memoirs of John Quincy Adams*, 407.

[34] Weld to Angelina Grimke Weld, Feb. 9, 1842, in Gilbert H. Barnes and Dwight L. Dumond (eds.), *Letters of Theodore Dwight Weld, Angelina Grimke Weld, and Sarah Grimke, 1822-1844* (New York, 1934), II, 916. See also n. 42, below, for information on New York jury trial law.

[35] *Herald*, quoted in *Liberator* Mar. 11, 1842. See also Massachusetts Anti-Slavery Society, *Eleventh Annual Report, January 25, 1843* (Westport, Conn., 1970, reprint of 1843 report), 13-17 for another attack on *Prigg*.

"treble the present number of abolitionists and serve to raise their zeal to a pitch, that will not exactly quiet the apprehensions of the South."[36] The *Philanthropist* at first thought its "effects may on the whole be beneficial to the fugitive slave," and that it was "a great gain for liberty." "Some additional legislation" would be "needed to guard liberty in the free States, from the potential loss of habeas corpus," but the optimistic reporter expected this to happen quite soon. He thought "the slaveholders are very much more dissatisfied with the result; far more so than the friends of liberty, wrong as the decision appears to them, in some of its aspects."[37] After two weeks of reflection, and a chance to read the entire opinion, this correspondent changed his mind. He now thought "Congress must be compelled" to give fugitives a jury trial "or our union is not worth two straws." The federal courts, once the "strongest bond of our Union" had now "become the most powerful lever to sunder it." Their decisions were "the tools of the most infamous despotism" which no one would respect. Echoing Garrison, he now predicted "The decision will do more than a thousand mobs, to weaken the public respect for laws and courts of justice."[38]

Aside from its utility as an organizing tool, abolitionists now saw little to cheer about. Garrison concluded that: "If a slaveholder may claim and hold his slave property in any of the States" there was "no reason why any man living in what are now called the *free States*, may not purchase and hold slaves in defiance of the State Constitution and laws." Garrison asked if the decision did not "in fact, establish the constitutionality of slavery in every State in the Union?"[39] The moderate New York *Tribune* termed it "the most important [Supreme Court] decision . . . for many years—perhaps ever," and deplored its results. A British anti-slavery paper reprinted the *Tribune's* story under the headline "A Crisis in the United States."[40]

Most abolitionists also feared that the case could lead to massive kidnapping of free blacks. Garrison's lieutenant, Wendell Phillips, explained to the Executive Committee of the American Anti-Slavery Society that under this decision "any Southern slavecatcher is empowered to seize and convey to the South, without hindrance or molestation on the part of the State, and without due process . . . any persons, irrespective of caste or complexion, whom he may choose to claim as runaway slaves." Although "the free colored population of the North" would be "specially liable to become the victims of this terrible power . . . all the other inhabitants are at the mercy of prowling

[36] *Liberator*, Mar. 11, 1842.

[37] *Philanthropist*, Mar. 9, 1842.

[38] *Ibid.*, Mar. 30, 1842.

[39] *Liberator*, Mar. 11, 1842.

[40] *Ibid.*, Mar. 18, 1842; and *Anti-Slavery Reporter and Aborigines Friend*, Apr. 20, 1842 (Ser. I, vol. 3), 58-59.

kidnappers, because there are multitudes of white as well as black slaves on Southern plantations, and slavery is no longer fastidious with regard to the color of its prey." Alvan Stewart, a non-Garrisonian lawyer, expressed similar fears. For him *Prigg* "transcended the decisions of the 17th [century], by Jeffreys, Scroggs and Pollexfen" as an example of "judicial tyranny." The *"truly fearful"* part of the decision was Story's concept of self-help, which in practice meant "the master may seize any person he sees fit," including those "born *free* and *white*" who had always lived in the North. The no longer sanguine correspondent for the *Philanthropist* exclaimed: "What! Shall a native of Ohio, be liable to be seized in the midst of his family, and on the oath of two perjured villians" be made a slave?[41]

Particularly obnoxious and frightening was the fact that Story's decision denied alleged fugitives the protection of a jury trial before being removed to the South. This was one aspect of the decision which led to an Albany, New York meeting which demanded a constitutional amendment to reverse *Prigg*. Only two years before, after years of struggling, the New York legislature had finally adopted a law which gave jury trials to alleged fugitives. Because of the lack of jury trial protection, Garrison determined that *Prigg* and the act of 1793 should be ignored. With his usual rhetoric he declared: *"It is not law*—for the entire system of slavery is at war with the rights of man . . . It is to be spit upon, hooted at, trampled in the dust. . ."* Garrison offered a resolution at one anti-slavery meeting which noted "the right of trial by jury is denied" by the decision "and slavery is declared to be the supreme law of the land." From this decision there was "no appeal to any higher judicatory, except the people on the ground of revoluntionary necessity."[42]

Wendell Phillips thought "As soon as that appalling decision . . . was enunciated . . . the people of the North should have risen *en masse* . . . and declared the Union at an end." A prospective victim of the law viewed the problem in more practical terms. Writing in the

[41] *Liberator*, Mar. 11, 1842; Wendell Phillips, *The Constitution: A Pro-Slavery Compact*, 106; Luther R. Marsh (ed.), *Writings and Speeches of Alvan Stewart on Slavery* (New York, 1860), 382-84; *Philanthropist*, Mar. 30, 1842.

[42] Frederick W. Seward (ed.), *Autobiography of William H. Seward, 1801-1834* (New York, 1877), 600; *New York Session Laws*, 1840, 174-77. See Morris, *Free Men All*, 49-84 for discussion of these laws. *Liberator*, Mar. 11, 1842; Wendell Phillips Garrison and Francis Jackson Garrison (eds.), *William Lloyd Garrison* (New York, 1889), III, 59: For similar resolutions see *Liberator*, Jan. 20, 1843. After the decision Charles Sumner attempted to convince Story that the act of 1793 was unconstitutional because it did not provide for a jury trial. Story left the impression that the matter would be reconsidered, but it never was. Wendell Phillips and other Garrisonians agreed that this made the law unconstitutional, even within the framework of a proslavery Constitution. Wendell Phillips to Charles Sumner, July 29, 1851, Sumner papers. See also the attack on the decision for denying jury trials by E. W. Clarke, in New-York Historical Society, Misc. MSS. Clarke, E. W. & Misc., Slavery Box 1.

Liberator, he urged something other than disunion or non-resistance on the part of Garrison's subscribers: "The only kind of free papers that could be effectual against a kidnapper's claim, would be a pair of wooden stocks and iron barrels, well loaded to the muzzle. . . . We are compelled . . . to protect ourselves."[43]

III

While Story's opinion provoked legitimate fears among blacks and abolitionists, it also displeased Chief Justice Taney, who feared that an anti-slavery interpretation of Story's *dicta* would negate the pro-slavery force of the decision. Thus, while concurring in the result and most of the holding, Taney expressly disagreed with two specific aspects of Story's opinion which could be used by those opposed to slavery. First was an apparently groundless fear that Story meant to declare all state legislation on fugitive slaves to be unconstitutional. Second was the more realistic fear that under Story's opinion state judges would refuse to enforce the law and thereby make it an ineffective remedy for masters.

The first fear stemmed from Story's assertion "that where Congress have exercised a power over a particular subject given them by the Constitution, it is not competent for state legislation to add to the provision of Congress upon the subject."[44] This, Taney said (and some abolitionists hoped), might mean that all state legislation on the subject was void. Taney went to great lengths to show that the Founding Fathers, some of who sat in the Congress which passed the law of 1793, expected the states to enforce the law with their own officers and helpful supplementary legislation. Taney pointed out that in Maryland and other slave states (and he might have added some free states as well) state officials were "by law required to arrest" runaways and to take necessary action to return them to their owners. These laws had "been almost daily in the course of execution in some parts of" Maryland. But now, he noted, "if the states are forbidden to legislate on this subject, and the power is exclusively 'in Congress, then these state laws are unconstitutional and void." This would mean that if state officials were "not justified in acting under the state laws, and cannot arrest the fugitive, and detain him in prison without having first received an authority from the owner, the territory of the state must soon become an open pathway for the fugitives escaping from other states." Taney, ever vigilant in protecting his section's interests, clearly rejected this view of the law: "I think the states are not prohibited; and that, on the contrary, it

---

[43] Phillips, *The Constitution: A Proslavery Compact*, 106-107, and *Liberator*, Mar. 18, 1842.

[44] *Prigg*, at 625. See also Ruggles letter to *Liberator*, Feb. 10, 1843, n. 27 above for one Garrisonian view of this.

is enjoined upon them as a duty to protect and support the owner when he is endeavouring to obtain possession of this property found within their respective territories."[45]

What Taney ignored in this attack on Story was that the two justices were fundamentally in agreement on state power to aid in the rendition of fugitive slaves. Story did not mean, nor did he declare, that all state legislation on the subject was void. His opinion only declared that supplemental legislation, requiring more than what the federal law required, was void. Story went out of his way to assert that the states retained the necessary police powers "to arrest and restrain runaway slaves, and remove them from their borders. . . . " Such police actions would be unconstitutional only if they were designed to "interfere with or to obstruct the just rights of the owner to reclaim his slave."[46] Despite Taney's protests, it does not appear that Story meant to interfere with those states wishing to aid in the rendition of fugitive slaves.

Where the two justices were in fundamental disagreement was over the question of states which did not wish to enforce the law. Taney believed that state officials were "enjoined" to enforce the law; if they did not enforce it, no one else would. He correctly observed that for other constitutional rights, particularly those found in Article IV, "it has always been held to be the duty of the states to enforce them." He noted that "in many states there is but one district judge, and there are only nine states which have judges of the Supreme Court." Thus, forcing claimants to rely on federal judges would virtually nullify the law. "Indeed," the Chief Justice declared, "if the state authorities are absolved from all obligation to protect this right, and may stand by and see it violated without an effort to defend it, the act of Congress of 1793 scarcely deserves the name of a remedy."[47]

Taney was "aware" that his "brethren of the majority do not contemplate these consequences and do not suppose that the opinion they have given will lead to them."[48] But, in the next eight years Taney's fears proved to be at least as justified as any optimism on the part of the majority. None of the slave states repealed their laws concerning fugitive slaves or ceased to enforce the federal act. A few Northern states also enforced the federal law, but in many free states magistrates and legislatures turned *Prigg* from a pro-slavery victory into an anti-slavery weapon.[49] The act of 1793 came to be viewed as a poor remedy

---

[45] *Prigg*, at 631-32, 627.

[46] *Prigg*, at 625.

[47] *Prigg* at 628-29; 630-31; 627.

[48] *Prigg*, at 632.

[49] One reason attacks on Justice Story ceased within a few years after the decision was his death in 1845. Charles Warren, *The Supreme Court in United States History* (Boston, 1922) II, 361, believes it was because anti-slavery enthusiasts came to the early "realization . . . of the effective weapon which had been placed in their hands."

by a majority of Congress, which in 1850 passed a new and harsher fugitive slave law. The act of 1850 responded to the exclusivity doctrine by creating a small federal bureaucracy throughout the states to enforce its provisions.

IV

The most direct Northern reaction to *Prigg* took the form of laws which prohibited state officials from enforcing the federal act. Such legislation was passed in Massachusetts (1843), Vermont (1843), Connecticut (1844), New Hampshire (1846), Pennsylvania (1847), and Rhode Island (1848).[50] While not specifically prohibiting officials from enforcing the federal law, Ohio, in 1843, repealed its 1839 act which required state officials to enforce that law.[51] In New York a strong personal liberty law, passed in 1840, remained on the books, despite attempts to repeal it.[52] When the Democratic governor William C. Bouck urged repeal in 1843, specifically because the law violated *Prigg*, a confident Theodore Dwight Weld wrote to his wife, "Let them do if they dare."[53] Anti-slavery sentiment was apparently strong enough so that a majority of assemblymen dared not. Despite *Prigg*, the New York law remained in force until the Civil War. After the passage of the Fugitive Slave Law of 1850 new personal liberty laws were passed in four more states: Maine (1855 and 1857), Ohio, (1857), Michigan (1857), and Wisconsin (1858) as well as the Minnesota Territory (1851).[54] In Kansas Territory a series of pro-slavery fugitive slave laws were repealed in

---

However, in 1847 Salmon Chase still did not see this as an effective anti-slavery tool. "I was surprised by what you said of Judge Story. How could he regard the Prigg decision as a triumph of freedom?" Chase agreed it contained "a dictum in favor of the doctrine that slavery is local" but felt "there will be [no] more regard paid to the dictum of the Prigg Case" than any other anti-slavery dictum. Chase was referring only to the U.S. Supreme Court, which he felt was controlled by the emerging "slave power." See n. 20, above. Also, generally on Chase, see Eric Foner, *Free Soil, Free Labor, Free Men: The Ideology of the Republican Party Before the Civil War* (New York, 1970), esp. 73-102. Another reason for an early decrease in attacks on Story may have been that his decision, however repugnant, confirmed the Garrisonian belief that the Constitution was really a pro-slavery document. Thus, Story could not be blamed for interpreting the Constitution as it really was. *Liberator*, Feb. 10, 1843.

[50] *Massachusetts Session Laws, 1843*, chaps. 5 and 69; *Vermont Session Laws, 1843*, chap. 15; *Connecticut Session Laws, 1844*, chap. 27; *New Hampshire Compiled Statutes*, 1853, chap. 238; *Pennsylvania Session Laws, 1847*, 206-08; *Rhode Island, Revised Statutes*, 1857, 532-576; See also, Morris, *Free Men All*, 219-224, for detailed discussion of some of these statutes, and for an extremely useful "check list" of personal liberty laws for all states.

[51] 41 *Ohio Laws* 13.

[52] *New York Session Laws, 1841*, C. 247.

[53] Barnes and Dumond, *Weld-Grimke Letters*, II, 963.

[54] *Maine Session Laws, 1855*, C. 182, and *1857*, C. 53; 54 Ohio Laws 170; However, these Ohio statutes were repealed in 1858, 55 Ohio Laws 10; Michigan, *Compiled Laws, 1857*, 1456, 1498; Wisconsin, *Revised Statutes, 1858*, Ch. 158; Minnesota, *Revised Statutes, 1851*, 23.

1858.[55] Additional legislation was passed in the New England states as well.[56] All of these acts were theoretically constitutional as long as they only served to eliminate state participation in the rendition of fugitive slaves.

Even without legislation, anti-slavery lawyers and judges found *Prigg* a useful tool for opposing the rendition of fugitive slaves. State judges were able to declare that they had no authority to hear cases involving fugitives, and to suggest claimants ought to seek a remedy in a federal court. Such a court might be hundreds of miles away and perhaps not even in session. The slave, of course, could be returned under the self-help rule, but without access to jails and without aid from local officials, it might be difficult or impossible for any owner to bring his property back home.[57]

The anti-slavery aspects of *Prigg* were applied by judges in cases involving fugitive slaves and slaves in transit through Northern states. With the notable exception of the Wisconsin courts in *Ableman v. Booth*,[58] Northern judges rarely directly challenged the supremacy of the federal government in its enforcement of the Fugitive Slave Laws of 1793 and 1850. As Robert Cover has shown, many state judges, like Lemuel Shaw of Massachusetts and Joseph Swan of Ohio, "not only perceived their primary obligation, as judges, to the Constitution, but they also affirmed the general principles of impersonal, neutral construction; adherence to recent precedent in spirit as well as holding; and obligation to make a good faith effort to effectuate the instrument's purpose even in the face of their own moral beliefs."[59] Thus, Shaw consistently refused to interfere in the rendition of fugitives in federal custody. Similarly, Swan refused to confront the federal government in the prosecution of those involved in the Oberlin-Wellington rescue.[60]

Direct confrontation with federal authority was not the only way state judges and legislatures could interfere with the rendition of fugitive slaves. As noted above, after 1842 many states passed personal liberty laws which, among other things, denied state judges any jurisdiction in fugitive slave cases, prohibited state police officials from participating in renditions, and barred the use of state facilities to hold fugitives. In states where such laws were not passed, it was possible for judges to hear fugitive slave cases, particularly under the 1793 act. When confronted

[55] *Kansas Session Laws, 1855*, c. 48; *Session Laws, 1858*, c. 62.

[56] Morris, *Free Men All*, 219-224.

[57] For examples of this see *Norris v. Newton*, 18 F.C. 322 (1850); *Graves v. State*, 1 Indiana 368 (1849); and *Vaughan v. Williams*, 28 F.C. 1115 (1845), all cases originating in Indiana, a notorious anti-black state, in which masters had difficulty bringing their fugitive slaves back with them and in which police officials were unable or unwilling to provide assistance.

[58] *Ableman v. Booth*, 21 Howard (U.S.) 506 (1858).

[59] Cover, *Justice Accused*, 171.

[60] *Ex parte Bushnell, Ex parte Langston*, 9 Ohio St. 77 (1859).

with such a case, a judge with anti-slavery sympathies had essentially three options: he could accept jurisdiction and decide the case on its merits according to the federal law; he could accept jurisdiction and free the alleged slave on the basis of natural law; or the judge could invoke the *dictum* of *Prigg* that he was not obligated to hear the case. Before 1850 the third course could mean that a master had no realistic remedy.

The first option, to accept jurisdiction and decide the case on its merits, fits into the positive law interpretation discussed in Professor Cover's *Justice Accused*. However, there are no instances in which Justices Shaw or Swan—the two state judges Cover cites to illustrate his thesis—took that position. In 1836, six years before *Prigg*, it appeared that Shaw might enforce the law against two alleged runaways. Fortunately, these two women ran from the courtroom during a complicated and chaotic hearing and were not recaptured. In the famous Latimer case, heard shortly after *Prigg*, Shaw complied with, but did not enforce, the federal law. Since Latimer's owner had a federal right to reclaim his slave without court interference under the self-help rule, Shaw rightly concluded he had no legal justification for interfering in the case. However, the logic of *Prigg* ultimately led to Latimer's freedom. Latimer was held in the city jail, under an agreement between the jailer and Latimer's owner. Public pressure forced the jailer to release Latimer to his master's custody but with no other facility available to restrain him, Latimer's owner conveniently cut his losses by selling the slave to a group of abolitionists who immediately freed him. Thus, Latimer's case underscored the anti-slavery potential of *Prigg*. Immediately after the case, the so-called "Latimer Law" was passed which prohibited state judges from taking cognizance of fugitive cases and barred the use of state facilities or the participation of state officials in such cases.[61] In the Sims and Burns cases[62] Shaw simply refused to confront federal authorities, but in none of these cases did he actually enforce the law and order a fugitive slave returned to the South.

Justice Swan, in *Ex Parte Bushnell*,[63] simply refused to oppose the federal government where it had jurisdiction. While his (and Shaw's) reluctance to challenge federal laws did not endear them to the abolitionists, their behavior must be seen in the context in which they operated. Both judges showed a marked inclination not to enforce the Fugitive Slave Law by granting certificates of removal. But both, particularly Shaw, were equally reluctant to disrupt the union through a direct confrontation with federal authority and power. Only the Wisconsin court, in *Ableman v. Booth*,[64] took that extreme position.

---

[61] For a discussion of Latimer Case see Leonard W. Levy, *The Law of the Commonwealth and Chief Justice Shaw* (New York, 1967) 72-108; also, n. 50, above.

[62] *Ibid.*

[63] See n. 60, above.

[64] See n. 58, above.

The second option, that of taking jurisdiction and then ignoring the positive law in favor of higher or natural law, was rarely taken. It would undoubtedly have been difficult for most judges to reconcile their judicial oaths with such actions. The best example of this type of decision was that of Justice Theophilus Harrington. In 1807, speaking for a unanimous Vermont Supreme Court, Harrington refused to return a fugitive slave to his New York owner, allegedly declaring: "If the master could show a bill of sale, or grant, from the Almighty, then his title to him would be complete: otherwise it would not." Although perhaps apocryphal, this unreported decision was viewed by abolitionists as an example of how judges ought to deal with the Fugitive Slave Law. The Garrisonian attorney Samuel E. Sewall thought it an important precedent for three reasons. First, it occurred only seventeen years after the federal Constitution was adopted, and thus reflected what people at the time may have thought the fugitive slave clause meant. Second, it was the unanimous decision of a state supreme court, and thus carried some weight. And finally, and most importantly, Sewall argued: "The decision was placed on a true and immovable foundation—the supremacy of God's law over all human Constitutions and laws."[65]

For judges opposed to slavery, but unwilling to accept—or at least implement—the higher law theory of the Garrisonians and Justice Harrington, there was a third option.[66] They could use *Prigg* as a way of freeing fugitive slaves by avoiding jurisdiction. This made them more daring than Chief Justice Shaw, but at the same time allowed them to maintain their judicial role. In cases involving slaves in transit and sojourning slaves, Northern judges also used *Prigg* to liberate bondsmen. This second use of *Prigg* was less important than the first because some states had freed slaves in transit before *Prigg*. Indeed, Justice Shaw had written the first major Northern court opinion freeing a

---

[65] *Liberator*, Jan. 6, 1843. Salmon P. Chase suggested that he would take an even more radical stand if he were a judge. In 1844 he told Lewis Tappan: "If I were a judge, with present views, and a *fugitive slave* in Ohio should bring an action against his *pursuing master* in Ohio for wages during the whole time of his servitude, he should have judgement. If I were a U.S. Judge and a Virginia Slave should bring an action before me against a Va. master the result would be the same." Chase to Lewis Tappan, Cincinnati, Apr. 3, 1844, Chase Papers, Library of Congress. Note on Chase provided by Louis S. Gerteis.

[66] A fourth option would have been to resign as a judge. In 1852 Salmon Chase suggested he might take this road, instead of the more radical one suggested in n. 65, above. He told Gerrit Smith: "For myself however, I have long *felt*, that I could not, in the exercise of judicial functions, should it ever be my fortune to be clothed with such, adjudge a man to be a thing, or doom a man whom God made free lifelong and absolute slavery. I should prefer to resign my seat." Chase to Gerrit Smith, Washington D.C., Aug. 9, 1852, Chase Papers. Again, I must thank Professor Gerteis for this information. That someone as articulate and committed as Chase should vacilate on what he would do if he were a judge, tends to show how difficult the fugitive slave issue was for judges, and how limited their options really were.

sojourner slave as early as 1836. This was the first step in a case line which would ultimately free virtually all slaves in transit or sojourn throughout most of the North.[67] Nevertheless, *Prigg* offered an extra bit of Supreme Court *dicta* in such cases for those judges unsure of the validity of early English and other American state precedents.

V

Northern judges further used *Prigg* as an anti-slavery tool by misreading—perhaps deliberately—Story's opinion. Story only declared that he doubted Congress had the constitutional power to compel state judges to enforce the federal act. Arguments in Northern courts soon restated this to mean that state officials *lacked any jurisdiction* over fugitive slaves. This line of reasoning was in fact first offered by Salmon P. Chase in his debut as an anti-slavery lawyer, five years before *Prigg*.

In 1837, a fugitive slave named Matilda was arrested in Cincinnati by the local sheriff who acted under a warrant issued by the county Court of Common Pleas. In arguing for her release, Chase claimed that Matilda's arrest was illegal because the federal act did not provide for arrests by any officers of the law, and more importantly, "because no act of congress could authorize the issuing of a state process, in the name of the state. . . ."[68]

In one of the earliest uses of states' rights by the anti-slavery movement, Chase stressed the federal nature of the Union, which separated the states from the national government. Congress could not authorize a state to arrest anyone "without a palpable violation of state rights," because the federal and state governments were "entirely distinct and independent."

Neither can control or regulate the action of the other. Neither can enlarge, diminish, or vary the powers or duties of the officers of the other. If then, the process, in the present case, was state process, it is plain that no act of congress could authorize the employment of it.

Anticipating what would be anti-slavery *dicta* in *Prigg*, Chase argued:

So far as the jurisdiction in cases of fugitive servants extends, the magistrate is a federal officer, and cannot, while acting in that capacity, issue state process. He cannot commit. No constable has authority to convey any person to jail by virtue of a commitment issued by him. No jailer is warranted in receiving any person into jail, or detaining him in custody, under such commitment.[69]

These arguments, unfortunately, convinced no one on the Court of Common Pleas and Matilda was returned to slavery. Indeed, Chase later

---

[67] On slaves in transit see Finkelman, "A More Perfect Union?" Shaw's decision was in *Commonwealth v. Aves*, 18 Pick, (Mass) 193 (1836).

[68] *Speech of Salmon P. Chase In the Case of the Colored Woman, Matilda* (Cincinnati, 1837), 11.

[69] *Ibid.*, 12, 15.

said his legal theory was "treated with ridicule or disregard." That same year Chase defended James G. Birney, an abolitionist who had helped Matilda in her abortive escape. Again Chase argued that "nothing in either" the United States Constitution or the Northwest Ordinance authorized "the legislature of any state to pass laws for the protection of the right of property in human beings." By this time Chase's legal theory may have gained some credibility, if not total acceptance, as the Ohio Supreme Court reversed Birney's conviction on a technicality concerning the wording of the indictment.[70] This made it "unnecessary to decide upon the other points, so laboriously argued . . . and of a character too important in their bearing upon the whole country to be adjudicated upon without necessity." However, in an unusual move, the Court had all of Chase's arguments printed with the opinion.[71] The idea that states could not enforce the fugitive slave law was still "treated with ridicule or disregard," but it had been brought before the legal community and published by the Ohio Supreme Court. Indeed, in freeing Birney, the Ohio court may have been reflecting the growing Northern distaste for enforcing the law. Within five years Northern judges would find *dicta* in *Prigg* allowing them to ignore it.

One of the first anti-slavery applications of *Prigg* occurred in Pennsylvania less than eight months after the decision was announced.[72] Oddly enough this case involved the extradition of a free man accused of helping five slaves escape from Maryland into Pennsylvania—almost the reverse of the facts in *Prigg*. For this act one Henry Jackson was indicted in Maryland and extradition papers were forwarded to Governor David Porter of Pennsylvania. Governor Porter in turn directed Judge Thomas Bell to issue a warrant for Jackson's arrest. This, Judge Bell refused to do. Instead, he wrote Governor Porter, explaining that under the Constitution and the extradition statute of 1793 (which included the Fugitive Slave Law) a state judge had no jurisdiction in an extradition case. He warned that if he were to issue the warrant he would first have to examine the law under which Jackson was indicted, implying he would not find this law valid in Pennsylvania. He further implied that *Prigg* made it unconstitutional for a state judge to enforce the Maryland law, and that the Maryland law itself might be unconstitutional.[73]

This case was curious for a number of reasons. First, Judge Bell mentioned *Prigg* twice in his letter, even though the case before him was not strictly concerned with fugitive slaves. Second, he acknowledged that previously it had always been the custom for Pennsylvania judges to issue warrants in extradition cases. Finally, Bell went out of his way to

---

[70] *James G. Birney v. The State of Ohio*, 8 Ohio 230 (1837).
[71] *Ibid.*
[72] *Ibid.*
[72] "Judge Bell's Letter," 2 Am. Law. J. 150 (1842).
[73] *Ibid.*, at 150-55.

indicate that if this case were brought before him he would examine the Maryland law and probably find for Jackson. It seems that Judge Bell was anxious to avoid any appearance of enforcing fugitive slave legislation.

In 1847 the Pennsylvania legislature finally took the time to respond to *Prigg* by passing a new personal liberty statute. In accordance with Story's ruling, it did not directly challenge federal authority over the rendition process. Instead it prohibited all state judges and officials from taking jurisdiction in fugitive slave cases. State jails and prison facilities were similarly denied to slave catchers. The act prohibited the kidnapping of free blacks or the taking of fugitive slaves under the self-help rule when done "in a riotous, violent, tumultuous and unreasonable manner." Finally, it took complete advantage of Story's narrow reading of Article IV to deny any rights to masters in transit. Before 1847 a master might bring a slave into Pennsylvania for up to six months, after which the slave would be free. This new act freed all slaves the moment their master brought them into the state.[74]

If Pennsylvania judges could no longer take cognizance of the federal Fugitive Slave Law, they nevertheless continued to hear cases involving fugitive slaves. In 1848, for example, a group of slaves successfully escaped from Maryland into Pennsylvania, where they were aided by an abolitionist named Kauffman. The owner, Mrs. Oliver, sued Kauffman and won in the Court of Common Pleas. In his appeal to the Pennsylvania Supreme Court[75] Kauffman "pleaded to the jurisdiction of the court." He argued that under *Prigg* only the federal courts had jurisdiction in fugitive slave cases, and any penalties under the Act of 1793 could only be levied by a federal court. He also argued, and was supported by *dicta* in *Prigg*, that there was no common law protection of slave property in Pennsylvania, and thus by aiding the runaway slaves he had committed no crime in Pennsylvania. Speaking for the Pennsylvania court, Justice Coulter agreed with Kauffman that Pennsylvania could give no legal protection to slave property. He pointed out that "even persuading the fugitives" to leave Maryland, which was what Mrs. Oliver claimed Kauffman had done, "would be no offence in Pennsylvania, whatever it might be in Maryland." Coulter asserted that his state could enforce Maryland's law as "a matter of comity" but "not as a matter of right or duty." He pointed out that Pennsylvania had tried to achieve proper interstate comity with its 1826 statute, but that act had been declared unconstitutional in *Prigg*. Thus, if Pennsylvania could not protect its free black citizens from kidnapping, it certainly could not be expected to protect the slave property of Maryland. Coulter concluded that the Pennsylvania court had no jurisdiction over the Act of 1793,

[74] *Pennsylvania, Session Laws of 1847*, 206-208 "An Act to Prevent Kidnapping . . . and to repeal certain slave laws."

[75] *Kauffman v. Oliver* 10 Pa. St. 541 (1849).

which offered Mrs. Oliver whatever remedy she might be entitled to. The judgment against Kauffman was reversed.[76]

In August, 1850, the *American Law Journal* described the case of *Commonwealth v. William Taylor*[77] as "more of the fruits of the wretched blunder committed by a majority of the judges of the Supreme Court of the United States in denying to the States the power to pass laws in fulfilment [sic] of their obligations to surrender fugitive slaves." Taylor and eight other Virginians discovered their escaped slaves in Harrisburg, Pennsylvania, where they were arrested for horse stealing. The slaves had indeed taken Taylor's horses, but only to help in their escape. The local court discharged them because "it did not appear that they took the horses with a felonious intent to convert the property to their own use." This ruling was itself an extraordinary example of a court interpreting law and fact in favor of fugitives.

As soon as the blacks were released they were attacked by Taylor and his friends. Local blacks soon entered the fracas and the court was "informed . . . a great riot had commenced and was in progress . . . a number of persons were engaged fighting within the jail walls, that much blood had been shed" and lives were in danger. All rioters found within the jail walls, including the Virginians, were arrested. Had the Pennsylvania judge been willing to incarcerate the slaves this riot would have been avoided. But, under *Prigg* the judge could, and did, decline to aid Taylor. This was the legally correct action under the Pennsylvania statute of 1847. Thus, the Virginians were arrested for riot and imprisoned for four months, while waiting trial. At a preliminary hearing a Judge Pearson noted that the masters were allowed to capture their fugitive slaves, but only if it could be done peaceably. This of course is what Story had declared in *Prigg*. At the trial it was determined that the Virginians had not used unnecessary violence in exercising their right of self-help and they were acquitted. What became of the slaves remains unclear, but the stress on the Union caused by this case and the anti-slavery use of *Prigg* was obvious. If masters were to risk four months in jail just to recapture their slaves, then the constitutional clause was hardly aiding the South. A new fugitive slave law was needed which would prevent "More Fruits of the Error in Prigg v. Penn.," as the *American Law Journal* subtitled its first article on the case.[78]

In *Commonwealth v. Auld*[79] and *Commonwealth v. Alberti*[80] slave

---

[76] Ibid., *passim,*; see also, *Oliver et al. v. Kauffman, Weakley, and Breckbill*, 18 F. C. 657 (1853).

[77] *Commonwealth v. William Taylor, et al.*, 10 Am. Law J. 90 (1850) and 10 Am Law J. 258 (1850).

[78] *Ibid.*

[79] *Commonwealth v. Auld*, 4 Clark (Pennsylvania) 507 (April, 1850).

[80] *Commonwealth v. Alberti*, 2 Parsons (Pennsylvania) 495 (1851).

catchers were sentenced to prison terms by Pennsylvania courts for kidnapping alleged fugitives who were really free blacks. In both cases the state courts took jurisdiction despite claims by the defendants that these cases came under the *Prigg* rule, and were subject solely to federal jurisdiction. In Auld's case the trial judge agreed that "the power to legislate on the subject of fugitive slaves belongs exclusively to Congress," but was unwilling to concede that "the legislature of Pennsylvania may not pass a law to protect the free negroes and mulattoes within her borders." Auld had kidnapped the Pennsylvania-born son of a fugitive slave, and for this he was convicted under the Pennsylvania law of 1847. Because Auld had acted under the constitutional right of self-help, on the assumption that his captive was a fugitive slave, the Pennsylvania court may have in fact had no legitimate jurisdiction over the case. However, the court asserted its jurisdiction on the assumption that the fugitive slave clause could not protect someone who had kidnapped a free black. This was, of course, possible only by reading Story's decision in the most narrow way. In *Commonwealth v. Alberti* two slave catchers received eight and ten year sentences for kidnapping free blacks whom they thought were runaways. Again, the Pennsylvania court acknowledged the right of peaceful recaption, but argued that it could only be used when bona fide slaves were taken. If free blacks were seized the slave hunters had to be prepared to pay for their mistakes.

Both of these cases underscored the dangerous tendencies of the right of recaption and the fragile protections Story's opinion gave free blacks. Had the slave catchers reached Maryland without detection, it is unlikely they would have been prosecuted and there is a good chance that the free blacks would have been enslaved for life. By hearing these cases, the Pennsylvania courts were in effect claiming the right to decide if blacks claimed as fugitives were in fact runaway slaves. If they were not, then their captors could be prosecuted. If they were, then the state would no longer have jurisdiction over the matter. But the speedy return of fugitives would have turned into a lengthy process involving perhaps a jury trial in Pennsylvania. The state could have decided to intervene every time an alleged fugitive claimed to be free, on the ground that *Prigg* dealt only with fugitives. This would have meant a very narrow reading of *Prigg* was being used to overturn the general aim of the decision. Given this possibility, it is likely these cases might have been reversed in federal courts, but they were never appealed. Thus, the Pennsylvania courts were able to give some protection to free blacks, as seen in the *Auld* and *Alberti* cases, and to discourage slave catchers, as in William Taylor's case. All of this was accomplished while the courts claimed to be adhering to the principles and *dicta*, if not necessarily the spirit and intent, of *Prigg*.

Prigg was also used to oppose slavery in New York, Ohio, Indiana, and Illinois. Although cases from these states are few in number, they indicate the willingness of judges to interfere in the rendition process where possible, to free slaves in transit within their jurisdiction, and to at least pronounce their opposition to slavery in appropriate cases.

In October, 1846, a fugitive slave named George Kirk was discovered aboard the brig *Mobile* while en route to New York. Kirk was chained and "closely confined" when the ship docked. It was the intention of the captain, Theodore Buckley, to return Kirk to Georgia, which under Georgia law he was required to do. Kirk was brought before a Court of Oyer and Terminer headed by Circuit Judge J.W. Edmonds on a writ of habeas corpus.[81] Edmonds concluded that Buckley had to release Kirk because the Georgia statutes could not be enforced in New York and because the right of recaption was only available to a master or his authorized agent, neither of which Buckley was. Here again, a very narrow reading of *Prigg*, that an "agent" had to have specific authorization from the master, was used to release a slave.

In his opinion Edmonds hinted at what appeared to be an alternative procedure: a New York statute which allowed ships' captains to bring stowaway fugitives before the mayor, who was authorized to issue certificates of removal. However, Edmonds indicated that this law might violate the *Prigg* decision. Immediately after this hearing Kirk was seized and brought before the mayor, who issued a certificate of removal under the New York law. This was quickly appealed to the only circuit judge in the city, J. W. Edmonds. As in the first case, Kirk was represented by the abolitionist attorney, John Jay. Edmonds issued a second writ of habeas corpus, which was directed at the mayor, because he had issued the certificate of removal. One day later a court of sessions, consisting of Judge Edmonds, the city recorder, and the mayor, heard the case. Technically, this meant the mayor had to rule on the validity of his own certificate of removal, while Edmonds had to rule on his own writ of habeas corpus.[82]

Edmonds began his second opinion by distinguishing the case from the "former occasion" where "no principle of law was involved." The first time he heard the case Edmonds had only to determine if Buckley had a factual claim to Kirk, and decided he did not. This time Buckley's claim was correctly made under the New York statute. It was for Edmonds to determine the constitutionality of that law. Edmonds analyzed *Prigg* from a number of angles. He discussed Congressional power and exclusivity of jurisdiction and concluded that New York could not legislate on the question of fugitive slaves. Disclaiming any interest in anti-slavery, he explained: "I only discharge my duty—obey, indeed merely one of its plainest and most simple dictates—by declaring that the rule of law thus laid down by the highest judicial tribunals in the

---

[81] *In the Matter of George Kirk, a Fugitive Slave,* 1 Parker Cr. R. (N.Y.) 67 (1846).; also in 9 Monthly L. Rep. 355; 9 Monthly L. Rep. 361.

[82] *In the Matter of George Kirk,* 9 Monthly L. Rep. 361, 362.

country, and whose decisions I am bound to respect and enforce, is applicable to the statute in question, and being applicable render the statute null and void, and the arrest and detention of Kirk under it improper."[83] Under the constitutional cover of *Prigg*, Judge Edmonds saw no alternative but to free a fugitive slave. As Taney feared, the exclusivity rule could be a potent two-edged sword.

One year later Judge Edmonds heard the case of Joseph Belt, an alleged fugitive from Maryland.[84] Belt had been captured on a New York City street and held incommunicado for two days while his captors waited for passage to Maryland. In the meantime, a writ of habeas corpus brought the case before Edmonds, where the ubiquitous John Jay, accompanied by a district attorney, argued for Belt's liberty. Belt's alleged owner claimed that under *Prigg* Edmonds had no jurisdiction in the case. Jay countered that the self-help right stopped short of "breach of the peace or illegal violence," as Story had declared in the same case. Edmonds used some of this argument to free Belt. He noted that Belt's captors had made neither a claim under the Fugitive Slave Law of 1793 nor taken Belt before a federal judge to obtain a certificate of removal. Instead, they secretly held Belt for two days. "If he can do this for two days," Edmonds declared, then "he can [do it] for two years or twenty. To justify this, would warrant every slaveholder in the nation to hold his slaves in this state as long as he pleases, notwithstanding slavery was unknown to our laws." This Edmonds could not allow. Edmonds would not decide if Belt was actually a fugitive slave; that was beyond his jurisdiction. Instead, he freed Belt from the illegal restraint under which he was held. Once again, the rights of a master appear to have been ignored or nullified by a New York judge who exploited *Prigg* for anti-slavery purposes.[85]

A final New York case involved slaves in transit with their owners.[86] In 1852 the Lemmon family left Virginia for New York, where they planned to secure direct passage to New Orleans. With them were eight slaves whom they placed in a hotel room. The slaves were discovered by Louis Napoleon, a free black who had discovered George Kirk six years before. As in Kirk's case, Napoleon secured a writ of habeas corpus, which began an eight year struggle in the New York courts. Lemmon's slaves were freed by a Superior Court judge and his decision was upheld by two both levels of New York's appellate courts. The initial decision rested on the 1840 New York statute which declared all slaves in the state to be free. Although this statute had been passed before *Prigg*, the later decision affirmed the right of a state to pass such a statute, because the

---

[83] *In the Matter of George Kirk*, 1 Parker Cr. R. (N.Y.) 67, 76, 79, 83, 94.

[84] *In the Matter of Joseph Belt, an Alleged Fugitive From Service in the State of Maryland*, 1 Parker Cr. R. (N.Y.) 169 (1848).

[85] *Ibid.*, at 181-82.

[86] *Lemmon v. The People*, 20 New York 562 (1860); also, n. 52, above.

constitution protected only property in fugitive slaves, and allowed the states to legislate on other aspects of the peculiar institution. In this sense, Story's localization of slavery was a "triumph of freedom." Indeed, Story's opinion was cited to support the contention by the New York Court of Appeals that "no nation is bound to recognize the state of slavery as to foreign slaves found within its territorial dominions, when it is in opposition to its own policy and institutions. . . ."[87] Although hardly the only, or most important, constitutional precedent in the *Lemmon* case, *Prigg* provided support for a decision that freed slaves in transit.

As noted earlier, the use of ideas found in *Prigg* began in Ohio long before Justice Story's opinion. Not surprisingly, Salmon P. Chase was quick to use the exclusivity doctrine after *Prigg*. He also used the arguments which would later be used in *Lemmon*, that *Prigg* supported the right of states to free slaves in transit. Both arguments were used in *State v. Hoppess*,[88] which involved a slaveowner in transit whose steamboat had docked at Cincinnati. While waiting for another ship, Hoppess' slave, Watson, casually walked away from the wharf. Hoppess soon seized him and took him before Judge N.C. Read of the Ohio Supreme Court to obtain a certificate of removal, and thus avoid any legal problems with taking his slave out of Ohio. The omnipresent Chase was there to represent Watson.

Chase argued that Watson had been voluntarily brought into Ohio and was free. He supported this by a narrow reading of *Prigg* and the Fugitive Slave Law. Watson might have escaped from his master while *in* Ohio, but he did not escape *into* Ohio. Chase also argued, directly citing *Prigg*, that Congress had no power to invest a state judge with any authority, and therefore Judge Read ought not enforce the federal law even if he determined Watson was a fugitive. Ultimately, Read decided that in a technical sense Watson had not been brought to Ohio by his master because the wharf area was open to all interstate traffic and thus state laws affecting status did not apply there. This was decidedly pro-slavery and ran counter to settled riparian law. Judge Read did not issue a certificate of removal but Hoppess was allowed to take Watson with him under the self-help rule. Although this decision did not free Watson, Judge Read did conclude that a slave voluntarily brought into Ohio (beyond the wharves) would be free and that under *Prigg* the master would have no claim upon him.[89]

Anderson v. Poindexter[90] proved to be more than just a moral victory.

---

[87] *Ibid.*, at 622-23.

[88] *State v. Hoppess in the Matter of Watson, Claimed as a Fugitive from Service,* 2 West Law J. 279 (1845)

[89] *Ibid.;* also see 2 West Law J. 333.

[90] *John Anderson v. Henry Poindexter and Others,* 6 Ohio St. 622 (1856). *Prigg* was of course not always used in an anti-slavery manner by Ohio courts. In *William R. Richardson*

Poindexter was a Kentucky slave who arranged to purchase himself from Anderson. To accomplish this Poindexter moved to Ohio, where three white friends signed notes as sureties. When Poindexter and his friends defaulted on the notes, Anderson sued. He lost when the Ohio Supreme Court ruled that Anderson had abandoned any claim to Poindexter by voluntarily allowing the slave to come to Ohio. Thus, the notes were void for "a want of consideration." In an elaborate concurrence, Justice Swan quoted Story's opinion that "the state of slavery is deemed to be a mere municipal regulation, founded upon and limited to the range of the territorial laws." He also cited *Prigg* to show that the Fugitive Slave Law could not apply to cases such as this one.[91] Salmon Chase's anti-slavery constitutionalism had finally been accepted by his home state's highest court.

Although sitting in notoriously negrophobic states, judges in both Indiana and Illinois used *Prigg* as an anti-slavery tool.[92] In *Freeman v. Robinson*[93] a free black in Indiana successfully sued a federal marshall for false arrest and assault. Before the Indiana Supreme Court, Marshall Robinson argued that he had acted under the Fugitive Slave Law and that state courts had no jurisdiction in this area. This was a correct interpretation of *Prigg* and the Indiana court agreed with him. However, the court went on to note that *Prigg* only dealt with the arrest of fugitive slaves which, as his named implied, Freeman was not. Since Robinson had exceeded his authority in his treatment of Freeman and since Freeman was not a fugitive slave the Indiana court sustained its jurisdiction over the case. The judgment against Robinson was affirmed.

A few weeks after *Prigg* was announced, the Cincinnati *Philanthropist* reported the case of a black named Daniel who was arrested as a fugitive slave under an Illinois law which authorized county sheriffs to detain

---

v. Huron Beebe, 9 Monthly L. Rep. 316 (1846), the Ohio Supreme Court ordered the release of Richardson, who was held by Sheriff Beebe for violating Ohio's personal liberty laws. The Court ruled that *Prigg* invalidated this law and it was not necessary for Richardson to bring a black to a state court before taking that black out of Ohio. Since no one disputed that the man removed from Ohio was a fugitive slave, the Court concluded Richardson had acted legally, under the self-help rule of *Prigg.*

[91] *Ibid.,* at 646-47.

[92] Leon F. Litwack, *North of Slavery: The Negro in the Free States, 1790-1860* (Chicago, 1961); V. Jacque Voegeli, *Free But Not Equal: The Midwest and the Negro During the Civil War* (Chicago, 1967); and Eugene H. Berwanger, *The Frontier Against Slavery: Western Anti-Negro Prejudice and the Slavery Extension Controversy* (Urbana, 1967). See also the following legal cases: *Glenn et al. v. The People,* 17 *Illinois* 104 (1855); *Nelson (a mulatto) v. The People,* 33 Illinois 390 (1864); *Hatwood v. State,* 18 Indiana 492 (1862).

[93] *Freeman v. Robinson,* 7 Indiana 321 (1855). For a pro-slavery use of *Prigg* in Indiana, see *Graves and Others v. The State,* 1 Indiana 368 (1849), where the state court voided a state statute requiring a rendition procedure in addition to, or instead of, that found in the federal law. Even in this case, however, it appears that the trial judge may have used *Prigg* as an anti-slavery weapon, since he refused to take cognizance of the master's claim under the federal law. Instead he dismissed a warrant for the fugitive's arrest, perhaps for lack of jurisdiction.

suspected runaways for over a year, while advertizing for their masters.[94] Judge Samuel Treat of the Illinois Supreme Court ordered Daniel released and declared this Illinois law to be in violation of the United States Constitution, as interpreted in *Prigg*. This case apparently had no effect on the Illinois law, perhaps because it was not appealed and went unreported, but it may have been the first anti-slavery use of *Prigg*.

In 1849 the Illinois law received a more complete court test in the case of Hempstead Thornton.[95] Thornton was arrested by the sheriff of Sangamon County who had received a dispatch from St. Louis which appeared to describe Thornton with some accuracy. Nevertheless, Treat, who was now Chief Justice, ordered Thornton released and again declared the old statute unconstitutional. He found *Prigg* "conclusive on the invalidity of this section of our statute. It is void, because it assumes to legislate upon a subject matter over which congress has exclusive jurisdiction." Thornton was discharged and the fears of Chief Justice Taney, that *Prigg* would be used to invalidate helpful state legislation, proved to be justified.[96]

In 1857 the Illinois Central Railroad was sued for the loss of a slave who escaped from a train he boarded in Illinois, after first escaping from Missouri. The Illinois court cited *Prigg* to show that the owner had no property in the slaves, once the slave had reached Illinois. At that point all the owner had was a right to reclaim the fugitive and take him back to Missouri, where he would once again be a slave. This was similar to the reasoning of the Pennsylvania court in *Oliver v. Kauffman*. The Illinois court also cited *Prigg*, as had the Pennsylvania court, to show that any claim for the value of the slave had to be made in federal, and not state, court. Without concurrent jurisdiction over fugitive slaves, Illinois could do nothing to support or oppose the claims of the master. Once again, *Prigg* was used to frustrate a slaveowner.[97]

VI

Almost from the moment of its passage the Fugitive Slave Law of 1793 was unsatisfactory to the South. In 1796 Congress considered revising the act and further proposals for a new act, always from the South and always to strengthen the law, came in 1801, 1802, and annually from 1817 to 1822. After that there were no legislative attempts to revise the law until after *Prigg*. However, throughout this period the inadequacies of the 1793 act bothered Southerners.[98]

---

[94] *Philanthropist*, Mar. 16, 1842. *Illinois Revised Statutes, 1845*, C. 74. This Illinois statute apparently was first passed in 1819, *Illinois Session Laws, 1819*, p. 354.

[95] *Thornton's Case*, 11 Illinois 332 (1849).

[96] *Ibid.*, at 335-36.

[97] *Thomas Rodney v. The Illinois Central Railroad Company*, 19 Illinois 42 (1857).

[98] Marion Gleason McDougall, *Fugitive Slaves* (Boston, 1892), 16-25.

Before 1842 many Northern states attempted to balance the desire to protect free blacks with the needs of their Southern neighbors. Northern states often required their officials to issue certificates of removal when ownership of a fugitive was proved. These were good faith efforts to protect the rights of free blacks and the property rights of Southerners, and to provide an orderly system of rendition. That such negrophobic states as Indiana and Ohio, as well as other free states, passed laws to protect free blacks suggests the Northern commitment to freedom was at least as strong as the prevailing racial prejudice.[99] This position is illuminated by the actions of the courts and state legislatures after *Prigg*. Not all Northern states passed personal liberty laws in this period nor did all judges avail themselves of the anti-slavery tendencies in *Prigg*, but enough states and courts acted in this manner to threaten the South.

Thomas Hart Benton thought the Pennsylvania personal liberty law of 1847, which was in direct response to *Prigg*, was "a new starting-point in the anti-slavery movements of [the] North," which "led to the new fugitive slave recovery act of 1850."[100] This new movement had, of course, begun much earlier but *Prigg* accelerated this movement toward anti-slavery, particularly among judges, legislators, and lawyers. Even judges and legislators who were not abolitionists took advantage of *Prigg* to disclaim any responsibility for the rendition of fugitive slaves. When forced to choose between the implied responsibilities of the Constitution and the immediate prospect of free blacks being kidnapped, most Northerners chose to support freedom. In this sense, Story's decision became "a triumph of freedom," not because he suggested it might be constitutional for state officials to ignore the Fugitive Slave Law, but because he made it impossible for state officials to enforce that law with equal respect for property rights and due process. Story inadvertently forced Northerners to make the difficult choice between harmony within the Union and the cherished liberties of free men. With increasingly regularity Northerners generally chose the latter.

[99] For Ohio statutes, see n. 51 and n. 54, above. For Indiana see protections found in state fugitive slave laws and prohibitions against kidnapping, in *Indiana Revised Statutes, 1838*, C. 26, C. 46, C. 73. While willing to protect its Negro population from kidnapping, Indiana also prohibited the immigration of any more blacks into the state. See *Indiana Constitution, 1851*, Art. XIII.

[100] Thomas Hart Benton, *Thirty Years View*, (New York, 1858), II, 777.

STATE CONSTITUTIONAL PROTECTIONS OF LIBERTY AND THE ANTEBELLUM NEW JERSEY SUPREME COURT: CHIEF JUSTICE HORNBLOWER AND THE FUGITIVE SLAVE LAW

Paul Finkelman*

In an era when the United States Supreme Court is contracting civil liberties and civil rights, the role of state courts may be expanding. Lawyers are beginning to turn to state courts to defend civil rights and to protect fundamental liberty. As long as they rely on their own constitutions, using "adequate and independent state grounds,"[1] state courts can expand liberties above the minimum floor set by the United States Supreme Court's interpretation of the federal constitution.[2] It is likely that attorneys will increasingly ask state judges to protect individual liberty and civil rights beyond the level required by the United States Supreme Court and the federal constitution. As lawyers turn to state courts to protect liberty, legal historians will no doubt turn to the history of state constitutional law to better understand the background of state protected liberties.[3] More-

* Associate Professor, Virginia Polytechnic Institute and State University. Research for this article was funded by a grant from the New Jersey Historical Commission. The author thanks William M. Wiecek and Robert J. Cottrol for their helpful comments on this paper, my former research assistant at Brooklyn Law School, Philip Presby, Mary R. Murrin of the New Jersey Commission, the staffs of the New Jersey Historical Society, the New Jersey State Archives, the Library of Congress, and the Rare Book and Manuscript Library, Columbia University for their help in expediting this research. Earlier versions of this paper were given at the Seminar for New Jersey Historians at Princeton University; Seton Hall Law School; and the Organization of American Historians.

1. The concept first arose in Murdock v. Memphis, 87 U.S. (20 Wall.) 590 (1874). *See also* Martha Field, *Sources of Law: The Scope of Federal Common Law*, 99 HARV. L. REV. 881, 919-921 (1986); LAWRENCE TRIBE, AMERICAN CONSTITUTIONAL LAW 162-173 (2d ed. 1988).

2. If a state judge relies upon the United States Constitution to protect liberties, then the United States Supreme Court can reverse the state court's decision by interpreting the federal Constitution. When a state court relies solely upon its state constitution to protect fundamental liberties, however, the United States Supreme Court cannot reverse the state court unless the state court's action actually violates rights guaranteed by United States Constitution.

3. *See, e.g.*, the essays in TOWARD A USABLE PAST: LIBERTY UNDER STATE CONSTITUTIONS (Paul Finkelman & Stephen Gottlieb eds., 1991) [hereinafter TOWARD A USABLE PAST].

over, as state courts seek to guarantee equal protection under their own constitutions, they may also look to their state's history for guidance.[4]

The history of the modern New Jersey Supreme Court offers much for scholars and attorneys interested in the development of liberty at the state level. The post-World War II New Jersey court has a well earned reputation as a leader among state courts in protecting individual rights and liberties.[5] Three decades ago Justice William J. Brennan, then a five year veteran of the United States Supreme Court and a former Chief Justice of New Jersey, encouraged state courts to use state bills of rights to extend individual liberties "beyond that required by the national government by the corresponding federal guarantee."[6] A decade and a half later, with the Warren Court era coming to an end, Brennan warned that "our liberties cannot survive if the states betray the trust the Court has put in them."[7]

Justice Brennan was not the first New Jersey jurist to find state law more protective of fundamental rights than federal law. In 1836, Chief Justice Joseph C. Hornblower interpreted the New Jersey constitution to set free a black man claimed as a fugitive slave in *State v. The Sheriff of Burlington*.[8] Obviously, there is no direct no connection between Hornblower and the modern New Jersey court. Nevertheless, Hornblower's decision in *The Sheriff of Burlington* has more than antiquarian value for lawyers and judges today.

The case is a precedent which demonstrates that New Jersey's legal history supports a tradition of expanding liberty at the state level. In *Sheriff of Burlington*, Chief Justice Hornblower found that the New

---

4. *See, e.g.*, Robert F. Williams, *Equality Guarantees in State Constitutional Law*, 63 TEX. L. REV. 1195 (1985); Ellen A. Peters, *Common Law Antecedents of Constitutional Law in Connecticut*, in TOWARD A USABLE PAST, *supra* note 2, at 189.

5. *See generally*, G. ALAN TARR, STATE SUPREME COURTS IN STATE AND NATION (1988); SUSAN P. FINO, THE ROLE OF STATE SUPREME COURTS IN THE NEW JUDICIAL FEDERALISM (1987).

6. WILLIAM J. BRENNAN, JR., THE BILL OF RIGHTS AND THE STATES 20 (1961).

7. William J. Brennan, Jr., *State Constitutions and the Protection of Individual Rights*, 90 HARV. L. REV. 489, at 503 (1977).

8. Case file No. 36286 (1836) (New Jersey State Archives). This unreported case file refers to the matter as Nathan, Alias Alex. Helmsley v. State.

Although unreported, an incomplete report of the case was published as a news item and then circulated as a pamphlet as *Opinion of Chief Justice Hornblower on the Fugitive Slave Law*, *reprinted in* Series II, 1 SLAVERY, RACE AND THE AMERICAN LEGAL SYSTEM, (Paul Finkelman ed., 1988) [hereinafter *Hornblower Opinion*]. The text of this pamphlet, the best report of the case in existence, is *exactly* the same as an article appearing in the NEW YORK EVENING POST on August 1, 1851. The type and fonts for both also seem to be identical. It appears that the pamphlet was printed from the fonts of the *Post*, and logically, it would have been published by the *Post*.

Jersey Constitution provided greater protections of liberty than did the federal constitution. Chief Justice Ellen Peters of Connecticut has recently argued that early state constitutional history can provide useful support for those justices "on state courts who have become committed to assigning independent constitutional weight to our state constitutions, particularly with regard to the protection of civil rights and liberties."[9] Hornblower's opinion might provide such support for the modern New Jersey court.

Even if the case is irrelevant as a precedent, it is certainly instructive of the ways that state judges might use their own constitutions and laws to protect fundamental rights. At the same time, the case illustrates that timidity on the part of a state judge can undermine liberty on a large scale; Hornblower's failure to publish his opinion is a tragic reminder that even the best intentioned judges can sometimes undermine their own values by a failure of will and determination.

Finally, an examination of New Jersey slave law helps place the state's present-day race relations into a larger context. What little is known of New Jersey's legal history of race relations tends to be negative. New Jersey was the last of the northern states to pass legislation ending slavery, and even then its 1804 gradual emancipation act did not protect black rights as well as similar laws in neighboring states.[10] As late as 1845, the New Jersey Court of Errors, in *State v. Post*,[11] held slavery permissible in the state. Scholars often refer to *Post* to illustrate a free state which failed to give equal protection to its black residents.[12] Indeed, antebellum New Jersey was one of the Northern States most hostile to blacks.[13] Nevertheless, Chief Justice Joseph C. Hornblower's opinion in *The Sheriff of Burlington* suggests that New Jersey had countervailing trends. Moreover,

---

9. Peters, *supra* note 4, at 189.

10. Arthur Zilversmit, *Liberty and Prosperity: New Jersey and the Abolition of Slavery*, 88 N.J. HIST. 215, 221-26 (1970), *reprinted in* SLAVERY IN THE NORTH AND THE WEST 485, 491-96 (Paul Finkelman ed., 1989).

11. 20 N.J.L. 368 (N.J. 1845), *aff'd.*, 21 N.J.L. 699 (N.J. 1848) (holding that the "free and equal" clause of the state constitution of 1844 did not emancipate the approximately 700 slaves remaining in the state).

12. *See, e.g.*, Williams, *supra*, note 4, at 1204; 63 *Tex. L. Rev.* 1195 (1985); William P. Marshall, *An Advance in Tradition*, 53 U. CHI. L. REV. 1508, 1510 (1986); Aviam Soifer, *Status, Contract, and Promises Unkept*, 96 YALE L.J. 1916, 1918 n.8 (1987); ROBERT M. COVER, JUSTICE ACCUSED: ANTISLAVERY AND THE JUDICIAL PROCESS 55-60 (1975).

13. *See* Lee Calligaro, *The Negro's Legal Status in Pre-Civil War New Jersey*, 85 N.J. HIST. 167 (1967), *reprinted in* RACE AND LAW BEFORE EMANCIPATION 41 (Paul Finkelman ed., 1992); PAUL FINKELMAN, AN IMPERFECT UNION: SLAVERY, FEDERALISM AND COMITY (1981); Paul Finkelman, *Prelude to the Fourteenth Amendment: Black Legal Rights in the Antebellum North*, 17 RIGHTS L.J. 415 (1986) [hereinafter *Prelude*]; LEON LITWACK, NORTH OF SLAVERY (1961).

Hornblower's failure to publish his opinion underscores the possibility that, with bold judicial action, Hornblower might have helped lead New Jersey in a more egalitarian direction. Hornblower's opinion and subsequent New Jersey legislative action suggest that for a brief moment the state was a leader in providing due process for blacks. *The Sheriff of Burlington*, the main focus of this article, was one of the most antislavery opinions issued by any antebellum northern judge. It stands in sharp contrast to *State v. Post*, and helps illustrate the enormous complexity of northern antebellum race relations.[14] It also can serve as a historical model for New Jersey justices seeking an egalitarian past under their own constitutional heritage.

With these possibilities and caveats in mind, we can turn to a general examination of the legal history of slavery in New Jersey and a more detailed investigation of the case of Alexander Helmsley and the strange career of Chief Justice Hornblower's extraordinary attack on the first federal Fugitive Slave Law.

I. AN OVERVIEW OF THE HORNBLOWER OPINION

In 1836 Chief Justice Hornblower ordered the release of Alexander Helmsley, a black man held as a fugitive slave in Burlington, New Jersey. In deciding this case, Hornblower wrote a strongly abolitionist opinion which suggested that the federal Fugitive Slave Law of 1793 was unconstitutional. Hornblower did not declare the federal law void, in part because this was unnecessary. Helmsley had been seized and incarcerated under a state law. Thus, finding this New Jersey law invalid under the state constitution enabled Hornblower to order Helmsley's release. Hornblower did not have to explicitly address the constitutionality of the federal statute because neither the sheriff who held Helmsley nor the slaveowner who claimed him raised the federal law of 1793. Hornblower did not read his elaborate opinion from the bench, but summarized his conclusions. Nor did Hornblower have the opinion published in either in the official reports or as a pamphlet.

Some newspapers, especially the antislavery press, reported Hornblower's decision. As far west as Ohio the antislavery attorney Salmon P. Chase, a future Chief Justice of the United States Supreme Court, cited it for authority in a fugitive slave case,[15] although Chase's citation was

---

14. For further discussion of the complexity in a variety of states, see *Prelude, supra* note 13.

15. Letter from Salmon P. Chase to Chief Justice Hornblower (April 3, 1851) (in Hornblower Papers, Box 2, New Jersey Historical Society (NJHS)).

probably an exception. Hornblower's unreported decision and unpublished opinion were initially of little use to antislavery lawyers and activists. In 1838, William Jay, the abolitionist attorney and antislavery constitutional theorist, was unaware of Hornblower's decision.[16] This illustrates the initial obscurity of Hornblower's decision, because Jay lived in Westchester County, New York, close to Hornblower, and because Hornblower was a personal friend of William Jay's late father, former Chief Justice John Jay.[17]

In 1851 the Hornblower opinion was resurrected from obscurity and published in the *New York Evening Post* and in pamphlet form. The new Fugitive Slave Law of 1850[18] revived interest in Hornblower's old opinion, because its principles applied equally to both this law and the 1793 act. Antislavery editors, activists, and politicians all saw the applicability of Hornblower's conclusions to the debate over the constitutionality of the Fugitive Slave Law of 1850. The previously unpublished opinion was cited in the 1850s, occasionally as a legal precedent,[19] but more importantly as an intellectual, moral, and political argument against the Fugitive Slave Law. The very fact that Hornblower had not published his opinion in 1836 made his arguments more valuable in the 1850s. First, Hornblower had not been an abolitionist when he wrote the opinion, and second, he had written it before fugitive slave rendition was a major political issue. Thus, the Hornblower opinion was an example of a dispassionate approach to fugitive slaves by a respected state chief justice, untainted by abolitionism. The opinion is an important example of the connection between court cases, legal theory, and antislavery politics. To understand this case, a short discussion of New Jersey's policy for dealing with the problems posed by fugitive slaves entering the state is in order.

Chase cited Hornblower's opinion before the Cincinnati Court of Common Pleas in the case of Matilda. SALMON P. CHASE, SPEECH OF SALMON P. CHASE IN THE CASE OF THE COLORED WOMAN, MATILDA 18 (Cincinnati, Pugh and Dodd, 1837).

16. Letter from William Jay to Joseph C. Hornblower (July 11, 1851) (Jay Family Papers, Rare Book and Manuscript Library, Columbia University (letters from this collection are cited and quoted with permission of the library)). Jay wrote, "In 1838 the question occurred to me, under what constitutional grant of power Congress has passed the fugitive slave law of 1793 [sic]. I was not aware that the question had been mooted before."

17. Letter from William Jay to Hornblower (August 12, 1851) (Jay Family Papers, Rare Book and Manuscript Library, Columbia University).

Jay thanked Hornblower for his support: "Your commendation is necessarily valuable to all who are honored by it, but to me it is peculiarly so, as coming from my Father's friend." *Id.*

18. 9 Stat. 462.

19. *E.g., ex parte* Bushnell, *ex parte* Langston, 9 Ohio St. 77, 205, 227, 321 (Ohio 1859).

II. FUGITIVE SLAVES AND ENDING SLAVERY IN NEW JERSEY

The problem of fugitive slaves in New Jersey cannot be divorced from other aspects of slavery in the state partly because New Jersey was the last northern state to abolish slavery. Thus, during much of the antebellum period New Jersey was concerned about intrastate fugitives, as well as those escaping from southern bondage. This is just one of the peculiar aspects of New Jersey's relationship with the peculiar institution.[20]

During the colonial period New Jersey was the home of one of America's most important early antislavery activists, John Woolman. In 1786 Elias Boudinot and Joseph Bloomfield organized New Jersey's first antislavery society. These men were not idealists, isolated from the mainstream, but leaders in state and national politics. Boudinot was twice president of the Continental Congress, a signatory to the peace treaty with Great Britain in 1783, and a three term Congressman under the new United States Constitution. Bloomfield was an admiralty judge, state attorney general, Governor of New Jersey from 1801 to 1812, general in the War of 1812, and a Congressman.[21] Despite this early antislavery leadership, New Jersey was the last northern state to take steps to abolish slavery. New Jersey did not enact a gradual emancipation statute until 1804,[22] nearly a quarter of a century after Pennsylvania adopted the nation's first gradual emancipation act.[23]

There is also a striking contrast on state-wide abolition between New Jersey and New York. New York was also slow to join the "first emancipation,"[24] passing its act in 1799.[25] But, New York quickly made up for lost time. In 1817 New York adopted a law freeing all its slaves on July

---

20. There is no good history of slavery in New Jersey. Helpful early studies include: HENRY SCHOFIELD COOLEY, A STUDY OF SLAVERY IN NEW JERSEY (Baltimore, Johns Hopkins Press, 1896); Marion Thompson Wright, *New Jersey Laws and the Negro*, 28 J. NEGRO HIST. 156-99 (1943); Simeon F. Moss, *The Persistence of Slavery and Involuntary Servitude in a Free State (1685-1866)*, 35 J. NEGRO HIST. 289-314 (1950).

The most important recent contribution to this literature is Zilversmit, *supra* note 10, at 215-26. Also useful is Francis D. Pingeon, *Dissenting Attitudes Toward the Negro in New Jersey — 1837*, 89 N.J. HIST. 197-220 (1971).

21. The society did not draft a Constitution until 1793, when members of the older Pennsylvania Abolition Society came to Burlington, New Jersey, for the formal signing of the Constitution of the New Jersey Society. ARTHUR ZILVERSMIT, THE FIRST EMANCIPATION: THE ABOLITION OF SLAVERY IN THE NORTH 173 (1967).

22. An Act for the Gradual Abolition of Slavery, Act of February 15, 1804, *in* LAWS OF THE STATE OF NEW JERSEY 103-09 (Joseph Bloomfield ed., 1811).

23. An Act for the Gradual Abolition of Slavery, Act of March 1, 1780, *in* LAWS OF THE COMMONWEALTH OF PENNSYLVANIA 492-93 (Philadelphia, Bioren, 1810).

24. The phrase is derived from ZILVERSMIT, *supra* note 21.

25. New York Laws, 1799, Ch. LXII.

4, 1827.[26] Meanwhile, in New Jersey slavery lingered. In 1845 abolitionists tried to end the institution through litigation, but the state supreme court rejected their arguments; only the aged Chief Justice Hornblower supported them.[27] In 1846 New Jersey took a small step towards finally ending slavery. A new law changed the status of the state's remaining slaves to servants for life.[28] Although a "free state," some New Jersey blacks were still in servitude when the Civil War began. These superannuated blacks remained in a state of semi-bondage until the adoption of the Thirteenth Amendment ended all involuntary servitude in the nation.

Moreover, New Jersey was not always considered a safe haven for escaped slaves. Bondsmen from Delaware and Maryland who came into New Jersey were well advised (provided they could find advice) to continue north. In 1846 the state's only antislavery paper complained that New Jersey "still continues to be the hunting ground of the kidnapper."[29] Conversely, in the 1830's, Negrophobes in southern Cumberland County complained that they were about to be overrun by fugitive slaves. These "vicious intruders," as one racist politician called them, allegedly threatened the stability of the entire county, if not the state.[30]

Nathan Helmsley, whom Chief Justice Hornblower released from custody, illustrates the complex circumstances surrounding the treatment of fugitive slaves in New Jersey. When he resolved to leave his bondage in Maryland, Helmsley recalled, "I started for New Jersey, where, I had been told, people were free, and nobody would disturb me."[31] After his arrival, Helmsley relocated a few times to avoid capture. He managed to live in the state for a number of years before a slave catcher finally discovered and seized him. As the Helmsley case suggests, New Jersey was neither entirely hostile to fugitive slaves nor especially welcoming. New Jersey was no Vermont or New Hampshire; but neither was it a Maryland or a Virginia. Ironically, it was in this atmosphere that Chief Justice Hornblower would issue the most radically antislavery opinion in the North before the 1850's.

---

26. 1817 N.Y. Laws Ch. CXCCVII.

27. *See* State v. Post and State v. Van Beuren, 20 N.J.L. (1 Spenc.) 368 (N.J. Sup. Ct. 1845). *See also* Dan Ernst, *Legal Positivism, Abolitionist Litigation, and the New Jersey Slave Case of 1845*, 4 L. & Hist. Rev. 337 (1986).

28. Statutes of the State of New Jersey: Revised and published Under the Authority of the Legislature 567-72 (Phillips & Boswell, 1847), *reprinted in* Digest of the Law of New Jersey 801-10 (Lucius Q.C. Elmer ed., 3d ed. 1838).

29. Boonton, New Jersey Freeman, February 11, 1846, *quoted in* Clement A. Price, Freedom Not Far Distant 92 (1980).

30. Pingeon, *supra*, note 20, at 198-99.

31. Benjamin Drew, A North-Side View of Slavery. The Refugee: Or the Narratives of Fugitive Slaves in Canada 33-34 (New York Negro Univ. Press, 1868) [hereinafter Drew, North-Side View].

III. NEW JERSEY, SLAVERY, AND EARLY NATIONAL POLITICS

Despite New Jersey's slow movement towards abolition, the state's representatives in the new Congress often opposed slavery and supported the rights of free blacks. In 1793, however, all four of New Jersey's Congressmen — Elias Boudinot, Abraham Clark, Jonathan Dayton, and Aaron Kitchell — voted for the Fugitive Slave Law.[32] None of these men supported slavery. In fact, Boudinot and Dayton were known as strong opponents of slavery. The New Jersey Congressmen probably did not see their votes as proslavery. The history of the first fugitive slave law suggests that its supporters thought the law was a fair compromise between the need of slaveowners — (including those from New Jersey) to recover their fugitives, and the need of the northern states to protect their free inhabitants from kidnapping.[33] Within a few years it became clear that the Fugitive Slave Law of 1793 offered little protection to northern free blacks. In 1797 New Jersey Congressman Isaac Smith argued in favor of federal legislation to protect free blacks from kidnapping. Smith argued that it was impossible for the states to protect free blacks living within their jurisdictions from kidnapping; a kidnapper could escape arrest and prosecution upon reaching another jurisdiction. Smith was particularly worried about those free blacks who might be kidnapped and taken to the West Indies. He wanted a federal inspection law to prevent this, and could see no reason why such legislation would give "offence or cause of alarm to any gentleman."[34]

Later in this session Congressman Kitchell spoke in favor of a petition from a group of African-Americans in Philadelphia who claimed to be free, but who felt threatened by the Fugitive Slave Law of 1793. During this debate southerners argued that these blacks were in fact fugitive slaves, and that their petition was unworthy of consideration by the House. Kitchell believed that the status of the petitioners was irrelevant. He argued that Congress should accept any petition if there was merit to the claim. The only question for him was "whether a committee shall be appointed to inquire on the improper force of law" used against blacks living in the North.[35]

The House of Representatives ultimately refused to modify the Fugitive Slave Law or receive the petition of the Philadelphia blacks. The House vote was not entirely sectional; a number of congressmen from New

32. 2 ANNALS OF CONG. 861 (1793) (debate of February 5, 1793).
33. Paul Finkelman, *The Kidnapping of John Davis and The Adoption of the Fugitive Slave Law of 1793*, 56 J.S. HIST. 397 (1990).
34. 4 ANNALS OF CONG. 1767 (1797) (debate of Jan. 2, 1797).
35. *Id.*, at 2024.

England and New York voted with southerners on both issues. Firm support for the rights of free blacks came from Pennsylvania, Delaware, and New Jersey.[36] This opposition to slavery continued through the 1790's.

The relationship between slavery and national politics changed with the Jeffersonian Revolution of 1800. After 1800, New England Federalists led the opposition to slavery, while New Jersey's congressional delegation receded into the background on this issue. Aaron Kitchell, a leader of the Jeffersonians in New Jersey, shared with Jefferson a Negrophobia[37] typical of many Democrats of the era.[38] After 1801 he usually sided with his southern allies, who became increasingly proslavery.[39] Opposition to fugitive slave rendition in New Jersey would not reemerge until the 1820's and 1830s. The most significant figure of the opposition was Chief Justice Joseph C. Hornblower, who viewed himself as a political and intellectual descendant of the previous generation's Federalist Party.

---

36. These states, along with Virginia, had been the only ones to consistently oppose the slave trade compromise at the Constitutional Convention. Paul Finkelman, *Slavery and the Constitutional Convention: Making a Covenant With Death, in* BEYOND CONFEDERATION: ORIGINS OF THE CONSTITUTION AND AMERICAN NATIONAL IDENTITY 188-225 (Richard Beeman et al. eds., 1987).

37. For various discussion of Jefferson's Negrophobia see JOHN C. MILLER, WOLF BY THE EARS (1977); William Cohen, *Thomas Jefferson and the Problem of Slavery,* 56 J. AMERICAN HISTORY 503 (1969); WINTHROP JORDAN, WHITE OVER BLACK: AMERICAN ATTITUDES TOWARD THE NEGRO, 1550-1812, at 429-81 (1968); David Brion Davis, *Slavery in the Age of Revolution* 164-212 (Ithaca, Cornell Univ. Press, 1975). In *Notes on the State of Virginia* Jefferson argued that blacks' ability to "reason" was "much inferior" to whites, while "in imagination they are dull, tasteless, and anomalous," and "inferior to the whites in the endowments of body and mind." Jefferson conceded blacks were brave, but this was due to "a want of fore-thought, which prevents their seeing a danger till it be present." Jefferson could assert the equality of mankind only by excluding blacks from the picture. He admitted some qualms at reaching a "conclusion [that] would degrade a whole race of men from the rank in the scale of beings which their Creator may perhaps have given them." Nevertheless, he articulated his "suspicion" that blacks might be "originally a distinct race, or made distinct by time and circumstances" and that because of this they were "inferior to whites in the endowments of both body and mind." THOMAS JEFFERSON, NOTES ON THE STATE OF VIRGINIA 138-43 (William Peden, ed., 1954). Throughout his life he opposed freeing slaves if they would remain in white society and he constantly expressed his fears of blacks and slavery.

38. ZILVERSMIT, *supra* note 21, quotes Kitchell as declaring: "The great evil of slavery was introducing a race of people of different colour from the mass of the people. If they were the same colour, time might assimilate them together." *Id.* at 225.

39. While beyond the scope of this article, the change in direction for New Jersey after 1801 suggests that the slaveholding majority in the Jeffersonian party, which became the Democratic Party, led to the creation of northern doughfaces long before the antebellum period. A "doughface" was a term of derision applied to northern Democrats who supported slavery. Critics described their faces of "dough" to be shaped by the desires of southerners.

IV. Regulating Slaves and Freemen

The history of New Jersey's statutory regulation of slavery reveals the contradictions within the state on the issue. In 1786, New Jersey virtually abolished the further importation of slaves from Africa and from other states by establishing fines for slaves brought into the state.[40] Illegally imported slaves, however, were not freed.[41] The statute also prohibited free blacks from moving to New Jersey (which was common in the laws of the *slave* states at this time).[42] These aspects of the 1786 law characterize a state more interested in slowing the growth of its black population than in promoting liberty. This analysis is qualified, however, by the statute's provisions which encouraged private manumission and decent treatment of slaves within the state.

The statute contained an important incentive for masters who wanted to free their slaves, but who could not afford to support them in the future. It, therefore, allowed for private manumission without requiring the owner to give a bond to guarantee that the ex-slave would not become a public charge. The statute also permitted ex-slaves to remain in the state, which encouraged manumission from owners who did not want to force their slaves to choose between freedom and having to abandon friends and family. Finally, the law subjected owners to penalties if they mistreated their bondsmen.[43] This step both humanized slavery and discouraged slaveholding.

In 1788, the New Jersey legislature further restricted the slave trade and attempted to prevent the kidnapping of free blacks by prohibiting the removal of slaves from the state without their consent.[44] The 1788 Act also required slaveowners to teach their young slaves to read and write.[45] This statute contrasted sharply with the laws of the antebellum South, which generally made it a criminal offence to teach a slave to read.[46] While the

---

40. Act of March 2, 1786, *in* Acts of the Tenth General Assembly of New Jersey . . . Second Sitting (Trenton, 1786). The fines were fifty pounds for slaves imported from Africa since 1776 and twenty pounds for other blacks. Zilversmit, *supra* note 21, argues that the "fines imposed on violators were low." *Id.* at 153. It is not clear if this judgment is fair. Visitors and transients were exempt from the duty, as long as they removed the slave from the state. *See also*, Henry S. Cooley, A Study of Slavery in New Jersey 18-19 (Johns Hopkins Press, 1896).
41. In State v. Quick, 2 N.J.L. 393 (N.J. Sup. Ct. 1807), the New Jersey court refused to free a slave who was illegally transported from New York into New Jersey.
42. *Id.*
43. For a discussion of this Act, see Cooley, *supra* note 40, at 18-19.
44. Act of Nov. 25, 1788, *in* 13 N.J. Acts 1788, 486-88.
45. *Id.*
46. For one example of a southerner tried for teaching free blacks to read, see The Personal Narrative of Mrs. Margaret Douglass, A Southern Woman, Who Was

literacy provision was certainly "a step in preparing them for freedom,"[47] the New Jersey legislature was not ready to adopt a gradual emancipation scheme.[48]

These statutes made New Jersey law appear moderately antislavery.[49] The New Jersey legislature's actions were consistent with Madison's claim that New Jersey did not threaten slavery in the South.[50] His claim received further support in 1790, when the legislature refused to adopt a gradual emancipation statute. The legislature concluded that private manumission would soon end slaveholding; thus legislators saw no need for a law on the subject. Indeed, the legislature perversely argued that a gradual emancipation bill would actually delay the end of slavery in the state, and would "do more hurt than good, not only to the citizens of the State in general, but the slaves themselves."[51] There was, however, little evidence to support this conclusion.[52]

In 1798 New Jersey adopted a new comprehensive slave code as part of a general revision of the state's laws. It did not lead to an end to slavery, but modified how slaves and free would be treated in New Jersey. One significant change allowed free blacks from other states to enter New Jersey, as long as they could produce proof of their freedom.[53] This provision made New Jersey virtually unique among slave states because it allowed the unrestricted immigration of free blacks.[54]

The 1798 law also regulated fugitive slaves who entered the state and

---

IMPRISONED FOR ONE MONTH IN THE COMMON JAIL OF NORFOLK, UNDER THE LAWS OF VIRGINIA, FOR THE CRIME OF TEACHING FREE COLORED CHILDREN TO READ (John P. Jewett, 1854) *reprinted in* Series IV, 2 SLAVERY, RACE, AND THE AMERICAN LEGAL SYSTEM 1700-1872, at 373 (Paul Finkelman ed., 1988).

47. ZILVERSMIT, FIRST EMANCIPATION, *supra* note 21, at 159.

48. For an excellent analysis of New Jersey's gradual emancipation, see Zilversmit, *Liberty and Prosperity*, *supra* note 10, at 215-26.

49. *See* ROBERT MCCOLLEY, SLAVERY IN JEFFERSONIAN VIRGINIA (1972). However, no one would describe late Eighteenth Century Virginia as "antislavery," although Virginia also limited the importation of slaves and permitted manumission. An Act to Authorize the Manumission of Slaves, Laws of Virginia, 1782, Ch. LXI.

50. ROBERT YATES, THE NOTES OF THE SECRET DEBATES OF THE FEDERAL CONVENTION OF 1787, *reprinted in* THE DEBATES OF THE SEVERAL STATE CONVENTIONS ON THE ADOPTION OF THE FEDERAL CONSTITUTION, AS RECOMMENDED BY THE GENERAL CONVENTION AT PHILADELPHIA IN 1787, at 424-25 (Jonathan Elliot ed., 1836).

51. The Assembly Journal is quoted in COOLEY, *supra* note 40, at 25.

52. ZILVERSMIT, FIRST EMANCIPATION, *supra* note 21, at 161-62.

53. An Act Respecting Slaves, 1798 N. J. Laws, 307, § 27.

54. This law is cited by LEON F. LITWACK, NORTH OF SLAVERY 70 (1961), as an example of northern Negrophobia. However, New Jersey was a *slave* state at the time it adopted the law. For a slave state, this was an unusually progressive law. *See also Prelude, supra* note 13, at 432-34.

those who fled within the state.[55] The law supplemented the federal Fugitive Slave Law of 1793 by providing mandatory rewards for anyone seizing a runaway slave, and by holding liable for the full value of the slave anyone harboring or assisting the escape of a fugitive slave.[56]

In 1804, the state finally passed a gradual emancipation statute, which gave freedom to the children of all slaves born in New Jersey, but required that they serve as apprentices, the females until age twenty-one, the males until age twenty-five.[57] The legislature fine-tuned this law over the next seven years, but none of these amendments and changes significantly altered the status of slaves or affected fugitives in the state.[58]

New Jersey adopted a comprehensive revision of its slave laws in 1821. The provision of the 1798 law regarding fugitives remained intact. However, the 1821 law severely punished anyone unlawfully removing a slave or black from the state. This new provision partially resulted from petitions from Middlesex County calling for a law to "prevent kidnapping and carrying from the State blacks and other people of color."[59] New Jersey residents could not sell their slaves to out-of-state buyers, and owners who permanently left the state could take their slaves with them only under certain circumstances.[60] Persons selling a slave for illegal export were fined between five hundred and a thousand dollars, or sentenced to from one to two years at hard labor, or both. Purchasers and exporters were fined from one to two thousand dollars and sentenced to from two to four years at hard labor. Officials were empowered to search ships for blacks who were being forced out of the state, and those who

---

55. An Act Respecting Slaves, *in* 1798 N.J. LAWS 307, §§ 27, 4 to 7.

56. *Id.*

57. An Act for the Gradual Abolition of Slavery, Act of February 15, 1804, *in* LAWS OF THE STATE OF NEW JERSEY 103-09 (Joseph Bloomfield, ed. 1811).

58. An Act for the Gradual Abolition of Slavery, Act of February 15, 1804; An Act to Repeal the Third Section of an Act Entitled "An Act for the Gradual Abolition of Slavery," Passed the Fifteenth Day of February, Eighteen Hundred and Four; Act of March 8, 1806; An Additional Supplement to the Act Entitled "An Act for the Gradual Abolition of Slavery," Passed the Fifteenth Day of February, Eighteen Hundred and Four; Act of November 28, 1808; An Act Concerning the Abolition of Slavery; Act of February 22, 1811; An Act Supplementary to the Act Respecting Slaves, LAWS OF THE STATE OF NEW JERSEY 103-09, 141-143 (Joseph Bloomfield, ed., 1811).

59. Marion Thompson Wright, *New Jersey Laws and the Negro*, 28 J. NEGRO HIST. 156, 179 (1943).

60. An Act for the Gradual Abolition of Slavery, and For Other Purposes Respecting Slaves, 1820 N.J. LAWS 74-80 at §§ 11-21. Masters moving out of the state could take slaves with them, only if they had lived in the state for the previous five years, owned the slave during that time, and the slave consented to the move. There did not appear to have been any suits arguing that this statute was an unconstitutional taking of private property without compensation. *Id.*

resisted a search faced the same penalties as exporters.[61] The law did not apply to bona fide transients from other states, nor presumably to masters recovering fugitives.[62] But, the law did make fugitive slave rendition more difficult because the master or his agent had to make sure that the proper documentation was available before a removal took place.

The laws of 1788, 1798, 1804, and 1821 reflected the tension between the need to support the constitutional claims of southerners and the almost universal belief in the North that slave catching was a dirty business, to be avoided by decent people.[63] Indeed, throughout the North fugitive slaves often gained the sympathy of people who opposed abolitionists, believed in supporting the Union at all costs, and supported the South in politics. Thus, New Jersey's citizens usually did not support the return of fugitive slaves. Moreover, as the statute of 1798 indicates, they felt an obligation to protect both the liberty of their free black neighbors and to provide basic rights for the slaves living within their midst.

At the same time, however, unlike every other "free" state, New Jersey had a substantial slave population as late as the 1830s. The New Jersey legislature and no doubt many of the citizens of the state were inclined to protect the property rights of their slaveholding neighbors. Thus, in New Jersey a tension existed between protecting local slaveowners, whose human chattel might escape, and protecting free blacks living in New Jersey. The early New Jersey cases dealing with fugitive slaves illustrate this tension.

In 1795, in *State v. Heddon*,[64] the New Jersey Court of Errors heard the case of Cork, a black man who was freed during the Revolution but who was later imprisoned in Essex county as a runaway slave. A man named Snowden claimed ownership. In a habeas corpus proceeding, the court ruled that Snowden's claim to Cork was insufficient and released the alleged slave.[65]

Heddon illustrates that before 1804 New Jersey and other slave states treated blacks similarly. Officials presumed Cork was a slave, and arrested him when he appeared to be wandering about without a master. The New Jersey court never declared Cork a freeman, but only determined that

---

61. *Id.*
62. On slave transit in New Jersey, see PAUL FINKELMAN, AN IMPERFECT UNION: SLAVERY, FEDERALISM, AND COMITY 71, 76-77, 83 (1981).
63. Many southerners also considered slave catching a dirty business; but for southerners it was a necessary one.
64. 1 N.J.L. 328 (N.J. 1795).
65. *Id.* at 331 (Heddon was the jailer who held Cork).

Snowden was not his owner. Since no one else claimed him, the court ordered Cork's release from jail.

The Gradual Emancipation Act of 1804 did not end New Jersey's willingness to help return fugitive slaves. In *Nixon* v. *Story's Administrators*,[66] the trial court awarded judgment against a man who had carried slaves from New Jersey to Pennsylvania. Although the Court of Errors reversed the verdict on technical grounds, the trial court's judgment reveals the New Jersey state courts' willingness to aid slave owners seeking their runaways.[67]

In *Gibbons* v. *Morse*,[68] and again in *Cutter* v. *Moore*,[69] the New Jersey courts decided in favor of masters seeking damages from ship owners or captains who had enabled slaves to escape by giving them passage. In these cases, the courts continued to enforce the provisions of the 1798 law which punished those who helped slaves escape. In both cases the plaintiffs did not allege any intent to help the slaves escape. Neither case involved the actions of abolitionists trying to undermine slavery; such a political motive was never an issue in these civil suits. Rather, the cases involved the acts of common carriers who negligently allowed slaves to escape. In both cases the slave owners recovered for the value of their lost slaves.[70]

For all blacks in New Jersey whether free people, local slaves, or fugitives, *Gibbons* and *Cutter* set ominous precedents. In *Gibbons*, the trial judge "charged the jury, that the colour of this man was sufficient evidence that he was a slave."[71] In upholding the jury's verdict, the New Jersey Court of Errors also affirmed the rule that "the law presumes every man that is black to be a slave."[72] *Cutter* explicitly reaffirmed the *Gibbons* holding.[73] Unlike other Northeastern states, New Jersey accepted the Southern rule that all blacks were slaves until they proved otherwise.[74]

---

66. 3 N.J.L. 545 (N.J. 1813).

67. *Id.*

68. 7 N.J.L. 253 (N.J. 1821).

69. 8 N.J.L. 219 (N.J. 1825).

70. *Gibbons* 7 N.J.L., at 254; *Cutter* 8 N.J.L. at 225.

71. *Gibbons* 7 N.J.L., at 270.

72. *Id.* This point is further dramatized by the headnotes to the official report of the case, which stated the rule. "In New Jersey, all black men are presumed to be slaves until the contrary appears." *Id.* at 253.

73. *Cutter* 8 N.J.L., at 225.

74. In Boice v. Gibbons, N.J.L. 324 (N.J. 1926), the New Jersey court retreated slightly from this position, implying that being black might not lead to a *prima facie* assumption of slavery. *See also* Fox v. Lambson, 8 N.J.L. 366 (N.J. 1826).

V. THE NEW JERSEY PERSONAL LIBERTY LAW OF 1826

New Jersey fundamentally altered its approach to fugitive slave rendition in 1826 with the adoption of a new statute regulating fugitive slaves.[75] The new law required a claimant to petition a judge for a warrant ordering a county sheriff to arrest the alleged fugitive slave. The judge would then hold a hearing. If convinced that the person before him was a fugitive slave, he would issue a certificate of removal. The law was designed to provide more protection for blacks living in New Jersey than the federal Fugitive Slave Law of 1793 provided. As Chief Justice Joseph C. Hornblower noted in 1836, the New Jersey law was "more humane and better calculated to prevent frauds and oppression" than the federal statute.[76] Hornblower would also conclude, however, that this law provided inadequate protection against "frauds and oppression."

Shortly after New Jersey adopted its 1826 Act, Pennsylvania and New York passed similar laws. These laws represented "a voluntary effort to find a workable balance between a duty to protect free blacks and the obligation to uphold the legitimate claims of slave owners."[77] These laws also represented a direct challenge to federal supremacy on the subject of fugitive slave rendition. These statutes added requirements to the rendition process that had been set out in the federal law of 1793. In 1842, the United States Supreme Court declared these additional requirements unconstitutional in *Prigg v. Pennsylvania*.[78] Prior to *Prigg*, however, these laws provided additional protection for free blacks and fugitive slaves in New York, Pennsylvania, and New Jersey. These laws are also early examples of state legislatures finding independent and separate state grounds for protecting the liberty of their citizens. The Hornblower opinion similarly reflects the Nineteenth Century notion that the states, and not the federal government, were the primary guarantors of individual rights.[79] The case also underscores that in antebellum America the federal government,

---

75. A Supplement to an Act entitled "An Act Concerning Slaves," 1826 N.J. LAWS 90.

76. *Hornblower Opinion, supra* note 8, at 4.

77. THOMAS D. MORRIS, FREE MEN ALL: THE PERSONAL LIBERTY LAWS OF THE NORTH, 1780-1861, at 57 (1974). Unfortunately, Morris did not discuss or analyze the New Jersey law.

78. Prigg v. Pennsylvania, 41 U.S. (16 Pet.) 539 (1842).

79. In the Constitutional Convention, James Wilson of Pennsylvania asserted that one purpose of the states was "to preserve the rights of individuals." Similarly, Oliver Ellsworth of Connecticut explained that state governments should be looked to "for the preservation of his rights." 1 RECORDS OF THE FEDERAL CONVENTION OF 1787, at 354, 492 (Max Farrand ed. 1966). Significantly, perhaps, both Wilson and Ellsworth subsequently served on the United States Supreme Court.

predicated on a proslavery constitution and largely dominated by slave-owners, posed a greater danger to individual rights than the northern states.

VI. The Hornblower Decision

State v. The Sheriff of Burlington, an unreported case heard by the New Jersey Supreme Court in 1836, determined the meaning of the 1826 law. The case involved Alexander Helmsley, a black man living near Mount Holly, New Jersey, his wife Nancy Helmsley, and their three children. Around 1820, Helmsley, then called Nathan Mead, had escaped from bondage in Maryland. In New Jersey he married a woman who had been freed in Maryland "by word of mouth," although she had no free papers. The Helmsleys found work and raised a family of free-born children.[80]

In 1835, John Willoughby, a Maryland attorney, purchased Helmsley "running" from the executor of Helmsley's deceased master. Another Maryland attorney, R.D. Cooper, claimed Nancy and the children as his own slaves.[81] On October 24, 1835 Willoughby and Cooper secured the Helmsleys' arrest on a warrant issued by Burlington County Judge George Haywood, and had them placed in the county jail. Two days later, the Helmsleys were brought before Judge Haywood on a writ of habeas corpus, which he also issued. Following the habeas corpus hearing, Judge Haywood recommitted Alexander Helmsley to jail, while apparently releasing his wife and children. At this point, Helmsley's attorney applied to Chief Justice Hornblower for a writ of habeas corpus to bring the case before the New Jersey Supreme Court. Hornblower did not immediately issue the writ. Thus, Helmsley remained in jail until November 24, when he was brought before Judge Haywood under a second writ of habeas corpus. Once again Judge Haywood ordered the alleged fugitive returned to the jail.

Throughout proceedings, the Helmsleys' friends provided the unfortunate family with abolitionists attorneys. The hearings before Judge Haywood raised numerous questions about the identity of the arrested blacks and whether they had been previously manumitted.[82] A trial on the

---

80. Drew, North-Side View, *supra* note 31, at 33-34. Like many other fugitive slave cases, Helmsley's case was complicated by the length of time Helmsley had lived in New Jersey, the roots he had put down, and the fact that his children had been born in the free state, and thus were free persons.
81. *Upholding Slavery*, 20 The Friend 281-82 (June 11, 1836).
82. Helmsley admitted he was a fugitive slave after Chief Justice Hornblower had released him and he had moved to Canada.

status of Helmsley finally began on December 9. After intermittent proceedings over a two week period, Haywood finally declared Helmsley to be the claimants' slave, and ordered him held in jail until he could be remanded to his owners.[83]

In early December, before Judge Haywood reached his decision on the merits of the case, Helmsley's attorneys filed for a writ of certiorari to bring the case before the New Jersey Supreme Court.[84] Unfortunately, the extant court papers do not indicate the exact procedural developments. The remaining record does show, however, that in February 1836 Chief Justice Hornblower finally issued the writ of habeas corpus that Helmsley's attorney had applied for in November.[85]

On March 3, 1836, the New Jersey Supreme Court determined Helmsley's status. At this point the Helmsleys' abolitionist attorneys deferred to more prominent counsel, William Halsted and Theodore Frelinghuysen. Halsted had previously been the official reporter for the New Jersey Supreme Court. Frelinghuysen, the mayor of Newark, was a former United States Senator. Frelinghuysen was also a leader of the American Colonization Society, and not disposed to abolition. Nevertheless, he vigorously supported the claims of this black family, which suggests the potency of claims to freedom by blacks living in the North.

Hornblower began his analysis of the case by noting that the New Jersey law of 1826 was in conflict with, although not "in direct opposition to," the federal law of 1793.[86] The two laws prescribed "different modes of proceeding" and so he concluded that "[b]oth cannot be pursued at one and the same time, and one only . . . must be paramount."[87]

Hornblower concluded that the federal law provided for a "summary and dangerous proceeding" and afforded "little protection or security to the free colored man, who may be falsely claimed as a fugitive from labor."[88] The New Jersey law was "more humane." The question for the court was which law should be paramount.[89]

While acknowledging that the United States Constitution made federal laws the "supreme law of the land," Hornblower asserted that this

---

83. Application for writ of habeas corpus, in Helmsley Case file. *Upholding Slavery*, *supra* note 81. Portions of this article are reprinted as *"Important Decision,"* in THE LIBERATOR, July 30, 1836, at 124.

84. *Upholding Slavery, supra* note 81. This writ was in addition to the request for the writ of habeas corpus filed in November.

85. Application for writ of habeas corpus in Helmsley Case File.

86. *Hornblower Opinion, supra* note 8, at 1.

87. *Id.*

88. *Id.*

89. *Id.* at 4.

was true only if the law was "made in pursuance thereof" to the Constitution. In other words, if Congress had "a right to legislate on this subject" the New Jersey law was "no better than a dead letter." Hornblower, however, was unwilling to acknowledge that the Congress had exclusive power to legislate on this subject. Instead, he carefully analyzed Article IV of the Constitution.[90]

Hornblower compared the Full Faith and Credit Clause of Article IV, Section 1 with the Fugitive Slave Clause of Section 2. The first provision explicitly gave Congress the power to "prescribe the manner in which" acts, records, and proceedings of one state would be proved in another.[91] Similarly, Hornblower noted that Section 3 also explicitly empowered Congress to pass legislation.[92] But, no such language existed in Section 2 of Article IV. This led him to conclude that "no such power was intended to be given" to Congress under Section 2. Indeed, Hornblower argued that Congressional legislation over the Privileges and Immunities Clause or over intestate rendition "would cover a broad field, and lead to the most unhappy results." Such legislation would "bring the general government in conflict with the state authorities, and the prejudices of local communities." In a reference to the emerging proslavery argument in the South, Hornblower also noted that in "a large portion of the country, the right of Congress to legislate on the subject of slavery at all, even in the district [of Columbia] and territories over which it has exclusive jurisdiction, is denied." Thus, Hornblower found that Congress lacked the "right to prescribe the manner in which persons residing in the free states, shall be arrested, imprisoned, delivered up, and transferred from one state to another, simply because they are claimed as slaves." Hornblower warned that the "American people would not long submit" to such an expansive view of Congressional power.[93]

This analysis seemed to lead to only one conclusion: that the federal law of 1793 was unconstitutional. But, Hornblower insisted that it was not his "intention to express any definitive opinion on the validity of the act of Congress."[94] He thought he could avoid this grave responsibility because

---

90. *Id.*

91. "Full Faith and Credit shall be given in each State to the public Acts, Records, and judicial Proceedings of every other State; And the Congress many by general Laws prescribe the Manner in which such Acts, Records and Proceedings shall be proved, and the Effect thereof." U.S. CONST., art. IV, § 1.

92. "The Congress shall have Power to dispose of and make all needful Rules and Regulations respecting the Territory or other Property belonging to the United States. . . ." U.S. CONST., art. IV, § 3, cl. 2.

93. *Hornblower Opinion, supra* note 8, at 4-5.

94. *Id.* at 5.

the case before him had been brought "in pursuance of the law of this state."[95] However, Hornblower's position on the constitutionality of the federal law was unambiguous. He explicitly argued that Congress lacked power to pass such a law.[96] The rest of the opinion considered the constitutionality of New Jersey's 1826 statute. Though he never addressed the federal law again, Hornblower's discussion of the state law implied that the federal law of 1793 was also unconstitutional because it did not guarantee a jury trial to putative slaves, and thus violated the basic protections of due process found in the Constitution and the Bill of Rights.

Hornblower began his examination of New Jersey's 1826 law by asserting, rather than debating, "the right of state legislation on this subject." He merely assumed the state had such a right.[97] But, the right to pass a law regulating fugitive slave rendition did not automatically make such a law constitutional. Hornblower complained that the 1826 law authorized "the seizure, and transportation out of this state, of persons residing here, under the protection of our laws." He noted that these blacks might be "free-born native inhabitants, the owners of property, and the fathers of families." Yet, "upon a summary hearing before a single judge, without the intervention of a jury, and without appeal" they could be removed from the state. Rhetorically he asked, "Can this be a constitutional law?"[98]

Hornblower pointed out the possibilities of fraud and deception under the 1826 law, and noted that a black person "may be falsely accused of escaping from his master, or he may be claimed by mistake for one who has actually fled." Hornblower held that these were issues of fact; the New Jersey Constitution *required* that factual questions be determined by jury.[99]

Hornblower agreed that the Fugitive Slave Clause of the United States Constitution had to "be executed fully, fairly, and with judicial firmness and integrity;" however, the clause did not require that "the person *claimed* shall be given up." It required only that a person who actually owed service or labor "be given up" to his or her master. The question of whether the person before the Court actually owed service or labor was a factual one that only a jury could determine.[100]

Hornblower carefully distinguished between the Fugitives from

---

95. *Id.*
96. *Id.*
97. *Id.*
98. *Id.*
99. *Id.* at 6.
100. *Id.*

Justice Clause of Article IV of the Constitution[101] and the Fugitive Slave Clause.[102] Hornblower believed that the former required the surrender of an alleged criminal "on demand of the EXECUTIVE authority of the state" because the person delivered was "charged with a crime." However, a criminal charge did not guarantee a conviction. An accused person was "to be delivered up, not to be punished, not to be detained for life, but to be *tried*, and if acquitted, to be set at liberty."[103]

Alleged fugitive slaves received different treatment. They would not get a trial when returned to the claimant, but would be immediately condemned to a lifetime of bondage. With eloquent passion, Hornblower defined the issue as "whether he is to be separated forcibly, and for ever, from his wife and children, or be permitted to enjoy with them the liberty he inherited, and the property he has earned. Whether he is to be dragged in chains to a distant land, and doomed to perpetual slavery, or continue to breathe the air and enjoy the blessings of freedom." Hornblower had no difficulty declaring the law of his own state to be "unconstitutional on the ground that it deprives the accused of a trial by jury."[104]

Hornblower still had one more hurdle to overcome, before he could free the slaves before him. Although only a handful of cases involving fugitive slaves had come before American courts by this time,[105] one of the few precedents on this subject complicated Hornblower's decision. In 1819 the prestigious chief justice of Pennsylvania, William Tilghman, decided *Wright v. Deacon*,[106] a similar case involving an alleged fugitive slave held in a Pennsylvania jail. The incarcerated black had argued that under both the Pennsylvania and the United States constitutions he was entitled to a jury trial.[107]

Chief Justice Tilghman rejected this plea and asserted that "our southern brethren would not have consented to become parties to a constitution under which the *United States* have enjoyed so much

---

101. "A Person charged in any State with Treason, Felony, or other Crime, who shall flee from Justice, and be found in another State, shall on Demand of the executive Authority of the States from which he fled, be delivered up, to be removed to the State having Jurisdiction of the Crime." U.S. CONST., art. IV, § 2, cl. 2.

102. "No Person held to Service or Labour in one State, under the Laws thereof, escaping into another, shall, in Consequence of any Law or Regulation therein, be discharged from such Servitude or Labour, but shall be delivered up on Claim of the Party to whom such Service or Labour may be due." U.S. CONST., art. IV, § 2, cl.3.

103. *Hornblower Opinion, supra* note 8, at 6.

104. *Id.* at 6, 7.

105. The United States Supreme Court would not decide a case involving fugitive slaves until six years later in Prigg v. Pennsylvania, 41 U.S. (16 Pet.) 53 (1842).

106. Wright v. Deacon, 5 Serg. & Rawle 62 (Pa. 1819).

107. *Id.* at 63.

prosperity, unless their property in slaves had been secured."[108] Tilghman's interpretation of the Framers' "original intent," like so much modern intentionalist analysis,[109] had no basis in fact.[110] This mattered little to Tilghman, who reasoned that "the whole scope and tenor of the constitution and act of Congress" led to the conclusion "that the fugitive was to be delivered up, on a summary proceeding, without the delay of a formal trial in a court of common law."[111] Tilghman naively believed, or disingenuously claimed to believe, that any slave who "had really a right to freedom" could "prosecute his right in the state to which he belonged."[112] Thus, Tilghman would not release the alleged slave or grant him a jury trial.

Although *Wright* did not bind Hornblower, he could not ignore the decision because Tilghman was a prestigious judge from an important neighboring state court.[113] Hornblower boldly rejected it. He reiterated his demand for due process by attacking Tilghman's belief that an alleged fugitive could "be transported" to another state because "he will there have a fair trial." Hornblower declared, "[s]o long as I sit upon this bench, I never can, no I never will, yield to such a doctrine." Indignantly, the Chief Justice asserted:

> What, first transport a man out of the state, on the charge of his being a slave, and try the truth of the allegation afterwards — separate him from the place, it may be, of his nativity — the abode of his relatives, his friends, and his witnesses — transport him in chains to Missouri or Arkansas, with the cold comfort that if a freeman he may there assert and establish his freedom! No, if a person comes into this state, and *here* claims the servitude of a human being, whether white or black, *here* he must prove his case, and here prove it according to law.[114]

With this opinion Hornblower established a right to a jury trial for any person claimed as a slave in New Jersey. He also overruled any vestiges of

---

108. *Id.*

109. For a discussion of the failure of intentionalists to be good historians, see Paul Finkelman, *The Constitution and the Intentions of the Framers: The Limits of Historical Analysis*, 50 U. PITT. L. REV. 349-98 (1989).

110. The fugitive slave clause was added to the Constitution late in the Convention, with little debate and with no demands made by southerners for it. Rather, it seems to have been something that a few southerners wanted, and that no northerners opposed. *See* Paul Finkelman, *Slavery and the Constitutional Convention, supra* note 33 at 119-223.

111. *Wright,* 5 Serg. & Rawle, at 64.

112. *Id.*

113. Hornblower, however, did ignore a similar case from New York. *See* Jack v. Martin, 12 Wend. 311 (N.Y. Sup. Ct.) *aff'd*, 14 Wend. 507 (N.Y. 1835).

114. *Hornblower Opinion, supra* note 8, at 6.

the notion that, in New Jersey, blacks were presumed to be slaves. Finally, Hornblower established himself, and his court, as perhaps the most antislavery in the nation. Ironically, although New Jersey was the northern state with the largest number of slaves, its Supreme Court had staked out the most progressive position on the rights of blacks claimed as fugitive slaves.[115]

VII.   THE HORNBLOWER OPINION AND PERSONAL LIBERTY IN THE NORTH

Hornblower's opinion was a remarkable response to the problem of fugitive slaves. It was the first case where a state supreme court justice demanded due process protections and jury trials for alleged fugitive slaves.[116] Hornblower had rejected the reasoning and analysis of the Pennsylvania Supreme Court. Similarly, he had ignored an important (and recent) New York case, even though that case might have bolstered his position that New Jersey need not follow the federal law of 1793.[117] Hornblower's opinion was as radical as anything the new abolitionist movement demanded. Equally significant, Hornblower was ahead of moderate antislavery politicians on this issue. A comparison with other states illustrates the radical position of Hornblower.

In 1826 Pennsylvania had adopted a personal liberty law which resembled the New Jersey law of that year.[118] Although the Pennsylvania

---

115. Shortly after the case Helmsley moved to St. Catherines, Ontario, apparently believing that in the long run the British crown would provide greater protection of his liberty than would Supreme Court of New Jersey. There he became a minister and eventually bought property. *See* DREW, NORTH-SIDE VIEW, *supra* note 31, at 32-40 (narrative account of Rev. Alexander Helmsley).

116. About the same time, *the Liberator* reported that United States Supreme Court Justice Henry Baldwin decided a case in Pennsylvania in which he held that an alleged fugitive slave was entitled to a jury trial. *The Liberator* did not give the name of this case, and I have been unable to locate any records of it. THE LIBERATOR, April 16, 1836, at 62. In Prigg v. Pennsylvania, 41 U.S. 539, 636 (16 Pet.) (1842), Justice Baldwin indicated that he doubted the constitutionality of the 1793 Federal Fugitive Slave law. Baldwin did not explain his hesitancy to support the law, but it may have been because the law did not guarantee a jury trial. If so, then the *Liberator* story may in fact have some basis.

117. In Jack v. Martin, the New York Court for the Corrections of Errors denied federal power over fugitive slave rendition, while acknowledging the state's obligation to return fugitives under the Constitutional Clause in Article IV. 14 Wend. 507 (N.Y. 1835). Despite the different outcomes of the two cases, Hornblower's position was relatively close to the New York position. In finding the New Jersey law in violation of the state constitution, Hornblower implied that he might uphold a valid rendition law adopted by his state. *See Hornblower Opinion, supra* note 7, at 4.

118. An Act to Give effect to the provisions of the Constitution of the United State Relative to Fugitives From Labor, For the protection of Free People of Color, and to Prevent Kidnapping, 1826 Pa. Laws.

Abolition Society thought this law was "a manifest improvement upon the previously existing laws," the law hardly offered blacks due process.[119] Under the Pennsylvania law, a single magistrate, without the aid of a jury, would decide the status of an alleged slave. Although the law has been correctly characterized as "a compromise between what were considered the demands of the fugitive slave clause, and the responsibility to protect the personal liberty of free blacks," the 1826 act did not guarantee a jury trial, or indeed a trial of any kind, on the issue of freedom.[120] Unlike New Jersey, Pennsylvania was unwilling to move from this position in the 1830s. In 1837, a year after Hornblower's decision, the Pennsylvania legislature overwhelmingly defeated a bill to provide jury trials in fugitive slave cases. In the Pennsylvania Senate only ten of thirty-one senators present voted in favor of the bill. The House defeated the proposal by a vote of seven to ninety-three.[121]

In 1835, Massachusetts eliminated the common law remedy of the writ of *de homine replegiando* from its books. This writ had allowed alleged fugitives to try their claim to freedom before a jury. With the writ gone, and no provision for jury trial on the books, alleged fugitives in Massachusetts were at the mercy of a single magistrate and the federal law of 1793.[122]

New York presented a more complicated situation. In 1828, the state adopted a procedure to allow the return of fugitive slaves after a hearing before a judge. However, another statute[123] permitted alleged fugitives to apply for a writ *de homine replegiando*, which would have brought the question of their status before a jury.[124] In *Jack v. Martin*, the New York Supreme Court declared unconstitutional the law allowing a writ *de homine replegiando* in fugitive slave cases.[125] On appeal to the New York Court for the Correction of Errors, Chancellor Reuben Walworth held that the writ should apply to alleged slaves.[126] However, Walworth and the rest of the court ruled that Jack was a fugitive slave, and remanded him to his owner. Thus, after 1835 it was impossible to know the exact status of jury trials for alleged fugitives seized in New York. In 1838, New York abolitionists questioned candidates for governor on whether they sup-

---

119. MORRIS, *supra* note 77, at 52.
120. *Id.* at 53.
121. THE LIBERATOR, March 24, 1837, at 52 (reprinting story from the *Harrisburg Keystone*).
122. MORRIS, *supra* note 77, at 64-65.
123. *Id.* at 55-57.
124. Jack v. Martin, 12 Wend. 311, 327 (N.Y. 1834).
125. Jack v. Martin, 14 Wend. 507, 512 (N.Y. 1835).
126. Paul Finkelman, *The Protection of Black Rights in Seward's New York*, 34 CIV. WAR HIST. 211-234 (1988).

ported a jury trial in fugitive slave cases. The Democratic candidate ignored the questions while the victorious William H. Seward was evasive. Not until 1840 would Seward sign into law a bill guaranteeing a jury trial for fugitive slaves.[127]

Within a year of Hornblower's opinion the New Jersey legislature adopted a law regulating the return of fugitives from the state.[128] The law sailed through the legislature, with minimal discussion in the House and almost no debate in the Council. This statute allowed for a summary hearing before a state court, but rather than one judge deciding the case, a panel of three judges would convene. The law also provided that "if either party shall demand a trial by jury, then it shall be the duty of the said judge, before whom such fugitive shall be brought," to impanel a jury to determine the black's status. This was the first statute in the North to guarantee a jury trial for fugitive slaves. It placed New Jersey in the forefront of the emerging movement to protect free blacks and alleged fugitive slaves.[129]

In 1842, in *Prigg* v. *Pennsylvania*, the United States Supreme Court ruled that state laws which interfered with the rendition of fugitive slaves were unconstitutional. Justice Joseph Story, who upheld the constitutionality of the 1793 law, reasoned that the federal law preempted the entire question, and concluded that no state could make additional regulations for the return of fugitives.[130] Story based some of his decision on the same sort of incorrect historical analysis[131] that Judge Tilghman had used in *Wright v. Deacon*.[132] This ruling of course undermined Hornblower's opinion and

---

127. A Further Supplement to an act entitled "An Act Concerning Slaves," 1837 N.J. LAWS 134.

128. A Further Supplement to an act entitled "An Act Concerning Slaves," 1837 N.J. LAWS 134. N.J. ASSEMBLY MINUTES, 1836-37, at 331-32; N.J. COUNCIL MINUTES, 1836-37, at 192, 210-11.

129. This may be one of the earliest uses of the "preemption doctrine" in federal constitutional law, predated, perhaps, only by Gibbons v. Ogden, 22 U.S. 1 (1824).

130. For a full discussion of Story's opinion, and its implications, see Paul Finkelman, Prigg v. Pennsylvania *and Northern State Courts: Anti-Slavery Use of a Pro-Slavery Decision*, 25 CIV. WAR HIST. 5-35 (1979).

131. Story wrote:
Historically, it is well known, that the object of this clause was to secure to the citizens of the slave-holding states the complete right and title of ownership in their slaves, as property, in every state in the Union into which they might escape from the state where they were held in servitude. The full recognition of this right and title was indispensable to the security of this species of property in all the slave-holding states; and, indeed, was so vital to the preservation of their domestic interests and institutions, that it cannot be doubted, that it constituted a fundamental article, without the adoption of which the Union could not have been formed.
Prigg, 41 U.S. (16 Pet.) 536, 611 (1842).

132. 5 Serg. & Rawle 62 (Pa. 1819).

the 1837 statute. Nevertheless, when New Jersey revised its statutes in 1846 the legislature included the 1837 act.[133]

VIII. THE HORNBLOWER OPINION AND ANTISLAVERY LEGAL THEORY

Although the Hornblower opinion had some impact on New Jersey law, it had little immediate effect on the rest of the nation. The opinion was never officially reported, because, as Hornblower later explained, "it being thought best on a conference between my associates and myself not to agitate the public mind on the question of the constitutionality of the Act of Congress of 1793, then in force."[134] As an unpublished opinion, it could not provide a useful legal precedent for abolitionist attorneys. Only after it was published as a pamphlet in 1851 did the opinion become nationally significant — and then mainly as a political precedent. Moreover, Hornblower's failure to publish the opinion eventually undermined its value in New Jersey. Although the opinion probably set the stage for the adoption of New Jersey's personal liberty law of 1837,[135] as knowledge of it diminished, its utility as a precedent disappeared.

The failure to officially publish the opinion limited access to newspaper accounts of the case, which had two consequences. First, as previously mentioned it undermined the opinion as a precedent. Second, it led to conflicting interpretations of exactly what the opinion said.

The first newspaper account of the case was in *The Friend*, published in Philadelphia by antislavery Quakers. This report did not appear until June, 1836, three months after the decision.[136] A month later the nation's leading antislavery newspaper, *The Liberator*, reprinted this article, under the headline "Important Decision." *The Liberator* favorably quoted one of Helmsley's original abolitionist attorneys, who declared "this day" was "the brightest that has dawned upon this unfortunate race of beings since the year 1804, and the proudest which has occurred in our judicial history, since we became a state."[137]

At about the same time another abolitionist periodical, *The Emanci-*

---

133. An Act Concerning Fugitive Slaves, STATUTES OF THE STATE OF NEW JERSEY. REVISED AND PUBLISHED UNDER THE AUTHORITY OF THE LEGISLATURE 567-72 (Trenton: Phillips & Boswell, 1847).

134. Letter from Hornblower to J. C. Ten Eyck (April, 1860) (in Hornblower Papers, Box 1, (NJHS)).

135. Act of Feb. 15, 1837. A Further Supplement to an act entitled "An Act Concerning Slaves." 1837 N.J. LAWS 134.

136. *Upholding Slavery*, 20 THE FRIEND 281-82 (June 11, 1836).

137. *Important Decision*, THE LIBERATOR, July 20, 1836, at 124.

pator, reprinted the original article from *The Friend*. The *Emancipator* article concluded by summarizing three major points of Hornblower's decision: (1) that the federal fugitive slave law of 1793 was unconstitutional; (2) that all people in New Jersey had a right to a jury trial; and (3) that "the color of a person should be no longer considered as presumptive evidence of slavery" in New Jersey.[138] Meanwhile, the *New York Evening Star* also wrote about the decision. The *Evening Star*, basing its assessment of the case on the story in the *Emancipator*, editorialized that under this decision New Jersey had become "an asylum of fugitive slaves" where owners lacked "any hope of recovering such property."[139]

Both newspaper reports were somewhat inaccurate. Hornblower had not declared the federal law of 1793 unconstitutional, although his opinion certainly led to that conclusion. The *Emancipator's* assertion that fugitive slaves were entitled to a jury trial and that blacks were presumptively free did accurately reflect Hornblower's opinion. However, the view of the *Evening Star* — that New Jersey had become an "asylum" for fugitive slaves — was clearly an exaggeration, although if Hornblower's decision had been vigorously adopted throughout the state, slave catching would have become quite difficult.

In August the *Newark Daily Advertiser* commented on the decision in less flattering terms.[140] Unhappy with the decision and with public perceptions of it, the *Daily Advertiser* began its comment by quoting briefly from the stories in *The Emancipator* and the *New York Evening Star*.[141] The *Daily Advertiser* believed these newspaper reports had created an erroneous impression that needed to be countered.

But, if the reports of the case in *The Emancipator* and the *New York Evening Star* were incorrect, so too was the report in the *Daily Advertiser*. This paper stated that the "only point *decided* by the Court was, that upon the facts of the case, . . . the prisoner was entitled to be discharged *out of jail*." The paper conceded that all blacks in the state were presumed free, but inaccurately denied that Hornblower had spoken to this point. The *Daily Advertiser* stressed the unpublished status of Hornblower's opinion, and declared that it was therefore not a precedent. The paper complained

---

138. *Important Decision*, NEWARK DAILY ADVERTISER, Aug. 18, 1836 (quoting *The Emancipator*).

139. *Id.* (quoting the *New York Evening Star*). I have been unable to locate this story in any microfilm editions of the *New York Evening Star*. This leads me to conclude that the microfilm editions of the *Star* are incomplete, or that the *Advertiser* mistakenly quoted the *Star*, when in fact it should have attributed the quotation to another paper.

140. NEWARK DAILY ADVERTISER, Aug. 18, 1836.

141. The *Daily Adver.iser* was apparently unaware that the story in *The Emancipator* had originally appeared in *The Friend*.

that "an obscure partizan press" (like the *Emancipator*) published misleading articles about the law by "catching reports of cases . . . from the lips of lookers-on, and spreading them before the world as decisions." The *Daily Advertiser* feared that other papers would make the same mistake as the *Evening Star* and believe the report in the *Emancipator* which would lead to a "kindling [of] prejudice and passion" in "the Southern States, against one of the most respectable legal tribunals in the country."[142]

The fears of the *Daily Advertiser* were unfounded. Because Hornblower's opinion was unreported, few in the state knew of it. Moreover, shortly after the decision, abolitionists in New Jersey discovered that their victory was incomplete. In deciding the case, Chief Justice Hornblower had declared the state act of 1826 unconstitutional. Other judges in the state apparently accepted this finding, but with ironic results.

While declaring the state law void under the New Jersey Constitution, Hornblower did not rule on the constitutionality of the federal law — in part because he did not have to, and in part because he apparently did not want to directly confront the national government. The result left New Jersey's free blacks and fugitives slaves in a worse position than before the decision. The 1826 New Jersey law had offered fugitive slaves more protection than the federal law, although not as much as Hornblower demanded. But with the 1826 act no longer in force, slave catchers could still use the federal law of 1793.

The irony of Hornblower's opinion revealed itself in August, 1836 when a Severn Martin, a black man living in Burlington, New Jersey, was arrested as a fugitive slave and brought before a county magistrate. Martin had lived in the area for seventeen years and there was little evidence that he was a slave. Only the "energy and judgment displayed by the Mayor" prevented a riot when several hundred people "attempted to rescue" Martin.[143] With calm restored, a magistrate, applying the rather loose evidentiary standards of the federal law of 1793, remanded Martin to the man who claimed to be his owner. The claimant quickly removed Martin. He subsequently gained his freedom when his New Jersey friends raised $800 to purchase him.[144]

---

142. NEWARK DAILY ADVERTISER, Aug. 18, 1836.

143. NEW JERSEY EAGLE, Aug. 19, 1836.

144. *The Slave Case*, BURLINGTON GAZETTE, Aug. 20, 1836, partially reprinted as *The Slave Case*, NEW JERSEY STATE GAZETTE, Aug. 26, 1836. BURLINGTON GAZETTE, Sept. 10, 1836; *Severn Martin, Case of Severn Martin*, THE LIBERATOR, Sept. 17, 1836, at 151. The *New Jersey Eagle*, a Democratic paper in Newark praised the outcome of this case, and suggested that purchasing the slave, as was done by the people of Burlington

Because this "atrocious case occurred in New Jersey," the Philadelphia paper *Human Rights* rhetorically asked "what has become of the decision of Chief Justice Hornblower?" The paper concluded that the decision was "inoperative" because it had declared the state law, but not the federal law, unconstitutional, even though the latter also denied a right to trial by jury.[146] The New Jersey legislature remedied this problem at its next session, when it passed the 1837 law giving alleged fugitive slaves greater legal protections than they had previously enjoyed, including the right to demand a jury trial.[146]

IX. The Resurrection of the Hornblower Opinion

Because Hornblower's opinion was never officially reported, judges and abolitionist lawyers generally did not cite the decision in other fugitive slave cases. One exception was Salmon P. Chase, the "attorney general for fugitive slaves," who cited a newspaper account of Hornblower's opinion in attempting to free the slave Matilda in 1837.[147] At the time, however, Chase had not seen a complete report of the opinion. With the emergence of a new fugitive slave law in 1850, Hornblower and his 1836 opinion gained new fame.

In April, 1851, Chase, by this time a U.S. Senator, sent Hornblower a copy of his brief[148] to the United States Supreme Court in the fugitive slave case of *Jones v. Van Zandt.*[149] Chase also sent Hornblower a copy of a speech he had given on the new fugitive slave law. Chase did not know Hornblower, but Chase often sent copies of his speeches and legal arguments to strangers who might agree with his position.[150] In his letter, Chase mentioned that he had cited the 1836 *Sheriff of Burlington* opinion

---

"should be imitated in all similar cases; instead of attempting to defraud the rightful owner of his property." *As It Should Be,* NEW JERSEY EAGLE, Aug. 26, 1836.

145. *Human Rights, quoted in,* THE LIBERATOR, Sept. 17, 1836, at 151.

146. A Further Supplement to an act entitled "An Act Concerning Slaves." Act of Feb. 15, 1837 N.J. LAWS, 134.

147. *Speech of Salmon P. Chase, in the Case of the Colored Woman, Matilda reprinted in* 2 SOUTHERN SLAVES IN FREE STATE COURTS: THE PAMPHLET LITERATURE No. 1, at 1 (Paul Finkelman ed., 1987). Chase quoted from the story about Hornblower's decision in THE LIBERATOR, July 30, 1836, at 124, but did not cite to the story.

148. This brief was published in pamphlet form as SALMON P. CHASE, RECLAMATION OF FUGITIVES FROM SERVICE *reprinted in* 1 FUGITIVE SLAVES AND AMERICAN COURTS: THE PAMPHLET LITERATURE No. 2, at 341 (Paul Finkelman ed., 1988).

149. 46 U.S. (5 How.) 215 (1847).

150. PAUL FINKELMAN, SLAVERY IN THE COURTROOM 74 (1985).

in Matilda's case, and Chase asked Hornblower for a copy of that opinion.[151]

Hornblower immediately responded with a gracious and lengthy letter thanking Chase for the material he had sent. He praised the "noble stand" the Ohio Senator had "taken in behalf of right; in behalf of law; of justice; humanity, of the Constitution, of patriotism, of philanthropy, of universal emancipation of the human race in body & mind, and of all that is calculated to elevate our fellow men, to the dignity of manhood." Hornblower complained that the "sacred . . . soil of New Jersey, consecrated by the blood of our fathers, in their struggles for human liberty, is now desecrated by the feet of bloodhounds pursuing their victims" and that "Jerseymen" and all "other free Americans" faced fines or imprisonment if they refused to "join in the chase."[152]

Hornblower concluded his four page letter by explaining to Chase that in Helmsley's case he had prepared a long opinion, but did not actually read it from the bench. Instead, he orally summarized of his points. Although it now lay in his "mass of miscellaneous unfinished" writings, Hornblower promised to find the opinion and send it to Chase.[153]

Shortly after Chase asked for a copy of the opinion, William Dayton, a former United States Senator from New Jersey, also asked for a copy. Dayton had served on the Senate judiciary committee during the debates over the Fugitive Slave Law of 1850, and he regretted that he had not had access to Hornblower's opinion then.[154]

Whether Hornblower sent either Chase or Dayton a complete copy of the opinion is unclear. However, in the spring and summer of 1851, the long-dormant opinion was revived. In the early summer of 1851 an antislavery convention in Ohio read Hornblower's opinion and ordered it published.[155] The convention may have obtained the text of the opinion from Chase (who was from Ohio) or some old newspaper account.

Meanwhile, portions of Hornblower's letter to Chase were reprinted in newspapers, and were "extensively disseminated by the press."[156] The

---

151. Letter from Salmon P. Chase to Hornblower (April 3, 1851) (in Hornblower Papers, Box 2, NJHS).

152. Letter from Hornblower to Chase (April 9, 1851) (in Salmon P. Chase Papers, Library of Congress).

153. *Id.*

154. Letter from William L. Dayton to Hornblower (September 9, 1851) (in Hornblower Papers, box 2, NJHS). Dayton would be the Republican candidate for Vice President in 1856, and serve as New Jersey's attorney general from 1857 to 1861, when Lincoln appointed him Minister to France.

155. N.Y. Evening Post, Aug. 1, 1851.

156. Letter from William Jay to Hornblower (July 17, 1851) (typescript in the Jay

excerpts from the letter included references to the *Sheriff of Burlington* case. These newspaper accounts prompted William Jay to write Hornblower praising him for his antislavery position. Jay, the son of Chief Justice John Jay, was especially pleased to find a "gentleman moving in" Hornblower's "sphere" — that is, to say a bona fide upper class American Brahmin — who also opposed slavery.[157] Hornblower then offered to send a copy of his opinion to Jay, which he did by the end of July.[158]

Hornblower sent the original manuscript opinion to Jay, who excitedly read it and then sent it to New York City for publication. On July 30, 1851 the opinion appeared on the front page of the *New York Evening Post*. Jay also arranged for publication and distribution of the opinion in pamphlet form.[159] Jay told Hornblower he could have "as many copies of the pamphlet as [he] might desire," since the pamphlet had been published for "gratuitous distribution."[160]

Printed with the opinion were a short unsigned commentary (written by Jay) quoting Massachusetts Senator Daniel Webster's "Seventh of March Speech,"[161] and a short attack on Webster. The commentary was followed by an extract from a letter from Hornblower to Jay[162] which also attacked Webster and the Fugitive Slave Law of 1850.

The commentary, and the quotations from Webster and Hornblower, supported the position that fugitive slave rendition should be a state matter. The pamphlet quoted Webster's "Seventh of March" speech where he declared:

> "I have always thought that the constitution addressed itself to the legislatures of the states themselves, or to the states themselves. It says that

---

Family Papers, on file in the Rare Book and Manuscript Library, Columbia University. Letters from this collection are cited and quoted with permission of the library. The letter of July 17 is misdated on the typescript as 1850).

157. Letters from William Jay to Hornblower (July 11, 1851, July 17, 1851, July 21, 1851 and July 29, 1851).

158. Letters from William Jay to Hornblower (July 21, 1851) (thanking Hornblower for a copy of the manuscript opinion); (July 29, 1851) (indicating the opinion has been "forwarded to . . . New York, & it will I trust be soon in print.").

159. *See supra*, note 8.

160. Letter from Jay to Hornblower (Sept. 3, 1851).

161. *Cong. Globe*, 31 Cong., 1 Sess. app. at 269-76. Webster gave this speech on March 7, 1850 in support of the Compromise of 1850 and the proposed Fugitive Slave Law. The speech shocked many northerners, who expected Webster to represent the overwhelmingly antislavery sentiments of Massachusetts. *See* DAVID POTTER, THE IMPENDING CRISIS 1848-1861, at 101-02 (1976); MAURICE BAXTER, ONE AND INSEPARABLE: DANIEL WEBSTER AND THE UNION 413-27 (1984).

162. Letter from Jay to Hornblower (July 29, 1851) (Jay Family Papers); Letter from Hornblower to Chase (September 16, 1851) (in Chase Papers, L.C.); *The New York Evening Post*, July 30, 1851, and the *Hornblower Opinion*, at 7.

those persons escaping into other states[] shall be delivered up, and I confess I have always been of opinion that it was an injunction upon the states themselves."[163]

Jay quoted Webster on this issue to make two points. First, if the "constitution addressed . . . the states," then the federal laws of 1793 and 1850 were unconstitutional (as Hornblower had intimated in 1836), and the states should protect the rights and freedom of blacks through appropriate legislation. While not using the term, Jay's point was that 'adequate and independent state grounds' existed to protect free blacks from kidnapping and to insure that alleged fugitive slaves received due process. Second, if this position was correct, then Webster, who had become an anathema to many Northerners — a "monster,"[164] a "fallen angel,"[165] "incredibly base and wicked"[166] — was further exposed as a hypocrite whose only concern was his political ambition.[167]

Jay and his fellow abolitionists gave away this pamphlet because they believed that Hornblower's opinion was an invaluable asset to their antislavery constitutionalism.[168] Unlike most antislavery propaganda, this assault on the fugitive slave laws was not written by an abolitionist. Rather, the opinion came from the respected chief justice of a very conservative northern state. This increased the opinion's credibility and its potential impact on northern society.

Even before the *Evening Post* printed the full text of Hornblower's manuscript, the opinion was apparently circulating within the antislavery

---

163. *Hornblower Opinion, supra* note 8, at 7.

164. DAVID POTTER, THE IMPENDING CRISIS 1848-1861, at 132 (1976).

165. In the poem *Ichabod* the poet John Greenleaf Whittier wrote:
Of all we loved and honored, naught
    Save power remains;
A fallen angel's pride of thought,
    Still strong in chains.
All else is gone; from those great eyes
    The soul has fled:
When faith is lost, when honor dies,
    The man is dead!
JOHN G. WHITTIER, THE POLITICAL WORKS OF WHITTIER 186-87.

166. DAVID POTTER, THE IMPENDING CRISIS 1848-1861, at 132 (Hyatt H. Waggoner ed., 1975).

167. "His more enduring reputation is probably the one originated by the antislavery 'Conscience Whigs' of Webster's party. They pictured him as a fallen Lucifer, who, in his support of the Fugitive Slave Law in the compromise package of 1850, had sold out all his principles to his own ambitions for the Presidency and to his commercial clients." Robert W. Gordon, *The Devil and Daniel Webster*, 94 YALE L.J. 445, 455 (1984).

168. *See generally* WILLIAM M. WIECEK, THE SOURCES OF ANTISLAVERY CONSTITUTIONALISM, 1760-1848 (1977).

movement. The potential impact of Hornblower's denunciation of the Fugitive Slave Law of 1793 and his support of due process for blacks became clear in the wake of the adoption of the Fugitive Slave Law of 1850. Finally, in early August 1851, Jay's pamphlet printing of the opinion began to circulate. Although they had asked Hornblower for a copy of the opinion before Jay did, neither Chase nor Dayton may have seen the full opinion before Jay had it published that August 1851.

After reading the full opinion, Chase complimented Hornblower and expressed his regret that the opinion had not been "printed and generally circulated" when first delivered, because it would "certainly have done much good." Chase thought that Hornblower's opinion might have prevented the "promulgation of the consolidation doctrines of constitutional construction" accepted by many "from whom better things might have been expected."[169]

The flurry of activity surrounding the opinion dissipated in 1851, but reemerged during the crisis over the Kansas-Nebraska Act in 1854. That year the *Trenton State Gazette* reprinted the opinion as a front page story.[170] It noted that "although delivered before the passage of the fugitive law of 1850, its arguments are such as will apply to that and all other laws passed by Congress for the rendition of fugitives." The paper endorsed Hornblower's argument that a jury trial was necessary for the return of a fugitive slave.

A few months later, Horace Greeley's *New York Tribune* cited the Hornblower opinion to argue that judges should oppose the Fugitive Slave Law of 1850, which the paper believed violated "reason and the vital principles of the Constitution."[171] The Tribune praised the Wisconsin Supreme Court for declaring the law unconstitutional in the case that would eventually be heard by the United States Supreme Court in *Ableman v. Booth*.[172] The paper noted that "Chief Justice Hornblower of New Jersey, sometime ago led the way in an elaborate opinion denying the power of Congress to legislate on the subject of fugitive slaves."[173]

In the legal conflicts caused by the Fugitive Slave Law of 1850, the

---

169. Letter from Chase to Hornblower (Oct. 21, 1851) (on file in Box 2, Hornblower Papers, NJSH).

170. TRENTON STATE GAZETTE, June 15, 1854 (reprinting the Hornblower Opinion from the N.Y. EVENING POST, Aug. 1, 1851). The article in the *New York Evening Post* is identical to the seven page pamphlet, cited as *Hornblower Opinion. See supra* note 7.

171. *The Fugitive Law Beginning to Tumble*, N.Y. TRIB., July 12, 1854, at 4.

172. *Id.* The Wisconsin case of *In re* Booth and Rycraft, 3 Wis. 157 (1854), held that Congress lacked the authority to pass the fugitive slave law of 1850. This decision was appealed, and reversed, in Ableman v. Booth, 63 U.S. (21 Haw.) 506 (1858).

173. *The Fugitive Law Beginning to Tumble*, N.Y. TRIB., July 12, 1854, at 4.

Ohio Supreme Court saw Hornblower's opinion as a valid precedent, although members of that court disagreed on its meaning. Both majority and dissenting judges cited Hornblower's opinion in *Ex parte Bushnell, Ex parte Langston,*[174] a case growing out of the famous Oberlin-Wellington rescue.[175] Simeon Bushnell and Charles Langston were in jail, under federal process, for their role in rescuing a fugitive slave. Concurring in the decision not to order the release of Bushnell and Langston, Justice Peck noted that in 1836

"Ch. J. Hornblower, of New Jersey . . . expressed doubts as to the validity of the act of 1793, on the ground of a want of constitutional power to pass it, and also of the validity of the act of New Jersey; but declined to declare either law invalid, and finally discharged the prisoner, because the proceedings did not conform to the requirements of the act of the State of New Jersey."[176]

In dissent, Justice Jacob Brinkerhoff, an abolitionist disciple of Salmon P. Chase, found that Hornblower's opinion, along with Chancellor Walworth's New York opinion in *Jack v. Martin,* "shows that the question [of federal power to pass a fugitive slave law] is not settled."[177] Justice Sutliff also dissented, and cited both Hornblower and Walworth for the proposition that the Fugitive Slave Clause of the United States Constitution "vests no power in the federal government" to adopt legislation.[178]

In 1860, the Senate debated the Hornblower opinion. In March 1860, Ohio Senator Benjamin F. Wade conceded that Congressional jurisdiction over fugitive slave rendition had been accepted, "the courts having adjudicated that point against my opinions," but he argued that "no lawyer would agree with the courts, were it a case of the first impression." He disputed that American courts had been unanimous on this question, as Senator Robert Toombs of Georgia had asserted. Wade stated that "Judge Hornblower, of New Jersey, on *habeas corpus,* held the law [of 1793] unconstitutional, and discharged the fugitive for that reason."[179] Wade slightly exaggerated Hornblower's holding. Hornblower never reached the constitutionality of the federal law, because the case came before him under the state statute.

Less than a month later, New Jersey's Senator John C. Ten Eyck

---

174. 9 Ohio St. 77 (1859).
175. Jacob R. Shipherd, History of the Oberlin-Wellington Rescue (Boston, John F. Jewett and Co. 1859).
176. 9 Ohio St., at 205 (Peck, J., concurring).
177. 9 Ohio St., at 321 (Brinkerhoff, J. dissenting).
178. 9 Ohio St., at 321 (Sutliff, J. dissenting).
179. Cong. Globe, 36th Cong., 1st Sess. App. at 152 (debate of March 7, 1860).

attempted to clarify the facts of the *Sheriff of Burlington* case. He told the Senate that Hornblower had not in fact declared the 1793 law unconstitutional, but had freed the slaves before him "on the ground of defective evidence."[180] This was also an incorrect statement of the case.

The speeches by Wade and Ten Eyck led to some correspondence between Hornblower and his senator. In a letter to Ten Eyck, Hornblower reaffirmed his position in the case and his opposition to remanding fugitive slaves without jury trials. Hornblower also noted that the two other judges on the court, "both of them my *political* opponents," agreed with him. One of his opponents, Judge Ford, was himself a slaveholder with family ties to South Carolina. Nevertheless, the New Jersey justices were unanimous in their decision to discharge the Helmsleys. Hornblower believed that Senator Ten Eyck, or Hornblower's "friend," the more radical Benjamin Wade, should bring these facts before the Senate.[181]

By 1860, the Hornblower opinion had become part of the Union's growing crisis. In 1836, Hornblower had argued that the powers of Congress in Article IV were strictly limited. These powers did not include the right to legislate over fugitive slaves. This right, he believed, was reserved for the states. Hornblower's position, however, had been rejected by the Congress in 1793, by the Supreme Court in 1842, and again by the Congress in 1850.

In 1860, the eighty-three-year-old Hornblower suggested that the defeat of his position might yet help promote the antislavery movement. Hornblower urged Ten Eyck, or some other senator, to "introduce a bill in Congress to secure to citizens of this or any other state the same 'immunities', they enjoy here, in every other state, or in other words, to carry into effect the provision of that section."[182] Hornblower's logic was clear. *If* Congress had the power to pass legislation to enforce the Fugitive Slave Clause of Article IV of the Constitution, then Congress also had the power to enforce the Privileges and Immunities Clause of Article IV. Hornblower believed that such a bill would "add fuel to the fire already burning in the South [and] what is now comparatively a small combustion will become a volcano."[183] The retired justice may by this time have regretted not publishing his 1836 decision, for he no longer thought that

---

180. CONG. GLOBE 36th Cong., 1st Sess., Pt. 2 1486 (debate of April 2, 1860).

181. Letter from Hornblower to John C. Ten Eyck (Apr., 1860) and letter from Hornblower to Ten Eyck (Apr. 16, 1860) (both on file at Hornblower Papers, Box 1, NJHS).

182. Letter from Hornblower to John C. Ten Eyck (Apr. 16, 1860) (on file at Hornblower Papers, Box 1, NJHS).

183. *Id.*

deference to the South, or federal power, was the answer to the problem of slavery in the nation.

THE FUGITIVE SLAVE LAW:
A Double Paradox [1]

Larry Gara

THE FUGITIVE Slave Law of 1850, as one of the compromise measures of that year, was meant to help quiet the explosive slavery issue and to remove it from the realm of political discussion. Instead, the law operated to keep the slavery question alive and to assure its inclusion in the political debates of the 1850's. This irony of political life was matched by another: that a measure which substantially increased the power of the general government was demanded by a section whose spokesmen consistently relied upon the arguments of state sovereignty for the protection of their interests.[2] The law was actually as much concerned with constitutional obligations as with the problem of returning fugitive slaves. Yet by its very nature it was a concession to nationalism, and a recognition by the South that when problems exceeded the ability of states to solve them the power of the national government should be brought into play.

The fugitive slave issue became an explosive one in the Southern states after the 1842 Supreme Court decision in *Prigg* v. *Pennsylvania*. In that decision the majority of the court declared unconstitutional a Pennsylvania personal liberty law because it interfered with the federal fugitive slave act of 1793. The court held that the constitutional obligation to return fugitive slaves was exclusively a federal responsibility, and this part of the decision opened the way for a new series of personal liberty laws which usually forbade state officials from participating in the arrest or return of runaways from slavery. Since the 1793 statute depended upon enforcement by state officials, the Northern

[1] This article is based, in part, upon research made possible by a grant from the Penrose Fund of the American Philosophical Society. In slightly modified form the article was read at the annual meeting of the Mississippi Valley Historical Association in Cleveland, May 1, 1964.

[2] Arthur Bestor has pointed out the constitutional significance of the doctrine of state sovereignty and asserted that in its last analysis it was a docrine of power rather than of rights and operated to make slavery a national rather than a local institution. See Bestor, "State Sovereignty and Slavery: A Reinterpretation of Proslavery Constitutional Doctrine, 1846-1860," *Journal of the Illinois State Historical Society*, LIV (1961), 117-180.

state laws rendered it largely ineffective. Not surprisingly, a demand for new federal legislation followed from Southern spokesmen.[3]

The issues at stake were far more important than the monetary value of any slaves who might escape north.[4] A fugitive slave recaptured was worth little as a chattel and slave dealers found such "property" difficult to sell even at greatly reduced prices. In 1850 Virginia's Senator James Murray Mason opposed a clause in the proposed fugitive slave measure which provided a possible jury trial for a fugitive in the state from which he had fled. Mason's objection was that such a requirement would prevent the master from selling the runaway immediately after recapture. Such quick sale was usually advisable, said Senator Mason, "first, on account of the example, and, secondly, because by absconding he has forfeited the confidence of his owner."[5]

The example of a successful flight was indeed a serious problem for those who claimed title to slave property. Abolitionists and slave-owners alike recognized that the influence of escapes on those remaining in slavery was considerable. In 1857 J. Miller McKim, a Philadelphia abolitionist, reported an increased number of escapes and remarked that "the tenure by which slave property is held all along our borders, is greatly weakened by these multiplying flights. Human chattels, even when but partially enlightened, constitute a very uncertain sort of possession." Dr. Robert Collins, the owner of Ellen Craft, who had fled from slavery, expressed similar sentiments. "Every slave who gains his freedom by flight from the south, and by protection from the north," he said, "presents his fellow slaves the temptation to follow in his footsteps and find the same freedom."[6]

Although fears of a mass exodus from slavery, always uppermost in the minds of the slaveholders, proved largely unfounded, Southern political leaders could not afford to ignore them. Such apprehension often seemed justified in the border states where the majority of successful escapes from slavery originated. In arguing for passage of the 1850 Fugitive Slave Law, Kentucky's Henry Clay pointed out that with

---

[3] Henry Steele Commager (ed.), Documents of American History (6th ed.; New York, 1958), pp. 292-295; Julius Yanuck, "The Fugitive Slave Law and the Constitution" (Ph.D. dissertation, Columbia University, 1953), p. 21.

[4] The number and actual value of slaves who escaped north is very difficult to determine. Southern spokesmen often exaggerated the monetary loss to the South, and official census figures undoubtedly underestimated the number when they indicated that about a thousand slaves a year escaped. For a discussion of this point see Larry Gara, The Liberty Line: The Legend of the Underground Railroad (Lexington, 1961), pp. 36-40.

[5] Congressional Globe, 31 Cong., 1 sess., Appendix, pt. 1, p. 649.

[6] J. Miller McKim, "The Slave's Ultima Ratio," in The Liberty Bell. By Friends of Freedom (Boston, 1858), pp. 326-327; Dr. Robert Collins to J. S. Hastings, Apr. 8, 1851, Theodore Parker Scrapbook, Boston Public Library.

the possible exception of Virginia, his state suffered more than any other "by the escape of slaves to adjoining States." He charged further that it was "at the utmost hazard and insecurity of life itself" that a Kentuckian could cross the Ohio river "and go into the interior and take back the fugitive slave to the State from which he has fled."[7]

Slaveholders tended to blame abolitionist agitation and Northern interference for slave escapes and it was in relation to this phase of the problem that the very significant constitutional issues emerged. Article IV, Section Two, of the Constitution clearly implied that fugitives from labor who escaped into another state should be delivered to their masters, though the word "slave" was carefully avoided. In light of this constitutional obligation spokesmen for the South argued that the Northern states' personal liberty laws involved a breach of faith more serious than the mobs which attempted to rescue recaptured fugitives. In 1848 a committee of the Virginia legislature expressed the sentiments of many Southern groups when it proclaimed that "the south is wholly without the benefit of that solemn constitutional guaranty which was so sacredly pledged to it at the formation of this Union." In his Seventh of March speech Daniel Webster agreed with many of his Southern colleagues that, in the matter of the return of fugitive slaves, "the South is right, and the North is wrong."[8]

To nineteenth-century Americans such constitutional questions were more than abstractions. They were truly vital issues—issues which, when added to such other divisive questions as economic interests, moral viewpoints and sectional pride, became highly explosive. Few questions were argued more heatedly than the nature of the government and the role of supposedly sovereign states within that government in the years before the Civil War. Furthermore, the debate took place at the same time that the industrial and transportation revolutions were raising new questions in the minds of many Americans concerning the nature of representative forms of government and the issues of central versus local self-government. It is in this light that the South's interest in a more stringent fugitive slave measure assumes importance far beyond that of the slaveholder's interest in returning individual fugitives. Even though the owner of an escaped slave might not particularly care to have him back in slavery he considered it his *right* to recapture him if he wished and the Northern states had an obligation guaranteed by the Constitution to assist him.

[7] *Congressional Globe*, 31 Cong., 1 sess., pt. 1, p. 123.
[8] *Report of the Select Committee Appointed under a Resolution of the House to Enquire into the Existing Legislation of Congress upon the Subject of Fugitive Slaves, and to Suggest such Additional Legislation as may be Proper* ([Richmond, 1848], Virginia General Assembly, 1848-1849 [House of Delegates], Document No. 50), p. 11; *Congressional Globe*, 31 Cong., 1 sess., p. 481.

The Fugitive Slave Law of 1850 was supposed to proffer the resources of the federal government towards that end.[9]

Even those who supported the new law admitted it was severe. The pro-compromise Cincinnati *Enquirer*, for example, deplored the absence of any provision for the alleged fugitive to testify on his own behalf.[10] The law created a new official, a commissioner, with special responsibility to enforce its provisions. Alleged fugitives could be arrested with or without warrants, were given only summary hearings, and could be returned on the sworn testimony of the masters or their agents. Any citizen could be summoned to aid in the capture of a fugitive slave and interference with the law was punishable by a fine of up to one thousand dollars and six months' imprisonment.[11] Opponents of the law correctly charged that the suspected fugitive was denied all semblance of due process of law, though this had also been a feature of the earlier statute. Years later Supreme Court Justice John M. Harlan noted that "Congress omitted from it nothing which the utmost ingenuity could suggest as essential to the successful enforcement of the master's claim to recover his fugitive slave."[12]

The law was the major concession to the South in the 1850 compromise measures. Southern moderates voiced the hope that it would be accepted in the North and enforced in such a way as to quiet the complaints of the more extremist spokesmen for Southern rights. "This law alone is worth far more to the slave-holders of the South than the running of the Missouri Compromise line through California, or anything of the kind could have been," commented a Kentucky newspaper. When the bill passed the Senate a Virginia editor voiced his belief "that a mob would respect the U.S. marshal, armed with all the power of the general government," and that the law "would be efficient in securing the constitutional rights of the slave power."[13]

Overlooked by many Southerners was the fact that the new Fugitive Slave Law involved a considerable expansion of federal power. Just as interest groups in other sections were looking to the federal government for such forms of aid as protective tariffs, internal improvement projects, and free homesteads, the South was demanding that federal power be used in order to protect its interests within the Union. Indeed, many Southern leaders insisted that strict enforcement of the

---

[9] Although some abolitionists denied that the North had any constitutional obligation to return fugitive slaves, the majority of them preferred to rely on the "higher law" docrine to justify interference with the federal statute.

[10] Cincinnati *Enquirer*, Dec. 4, 29, 1850.

[11] Commager, *Documents*, pp. 321-323.

[12] Quoted from Justice Harlan's dissent in the Civil Rights Cases, 1883, in Yanuck, "Fugitive Slave Law and the Constitution," p. 64.

[13] Frankfort (Ky.) *Commonwealth*, Oct. 8, 1850; Richmond *Enquirer*, Aug. 30, 1850.

Fugitive Slave Law should be a test of the North's sincerity in relation to its constitutional obligations. Missouri's Governor Austin A. King observed that "all assaults upon that law—all efforts to prevent its execution—all movements to deprive the South of its benefits, . . . are aimed directly at the constitution, and consequently at the perpetuity of the Union." A St. Louis editor asserted that

If there be not the moral power in the free States to maintain that law—if there be not the moral and physical power in the General Government to enforce it, . . . then will the Southern States be compelled, in defence of their rights, . . . to dissolve all connection with the Union, and follow, alone, such destiny as their own courage, and genius, and trust in God, shall mark out for them.[14]

Nevertheless, at least a few Southern spokesmen were wary of the South's calling upon the physical power of the general government to protect its interests, and saw in the law a dangerous admission of national supremacy. "If Congress can legislate at all between the master and slave in a State, where can its power be stayed?" asked a group of delegates to a Southern convention. "It can abolish slavery in the States," they warned.[15] The extremist Charleston *Mercury* deplored the new power assumed by Congress in the law, and went so far as to support a Massachusetts statute which clashed directly with the federal measure. According to the *Mercury*, the Fugitive Slave Law demonstrated that in contesting an aggressive adversary "we lose the landmarks of principle—to obtain an illusive triumph, we press the Government to assume a power not confirmed by the instrument of its creation. . . ." The Charleston *Standard* maintained that the matter of returning fugitives involved a compact between sovereign states, and had nothing to do with Congress. "And instead of clinging to this provision of the compromise act as a compensation for its other most objectionable features," commented the editor, "it might be well for us to consider whether we have not, in fact, made a concession more fatal to our separate and distinct political existence, than even the founders of the Constitution themselves were prepared to make."[16]

Though some extremist politicians and writers may have been regarded as purveyors of gloom by their contemporaries, they were nearer the truth than their more moderate countrymen. Ultimately, the Fugitive Slave Law, by recharging the highly emotional slavery debate,

---

[14] St. Louis *Daily Union*, Jan. 4, 1851; St. Louis *Intelligencer*, Oct. 26, 1850.
[15] *Address to the People of Maryland, Virginia, North Carolina, South Carolina, Georgia, Florida, Alabama, Tennessee, Kentucky, Louisiana, Texas, Missouri, Mississippi, and Arkansas* (n.p., n.d.).
[16] New York *National Anti-Slavery Standard*, Oct. 6, 1855, quoting the Charleston *Mercury*; Salem (Ohio) *Anti-Slavery Bugle*, Dec. 24, 1853, quoting the Charleston *Standard*.

helped to bring on the Civil War with its eventual victory for national unification. It was a result not anticipated by the architects of the compromise whose Northern and Southern supporters hailed the statute as a triumph for moderation and pro-Union sentiments which would stifle extremism everywhere. When the measure passed the Senate the Richmond *Enquirer* commented that its passage by a strong vote "should naturally have the effect of inducing a better feeling and aiding the adjustment of the alarming difficulty." In the spring of 1851 a Buffalo newspaper noted that opposition had nearly subsided "except in purely Abolition quarters, and we shall soon see the Adjustment Measures, as a whole, not merely acquiesced in, but heartily sustained all over the country." A year after the law went into effect Senator Stephen A. Douglas asserted that "the whole country is acquiescing in the compromise measures—everywhere, North and South. Nobody proposes to repeal or disturb them."[17]

Those who made such sanguine predictions had to overlook many signs which indicated quite a different future from that prophesied by Senator Douglas. Regarded in the abstract, and considering the terrible alternatives of disruption or civil conflict, the compromise as a whole undoubtedly received the support of a majority of the people. But the Fugitive Slave Law was another matter. It enabled the abolitionists once again to link their cause with that of civil liberties and to reach large numbers of people untouched by the purer antislavery arguments. Southerners considered it their inalienable right to have runaway slaves returned, but Northerners viewed the demand as an affront to their pride. Returning men to slavery was nasty business and a measure which attempted to require it was very much out of step with public opinion in the states where slavery itself did not exist. Some Southern leaders recognized the problem. Early in 1850, before the passage of the law, Senator Jefferson Davis commented, "I feel that the law will be a dead letter in any State where the popular opinion is opposed to such rendition." Mississippi's Congressman Jacob Thompson also believed that the new statute would "prove a mere mockery." He thought the older law was "full and strong enough, if the States of the North would comply, or were disposed to comply with their constitutional obligations."[18]

A segment of Northern press reaction to the law confirmed Congressman Thompson's fears. An Ohio editor lamented that "We are all Slave-Catchers," pointing out that all were now compelled by law to

---

[17] Richmond *Enquirer*, Aug. 30, 1850; Wilmington *Delaware State Journal*, Mar. 25, 1851, quoting the Buffalo *Commercial Advertiser*; Stephen A. Douglas, *Remarks of Mr. Douglas of Illinois . . . Delivered in the Senate of the United States, December 23, 1851* (Washington, 1851), pp. 14-15.

[18] *Congressional Globe*, 31 Cong., 1 sess., Appendix, pt. 1, pp. 150, 660.

render aid to the *legal* kidnappers." A Massachusetts paper could find no language strong enough "to express the contempt with which we regard the miserable-tools, sycophants and traitors whose votes have brought about this result." Even the moderate New York *Courier and Enquirer* predicted that the measure "will not substantially aid the recovery of fugitive slaves, while it will deepen and strengthen the prevalent feeling upon that subject."[19]

The abolitionists capitalized upon and widened the already strong Northern sentiment against returning fugitives to slavery. In countless meetings they passed resolutions promising resistance to the law and solemnly vowed that as individuals, as Milwaukee's Sherman M. Booth expressed it, they would "trample this law under foot, at the first opportunity."[20] They made certain that any fugitive slave incident was widely publicized through demonstrations, special meetings, and publications. They petitioned for the law's repeal and organized special vigilance committees to prevent its successful enforcement. They usually referred to the law in such terms as "the bloodhound bill," "the infamous law," the "slave-catching bill," or the "enactment of hell."

The abolitionists quickly recognized that the "infamous law" had a significance far greater than the relatively small number of fugitive slaves it was designed to return. In 1853 the Massachusetts Anti-Slavery Society reported that events of the previous year had confirmed that the fugitive slave act "was but an electioneering trick, not designed nor expected to be of material advantage to the Slaveholders." It was a bid for Southern votes and "was meant rather as a homage to the Slave Power than as a Remedy from which intelligent Slaveholders hoped for much relief from the flight to which this form of riches was peculiarly exposed." The report noted that though the number of escapes from slavery had increased, there had been few arrests. William Jay pointed out that in a period of two years and nine months, not fifty slaves had been recovered under the act, an average of less than eighteen slaves a year. "Poor compensation this to the slaveholders," he concluded, "for making themselves a bye-word, a proverb, a reproach to Christendom—for giving a new and mighty impulse for abolition. . . ."[21]

In light of the number of fugitive slaves remanded under the law, it was indeed poor compensation for the slaveholders. In a decade of enforcement only about two hundred escaped slaves were returned

[19] Press comments quoted in Salem *Anti-Slavery Bugle,* Oct. 5, 1850.
[20] Milwaukee *Daily Free Democrat,* Oct. 5, 1850.
[21] *Twenty-first Annual Report Presented to the Massachusetts Anti-Slavery Society, by Its Board of Managers, January 26, 1853* (Boston, 1853), p. 43; William Jay, "The Fugitive Slave Act," in Julia Griffiths (ed.), *Autographs for Freedom* (Auburn and Rochester, 1854), p. 39.

south. Despite the lack of procedural legal protection for the fugitives, most government officials were scrupulous in preventing the use of the law to enslave Negroes not actually named in the warrants. About thirty persons were arrested as alleged fugitives and later released on the basis of mistaken identity.[22] Nevertheless, one abolition newspaper charged that the only ones to benefit from the law were the professional slave-catchers who, after 1850, were able "to do openly, what they were before compelled to do in the dark." Abolitionists also contended that the law encouraged the kidnaping of free Negroes and "built up a regular NORTHERN SLAVE TRADE" which threatened "to victimize every person in whom a suspicion of African blood" existed, and would assuredly not stop with them.[23]

Pride in Northern concepts of civil liberties, along with a justified concern for protecting free Negroes from being taken into slavery, led a number of Northern states to enact a new series of personal liberty laws. On the surface the laws provided legal protection for free Negroes but they were also designed to impede the enforcement of the federal statute. Many lengthy legal disputes resulted when state officials, concerned with the enforcement of the personal liberty laws, clashed with federal officials trying to enforce the Fugitive Slave Law. In 1854 Wisconsin's supreme court went so far as to declare the federal law unconstitutional. The personal liberty laws were based upon the same concept of state sovereignty which Southern spokesmen were using for other purposes. When discussing such a proposed bill in the New York assembly, Gerrit Smith argued that the time had come "for New York, in her sovereign capacity, to assert her independence as a sovereign State, and, by positive enactment, pass such laws as shall protect all persons coming within her jurisdiction."[24]

The new personal liberty laws were political manifestations of growing anti-Southern sentiment in the Northern states. They were a reaction to a measure which a group of abolitionists characterized as "a reproduction, on the soil of Massachusetts, New York, and Ohio, of the most diabolical features of the slave code, and that, too under the Federal authority." Although very few people actually were called upon to help send fugitives back into slavery, the law brought the issue home in a way that nothing else had done. Numerous ministers used it to further antislavery doctrine. The Reverend B. M. Hall told his congregation that "it is the duty of every Christian citizen to obey God rather than man," and to resist peacefully the execution of "this

[22] Samuel May, Jr., *The Fugitive Slave Law and Its Victims* (Anti-Slavery Tracts, n.s. no. 15, rev. and enlarged ed.; New York, 1861).
[23] Chicago *Western Citizen*, Jan. 7, 1851; May, *Fugitive Slave Law*, p. 55.
[24] New York *National Anti-Slavery Standard*, Apr. 7, 1860.

unjust and unconstitutional law." A New England minister likened closing one's door to the fugitive slave to shutting out "your Saviour himself." He told his congregation that were a fugitive to come to him he would defy the authorities and render assistance, urging them to do the same, "and trust God with the result." After his sermon one Sunday a minister in Painesville, Ohio, announced that five fugitive slaves, including two infants, had just arrived and needed money for their journey to Canada. Anyone contributing to the fund, he warned dramatically, would be liable to the penalties of the Fugitive Slave Law. The congregation promptly gave thirty dollars. The local newspaper commented: "Heartless politicians and 'lower law' priests will soon learn that there is a higher law than man-enslaving, woman-whipping, baby-stealing and God-defying enactments."[25]

Such strong reactions were typical. No other issue related to slavery stirred people in quite the same way. From time to time abolitionists had aroused a certain amount of popular support for their cause by associating it with the right of petition or some other issue. Yet for the most part the slavery question remained an abstraction until fugitive slave incidents brought it into the realm of the emotions. A frightened, shivering fugitive aroused a sympathetic response even from those who theoretically accepted the compromise measures. Some of the abolitionists were well aware of the significance of the fugitive issue. "There are only a few, unfortunately," said J. Miller McKim, "who can understand an abstract idea or comprehend a general principle. . . . To make our anti-slavery idea fully understood we must put legs on it."[26]

Abolitionists called attention to arrests under the law, and special vigilance committees worked overtime to prevent rendition when possible, and to publicize those that could not be prevented. They sometimes arranged for the purchase of fugitives who had been captured and returned to slavery. Anthony Burns and other former slaves frequently spoke to antislavery audiences and attracted large numbers of listeners from outside the ranks of the dedicated abolitionists. Such incidents as the rescue in 1851 of William Henry, or "Jerry," from his captors in Syracuse provided the occasion for special protest meetings. The complicated legal struggle growing out of the government's unsuccessful attempt to punish the rescuers aroused additional interest.

---

[25] "Address of the Convention of Radical Political Abolitionists," in *Proceedings of the Convention . . . Held at Syracuse, New York, June 26th, 27th, and 28th, 1855* (New York, 1856), pp. 31-32; B. M. Hall, *The Fugitive Slave Law. A Sermon* (Schenectady, 1850), pp. 18-19; Kazlitt Arvine, *Our Duty to the Fugitive Slave* (Boston, 1850), pp. 20-21; New York *National Anti-Slavery Standard,* Oct. 15, 1852.

[26] J. Miller McKim to Mrs. Chapman, Dec. 11, 1857, Weston Papers, Boston Public Library.

Following a large anti-Fugitive Slave Law convention, and while the legal cases were still pending, Samuel J. May reported that

The sentiment of our City and County is nobly right on the question which the rescue has raised. Men that I supposed cared not at all for the enslavement of our colored countrymen, have taken pains to express to me their detestation of the attempt to rob Jerry of his liberty.

To keep the issue alive in Syracuse abolitionists annually celebrated the Jerry rescue with as much fanfare as they could muster.[27]

Rescues of fugitive slaves provided exciting moments, and those who participated in one or two such affairs or assisted only a few fugitive slaves along their way to Canada added their emotional experiences to an already widespread antislavery commitment in the North. Levi Coffin and other abolitionist veterans recalled in later years the effectiveness of the presence of a fugitive slave in arousing a sympathetic response. Oftentimes the humanitarian reaction was not consciously antislavery but rather another example of practical behavior overriding abstract principles.

Uncle Tom's Cabin also helped "put legs" on the antislavery principles. The novel was a reaction to the Fugitive Slave Law and, according to a contemporary commentator, it "served its purpose. What truth could not accomplish, fiction did, and Harriet Beecher Stowe has had the satisfaction of throwing a firebrand into the world, which has kept up a furious blaze ever since." The demand for the novel seemed unlimited and its sales quickly broke all previous records for fiction. By personifying various aspects of slavery and creating stereotyped characters, Mrs. Stowe touched the emotions of millions of readers. Numerous artists found it profitable to make pictorial reproductions and statues of the novel's characters. In 1853 the *Liberator* commented that in Boston and the larger towns, people had become "accustomed to see Uncle Toms, Evas and Topseys without number, in engravings of various degrees of merit and price."[28]

Numerous dramatic troups added *Uncle Tom's Cabin* to their repertoires and thus brought the message to many who had not read the book. One of these productions was playing in Milwaukee at the time that Sherman M. Booth was being held by United States authorities for rescuing Joshua Glover, a fugitive slave. Booth's newspaper, the *Daily*

[27] Samuel J. May to Charlotte G. Coffin, Oct. 15, 1851, William Lloyd Garrison Papers, Boston Public Library; New York *National Anti-Slavery Standard*, Sept. 16, 1852.

[28] F. G. de Fontaine, *American Abolitionism, from 1787 to 1861. A Compendium of Historical Facts, Embracing Legislation in Congress and Agitation without* (New York, 1861); John Herbert Nelson, *The Negro Character in American Literature* (*Bulletin of the University of Kansas Humanistic Studies*, vol. IV, no. 1; Lawrence, 1926); Boston *Liberator*, Dec. 23, 1853.

Free Democrat, called attention to the fact that the drama was "preaching up the old Patrick Henry Doctrine of Liberty or Death—the very doctrine carried out by the people at the Court-House in rescuing Glover." It noted that the play justified a fugitive's shooting down slave-catchers rather than return to slavery, and suggested that the approving audience should be arrested at once and tried for riot. "They are in the same category with us," continued the editorial, "and when the Judge has disposed of them he should get up an indictment against Human Nature, which is a Great Incendiary—always taking the part of the oppressed."[29]

The Booth case succeeded in calling attention to the harsh law and gave new weight to the abolitionist view of events. "The object of this prosecution is to establish the law of Slavery and kidnapping on the free soil of Wisconsin," commented Booth's paper, "and to make this a Slave State. . . . The people of this State are to be taught that they are the slaves of the Slave Power." Although the government prosecuted only about a dozen cases under the Fugitive Slave Law, each of them contributed to a growing popular reaction against enforcement. The court cases also inspired protest demonstrations, special publications, and countless petitions. According to an antislavery society report, the Oberlin-Wellington rescue and the prosecutions growing out of it "stimulated discussion, roused popular feeling, extended and deepened the abhorrence felt toward Slave-Catching . . . and called forth many an emphatic utterance of that sentiment from pulpit, and press, and public meeting."[30]

The renditions, rescues of arrested fugitives, and prosecutions played a major role in bringing the whole slavery question home to the people of the free states. When combined with such other related issues as the Nebraska Bill and slavery in the territories, the Brooks-Sumner affair, and the troubles in Kansas, the Fugitive Slave Law added fuel to a fire which was burning the remaining ties between the sections. Many moderates in the North who had supported the 1850 compromise measures found themselves unable to support the law and what it came to mean. It became the abolitionists' most powerful propaganda weapon and reopened the whole slavery question with an intensity previously unknown.

For those Southerners who had demanded the law with its enlarged concept of national power, nothing was gained. Instead of strengthening it weakened the position of the southern Unionists who had supported

[29] Milwaukee *Daily Free Democrat,* Mar. 16, 1854.
[30] *Ibid.; The Anti-Slavery History of the John Brown Year; Being the Twenty-Seventh Annual Report of the American Anti-Slavery Society* (New York, 1861), p. 71.

it. Few slaves were returned and often those few renditions required considerable outlays of time and money. The return of Anthony Burns cost a total of more than $20,000, which caused a Virginia editor to comment that "under the Massachusetts style of doing business, it is a law without a sanction, and, except for the mere principle which it asserts, it is not worth a copper to the South."[31] By 1860 it was clear that the principle it asserted was also worthless.

[31] New York *National Anti-Slavery Standard*, July 21, 1855, quoting the Petersburg (Va.) *Intelligencer*.

THE *BOOTH* CASES: FINAL STEP TO THE CIVIL WAR

Jenni Parrish*

I. Introduction

Nineteenth-century American history recounts that the slaveholding South's desire to secede from the Union was based on the North's growing hostility to slavery. The unionist North wanted to preserve the country but abolish slavery. Thus, economic, social, and political factors combined to create a Southern Confederacy, which fired the first shot at Fort Sumter and started the Civil War.

The traditional analysis of the American legal system's involvement in this crisis focuses on the *Dred Scott*[1] decision. This is the case most often scrutinized in any discussion of slavery in nineteenth-century America.[2] The *Dred Scott* decision in 1857 was, however, neither the first nor the last pronouncement of the Taney Court on slavery and related issues. In 1842, *Prigg v. Pennsylvania*[3] upheld the constitutionality of the Fugitive Slave Law of 1793 and invalidated Pennsylvania's personal liberty law of 1826. In 1859, the consolidated cases of *Ableman v. Booth* and *United States v. Booth*,[4] also authored by Taney, determined that the Fugitive Slave Law of 1850 was constitutional and that a state cannot invalidate a federal law.

---

* Professor of Law and the Director of Legal Information Center, Hastings College of the Law, University of California.

1. Scott v. Sandford, 60 U.S. (19 How.) 393 (1857); *see infra* text accompanying notes 161-69.

2. *See, e.g.*, DON E. FEHRENBACHER, THE DRED SCOTT CASE: ITS SIGNIFICANCE IN AMERICAN LAW AND POLITICS vii (1978):

> Scott v. Sandford . . . remains to this day the most famous of all American judicial decisions . . . . The principle reason for the prominence of the decision in American historical writing is the belief that it became a major causal link between the general forces of national disruption and the final crisis of the Union in 1860-61. Scholars have tended to be emphatic in affirming the connection but vague about its mechanics . . . . The Dred Scott decision by itself apparently caused no significant number of changes in political allegiance. Yet it was a conspicuous and perhaps an integral part of a configuration of events and conditions that did produce enough changes of allegiance to make a political revolution and enough intensity of feeling to make that revolution violent.

Id. at 561-62, 567.

3. Prigg v. Pennsylvania, 41 U.S. (16 Pet.) 539 (1842).

4. Ableman v. Booth, 62 U.S. (21 How.) 506 (1859).

Prigg stiffened the free states' resistance to enforcement of the 1793 Fugitive Slave Law.[5] *Dred Scott's* denial of citizenship and personhood[6] to African-Americans took the country another step toward violent resolution of the slavery controversy.

The *Booth* decision was the next logical step for the states: open resistance from a state supreme court, a state legislature, and a state's citizenry to the Fugitive Slave Law of 1850. It is important because the actions of people in the new, free state of Wisconsin in the decade prior to the Civil War amounted to the kind of secessionist behavior typically associated in American historical consciousness with the Southern slave states. Wisconsin was ready to secede from the Union over the removal of a fugitive slave from its borders. Such removal was a fairly ordinary occurrence throughout the United States in 1859.[7]

This Article begins by telling the fascinating, but complex, Glover/Booth story with all its legal twists and turns.[8] After detailing some previously unexplored aspects of the case, this Article describes the broader legal and historical context, considers the motives of the state and federal judiciary, and discusses the attitudes of the Wisconsin populace toward African-Americans. Finally, this Article draws conclusions about the place of the Booth story in nineteenth-century United States history. This Article lifts *Booth* out of obscurity, places it in the national context of 1850's America, and concludes by speculating as to the reasons for this unjustified obscurity over the last one-hundred thirty years. The objective is to articulate the importance of this case in pre-Civil

---

5. *See* FEHRENBACHER, *supra* note 2, at 43-47.

6. *See* FEHRENBACHER, *supra* note 2, at 363.

7. STANLEY W. CAMPBELL, THE SLAVE CATCHERS 6, app. at 207 (tbl. 12) (1970) (noting that United States Census reported number of slaves who had escaped into free states in 1850 was 1011; number of fugitive slave cases documented during period 1850-1860 totaled 332).

8. The facts of the story were pieced together from a number of sources. *See* titles cited *infra* notes 18, 117-120. The most coherent source by far is A.J. Beitzinger, *Federal Law Enforcement and the Booth Cases*, 41 MARQ. L. REV. 7 (1957). Professor Beitzinger was particularly diligent in mining the archival sources in Washington, D.C., and his article clarifies many of the details of this complicated saga. However, Professor Beitzinger views the Booth story "purely as a law enforcement problem." *Id.* at 7. *Booth* is a law enforcement problem only in the sense that the Civil War was a law enforcement problem. Such a narrow frame of reference does an injustice to a very complex legal historical episode with broad-based philosophical and moral underpinnings. The question was not simply how to enforce the fugitive slave laws. The bigger questions were why these laws were still considered valid at the mid-point of the nineteenth century and why the national American conscience had not evolved further by that time.

War slavery litigation. What begins as the tale of a captured fugitive slave quickly becomes the story of an outraged public consciousness making demands of an only partially responsive legal system. That system was substantially rooted in judicial conservatism (with its adherence to precedent and a view of the Supreme Court as operating above the political fray) as much as political conservatism.

II. THE STORY OF JOSHUA GLOVER

Joshua Glover[9] was an African-American who for several years lived and worked at a saw mill four miles outside Racine, Wisconsin. On the evening of Friday, March 10, 1854, he was playing a game of cards with a few friends when there came a knock at the door.[10] Glover told his friends not to open the door until the identity of those outside was determined.[11] One of his companions, a mulatto named Turner, later considered a confederate of the visitors, opened the door.[12] There stood Bennami Garland, from St. Louis, Missouri, who claimed Joshua Glover was his runaway slave;[13] deputy United States Marshals Charles Cotton of Milwaukee and John Kearney of Racine; and five other men. Although Cotton (acting in the absence of the U.S. Marshal, Stephen Ableman) supposedly had a warrant for Glover's arrest issued by Federal District Judge Andrew G. Miller,[14] none of the histori-

---

9. The said Joshua Glover is described in said affidavit to be forty-four or forty-five years of age, about five feet six or eight inches high, spare built, with rather long legs, very prominent knuckles, has large feet and hands, has a full head of wool, eyes small and inflamed, is of dissipated habits, is of rather an ashy black color. . . . [He] . . . had one of his shoulders stiff from dislocation, and had stooping shoulders and a slow gait.

In re Booth, 3 Wis. 144, 150, 155 (1854).

10. *High-Handed Outrage! Attempt to Kidnap a Citizen of Racine by Slave-Catchers*, RACINE ADVOCATE, Mar. 20, 1854, at 1 [hereinafter *High-Handed Outrage*].

11. *Id.*

12. *Id.* "His inhuman perfidy in this transaction has branded him with a mark that will last longer than the color of his skin." *Id.*

13. *In re Booth*, 3 Wis. at 155. Glover was alleged to have been the foreman of Garland's farm four miles outside St. Louis until his escape in the spring of 1852. Garland bought Glover on January 1, 1849. *Id.*

14. The warrant for Joshua Glover's arrest is reproduced at 3 Wis. at 149-50. For an even more detailed account of this entire episode, see PARKER M. REED, THE BENCH AND BAR OF WISCONSIN 496-504 (1882). Reed is the only commentator who spends much time discussing the fact that a warrant was issued. *Id.* at 497-98. However, the author could find no commentator who states that Glover was shown the warrant.

cal accounts states that the warrant was produced at Glover's home.

Glover was bludgeoned, manacled, and taken bleeding to the wagon waiting outside.[15] Initially, they rode toward Racine but the prospect of facing angry citizens caused them to make a detour.[16] Avoiding the main highway, Glover, Garland, and Cotton headed north to Milwaukee where they arrived early the next morning.[17] Joshua Glover was placed in the county jail pending a hearing before Judge Miller.[18]

That same morning the people of Racine gathered together at the ringing of the courthouse bell and adopted a resolution that stated in part:

-Resolved, that we look upon the arrest of said Glover as an outrage upon the peaceful rights of this assembly, it having been made without the exhibition of any papers, by first clandestinely knocking him down with a club, and then binding him by brute force and carrying him off.

-Resolved, that we, as citizens of Racine, demand for said Glover a fair and impartial jury trial, in this, the state where he has been arrested, and that we will attend in person to aid him, by all honorable means, to secure his unconditional release, adopting as our motto the Golden Rule.

-Resolved, that inasmuch as the Senate of the United States has repealed all compromises heretofore adopted by the Congress of the United States, we as citizens of Wisconsin are justified in declaring, and do hereby declare, the slave-catching law of 1850 disgraceful and also repealed.[19]

A delegation of one hundred men was appointed to go to Milwaukee and represent the sentiments of the Racine citizens.[20] They arrived in Milwaukee about 5:00 p.m. and joined the throng of

---

15. *High-Handed Outrage, supra* note 10, at 1.

16. REUBEN G. THWAITES, THE STORY OF WISCONSIN 249 (1890).

17. *Id.*

18. 3 Wis. at 156. With some minor variations, most commentaries agree on the facts as outlined here. *See, e.g.,* JAMES I. CLARK, WISCONSIN DEFIES THE FUGITIVE SLAVE LAW 106-07, 113 (1955); CARL SCHURZ, THE REMINISCENCES OF CARL SCHURZ II 105-15 (1907); THWAITES, *supra* note 16, ch. IX.

19. *High-Handed Outrage, supra* note 10, at 1; *see also* DANIEL HOWE, POLITICAL HISTORY OF SECESSION 236-38 (1914).

20. Vroman Mason, *The Fugitive Slave Law in Wisconsin with Reference to Nullification Sentiment, in* PROCEEDINGS OF THE STATE HISTORICAL SOCIETY OF WISCONSIN 117, 124 (1895).

5,000 people reported to have gathered on the courthouse square.[21] One of the Milwaukee citizens most influential in gathering together this huge crowd was Sherman M. Booth, the fiery abolitionist editor of the *Free Democrat*, a local newspaper.[22] Although he would later deny it,[23] Sherman Booth was said to have rushed through the streets on horseback shouting, "Freemen to the rescue! Slave-catchers are in our midst! Be at the courthouse at two o'clock."[24] On the other hand, at least one commentator reported that Booth actually "counseled the people against violence."[25]

At the request of Booth's attorneys, Milwaukee County Court Judge Jenkins issued a writ of habeas corpus for the release of Joshua Glover, but the sheriff refused to serve it,[26] acting under the influence, if not the direct orders, of Federal District Judge Miller.[27] Judge Miller also postponed the hearing on the writ until Monday, hoping that by then the crowd would have dispersed or the military would have arrived.[28] There is some evidence that the soldiers in a battalion stationed nearby had peremptorily "declined to do duty."[29]

The sheriff's refusal to act on the writ was transmitted to the crowd at the courthouse, who had been listening to the oratory of "the most eloquent and influential members of the Milwaukee bar."[30] By 6:00 p.m. the crowd would no longer be contained.[31] They were particularly incensed at the prospect of Glover being held in jail over the Sabbath.[32] With a battering ram ("the writ of

---

21. *High-Handed Outrage, supra* note 10, at 1. According to the UNITED STATES CENSUS OF 1850, the total population of Milwaukee was 20,061. The total population of Racine City was less than 6000. If the newspaper account is accurate, this was a phenomenally large crowd. Another account describes it as "the largest public meeting ever held in the place . . . ." REED, *supra* note 14, at 497.

22. Mason, *supra* note 20, at 124.

23. JOHN B. WINSLOW, STORY OF A GREAT COURT 73 (1912) (citing a speech made by Booth in Madison, Mar. 12, 1897) [hereinafter WINSLOW, GREAT COURT]. John Winslow reproduces most of Booth's speech in *Special Address: The Booth Case—A Chapter from the Judicial History of Wisconsin*, 29 PROC. OF THE ILL. ST. B. ASS'N 43, 49-50 (1905) [hereinafter Winslow, *Special Address*].

24. Beitzinger, *supra* note 8, at 10; CLARK, *supra* note 18, at 6.

25. Reed, *supra* note 14, at 499.

26. *High-Handed Outrage, supra* note 10, at 1.

27. *High-Handed Outrage, supra* note 10, at 1.

28. Beitzinger, *supra* note 8, at 10.

29. Beitzinger, *supra* note 8, at 11.

30. *High-Handed Outrage, supra* note 10, at 1.

31. *High-Handed Outrage, supra* note 10, at 1.

32. *High-Handed Outrage, supra* note 10, at 1.

'open sesame' ") they broke into the county jail, freed Glover, and cheered as he climbed onto a wagon and left for Racine.[33] Shortly thereafter, Glover left for Canada via the Underground Railroad.[34] Nothing more was ever reported about Joshua Glover.

Bennami Garland, the slaveowner, was arrested on the charge of assault and battery by the Sheriff of Racine County, but Judge Miller released him on a writ of habeas corpus.[35] The local newspapers characterized this action as a violation of states' rights.[36]

A number of other Milwaukee and Racine citizens also were arrested because they aided Joshua Glover's escape. In the end, only Sherman Booth and John Rycraft were brought to trial.[37]

III.   The Trials of Sherman Booth

Sherman Booth was arrested on March 15, 1854, charged with violating the Fugitive Slave Act of 1850, and brought before the U.S. Commissioner, Winfield Smith.[38] Smith required bail to insure Booth's appearance before the district court in its July session.[39] Booth initially paid the bail, but two months later decided he would rather go to jail, probably hoping to bring a test case in state court on the constitutionality of the federal law.[40] He was then placed in the county jail on May 26, 1854, on the charge of unlawfully aiding, abetting, and assisting Joshua Glover in his escape.[41]

The next day Sherman Booth applied to Abram D. Smith, one of the three justices of the Wisconsin Supreme Court, for a writ of habeas corpus.[42] The federal marshal, Ableman, was not certain

---

33. *High-Handed Outrage, supra* note 10, at 1. "As he went through the streets he aroused the enthusiasm of the crowds to a still higher pitch by holding up his manacled hands and shouting, 'Glory, Hallelujah!' " Howe, *supra* note 19, at 230.

34. Howe, *supra* note 19, at 230.

35. *High-Handed Outrage, supra* note 10, at 1.

36. *Review of Judge Miller's Decision in the Garland Case*, Racine Advocate, Mar. 27, 1854. "Garland later recovered a judgment against Booth in the federal court for the value of the escaped slave. The collection of this judgment ruined Booth financially." Horace H. Hagan, *Ableman v. Booth*, 17 A.B.A. J. 19, 20 n.12 (1931).

37. *See infra* note 287.

38. Mason, *supra* note 20, at 128. The office of United States Commissioner was created in the 1850 Fugitive Slave Act. *See infra* text accompanying notes 151-59.

39. Mason, *supra* note 20, at 129.

40. Beitzinger, *supra* note 8, at 11; Winslow, Great Court, *supra* note 23, at 74.

41. Mason, *supra* note 20, at 129.

42. *In re* Booth, 3 Wis. 13, 14 (1854).

whether he should comply with the state writ.[43] On the advice of
U.S. District Attorney Sharpstein, he did comply, probably hoping
to avoid a riot.[44] At the hearing, Justice Smith expressed a desire
to consider the constitutionality of the Fugitive Slave Act.[45] While
this took the U.S. District Attorney by surprise,[46] Booth's attorney,
Bryon Paine,[47] gave a long and eloquent indictment of the 1850
Fugitive Slave Act, concluding that it was unconstitutional.[48]
Sharpstein's hastily prepared counterarguments were simply no
match for Paine.[49]

Justice Smith ordered Booth released from jail and declared
the Fugitive Slave Law of 1850 unconstitutional.[50] Sharpstein then
petitioned the Wisconsin Supreme Court to review Smith's decision
on certiorari.[51] In a 2-to-1 decision, Justices Whiton and Smith
found the warrant for Booth's arrest was defective because it did
not precisely state that Booth had aided a fugitive from labor to
escape from custody.[52] They also agreed that the 1850 law was
unconstitutional.[53] Justice Crawford defended the law's constitutionality.[54]

Booth's freedom was shortlived. The federal district court of
Wisconsin had started its summer session and the grand jury indicted both Sherman Booth and John Rycraft[55] for aiding and abetting Glover's escape.[56] After their arrest, both men applied to the
Wisconsin Supreme Court for a writ of habeas corpus, which the
court denied.[57] The court reasoned that because jurisdiction was
then firmly established with the federal court, no justification ex-

---

43. Beitzinger, *supra* note 8, at 12.
44. Beitzinger, *supra* note 8, at 12.
45. Beitzinger, *supra* note 8, at 12.
46. Beitzinger, *supra* note 8, at 12.
47. Of Byron Paine it was said that he "drank in abolitionism with his mother's
milk." WINSLOW, GREAT COURT, *supra* note 23, at 74.
48. 1 JOHN BERRYMAN, HISTORY OF THE BENCH AND BAR OF WISCONSIN 138-43
(1898) (Payne's statements printed in part); *see also* WINSLOW, GREAT COURT, *supra* note
23, at 76-77.
49. Beitzinger, *supra* note 8, at 12.
50. *In re* Booth, 3 Wis. 13, 46 (1854).
51. Beitzinger, *supra* note 8, at 12.
52. *In re* Booth, 3 Wis. 13, 54, 60 (1854).
53. *Id.* at 67-68.
54. *Id.* at 76.
55. The commentaries are inconsistent in the spelling of Rycraft (or Ryecraft). Here
the Wisconsin Supreme Court's spelling (Rycraft) is adopted for uniformity's sake.
56. Beitzinger, *supra* note 8, at 13.
57. *Ex parte* Booth, 3 Wis. 134 (1854).

isted for interfering with it.[58]

In September 1854, United States Attorney General Caleb Cushing appealed the Wisconsin court's decision declaring the 1850 Fugitive Slave Law unconstitutional to the Supreme Court of the United States.[59] The two issues presented were: 1) the constitutionality of this controversial law, and 2) the appropriate jurisdictional limits to be placed on a state with regard to issuance of writs of habeas corpus for federal prisoners.[60] Chief Justice Taney issued a writ of error requiring a return by the first Monday of December 1854.[61]

Judge Miller heard Rycraft's case in November 1854 and Booth's in January 1855.[62] Both men were found guilty of aiding, assisting, and abetting Glover's escape.[63] Rycraft was sentenced to ten days in the Milwaukee County jail and fined $200.[64] Booth was sentenced to thirty days in the county jail and fined $1000.[65]

Booth and Rycraft, undoubtedly spurred on by popular support,[66] petitioned the Wisconsin Supreme Court for two writs of habeas corpus—one for the federal marshal, Ableman, and the other for the county sheriff.[67] On January 30, 1855, the county sheriff and 2000 well-wishers marched the prisoners to the Milwaukee railroad station, where they departed for the state supreme court hearing in Madison.[68] After the hearing, Booth and Rycraft were released.[69] The court reasoned that the indictment failed to describe adequately Glover's status and therefore did not set forth an offense punishable by federal law.[70] By this action, the Wisconsin Supreme Court contradicted its earlier decision relating to non-

---

58. *Id.* at 137.
59. Beitzinger, *supra* note 8, at 14.
60. Beitzinger, *supra* note 8, at 14.
61. Beitzinger, *supra* note 8, at 14.
62. Beitzinger, *supra* note 8, at 14-15.
63. Beitzinger, *supra* note 8, at 14-15.
64. Beitzinger, *supra* note 8, at 64.
65. Beitzinger, *supra* note 8, at 64.
66. Beitzinger, *supra* note 8, at 16; WINSLOW, GREAT COURT, *supra* note 23, at 78 ("This conviction aroused intense feeling all over the State.").
67. Beitzinger, *supra* note 8, at 16.
68. Beitzinger, *supra* note 8, at 16.
69. Beitzinger, *supra* note 8, at 16.
70. *In re* Booth & Rycraft, 3 Wis. 144, 167-68 (1854); *see* discussion *infra* note 270 and accompanying text.

interference with federal court proceedings.[71]

Considering the strong sentiment of the Wisconsin populace and its state judiciary, federal Judge Miller confined himself to delivering a statement condemning the actions of the Wisconsin Supreme Court.[72] He predicted that if such rebellious actions were allowed to stand as precedent, any state judge could ignore federal court decisions and decide that any act of Congress was unconstitutional, thus opening the jail doors for the federal prisoners in the states.[73]

The U.S. District Attorney Sharpstein secured a copy of the state supreme court record from the clerk of the court.[74] He did so in anticipation of the court refusing to comply with any future request from Chief Justice Taney that the record be sent up to the Supreme Court,[75] a well founded fear. The state court forbade the clerk to make a return or to enter the writ of error in the state court's records.[76] This action flew in the face of the Wisconsin court's own assertion two years earlier, when it considered the first habeas corpus writ, that the Supreme Court of the United States "has the power finally to decide all questions growing out of an alleged violation of the constitution of the United States by an act of Congress."[77]

In March 1856, Attorney General Cushing requested and received a postponement on the hearing of the second *Booth* case.[78] However, Chief Justice Taney insisted that the Wisconsin Supreme Court once again be requested to comply with the order to respond to the United States Supreme Court's writ of error.[79] He also decided that both *Booth* cases would be consolidated and heard in the next term.[80] By March 1857, it was clear that the Wisconsin court again would refuse to accept the high court's writ of error, and so

---

71. Beitzinger, *supra* note 8, at 16, 18 n.51; *see also* 3 Wis. 144, 170-71. The earlier decision was *Ex parte* Booth, 3 Wis. 134 (1854).

72. Beitzinger, *supra* note 8, at 17 n.46.

73. Beitzinger, *supra* note 8, at 17 n.46.

74. Beitzinger, *supra* note 8, at 18.

75. United States v. Booth, 59 U.S. (18 How.) 476 (1856); Beitzinger, *supra* note 8, at 18.

76. United States v. Booth, 59 U.S. (18 How.) 476, 477-78 (1856); *see* Mason, *supra* note 20, at 138.

77. *In re* Booth, 3 Wis. 1, 66 (1854).

78. Beitzinger, *supra* note 8, at 19.

79. Beitzinger, *supra* note 8, at 19.

80. Beitzinger, *supra* note 8, at 19.

the unofficial copy of the record obtained earlier by Sharpstein was used.[81]

The United States Supreme Court finally considered the *Booth* cases jointly in January 1859.[82] Chief Justice Taney's decision upheld the Fugitive Slave Law of 1850[83] and severely castigated the Wisconsin Supreme Court throughout his opinion.[84] The Court reversed and remanded the case to the Wisconsin Supreme Court throughout his opinion. This so infuriated the people of Wisconsin that the state legislature passed resolutions denouncing the Supreme Court's action as "an arbitrary act of power . . . without authority, void and of no force" and urging "positive defiance" by the states as the "rightful remedy."[85]

In the summer of 1859, the Wisconsin Supreme Court reconsidered *Booth*. Two events probably influenced the tone of that decision. First, the composition of the Wisconsin Supreme Court changed.[86] Byron Paine (formerly Booth's attorney) was elected to replace Abram Smith.[87] The very conservative Luther Dixon succeeded to the Chief Justiceship when Whiton died.[88] Orasmus Cole, the third justice, had participated in the second *Booth* decision, but not the first.[89]

Secondly, Sherman Booth was tried for the seduction of Caroline Cook, a fourteen-year-old girl.[90] Although Booth supposedly made two pre-trial confessions, the jury could not agree on a verdict and Booth was freed.[91] His public image, however, would never be quite as pure as before this highly publicized trial.[92]

On March 1, 1860, Judge Miller issued an order for Booth's rearrest after a prolonged deferral of action because of fear of repri-

---

81. United States v. Booth, 59 U.S. (18 How.) 476 (1856); Ableman v. Booth, 59 U.S. (18 How.) 479 (1856).

82. Ableman v. Booth, 62 U.S. (21 How.) 506 (1859).

83. *Id.* at 526.

84. *Id.*

85. 1859 Wis. Laws 247-248. The resolution is virtually identical to the Kentucky nullification resolution of 1799. 1799 Ky. Acts 207-10.

86. Beitzinger, *supra* note 8, at 22.

87. DICTIONARY OF WISCONSIN BIOGRAPHY 277, 330 (1960).

88. *Id.* at 102-03.

89. *Id.* at 82 (Orasmus Cole was not elected as associate justice until 1855).

90. THE TRIAL OF SHERMAN M. BOOTH FOR SEDUCTION (1859).

91. *Id.* at 294; Beitzinger, *supra* note 8, at 22-23.

92. Beitzinger, *supra* note 8, at 22-23; *see also* RICHARD CURRENT, THE HISTORY OF WISCONSIN II 271-74 (1976); A.J. Beitzinger, *Edward George Ryan—19th Century Lawyer*, 1956 WIS. L. REV. 248, 263-68 (1956) (describing seduction trial).

sals from a Wisconsin antislavery populace.[93] Booth was placed in the federal customs house at Milwaukee.[94] The Wisconsin Republican party, which dominated the press, took up Booth's cause once more.[95]

On March 6, 1860, Booth again applied to the Wisconsin Supreme Court for a writ of habeas corpus.[96] Rumors circulated of a possible clash between the state militia trying to enforce such a writ and federal troops trying to block its enforcement.[97] However, the state supreme court refused to grant the writ.[98]

Booth's term of imprisonment expired on March 23, 1860.[99] He remained in the customs house, however, because he refused to pay the fine.[100] He also filed a suit for false imprisonment against Judge Miller and the new U.S. Marshal, John Lewis.[101] During the rest of the spring and into the summer Booth wrote a number of inflammatory letters regarding his imprisonment, which were published in newspapers statewide.[102] A second application for a writ of habeas corpus was made to the Wisconsin Supreme Court and again it was denied.[103]

On August 1, 1860, a group of armed men succeeded in breaking Booth out of the customs house.[104] He was taken to Waupun, Wisconsin where Hans C. Heg, the state prison commissioner, took him into protective custody.[105] Two days later, a federal deputy marshal went to the state prison to rearrest Booth, but the Commissioner refused to give him up.[106] On August 5, Booth traveled to Ripon, Wisconsin to make a speech and was escorted to the hall by two-hundred armed men.[107] Federal Deputy Marshal Frank

---

93. Beitzinger, *supra* note 8, at 26.
94. Beitzinger, *supra* note 8, at 26.
95. Beitzinger, *supra* note 8, at 26; *see also* HOWE, *supra* note 19, at 236 ("Indignation meetings were held in many places in Wisconsin.").
96. Ableman v. Booth, 11 Wis. 517, 555 (1860).
97. Beitzinger, *supra* note 8, at 27; HOWE, *supra* note 19, at 236; George W. Carter, *The Booth War in Ripon*, in PROCEEDINGS OF THE STATE HISTORICAL SOCIETY OF WISCONSIN 161, 164-65 (1902).
98. *Ableman*, 11 Wis. at 517, 558.
99. Beitzinger, *supra* note 8, at 27.
100. Beitzinger, *supra* note 8, at 27.
101. Beitzinger, *supra* note 8, at 27.
102. Beitzinger, *supra* note 8, at 27; Carter, *supra* note 97, at 165.
103. Beitzinger, *supra* note 8, at 28.
104. Beitzinger, *supra* note 8, at 28.
105. Beitzinger, *supra* note 8, at 28.
106. Beitzinger, *supra* note 8, at 29.
107. Beitzinger, *supra* note 8, at 29.

McCarty and two assistants tried to arrest him onstage, but the crowd surged forward and forcibly ejected the three officers.[108]

On August 29, the very persistent Deputy Marshal McCarty and five assistants stealthily approached the house near Ripon where Booth was staying, hoping to take him by surprise.[109] They were met, however, by sixty to seventy armed men and forced to retreat.[110] "McCarty said he was getting disgusted with the whole business anyway, and would return the warrant to the court unexecuted."[111] A second federal officer also tried to take Booth but was seized by a mob, who paraded him through the streets of Ripon with a yoke on his head.[112]

Finally, on October 8, 1860, Marshall Lewis captured Booth, returning him to the Milwaukee customs house where he remained for over three months.[113] After Lincoln's election, Booth applied to the outgoing President Buchanan for a pardon.[114] On the day before Lincoln's inauguration, March 4, 1861, Buchanan granted the pardon, thus ending the saga.[115]

IV. THE UNEXPLORED QUESTIONS

While the drama of this story stands out even in a dramatic historical time, it still raises numerous questions. The first line of inquiry is suggested in the opening sentences of a speech printed in the *Michigan Law Review* in 1913:

---

108. Beitzinger, *supra* note 8, at 29; Carter, *supra* note 97, at 166-67 ("It must be conceded that the proceeding was somewhat disrespectful to the marshal and liable to be construed as against the peace and dignity of the United States of America.").

109. Beitzinger, *supra* note 8, at 30.

110. Beitzinger, *supra* note 8, at 30.

111. Carter, *supra* note 97, at 170.

112. Beitzinger, *supra* note 8, at 30. This second federal officer is not mentioned in Carter's highly detailed account of this period, *The Booth War in Ripon*, *supra* note 97.

113. Beitzinger, *supra* note 8, at 31.

114. HOWE, *supra* note 19, at 238.

115. Beitzinger, *supra* note 8, at 32. "Probably both Stanton [the U.S. Attorney General] and the President thought that the rebellion in the South was all that the Administration could manage without encouraging another in Wisconsin. So on the last day of Buchanan's Administration, Booth was pardoned." HOWE, *supra* note 19, at 238. Thomson, however, credits Judge Miller with procuring the pardon:

> He wrote to Buchanan without solicitation from any quarter that it would be a graceful ending of "this unfortunate affair" if the President would issue to Booth immediately an unconditional pardon, on his retirement from the office of chief magistrate. Buchanan immediately replied, thanking Judge Miller for the suggestion, and assuring him that he would act upon it.

A.M. THOMSON, A POLITICAL HISTORY OF WISCONSIN 101 (1898).

Probably most well informed persons of the present generation associate the notion, once maintained, that a state might secede or nullify an act of Congress, with the South and its earlier statesmen . . . . Yet it seems to be well authenticated that . . . the first formal and definite effort at nullification under solemn judicial sanction was made by the state of Wisconsin . . . .[116]

Why have the *Booth* cases remained so obscure if they truly are such a significant historical event? Why are they not well known as the first instance of secession? Why have they not enjoyed the popularity in the American public's consciousness of the history of slavery that the *Dred Scott* case has?[117]

The second line of inquiry relates to why Sherman Booth was singled out for persecution/prosecution when the actions of freeing Glover and resisting the enforcement of the Fugitive Slave Act of 1850 were so obviously a concerted effort on the part of a great many people in Wisconsin, including legislators and judges. Was Booth's behavior so inflammatory as to make him a natural target for exemplary prosecution?

The third line of inquiry concerns the motivations of all the judges involved. State and national politics unquestionably entered into the deliberations, for the state supreme court justices were

---

116. S.S. Gregory, *A Historic Judicial Controversy and Some Reflections Suggested by It*, 11 MICH. L. REV. 179 (1913); *see also* HOWE, *supra* note 19, at 238 ("Here then we have the Legislature, the Governor, the Supreme Court, and the people of Wisconsin committed to nullification as rank as anything of the kind ever advocated by Calhoun or the authorities of South Carolina.").

117. "*Dred Scott* had greater political implications, but *Ableman v. Booth* was the nail in the coffin of a legal strategy that had preoccupied the antislavery bar for almost the entire period of militant abolitionist activity." ROBERT COVER, JUSTICE ACCUSED 187 (1975).

"The [*Booth*] opinion was pronounced by Chief Justice Taney, but not until after his opinion in the *Dred Scott* case, which had greatly weakened the respect felt in the North for any opinion given by him involving the interests of slavery." HOWE, *supra* note 19, at 233.

What is curious is how often the *Booth* cases are overlooked. In a very insightful essay on Taney, *Roger Taney and the Limits of Judicial Power* in THE AMERICAN JUDICIAL TRADITION (1976), G. Edward White discusses the major cases of the Taney period, citing Dred Scott v. Sandford, 60 U.S. (19 How.) 393 (1857), Strader v. Graham, 51 U.S. (10 How.) 82 (1850), Prigg v. Pennsylvania, 41 U.S. (16 Pet.) 539 (1842), and Groves v. Slaughter, 40 U.S. (15 Pet.) 449 (1841), but there is no mention of *Ableman v. Booth*. But see ROBERT COVER, JUSTICE ACCUSED, at 166 n. (1975), where the author describes *Prigg, Booth,* and *Dred Scott* as "the three most important Supreme Court decisions on slavery."

Finally, though the *Booth* cases have received insufficient recognition nationally, they have been regarded as the leading historical Wisconsin cases among the members of the legal community in the state. Evan A. Evans, *Fifteen Important Decisions of the Wisconsin Supreme Court*, 23 MARQ. L. REV. 71 (1939).

elected officials. Neither Judge Miller nor Chief Justice Taney were elected,[118] however, so other explanations must be sought for their judicial behavior. The biographical information on each judge and justice given below may provide some insight into their motivations.

The *Booth* cases have been cited in numerous court decisions and legal or historical books and articles to support propositions about federalism,[119] the proper and improper use of writs of habeas corpus,[120] fugitive slave legislation and the problems of enforcing it,[121] and Wisconsin's development as a state that has always gone its own way.[122] None of them, however, combine an examination of the facts with an analysis of the opinions set in their historical context.

The *Booth* cases constituted the final rung on the ladder leading to the Civil War.[123] They also demonstrate that "hard cases make bad law."[124] The resolution of legal disputes at such great variance with public opinion càn serve as a focal point for the onset of cataclysmic political upheaval.

V. BACKGROUND TO THE *BOOTH* CASES

An understanding of the *Booth* cases and their historical importance requires a sense of both the legal framework and the major preceding historical events. These include the fugitive slave clause of the Constitution,[125] the 1793 Fugitive Slave Law,[126] *Prigg*

---

118. U.S. CONST. art. III, § 1: "The Judges, both of the supreme and inferior Courts, shall hold their Offices during good Behaviour . . . ."

119. *See, e.g.,* Richard S. Arnold, *State Power to Enjoin Federal Court Proceedings,* 51 VA. L. REV. 59, 65 n.35 (1965); Burt Neuborne, *The Myth of Parity,* 90 HARV. L. REV. 1105, 1111 *passim* (1977); *Interposition vs. Judicial Power: A Study of Ultimate Authority in Constitutional Questions,* 1 RACE REL. L. REP. 465, 492 (1956).

120. *See* ROLLIN C. HURD, A TREATISE ON THE RIGHT OF PERSONAL LIBERTY AND ON THE WRIT OF HABEAS CORPUS 649 (1858).

121. *See* HOWE, *supra* note 19, at 229; THOMAS D. MORRIS, FREE MEN ALL 173-80 (1974).

122. *See* CLARK, *supra* note 18; Mason, *supra* note 20; John Sundquist, *Construction of the Wisconsin Constitution—Recurrence to Fundamental Principles,* 62 MARQ. L. REV. 531, 532 (1979).

123. 2 JOHN BERRYMAN, HISTORY OF THE BENCH AND BAR OF WISCONSIN 2 (1898) (They "contributed not a little to preparing the way for the conflict of arms between the free and slave states in 1861.").

124. Northern Sec. Co. v. United States, 193 U.S. 197, 400 (1904) ("Great cases like hard cases make bad law.").

125. U.S. CONST. art. IV, § 2 (modified by Thirteenth Amendment).

126. Act of Feb. 12, 1793, ch. 7, 1 Stat. 302.

v. *Pennsylvania*,[127] the 1850 Fugitive Slave Law,[128] and *Dred Scott*.[129] Some knowledge of Wisconsin's history is also important to understand why the people, the legislature, and the judiciary took the stands they did. With a brief explanation of these factors, a closer look at the opinions of the judges reveals both more and less judicial wisdom than one might have expected.

The first important facet is the fugitive slave clause of the Constitution, Article IV, section 2. It states:

> No person held to service or labor in one state, under the laws thereof, escaping into another, shall, in consequence of any law or regulation therein, be discharged from such service or labor, but shall be delivered upon claim of the party to whom such service or labor may be due.

The difficulty with this clause is that it left certain concepts undefined. How was the "delivery" to take place? What constituted a proper "claim?" With a sizeable slave population,[130] clarifying and enabling legislation was definitely needed.

The first clarifying law was "An act respecting fugitives from justice, and persons escaping from the service of their masters" passed on February 12, 1793.[131] It required that a number of specific procedures be followed. An indictment or affidavit issued by a magistrate and certified by the governor of the state or territory from which the fugitive had fled had to be produced to the executive authority of the state in which the fugitive had been found.[132] The latter state authority was required to assist in the fugitive's arrest and to deliver the fugitive to the agent of the originating state's executive.[133] The Act specified a fine and term of imprisonment for anyone assisting in the fugitive's escape.[134] The Act further described judicial proceedings and necessary proof.[135]

The first major case interpreting the 1793 Act was *Prigg v.*

---

127. Prigg v. Pennsylvania, 41 U.S. (16 Pet.) 539 (1842).

128. Act of Sept. 18, 1850, ch. 60, 9 Stat. 462, *repealed by* Act of June 28, 1864, ch. 166, 13 Stat. 200.

129. Scott v. Sandford, 60 U.S. (19 How.) 393 (1857).

130. In 1790, the U.S. census showed the "free colored population" to be 59,466 and the slave population to be 697,897. By 1860, the U.S. census showed the figures to be 487,970 free colored and 3,953,760 slaves.

131. Act of Feb. 12, 1793, ch. 7, 1 Stat. 302.

132. *Id.* § 1.

133. *Id.*

134. *Id.* § 2.

135. *Id.* § 3.

Pennsylvania,[136] in which the Supreme Court upheld its constitutionality. Edward Prigg, acting as agent for Maryland slaveowner
Margaret Ashmore, went to Pennsylvania and applied for a warrant to remove Margaret Morgan, Ashmore's alleged fugitive
slave.[137] Prigg secured the warrant and brought Morgan before the
justice of the peace in Pennsylvania as required under the 1793
Act.[138] The justice of the peace refused to deal with the case.[139]
Prigg then took Morgan and her two children back to Maryland
and subsequently was indicted in Pennyslvania for kidnapping.[140]
His conviction was upheld by the Pennsylvania Supreme Court but
reversed by the U.S. Supreme Court in 1842.[141] The decision had a
much greater impact than the simple freeing of a convicted kidnapper. In addition to upholding the 1793 Fugitive Slave Act, it also
declared unconstitutional the 1826 Pennsylvania personal liberty
law,[142] casting into doubt the personal liberty laws of many other
northern states. The majority opinion, written by Justice Story,
stated that enforcement of the federal law was largely the responsibility of federal authorities.[143] Given the scarcity of federal officials
in some of the other states, enforcement of such an unpopular federal law without the assistance of state officials became far more
difficult.[144] While state officials were not absolutely prohibited
from enforcing the federal law, and indeed could arrest runaway
slaves as part of their general police power, Story maintained that
the states could not be coerced into doing so.[145] This point would
be revisited in the *Booth* controversy. Chief Justice Taney, often
considered a proponent of state independence of thought and action, nonetheless disagreed with this part of Story's opinion, recognizing the federal government's need to enlist the aid of state

---

136. Prigg v. Pennsylvania, 41 U.S. (16 Pet.) 539 (1842).
137. *Id.*
138. *Id.*
139. *Id.*
140. *Id.*
141. Judgment against Edward Prigg rendered in the York County Court of Oyer
and Terminer was taken to the Pennsylvania Supreme Court on a writ of error in May term
1840. There it was affirmed *pro forma* and the case was carried to the Supreme Court of
the United States. *Id.* at 558.
142. Law of Mar. 25, 1826, ch. 5777, 9 Pa. Laws. 95.
143. *Prigg*, 41 U.S. at 615-16.
144. FEHRENBACHER, *supra* note 2, at 45 ("Various northern legislatures enacted
laws forbidding state officials to participate in the recovery of fugitive slaves.").
145. *Prigg*, 41 U.S. at 615-16, 625.

officials.[146] Many state officials ultimately chose not to assist in the enforcement of a law they found odious.[147]

Finally, *Prigg* is noteworthy because, "among other things, this was the first Supreme Court opinion in which slavery was explicitly recognized as a constitutionally protected institution with special privileges within the Union."[148] It certainly struck a nerve in the free states, notably Wisconsin, where several of the *Booth* opinions, especially those of Justice Smith, include critical analyses of *Prigg*.[149]

After *Prigg* exposed some of the inadequacies of the 1793 Fugitive Slave Act, particularly regarding enforcement, dissatisfaction began to grow, especially among the Southern states.[150] On September 18, 1850, Congress, responding to this pressure, passed "An Act to amend, and supplementary to, the Act entitled 'An Act respecting Fugitives from Justice, and Persons escaping from the Service of their Masters, approved February twelfth, one thousand seven hundred ninety-three.' "[151]

The 1850 Act was an attempt to resolve the uncertainties in the 1793 Act discovered in the intervening fifty-seven years.[152] It created commissioners as judicial officers to execute the judicial powers and duties of the law.[153] Their jurisdiction was made concurrent with the judges of circuit and district courts of the United States.[154] A stiff one thousand dollar penalty was prescribed for

---

146. "I think, the states are not prohibited; and that, on the contrary, it is enjoined upon them as a duty, to protect and support the owner, when he is endeavouring to obtain possession of his property found within their respective territories." 41 U.S. at 627. For a discussion of the Taney Court's attitude toward state-federal relations, see FEHRENBACHER, *supra* note 2, at 228-35.

147. Paul Finkelman, *Prigg v. Pennsylvania and Northern State Courts: Anti-Slavery Use of a Pro-Slavery Decision*, 25 CIVIL WAR HIST. 5, 9-10 (1979).

148. *Id.* at 10.

149. *In re Booth*, 3 Wis. at 49-52, 66-67, 107 (1854); *In re* Booth, 3 Wis. 144, 191 (1854); see also TITUS HUTCHINSON, JURISDICTION OF COURTS, THAT OF STATE COURTS ORIGINAL, THAT OF UNITED STATES COURTS DERIVATIVE (1855), for an interesting contemporary discussion of the *Booth* cases and *Prigg*.

150. *See* Allen Johnson, *The Constitutionality of the Fugitive Slave Acts*, 31 YALE L.J. 161 (1921).

151. Act of Sept. 18, 1850, ch. 60, 9 Stat. 462, *repealed by* Act of June 28, 1864, ch. 166, 13 Stat. 200. For a discussion of both the 1793 and 1850 Fugitive Slave Acts, see Johnson, *supra* note 150.

152. *See* Johnson, *supra* note 150, at 169-70.

153. Act of Sept. 18, 1850, ch. 60, § 1, 9 Stat. 462, *repealed by* Act of June 28, 1864, ch. 166, 13 Stat. 200.

154. *Id.* § 4.

any United States marshal who did not execute a warrant issued under this Act.[155] Commissioners were authorized to appoint a *posse comitatus* to execute warrants, "and all good citizens [were] hereby commanded to aid and assist in the prompt and efficient execution of this law."[156]

The hearing procedures specifically indicated that the alleged fugitive would not be allowed to testify.[157] Persons who helped the alleged fugitive escape faced stiffer penalties under the 1850 Act[158] than under the 1793 Act.[159] The Commissioner was entitled to a fee of ten dollars for granting the certificate, but only five dollars if the claimant's proof was insufficient to warrant granting a certificate.[160] As one commentator succinctly put it: "[F]eatures unnecessarily irritating enhanced the unpopularity of an intrinsically distasteful law."[161] Sherman Booth was prosecuted under this law four years after its passage.[162]

The intervening decision in *Dred Scott* has only indirect relevance to the *Booth* cases. *Dred Scott* encompassed eleven years of litigation, culminated in the 1857 Supreme Court opinion, and preceded by two years the Supreme Court's *Booth* decision.[163] However, none of the Wisconsin or federal *Booth* opinions cites *Dred Scott*. Nevertheless, it was an influential opinion and is so reflective of the biases of the time[164] that it must be considered as part of the context of the *Booth* cases.

Dred Scott, his wife, and two daughters were slaves owned by an Army doctor, John Emerson.[165] Although Missouri residents, they accompanied the doctor into the free state of Illinois and later into the free Wisconsin Territory.[166] Dred Scott waited, however, until his return to the slave state of Missouri to sue for his freedom,

---

155. *Id.* § 5.
156. *Id.*
157. *Id.*
158. *Id.*
159. Act of Feb. 12, 1793, ch. 7, § 4, 1 Stat. 302, 305 (provided for a fine not exceeding $1000, imprisonment not exceeding six months, and civil damages of $1000).
160. Act of Sept. 18, 1850, ch. 60, § 8, 9 Stat. 462, 464, *repealed by* Act of June 28, 1864, ch. 166, 13 Stat. 200 (provided for a fine of $500).
161. 1 BERRYMAN, *supra* note 48, at 28.
162. *In re* Booth, 3 Wis. 13 (1854).
163. *See infra* note 169 for commentary on *Dred Scott*.
164. Carter, *supra* note 97 at 161; WESTEL W. WILLOUGHBY, THE SUPREME COURT OF THE UNITED STATES 95 (1890).
165. Scott v. Sandford, 60 U.S. 393, 397-98 (1857).
166. *Id.* at 397.

after trying unsuccessfully to purchase it.[167] Eventually the case went to the Supreme Court, which held that Scott was not entitled to his freedom.[168] The commentary on the case is voluminous,[169] underscoring the fact that it is unquestionably the most important opinion authored by Roger Brooke Taney, and probably the one most damaging to his judicial reputation. Its importance for *Booth* lies in its proslavery cast. While *Dred Scott* specifically stated that African-Americans were not citizens, its implication was that they were not even persons.[170] This harsh attitude would later motivate the Wisconsin citizenry in 1859 to stand up for fair treatment for one of their own residents, Joshua Glover, regardless of his color.

Finally, one cannot ignore the social and political environment of Wisconsin. Proslavery sentiment existed in western and particularly in southwestern Wisconsin during its territorial days.[171] Generally, however, the territory was antislavery in orientation, with Racine County being the center of such sentiment.[172] The first abolition society was formed there in 1840, eight years before statehood.[173] In 1842, a territorial antislavery party was formed; in 1843, the first abolitionist newspaper in the territory, the *Wisconsin Aegis*, was established in Racine.[174] Its successor, the *American Freeman*, established in 1843, became famous because of its editor, Sherman M. Booth.[175]

Antislavery public opinion crystallized in 1850 with the passage of the Fugitive Slave Law.[176] Another shock to the public consciousness came early in 1854 with the repeal of the Missouri Compromise in the passage of the Kansas-Nebraska Act.[177] The

---

167. FEHRENBACHER, *supra* note 2, at 250.

168. 60 U.S. 393, 453.

169. Especially noteworthy are: FEHRENBACHER, *supra* note 2; DON E. FEHRENBACHER, SLAVERY, LAW AND POLITICS (1981) (abridged version of DRED SCOTT) [hereinafter SLAVERY, LAW AND POLITICS]; and WALTER EHRLICH, THEY HAVE NO RIGHTS (1979). Fehrenbacher's abridged work and Ehrlich's book both contain extensive bibliographies.

170. FEHRENBACHER, *supra* note 2, at 363.

171. Kate E. Levi, *The Wisconsin Press and Slavery*, 9 WIS. MAG. OF HIST. 423 (1926).

172. *Id.*

173. *Id.*

174. *Id.*

175. *Id.* at 425; *see also* Winslow, *Special Address*, *supra* note 23, at 46; *An Abolitionist in Territorial Wisconsin*, 52 WIS. MAG. OF HIST. 3 (1968-69).

176. Mason, *supra* note 20, at 120.

177. Act of May 30, 1854, Ch. 59, 10 Stat. 277. For a brief discussion of the impact of the Kansas-Nebraska Act in Wisconsin, see CLARK, *supra* note 18, at 15. For an inter-

Glover/Booth incidents revealed Wisconsin's answer to these measures.

While antislavery sentiment was strong, familiarity with the black man was more theoretical than real in early Wisconsin. In 1850 there were 635 free blacks and no slaves out of a total state population of 305,391.[178] By 1860, the black population had nearly doubled (1,171).[179] Racism did exist in Wisconsin.

> When the first state constitutional convention assembled in Madison in 1846, a young Irishman, destined to achieve eminence as Chief Justice of the state supreme court, addressed the delegates on the subject of Negro suffrage. In detail, Edward G. Ryan pictured the abject social condition and habits of the colored people of New York City. There, he proclaimed, "Every negro was a thief and every negro woman far worse." Defiantly he challenged any gentleman present to refute his words.[180]

The attainment of suffrage for black Wisconsin citizens illustrates the strength of racism in this antislavery state.[181] The first state constitutional convention, held in Madison in 1846, debated suffrage for African-Americans.[182] After a great deal of political wrangling, the delegates finally attached to the constitution a resolution on suffrage for men of color. A separate ballot was required on which a majority of all those voting in the general election had to vote affirmatively in order for this resolution to pass.[183] The constitution was defeated 20,233 to 14,119.[184] The suffrage question was defeated by a vote of 14,615 to 7,664.[185]

The second constitutional convention met in Madison in 1847-48.[186] Edward Whiton, another future Chief Justice of the state supreme court, debating in favor of the postponement of the suffrage question, said: "If that race become[s] enlightened sufficient

---

esting, though hardly impartial, discussion of this legislation, "wicked as a covenant with hell," see FRANK A. FLOWER, HISTORY OF THE REPUBLICAN PARTY 81-96 (1884).

178. ZACHARY COOPER, BLACK SETTLERS IN RURAL WISCONSIN 4 (1977).

179. *Id.*

180. Leslie H. Fishel, *Wisconsin and Negro Suffrage*, 47 WIS. MAG. OF HIST. 180 (1963) (citations omitted).

181. For background on suffrage for African-Americans in Wisconsin, see *id.* and CURRENT, *supra* note 92, at 148.

182. Fishel, *supra* note 180, at 181-82.

183. Fishel, *supra* note 180, at 182, 184.

184. Fishel, *supra* note 180, at 183.

185. Fishel, *supra* note 180, at 183.

186. Fishel, *supra* note 180, at 183.

to entitle them to a right to vote, in heaven's name, let them have it."[187] Ultimately this convention left it to the state legislature to decide when to put African-American suffrage on the ballot in a general election.[188] The constitution passed and Wisconsin became the thirtieth state in 1848.[189]

The following year's general election had the suffrage question on the ballot.[190] Even though a majority of those voting on this single issue (5,265 to 4,075) voted affirmatively, this was not a majority of the 31,759 votes cast overall, and therefore the resolution failed.[191] The issue arose again in the general election of 1857 and was soundly defeated, 40,915 to 23,074.[192] The Civil War did not make a difference. When the issue was again raised in the 1865 election, the fact that black men had fought in the Civil War and paid taxes did not matter enough; the suffrage issue was defeated by a 9000-vote margin.[193]

One black Wisconsin citizen, Ezekiel Gillespie, had tolerated enough. Represented by Byron Paine, formerly Sherman Booth's attorney and formerly a state supreme court justice, he sued Henry Palmer, the inspector of elections in the Milwaukee ward where he lived.[194] Palmer had refused to allow him to vote in the 1865 election.[195] The case reached the Wisconsin Supreme Court in 1866.[196] Paine argued that the resolution passed by the state constitutional convention in 1848 with regard to a majority of the electorate deciding on African-American suffrage meant a majority of those voting on that particular issue, not a majority voting in the election as a whole.[197] Whether due to Paine's brilliant style, the defendant's lackluster style, the political climate in the state, or all of the above, the supreme court ruled in favor of Ezekiel Gillespie, and African-Americans in Wisconsin finally won the franchise.[198]

By the mid-nineteenth century, Wisconsin was an environ-

---

187. Fishel, *supra* note 180, at 183 (citation omitted).
188. Fishel, *supra* note 180, at 184.
189. Fishel, *supra* note 180, at 184.
190. Fishel, *supra* note 180, at 184.
191. Fishel, *supra* note 180, at 185.
192. Fishel, *supra* note 180, at 188.
193. Fishel, *supra* note 180, at 193.
194. Fishel, *supra* note 180, at 194-95.
195. Fishel, *supra* note 180, at 194.
196. Gillespie v. Palmer, 20 Wis. 572 (1866).
197. *Id.* at 584; Fishel, *supra* note 180, at 195.
198. 20 Wis. at 572, 590; Fishel, *supra* note 180, at 196.

ment of contrasts—antislavery for the most part but hardly racially unbiased.[199] However, according to the citizens of Wisconsin, one African-American deserved fair treatment; his name was Joshua Glover.

VI. The Wisconsin Court and Its Opinions

The justices of the Wisconsin Supreme Court were not simply local citizens elevated to the bench and confronted with difficult moral and legal issues. They were, in fact, a worldly group in terms of legal training and experience. Their *Booth* opinions show erudition worthy of some of the better known state jurists of the nineteenth century.

Wisconsin became a state on May 29, 1848.[200] Initially, the state was divided into five circuits, each with its own elected judge.[201] A sixth circuit was added in 1850.[202] These judges sat together annually as a supreme court.[203] The state constitution provided for reorganization of the judiciary after five years if the circuit court/supreme court arrangement proved unsatisfactory.[204] With the growth of the population, this double duty became too burdensome and a separate supreme court was created.[205] The chief justice and two associate justices were elected in September 1852, with staggered terms.[206] Edward Whiton, a circuit court judge since 1848, was elected Chief Justice, and Abram Smith and Samuel Crawford were elected Associate Justices.[207] At the time of the Glover/Booth incidents in 1854, this was still a very new court in a very new state.

None of these three justices was born in Wisconsin.[208] Abram D. Smith studied and practiced law in New York prior to his arri-

---

199. For a more complete discussion of the antislavery-but-racist mind-set of many people in the free states prior to the Civil War, see Eric Foner, Free Soil, Free Labor, Free Men (1970). For a discussion of the rise of the antislavery Republican party in Wisconsin, see Theodore C. Smith, *The Free Soil Party in Wisconsin*, Proceedings of the State Historical Society of Wisconsin 97-162 (1894) and Current, *supra* note 92.

200. Reed, *supra* note 14, at 29.

201. Reed, *supra* note 14, at 29.

202. Reed, *supra* note 14, at 30.

203. Reed, *supra* note 14, at 29.

204. Reed, *supra* note 14, at 30.

205. Reed, *supra* note 14, at 32.

206. Reed, *supra* note 14, at 30-31.

207. Reed, *supra* note 14, at 29-31.

208. For more information on the three justices, see Timothy Higgins, *Justices of the Wisconsin Supreme Court*, 1949 Wis. L. Rev. 738 (1949).

val in Wisconsin in 1842, when he set up practice in Milwaukee.[209] Chief Justice Edward V. Whiton was a member of the bar in his native Massachusetts prior to settling in Janesville, Wisconsin, where he set up practice in 1837.[210] He was a member of both houses of the territorial legislature (1838-46), a delegate to the second state constitutional convention (1847-48), a state circuit judge (1848-53) and the first Chief Justice of the reorganized Wisconsin Supreme Court from 1853 until his death in 1859.[211] Samuel Crawford received an excellent education in his native Ireland, then studied law in New York and Illinois before setting up practice in New Diggings, Wisconsin in 1844.[212]

Despite a highly volatile political environment, and a new court, the opinions in the *Booth* cases were remarkably well reasoned and written. Although Justice Smith occasionally bent matters to create a more sympathetic perspective in the reader, he was doing neither more nor less than did Chief Justice Taney. But Taney was not an elected official, and thus did not have to assume responsibility for his opinions in quite the same way as did these state jurists.

The first Wisconsin opinion in the *Booth* line[213] of litigation was Judge Smith's decision regarding Sherman Booth's first petition for a writ of habeas corpus. It asserted a number of principles that would be vehemently argued or pointedly ignored in subsequent opinions. First, he questioned Booth's motives in seeking this writ during the court's vacation instead of during the term that coincided with Booth's arrest.[214] He expressed his own inadequacy to deal with this case, a sentiment common to nineteenth-century jurists deciding issues related to slavery.[215] He also stated: "I do

---

209. DICTIONARY, *supra* note 87, at 330.
210. DICTIONARY, *supra* note 87, at 374-75.
211. DICTIONARY, *supra* note 87, at 375.
212. WINSLOW, GREAT COURT, *supra* note 23, at 43-44.
213. *In re* Booth, 3 Wis. 13 (1854).
214. *Id.* at 20.
215. *Id.* at 31. This sentiment is reminiscent of Judge Ruffin's remarks in State v. Mann, 13 N.C. (2 Dev.) 263, 264 (1829): "The struggle . . . in the Judge's own breast between the feelings of the man and the duty of the magistrate is a severe one, presenting strong temptation to put aside such questions, if it be possible." Both Smith and Ruffin, however reluctant they may have been, wrote important and controversial opinions on the issue of slavery.

For an interesting discussion of the judges' dilemma in reconciling their moral qualms with the enforcement of the Fugitive Slave Acts, see H.L.A. Hart, *Law in the Perspective of Philosophy: 1776-1976*, 51 N.Y.U. L. REV. 538, 548-51 (1976).

not admit the right . . . merely to experiment upon my opinions
. . . ."[216] Despite his misgivings and modesty, however, the justice
had something to say and was not to be deterred.

Justice Smith saw no jurisdictional conflict because United
States commissioners ("irresponsible and unimpeachable"[217]) did
not have "exclusive or ultimate jurisdiction."[218] This was the first
step in his attack on the validity of the 1850 Fugitive Slave Law
that granted the commissioners jurisdiction in cases such as
Glover's.[219]

He then reached the major point over which Wisconsin and
the United States Supreme Court would disagree—the question of
who had jurisdiction to investigate and decide the kinds of questions presented by the *Booth* cases.[220] He stated:

> Every jot and tittle of power delegated to the federal gov-
> ernment will be acquiesced in, but every jot and tittle of power
> reserved to the states will be rigidly asserted, and as rigidly
> sustained.
>
> It is only by exacting of the federal government a rigid con-
> formity to the prescribed limitation of its powers, and by the
> assertion and exercise on the part of the states of all the powers
> reserved to them, and a due regard by both of their just and
> legitimate sphere, that obedience can be rightfully exacted of the
> citizen, to the authority of either.[221]

As a theoretical matter, Chief Justice Taney would probably
have agreed with the sentiment expressed here. It would be his
assertion five years later that this state supreme court simply exceeded its legitimate authority.[222]

Justices Smith and Taney appeared to agree on two points.
First, the Constitution of the United States was the fundamental
law of the land and was to be upheld by all citizens.[223] Second,
Smith, without elaborating, asserted his agreement with Taney's

---

216. *In re Booth*, 3 Wis. at 25.

217. *Id.* at 21.

218. *Id.* at 20.

219. Act of Sept. 18, 1850, ch. 60, 9 Stat. 462, *repealed by* Act of June 28, 1864, ch.
166, 13 Stat. 200.

220. *In re Booth*, 3 Wis. at 20-22.

221. *Id.* at 22.

222. Ableman v. Booth, 62 U.S. (21 How.) 506 (1859); *see also* Passmore Williamson's Case, 26 Pa. 9 (1855) (holding that state supreme court cannot grant writ of habeas
corpus to abolitionist cited and imprisoned for contempt in federal court proceeding regarding freeing of slaves brought into free jurisdiction).

223. *In re Booth*, 3 Wis. at 23.

concurrence in *Prigg v. Pennsylvania*.[224]

There were two major reasons why Justice Smith ordered Booth's release. First, Garland did not make a proper claim on Glover as his fugitive slave, as required under the 1850 Fugitive Slave Act.[225] Unless such a claim was established, the status of the alleged fugitive was identical to any other (white) citizen of Wisconsin.[226] Second, the fugitive slave law was unconstitutional because it violated the Due Process Clause of the Constitution.[227]

He ended the opinion by asserting that there existed no authoritative judicial guide to the 1850 Act.[228] Smith also suggested to the Supreme Court that it review its own decision in *Prigg v. Pennsylvania*.[229]

After Justice Smith ordered Booth discharged, the Supreme Court granted certiorari to correct any error in the prior opinion.[230] In the second part of this opinion, the Wisconsin Supreme Court, by a vote of 2 to 1, upheld the granting of the petition for the writ of habeas corpus.[231] Whiton wrote the majority opinion, Crawford the dissent, and Smith a concurring opinion in which he restated his views even more vehemently.[232]

Chief Justice Whiton's opinion was concise compared with either of Smith's opinions. Whiton addressed several questions deserving comment. First, should the writ have been issued by a state supreme court justice when the prisoner was detained by virtue of legal process conducted by a United States Commissioner?[233] Whiton began his affirmative answer with a definition of comity, but immediately distinguished this case from one in which comity would apply.[234] "We do not see how these commissioners can properly be called officers of the *courts* of the United States . . . . Nor do we think that they can, with any propriety, be called judi-

---

224. *Id.* at 52 ("Time will not permit a further review of this case."); *see supra* text accompanying notes 143-48 for a discussion of *Prigg v. Pennsylvania*.
225. *In re Booth*, 3 Wis. at 29.
226. *Id.*
227. *Id.* at 47-49.
228. *Id.* at 53.
229. *Id.* at 52.
230. *Id.* at 54.
231. *Id.*
232. *Id.* at 54, 72, 86.
233. *Id.* at 57.
234. *Id.* at 57, 59.

cial officers."[235] To apply comity here would require that the case was pending before a United States district court, a fact that was not shown.[236] The state supreme court appropriately issued the writ.[237]

The second important question Chief Justice Whiton considered was whether the prisoner was discharged in accordance with law.[238] He held that it was lawful after asserting that the warrant was defective because it failed to show why Joshua Glover was in custody.[239] Even if the warrant was not defective, the arrest was still unlawful because the 1850 Fugitive Slave Act under which he was arrested was unconstitutional.[240] The plaintiff in error, Marshal Ableman, had asserted that because the 1793 Act had been held constitutional by the United States Supreme Court in *Prigg*,[241] it followed that the 1850 Act was also constitutional. The court was not persuaded.[242]

After giving the obligatory lament, wishing it did not have to decide these questions, the court held the 1850 Act unconstitutional because 1) it gave commissioners judicial powers[243] and 2) it denied the alleged fugitive due process and a trial by jury.[244]

Chief Justice Whiton denied the validity of comparing the situation of a fugitive from labor with that of a fugitive from justice.[245] With a fugitive from justice, all that was determined by the state official was that he should return to the state from whence he fled for a determination of his guilt.[246] However, for a fugitive from labor, his status was adjudged before extradition.[247] Furthermore, the accused was found to be a slave without a chance to say anything in his own behalf, call witnesses, or in general have an opportunity to be heard.[248]

Justice Crawford, although harboring doubts about the 1850

---

235. *Id.* at 57.
236. *Id.* at 59.
237. *Id.* at 60-61.
238. *Id.* at 61.
239. *Id.* at 62.
240. *Id.*
241. *Id.* at 62-63.
242. *Id.*
243. *Id.* at 67.
244. *Id.*
245. *Id.* at 83.
246. *Id.*
247. *Id.* at 70-71.
248. *Id.* at 70.

Act, dissented.[249] He stated: "The force of argument . . . has failed to produce that conviction which should justify a court, or judge, to pronounce a legal enactment void, because unconstitutional, and I am therefore unable to concur in the opinion that this law is unconstitutional."[250]

Justice Smith concurred in an incredibly long opinion (48 pages), much of which simply restated his earlier views.[251] Some points, however, deserve attention.

Justice Crawford's dissent evidently stung Smith badly, for he stated that Crawford was equating "a dignified judicial subordination" with "requiring absolute and unqualified submission on the part of the states."[252] Smith was distressed by the underlying notion that because state officials, including the judiciary, cannot be relied on to execute their constitutional duties, federal officers must execute those duties.[253]

Smith asserted that the only issue before the Court in *Prigg v. Pennsylvania* was the constitutionality of the Pennsylvania law.[254] The question was not: Does Congress have exclusive power to legislate in regard to fugitive slaves, *or* do the states have concurrent power to legislate on the same matter?[255] Because these questions were not before the Wisconsin court, the U.S. Supreme Court's observations were merely dicta.[256]

In light of Chief Justice Taney's later opinion, one of Smith's most interesting statements was that an important rule of legal interpretation, found in Story's *Commentaries*, had been violated.[257] This rule dictated that one not "enlarge the construction of a given power beyond the fair scope of its terms" just because it was inconvenient to stay within its bounds.[258] Justice Smith applied the rule to the Booth situation, stating:

> The states have agreed that escaping slaves shall not be discharged from service or labor by the operation of their own

---

249. *Id.* at 72 (Crawford, J., dissenting).
250. *Id.* at 80.
251. *Id.* at 86-134 (Smith, J., concurring).
252. *Id.* at 98.
253. *Id.*
254. *Id.* at 108.
255. *Id.*
256. *Id.* at 109.
257. *Id.* at 110.
258. *Id.* (referring to JOSEPH STORY, COMMENTARIES ON THE CONSTITUTION OF THE UNITED STATES I 409-10 (1833)).

laws, but that when claimed within their territory, and the claim established, shall be delivered up. This is the extent of the obligation. Is it not to enlarge the scope of its terms, to hold . . . that they have thrown open their territories to incursion by fugitive hunters, and relinquished all power to protect their own people from false charges of escape, or of the obligation of service? or from assault and outrage during the search?[259]

Smith dwelled at length on the fact that the slave, while chattel in a slaveholding state, is a "MAN . . . . a PERSON" in Wisconsin.[260]

Smith maintained that *Prigg* overturned the long-established principle that all powers not delegated to the federal government are reserved to the states.[261] Smith interpreted *Prigg* as holding that powers not specifically reserved for the states belong to the federal government and that these federal powers can be expanded at will.[262] "Fealty to the doctrines of this case is treason to the law of all preceding cases."[263] Given the perceived proslavery stance of the federal government, as exemplified by the *Prigg* decision, Smith was compelled to comment bitterly: "The rights, interests, feelings, . . . of the free states are as nothing, while the mere pecuniary interests of the slaveholder are everything."[264]

He concluded his concurrence with a long critique of *Prigg v. Pennsylvania.*[265] The Supreme Court did not deal with the fact that Margaret Morgan's children were taken with their mother into Maryland.[266] One of the children had been born in Pennsylvania more than a year after the mother's escape from Maryland.[267]

---

259. *In re Booth*, 3 Wis. at 110-11 (Smith, J., concurring).
260. *Id.* at 113.
261. *Id.* at 115-17.
262. *Id.*
263. *Id.* at 117.
264. *Id.* at 123. Such extreme language, representing an extreme view of the impasse over slavery rapidly approaching in the United States, has been expanded elsewhere. One commentator has noted: "By the eve of secession, on the important issues of slavery, comity, and federalism, the most extreme courts in the North and those in the South acted as though they were in separate nations—and they soon would be." PAUL FINKELMAN, AN IMPERFECT UNION 286 (1981). The clerk of the Supreme Court of the United States, William Thomas Carroll, has reported that on delivery of a copy of the Court's opinion in *Ableman v. Booth* to President Buchanan, the President remarked that "[T]he Supreme Court and the Executive should stand shoulder to shoulder in such a crisis, that united they might be able to resist the fanaticism of both the North and the South . . . ." Memorandum of William Thomas Carroll, dated Apr. 28, 30, 1859, *cited in* A.J. Beitzinger, *Chief Justice Taney and the Publication of Court Opinions*, 7 CATH. U. L. REV. 32, 34 (1958).
265. *In re Booth*, 3 Wis. at 123 (Smith, J., concurring).
266. *Id.* at 129.
267. *Id.*

Smith's analysis of *Prigg* was that either the condition of the slave mother attached to the child regardless of the child's place of birth, or that the Court simply overlooked this "little humanity."[268]

Finally, in case his position had been misunderstood, Justice Smith stated:

[The states] will never consent that a slave owner, his agent, or an officer of the United States, armed with process to arrest a fugitive from service is clothed with entire immunity from state authority; to commit whatever crime or outrage against the laws of the state, that their own high prerogative of *habeas corpus* shall be annulled, their authority defied, their officers resisted, the process of their own courts condemned, their territory invaded by federal force, the houses of their citizens searched, the sanctuary of their homes invaded, their streets and public places made the scene of tumultuous and armed violence, and state sovereignty succumb, paralyzed and aghast, before the process of an officer unknown to the constitution, and irresponsible to its sanctions. At least, such shall not become the degradation of Wisconsin, without meeting as stern remonstrance and resistance as I may be able to interpose, so long as her people impose upon me the duty of guarding their rights and liberties, and of maintaining the dignity and sovereignty of their state.[269]

After the Wisconsin Supreme Court opinion, the federal grand jury indicted Booth and Rycraft for aiding and abetting Glover's escape.[270] One question to consider is why they were indicted in the first place, given the strong public sentiment against the 1850 Fugitive Slave Act and the public arousal over Joshua Glover's capture. A possible answer is found in Parker Reed's 1882 edition of the *Bench and Bar of Wisconsin*:

The motion of [Booth's] counsel that the indictment should be set aside, on the ground, as shown by the affidavits of four witnesses, that two of the grand jury which had indicted him were strongly prejudiced against the defendant, and had expressed themselves in favor of his conviction, was overruled.[271]

With the indictment pending against him, Sherman Booth once again petitioned the Wisconsin Supreme Court for a writ of habeas corpus.[272] This time the writ was denied in an opinion writ-

---

268. *Id.* at 130.
269. *Id.* at 133-34 (Smith, J., concurring).
270. *Ex parte* Booth, 3 Wis. 134, 135-36 (1854).
271. REED, *supra* note 14, at 501.
272. *Ex parte Booth*, 3 Wis. at 135.

ten by Chief Justice Whiton with a concurrence by Justice Smith.[273] The rationale of the court in taking this politically unpopular step was that once the district court obtained jurisdiction, its jurisdiction was exclusive and the Wisconsin court could not interfere.[274] In response to Booth's assertion that no court can have jurisdiction to try a person for an alleged violation of a void statute, Whiton said that the district court must determine all questions presented by the case, including the question of its own jurisdiction.[275]

Justice Smith felt compelled to distinguish this habeas corpus petition from the first one Booth requested.[276] The granting of the first petition was no bar to new proceedings in the federal court: "His discharge is by no means an acquittal."[277] If state and federal courts wrested cases from each other for fear that the other tribunal would not properly decide matters, this would show an unseemly want of confidence among judicial brethren.[278] Smith declared that the Wisconsin Supreme Court's decision on the unconstitutionality of the 1850 Fugitive Slave Act was not binding on the federal court.[279] But he also suggested that Booth could use the state pronouncement as part of his defense in federal court.[280]

Booth paid bail and was released from jail after ten days.[281] Booth and Rycraft were to be tried together in federal district court in November 1854, but a case of typhoid fever prevented Booth's appearance and Rycraft was tried separately.[282]

To understand the federal position on these matters, it is helpful to look at Judge Miller's charge to the jury in Rycraft's case.[283] "This being a national court, you are a national jury, equally removed, with the judge, from all local influences."[284] As a state-

---

273. *Id.* at 136, 138.
274. *Id.* at 137.
275. *Id.* at 137-38.
276. *Id.* at 138.
277. *Id.* at 140.
278. *Id.* at 141.
279. *Id.* at 143.
280. *Id.* at 144. One commentator has speculated about this denial of the writ of habeas corpus: "One cannot help suspecting that the members of the court indulged the hope that no Wisconsin jury could be found, which would convict Booth, and that the whole affair would soon be moot, by reason of his triumphant acquittal." Hagan, *supra* note 36, at 22.
281. REED, *supra* note 14, at 501.
282. REED, *supra* note 14, at 501.
283. United States v. Rycraft, 27 F. Cas. 918 (D.C.C. Wis. 1854).
284. *Id.* at 919.

ment of a goal to which the jurors should strive, Judge Miller's point was plausible. But as a statement of reality, this was simply untrue. Given the law enforcement difficulties Judge Miller had already faced, he, most of all, was aware of the heavy weight of local political influences.

The following excerpt is even more problematical:

> This is a prosecution for the public offence of resisting a lawful process . . . . The judge has lawful authority to issue this process . . . . It was lawfully served by the deputy marshal; Glover was thereby in the custody of the law, from which he escaped before he was delivered.[285]

It is uncertain what the term "lawful" meant to Judge Miller. When slaveowner Garland had requested a writ of habeas corpus after his arrest for assault and battery on Glover, Miller granted the petition on the reported rationale that Garland "could not be interfered with by any legal process by the state, and that in the execution of his slave warrant he was justified in using any violence, even to the taking of life, if necessary, to secure his slave, and that no state process could interrupt such violence."[286] Though slave jurisdictions considered physical violence against slaves an acceptable form of "correction,"[287] Wisconsin was a free state and not accustomed to this type of behavior against one of its quiet, peaceful residents. Furthermore, the 1850 Fugitive Slave Act nowhere states or implies that this kind of violence was lawful in taking an alleged fugitive slave. Indeed, if it were permissible under the law, why would there be such elaborate provision on the issuance of the certificate to the slaveowner/claimant? It is doubtful that Justice Smith would have agreed with Judge Miller's concept of "lawful process."

A third troublesome point made by Judge Miller in this jury charge was: "If, as from the defendant's evidence, he was associated with that committee which was engaged in impeding or obstructing the process, he must take the consequences. They are all indictable."[288]

The fact is that very few were indicted and only Rycraft and

---

285. *Id.* at 922.
286. REED, *supra* note 14, at 500.
287. State v. Mann, 13 N.C. (2 Dev.) 263, 266 (1829) ("The power of the master must be absolute to render the submission of the slave perfect.").
288. *Rycraft*, 27 F. Cas. at 923.

Booth were actually convicted and punished.[289] Booth was ultimately pardoned by the President.[290] The question this raises is the ultimate nightmare of the lawmaker: How does the system deal with massive civil disobedience of an unpopular and arguably immoral and unconstitutional law? This is certainly not the only case in the decade preceding the Civil War in which groups of citizens undertook to emasculate this "intrinsically distasteful law."[291]

When Booth recovered from his illness, his case came to trial in January 1855.[292] The trial lasted five days and the jury deliberated its verdict for seven hours.[293] They found Booth not guilty on the first three counts for resisting United States process and guilty on the two counts regarding aiding Joshua Glover's escape.[294] Three jurors adopted a resolution that made it clear that while they saw conviction of Booth as inevitable, they were not morally comfortable with their role in the enforcement of the Fugitive Slave Law.[295] They ended their resolution by requesting the court's

---

289. "From the legal point of view the men who helped Glover to escape were undoubtedly guilty . . . . But their case was really that of the people of Wisconsin, and a people can neither be indicted nor put on formal trial." JOHN N. DAVIDSON, NEGRO SLAVERY IN WISCONSIN AND THE UNDERGROUND RAILROAD 238 (1896). "Because he was the most conspicuous member of the movement to free Glover, Booth was arrested . . . ." MORRIS, *supra* note 121, at 174.

It is not as though the other participants were not known.

A much more appropriate subject for the slaveholder's wrath would have been Edward P. Allis, the founder of the great iron works in Milwaukee, and a candidate for Governor of Wisconsin on the radical greenback ticket in 1877. Mr. Allis had hold of the piece of square timber which was used as a battering-ram when the door of the jail was smashed in and the slave taken out . . . . Booth made a propitiation for the sins of all the Abolitionists in Wisconsin . . . .

THOMSON, *supra* note 115, at 96-97.

290. *See supra* notes 115-16.

291. For a discussion of *Bushnell,* see 1 BERRYMAN, *supra* note 47, at 28. *See Ex Parte* Bushnell, 9 Ohio St. 77 (1859); Carter, *supra* note 97, at 163; COVER, *supra* note 117, at 188-89, 223, 253-54. The case of the fugitive slave Anthony Burns has been described in a number of publications, including David R. Maginnes, *The Case of the Court House Rioters in the Case of the Fugitive Slave Anthony Burns, 1854,* 56 J. OF NEGRO HIST. 31 (1971), and JANE PEASE & WILLIAM PEASE, THE FUGITIVE SLAVE LAW AND ANTHONY BURNS (1975).

For a theoretical discussion of nullification as "a socially useful part of the total legal process, . . . or as mere law-breaking . . . ," see Robert C. Binkley, *Nullification and the Legal Process,* 14 MASS. L.Q. 109 (1928-29).

292. REED, *supra* note 14, at 501.

293. REED, *supra* note 14, at 501.

294. REED, *supra* note 14, at 501-02.

295. REED, *supra* note 14, at 501-02.

clemency.[296]

Both Booth and Rycraft were sentenced to brief stays in the county jail and fines of $1,000 and $200, respectively.[297] On January 26, 1855, both men petitioned the Wisconsin Supreme Court for writs of habeas corpus.[298] These were granted, with all three justices filing opinions justifying this inconsistent and dangerous course of action because of its blatant challenge to federal authority.[299]

Chief Justice Whiton's brief opinion simply stated that the state supreme court should have the power to release its citizens from illegal imprisonment.[300] The federal court should have realized it had no jurisdiction because the federal law in question was a nullity.[301]

Justice Crawford, while somewhat cautious in his earlier opinion regarding Booth's first petition for a habeas writ,[302] now maintained that the district court did not have jurisdiction in this case because the indictment did not describe Glover as a fugitive from labor.[303] He ignored the fact that the warrant for Glover's arrest, which described him as a fugitive from labor, was reproduced in the indictment.[304] More incredible still, in light of the Wisconsin court's previous assertions, was the following:

> If either [state or federal courts], indeed, should assume to act in
> derogation of the prerogative of the other, a means of correcting

---

296. REED, *supra* note 14, at 502. At least three petit jurors felt empathy as indicated by the following resolution, which they adopted after Booth's indictment:

> That while we feel ourselves bound by a solemn oath to perform a most painful duty, in declaring the defendant guilty of the above charge, and thus making him liable to the penalties of a cruel and odious law, yet at the same time, in so doing, we declare that he performed a noble, benevolent and humane act, and we thus record our condemnation of the fugitive slave law, and earnestly commend him to the clemency of the court.

REED, *supra* note 14, at 502. Another commentator also describes them as "an unwilling jury." HOWE, *supra* note 19, at 232.

297. Beitzinger, *supra* note 8, at 15.

298. *In re* Booth, 3 Wis. 144, 146 (1854).

299. *Id.* at 171-72.

300. *Id.* at 160-61.

301. *Id.* at 160.

302. Justice Crawford's earlier opinion is at *In re Booth*, 3 Wis. at 72 (Crawford, J., dissenting).

303. *In re Booth*, 3 Wis. at 167-68.

304. *Id.* at 148-50. This text includes the warrant for Glover's arrest. *Id.* at 149 ("Whereas Bennami S. Garland hath made affidavit . . . that one Joshua Glover, a negro man, owes him labor and service, according to the laws of Missouri . . . .").

the evil would be very necessary, but we are not without that corrective. An unwarrantable infraction of the jurisdiction of the state tribunals by the federal courts, would call forth an assertion of their prerogatives and power by the state courts, and if in this the latter were wrong, a peaceful means of redress is afforded by a resort to the court of *dernier resort,* the supreme court of the United States, whose decision should and would be acquiesced in by all parties.[305]

The major principle asserted by Justice Smith was that the state supreme court had the power to inquire into the legality of inferior federal court proceedings that led to the imprisonment of a citizen of the state, and "the power to inquire includes the power to decide."[306] To the query of whether such interference might cause confusion in the interpretation of the Constitution, his response was to analogize that situation to the checks and balances system of the federal government, where a federal court can convict a person only to have that person pardoned later by the federal executive.[307] If interference does not cause havoc in the latter situation, why should it in the former?[308] Smith then speculated that it is safer to resist unconstitutional power at its onset "than to wait until the evil is so deeply and firmly rooted that the only remedy is revolution."[309] This prediction of war would be echoed in Taney's opinion.[310]

What started with Justice Smith granting the first habeas corpus writ to Booth hardened over eight months into a vehement antislavery, antifederalist stance. Could these justices have backed down at this point? Justice Crawford was defeated in his 1855 bid for reelection mainly because he was not willing to take a strong antislavery stance in the *Booth* case.[311] If Smith and Whiton had not already been prone to strong antislavery sentiments, a desire to maintain a long tenure on the bench might have pushed them in that direction.

Judge Andrew Miller, appointed for life, did not operate under

---

305. *Id.* at 171.
306. *Id.* at 175.
307. *Id.* at 181.
308. *Id.*
309. *Id.* at 182.
310. *Ableman,* 62 U.S. at 520-21.
311. *See* DICTIONARY, *supra* note 87, at 89; WINSLOW, GREAT COURT, *supra* note 23, at 87. For a thoughtful discussion on the judges-as-politicians idea, see Joseph Schafer, *Stormy Days in Court—the* Booth *Case,* 20 WIS. MAG. OF HIST. 89, 108-10 (1936).

these constraints.[312] Andrew G. Miller was a native of Pennsylvania, where he practiced law from 1822 to 1838 and held office as state attorney general for part of that time.[313] In 1838, President Van Buren commissioned him an associate justice of the Wisconsin territorial supreme court.[314] He served in that capacity until 1848, when he was appointed judge of the federal district of Wisconsin.[315] He maintained that appointment until the district was split in 1870; he then continued as judge for the eastern district until 1873.[316]

While one commentator has described Miller's demeanor throughout the *Booth* litigation as firm and courageous, he also noted that Miller's decisions were "virtually the end of the law for litigants"[317] because the expense of an appeal was prohibitive for many citizens. Given such power vested in one man, it must have been particularly difficult for him to accept the recalcitrance of his judicial cousins on the state supreme court. Chief Justice Ryan would say of him posthumously: "[T]here was something grand in the lonely self-reliance and steadfastness of the man . . . ."[318]

VII. CHIEF JUSTICE TANEY'S OPINION

By 1859, the tug of war between the state and federal judiciary over the *Booth* cases was firmly established. It was time for a higher judicial statement. Chief Justice Taney authored the Court's opinion.[319]

The opinion is only twenty-one pages in length, a middling size Taney opinion.[320] The first eight pages are a recounting of the history of the case.[321] In the remaining thirteen pages, Justice Taney made assertions that do not survive scrutiny and offers few legal or historical references to support his analysis.

The first shortcoming is his statement that the supremacy of the state courts over the federal courts in cases arising under the

---

312. 2 BERRYMAN, *supra* note 123, at 2 ("The large and nearly absolute power vested in the district judge could not fail to excite the jealousy of lawyers and their clients . . . .").
313. 2 BERRYMAN, *supra* note 123, at 4.
314. 2 BERRYMAN, *supra* note 123, at 4.
315. 2 BERRYMAN, *supra* note 123, at 4.
316. 2 BERRYMAN, *supra* note 123, at 4-5.
317. 2 BERRYMAN, *supra* note 123, at 1.
318. 2 BERRYMAN, *supra* note 123, at 7.
319. Ableman v. Booth, 62 U.S. (21 How.) 506, 507 (1859).
320. His majority opinion in *Dred Scott* was 56 pages long; in *Prigg v. Pennsylvania*, Justice Taney's dissent was 8 pages long.
321. *Ableman*, 62 U.S. at 507-14.

Constitution and federal laws had been asserted in *Booth* by a state supreme court for the first time.[322] This ignores the numerous habeas corpus cases in the early nineteenth century regarding minors in the armed forces.[323] The practice was long established that a state court could issue the writ for a person held in the custody of a federal officer.[324] Taney's opinion in *Ableman v. Booth* was the first Supreme Court challenge to such state action.

The second difficulty with Taney's opinion lies in his assertion that if Wisconsin could disregard the 1850 Fugitive Slave Law, then it could disregard any federal law.[325] If Wisconsin could do this, so could other states. Therefore, "it is very certain that the State courts would not always agree in opinion; and it would often happen, that an act which was admitted to be an offense, and justly punished, in one State, would be regarded as innocent, and indeed as praiseworthy, in another."[326] The majority decision in the subsequent 1870 Wisconsin Supreme Court case of *In re Tarble*[327] was written by Justice Byron Paine, Booth's attorney throughout the 1850's litigation. Justice Paine took this occasion to engage in a lengthy defense of the Wisconsin *Booth* opinions.[328] According to Paine, the Wisconsin court never claimed authority to annul a federal court judgment, but was simply acting under the familiar principle that

> whenever, in any court, in a case in which it has jurisdiction, the validity of the judgment of any other court is drawn collaterally in question, it must decide whether the court rendering it had

---

322. *Id.*
323. Dallin H. Oaks, *Habeas Corpus in the States—1776-1865*, 32 U. CHI. L. REV. 243, 274-75 (1965).
324. *Id.*
325. 62 U.S. at 514-15.
326. *Id.* at 515.
327. *In re* Tarble, 25 Wis. 390 (1870), *rev'd*, 80 U.S. (13 Wall.) 397, 412 (1871); *see also* HURD, *supra* note 120, Book II, ch. 1, § 5; *Concurrent Jurisdiction of the Federal and State Courts; see also Collier's Case—Jurisdiction of Federal and State Courts*, 6 OP. ATT'Y GEN. 103 (1853); WILLIAM F. DUKER, A CONSTITUTIONAL HISTORY OF HABEAS CORPUS 153-55 (1980); WILLIAM NELSON, ROOTS OF AMERICAN BUREAUCRACY, 1830-1900, at 73, 76 (1982).

It seems highly relevant to note that the broad assertion of federal power and state helplessness concerning habeas corpus jurisdiction in *Ableman v. Booth* (1859) had to be reasserted after the Civil War in *Tarble's Case* . . . (1872). It is as if the unambiguous language of *Booth* could not be trusted because of its intimate connection with slavery and with the court that had rendered *Dred Scott*.

COVER, *supra* note 117, at 187 n. (1975).
328. *In re Tarble*, 25 Wis. at 390-412.

jurisdiction. This familiar doctrine has never been more strongly asserted or acted on than by the Supreme Court of the United States.[329]

Paine may have been overly defensive and simplistic in his explanation of the Wisconsin court's actions; Taney, to prove a point, may have been painting too harsh a picture of the Wisconsin court's attitude. Taney's reasoning, however, ignored the uniquely volatile nature of slavery and the futility of regulating, by manmade law, an institution that many Americans viewed as violative of a higher law. It did not necessarily follow that offenses in one state would be praiseworthy in another, but the greatest potential for this existed with regard to slavery.

Taney next asserted that the Wisconsin Supreme Court justices did not state from whence they derived the power to review a federal court decision.[330] He chose to ignore their opinions because Justice Smith explicitly stated that they were following the rule that powers not specifically reserved for the federal government by the Constitution remain within the states' realm.[331]

Taney repeatedly referred to violence, force of arms, revolution, and similar phrases to suggest the dire consequences of not submitting to the authority of the federal government and its tribunals.[332] However, he later recommended that a federal officer in a similar situation in the future should use force to resist state attempts to interfere with his prisoner.[333] If one expected a temperate judicial statement from the Supreme Court in the volatile year of 1859, there was no evidence of it in the opinion. Taney ended the opinion by flatly stating that the fugitive slave law was constitutional.[334]

Some commentators consider Taney's opinion in *Ableman v. Booth* praiseworthy.[335] In contrasting the unanimity of the Court

---

329. *Id.* at 396.

330. *Ableman*, 62 U.S. at 514.

331. *In re Booth*, 3 Wis. at 115-17. For more discussion of Taney's ignoring the Tenth Amendment's reservation of nondelegated powers to the states, see DUKER, *supra* note 327, at 152-53.

332. *Ableman*, 62 U.S. at 517, 519-21.

333. *Id.* at 524.

334. *Id.* at 526.

335. *See* Winslow, *Special Address*, *supra* note 23, at 56, where this extremely pro-Wisconsin author states: "The issue was of supreme importance, and the opinion was one worthy of the issue and of the distinguished jurist who wrote it." Hagan states: "In force, loftiness of tone and lucid logic, it is not surpassed by any judicial pronouncement in our

in *Booth* and its diversity of opinions in *Dred Scott*, one commentator noted:

> The Booth opinion marked the Chief Justice at his best, without any of the striving after extreme effect or the rewriting of American history for the making of a constitutional point which had characterized his derided treatment of Dred Scott. It was thoughtful, measured, and disciplined to the last degree.[336]

Although *Booth* was not the extreme opinion *Dred Scott* was, it nonetheless sprang from the same mind that refused to understand how intolerable slavery had become to a large part of the American population. Rather than attempt to conciliate that part of the population, Taney chose to threaten them with force if they did not subordinate themselves to superior federal law. In modern parlance, "he just didn't get it."

With the reversal of the Wisconsin Supreme Court decisions by the United States Supreme Court, the final scene in the drama shifted back to Wisconsin. The people in the state were so outraged that the legislature was prompted to enact joint resolutions on March 19, 1859 voiding this assumption of jurisdiction by the federal judiciary, accusing the federal government of despotism, and calling for a "positive defiance" as the "rightful remedy."[337]

VIII. WISCONSIN'S FINAL OPINION

When the Supreme Court of Wisconsin considered the cases on remand,[338] the composition of the court had changed since its prior consideration of the *Booth* litigation.[339] Byron Paine, formerly counsel to Sherman Booth, had been elected to the court but abstained from participating in the decision.[340] Chief Justice Luther Dixon held that the Supreme Court of the United States did have appellate jurisdiction over the highest state courts.[341] Justice

---

annals and, in fact, is equalled only by Marshall's mighty opinion in *McCulloch v. Maryland*." Hagan, *supra* note 36, at 23.

336. CARL B. SWISHER, THE TANEY PERIOD 1836-64, at 662 (1974).

337. *See supra* note 86; *see also* Mason, *supra* note 20, at 143 ("These resolutions, and the personal liberty law of 1857 [1857 Wis. Laws 12], were Wisconsin's strongest formal protests against the fugitive slave law."). For a history of the passage of the Wisconsin Personal Liberty Law, and the accompanying resolutions, see MORRIS, *supra* note 121, at 176-80.

338. Ableman v. Booth, 11 Wis. 517 (1859).

339. Beitzinger, *supra* note 8, at 21-22.

340. *Ableman*, 11 Wis. at 518.

341. *Id.* at 540.

Cole disagreed, but declined to file an opinion.[342] Given Paine's
views as expressed in *Tarble*[343] eleven years later, it seems fair to
state that the Wisconsin Supreme Court, while officially agreeing
with the federal high court and thus bringing this litigation to an
end, in fact still disagreed with the Supreme Court of the United
States in a 2-to-1 decision.

Justice Dixon made it clear that this opinion was entirely the
result of his own research and thought, even lamenting the "want
of those arguments of . . . counsel by which courts are usually so
much enlightened . . . ."[344] He was embarrassed by this and by the
court's decision five years earlier to refuse to make a return to the
United States Supreme Court's writ of error.[345] He reiterated that
he had given this matter great study and thought ("my sole purpose
has been to be right . . . ."[346]) and then proceeded to explain that
this was not the federal usurpation of state powers.

Dixon noted that the 25th section of the Judiciary Act stated
that the Supreme Court did have appellate power over the state
court because a Constitutional question was involved.[347] He then
cited Article III, section 2 of the Constitution, the pertinent and
controversial sentence being: "The judicial power shall extend to
all cases in law and equity arising under this constitution . . . ."[348]
He next cited Supreme Court cases[349] dispositive of the question
whether "*all* cases in law and equity" meant inferior federal court
cases only or cases in both federal and state courts.[350] The latter
was the proper construction.[351] This proposition was further bolstered by a quotation from Kent's *Commentaries* stating that federal disposition of such cases would prevent state prejudices and
jealousies from obstructing justice and would "preserve uniformity
of decision throughout the United States."[352]

In response to the opposing viewpoint that "cases" meant any

---

342. *Id*. at 518.
343. *In re* Tarble, 25 Wis. 390 (1870).
344. *Ableman*, 11 Wis. at 521.
345. *Id*.
346. *Id*. at 522.
347. *Id*. at 524-25.
348. *Id*. at 525 (citing U.S. CONST. art. 3, § 2).
349. *Id*. at 527 (citing Martin v. Hunter's Lessee, 14 U.S. (1 Wheat.) 304 (1816);
Cohens v. Virginia, 19 U.S. (6 Wheat.) 624 (1821)).
350. *Id*. at 527.
351. *Id*.
352. *Id*. at 534.

suits commenced in an inferior federal court possessing original jurisdiction, Justice Dixon stated:

> The radical defect of this doctrine is that, by giving this narrowed meaning in the word *"cases,"* it almost entirely cuts off,
> ... the power of the federal courts with which the advocates of this doctrine themselves admit it was the intention of the framers to invest them by the clause in question, and vests it *exclusively* in the state courts.[353]

Dixon concluded by admitting he had written a longer opinion than he had intended ("The subject is one of much interest, and it is difficult to know where to stop."[354]). However, he could not resist appending a pamphlet authored by an unnamed but "eminent" member of the Milwaukee bar who supported his view of the case.[355]

Jurisdiction was about to be taken away from both federal and state courts and lodged on the battlefield. Those efforts to be right, no matter how vigorously executed or how sincerely meant, became trivial in light of the events to come.

IX. CONCLUSION

At its simplest, the *Booth* story is about a fugitive slave, Joshua Glover, who got away. The fact that it was far more complicated than that has to do with the timing—i.e., 1854-1860, the era of *Dred Scott* and the hardening of attitudes on both sides of the Mason-Dixon line. It has to do with geography—i.e., the fact that this took place in the relatively new state of Wisconsin, a state with a distinctly antislavery bias. And it has to do with the subject matter—i.e., slavery, the legally condoned ownership of one human being by another human being.

The *Booth* cases deserve a more prominent place in America's historical consciousness of the nineteenth century than they currently hold. A part of this country eventually seceded because of the antislavery cast of the federal government, particularly after the election of President Lincoln in 1860. But what has been forgotten is that there was an equally vehement segment of the population so offended by the perceived proslavery bias of both the federal gov-

---

353. *Id.* at 535-36.
354. *Id.* at 540.
355. *Id.* at 540-55.

ernment and the Supreme Court that it too was ready to secede, and nearly did so.

Though one cannot prove in an empirical sense just why the *Booth* cases remained so obscure, one can certainly speculate. Several theories might be advanced to explain their relative obscurity. First, the major part of the controversy took place on the western frontier and the state supreme court decisions were authored by justices who, while competent, do not rank among the better-known state jurists of the nineteenth century.

Second, much of the action was overshadowed by *Dred Scott.* Perhaps Taney wrote a shorter, less strident opinion in *Booth* because he could not face another national outcry such as the one that had accompanied *Dred Scott.* Furthermore, in *Booth*, the slave Glover had long since made his way to freedom and anonymity. The same could not be said of Dred Scott. Third, the Civil War was so near at the time the *Booth* cases came to a close that the public consciousness could no longer be shocked.

Finally, history is always written by the victors. Inevitably, all the morally correct perspectives are aligned on the victor's side and all the morally incorrect views on the side of the defeated. Preserving the Union and abolishing slavery were among the chief motivations for the Northern pursuit of war. Asserting the right of states to secede and preserving slavery were Southern motives. Because the *Booth* story does not fit neatly in this schema, it has been forgotten.

It is time to reassess the importance of the *Booth* cases. There was always a tension between slave and free jurisdictions regarding the appropriate way, legally, socially, and morally, to treat slaves. In 1859, the Mississippi Supreme Court criticized Ohio for granting citizenship to African-Americans:

> Suppose that Ohio, still further afflicted with her peculiar philanthropy, should determine to descend another grade in the scale of *her peculiar* humanity, and claim to confer citizenship on the chimpanzee or the ourang-outang [sic] (the most respectable of the monkey tribe), are we to be told that "comity" will require of the States not thus demented, to forget their own policy and self-respect, and lower their own citizens and institutions in the scale of being, to meet the necessities of the mongrel race thus attempted to be introduced into the family of sisters in this confederacy? The doctrine of comity is not thus un-

reasonable.[356]

This extreme Southern judicial view was difficult enough for the citizens of Northern states to accept. But when the U.S. Supreme Court entered the picture on the side of slaveholding interests, a violent end became inevitable.

In 1842, *Prigg* affirmed the constitutionality of the Fugitive Slave Law of 1793. In 1857, *Dred Scott* denied citizenship and personhood to slaves. In 1859, *Booth*, in its announcement of the constitutionality of the 1850 Fugitive Slave Law, made clear that open resistance and civil disobedience on a massive scale was to be the ultimate conclusion to the struggle. The Wisconsin judiciary backed down and wrote a final conciliatory opinion acknowledging the supremacy of the federal government in that case. But what if a Southern sympathizer had been elected President in 1860? What if another Joshua Glover had been taken from Wisconsin by his former slave master? How long would the Wisconsin populace have complied with this state of affairs? The *Booth* story suggests both that the tensions were too great by 1860 to avoid war and that the importance of who fired the first shot is negligible. *Booth*, with *Prigg* and *Dred Scott*, is also an indicator of what happens when a government strays too far from the moral principles of a large segment of the populace. In that, there is a lesson for all time.

---

356. Mitchell v. Wells, 37 Miss. 235, 264 (1859) (emphasis added). In his dissenting opinion, Justice Handy succinctly stated the southern secessionist view:

> Whilst the confederacy [Union] continues, we cannot justify ourselves as a State in violating its spirit and principles, because other States have, in some respects, been false to their duties and obligations. It may justify us in dissolving the compact, but not in violating our obligations under it whilst it continues.

Id. at 286 (Handy, J., dissenting).

Personal Liberty Laws and Sectional Crisis: 1850-1861

Norman L. Rosenberg

ALTHOUGH AMERICAN NEGRO SLAVERY came to be a uniquely southern institution, runaway slaves found no legal dividing line between slave and free states. The fugitive slave clause of the Constitution, which guaranteed the return of interstate fugitives "held to Service or Labour," gave southern slave codes extraterritorial validity, so that escape into a free state offered slaves no legal refuge from pursuit by their masters. During the 1850's rendition of slaves in northern states increasingly involved questions of states' rights and civil liberties. The use of federal officials to enforce the Fugitive Slave Act of 1850 appeared to support antislavery charges that an aggressive "slave power" conspiracy was invading, under the protection of the national government, the free soil of sovereign northern states as well as free western territories above the Missouri Compromise line. The summary procedures of a fugitive slave hearing seemed to violate traditional standards of Anglo-American justice and to substantiate claims that slaveholders were antirepublican power mongers.[1] A number of free state legislatures adopted statutes, so-called "personal liberty laws," which purported to counteract the use of federal power on behalf of slave interests and to insure state protection of the liberty of free Negroes by guaranteeing fugitive slave suspects rights such as trial by jury and *habeas corpus*. Southern spokesmen and most Northern Democrats charged that the liberty laws violated sacred constitutional obligations and threatened the property of citizens of slaveholding states.

Despite northern and southern concern over the issue of fugitive slaves during the 1850's, historians have not adequately examined the personal liberty laws passed in that decade. Neither the laws' antebellum critics nor later historians have even agreed upon which states enacted liberty bills.[2] An examination of the controversy surrounding

[1] Arthur E. Bestor Jr., "State Sovereignty and Slavery: A Reinterpretation of Proslavery Constitutional Doctrine, 1846-1860," *Journal of the Illinois Historical Society*, LIV (1961), 117-180; Larry Gara, "Slavery and the Slave Power: A Crucial Distinction," *Civil War History*, XV (1969), 5-18.

[2] The laws passed before 1850 have been given greater attention than those enacted after the Fugitive Slave Act of 1850. See Alexander Johnston, "Personal Liberty Laws," John J. Lalor (ed.), *Cyclopaedia of Political Science, Political Economy, and of the Political History of the United States* (Chicago, 1884), III, 162-163; Julius Yanuck, "The Fugitive Slave Law and the Constitution" (Ph.D. Dissertation, Columbia University, 1953), 32-34; Joseph Nogee, "The Prigg Case and

321

these laws adds another dimension to the extent of mutual hostility and suspicion that existed between the slave and free sections of the Republic in November, 1860.

Sectional conflict over the return of fugitive slaves originated in the ambiguity of the Constitution. Drafted hurriedly late in the Convention, the fugitive slave clause did not specify whether the return of runaway slaves was the responsibility of state or federal officials.[3] The Fugitive Slave Act of 1793 only complicated the problem of enforcement because its framers created no national apparatus to recover fugitive slaves. Slaveowners themselves were to seize their interstate runaways and to take them before a wide variety of state and national officers who, after a summary hearing, would issue a certificate authorizing their removal from the state.[4] Antislavery groups complained that kidnappers took advantage of the Act's flimsy procedural safeguards to sell large numbers of blacks into slavery, but calls for additional protection of free Negroes encountered southern demands for strengthening the fugitive law by requiring greater state assistance to slave claimants.[5] As a result, Congress passed no new legislation affecting fugitive slaves until 1850.

Even though Congress did not act, some northern states adopted various kinds of laws. Kidnapping laws, the earliest and most limited type of state legislation, established penalties for abduction of free blacks but did not affect legitimate claims by slaveholders.[6] A few northern legislatures passed a second type of statute which provided claimants with separate state procedures for rendition of runaways. Alternatives to the Fugitive Slave Act of 1793, these state fugitive slave laws did not seriously hamper the operation of the federal act and generally represented a compromise between southern desires for more state assistance and antislavery demands for greater protection of the liberties of free

---

Fugitive Slaves, 1842-1850," *Journal of Negro History*, XXXIX (1954), 185-205. For differing lists of the number of states with personal liberty laws, see, for example, Allan Nevins, *The Emergence of Lincoln* (New York, 1950), II, 29 and J. G. Randall and David Donald, *The Civil War and Reconstruction* (Boston, 1961), p. 122.

[3] Max Farrand, *The Records of the Federal Convention of 1787* (New Haven, 1911), II, 443, 446, 601-602, 628.

[4] William R. Leslie, "A Study in the Origins of Interstate Rendition: The Big Beaver Creek Murders," *American Historical Review*, LVII (1951), 63-76 examines the background and framing of the act; *U.S. Statutes at Large*, I, 302-305.

[5] For the arguments of antislavery congressmen, see *Annals of Congress*, 15 Cong., 1 sess., pp. 231, 245, 837-840; Jacobus Ten Broek, *The Antislavery Origins of the Fourteenth Amendment* (Berkeley, 1951), pp. 32-33, supports antislavery claims about the kidnapping of free blacks under the Fugitive Slave Act of 1793; for complaints by southern congressmen see *Annals of Congress*, 16 Cong., 1 sess., pp. 553, 606, 618, 1379-1380, 1717, 1863.

[6] New York (1808, 1819, 1828), Indiana (1816), Connecticut (1821), Ohio (1819, 1821, 1857), Pennsylvania (1820), Michigan (1827), Maine (1838), Wisconsin (1839); for convenient summaries of these laws see John C. Hurd, *The Law of Freedom and Bondage in the United States* (Boston, 1858-1862), II, 34, 44, 54-58, 70-71, 118, 122, 127, 138-139, 141.

blacks. Some of the provisions of these kidnapping and state fugitive slave laws were inconsistent with the federal act, but all free states recognized the right of slaveowners to recover their property through some simple legal procedure.

These two types of statutes—kidnapping and fugitive slave laws—were primarily objectionable because their provisions differed from those of the Fugitive Slave Act of 1793, not because they were hostile to national authority or to southern slaveholders.[7] More radical laws, which openly defied the national government and marshaled state power to aid fugitive slaves, were passed in 1840 by Whig-controlled legislatures in Vermont and in New York. Similar in their provisions, these laws "to extend the right of trial by jury" guaranteed fugitive suspects a trial, public funds to summon witnesses, and an attorney at state expense. Vermont, in effect, forbade use of the federal law by declaring illegal the removal of alleged fugitives under any procedure except their own. New York required claimants to post bond and to reimburse anyone found to be a free man.[8]

In 1842 the United States Supreme Court tried, but failed, to settle the confusion over the constitutionality of state laws affecting fugitive slaves. In *Prigg* v. *Pennsylvania*, a case involving a kidnapping prosecution against a slaveowner who had seized a runaway without complying with either Pennsylvania or federal law, the Court appeared to declare unconstitutional all state laws affecting the rendition process. The separate opinions of the Taney Court, however, only created judicial confusion, forcing state and lower federal courts to continue the task of defining the proper scope of state jurisdiction. Referring to the numerous conflicting state statutes, Justice Joseph Story, who wrote the "official" opinion of the Court, held that the power to legislate on fugitive slaves rested exclusively with the national government and that "any State law or State regulation, which interrupts, limits, delays, or postpones the right of the owner to immediate possession of the slave" was void. Story went on, however, to claim that even though states could not hinder a slaveowner, they were not constitutionally required to aid him by enforcing the Fugitive Slave Act of 1793. In what may have been a subtle antislavery maneuver, the Massachusetts Justice held that

[7] William R. Leslie discusses two of these state fugitive slave laws: "The Pennsylvania Fugitive Slave Act of 1826," *Journal of Southern History*, XVIII (1952), 429-445; and "The Constitutional Significance of Indiana's Statute of 1824 on Fugitives from Labor," *Journal of Southern History*, XIII (1947), 338-353. State fugitive slave laws were also passed in New Jersey (1826, 1837), Connecticut (1838, repealed 1844), Ohio (1839, repealed 1843). Hurd, *Law of Freedom and Bondage* II, 46-47, 64-67, 119-120.

[8] *Acts and Resolves Passed by the Legislature of Vermont at Their October Session, 1840*, pp. 13-15; *Laws of the State of New York, 1840*, pp. 174-177. Valuable background on events surrounding the passage of the New York law is found in William E. Seward, *An Autobiography from 1801 to 1834 with a Memoir of His Life, and Selections from His Letters, 1831-1846 by Frederick W. Seward* (New York, 1891), pp. 463-465; and in George Baker (ed.), *The Works of William E. Seward* (Boston, 1884), II, 413-414, 432-433, 449-518.

state judges could, "if they choose," act under the federal law "unless prohibited by state legislation." Chief Justice Roger B. Taney severely criticized Story's reference to possible prohibitory state legislation, predicting that withdrawal of state officials would cripple the Fugitive Slave Act.[9]

The Massachusetts legislature did take advantage of Story's dictum that a state might prohibit its judges from enforcing the act of 1793. A Massachusetts law of 1843, enacted in response to popular sentiment against the rendition of fugitive slaves in Boston, prohibited state officers from participating in fugitive slave cases and also forbade use of state jails for detention of suspects.[10] When the antislavery movement gathered momentum in the 1840's, the Massachusetts "Act for the Protection of Personal Liberty" became the model for laws passed in Vermont, Connecticut, New Hampshire, Pennsylvania, and Rhode Island.[11]

The precise effect of withdrawal of state participation by these personal liberty laws is difficult to measure. Undoubtedly extralegal, violent resistance to slave claimants had as much, if not more, to do with the breakdown of the Fugitive Slave Act than state legislation. Whatever their real impact on recovery of fugitives, leading northern jurists rejected the constitutionality of the laws and condemned their consequences. United States Supreme Court Justice Robert C. Grier advised his fellow Pennsylvanian James Buchanan that, because the statutes compelled state officers to disregard the fugitive slave clause of the Constitution, the Supreme Court would treat them "as entirely unconstitutional, null, and void." Liberty laws had an "evil" effect on domestic tranquility, Grier believed, encouraging "fanatics, fools and negroes to incite riots, insult, beat and murder, the owners of slaves."[12] Another Supreme Court Justice, Samuel Nelson of New York, told a federal grand jury that the laws were more dangerous than riots and slave rescues

[9] Story's opinion is in 16 *Peters* 417, pp. 417-433 (1842); Taney's opinion is in *ibid.*, pp. 433-440. See also William W. Story, *Life and Letters of Joseph Story* (Boston, 1851), II, 393-395; William R. Leslie, "The Influence of Joseph Story's Theory of the Conflict of Laws on Constitutional Nationalism," *Mississippi Valley Historical Review*, XXV (1948), 203-220; Joseph C. Burke, "What Did the Prigg Decision Really Decide?" *Pennsylvania Magazine of History and Biography*, XCIII (1969), 73-85. The best example of the judicial confusion resulting from the individual opinions of the Taney Court is the attempt of the Indiana courts to interpret the *Prigg* decision; see *Graves v. The State*, 1 *Ind. Rep.* 480 (1849), *Devant v. Michael*, 2 *Ind. Rep.* 396 (1850), and *Donnell v. The State*, 3 *Ind. Rep.* 368 (1852). The United States Supreme Court clarified its position somewhat in *Moore* v. *The People of Illinois*, 14 *Howard* 539 (1855).

[10] *Acts and Resolves of Massachusetts, 1843*, p. 33; Massachusetts General Court, *Joint Special Committee on Fugitives From Slavery* (House Report No. 41); Martin Duberman, *Charles Francis Adams* (Boston, 1961), pp. 80-86.

[11] Nogee, "The Prigg Case," 199-202; Yanuck, "Fugitive Slave Law," 32-34. In 1843, the Maine House of Representatives passed a personal liberty bill similar to the Massachusetts statute, but the Maine Senate rejected the bill. *Twelfth Annual Report Presented to the Massachusetts Anti-Slavery Society . . . January 24, 1844* (Boston, 1844), p. 17.

[12] Grier to Buchanan, Apr. 2, 1850, James Buchanan Papers, State Historical Society of Pennsylvania.

because they destroyed southern confidence in the North's willingness to fulfill constitutional requirements.[13] Southerners considered the liberty laws unconstitutional and used them as evidence of the need for strengthening the Fugitive Slave Act. Southern politicians, especially those from states near Pennsylvania, complained that liberty laws lured runaways northward. Protest meetings were held in Maryland; Virginia and Maryland representatives in Washington denounced "Northern nullification" and called for stricter federal legislation; Virginia issued an official report condemning the "deeper venom" and "more determined hostility" of the liberty laws; a South Carolina politician proposed retaliatory legislation directed against northern commerce within his state.[14]

Removal of state assistance through the personal liberty laws of the 1840's influenced the form of the Fugitive Act of 1850. Drafted by James Mason of Virginia, the new law strengthened enforcement by adding national officials and federal processes. Although Congress did not repeal the old procedures of the 1793 act, claimants no longer had to rely upon state officials and state courts. The new law authorized special federal fugitive slave commissioners to issue certificates of removal after a summary hearing. Congress allowed no jury trial, and alleged fugitives could not testify in their own behalf. Southern representatives successfully opposed amendments, such as William Seward's jury trial provision, that would have complicated or slowed the rendition process. Part of the Compromise of 1850, the fugitive law passed the Senate by a voice vote and the House of Representatives by a solid margin when a number of Northern Whigs left the chamber to avoid the final balloting.[15]

The Fugitive Slave Act, the most troublesome part of the Compromise, divided northern citizens. "Union meetings" strongly endorsed the law. James Buchanan told such a meeting that fugitive slaves did not deserve a jury trial since fugitive criminals enjoyed no such "privilege." "Surely," wrote Buchanan, "the fugitive slave is not entitled to superior privileges over the free white man." Daniel Webster appealed for support of the new act, blaming its passage upon the "theoretic, fanatical, and fantastical agitation" that had produced the personal liberty laws.[16] Many northerners rejected such counsel and denounced

[13] "Charge to a Grand Jury of the United States Circuit Court of New York, April 7, 1851," in American Law Journal, III (1851), 560-61.

[14] Cong. Globe. 30 Cong., 1 sess., pp. 610-611; ibid., 30 Cong., 2 sess., p. 188; Herman V. Ames (ed.), State Documents on Federal Relations: The States and the United States (Philadelphia, 1906), pp. 250-252; C. J. Faulkner to John C. Calhoun, July 15, 1847, in Chauncey S. Boucher and Robert P. Brooks (eds.), "Correspondence Addressed to John C. Calhoun, 1837-1849," Annual Report of the American Historical Association for the Year 1929 (Washington, 1929), pp. 385-387; L. M. Keitt to Calhoun, Oct. 1, 1847, ibid., p. 402.

[15] Yanuck, "Fugitive Slave Law," 40-59; Holman Hamilton, Prologue to Conflict: The Crisis and the Compromise of 1850 (Lexington, Ky., 1964), pp. 140-141, 161-162.

[16] John Bassett Moore (ed.), The Works of James Buchanan (Philadelphia, 1908-

the Fugitive Slave Act as the most odious portion of the Compromise. Opposition to the new law was closely linked to states' rights slogans and to the cause of civil liberty. Critics viewed the use of federal slave commissioners and United States marshals upon northern free soil as illegal encroachment upon sovereign state jurisdiction. Orators and pamphleteers criticized the absence of a jury trial, the use of *ex parte* evidence, and the substitution of a "mere" commissioner for a judge.[17]

Some opponents of the fugitive law turned directly to the states for a remedy. An Ohio state judge issued a writ of *habeas corpus* to release a fugitive slave suspect from federal custody, and a New York anti-slavery group brought suit against a United States marshal who aided slave claimants. The most extreme example of state defiance came in 1854 when the Wisconsin Supreme Court freed Sherman M. Booth, a Milwaukee abolitionist held by the federal government for leading a slave rescue, and declared the Fugitive Slave Act unconstitutional.[18] Despite judicial resistance in several states, only Vermont passed a new personal liberty law. Whig legislators, with the cooperation of Whig Governor Charles T. Williams, sneaked through a comprehensive liberty law on the last day of the 1850 session after many members had already left the capitol. Similar to Vermont's 1840 law, the new statute promised fugitive slave suspects jury trial, right of *habeas corpus*, defense counsel, and state payment of all legal fees.[19]

The law provoked immediate complaints in both North and South, the loudest protests coming from Virginia's Democratic governor, John B. Floyd. Floyd advocated a retaliatory state tax on all northern products until free states stopped interfering with the fugitive law. Floyd's suggestion, which was summarily rejected by cooler heads in the Virginia legislature, received an unfavorable reception throughout the rest of the South. Southern moderates received strong support from President Millard Fillmore who announced his determination to enforce vigorously the fugitive law and warned against attempts to nullify it through state legislation.[20]

1911), VIII, 401; Daniel Webster to "Mr. . . . . . . of Boston," in George T. Curtis, *Life of Daniel Webster* (New York, 1870), II, 426-427.

[17] Henry Wilson, *History of the Rise and Fall of the Slave Power in America* (Boston, 1871), II, 304-312; Russel B. Nye, *Fettered Freedom: Civil Liberties and the Slavery Controversy* (rev. ed., East Lansing, Michigan, 1963), pp. 267-270.

[18] *Trial of Henry W. Allen, U.S. Deputy Marshall for Kidnapping. . . .* (n.p., [1852?] pamphlet); *ex parte Robinson*, 20 Fed. Cas. 960 (1855); E. F. Hall, *et al.* (eds.), *Official Opinions of the Attorneys General of the United States* (Washington, 1852-1949), VI, 237-239, 713-714; Yanuck, "Fugitive Slave Law," 151-177, 195-203; *in re Booth*, 3 Wisc. 157 (1854).

[19] *The Acts and Resolves Passed by the Legislature of Vermont, at the October Session, 1850*, pp. 9-10; Boston *Evening Transcript*, Dec. 19, 1850; Richmond *Whig*, Dec. 27, 1850; Richmond *Enquirer*, Apr. 1, 1851.

[20] Richmond *Whig*, Dec. 10, 1850, Apr. 4, 1851; James D. Richardson (ed.), *A Compilation of the Messages and Papers of the Presidents, 1789-1897* (Washington, 1896-1899), V, 137-138; Avery O. Craven, *The Growth of Southern Nationalism, 1848-1861* (Baton Rouge, 1951), pp. 152-153; Allan Nevins, *Ordeal of the Union* (New York, 1947), II, 346-379.

Outside Vermont, legislators heeded Fillmore's warning and rejected calls for new personal liberty laws. This legislative moderation which characterized the early 1850's sprang from a concern for the grave constitutional issues, from a fear of sectional discord, and from a belief that there was general popular support for the Fugitive Slave Act. A petition drive by New York City blacks for additional protection against kidnapping did not attract support from white legislators. Attempts to enact a new Massachusetts liberty law, secretly drafted by Charles Sumner and Richard Henry Dana, failed in 1851 and again in 1852.[21] Whig Governor William Johnston saved the section of Pennsylvania's 1847 liberty law, which barred use of state jails, by vetoing a Democratic-sponsored repeal bill in 1851. The following year the Democrats successfully removed the jail provision after newly-elected Democratic Governor William Bigler assailed the ban as unconstitutional and as a serious irritant to relations between "the different sections of the country."[22] Bigler believed that there was substantial support for the Fugitive Slave Act in Pennsylvania and that the Democratic party would gain at the polls by attacking the antislavery opposition to the law.[23]

Northern citizens slowly had become reconciled to the Fugitive Slave Act of 1850, but passage of the Kansas-Nebraska Act in May, 1854, shattered this forbearance. Opponents of the Nebraska bill denounced the repeal of the Missouri Compromise line as an unprovoked attack upon freedom and liberty by the "slave power."[24] Enactment of the bill coincided with, and helped to spark, a violent confrontation over the return of a fugitive slave in Boston. The furor following the rendition of Anthony Burns captured national headlines and helped to link anger against the Nebraska bill with the fugitive slave issue.[25] Southern intrusion upon the supposedly free territory of Kansas seemed to be accompanied by invasion of the sacred free soil of sovereign northern states. In the wake of these events, support for, or deference to, the Fugitive Slave Act collapsed completely and many politicians began to echo antislavery claims that an aggressive, antilibertarian "slave power" threatened northern liberties, especially those of black residents. Southern provocations, it seemed, had to be confronted everywhere; liberty had

[21] *Civil Liberty Outraged* (New York, n.d. pamphlet). Robert F. Lucid (ed.), *The Journal of Richard Henry Dana, Jr.* (Cambridge, Mass., 1968), II, 416; Boston *Evening Transcript*, Apr. 7, 8, 9, May 2, 1851; *ibid.*, May 15, 1852.

[22] *Pennsylvania Archives, Fourth Series. Papers of the Governors, 1681-1902* (Harrisburg, 1900-1902), VII, 481-496, 519-521; *Laws of the General Assembly of the Commonwealth of Pennsylvania, 1852*, 295; extract of legislative debates printed in Richmond *Enquirer*, Apr. 1, 1851.

[23] William Bigler to Franklin Pierce, June 26, 1852, Franklin Pierce Papers (microfilm edition).

[24] James A. Rawley, *Race and Politics: Bleeding Kansas and the Coming of the Civil War* (Philadelphia, 1969), *passim*.

[25] Lucid (ed.), *Journal of Richard Henry Dana, Jr.*, II, 625-638; Sarah Forbes Hughes (ed.), *Letters and Recollections of John Murray Forbes* (Boston, 1899), 142-144; New York *Tribune*, May 28, 29, 30, 31, 1854.

to be vindicated. Garrison's Massachusetts Anti-Slavery Society urged individual citizens to resist slave claimants with force, but most northerners rejected the vigilante tactics employed in Boston.[26]

Members of the collapsing Whig and Free Soil parties joined leaders of the infant Republican and American parties to urge repeal or reform of the fugitive slave laws. Some politicians called for new personal liberty laws to meet the southern threat. Charles Sumner assured Massachusetts Republicans that he would work for repeal of the Fugitive Slave Act and advocated that the Bay State pass a new liberty law similar to the one rejected by the 1851 and 1852 legislatures. Horace Greely's *Tribune* and Henry J. Raymond's New York *Times*, while counselling against violent resistance, advised state legislatures to pass laws insuring the basic civil rights of fugitive slave suspects.[27] As a practical matter, these gestures of resistance to the rendition of fugitive slaves were one of the few ways northern legislators could express their outrage over the Kansas-Nebraska Act. Most advocates of state action did not contemplate real interposition or nullification but supported personal liberty laws primarily as a symbol of northern resistance to "aggression" by the "slave power."

In 1854 and early 1855, when northern legislatures met for the first time after the passage of the Kansas-Nebraska Act, anti-Nebraska politicians turned rhetoric into statutory reality in six states. Connecticut, Vermont, and Rhode Island passed personal liberty laws in 1854; Michigan, Maine, and Massachusetts adopted laws the following spring.[28] The acts differed in detail, but there was substantial interstate borrowing since antislavery leaders sought advice from allies in other states.[29] Some legislatures followed the post-Prigg pattern by prohibiting employment of state officials or facilities in fugitive slave cases.[30] As a protest against the summary nature of the fugitive slave hearing, other laws contained certain procedural guarantees: more favorable rules of evidence barring depositions and requiring oral testimony from two witnesses; jury trials; and special state defense attorneys.[31] Denial

[26] New York *Times*, May 30, 1854.

[27] Charles Sumner (ed.), *The Works of Charles Sumner* (Boston, 1870-1883), III, 453-461; New York *Tribune*, May 31, June 30, 1854; New York *Times*, May 29, 30, June 1, 1854.

[28] *Public Acts, Passed by the General Assembly of the State of Connecticut, May Session, 1854*, pp. 80-81; *Acts and Resolves Passed by the General Assembly of the State of Vermont at the October Session, 1854*, pp. 50-52; *Acts and Resolves of the General Assembly of the State of Rhode Island and Providence Plantations, June Session, 1854*, pp. 22-23; *Acts of the Legislature of the State of Michigan, 1855*, pp. 413-415; *Acts and Resolves of the State of Maine, 1855*, pp. 207-208; *Acts and Resolves of Massachusetts, 1855*, p. 924. See also *Acts of Michigan, 1855*, p. 202.

[29] See, for example, Charles Sumner to John Jay, Mar. 3, 1855, in Edward L. Pierce, *Memoir and Letters of Charles Sumner* (Boston, 1877-1893), III, 417.

[30] Rhode Island, Michigan, and Maine.

[31] Michigan and Massachusetts guaranteed jury trial; Vermont, Connecticut, and Michigan required testimony of two witnesses; Vermont and Connecticut barred the use of depositions; Michigan and Massachusetts provided state defense attorneys.

of state aid and erection of safeguards in state courts were worthless victories for blacks, however, because slave claimants could use the Fugitive Slave Act of 1850 which provided a wholly national system of enforcement. No state could bind federal courts or United States commissioners to requirements not contained in federal laws or procedures. The Massachusetts liberty law of 1855 raised the threat of more effective action by authorizing state interposition in fugitive slave cases. Massachusetts empowered state judges to issue writs of *habeas corpus* to release suspects from federal authorities and to hear claims under state law. Know-Nothing Governor Henry J. Gardner, believing that this removal provision raised serious constitutional issues, rejected the entire law, but a coalition of Know-Nothings and Republicans overrode his veto by a large margin.[32]

Defenders of personal liberty laws argued that the acts were legitimate answers to the repeal of the Missouri Compromise and to the deficiencies of federal fugitive slave laws. Most proponents of state action did not deny the binding validity of the Constitution's fugitive slave clause, but they did claim that there was no longer any obligation to obey the Fugitive Slave Act of 1850.[33] Passage of the Kansas-Nebraska Act, according to state Senator William H. Robertson of New York, "released the Free States from all obligations that may be expressed or implied in any compromise on the subject of slavery outside the Federal Constitution." United States Senator James Cooper of Pennsylvania defended the laws as proper "countervailing" legislation against southern aggression in the territories.[34] While most adopted this "tit-for-tat" argument without rejecting the supremacy of federal authority, some defenders of state action based their position upon the Virginia and Kentucky Resolutions of 1798 and 1799. Their constitutional arguments represented the classic linking of libertarianism and states rights. State governments had the right, indeed the duty, to redress all infringements upon fundamental individual freedoms, even if this meant opposing the authority of the national government. The Fugitive Slave Act of 1850, it was argued, violated one of the most basic state rights—the right to protect the personal liberty and safety of its black residents.[35] "Bluff

[32] *Acts of Massachusetts, 1855*, p. 924; *Liberator*, May 25, 1855; Boston *Evening Transcript*, May 1-30, 1855; Joel Parker, *Personal Liberty Laws, (Statutes of Massachusetts)* .... (Boston, 1861, pamphlet), pp. 31-33. Political opponents of Gov. Gardner, an ex-Whig elected on the American ticket, charged that his veto was a political maneuver to counter southern Democratic claims that abolitionists had infiltrated the American party. New York *Tribune*, July 28, 1855; Nevins, *Ordeal of the Union*, II, 396-397.

[33] One exception was the small group of New York abolitionists, including Frederick Douglass and Gerrit Smith, who advocated that states intervene to prevent the return of all fugitive slaves to the South. New York *Tribune*, July 2, 1855; *Radical Abolitionist*, Apr. 1856.

[34] New York *Tribune*, Mar. 24, 1855; *Cong. Globe*, 33 Cong., 2 sess., Appendix, p. 221.

[35] See, for example, Carl Schurz, *The Reminiscences of Carl Schurz* (New York, 1907-1908), II, 110-111; Sumner (ed.), *Works of Sumner*, III, 156-157, 356-357,

Ben" Wade of Ohio used the doctrines of 1798 and 1799 to claim not only that northern states had the power to pass personal liberty laws, but also that state courts had the final authority to determine the constitutionality of the Fugitive Slave Act. Surrender of the right of state review, according to Wade, would "yield up all the rights of the States to protect their own citizens" and "turn this government into a miserable despotism." Samuel P. Chase of Ohio and some abolitionist spokesmen repeated Wade's claim that a despotic central government was endangering state liberties.[36] The states rights position received its strongest support from the Wisconsin judges who declared the Fugitive Slave Act of 1850 unconstitutional and denounced attempts to appeal their decision to the United States Supreme Court.[37]

Southern leaders, championing the supremacy of national judicial and executive authority, quickly protested these new examples of state defiance of the fugitive slave laws. Senator Judah P. Benjamin of Louisiana charged that nullification doctrines had changed their locale: "South Carolina is now taken into the arms and affectionately caressed by Ohio, Vermont, Michigan, Wisconsin, and Connecticut."[38] Virginia Democrats, facing political competition from the fledgling American party, were particularly loud in their protests, painting the American party with the black brush of abolitionism because of Know-Nothing support for the 1855 Massachusetts liberty law.[39] A few southerners advocated nonintercourse or commercial boycott in retaliation, but most, believing that they had caught northern legislatures in clearly unconstitutional positions, attempted to avoid radical measures themselves. Slave state leaders recognized that almost all retaliatory proposals violated the full faith and credit clause of the Constitution and that the united front necessary for a successful economic boycott was impossible.[40] Several attempts at federal remedies, initiated by southern representatives or by their Northern Democratic allies, died in Congress. Representative Eli M. Shorter unsuccessfully proposed expelling the congressional delegations from states with personal liberty laws. Senator Charles Stuart of Michigan failed to win support for construction of a federal jail in his state to detain fugitive slave suspects barred from

---

410-411; New York *Tribune*, May 23, 1899; *Radical Abolitionist*, Sept. 1855; see also Bestor, "State Sovereignty," 137.

[36] *Cong. Globe*, 33 Cong., 2 sess., Appendix, pp. 213-214; American Anti-Slavery Society, *Annual Report . . . May 9, 1855* (New York, 1855), pp. 60-65.

[37] "Letter of Judge A. D. Smith to a Public Dinner in His Honor," Milwaukee *Free Democrat*, Apr. 15, 1857.

[38] *Cong. Globe*, 33 Cong., 2 sess., Appendix, pp. 219-220; see also the remarks of Maryland's James Bayard, *ibid.*, p. 243.

[39] Richmond *Enquirer*, May 18, 22, 24, 1855.

[40] Various retaliatory proposals are reprinted in the *Liberator*, June 22, July 27, 1855; Richmond *Enquirer*, July 6, Sept. 18, 1855; for arguments against retaliation see Richmond *Enquirer*, Sept. 21, 25, 1855. A retaliatory bill was introduced during the 1856 Alabama legislative session but was not passed. *Liberator*, Jan. 25, Feb. 8, 15, 1856.

state facilities by the 1855 personal liberty law. The Senate did pass a bill, sponsored by the Democratic leadership, designed to quash state suits against United States marshals executing the Fugitive Slave Act, but antislavery congressmen blocked the bill in the House.[41]

Although passage of the personal liberty laws following the Kansas-Nebraska Act provoked heated rhetoric in Congress and in state legislatures, the problem of fugitive slaves soon receded into the background. Antislavery politicians shifted their primary attention to opposing expansion of slavery into the territories and to "bleeding Kansas." Southern congressmen, despairing of getting any substantial revision of the fugitive laws, dropped their complaints. More importantly, the small number of fugitive slaves actually escaping to free soil worked against any drastic southern action and cooled northern sentiments. During the next four years a few slave state legislators or fire-eating newspaper editors raised their voices, but there was little mention of personal liberty laws in the South until the secession crisis of 1860-1861.[42]

Although after 1855 the fugitive slave issue was largely forgotten in Washington and remained only a secondary grievance in the slave states, supporters of liberty laws still continued their agitation in northern legislatures. Drives for new laws temporarily stalled in 1856; even in supposedly radical Massachusetts the desire for state interposition cooled perceptibly. Charles Sumner had hoped that the 1855 measure would provoke further complaints by southern senators, giving him an opening to excoriate the slave power. Instead, the 1856 Massachusetts legislature defeated an attempt to strengthen the liberty law, and a Democratic sponsored repeal bill gained enough momentum for Sumner to complain about an embarrassing "fire in the rear." The liberty law appeared to be headed for extinction until the outpouring of antisouthern feeling following the caning of Sumner by Preston Brooks. The law was retained as a symbol of Massachusetts' support for the martyred senator.[43]

The *Dred Scott* decision in 1857 gave the appeals of proponents of state action new life. The adverse northern reaction to the Supreme Court's voiding of the Missouri Compromise line and to Chief Justice Roger B. Taney's statement that Negroes were noncitizens, lacking rights that white men had to respect, not only revived the movement for personal liberty laws but also provoked demands for state measures

[41] *Cong. Globe*, 34 Cong., 1 sess., pp. 395-397 (Shorter Resolution); New York *Herald*, Feb. 23, 1855 (Stuart Resolution); *Cong. Globe*, 33 Cong., 2 sess., Appendix, pp. 226-227, 243 (Toucey Bill).

[42] Craven, *Growth of Southern Nationalism*, pp. 152-153 notes the decline of southern concern with the fugitive slave issue; for the most recent estimate of the small number of slaves escaping to free territory see Larry Gara, *The Liberty Line* (Lexington, Ky., 1961), pp. 36-40.

[43] Sumner to Theodore Parker, Jan. 9, 1856, in Pierce, *Memoir and Letters of Sumner*, III, 426; *Liberator*, May 30, 1856; Godfrey T. Anderson, "The Slave Issue as a Factor in Massachusetts Politics from the Compromise of 1850 to the Outbreak of the Civil War" (Ph.D. dissertation, University of Chicago, 1944), pp. 136-137.

that would counter the Chief Justice's denial of Negro citizenship.[44] An 1857 New Hampshire "act to secure freedom and the right of citizenship," which was sometimes mistaken for a liberty law, provided that African ancestry was not a bar to citizenship in the Granite State. The legislature also included a "sojourner clause" which declared that all slaves brought into New Hampshire by their masters would be considered free men. The statute was clearly not designed as a personal liberty law because it specifically recognized the right of slaveowners to reclaim runaway slaves under federal statutes. A similar bill passed the New York assembly but died in the senate.[45] Other northern legislatures adopted true personal liberty laws following the *Dred Scott* decision. Maine extended fugitive slave suspects the additional protection of a defense attorney.[46] Republican legislators in Ohio overrode Democratic and downstate opposition to pass a liberty law prohibiting use of state jails, but Ohio Democrats, after sweeping the fall elections, promptly repealed the measure and frustrated later attempts to pass a new liberty law.[47]

In 1857, Wisconsin also enacted a comprehensive personal liberty law which included provision for a jury trial, state defense attorney, and various procedural safeguards. This act was more the product of the continuing war between Sherman Booth and the federal government than a reaction against the *Dred Scott* decision. Following the Wisconsin supreme court's ruling in favor of Booth and against the validity of the Fugitive Slave Act, the new Republican party strongly backed the abolitionist editor. Wisconsin Republicans adopted a strong states rights platform, one of the purposes being to support Booth, who faced federal court suits stemming from his slave rescue. Republican sponsors of the 1857 liberty law closely linked its passage with attempts to prevent United States marshals from executing a lien obtained in a civil suit against Booth's printing equipment. The Wisconsin assembly underwrote state support of Booth and future slave rescuers to the extent of reimbursing them for any civil damages assessed by federal courts. The state senate rejected this section of the liberty bill but did agree to a clause declaring that no liens in cases involving violation of the Fugitive Slave Act could be executed in Wisconsin and that persons in

---

[44] *Dred Scott* v. *Sanford*, 19 Howard 393 (1857). The literature on the case is extensive; a good summary of northern reaction to the decision is Nevins, *Emergence of Lincoln*, I, 112-118.

[45] *Laws of the State of New Hampshire, Passed June Session, 1857,* pp. 1876-77; the New Hampshire Supreme Court later issued an advisory opinion distinguishing this statute from the personal liberty laws of other states. *In re Opinion of the Justices,* 41 N.H. 553 (1861). "Report of the Special Committee [New York Legislature] on the Dred Scott Decision," New York *Times,* Apr. 11, 1857.

[46] *Public Laws of the State of Maine, 1857,* p. 28; Maine also adopted a "sojourner law" in 1857, denying slaveowners the right to bring their slaves into the state. *Ibid.,* p. 38.

[47] *Acts . . . Passed by the General Assembly of Ohio . . . 1857,* p. 170; *Ibid. . . . 1858,* p. 10; Eugene Roseboom, *The Civil War Era, 1850-1873* (Columbus, Ohio, 1944), pp. 260, 326-327, 341-347.

Booth's situation could remove federal lien proceedings to state courts.[48] Although Booth used the liberty law to recover his equipment from the federal government, he finally ran out of state support and found himself in jail after the United States Supreme Court reversed the Wisconsin Court in the famous case of *Abelman v. Booth.*

Taney's opinion in the *Booth* case settled the question of whether states could, as provided in some of the personal liberty laws, use writs of *habeas corpus* to remove fugitive slave suspects from federal authorities. State courts could never, Taney held, issue a writ when they knew that the petitioner was held by the national government. Likewise, the return of a writ showing that the prisoner was in federal custody immediately stopped all state proceedings. The *Booth* decision involved removal of a white man charged with interfering with the fugitive laws, but Taney's opinion was stated broadly and upheld the supremacy of the federal courts and national executive to administer the Fugitive Slave Act of 1850 entirely free from state interference.[49] Following *Abelman v. Booth* there was no way a state liberty law could be effective unless a slave claimant was foolish enough to bring his case before state courts or unless a state court was rash enough to issue a writ of *habeas corpus* in defiance of federal authority.

Still, the *Booth* case did not stop the drive for personal liberty laws that had revived after the *Dred Scott* decision. Until, and even during, the secession crisis abolitionists and a few antislavery Republicans continued to press for state nullification with a new, broader type of personal liberty law. The first concentrated drive for such a law came in the 1857 New York legislature. During the session a coterie of "Radical Abolitionists" led by Gerrit Smith and Frederick Douglass used opposition to Taney's *Dred Scott* opinion to win Republican support for a bill stating that no person could be removed from New York as a fugitive slave under any law, state or federal. Assembly Speaker Dewitt C. Littlejohn, a special target of Gerrit Smith's lobbying, argued that New York had to take extreme action to protect individual liberties from abridgement by the southern-dominated Supreme Court. The Republican leader ridiculed protests that the bill would lead to a direct conflict with the federal government. "Will James Buchanan march troops into New York, to coerce us into submission?" he taunted the Democratic opposition.[50] The abolitionists' attempt to interpose, rhetorically

---

[48] This discussion of the personal liberty law issue in Wisconsin is primarily based upon the voluminous material in Booth's newspaper, the Milwaukee *Free Democrat*, Feb. 9-20, 1857. See also *General Acts Passed by the Legislature of Wisconsin, 1857*, pp. 12-14; James L. Sellers, "Republicanism and States Rights in Wisconsin," *Mississippi Valley Historical Review*, XVII (1930), 213-229; Vroman Mason, "The Fugitive Slave Law in Wisconsin with Reference to Nullification Sentiment," *Wisconsin Historical Society Proceedings, 1895*, 117-144.

[49] *Abelman v. Booth*, 21 Howard 506 (1859); Bestor, "State Sovereignty," 136-42.

[50] *Radical Abolitionist*, May, 1857; New York *Times*, Apr. 17, 1857; Milwaukee *Free Democrat*, Apr. 24, May 7, 1857.

at least, state authority against the national government failed by only twelve votes.

Gerrit Smith and Frederick Douglass advanced their bill proposing virtual rebellion against national authority with the long range goal of winning Republican support for radical political action against the slave power. Unlike the Garrisonians, the Radical Abolitionist party of New York believed that the slave power could be attacked through the Republican party. Douglass was encouraged that their first effort to radicalize the Republican party through the extreme liberty bill had been so successful, but any hope of converting many Republicans into abolitionists through personal liberty laws soon proved chimeric.[51] When the Republicans were a newly-formed opposition party, states' rights rhetoric and proposals fitted their crusade against the slave power, but as their political base expanded, party leaders sought to avoid identification with extreme measures of questionable constitutionality. The liberty bills advanced after 1857 did not purport to remedy particular defects in the fugitive slave laws but openly rejected the validity of a provision of the Constitution itself. Outright denial of the clear requirement of returning fugitive slaves did not appeal to practical Republican politicians, intent upon building a winning northern coalition for 1860.[52]

Despite declining Republican support, abolitionists organized elaborate campaigns for new personal liberty laws in most northern states. Never blessed with much popular approbation, abolitionist groups struggled to keep their crusade going in the face of waning interest, even in staunchly antislavery Massachusetts. Appeals for radical personal liberty laws provided one means of keeping alive agitation on the slavery question. For this reason, the loosely amalgamated Garrisonian groups, which had never been greatly interested in liberty laws, began advocating legislation that went beyond the enactment of procedural safeguards.[53]

William Lloyd Garrison had previously endorsed the usual liberty laws, but he had stressed the need for more sweeping measures that would totally reject the concept of property in man and the proposition that fugitives could be returned to slavery.[54] After 1857 his followers sought state laws "prohibiting the surrender of any human being claimed as a slave." Because of the collaboration among the scattered Garrisonian societies, proposals, methods of agitation, and the agitators themselves were often the same in different states. The state societies

[51] Douglass to Smith, Apr. 20, 1857, in Philip Foner, (ed.), *The Life and Writings of Frederick Douglass* (New York, 1950), 406-407.

[52] See, for example, Abraham Lincoln to Samuel Galloway, July 28, 1859 in Roy Basler, (ed.), *The Collected Works of Abraham Lincoln* (New Brunswick, N.J., 1953), 394; editorial of Springfield *Republican* reprinted in *Liberator*, Feb. 18, 1859; editorial of Boston *Daily Advertiser* reprinted in *Liberator*, Sept. 14, 1860.

[53] Aaron M. Powell, *Personal Reminiscences of the Anti-Slavery and Other Reforms and Reformers* (New York, 1899), p. 126; Irving Bartlett, *Wendell Phillips, Brahmin Radical* (Boston, 1961), pp. 205-207.

[54] See, for example, *Liberator*, June 1, 1855.

coordinated petition drives with local abolitionist groups. Clergymen were asked to circulate petitions and to support the radical bills in their sermons. Women's rights leaders, such as Susan B. Anthony and Lydia Maria Child, urged women to sign the petitions. Abolitionist orators traveled to state capitols throughout the North, appealing for action and arguing constitutional problems with legalistic legislators.[55] Two Garrisonian assemblymen, Parker Pillsbury in New Hampshire and Aaron M. Powell in New York, actively directed attempts to nullify the Fugitive Slave Act. Republican legislators were not totally hostile to the abolitionists' appeals, but no legislature ever passed one of these radical laws. Pillsbury failed to get his bill past a first reading at the 1859 New Hampshire session, and the New York assembly rejected several times Powell's extreme proposals based on the "higher law."[56] Abolitionists came closest to victory in Massachusetts, where Democrats, led by former United States Attorney General Caleb Cushing, and a few Republicans defeated by only three votes a Republican-abolitionist radical liberty law in 1859. A similar Massachusetts drive in 1860 collected over 20,000 signatures but attracted very little Republican support during a national election year.[57]

Failure to add any new personal liberty laws to northern statute books did not discourage leaders of these campaigns. Wendell Phillips, a chief abolitionist strategist, admitted that his reason for "pushing this special question" was primarily to bring the slavery issue before northern legislatures and Congress and only secondarily to protect the rights of fugitive slave suspects. "What we want is agitation," Phillips told Massachusetts abolitionists. He believed that these bills would bring "the insults and fury of the South" down upon overly cautious antislavery politicians, such as Henry Wilson, spurring "him to the vigor of action needful for his own honor and that of his state."[58] Other leaders of the American Anti-Slavery Society agreed that the drives were valuable. Oral presentations before state legislatures allowed abolitionist speakers to spread their gospel from prestigious platforms; the cam-

[55] Powell, *Personal Reminiscences*, pp. 172-173; *Liberator*, Feb. 18, 25, Oct. 14, Nov. 18, 1859; *ibid.*, Jan. 27, 1860; American Anti-Slavery Society, *Annual Reports . . . for 1857 and 1858* (New York, 1859), pp. 131-142; American Anti-Slavery Society, *Annual Report . . . for Year Ending May 1, 1859* (New York, 1860), p. 108; Gerrit Smith, *Speeches and Letters, 1843-1873* (n.p., n.d.), No. 37.

[56] On New Hampshire see *Liberator*, July 1, 1859. For the drives in New York see New York *Tribune*, Mar. 7, Apr. 13, 19, 21, 1859; *ibid.*, Feb. 4, 14, Mar. 1, 1860. Vermont and Massachusetts were the only states that passed new legislation. A Vermont Act of 1858 brought together the provisions of the 1850 and 1854 personal liberty laws. In addition, the Vermont legislature added a "sojourner clause" and another section declaring that African ancestry was no bar to state citizenship. *Acts and Resolves . . . of Vermont . . . October Session, 1858*, pp. 42-44. A Massachusetts law of 1858 repealed some ancillary provisions of the 1855 liberty law, but the legislators left intact the sections guaranteeing rights to fugitive slave suspects. *Acts and Resolves of Massachusetts, 1858*, p. 151.

[57] *Liberator*, Apr. 1, 8, 15, Nov. 11, Dec. 9, 1859; *ibid.*, Feb. 8, 1860.

[58] Speech of Wendell Phillips at 1859 Massachusetts Anti-Slavery Society Convention, reprinted in *Liberator*, Feb. 4, 1859.

paigns also permitted circulation of "valuable antislavery documents" among suspicious northern citizens.[59]

These campaigns attracted attention during legislative sessions, but the larger goal of provoking nationwide controversy was not realized. Southern politicians and newspaper editors complained about northern perfidy, but few revived talk of retaliation against states with liberty laws or of strengthened fugitive slave laws. Virginia Democrats, who claimed that slaves were still escaping into Pennsylvania, raised the loudest protests against the liberty laws. The 1859 Virginia legislature passed a resolution condemning personal liberty bills, and Governor John Letcher, a moderate, advocated sending emissaries to northern states to seek repeal of the laws.[60] Northern Democrats continued to support southern complaints; both the Douglas and Breckenridge Democratic platforms of 1860 condemned the laws as "hostile in character, subversive of the Constitution, and revolutionary in their effect." Republican leaders tried to sidestep the issue; Abraham Lincoln advised Republicans to stop "tilting against the Fugitive Slave law" to avoid "the charge of emnity to the Constitution."[61]

The personal liberty laws played no significant part in the 1860 elections, but Lincoln's victory suddenly revived them as a national issue. Disunionists in the Cotton States, although unsure which states had passed the odious measures, used the liberty laws to justify the validity of their course. Georgia's secessionist leader Robert Toombs called the statutes positive proof of the North's violation of the Constitution and declared that they were only the first step in a systematic campaign to exterminate slavery throughout the South.[62] Because of the laws' prominence in secessionist rhetoric, compromisers from both sections talked for a short time as if the laws held the key to peaceful reconciliation. Some southern unionists agreed with the fire-eaters' indictment of the liberty laws but lamely advocated commercial retaliation instead of secession to obtain their repeal. A number of spokesmen from the upper South and border states claimed that removal of the liberty laws would help prevent the breakup of the Republic.[63]

[59] American Anti-Slavery Society, *Annual Report . . . for the Year May 1, 1860* (New York, 1861), pp. 260-261.

[60] *Journal of Virginia House of Delegates, 1859-1860,* pp. 64, 166, 272.

[61] Kirk H. Porter and Donald Bruce Johnson (eds.), *National Party Platforms, 1840-1964* (Urbana ,Ill., 1966), pp. 30-31; Lincoln to Schuyler Colfax, July 6, 1859, Basler, (ed.), *Works of Lincoln,* III, 390-391.

[62] See, for example, "Declaration of Causes Which Induced the Secession of South Carolina," in Frank Moore, (ed.), *The Rebellion Record, A Diary of American Events* (New York, 1861-1868), I, 3-4; Dwight L. Dumond, (ed.), *Southern Editorials on Secession* (New York, 1931), pp. 237-238; Robert Toombs to E. B. Pullin and others, in U. B. Phillips (ed.), "The Correspondence of Robert Toombs, Alexander H. Stephens and Howell Cobb," *Annual Report of the American Historical Association for the Year 1911* (Washington, 1913), 520-521.

[63] Alexander H. Stephens to J. Henry Smith, Dec. 31, 1860, *ibid.,* 526; New York *Tribune,* Nov. 14, 17, Dec. 3, 1860; compromise proposal of Richmond *Enquirer* reported by Chicago *Tribune,* Nov. 27, 1860; proposal of John Minor Botts of Va.

In the North, outside the Republican party, there was widespread sentiment for immediate repeal. In his long-awaited, carefully prepared message of December 3, 1860, James Buchanan endorsed the southern position on the liberty laws, warning the northern states that failure to repeal the laws, which "willfully violated" a portion of the Constitution "essential to the domestic security and happiness" of the South, would justify "revolutionary resistance to the Government of the Union" by the slave states. Almost all Northern Democrats and backers of the Bell-Everett Constitutional Union ticket of 1860 clamored for withdrawal of the liberty laws.[64]

Republicans were much more divided. For different reasons a number of Republicans urged immediate repeal. Republican businessmen hoped such action would hold off secession, at least in the border states and upper South. A well-publicized meeting of leading New York City merchants supported instant repeal of all liberty laws, and a similar gathering in Philadelphia pledged a prompt search of Pennsylvania's statutes for any offending law.[65] Practical politicians, such as Schuyler Colfax and Governor Edwin Morgan of New York, were politically embarrassed by Democratic attacks on the liberty laws. These leaders, more concerned with avoiding the stigma of Republican nullification than with heading off war, wanted the laws expunged in order to lift the onus of unconstitutional legislation from the party, enabling it to approach the impending conflict with "clean hands."[66]

Republican proponents of repeal met resistance from several fronts within their own party. Only three Republican governors unequivocally advised their state legislatures to heed demands for repeal.[67] Some Republicans strongly opposed immediate action but hinted that removal of the laws would be possible if it were not done under the threat of secession or if the South offered something in return, such as a revised

reported by Chicago *Tribune*, Dec. 14, 1860; public letter of Gov. John Letcher of Virginia reprinted in New York *Tribune*, Dec. 1, 1860; public letter of John Bell of Ky. reprinted in New York *Tribune*, Dec. 12, 1860.

[64] Richardson (ed.), *Messages of the Presidents*, V, 626-653, esp. 629-630; P. Orman Ray (ed.), "Some Papers of Franklin Pierce, 1852-1862," *American Historical Review*, X, (1904), 365-366; Howard Perkins (ed.), *Northern Editorials on Secession* (Gloucester, Massachusetts, 1964; orig. ed., 1942), *passim*.

[65] *Proceedings of a Union Meeting, Held in New York: An Appeal to the South* (New York, 1860, pamphlet); *Cong. Globe*, 36 Cong., 2 sess., p. 121; Philip S. Foner, *Business and Slavery, New York Merchants and the Irrepressible Conflict* (Chapel Hill, 1941), pp. 228-231.

[66] Message of Gov. Edwin D. Morgan of New York, New York *Tribune*, Jan. 3, 1861; James A. Rawley, *Edwin D. Morgan, 1811-1883, Merchant in Politics* (New York, 1955), p. 124; Letter of George Ashmun (Chairman of 1860 National Republican Convention) in *Liberator*, Jan. 11, 1861; editorial of Springfield *Republican*, reprinted in *Liberator*, Nov. 30, 1860; Willard H. Smith, *Schuyler Colfax, The Changing Fortunes of a Political Idol* (Indianapolis, 1952), pp. 145, 149.

[67] William B. Hesseltine, *Lincoln and the War Governors* (New York, 1955), pp. 123-125. They were Andrew G. Curtin of Pa., Edwin Morgan of N.Y., Charles Smith Olden of N.J.

fugitive slave law.[68] Governor John A. Andrew of Massachusetts, a member of the politically powerful and strongly antislavery "Bird Club," was the most conspicuous leader who finally agreed to modification after rejecting outright repeal.[69] A good many Republicans absolutely refused to back down, arguing that the liberty laws were valid and should not be abandoned in the face of southern threats. Michigan's Governor Austin Blair, who had drafted his state's liberty law of 1855, refused to abandon it and publically defended its constitutionality. Charles Summer was indefatigable in urging Massachusetts Republicans to oppose the campaign for repeal instigated by the surviving leaders of the moribund Massachusetts Whig Party. Wendell Phillips, who personally rejected the Constitution, drew upon his early legal experience to give Massachusetts Republicans a long discourse on the constitutional intricacies of the liberty law question. Phillips and other abolitionists told Republican legislators to remain firm, assuring them that the laws were constitutional.[70]

During the first months of the secession winter, modification or repeal of the personal liberty laws remained a matter of serious discussion, but in the end only two states took positive action. Rhode Island Democrats, at the urging of national party officials, repealed the state's 1854 liberty law.[71] After complicated intraparty maneuvering and consultation with leaders throughout the North, Massachusetts Republicans modified their state's provisions on fugitive slaves. By the time they finally acted, however, the question of fugitive slaves and liberty laws was a dead issue.[72] Once the shock of secession had passed, national leaders realized the liberty law problem was a minor matter. Abraham Lincoln, for example, while steadfastly refusing to yield on the issue of expansion of slavery in the territories, supported repeal of all state statutes conflicting with the Fugitive Slave Act. Charles Francis Adams, whose membership on

[68] J. M. Forbes to Charles Francis Adams, Feb. 2, 1861, Adams Family Papers (microfilm edition); New York *Times*, Dec. 3, 4, 1860; Hartford *Courant*, Dec. 1, 1860.

[69] Gov. Andrews' message to the Massachusetts legislature in support of modification of the personal liberty law was the product of much consultation with Republican leaders in Massachusetts and in Washington. George Morey to Charles Francis Adams, Jan. 5, 1861, Adams Papers. See also the message of Gov. Israel Washbourne of Maine, New York *Tribune*, Jan. 7, 1861; Hesseltine, *Lincoln and War Governors*, pp. 110-111, 113-114.

[70] *Speech of Wendell Phillips Against Repeal of the Personal Liberty Bill [of Massachusetts]* (Boston, 1861, pamphlet); *Speech of Hon. P. Hitchcock of Geauga on the "Bill to Prevent Giving Aid to Fugitive Slaves"* in the House of Representatives *[of Ohio]* Feb., 23, 1861 (Columbus, Ohio, 1861, pamphlet); Thomas Wentworth Higginson to Charles Francis Adams, Dec. 22, 1860, Adams Papers; G. N. Fuller (ed.), *Messages of the Governors of Michigan, 1824-1927* (Lansing, 1925-1927), I, 439-441; Pierce, *Memoir and Letters of Sumner*, IV, 16-21; Sumner (ed.), Works, V, 450-467.

[71] *Letters, Speeches and Addresses of August Belmont* (New York, 1890), pp. 30-36; New York *Herald*, Jan. 23, 26, 28, 1861.

[72] *Acts and Resolves of Massachusetts, 1861*, pp. 398-399; Henry G. Pearson, *The Life of John A. Andrew* (Boston, 1904), I, 166; *Liberator*, Jan. 11, 1861.

the House of Representatives compromise committee made him the recipient of numerous inquiries on the liberty laws, advised several of his correspondents that repeal would count only "a feather's weight" in preventing dissolution of the Union.[73]

If the personal liberty laws counted only "a feather's weight" during the secession crisis, they were important during the 1850's. The conflict between the northern states and the federal government over rendition of runaway blacks represented in concrete microcosm the basic constitutional problem dominating the first seven decades of the Republic: the locus of ultimate political authority within the federal system. The arguments of advocates and opponents of personal liberty laws support the view that the constitutional issue was not a simple one of southern states' rights versus the northern doctrine of national supremacy. Antislavery Republicans such as Wade and Sumner and abolitionist theorists were the primary champions of states' rights. Southerners supported strong national action to recover fugitive slaves.

The liberty laws are also a gauge of antebellum attitudes toward the status of free blacks. Large numbers of northerners disliked the flimsy procedural guarantees which seemed to threaten the liberty and safety of free Negroes. In this respect the liberty laws reflected a general northern desire that free blacks have a certain minimal degree of civil protection. But, at the same time, debates over the laws reveal the limits of northern libertarianism. Supporters of liberty laws showed little concern that the bills offered almost no practical assistance to blacks since most fugitive slave suspects were held by federal authorities. Many proponents came to view enactment as an end in itself rather than as a means of effectively raising the black man above second class citizenship.[74]

Although the personal liberty laws were important to the conflict over the Constitution and civil liberties, their greatest significance lay in their use, by both sides, as symbols around which clustered all of the emotional issues which separated the two antagonistic sections of the Republic. Most proponents of the laws considered the statutes a form of symbolic resistance to southern violations of individual liberties, incursions upon the authority of free state governments, and aggressions in the territories. Commenting on Massachusetts' liberty law of 1855, an astute correspondent from the New York *Tribune* observed that the law was of little practical consequence. The idea that a serious collision would occur between Massachusetts and the federal government was "simply laughable." "The value of the law," he went on, "is that it is a protest, the strongest and most dignified that Massachusetts

---

[73] Lincoln to William Seward, Feb. 1, 1861, in Basler (ed.), *Works of Lincoln*, IV, 183; *ibid.*, 156-157; Charles Francis Adams to Dwight Foster, Dec. 31, 1860, Adams Papers.

[74] See also Leon Litwack, *North of Slavery: The Negro in the Free States, 1790-1860* (Chicago, 1961), *passim*.

is able to make against slavehunting on her soil."[75] Similarly, to the South the liberty laws symbolized northern disregard of fundamental constitutional obligations and of the Black Republicans' hostility to the rights and property of slaveholders. Personal liberty laws, though not a substantive "cause" of the war, were symptomatic of more basic divisions. Debates over the laws provided rhetorical outlets which reflected and deepened sectional antagonism.[76]

[75] New York *Tribune*, July 28, 1855.

[76] The author wishes to thank Professor James A. Rawley of the University of Nebraska who suggested this topic and provided guidance for an earlier version of this article.

KENTUCKY, CANADA, AND EXTRADITION:
THE JESSE HAPPY CASE

By Jason H. Silverman*

Writing in 1826 to Albert Gallatin, the American ambassador in London, Secretary of State Henry Clay described the number of successful fugitive slave escapes to Canada as a "growing evil [which] has produced some . . . and is likely to produce much more irritation . . . [for] the attempt to recapture them leads to disagreeable collisions." Clay further advised that the fugitive slaves were hardly an acquisition of which Canadians could be proud since the runaways were "generally the most worthless of their class." The Secretary of State concluded that all runaway slaves in Canada should be returned immediately to discourage any future escapes by American slaves.[1]

This problem of fugitive slaves plagued Southern slaveowners throughout the entire ante-bellum period. However, it most affected slaveholding states bordering free Northern states where the road to freedom in Canada was shorter, more enticing, and more likely to reach fruition. The states of Kentucky, Virginia, and Maryland all suffered greater loss of property in the form of runaway slaves than the slaveholding states of the Deep South.[2] In fact, the Louisville *Journal* estimated that the state of Kentucky lost at least $30,000 in runaway slave property every year.[3] Therefore, the border slaveholding states had more at stake when extradition requests arose. In the late 1830's, for example, Kentucky made three successive extradition requests that were to have international ramifications. The petitions for the return of escaped slaves Thornton Blackburn and Solomon Mosely set the stage for the extradition appeal in 1837 of Jesse Happy. In the latter case, the Canadian Government rendered legal decisions and established precedents that would affect the status and security of all fugitive slaves in Canada. Henceforth, all legal and diplomatic maneuvers to secure the return of American fugitive slaves residing in Canada prior to 1850 would be governed by the ruling in the Jesse Happy case. Unfortunately, the Jesse Happy case has received very little attention from historians. It is therefore the purpose of the present

---

*Jason H. Silverman, Ph.D. candidate, is an instructor in the Department of History at the University of Kentucky.
1 Letter reprinted in *Niles' Weekly Register*, June 19, 1826.
2 *New York Tribune*, August 28, 1851.
3 Louisville *Daily Journal*, January 24, 1850.

study to examine and evaluate a legal decision that had not only domestic but international consequences as well.

In 1793, the first Parliament of the Province of Upper Canada[4] enacted a law which stated that "No Negro or other person who shall come or be brought into this Province . . . shall be subject to the condition of a slave or to bounden involuntary service for life."[5] Every slave already residing in Upper Canada would remain in bondage at the discretion of the master, but any child born of a slave after passage of this statute would be free at the age of twenty-five. Upper Canada thus provided for the gradual abolition of slavery within its boundaries .

Coincidentally, the United States Congress passed the first Fugitive Slave Law in 1793. It empowered a slaveowner to hunt, seize, and then carry his fugitive property to the nearest district or circuit judge and, upon oral testimony, to receive a certificate warranting the slave's return.[6] The two neighboring countries had embraced mutually exclusive laws which symbolized their divergent viewpoints on the institution of slavery. When United States slaves heard of the Canadian asylum, many chose to seek freedom on British soil rather than risk extradition from another state of the Union.

Like their Southern brethren, however, the Commonwealth of Kentucky was dissatisfied with the fugitive slave law and actively advocated stronger and more efficient means of returning the runaways. Due in part to her geographical location (bordering the three Northern free states of Ohio, Indiana, and Illinois), Kentucky consistently requested assistance from the Federal Government in preventing successful slave escapes through the North into Canada. In 1817, Representative Richard C. Anderson of Kentucky co-authored a bill that called for deference to slaveholders in all fugitive slave cases. Anderson's bill proposed that the slaveowner be enabled to return the fugitive slave back to the state from which he escaped before initiating legal proceedings. The owner could then bring charges against the fugitive in the state from which he

---

4 Upper Canada was created in 1791 and constituted what is now the province of Ontario. Lower Canada, created the same year, was the present-day province of Quebec. From 1841-1867 they were Canada West and Canada East respectively. On March 29, 1867 under the British North America Act, the Dominion of Canada was created uniting Ontario, Quebec, New Brunswick, and Nova Scotia.

5 The Statute is (1793) 33 George III, c. 7 (U.C.) found in William R. Riddell, "The Slave in Canada," *Journal of Negro History* 5 (July, 1920), 318-19. For more information on blacks in Canadian history, see Robin W. Winks, *The Blacks in Canada* (New Haven, 1971).

6 John Hope Franklin, *From Slavery to Freedom: A History of Negro Americans* (New York, 1967). See also C.W.A. David, "The Fugitive Slave Law of 1793 and its Antecedents," *Journal of Negro History* 9 (January, 1924), 18-25; and Marion G. McDougall, *Fugitive Slaves, 1619-1865* (Boston, 1891).

fled where, it was argued, a fairer judgement could be rendered on the accused's guilt or innocence. Anderson believed this bill would serve to protect the slaveowner's rights and would result in greater return of fugitive slave property to slaveholding states. The bill provisionally passed both House and Senate but was tabled before concurrence of amendments.[7] Anderson's efforts in Congress thus proved fruitless, and consequently in 1821 the General Assembly of Kentucky requested that the Federal Government negotiate an extradition treaty with Great Britain for the return of fugitive slaves from Canada. Owing to the pressure of the Kentuckians, Secretary of State John Quincy Adams met with the British Ambassador in an attempt to reach an agreement. Nonetheless, the British Government refused to co-operate.[8]

From the Canadian viewpoint, the question concerning American extradition requests for fugitive slaves seems to have been answered first by John Beverly Robinson, Attorney General of Upper Canada, who stated in 1819 that

> ... the Legislature of this Province having adopted the Law of England as the rule of decision in all questions relative to property and civil rights, and freedom of the person being the most important civil right protected by those laws, it follows that whatever may have been the condition of these Negroes in the Country to which they formerly belonged, here they are free — For the enjoyment of all civil rights consequent to a mere residence in the country and among them the right to personal freedom as acknowledged and protected by the Laws of England ... must ... be extended to these Negroes as well as to all others under His Majesty's Government in this Province.[9]

He concluded by noting that any interference with the civil rights of Canadian residents would be prosecuted to the full extent of the law. Canada became a haven for the hunted.

However, the Parliament of Upper Canada passed an act in February of 1833 that provided for extradition of fugitive criminals from foreign countries. Under this statute, anyone in the province charged by the executive of a foreign country with "Murder, Forgery, Larceny or other crime which if committed within

7 *Annals of Congress*, 15th Congress, 1st Session, 1818, pp. 826-36, 837-40. See also Henry Wilson, *The Rise and Fall of the Slave Power in America*, (3 vols.; Boston, 1875), I, 74-78; and Stanley W. Campbell, *The Slave Catchers: Enforcement of the Fugitive Slave Law, 1850-1860* (New York, 1968), pp. 3-26.

8 *Annals of Congress*, 16th Congress, 2nd Session, 1821, pp. 941-42. See also Alexander L. Murray, "Canada and the Anglo-American Anti-Slavery Movement: A Study in International Philanthropy" (Ph.D. dissertation, University of Pennsylvania, 1960), pp. 117-20; and Campbell, *The Slave Catchers*, p. 9

9 *Canadian Archives Sundries*, U.C., 1819. See also Riddell, "The Slave In Canada," pp. 340-45; and William R. Riddell, "The Slave In Upper Canada," *Journal of Negro History* 4 (October, 1919), 372-95.

the province would have been punishable with death, corporal punishment, the pillory, whipping, or confinement at hard labour" could be arrested, detained, and ultimately returned at the discretion of the provincial Governor and his Executive Council.[10] This law obviously threatened the freedom of all runaway slaves from the United States: first, because many slaves indeed committed such crimes in the process of escaping; second, because slaveowners might bring false charges in order to regain their property. Three test cases came from the state of Kentucky which requested in rapid succession the extradition of runaway slaves Thornton Blackburn, Solomon Mosely, and Jesse Happy.

In the case of Thornton Blackburn and his wife, extradition was refused.[11] They had been taken into custody in Detroit in accordance with the United States Fugitive Slave Law and a certificate issued for their return as slaves to Kentucky. On the day he was to be transported to Kentucky, however, Thornton Blackburn was rescued by the aid of a violent mob and crossed into Canada where his wife had escaped in disguise a day earlier. Canadian authorities denied that Blackburn had taken part in rioting or forcible rescue since he was merely trying to escape slavery. By Canadian definition, then, Blackburn could not be charged with any of the offenses stipulated in the act of 1833 which would have required his extradition. The Attorney General of Upper Canada argued further that if Blackburn and his wife

> ... should be delivered up they would, by the laws of the United States be exposed to be forced into a state of slavery from which they had escaped two years ago when they fled from Kentucky to Detroit; that if they should be sent to Michigan and upon trial be convicted of the riot and punished, they would after undergoing their punishment be subject to be taken by their masters and continued in a state of slavery for life, and that, on the other hand, if they should never be prosecuted, or if they should be tried and acquitted, this consequence would equally follow.[12]

As a result, no extradition occurred in the Blackburn case.

---

10 The Statute is Act (1833), 3 Will IV, c. 7 (U.C.) found in Riddell, "The Slave In Canada," p. 345. The Executive Council was appointed by the Provincial Governor. For more on the extradition of fugitive slaves from Canada see Roman J. Zorn, "Criminal Extradition Menaces the Canadian Haven for Fugitive Slaves, 1841-1861," *The Canadian Historical Review* 38 (December, 1957), 284-94; and Alexander L. Murray, "The Extradition of Fugitive Slaves from Canada: A Re-evaluation," *The Canadian Historical Review* 43 (December, 1962), 298-314.

11 An exhaustive search through Kentucky local, regional, and state histories for information on Thornton Blackburn and Solomon Mosely has proved fruitless. In addition, neither is mentioned in the Governors' Papers located at the Kentucky State Historical Society, Frankfort.

12 Winks, *The Blacks In Canada*, p. 169. The quote is from the Report from Attorney General Robert S. Jameson in *Canadian Archives, State J.*, p. 137.

The next request from Governor James Clark of Kentucky concerned Solomon Mosely who stole his master's horse, rode the horse to Buffalo where he sold it, and escaped across the Niagara River to Canada. Mosely's lawyer made no attempt to deny the theft but chose to emphasize the ulterior motive of the Americans to return Mosely to slavery, noting that "four men have travelled 1500 miles at the expense of at least $400 to bring to justice a Slave charged with stealing a horse of only the value of $150."[13] Nevertheless, the Attorney General, Executive Council, and Lieutenant Governor of Upper Canada all agreed that the crime had been proved and was one of the offenses provided by the act of 1833 for extradition of fugitive criminals. Despite their abhorrence of slavery, Canadian officials could find no legal technicality upon which to deny extradition, so Mosely was ordered to be returned to Kentucky. His return was prevented by mob force which allowed him to escape, and Mosely lived free in England and Canada with no further legal action against him.[14]

The case of Jesse Happy brought a more definitive ruling on extradition as this matter received the careful consideration and attention of the Attorney General, Executive Council, and Lieutenant Governor of Upper Canada, the Secretary of State of the Colonies, the Foreign Secretary, and ultimately the Law Officers of the Crown. Jesse Happy escaped from Kentucky in 1833 on his master's horse. He left the animal and arranged for its recovery before crossing the border into Canada. Thomas Hickey,[15] the owner, subsequently reclaimed the horse. Two years later the Grand Jury of Fayette County, Kentucky, indicted Happy on the charge of horse stealing. Two more years passed before Thomas Hickey swore out an affidavit against Happy, in which Hickey did no more than describe the ex-slave.[16] Yet it was upon this indictment and affidavit that Governor Clark of Kentucky based his demand in August, 1837, for extradition of Jesse Happy as a fugitive criminal. A Canadian Justice of the Peace forthwith issued a warrant for Happy's arrest and detention on September 7, 1837. Consequently, Happy was taken into custody and confined in the Hamilton (Ontario) jail.

---

13 Murray, "Canada and the Anglo-American Anti-Slavery Movement," p. 125.
14 *Ibid.*, pp. 125-28.
15 Thomas M. Hickey, a Lexington native, became a Fayette County Circuit Court Judge in 1836. See Richard H. Collins. *History of Kentucky*, (2 vols.; Frankfort, 1966), I, 41.
16 *Commonwealth v. Happy* (1835), VI-C-124, Box 94, Drawer 835-37; Hickey Affidavit (1837), VI-C-124, Box 96, Drawer 851-58. Both are located in the Fayette County and Circuit Court Records housed at the State Archives and Records Center, Frankfort.

The Attorney General of Upper Canada, the Honorable Mr. Hagerman, rendered a routine decision the next day when he reported that the evidence pointed toward the accused's guilt and judged that legally the prisoner could be extradited. That Mr. Hagerman had misgivings concerning the case appeared in a postscript to the ruling in which he commented:

> It has been intimated to me that the accused is a fugitive slave and if delivered up will not only be subject to punishment for the felony charged against him but after such punishment shall have been inflicted he will be returned to Slavery—
> It also appears that the Indictment found by the Grand Jury of the State of Kentucky is certified on the 1st of June 1835 and that the offense appears to have been committed on the 18th May 1833.[17]

A cursory examination of the evidence apparently proved unsatisfactory to the Attorney General, who forwarded this report with postscript to the executive branch of the provincial government.

The Executive Council met on September 9 to deliberate the proper course of action in Happy's case. They reviewed the evidence, the Attorney General's report, and a report from Chief Justice Robinson concerning the statute of 1833.[18] Compared to the

---

17 Colonial Office Records, 42 Series, Volume 439, p. 182 (Hereafter cited as CO 42/439/182). The original records from the Colonial Office are located in the Public Record Office, London, England. However, for this study microfilmed copies were used, obtained from the Public Archives of Canada in Ottawa.
18 Chief Justice John Beverly Robinson, formerly Attorney General of Upper Canada and author of the Statute of 1833, detailed in an undated report the legal ramifications of that statute. He noted that the purpose of the act was to ensure reciprocity in the surrender of fugitive criminals, particularly between Upper Canada and the adjoining states of New York and Michigan. He disagreed that the one phrase allowing discretion by the Executive of said Providence was intended to be applied toward fugitive slaves. Taking a purely legalistic stance, he argued against the exemption of ex-slaves from the provisions of the statute by claiming
> We have not a right to say, and certainly not the power to insist, that slavery shall not be tolerated in [other] countries; and since we cannot abolish slavery there, I do not think that we can properly proceed towards accomplishing such a result . . . by deciding that slaves who murder their masters, or burn their houses, or steal their goods, shall find a secure refuge in this Province,—while the white inhabitants of the same Countries shall, under similar circumstances be surrendered, on the requisition of their Government.
Thus, Robinson disposed of the moral argument that returning the party to America would again subject him to the institution of slavery and negated the problem of double penalty since Canadian officials could take no legal responsibility toward any consequences to the party after trial. The Chief Justice then denied that if fraudulent charges came against one fugitive slave, such charges would be repeated in similar cases. He implied that presupposing insincere and unauthentic warrants on the part of the United States would result in similar reaction to Canadian requests for extradition of fugitive criminals. The danger, as he saw it, was in encouraging a breakdown in the exchange of criminals who might flee from one country and "could be secure of protection in the other against the consequences of their most atrocious crimes." Robinson concluded that, contrary to popular opinion, Canadian protection of a fugitive slave "is to stand between him and public justice . . . and if he ought to abide the test of a public trial, we cannot properly avert the possible consequences to him of a state of slavery which we had no hand in creating." Yet perhaps the Chief Justice's true sympathies appeared when he made the extra-legal remark that such protection of fugitive slaves would increase the migration of Negroes into Canada which "to say the least, it is not desirable to encourage." CO 42/439/199-204. See also Murray, "Canada and the Anglo-American Anti-Slavery Movement," p. 131.

Mosely case which was characterized by prompt and correct documentation, the case against Jesse Happy lacked credence since "The Alleged Offence purports to have been committed more than four years ago" with no legal recourse sought until August, 1837. In addition, the Executive Council felt uneasy about subjecting Happy to the possibility of double penalty. Concerned that the ulterior motive on the part of the former owner was to return the man to slavery, the Council professed that "Were there any Law by which after taking his trial and if convicted undergoing his sentence he would be restored to a State of Freedom — The Council would not hesitate to advise his being given up, but there is no such provision in the Statute [of 1833]." The Council hesitated to decide the matter as peremptorily as the Attorney General and therefore closed their report with a request for further information from Happy and a request for guidance on these questions from the government "as a matter of general policy."[19]

Sir Francis Bond Head, Lieutenant Governor of Upper Canada, received his Executive Council's report and determined to resolve the question of extradition of fugitive slaves by appealing to a higher court. In early October of 1837, he wrote to the Secretary of State for the Colonies, Lord Glenelg, requesting specific instructions for such cases. In a lengthy harangue which belied the author's attitude, the Lieutenant Governor argued:

> It is quite true that if a white man who has stolen a horse from the Commonwealth of Kentucky comes with it or without it to this Province, he is . . . liable to be given up on demand to the neighboring authorities, and it certainly does seem to follow that a black man ought not to expect, because our laws grant him personal freedom, that he should moreover claim from them emancipation from trial for crimes for which even British-born subjects would be held responsible; yet on the other hand, it may be argued that a slave escaping from bondage on his master's horse is a vicious struggle between two parties of which the slave owner is not only the aggressor, but the blackest criminal of the two — it is the case of the dealer in human flesh versus the stealer of horse-flesh. . . . The clothes and even the manacles of a slave are undeniably the property of his master, and it may be argued that it is as much a theft in the slave walking from slavery to liberty in his master's shoes as riding on his master's horse; and yet surely a slave breaking out of his master's house is not guilty of the same burglary which a thief would commit who should force the same locks and bolts in order to break in.[20]

He continued by declaring that the Canadian government would be justified in refusing extradition until American law would guar-

---

19 CO 42/439/190-192.
20 CO 42/439/170-173. See also Fred Landon, "The Fugitive Slave In Canada," *The University Magazine* 18 (Summer, 1919), 275-76.

antee the return of the subject to Upper Canada, thus precluding
the possibility of double indemnity. Sir Francis Bond Head included documentation for both the Mosely and Happy cases in his
communication to the Secretary of State to show impartiality in
his rulings, even though his true sentiment toward the morality
of extraditing fugitive slaves was clearly evident in his letter.

While awaiting a reply from the Secretary of State, the Executive Council of Upper Canada met again to consider the disposition
of Happy's case. The Council re-examined the evidence, particularly
Hickey's affidavit, and found new facts relating to the actual
events of the case. In addition, they considered new evidence wherein a witness corroborated Happy's claim that he carefully planned
the animal's return to the rightful owner. They then ruled "that
the horse may not have been stolen but merely wrongfully used for
the purpose of Escape." Even were he not a runaway slave, they
concluded, there was "so much doubt over the case that the Council
cannot report . . . that the Evidence is sufficiently satisfactory . . .
to recommend the delivery up of the Prisoner." It was implied that
they could not accept the indictment by Kentucky's Grand Jury on
face value in view of the contradiction of sworn statements by
Canadian residents. Their report reiterated the earlier request for
a legal ruling from a higher governmental authority on the subject
of extradition of fugitive slaves. It nevertheless, though, rendered
the Council's final decision to release Happy from custody based
on insufficient evidence.[21] This correspondence, forwarded to the
Lieutenant Governor, prompted the release of Jesse Happy from
the Hamilton jail in mid-November of 1837.

Meanwhile, Secretary of State Glenelg received the request for
advice and directed the problem to the Foreign Secretary, Lord
Palmerston. Noting that he was aware of no positive rule governing the extradition of fugitive slaves, Lord Glenelg submitted that
in his view each case should be decided at the discretion of the
officials involved. If his interpretation held true, Glenelg continued,
the suit on restitution of Jesse Happy should be refused on three
grounds: first, that Happy did not take the horse with felonious
intention and did not appropriate the property permanently; second, that no legal action had been pursued for four years after
perpetration of the alleged crime; and third, that "the punishments
to which Slaves are liable by law in the United States for offences
of this nature are such as our own principles of jurisprudence

---

21 CO 42/445/35-38.

compel us to regard as indefensible, and disproportioned to the crime."[22] Lord Glenelg thus supported the action taken in this instance by the Council and executive of Upper Canada.

Lord Palmerston agreed to lay both the general matter and the specific case before the Law Officers of the Crown. The opinion was handed down by Law Officers Sir John Campbell and Sir Robert Mousey Rolfe early in 1838.[23] As a general policy, they advised that "no Distinction should . . . be made between the Demand for Slaves or for Freemen." If the alleged offense "had been committed in Canada," warranting apprehension and prosecution in accordance with Canadian statutes, "then on the requisition of the Governor of the Foreign State, the accused party ought to be delivered up, without reference to the question as to whether he is, or is not, a Slave." However, the Law Officers stipulated that the evidence to be used in cases concerning extradition of fugitive slaves "must be evidence taken in Canada, upon which (if False) the Parties making it may be indicted for Perjury."[24] This would ensure against further examples of faulty, inaccurate, or incomplete documentation. In addition, the power of discretion could still be used by Canadian officials to refuse extradition whenever special circumstances so demanded. Noting the lack of evidence of criminality in the case of Jesse Happy—especially since the accused had no intention of appropriating the animal—the Law Officers ordered his release. The Officers did not discuss the moral ramifications of slavery as exemplified by the double penalty argument. They merely interpreted the legal technicalities fixed by the statute of 1833 and ignored the politics of abolition.

Lord Palmerston accepted this response from the Law Officers of the Crown without comment and forwarded the substance of their opinion to Lord Glenelg. Consequently, Lord Glenelg enclosed a copy of Palmerston's text in his March 9, 1838 reply to Sir George Arthur, Lieutenant Governor of Upper Canada. The new Lieutenant Governor used the opinions of the Law Officers as precedent-setting standards and as a general instruction "for the guidance of the local Government on future similar occasions."[25]

Instead, the Law Officers' ruling was strictly upheld in the

---

22 CO 42/439/176-179.
23 Sir John Campbell was Attorney General in the Law Offices of the Crown. See Winks, *The Blacks In Canada*, p. 171.
24 CO 42/453/84-87.
25 Public Archives of Canada, Record Group 7, G 1. Dispatches from the Colonial Office, 1841-1865. See also Murray, "Canada and the Anglo-American Anti-Slavery Movement," p. 133.

cases pursued after this decision. No further extradition charges against fugitive slaves appear in official records for almost five years until the Nelson Hackett case arose. Hackett, a slave in Arkansas, stole a horse, a coat, a saddle, and a gold watch, and escaped to Canada West.[26] His master pursued proper legal channels, and Canadian officials adhered to the standard set by the Law Officers in the Happy case. They granted extradition based on the reasoning that at least one of the aforementioned thefts had been committed with felonious intention. The other most noteworthy extradition case concerned a slave who killed a white master when escaping. All evidence indicated the slave's guilt, but he was acquitted because of a technically defective warrant.[27] The courts again followed the letter of the Law Officers' judgment in the Happy case by accepting only formally correct documentation.

Extradition of fugitive slaves from Canada to the United States involved an issue sensitive to both countries. The British Government had encouraged gradual abolition by their Act of 1793; in practice, that goal was reached by the 1820's in the Canadian provinces. Slavery was formally abolished in all British possessions in an act passed in 1833 to become effective in 1834.[28] Canadians seemed justifiably proud of this accomplishment and therefore "were generally hostile to American slavery," which continued to exist.[29]

Meanwhile, Southerners within the United States were trying desperately to maintain the institution of slavery by lobbying for more stringent domestic and international fugitive slave laws. Friction between American pro-and anti-slavery forces grew fiercer during the very decade when Britain abolished all slavery within her possessions. The argument between South and North concerning the return of fugitive slaves was merely extended into an argument between the American South and Canada once slaves

---

26 See above note 4. For more on the Hackett case, see Roman J. Zorn, "An Arkansas Fugitive Slave Incident and Its International Repercussions," *Arkansas Historical Quarterly* 16 (Summer, 1957), 133-40. See also Murray, "Canada and the Anglo-American Anti-Slavery Movement," pp. 143-44.

27 Riddell, "The Slave In Canada," pp. 355-57; Winks, *The Blacks In Canada,* p. 175. For more on this case, see Fred Landon, "The Anderson Fugitive Slave Case," *Journal of Negro History* 7 (July, 1922), 233-42.

28 C. Duncan Rice, *The Rise and Fall of Black Slavery* (Baton Rouge, 1975), p. 257; Riddell, "The Slave In Canada," p. 313; Winks, *The Blacks In Canada,* p. 110. For more on the anti-slavery sentiment in Canada see Robin W. Winks, " 'A Sacred Animosity': Abolitionism In Canada," in Martin Duberman (ed), *The Anti-slavery Vanguard: New Essays on the Abolitionists* (Princeton, 1965), pp. 301-42; and the following three articles by Fred Landon: "The Anti-Slavery Society of Canada," *Journal of Negro History* 4 (January, 1919), 33-40; "Abolitionist Interest In Upper Canada," *Ontario History* 44 October, 1952), 165-72; and "The Anti-Slavery Society of Canada," *Ontario History* 48 (Summer, 1956), 125-31.

29 Murray, "Canada and the Anglo-American Anti-Slavery Movement," p. 19.

realized the safety of Canadian asylum. However, few appeals for extradition of fugitive slaves, brought by Kentucky and other slaveholding states before Canadian authorities, were decided in the plaintiffs' favor. Moral issues aside, Canadian officials strictly complied with the legal opinion of their highest Law Officers as set forth in the Jesse Happy case. Through its extradition petitions, the slaveholding state of Kentucky had indirectly forced a definitive Canadian ruling on the return of refugee slaves. Ironically, Kentucky's extradition requests had now made it even more difficult than before for the Southern states to reclaim their "property."

Abolitionists and the Civil Rights Act of 1875

JAMES M. MCPHERSON

T HE Civil Rights Act of 1875 climaxed a decade of efforts by radical Republicans, particularly Charles Sumner, to incorporate the Negro's freedom and equal rights into the law of the land. In some respects the act was a hollow achievement, for the clause outlawing segregation in public schools—which its sponsors considered the most important part of the bill —was stripped away before passage, and the remaining provisions forbidding discrimination in public transportation, inns, theaters, and "other places of public amusement" were rarely enforced and soon ruled unconstitutional.[1] But despite its failure in practice, the Civil Rights Act of 1875 was a symbolic victory for the equalitarian ideals of Reconstruction and an historical bridge between the Fourteenth Amendment and the Civil Rights Act of 1964.

The leadership of Sumner, the political pressures of Negro voters, and the partisan maneuvering in Congress that preceded passage of the act of 1875 have been thoroughly chronicled.[2] But the role of the abolitionists has not been adequately recognized. Since the 1830s the attainment of equal rights for Negroes had been an essential corollary to the abolitionist crusade for freedom. After the final victory of emancipation in 1865, some abolitionists turned their attention to other causes and a few retired altogether from the arena of reform, but most remained in harness for the long pull toward racial equality. Although the American Anti-Slavery Society and its state auxiliaries were dissolved after the Fourteenth and Fifteenth amendments had placed the Negro's civil and political rights in the Consti-

Mr. McPherson is assistant professor of history in Princeton University.

[1] For the text of the act, see *U.S. Statutes at Large* [XVIII], 336-37; for the Supreme Court decision of 1883, see *Civil Rights Cases*, 109 U.S. 3.

[2] Edward L. Pierce, *Memoir and Letters of Charles Sumner* (4 vols., Boston, 1877-1893), IV, 499-504, 580-82; L. E. Murphy, "The Civil Rights Law of 1875," *Journal of Negro History*, XII (1927), 110-27; Alfred H. Kelly, "The Congressional Controversy over School Segregation, 1867-1875," *American Historical Review*, LXIV (April 1959), 537-63; Bertram Wyatt-Brown, "Cenotaph for Charles Sumner: The Civil Rights Law of 1875" (seminar paper, Department of History, Johns Hopkins University).

tution, many of the individual abolitionists still alive in the 1870s continued to view themselves as the principal keepers of the nation's racial conscience.[3] For several years they bent their main efforts toward passage of civil rights legislation that would give substance and meaning to the promises contained in the Fourteenth Amendment.

As early as 1863 Theodore Tilton, the brilliant young editor of the *Independent,* had expressed a sentiment widely shared by his fellow abolitionists: "Our war against this rebellion is . . . a war for social equality, for rights, for justice, for freedom." After the war, John T. Sargent, president of the Massachusetts Anti-Slavery Society, declared that abolitionists must continue their labors until the Negro was recognized as "a man among men, a brother among his kindred with every natural and legitimate right conceded him, and every social privilege guaranteed and his rightful position in the community fully integrated and *beyond a doubt established.*"[4] Aaron M. Powell, editor of the official organ of the American Anti-Slavery Society, wrote in 1870 that "the work of moral regeneration, not yet accomplished, must still go on. To this we summon all who have been trained and disciplined in the severe but most valuable school of anti-slavery experience." And Frederick Douglass, the veteran Negro abolitionist, proclaimed that

while all lucrative employments are closed to the colored race,—and the highest callings opened to them are of a menial character; while a colored gentleman is compelled to walk the streets of our largest cities like New York unable to obtain admission to the public hotels; while state-rooms are refused in our steamboats, and berths refused in our sleeping-cars, on account of color . . . the negro is not abolished as a degraded caste. . . . We need to-day every influence that served to put the fifteenth amendment on the national statute-book to help us put the same fully into every department of the nation's life.[5]

Douglass did not greatly exaggerate the prevalence of Jim Crow in post-Civil War America. In truth, racial segregation was more deeply rooted and pervasive in some parts of the North than it was in the South. In the decades before the war Jim Crow had become institutionalized in the North, while the existence of slavery had precluded the development of a similar pattern in the South. After the war segregation of the freedmen in schools and churches was quickly established, but in the areas of transportation and public accommodations the South groped its way only gradually

[3] James M. McPherson, *The Struggle for Equality: Abolitionists and the Negro in the Civil War and Reconstruction* (Princeton, 1964).
[4] *Independent,* June 25, 1863; *National Anti-Slavery Standard,* Dec. 19, 1868.
[5] *National Standard,* I (May 1870), 43; *New National Era,* Oct. 6, 1870.

toward Jim Crow. Not until the first decade of the twentieth century did racial segregation become completely institutionalized in the South.[6]

In the North, meanwhile, the impact of the Civil War had begun to break down the barriers of Jim Crow in transportation, public accommodations, and schools. The substantial contribution of Negro soldiers to Union victory and the dimly-felt commitment to equal rights as a northern war aim stimulated the abolition of segregation in many parts of the North during and after the war. Between 1863 and 1867 California, Illinois, Indiana, Iowa, and Oregon repealed their "black laws" which had prohibited Negro testimony in court against whites; Congress abolished racial discrimination in federal courts and outlawed segregation on the streetcars of the District of Columbia; New York, San Francisco, and Cincinnati put an end to Jim Crow on city streetcars; and the Pennsylvania legislature prohibited Jim Crow in public transportation throughout the entire state. Within a decade after the Civil War most northern states had outlawed segregation in public schools, and in 1865 Massachusetts anticipated the future by enacting a civil rights law forbidding racial discrimination in places of public accommodation.[7]

Although these achievements appeared impressive, they left large areas of segregation in the North untouched. Negroes contined to suffer discrimination in housing and employment. Public schools in many parts of New York, New Jersey, Pennsylvania, Ohio, Illinois, and Indiana—where the large majority of northern Negroes lived—remained segregated until the last two decades of the nineteenth century (Indiana did not completely abolish public school segregation until 1949). For a long time after the Civil War, hotels and restaurants in some parts of the North continued to refuse service to Negroes. Even in Massachusetts, the civil rights law of 1865 did not prevent occasional discrimination by hotels and restaurants, for the difficulties and expense of bringing suit against offenders discouraged many Negroes from seeking legal redress.[8]

[6] Leon F. Litwack, *North of Slavery: The Negro in the Free States, 1790-1860* (Chicago, 1961); C. Vann Woodward, *The Strange Career of Jim Crow* (2nd ed., New York, 1957). But see Richard C. Wade, *Slavery in the Cities: The South 1820-1860* (New York, 1964), 266-71, for evidence that free Negroes in some antebellum southern cities were segregated by both law and custom.

[7] For a more detailed discussion of these measures, see McPherson, *Struggle for Equality*, 228-37; and James M. McPherson, *The Negro's Civil War: How American Negroes Felt and Acted During the War for the Union* (New York, 1965), 245-70.

[8] Boston *Commonwealth*, Sept. 24, 1870; *Zion's Herald*, Dec. 8, 1870; *New National Era*, May 9, 1872. When James Bryce visited the United States in the 1880s, he found that in most parts of the North the Negro "is not received in a hotel of the better sort, no matter how rich he may be. He will probably be refused a glass of soda water at a

By 1870 Jim Crow on trains, steamboats, and streetcars was becoming rare in the North, but the incidence of such segregation was growing in the South. In the late 1860s and early 1870s there were several well-publicized Jim Crow incidents in the South involving prominent Negroes. In 1869 Lieutenant Governor Oscar J. Dunn of Louisiana was denied admission to a first-class railroad car in his own state. A year later J. Sella Martin, a Negro clergyman from New York who had recently been appointed a special agent of the Post Office department, was forcibly ejected from a first-class car while on duty in Alabama. In 1871 the captain of a privately-owned Potomac River steamboat refused to allow dinner to be served to Douglass, who was returning to Washington from Santo Domingo where he had served as assistant secretary of a government commission investigating the possibility of annexing that Caribbean republic.[9]

In 1872 Douglass traveled from Washington to New Orleans, where he presided over a national convention of colored men. Upon his return, Douglass reported that he and his companions were denied service in railroad restaurants and were frequently forced to ride in second-class cars amid filth and smoke, even though they had purchased first-class tickets. Gilbert Haven, a militant Massachusetts abolitionist who had been elected bishop of the Southern Conference of the Methodist Episcopal Church in 1872, wrote from Georgia two years later that the second-class cars in which Negro passengers must ride were "hideous pens." While traveling through the state, wrote Haven, "I went forward, by permission of the conductor . . . to see my friend and brother, the presiding elder of the Savannah district. He was in a dirty, ill-ventilated, close-packed, unswept car, as mean as mean could be. Yet he was paying first-class fare and two score of seats in my clean car were vacant."[10]

drug store. He is not shaved in a place frequented by white men, not even by a barber of his own colour." James Bryce, *The American Commonwealth* (3rd ed., 2 vols., New York, 1893-1895), II, 504. Even after several northern states had passed public accommodations laws in the 1880s and 1890s, Negroes continued to suffer discrimination in many parts of the North—the laws were often weak and unenforceable. Leslie H. Fishel, "The North and the Negro, 1865-1900: A Study in Race Discrimination" (doctoral dissertation, Harvard University, 1954), 285-99, 392-400.

[9] *National Anti-Slavery Standard*, May 29, 1869; Boston *Commonwealth*, Sept. 3, 1870; *National Standard*, April 1, 8, 1871. The incidents involving Dunn and Douglass were cited by Charles Sumner in a Senate speech supporting his civil rights bill on January 15, 1872. *The Works of Charles Sumner* (15 vols., Boston, 1875-1883), XIV, 372-74.

[10] Article by Douglass in *Independent*, May 2, 1872; article by Haven in *Independent*, Aug. 6, 1874. It should be noted that when Thomas Wentworth Higginson traveled through the South Atlantic states in 1878 he found little overt discrimination against colored people. Negroes voted in large numbers, he reported, and "I rode with colored people in first-class cars throughout Virginia and South Carolina, and in street cars in Richmond and Charleston." Higginson, "Some War Scenes Revisited," *Atlantic Monthly*,

The Negro citizens of Charleston made an effort in 1867 to break the color line in the city streetcars. Gilbert Pillsbury, a New England abolitionist who had come to South Carolina during the war and later became mayor of Charleston, supported the drive to prohibit streetcar segregation. This prohibition was accomplished by military order in the spring of 1867.[11] The following year one of the first measures enacted by the Reconstruction legislature of South Carolina, which contained several erstwhile abolitionists and northern Negroes, was a civil rights law forbidding discrimination in public accommodations. This law was never fully enforced, but the Negroes of South Carolina reportedly suffered less segregation than those of other southern states during Reconstruction.[12]

As in South Carolina, abolitionists battled discrimination at the local and state level wherever possible. Of course the major portion of this activity took place above the Mason-Dixon line, since most of the abolitionists, despite the exodus of large numbers of schoolteachers and missionaries to the South during the war and Reconstruction, continued to reside in the North. In 1869 Powell tried to obtain hotel rooms in New York City for some colored visitors from Massachusetts. He applied to the city's ten leading hotels and found only one of them willing to accommodate the Negroes.[13]

XLII (July 1878), 1-9, esp. 7. Higginson added, almost as an afterthought, that "In Georgia, I was told, the colored people were not allowed in the first-class cars; *but they had always a decent second-class car.*" Negroes in Georgia and other parts of the South who were forced to ride in dirty, smoke-filled second-class cars did not always consider them "decent." Higginson was a prominent supporter of President Rutherford B. Hayes' policy of federal noninterference in the South which was based on a faith in the good will of southern white leaders toward the Negro population, and during his trip Higginson tended to view matters through rose-colored glasses, seeing only those things that justified Hayes' southern policy and ignoring those that did not. See the forthcoming biography of Higginson by Tilden G. Edelstein.

[11] Boston *Commonwealth*, April 27, 1867; Gilbert Pillsbury to Aaron M. Powell, May 21, 1867, *National Anti-Slavery Standard*, June 8, 1867. Gilbert was the brother of the more famous abolitionist, Parker Pillsbury.

[12] *The Revised Statutes of the State of South Carolina* (Columbia, 1873), 739-41; Joel Williamson, *After Slavery: The Negro in South Carolina During Reconstruction, 1861-1877* (Chapel Hill, 1965), 279-80; article by Gilbert Haven in the *Independent*, Aug. 6, 1874. Negroes achieved the desegregation of public facilities in a few other parts of the South during Reconstruction, especially New Orleans, where even some of the public schools were integrated for a major part of the Reconstruction period. Louis R. Harlan, "Desegregation in New Orleans Public Schools during Reconstruction," *American Historical Review*, LXVII (April 1962), 663-75. But Joel Williamson has demonstrated that even in South Carolina, where Negroes constituted a majority of the population and the Republicans had complete control of governmental machinery, the civil rights law was only partially effective. Most hotels, inns, and restaurants refused to serve Negroes, and though numerous complaints were lodged against these facilities under the state civil rights law, "not a single conviction was ever recorded." Williamson, *After Slavery*, 283-88.

[13] New York *Tribune*. April 3, 14, 1869; *National Anti-Slavery Standard*, April 24, 1869.

Appalled by this situation, Powell and his fellow abolitionists mounted a publicity campaign against Jim Crow in New York. Immediately after the dissolution of the American Anti-Slavery Society in 1870, Powell organized the National Reform League, composed of veteran abolitionists, to carry on the struggle for equal rights. As editor of the *National Standard* (successor of the *National Anti-Slavery Standard*), Powell waged an unremitting campaign for the desegregation of hotels and restaurants in New York.[14] His efforts, and the efforts of like-minded citizens elsewhere in the state, were rewarded in 1873 when the legislature passed a public accommodations law.[15]

Segregation in public schools had always been a prime target of abolitionist attack. In the years following the Civil War abolitionists and Negroes renewed their drive to cleanse the schools of caste. "Clearly, in a nation like ours," wrote one abolitionist in 1867, "the majority have no right to exclude the children of the minority from the schools, even though they open others 'as good' for their use. Such a separation in childhood would breed two races of citizens, hostile in their interests, with jealousies towards each other, that would forever prevent the harmony necessary for prosperity, or for the safe administration of the laws." Wendell Phillips declared that "the education of all classes and conditions of children *together* is one of the most valuable elements of our School System and makes it the root of our Republican Institutions. If you separate sects, races, or classes and educate them . . . you lose one of the finest influences of the plan."[16]

By 1860 the public schools of New England, except for a few cities in Rhode Island and Connecticut, admitted both races on an equal basis. Under the leadership of Thomas Wentworth Higginson and George T. Downing, a wealthy Negro restaurateur and abolitionist, Rhode Island abolitionists carried on a struggle for the desegregation of public schools in Newport and Providence. Their efforts were climaxed by success in 1866 when the legislature outlawed school segregation throughout the state.[17] Between 1867 and 1874 the legislatures or courts of five additional northern states (Michigan, Connecticut, Iowa, Minnesota, and Kansas) abol-

[14] *National Standard*, May 1870, Oct. 1, 15, 22, 1870, April 29, May 13, 1871; Powell to George W. Julian, Feb. 24, 1871, Giddings-Julian Correspondence (Manuscript Division, Library of Congress).
[15] *Laws of the State of New York . . . 96th Session* (Albany, 1873), 303. Kansas enacted an antidiscrimination law in 1874. *General Statutes of Kansas, 1909* (Topeka, 1910), 643.
[16] *The Right Way*, Feb. 23, 1867; *National Anti-Slavery Standard*, Dec. 11, 1869.
[17] McPherson, *The Negro's Civil War*, 266-69; McPherson, *Struggle for Equality*, 228-29.

ished segregation in public schools.[18] But most schools in the cities and states where the majority of northern Negroes lived remained segregated during Reconstruction, and the newly-established public schools in the South were, with very few exceptions, separated by race.[19]

Abolitionists continued their antidiscrimination efforts in such northern states as New York, New Jersey, and Pennsylvania. Lucy Stone, a veteran abolitionist and an emerging leader of the women's rights movement, tried unsuccessfully to persuade public authorities in Newark to admit colored children to the white schools. An abolitionist schoolteacher in Westbury, New York, was fired by the school board because of her protests against segregation.[20] In 1873 the venerable Pennsylvania Society for Promoting the Abolition of Slavery (founded in 1775 by Benjamin Franklin) made an unsuccessful attempt to insert into the new Pennsylvania constitution a clause abolishing school segregation.[21] The failure of these efforts and the persistence of segregation in the schools of North and South alike prompted the abolitionists' concentration on a federal antidiscrimination law in the 1870s.[22]

By 1870 most abolitionists had become convinced that private, local, and state efforts to end Jim Crow were inadequate. A decade of war and reconstruction had furnished many precedents for action by the federal government in the field of race relations, and abolitionists once again urged

[18] Kelly, "The Congressional Controversy over School Segregation," 563n; *General Statutes of Kansas, 1909* (Topeka, 1910), 643. In 1901 the Kansas legislature empowered the school boards of cities with more than 15,000 population to provide separate elementary schools for Negro and white children if they wished to do so. *Ibid.*, 1633-34. Several cities established segregated schools under this law—hence the origin of *Brown v. Board of Education of the City of Topeka*, which resulted in the Supreme Court's desegregation decision in 1954.

[19] More than 70 percent of the northern Negroes lived in New York, Pennsylvania, New Jersey, Ohio, Indiana, and Illinois where the schools were not officially desegregated by state action before the 1880s. The colored schools in these states were usually inferior to the white schools in physical equipment, length of term, and quality of teaching. In some parts of the six states, however, colored children attended integrated schools in small towns and in areas of sparse Negro population. Fishel, "The North and the Negro, 1865-1900," 183-225.

[20] *National Anti-Slavery Standard*, May 22, 1869; *National Standard*, Dec. 16, 1871.

[21] Alberta S. Norwood, "Negro Welfare Work in Philadelphia, Especially as Illustrated by the Career of William Still, 1775-1930" (master's thesis, University of Pennsylvania, 1931), 65-66.

[22] Caroline Putnam to Charles Sumner, Feb. 13, 1870, Charles Sumner Papers (Houghton Library, Harvard University); *National Standard*, June 1870, pp. 120-21; *Independent*, Sept. 22, 1870. The American Missionary Association and the American Freedmen's Union Commission, two abolitionist-dominated societies which established hundreds of schools for freedmen in the South during and after the war, opened their schools to both races on an equal basis. In practice, however, few white southerners were willing to send their children to "nigger schools," and only about 1 percent of the students in these schools were white. McPherson, *Struggle for Equality*, 399-400.

Congress to adopt strong measures against the national sin of discrimination. The Boston *Commonwealth* (edited by Charles W. Slack, an abolitionist who had led the fight to abolish school segregation in Boston in 1855) declared that "the Republican party has not yet accomplished its work, and will not till a perfect civil rights bill secures to every ransomed citizen the full enjoyment of his personal liberty. The Republican party *must* take that next step in the order of its march." An abolitionist from Worcester demanded angrily: "Why sit supinely and let these insolent [hotel] proprietors . . . virtually trample upon the great Constitutional guarantees of the Government? . . . The hour for fawning, begging, and cringing has gone by. . . . It is necessary and proper that the *law* be appealed to, and that respectable, well-behaved persons of color are accorded the rights which belong to them as citizens."[23] Charles Stearns, a Massachusetts abolitionist who had gone to Georgia after the war to help the freedmen buy land, asked rhetorically: "At the South, any more than at the North, why should a colored child go miles from his dwelling in quest of a colored school, when a white one is to be found near at hand?" He urged federal aid for education in the South, coupled with a provision requiring desegregated schools in every state. And Sumner, the abolitionists' best friend in Congress, told a gathering of colored people in 1870 that "it remains that equal rights shall be secured in all the public conveyances, and on the railroads. . . . All schools must be opened to all, without distinction of color."[24]

During the war Sumner had sponsored legislation to abolish racial discrimination in the Post Office department, the federal courts, and on Washington streetcars. In the postwar decade he provided the leadership for the legislative struggle against segregation. On May 13, 1870 he introduced in the Senate a bill to prohibit discrimination by railroads, steamboats, public conveyances, hotels, restaurants, licensed theaters, public schools, juries, and church organizations or cemetery associations "incorporated by national or State authority." Offenders were to be tried by federal courts and punished with heavy fines or imprisonment.[25] The Boston *Commonwealth* declared that passage of Sumner's bill was "required to make us a homogeneous people," but Sumner's colleagues were cool toward the measure, and on July 7, 1870 Lyman Trumbull, chairman of the Senate judiciary committee, recommended its "indefinite postponement."[26]

[23] Boston *Commonwealth*, June 29, 1872; *National Standard*, Oct. 15, 1870.

[24] Charles Stearns, *The Black Man of the South, and the Rebels* (New York, 1872), 477-98, esp. 481. Sumner's speech was published in the *Independent*, April 14, 1870.

[25] *Cong. Globe*, 41 Cong., 2 Sess., 3434.

[26] Boston *Commonwealth*, May 28, 1870; *Cong. Globe*, 41 Cong., 2 Sess., 5314.

Sumner reintroduced his bill at the next session of Congress, but except for the articulate Negroes and the abolitionists, public opinion was indifferent or hostile. Douglass denounced southern Republicans who refused to support the bill and asked if they wished "their colored constituents to understand that it is a matter of no consequence to them whether colored people are forced to travel in a manner such as no lady in the land would allow her pet dog to travel?" He warned the Republican party not to take the Negro vote for granted: "The colored people are loyal and grateful, but they are *people,* and are ready to resent any undue disregard of their just expectations.[27]

Sumner made a determined bid for passage of the civil rights bill in the 1871-1872 session of Congress, and the abolitionists mobilized their journalistic and oratorical resources to aid his efforts. Theodore Tilton proclaimed through his new journal, the *Golden Age,* that "it is not enough to provide separate accommodations for colored citizens, even if in all respects as good as those of other persons; equality is not found in equivalent, but only in equality." Tilton answered doubts about the constitutionality of the bill with the argument that "a hotel is a legal [i.e., licensed] institution, and so is a common school. . . . Discrimination is an insult, and a hindrance, and a bar, which not only destroys comfort and prevents equality, but weakens all other rights. The right to vote will have new security when the equality of all citizens in public conveyances, hotels, and common schools is at last established." Douglass urged passage of the bill so that "the baleful influence upon the children of the colored race of being taught by separation from the whites that the whites are superior to them may be destroyed."[28] Abolitionists repeated and elaborated these arguments in editorials, letters to newspapers, and on the lecture circuit. Negroes and abolitionists in both North and South circulated petitions urging passage of the bill, and scores of these petitions bearing thousands of signatures soon found their way to the desks of congressmen.[29]

During this session of Congress the civil rights bill became embroiled in political maneuvers connected with the Liberal Republican movement and the amnesty issue. By the winter of 1871-1872 the "liberal" revolt within Republican ranks against Grantism had reached formidable proportions.

[27] *New National Era,* Jan. 26, March 23, 1871. The *Era* was edited and published by Douglass in Washington.
[28] *Golden Age,* Nov. 4, 1871; *New National Era,* May 2, 1872.
[29] *National Standard,* Sept. 23, Nov. 25, 1871, Jan., Feb., March, June, 1872; *Cong. Globe,* 42 Cong., 2 Sess., 2, 36, 84, 429-34; *Cong. Record,* 43 Cong., 1 Sess., 50, 76, 101, 187, 568, 1976, 3827; *Journal of the Senate,* 43 Cong., 1 Sess., 33, 40, 50, 55, 65, 72, 90, 97.

The Liberal Republicans hoped to attract support from southern whites and northern Democrats by advocating complete amnesty for those southerners who still suffered the political disabilities of the Fourteenth Amendment. The House passed an amnesty bill in 1871, but when the measure came up for consideration in the Senate in December, Sumner attached his civil rights bill as a rider. Sumner favored amnesty as well as civil rights, and his strategy was designed to unite the supporters of both measures behind a single bill. Several of Sumner's radical colleagues, who were lukewarm toward civil rights and hostile to amnesty, backed Sumner's rider in the hope that by uniting the opponents of each measure they could defeat both.[30]

In reply to a letter from Gerrit Smith urging passage of the civil rights rider, Senator Roscoe Conkling, who knew whereof he spoke, said that "the juggles, and tricks of this session exceed all of the kind I have seen before."[31] The abolitionists may or may not have been aware of the motives of Sumner's allies, but at any rate they strongly supported Sumner's belief that amnesty should be coupled with civil rights. "When a colored United States Senator or a colored [Lieutenant] Governor of a State cannot ride from New Orleans to Washington in a first-class car," stated the Boston *Commonwealth*, "it is no time to ask for the rebel leaders full restoration to political privileges." Smith, long an advocate of universal amnesty, said that "to accord such great kindness to our bitter and murderous foes, and at the same time to deny justice to the millions, who, notwithstanding our ages of cruelty to them, were our friends, allies, and saviors, is more than any of us should be reconciled to."[32]

In February 1872 and again in May the Senate, by the tie-breaking vote of Vice-President Schuyler Colfax, approved Sumner's civil rights rider. But both times a coalition of radicals, Liberal Republicans, and Democrats, of whom some opposed amnesty and the rest opposed civil rights, defeated the combined amnesty-civil rights bill.[33] Meanwhile the Liberal Republicans held their national convention and nominated Horace Greeley for president on a platform calling for "the immediate and absolute removal of all disabilities imposed on account of the rebellion."[34] Fearful of voter

[30] These complicated partisan maneuvers are described in Pierce, *Sumner*, IV, 499-503, and Kelly, "The Congressional Controversy over School Segregation," 547-51.
[31] Conkling to Smith, May 17, 1872, Gerrit Smith Papers (Syracuse University Library).
[32] Boston *Commonwealth*, Dec. 30, 1871; Smith to Conkling, May 10, 1872, Smith Papers. See also John G. Whittier to Sumner, Jan. 16, 1872; David L. Child to Sumner, March 16, 1872; Francis W. Bird to Sumner, March 27, 1872, Sumner Papers.
[33] *Cong. Globe*, 42 Cong., 2 Sess., 919, 928-29, 3268, 3270. The amnesty bill required a two-thirds majority.
[34] Thomas H. McKee, *The National Conventions and Platforms of All Political Parties, 1789 to 1901* (4th ed., Baltimore, 1901), 146.

defections on the amnesty issue, radical Republicans in the Senate separated the civil rights and amnesty measures, and with Sumner ill and absent the Senate passed an emasculated version of the civil rights bill (shorn of the clauses covering schools, juries, churches, and cemeteries) on May 22. Freed from the encumbrance of the civil rights rider, the amnesty bill was quickly adopted. Sumner arrived on the scene at the last minute and protested vigorously, but without avail, against the emasculation of his bill and the separation of amnesty and civil rights. Sumner's fears that the House would kill even the crippled civil rights bill, standing alone, proved justified.[35]

Abolitionists were disappointed and angered by the defeat of Sumner's bill. "What a marked difference in the unanimity of the Senate for Amnesty, and the division that was shown in the matter of Civil Rights!" exclaimed William Lloyd Garrison. "Is a Southern policy again to dominate the land? It looks like it."[36] Abolitionists continued to publicize and denounce Jim Crow incidents in an effort to arouse public concern and indignation. An official of the American Missionary Association, an abolitionist-dominated society for the education of the freedmen, pointed out that even the popular Fisk Jubilee Singers were frequently denied accommodations on their tours, in the North as well as in the South. "In some places we are refused altogether," he reported, "and in others grudgingly received and compelled to bear the inconvenience and humiliation of having our meals served, either before or after the regular time, or of being put away in a private room to eat as persons unclean."[37]

When Congress convened again in December 1872, supporters of civil rights urged reconsideration of Sumner's bill. In an editorial entitled "Give Us the Freedom Intended for Us," Douglass proclaimed that "the black man is not a free American citizen in the sense that a white man is a free American citizen; he cannot protect himself against encroachments upon the rights and privileges already allowed him in a court of justice without an impartial jury." Nor, he added, "can it be denied that the forcing of colored men to pay for what they do not get by railroad corporations or the refusal to allow the same accommodation to them as to other citizens . . . is an invidious discrimination amounting to an abridgment of citizenship rights."[38] But Sumner was ill during most of the short 1872-1873 session

[35] New York *Times*, May 10, 1872; New York *Herald*, May 11, 1872; *Cong. Globe*, 42 Cong., 2 Sess., 3260, 3728-38, 3932, 4321-22.
[36] Garrison to Sumner, May 27, 1872, Sumner Papers.
[37] George L. White to John G. Whittier, Nov. 20, 1872, John G. Whittier Papers (Essex Institute, Salem, Mass.).
[38] *New National Era*, Dec. 5, 1872.

of Congress, and without his leadership the civil rights bill languished.

Sumner returned to Congress in December 1873 for what was to be his final effort in behalf of racial equality. The growing demand of Negro voters, abolitionists, and northern liberals for civil rights legislation—plus President Grant's recommendation in his annual message to Congress of a law "to better secure the civil rights" of Negroes[39]—created a more favorable climate for Sumner's bill than at any previous time. The Republicans, most of whom were now committed, however reluctantly, to some kind of civil rights legislation, had more than a two-to-one majority in both houses of Congress.

Early in the session a new and menacing obstacle arose to confront Sumner's bill. The constitutional sanction for civil rights legislation was believed to rest in part on the section of the Fourteenth Amendment which prohibited states from abridging the "privileges or immunities" of United States citizens. In 1873 the Supreme Court, by a vote of five to four, had declared in the Slaughterhouse decision that the Fourteenth Amendment applied only to the privileges and immunities of national citizenship, and that the protection of the rights of state citizenship must be left to the states themselves.[40] The Court did not clearly define the respective spheres of state and national citizenship, but the opponents of civil rights legislation seized upon the Slaughterhouse decision to condemn Sumner's bill as an unconstitutional extension of federal power into the realm of states rights. Even the *Independent* (no longer edited by Tilton), hitherto a supporter of equal rights legislation, in February 1874 came out against Sumner's bill on the grounds that the "rights" enumerated in the measure were those of state, not national citizenship.[41]

Sumner's allies in Congress quickly took up the challenge, and at least one of them turned to the "equal protection" clause of the Fourteenth Amendment to justify the bill.[42] Abolitionists joined in the argument and concentrated most of their fire on the *Independent* which had once been the most powerful abolitionist journal. Taken aback slightly, editor Henry C.

[39] James D. Richardson, ed., *Messages and Papers of the Presidents* (20 vols., Washington, 1897-1913), X, 4209.
[40] 16 Wallace 36.
[41] *Cong. Record,* 43 Cong., 1 Sess., 376, 380-81, 405-06, 419-20, 453-54; *Independent,* Feb. 5, 1874. The *Nation,* which had previously supported the civil rights bill, declared in 1874 that the bill was "so unconstitutional that probably not ten respectable lawyers in the country could be found who would be willing to father it." *Nation,* XIX (Dec. 3, 1874), 357.
[42] *Cong. Record,* 43 Cong., 1 Sess., 412. Sumner had argued in 1872 that the equal protection clause gave Congress the power to enact civil rights legislation. *Speeches of Charles Sumner on the Civil Rights Bill in the Senate* (Washington, 1874), 10-21.

Bowen clarified his position by explaining that he favored integration, but he did not see how, under the Constitution, the federal government could prevent individuals or corporations from discriminating against Negroes. Such discrimination was a matter for state action, and if the state chose not to act there was nothing the federal government could do about it.[43] Downing, the Negro abolitionist from Rhode Island who was now proprietor of the House of Representatives restaurant in Washington, replied angrily to Bowen's assertion. "The very nice concern you manifest for state rights," he told Bowen, "might receive more consideration did it not oppose efforts in behalf of *personal rights.*" Downing advanced an argument for federal civil rights legislation which has a modern ring. "If an inn," he wrote,

having its right to exist by virtue of state authority, being a creature of the state, in fact regulated by it, "shall make any discrimination between citizens of the United States on account of race, color, or previous condition of servitude," it may be said the *state* does the discriminating; and Congress may, under the fourteenth amendment to the Constitution, if not by virtue of any other section, legislate against the same.[44]

Other abolitionists amplified Downing's argument. Smith believed that the Constitution should be adapted to human rights, not vice versa. "A constitution, which is not built upon the recognition of our common humanity, is entitled to no respect," he said. "The right to our manhood and to the conditions of maintaining our manhood (such conditions, for instance, as are contained in the Civil Rights Bill) is not derived from the constitution. It comes . . . from the law of human nature and of God."[45] From his bishopric in Atlanta, Haven recounted numerous examples of segregation on the streetcars of Atlanta, the railroads and railroad stations of Georgia and Tennessee, and in the schools of the South. "Now there is no cure for this evil except by [federal] law," declared Haven. "Law alone abolishes a seated evil. Moral suasion never killed so much as a mosquito sin. It has been said the schools in the South would be ruined if this law should prevail. That is not true. But perhaps they had better be ruined than perpetually to train little children and youth to abhor each other who have no natural antipathies."[46]

In addition to raising the constitutional issue, opponents of Sumner's bill echoed the argument of southern educators that forced mixing of races in

[43] *Independent,* Feb. 19, 26, June 4, 1874.
[44] *Ibid.,* March 12, 1874.
[45] Gerrit Smith, *Equal Rights for Blacks and Whites,* letter to George Downing, March 6, 1874, published as broadside (Peterboro, 1874).
[46] *Independent,* Feb. 26, March 26, 1874.

the schools would destroy public education in the South.[47] As a result of these attacks on the bill, the outlook for civil rights legislation dimmed. Then on March 11, 1874 Charles Sumner succumbed to his final illness. On his deathbed, Sumner is reported to have told Judge Ebenezer R. Hoar: "You must take care of the civil-rights bill,—my bill, the civil-rights bill, —don't let it fail!"[48] Two months later the Senate finally passed an exceptionally strong version of Sumner's bill, minus only the clause relating to churches.[49] Adoption of the law was probably intended as a memorial to the dead senator, but the House, perhaps less affected by Sumner's passing, refused to concur in the Senate's action before adjournment.

Angry, discouraged, but not hopeless, abolitionists redoubled their efforts to mobilize support for House passage of the bill at the next session of Congress. A speaker at a reunion meeting of old abolitionists in Chicago told the assembled veterans of the antislavery crusade that "we do not regard our duty as done until [Negroes] enjoy the same social rights and privileges which are accorded to ourselves. . . . So long as the freedmen are excluded from the public schools, equal seats in the railroad cars and churches, and places of amusement and hotels, our work is not done."[50] In the summer of 1874 Charles C. Fairchild, an abolitionist member of the faculty of integrated Berea College in Kentucky, presented a reasoned and eloquent plea for passage of the civil rights bill. "The social standing and progress of the colored people [is] a matter of national importance," said Fairchild. "The Fourteenth Amendment was an express national recognition of this peculiar responsibility, and to reject this bill would be to reject the spirit and intent, at least, of that amendment." Fairchild could not accept the common argument that the roots of race prejudice and segregation in the South were so deep as to be ineradicable. "This prejudice is not so intangible," he wrote. "It is not inborn, but an educated prejudice, and a little compulsory education of a different nature will do much to remove it. . . . Progress in the matter of public conveyances and of schools [in the North] has been a constant illustration of this. . . . The social waters have always been greatly disturbed; but in a short time they ran quietly through a channel which contained one less obstacle." Fairchild also dealt with the objection that equality could only be earned by merit. He admitted that the civil rights law could not create merit,

[47] *Cong. Record,* 43 Cong., 1 Sess., 377, 405, 4089, 4114-15; *Nation,* XVIII (May 28, 1874), 339; J. L. M. Curry, *A Brief Sketch of George Peabody and a History of the Peabody Education Fund through Thirty Years* (Cambridge, 1898), 64-65.

[48] Pierce, *Sumner,* IV, 598.

[49] *Cong. Record,* 43 Cong., 1 Sess., 3451, 4175-76.

[50] Chicago *Tribune,* June 12, 1874.

but it can create circumstances which will tend to bring forth merit. At present in schools, churches, hotels, and cars the most prominent thing taught a colored man is that he is a "nigger." A man might as well place a flowering plant in a dark corner of his cellar and say that when it came into full fresh bloom he would bring it up into the sunlight and air as to place a young man under such rasping and degrading tutelage and say that when he had attained a generous and delicate culture that merit would be recognized.[51]

The election campaign of 1874 produced fierce outbreaks of violence against Negro voters in several southern states. Commenting on these events, the Boston *Commonwealth* stated that "there has been too much shilly-shallying about the civil rights bill. It is seen everywhere that no Southern hate has been placated by deferring action on that bill. The Republicans had better stake the enhanced devotion of the blacks by passing that bill than longer hope to conciliate a set of worthless Southerners by refraining from so doing."[52] Due mainly to economic depression, political corruption, and the turbulence of southern politics, more than half of the Republican incumbents of the House of Representatives were defeated in the election of 1874 and were therefore lame ducks in the 1874-1875 session of Congress.[53]

As the legislators convened in Washington in December 1874, abolitionists were dismayed by indications that the House would not pass the civil rights bill unless the school clause was stricken out. Elizur Wright, an abolitionist veteran of forty years' standing, was disgusted to "see even the foremost 'republican' politicians going back on the Civil Rights Bill, with their crocodile tears for Sumner yet moist on their handkerchiefs." Phillips warned that abandonment of the school clause would be "a surrender of the principle for which the war was waged. . . . If the war settled anything it settled this: that neither law nor constitution here can *recognize race* in any way, or in any circumstances." Segregated schools, he said, even if "equal" in theory, would never be equal in fact. "Herd together the children of the poor, no matter whether colored poor or those of any other race —whose parents have not the education to see defects, or the influence to

[51] *Independent*, June 25, 1874. Charlotte Forten, a Negro abolitionist from Philadelphia who had taught in the integrated public schools of Salem, Mass. before the Civil War and had gone to South Carolina as a teacher of the freedmen during the war, returned to the Palmetto State for a visit in 1874. She wrote that the success of racial integration in the University of South Carolina during Reconstruction was proof that race mixing could work even in the deep South. Boston *Commonwealth*, Aug. 22, 1874.
[52] Boston *Commonwealth*, Oct. 17, 1874.
[53] William B. Hesseltine, *Ulysses S. Grant, Politician* (New York, 1935), 367-71. Grant was reported to believe that popular hostility to the civil rights bill, especially in the South and border states, was partly responsible for the Republican defeat. New York *Tribune*, Nov. 7, 1874.

secure attention to their complaint—and how long will the schools continue equal?" asked Phillips. "The negro child loses if you shut him up in separate schools, no matter how accomplished his teacher or how perfect the apparatus furnished the school. . . . Just this deprivation and inequality the fourteenth amendment was intended to prevent when it secured to all 'United States citizens' the same 'privileges and immunities' and 'the equal protection of the laws.' "[54]

Despite the eloquent protests of abolitionists and of a handful of congressmen, the House cut out the school and cemetery provisions and passed the emasculated version of Sumner's civil rights bill on February 4, 1875.[55] On the road to passage by the House, the bill had become the political stalking-horse of a complicated maneuver by Benjamin F. Butler to secure suspension of the rules in order to pass enforcement legislation for the South, an army appropriation bill, and a railroad subsidy bill. All of this legislation was defeated except the civil rights bill, which as it emerged from the House was in part the child of political expediency and cynical partisanship.[56] Moreover, 90 of the 162 Republicans who voted for it had been retired by the voters at the previous election.[57] Under such circumstances, the chances that the Civil Rights Act would be a meaningful contribution to desegregation in the South were rather slight.

The Senate concurred in the House bill on February 27, and the Civil Rights Act of 1875 became law when President Grant affixed his signature on March 1.[58] Abolitionists were far from jubilant over this hollow victory. The Boston *Commonwealth* called the act an "apology for the civil rights bill" because "the most important feature," the school clause, had been stricken out. "What should have been a great measure of justice," said the *Commonwealth*, "has, by this action, proved of the very least consequence. . . . To let the colored people ride in cars, stop at hotels, and go to places of amusement, while they are denied equal school education . . . can bring no satisfaction to a thoughtful and logical mind." Garrison stated flatly that "I

[54] Elizur Wright to Gerrit Smith, Dec. 23, 1874, Elizur Wright Papers (Manuscript Division, Library of Congress); letter from Wendell Phillips published in the Boston *Advertiser*, Jan. 11, 1875. See also Boston *Commonwealth*, Dec. 5, 1874 and two printed circulars by Gerrit Smith: *To Thyself be True* (Nov. 23, 1874), and *Will the American People Never Cease to Oppress and Torture the Helpless Poor?* (Dec. 12, 1874).
[55] *Cong. Record*, 43 Cong., 2 Sess., 996-1011.
[56] The complex political maneuvers preceding House passage of the bill are described in Wyatt-Brown, "Cenotaph for Charles Sumner," 17-30, and Kelly, "The Congressional Controversy over School Segregation," 556-62.
[57] Murphy, "The Civil Rights Law of 1875," 123-24.
[58] *Cong. Record*, 43 Cong., 2 Sess., 1861-70; *U.S. Statutes at Large*, XVIII, 336-37.

would prefer to have the bill defeated as it stands, rather than adopted with the sanction of separate schools."[59]

Few people in the North seemed to take the Civil Rights Act seriously. The Chicago *Tribune* called it a "harmless" and "unnecessary" bill, and the Washington *National Republican* described it as a "piece of legislative sentimentalism." The *Nation* considered it "amusing" and "tea-table nonsense." The Washington correspondent of the Boston *Commonwealth* predicted that the federal government would make little effort to enforce the act; moreover, he expected the Supreme Court to declare it unconstitutional, for in the Slaughterhouse decision the Court had already expressed the opinion "that the general government has nothing to do with human life and personal rights within the States, which may take care of them or not, as suits their taste or convenience."[60]

The Civil Rights Act had little impact on "southern customs." In August 1876, more than a year after passage of the bill, Benjamin Tanner, a Negro Methodist clergyman who traveled widely in the South in connection with his pastoral duties, complained that he was nearly always shunted off into second-class or segregated accommodations. "The fact is," he reported, "pushing the colored people off to themselves is the practice of all the South. . . . In Atlanta everything is separate. You go to the depot, and you find three sets of rooms—*to wit*, 'Ladies' Rooms', 'Gentlemen's Rooms' and 'Freedmen's Rooms'! You enter the cars, and the same heathen rule bears sway, only to be broken when white men wish to smoke, and then they come into the 'Freedmen's Car.' " In 1883, after the Civil Rights Act had been in effect for eight years, the New York *Tribune* noted that it had been pretty much a dead letter from the beginning: "The few isolated efforts made to enforce it by legal process have hardly served to call attention to its existence." Few Negroes could afford to bring suit for damages under the law, said the *Tribune*, and most colored people were reluctant to force themselves into white theaters, inns, and other places of public accommodation.[61] Segregation in the South did not become a rigidly closed

[59] Boston *Commonwealth*, Feb. 13, 1875; letter from Garrison published in the Washington *Chronicle*, Feb. 5, 1875. See also C. T. Garland to Garrison, Jan. 26, Feb. 5, 16, 1875, William Lloyd Garrison Papers (Boston Public Library).

[60] Chicago *Tribune*, Feb. 6, 1875; Washington *National Republican*, March 1, 1875; *Nation*, XX (March 4, 1875), 141, (June 3, 1875), 370; Boston *Commonwealth*, Feb. 13, March 13, 1875. The text of the Slaughterhouse decision is in 16 Wallace 36 ff.

[61] *Independent*, Aug. 17, 1876; New York *Tribune*, Oct. 17, 25, 1883. In a paper presented to the American Historical Association on December 29, 1964, John Hope Franklin concluded, after a careful survey of the evidence, that "the Civil Rights Act was never effectively enforced." Doubts about its constitutionality, the passive role of the

system for another two decades, but already by 1880 it was a way of life for most Negroes, and the Civil Rights Act of 1875 had little effect in stopping the steady march of Jim Crow.

The Supreme Court, asserting that the adjustment of social relations of individuals was beyond the power of Congress, declared the Civil Rights Act unconstitutional in 1883. The *Nation* noted that the country's general approval of the decision showed "how completely the extravagant expectations as well as the fierce passions of the war have died out."[62] Those few abolitionists still alive did not approve of the decision. Phillips declared angrily that the Court was "governed by a pro-slavery bias," and Douglass condemned the decision as "a blow . . . struck at human progress." Even though the law had seldom been enforced, its existence was a symbol of the nation's equalitarian aspirations, and its nullification by the Supreme Court, said Douglass, was "one more shocking development of that moral weakness in high places which has attended the conflict between the spirit of liberty and the spirit of slavery from the beginning."[63]

The high hopes for a future of racial justice which abolitionists had expressed at the end of the war were betrayed by the moral indifference and sordid politics of the Gilded Age. The circumstances surrounding the congressional debate and final passage of the Civil Rights Act doomed it to impotence from the outset. The conservative reaction against radical Reconstruction was well under way by the time the bill was passed, and this reaction, coupled with widespread doubts about the constitutionality of the act even before 1883, rendered it virtually unenforceable. The vision of Sumner and the abolitionists was a hundred years ahead of its time, and it remains for the twentieth century to give substance to the ideals of the Civil Rights Act of 1875.

Department of Justice, and widespread white resistance to equal accommodations for Negroes in both North and South were the major reasons for nonenforcement of the act. John Hope Franklin, "The Enforcement of the Civil Rights Act of 1875."

[62] *Nation*, XXXVII (Oct. 18, 1883), 326.

[63] Clipping of a published letter by Phillips, dated Oct. 30, 1883, in the Stephen S. Foster Papers (American Antiquarian Society, Worcester); Philip S. Foner, *The Life and Writings of Frederick Douglass* (4 vols., New York, 1950-1955), IV, 393.

ABOLITIONIST POLITICAL AND CONSTITUTIONAL THEORY AND THE RECONSTRUCTION AMENDMENTS

David A.J. Richards *

I. INTRODUCTION

It is by now a familiar and well-evidenced historical claim that the Reconstruction Amendments were an outgrowth of the abolitionist political and constitutional theory of the antebellum period;[1] but such reasonable historical consensus on this matter does not, *pari passu*, tell us how this historical claim should guide our interpretation of the Reconstruction Amendments. Three main problems arise with such a simplistic interpretation. First, abolitionist political and constitutional theory was internally complex. It can be divided into at least three antagonistic schools of thought—radical disunionism, moderate antislavery and radical antislavery.[2] Presumably, however, good historical argument could discriminate among the various strands of abolitionist thought, and identify the one among them that crucially shaped the terms of the Reconstruction Amendments.

But second, even if we had such good historical analysis, the terms of such an abolitionist theory could be understood at various levels, some quite abstract and others quite concrete; complex internal disagreements

* Professor of Law, New York University Law School; A.B., 1966, Harvard College; D. Phil., 1970, Oxford University; J.D., 1971, Harvard Law School.

1. *See generally* MICHAEL K. CURTIS, NO STATE SHALL ABRIDGE: THE FOURTEENTH AMENDMENT AND THE BILL OF RIGHTS (1986); HOWARD J. GRAHAM, EVERYMAN'S CONSTITUTION (1968); HAROLD M. HYMAN, A MORE PERFECT UNION: THE IMPACT OF THE CIVIL WAR AND RECONSTRUCTION ON THE CONSTITUTION (1973); HAROLD M. HYMAN & WILLIAM M. WIECEK, EQUAL JUSTICE UNDER LAW: CONSTITUTIONAL DEVELOPMENT 1835-1875 (1982); ROBERT J. KACZOROWSKI, THE NATIONALIZATION OF CIVIL RIGHTS: CONSTITUTIONAL THEORY AND PRACTICE IN A RACIST SOCIETY 1866-1883 (1987); ROBERT J. KACZOROWSKI, THE POLITICS OF JUDICIAL INTERPRETATION: THE FEDERAL COURTS, DEPARTMENT OF JUSTICE AND CIVIL RIGHTS, 1866-1876 (1985); WILLIAM E. NELSON, THE FOURTEENTH AMENDMENT: FROM POLITICAL PRINCIPLE TO JUDICIAL DOCTRINE (1988); JACOBUS TEN BROEK, EQUAL UNDER LAW (2d ed. 1969) (originally published as THE ANTISLAVERY ORIGINS OF THE FOURTEENTH AMENDMENT (Univ. of Cal. Press 1951)); Robert J. Kaczorowski, *Revolutionary Constitutionalism in the Era of the Civil War and Reconstruction*, 61 N.Y.U. L. REV. 863 (1986); Robert J. Kaczorowski, *Searching for the Intent of the Framers of the Fourteenth Amendment*, 5 CONN. L. REV. 368 (1972-73).

2. For a good historical study of these various movements, see WILLIAM M. WIECEK, THE SOURCES OF ANTISLAVERY CONSTITUTIONALISM IN AMERICA, 1760-1848 (1977).

will appear at all these levels, and it is not obvious what weight, if any, we should accord any one of them in the interpretation of the Reconstruction Amendments today. For example, some abolitionists were remarkably critical of American racism; others were less critical, and members of the Reconstruction Congress thus held diverse views about the degree to which the substantive terms of the amendments (like equal protection) should be understood to condemn concrete practices like state-sponsored segregation.[3] Senator Charles Sumner and some others regarded such segregation as inconsistent with equal protection;[4] most others arguably did not.[5] Whose concrete convictions should prevail in shaping constitutional interpretation today?

Finally, the interpretation of the Reconstruction Amendments must make sense of their interpretation over time, including our contemporary sense of grave interpretive mistakes like *Plessy v. Ferguson*[6] and corrections thereof like *Brown v. Board of Education*.[7] The best interpretation of such evolving interpretive practice cannot reasonably be understood as some simplistic tracking of a prior concrete historical understanding—indeed, on such a view *Plessy* would be right and *Brown* wrong.[8] Rather, our evolving and self-correcting interpretive experience must be understood in some other way in which various factors, including history, must be given appropriate weight in the larger interpretive project of American constitutionalism.

To address these questions reasonably, we need to ask meta-interpretive questions about constitutional interpretation as a complex, historically self-conscious practice of understanding the supreme law of the Constitution in the United States and the role the Reconstruction Amendments play or should be understood to play in that project. American constitutionalism is a complex genre of historically evolving interpretive practices aspiring to narrative integrity centering on the text and institutions that express a people's self-conscious historical struggle to achieve a politically legitimate government which would guarantee all persons equal human rights.[9] The Reconstruction Amendments express

---

3. *See* NELSON, *supra* note 1, at 133-34.

4. *See id.*

5. *See id.* at 134-36.

6. 163 U.S. 537 (1896).

7. 347 U.S. 483 (1954).

8. For a notable example of an approach under which *Brown* is wrongly decided, see RAOUL BERGER, GOVERNMENT BY JUDICIARY: THE TRANSFORMATION OF THE FOURTEENTH AMENDMENT 230-45 (1977).

9. On the role of integrity in legal interpretation in general, and constitutional interpretation in particular, see generally RONALD DWORKIN, LAW'S EMPIRE (1986).

the greatest struggle of the American people since the founding to remember and recover the narrative thread of that story. I shall argue that the study of abolitionist political and constitutional theory enables us to clarify the place of these amendments in our constitutionalism because it offers an enriched understanding of both that struggle and its resolution in a permanent constitutional legacy to posterity. The Reconstruction Amendments address central defects in the legitimacy of the Constitution as supreme law as it had been interpreted in the antebellum period— a period very similar in methodological spirit to the revolutionary constitutionalism that the Founders of 1787 had brought to bear on the British Constitution. Abolitionist political and constitutional theory was the vehicle of this critical reflection on our constitutionalism. Therefore, study of these theories advances understanding of what our traditions are and how we should think about the proper interpretive attitude to be taken as to the role of these amendments in the preservation and legitimacy of the Constitution as supreme law.

II. ANTEBELLUM CONSTITUTIONAL AND POLITICAL THEORY

The appropriate framework for an analysis of these matters must be the growing sense of crisis in constitutional legitimacy during the antebellum period. This was initially marked by the claims of the success of Calhoun's proslavery constitutionalism[10] and then by its cumulative political successes. The success of Calhoun's constitutionalism is seen first in Congress's repeal of the Missouri Compromise in the Kansas-Nebraska Act of 1854 sponsored by Stephen Douglas's theory of popular sovereignty,[11] and then in the Supreme Court's adoption of the central claims of Calhoun's constitutionalism in *Dred Scott v. Sandford*.[12] The narrow issue of constitutional interpretation common to both these matters was the power or lack of power of Congress to forbid slavery in the territories. But the deeper question of constitutional legitimacy, posed by Lincoln among others,[13] was the interpretive attitude taken by Douglas and Taney to the text of the Constitution of the United States. This atti-

---

10. *See* JOHN C. CALHOUN, A DISQUISITION ON GOVERNMENT: AND SELECTIONS FROM THE DISCOURSE 44-45 (G. Gordon Post ed., 1943) (1853). For useful commentary, see AUGUST O. SPAIN, THE POLITICAL THEORY OF JOHN C. CALHOUN (1951).

11. *See* DAVID M. POTTER, THE IMPENDING CRISIS 1848-1861, at 145-76 (1976).

12. 60 U.S. (19 How.) 393 (1857). For commentary, see DON E. FEHRENBACHER, THE DRED SCOTT CASE: ITS SIGNIFICANCE IN AMERICAN LAW AND POLITICS 46-47, 126, 140-41 (1978); POTTER, *supra* note 11, at 267-96.

13. *See, e.g.*, Abraham Lincoln, Fifth Joint Debate at Galesburg (October 7, 1858), *in* THE LINCOLN-DOUGLAS DEBATES 206, 219-20 (Robert W. Johannsen ed., 1965) (arguing blacks were included in Declaration of Independence).

tude disengaged its interpretation from the Lockean political theory of the Declaration of Independence, namely, that all persons subject to political power have inalienable human rights. Calhoun, in contrast to other Southern constitutionalists like John Taylor of Caroline,[14] had radically defended his positivistic reading of the Constitution on grounds of a self-conscious repudiation of the very idea of inalienable human rights, and thus consistently argued that the Constitution should not be interpreted, either at the state or federal level, as a document with a vision of equal human rights.[15] Lincoln and others granted that the best interpretation of the history and text of the Constitution protected slavery in the states that had it. They distinguished, however, this short-term political compromise from the more long-term ambition of the Constitution to protect human rights—requiring federal power to protect human rights by forbidding slavery in the federal territories and thus over time encouraging slavery's gradual abolition by the states that retained it.[16] Such an interpretation would put slavery, as Lincoln argued that the Founders intended, "in the course of ultimate extinction."[17] By contrast, Calhoun's radical rights skepticism disallowed an interpretive attitude which was sensitive to the ultimate long-term obligation of a constitutional government to respect the equal human rights of all persons subject to its political power.

Although the issue in dispute was ostensibly a matter of constitutional interpretation, in substance, the issue was the very legitimacy of the Constitution as the supreme law of the land. The Constitution, as supreme law, must have a basis that renders a respect for its terms more legitimate than the laws over which it reigns supreme. Rights-based political theory gave a natural and plausible substantive basis for such legitimacy. The Constitution, when properly interpreted, was consistent with this political theory, which secured conditions of respect for human

---

14. Taylor had offered a Jeffersonian rights-based theory of the Constitution that gave a central role to the states in the protection of human rights and a correspondingly narrow role to the federal government. *See* JOHN TAYLOR, NEW VIEWS OF THE CONSTITUTION OF THE UNITED STATES (Leonard W. Levy ed., 1971) (1823); JOHN TAYLOR, CONSTRUCTION CONSTRUED AND CONSTITUTIONS VINDICATED (Leonard W. Levy ed., 1970) (1820).

15. For Calhoun's most explicit attack on the Declaration of Independence as embodying "the most dangerous of all political errors," and Jefferson's "utterly false view," see John C. Calhoun, Speech on the Oregon Bill, before the Senate (June 27, 1848) *reprinted in* IV THE WORKS OF JOHN C. CALHOUN 511, 512 (Richard K. Cralle ed., New York, D. Appleton & Co. 1861).

16. *See* Abraham Lincoln, Address at Jonesboro (September 15, 1858), *in* THE LINCOLN-DOUGLAS DEBATES, *supra* note 13, at 132.

17. *See* Abraham Lincoln, First Joint Debate, Ottawa (August 21, 1858), *in* THE LINCOLN-DOUGLAS DEBATES, *supra* note 13, at 55.

rights. This alone rendered any exercise of political power legitimate, and thus the claim of constitutional supremacy rested on the background political theory which defined when an exercise of coercive power was legitimate. The Constitution was supreme law because it enforced political power that de-legitimated exercises of a restrictive political theory which were inconsistent with its demands.

But how could one interpret the text and history of the Constitution of the United States as consistent with this political theory in light of its putative toleration of slavery, an institution resting on the abridgement of basic human rights? One response to this question was common to a proslavery radical like Calhoun and abolitionist radical disunionists like William Lloyd Garrison[18] and Wendell Phillips:[19] namely, abandon any attempt to interpret the Constitution in terms of rights-based political theory. Calhoun, who was skeptical of rights as defensible political values, did not conclude that the Constitution was illegitimate; rather he rested its legitimacy on other grounds, namely, a Hobbesian theory of state sovereignty.[20] Garrison and Phillips, however, believed in respect for human rights as ultimate political values and concluded that the Constitution, if not based on human rights, was illegitimate. The question became, was there a way that the Constitution could be regarded as legitimate on the basis of rights-based political theory?

The goal of giving an affirmative answer to this question motivated complex forms of internal and external criticism of the Constitution by various forms of abolitionist political and constitutional theory. By internal criticism, I mean the criticism of mistaken interpretations of the Constitution on the ground that the interpretations failed to elaborate properly the principles of the Constitution itself. By external criticism, I mean criticism of the Constitution, even properly interpreted, as inconsistent with enlightened critically defensible political values like respect for human rights. Thus, both advocates of moderate and radical antislavery internally criticized *Dred Scott v. Sandford*[21] as a mistaken interpretation of relevant constitutional principles. Although many advocates of moderate antislavery externally criticized slavery as a moral and polit-

---

18. *See* WILLIAM LLOYD GARRISON, SELECTIONS FROM THE WRITINGS AND SPEECHES OF WILLIAM LLOYD GARRISON (photo. reprint 1968) (Boston, R.F. Wallcut 1852).

19. *See* Wendell Phillips, *Introduction* to THE CONSTITUTION: A PRO-SLAVERY COMPACT 3-7 (photo. reprint 1969) (Wendell Phillips ed., New York American Anti-Slavery Society 1844); WENDELL PHILLIPS, CAN ABOLITIONISTS VOTE OR TAKE OFFICE UNDER THE UNITED STATES CONSTITUTION? (New York, American Anti-Slavery Society 1845).

20. For a good account of Calhoun's theory of sovereignty, see SPAIN, *supra* note 10, at 164-83.

21. 60 U.S. (19 How.) 393 (1857).

ical wrong, moderate—in contrast to radical—antislavery did not, however, take the same negative view of the interpretive claim that slavery was constitutional in the states that had adopted it.[22] Such forms of both internal and external criticism of the Constitution were grounded in the tension acutely experienced by all of these abolitionists between the Constitution and what they took to be its governing rights-based political theory. On the one hand, the text and history of the Constitution apparently contemplated the legitimacy of slavery at least at the state level;[23] on the other hand, the rights-based theory of the Constitution condemned slavery as a violation of inalienable human rights.[24] Various forms of abolitionist constitutional and political theory relieved this tension in different ways.

Perhaps the most plausible interpretive position was that of the moderate antislavery movement.[25] Fair interpretive weight' was accorded the text and history legitimizing slavery in the states as a reasonable short-term compromise with an already entrenched institution that the states could fairly be expected to abolish in due course. On the other hand, fair interpretive weight was accorded the background political theory of human rights by forbidding any legitimization of slavery by the federal government in service of the long-term goal of respect for human rights everywhere in the United States—including eventual abolition of slavery by the states. The moderate antislavery theme—liberty national, slavery local or sectional—thus gave full interpretive scope to the political theory of human rights only at the national level; at the state level, the political theory afforded a ground for external criticism and set a long-term national goal of encouraging abolition.[26]

---

22. For a good general study on the diverse forms of political abolitionism, see RICHARD H. SEWELL, BALLOTS FOR FREEDOM: ANTISLAVERY POLITICS IN THE UNITED STATES 1837-1860 (1976).

23. See U.S. CONST. art. I, § 2, cl. 3 ("Representatives and direct Taxes shall be apportioned among the several States . . . according to their respective Numbers, which shall be determined by adding to the whole Number of free Persons . . . and excluding Indians not taxed, three fifths of all other Persons.").

24. See, e.g., THOMAS JEFFERSON, NOTES ON THE STATE OF VIRGINIA 162-63 (William Pedea ed., 1982) (1781).

25. For a seminal statement of the view, see Salmon P. Chase, The Address of the Southern and Western Liberty Convention (June 11 & 12, 1845), in SALMON P. CHASE & CHARLES D. CLEVELAND, ANTI-SLAVERY ADDRESSES OF 1844 AND 1845, at 1 (photo. reprint 1969) (n.p., Sampson Low, Son, and Marston 1867).

26. For a statement of this moderate antislavery theme, see CHASE & CLEVELAND, supra note 25, at 84-85.

In contrast, advocates of radical antislavery, for example William Goodell,[27] Lysander Spooner[28] and Joel Tiffany,[29] accorded the political theory of human rights decisive interpretive weight at both the national and state levels. The interpretive implausibility of this approach was the Constitution it claimed to be interpreting, in particular, the text and history of the Constitution bearing on the legitimacy of slavery at the state level. The interpretive primacy of political theory was sustained and defended by the most theoretically profound advocate of this position, Lysander Spooner, by denying any weight to the constitutional text or history in conflict with the claims of rights-based political theory. The clauses of the Constitution apparently recognizing state-endorsed slavery were to be interpreted not to recognize slavery on the theory that any interpretation should be accorded the words, no matter how textually strained, that did not recognize slavery.[30] Furthermore, history was to be disowned altogether, as a valid ground for interpretation, in favor of focusing exclusively on the text itself—a text to be interpreted anti-positivistically in whatever way gave best effect to rights-based political theory.[31] The Constitution was to be interpreted in this way because, otherwise, the Constitution could not be regarded as the supremely legitimate law of the land. If slavery in the states which condoned it was constitutional, such a constitutional claim would be a politically illegitimate abridgement of human rights, indeed a just ground for the right to revolution. As Joel Tiffany starkly put the radical antislavery point, "give us *change* or *revolution.*"[32] To avoid such a crisis in constitutional legitimacy, the Constitution was to be interpreted in the mode called for by radical antislavery.

Both advocates of moderate and radical antislavery shared a common interest in analyzing how the interpretation of the Constitution could have been so decadently unmoored from its basis in the political theory of human rights—a national decadence reflected in the political

---

27. WILLIAM GOODELL, VIEWS OF AMERICAN CONSTITUTIONAL LAW IN ITS BEARING UPON AMERICAN SLAVERY (photo. reprint 1971) (Utica, Lawson & Chaplin, 2d ed. 1845).

28. LYSANDER SPOONER, THE UNCONSTITUTIONALITY OF SLAVERY (n.p. 1860).

29. JOEL TIFFANY, A TREATISE ON THE UNCONSTITUTIONALITY OF AMERICAN SLAVERY (photo. reprint 1969) (n.p. 1849).

30. Since the word "slave" was never expressly used, but rather "three fifths of all other Persons," *see* U.S. CONST. art. I, § 2, cl. 3, or "Migration or Importation of Such Persons," *see* U.S. CONST. art. I, § 9, cl. 1, or "Person[s] held to Service or Labour," *see* U.S. CONST. art. IV, § 2, cl. 3, the radicals ascribed to these texts meanings that did not protect slavery. For example, Spooner argued that the Three-fifths Clause applied not to Southern slaves, but mainly to resident aliens. *See* 1 SPOONER, *supra* note 28, at 73-81.

31. *See* 2 SPOONER, *supra* note 28, at 146.

32. TIFFANY, *supra* note 29, at 99.

successes of Calhoun's proslavery constitutionalism. The nerve of their analysis—the "slave power conspiracy"[33]—was an elaboration of the Founders' theory of faction,[34] only now applied to a form of faction that had been fostered by the Constitution itself. The theory of faction had identified pervasive tendencies of group psychology in politics to protect the interests of some political group at the expense of denying fair respect for the rights and interests of outsiders.[35] Madison had argued in *The Federalist* that the Constitution had structured the exercise of republican political power in order to better ensure that such factions would not achieve their mischievous ends at the expense of the governing political theory of republican constitutionalism—respect for human rights and pursuit of the public interest.[36] The antislavery analysis of America's constitutional decadence was that the Constitution, through augmenting the political power of the slave states by the Three-Fifths Clause,[37] had so constitutionally entrenched the political power of slave-owning interests that their power as an effective political faction had flourished to the degree that, inconsistent with the aims and theory of Madisonian constitutionalism, these factions actually had subverted the Constitution.

Radical antislavery gave a distinctively deep moral and constitutional analysis of the sources of the constitutional decadence in the Constitution and what would be required to remedy the underlying constitutional pathology. The premise of its distinctive approach was its view of the proper understanding of the relationship of Lockean political theory to constitutional interpretation. The foundation of this view had been laid earlier by the abolitionist Theodore Weld in his analysis of the wrongness of slavery; Weld's analysis invoked the Lockean political theory that legitimate government must protect equal rights. He made a similar appeal in explaining why Congress had the power to abolish slavery in the District of Columbia:

> It has been shown already that *allegiance* is exacted of the slave. Is the government of the United States unable to grant *protection* where it exacts *allegiance*? It is an axiom of the civi-

---

33. For a useful study of this idea, see DAVID B. DAVIS, THE SLAVE POWER CONSPIRACY AND THE PARANOID STYLE (1969).

34. THE FEDERALIST No. 10 (James Madison) (defining faction as some number of citizens united by common interest adverse to rights of other citizens or community). For further discussion of the Founders' theory of faction, see DAVID A.J. RICHARDS, FOUNDATIONS OF AMERICAN CONSTITUTIONALISM 32-39 (1989).

35. *See* RICHARDS, *supra* note 34, at 32-39.

36. *See* THE FEDERALIST No. 10 (James Madison). For further discussion, see RICHARDS, *supra* note 34, at 105-30.

37. *See* U.S. CONST. art. I, § 2, cl. 3.

lized world, and a maxim even with savages, that allegiance and protection are reciprocal and correlative. Are principles powerless with us which exact homage of barbarians? *Protection is the CONSTITUTIONAL RIGHT of every human being under the exclusive legislation of Congress who has not forfeited it by crime.*[38]

This view assumed that black Americans, slave or free, were working members of the American political community and, as such, subject to its governing Lockean principles of a fair balance of rights and obligations as a condition of allegiance. But many Americans, Lincoln being one of them, wanted to distinguish the question of abolishing slavery in order to recognize the natural rights of slaves from the question of further empowering the slaves with rights of membership in the American political community.[39] This explains the view of moderate antislavery that the best theory of the Constitution would allow the national government to achieve its goals of respect for human rights by the long-term abolition of slavery and colonization of the freedmen abroad—thereby not including them in the American political community. They were able to take this view by ascribing decisional powers of the rights of American citizenship to the states alone; thus, the national government might constitutionally achieve the long-term abolition of slavery and colonize the freedmen abroad without violating any nationally guaranteed constitutional rights of the freedmen. But, if one believed, like Weld and many more radical abolitionists, that Lockean political theory guaranteed black Americans, slave and free, both their natural rights and their rights to citizenship, moderate antislavery constitutional theory reconciled the Constitution and its background political theory in an unappealing way. The distinction between national and state power over slavery, fundamental to the moderate antislavery view, could sensibly interpret the Constitution as serving its political theory of respect for equal rights only if national power could be read as achieving such rights by abolition and colonization. But, if Weld and the abolitionists were right, that interpretation of the Constitution would violate the rights of black Americans—earned by years of unremunerated labor in service of the national interest—to be free and to be citizens. Was there an interpretation of the Constitution that might better reconcile it with its background political theory?

---

38. Theodore Weld, *The Power of Congress over Slavery in the District of Columbia* (New York, American Anti-Slavery Society 1838), *reprinted in* TEN BROEK, *supra* note 1, at 278.

39. *See, e.g.*, Abraham Lincoln, Speech on the Kansas-Nebraska Act (October 16, 1854), *in* ABRAHAM LINCOLN: SPEECHES AND WRITINGS 1832-1858, at 307-08, 315-16 (Don E. Fehrenbacher ed., 1989).

Radical antislavery constitutional theory responded to this question, as we have seen, by interpreting the Constitution to forbid slavery both at the national and state levels. Radical antislavery theory agreed with moderate antislavery that the proper interpretive attitude towards the United States Constitution must be Lockean political theory, but disagreed about the best account of such theory—in particular, about what rights black Americans in fact had in light of the wrongs inflicted on them by American slavery and racism. Taking the view of political theory that radical antislavery did, the moderate antislavery reading of the Constitution, in terms of a federal-state dichotomy on the slavery issue, could not be reasonably justified in light of protecting both human rights and the public interest. Such an interpretation would allow abolition on terms which violated the rights of black Americans as citizens. The better interpretation—the one that over-all enabled the Constitution to be read more coherently as in service of its political theory—was one that made all participants in the American political community national citizens and therefore bearers of the equal human rights of such citizenship.[40] Under radical antislavery, the national government—both the judiciary and Congress—thus had power to achieve the abolition of slavery, but, in stark contrast to moderate antislavery, only on terms that recognized the rights of black Americans to be both free and equal citizens.

Radical antislavery was, as we have seen, self-consciously proposed as an interpretive theory. However, its real force was its profound external criticism of the Constitution on the very grounds central to the distinctive methodologies of American revolutionary constitutionalism. In effect, the United States Constitution, constructed on the basis of a complex empirical and normative assessment of the genre of republican constitutionalism, was subjected to a comparably profound criticism by radical antislavery in terms self-consciously inspired by the critical achievement of the founding itself.

III.   AMERICAN REVOLUTIONARY CONSTITUTIONALISM AND THE RECONSTRUCTION AMENDMENTS

It is fundamental to the American legal and political experience that its revolutionary and constitutional project was conceived as a common enterprise.[41] Leading advocates of the American Revolution such as

---

40. Joel Tiffany generalized these arguments into a general constitutional principle "for the equal protection of all, individually and collectively." TIFFANY, *supra* note 29, at 87.

41. The following discussion of American revolutionary and constitutional thought is an abbreviated summary of the lengthy treatment of these matters in RICHARDS, *supra* note 34.

John Adams and Thomas Jefferson clearly saw constitutionalism at both the state and national levels as the test of the very legitimacy of the revolution. Accordingly, Jefferson wrote no less than three constitutions for Virginia, and Adams was the main author of the Massachusetts constitution of 1780 that was centrally used by the Founders in 1787.[42] The success of American constitutionalism was, for Adams and Jefferson, literally the test of the legitimacy of the revolution.

American revolutionary constitutionalism contained six critical ingredients—namely: (1) the Lockean political principles of the revolution; (2) the relationship of those principles to what Americans regarded as the pathological misinterpretation of the British Constitution by the British Parliament; (3) the analysis of political pathologies, for example, the theory of faction, in light of the history of British constitutionalism and the larger practice of republican and federal experiments over time; (4) the use of such comparative political science in constructing new structures of government free of the mistakes both of the British Constitution and republican and federal experiments in the past; (5) the weight placed on the experiments in the American states and in the nation between 1776 and 1787 in thinking about institutional alternatives; and (6) the historically unique opportunity self-consciously recognized and seized by Americans in 1787 to develop a novel republican experiment that established a new government which was more politically legitimate than the arguments of ordinary politics.

Radical antislavery brought the same critical ingredients of American revolutionary constitutionalism to bear when it criticized the Constitution in light of its antebellum decadence. First, the distinctive depth of its analysis derived from the remarkable moral independence of its articulation, on the basis of Lockean political theory, of basic human and constitutional rights of all persons subject to the political power of the United States.[43] Second and third, that perspective enabled radical antislavery to interpret the pathological misinterpretations of the Constitution as grounded not only in the slave power conspiracy,[44] but in the pathological construction of American racism that the Constitution had fostered,[45] in effect legitimatizing the monstrous faction of white

---

For pertinent supporting arguments and citations, I refer the reader, in the text that follows, to that discussion, not repeating here the citations contained there.

42. *See id.* at 19-20, 95, 106, 123, 124, 141.

43. *See generally* TIFFANY, *supra* note 29, at 271 (criticizing interpretations that read Constitution as favoring slavery).

44. *See* DAVIS, *supra* note 33.

45. For the seminal analysis along these lines, see L. MARIA CHILD, AN APPEAL IN FAVOR OF AMERICANS CALLED AFRICANS (photo. reprint 1968) (New York, John S. Taylor

supremacy that Chief Justice Taney explicitly embraced as the proper measure of constitutional rights in *Dred Scott v. Sandford*.[46] Fourth and fifth, comparative reflection on the earlier abolition of slavery by Britain and the growing power of slave-holding interests in American politics, both state and national, led the radical antislavery movement to identify the crucial error of American constitutional design as the failure to take seriously Madison's original constitutional suggestions that the nation have the power to secure that states could not violate a nationally articulated conception of human rights and the public interest.[47] Madison's theory of faction focused on local interests at the state level as the loci of faction, and called for nationally representative institutions as a way of detoxifying the evils of local factions.[48] However, the most precisely oppressive of state factions—slavery at the state level—had been constitutionally immunized from national scrutiny in terms of enforceable standards of human rights and the public interest. This lacuna had, in the view of radical antislavery, over time led to the degradation of the Constitution by the worst form of factionalized insularity and oppression as reflected in the political appeal to Douglas and Taney, among many others, of Calhoun's proslavery constitutionalism with its denial of the role of rights-based political theory in constitutional interpretation. Finally, the appropriate remedy must accordingly be a conception of national institutions with adequate competence and power to ensure that the states, like the national government, respect the human rights of all Americans.

IV. RADICAL ANTISLAVERY AND THE RECONSTRUCTION AMENDMENTS

Radical antislavery offered its analysis as internal interpretive criticism of dominant antebellum views of constitutional interpretation. It

---

1833). At the Constitutional Convention, Madison had himself described racism as one of the worst forms of faction: "We have seen the mere distinction of colour made in the most enlightened period of time, a ground of the most oppressive dominion ever exercised by man over man." James Madison, Speech Before the Constitutional Convention (June 6, 1787), *in* 1 RECORDS OF THE FEDERAL CONVENTION OF 1787, at 135 (Max Farrand ed., 1966).

46. 60 U.S. (19 How.) 393 (1857). "[T]hey [blacks] had no rights which the white man was bound to respect." *Id.* at 407.

47. Joel Tiffany, for example, sharply posed the crisis of American constitutionalism in terms of the despotic powers of the states at home. *See* TIFFANY, *supra* note 29, at 55-56. It was not the states that required protection "but the *individual*, crushed, and overwhelmed by an insolent, and tyrannical majority, that needed such a guaranty; and to him, as a citizen of the United States, whether in the majority, or minority, is that guaranty given, to secure him, not only from *individual*, but also from *governmental* oppression." *Id.* at 110.

48. *See* RICHARDS, *supra* note 34, at 36-37.

was, however, regarded as a marginal view of constitutional interpretation even among mainstream political abolitionists, most of whom gravitated to moderate antislavery as the best theory of constitutional interpretation.[49] In the wake of the Civil War, the analysis of radical antislavery occupied center stage in the critical reflection on American constitutionalism culminating in the Reconstruction Amendments because it afforded the most reasonable analysis and diagnosis of the nation's constitutional crisis and its solution.[50] By the end of the Civil War, slavery had effectively been ended in the South, and the new task became forging a moral and constitutional vision that would memorialize the fruits of that war in an enduring legacy of constitutional principle for posterity. Both the North and the South had come to interpret the Civil War as a controversy over the meaning of American revolutionary constitutionalism ultimately justified by appeal to the right to revolution when constitutional structures had proven radically inadequate to their ultimate normative values. From the perspective of the Reconstruction Congress, Southern secession was based on a perverse interpretation of American revolutionary constitutionalism that appealed to the Constitution to justify the entrenchment of slavery, the ultimate violation of basic human rights, against any possibility of inhibition by the federal government under moderate antislavery's reasonable interpretation of the Constitution of 1787. Proslavery constitutionalism, when carried to this extreme, had become the systematic instrument for the permanent abridgement of basic human rights, and the Civil War was thus justified on the same grounds as the American Revolution had been justified against a decadent form of British constitutionalism—namely, to protect human rights and to forge constitutional forms more adequate to this ultimate moral vision of legitimate government.

If the legitimacy of the American Revolution required a form of constitutionalism, in contrast to the corrupt British Constitution, adequate to its normative demands, the legitimacy of the Civil War required a comparably profound reflection on constitutional decadence adequate to its demands for a rebirth of rights-based constitutional government. Radical antislavery's critical analysis of antebellum constitutional decadence met this need because it was the most profound such reflection culturally available in the genre of American revolutionary constitution-

---

49. For a good general treatment, see SEWELL, *supra* note 22, at 3-23.

50. I explore the argument merely sketched in this paragraph at much greater length in a work in progress, David A.J. Richards, Conscience and the Constitution: Abolitionist Dissent, The Second American Revolution and the Reconstruction Amendments (unpublished manuscript, on file with the author).

alism forged by the Founders of 1787. Its great appeal for the American constitutional mind was both its radical insistence on the primacy of the revolutionary political theory of human rights central to American constitutionalism and its brilliant reinterpretation of the ingredients of such constitutionalism in light of that political theory and the events of antebellum constitutional decadence and civil war. In light of its analysis, radical antislavery supplied the most reasonable interpretation of the Civil War as the second American Revolution, and offered, consistent with the genre of American revolutionary constitutionalism, remedies that plausibly could be and were regarded as the most justifiable way to correct central defects in the Constitution of 1787, defects some of which had been acknowledged by leading founders like Madison in 1787.[51] The Reconstruction Amendments, the most radical change in constitutionalism in our history, could thus be plausibly understood as a wholly reasonable conservative way to preserve the legitimacy of the long-standing project of American revolutionary constitutionalism.

The Reconstruction Amendments contain both negative and positive features: the abolition of slavery and involuntary servitude (Thirteenth Amendment) and the prohibition of racial discrimination in voting (Fifteenth Amendment); the affirmative requirements of citizenship for all Americans and nationally defined and enforceable guarantees applicable against the states of equal protection, privileges or immunities, and due process of law (Fourteenth Amendment). The political theory of these prohibitions and requirements was Lockean political theory as it had been articulated and applied in the antebellum period by radical antislavery: all political power, now including the power of the states, could be legitimate only if it met the requirement of extending to all persons subject to such power respect for their inalienable human rights and the use of power to pursue the public interest. And their constitutional theory was, in light of the critical analysis of antebellum decadence of radical antislavery, what such requirements of politically legitimate power clearly required—nationally articulated, elaborated and enforceable constitutional principles that would preserve or tend to preserve the required respect for rights and pursuit of the public interest. These guarantees thus textually included the central normative dimensions distinctive of radical antislavery: the demand that all persons subject to the burdens of allegiance to the political power of the United States be accorded both their natural rights as persons and their equal rights as citizens, based on the fundamental egalitarian requirement of politically

---

51. *See* RICHARDS, *supra* note 34, at 37-38.

legitimate government as stated by the Equal Protection Clause. If the Constitution of 1787 had made remarkably little textual reference to its background political theory, the Reconstruction Amendments textually affirmed and enforced that political theory with notable focus on the forms of political pathology that had motivated antebellum constitutional decadence—the untrammelled state power over abridgement of human rights that had given rise to the political pathologies of the slave power conspiracy in general and American racism in particular.[52] Both the Thirteenth Amendment's prohibition of slavery and the Equal Protection Clause of the Fourteenth Amendment's prohibition of racist subjugation were thus negative corollaries of the affirmative principle of equal respect for the rights of all persons subject to political power, and therefore required the national articulation, elaboration and enforcement of constitutional principles that defined the supreme law of the land because they secured the politically legitimate terms for the exercise of any political power.

The Reconstruction Amendments, thus understood, responded to the gravest crisis of constitutional legitimacy in our history, and are best understood and interpreted as negative and affirmative constitutional principles responsive to that crisis and any comparable crisis in the legitimacy of the Constitution as supreme law. Our interpretive attitude today to these amendments must make the best sense of them in light of the genre of American revolutionary constitutionalism that they assume and critically elaborate in service of the narrative integrity of the story of the American people and their struggle for a politically legitimate government that respects human rights. I have here argued that abolitionist political and constitutional theory played a crucial role in telling this story, and our interpretive attitude today should take account of this theory as part of an enriched sense of what our constitutional tradition is and how it should be carried forward on the terms that do justice to it.

It cannot do justice to this enriched understanding of our interpretive responsibilities to trivialize our interpretation of the Reconstruction Amendments to some fictive search for the concrete exemplars to which some suitably described majority of the Reconstruction Congress or the ratifying states or, for that matter, advocates of radical antislavery would or would not have applied the relevant clause under interpretation. The political and constitutional theory of the Reconstruction Amendments

---

52. For a good statement of this general concern at the time of the introduction of the Thirteenth Amendment on the floor of the House of Representatives, see Speech of Representative Henry Wilson (Mar. 19, 1864), *in* CONG. GLOBE, 38th Cong., 1st Sess. 1199-1204 (1864).

was rooted in the radically anti-positivist jurisprudence of radical anti-slavery. It responded to the antebellum crisis of constitutional legitimacy by requiring an interpretive attitude to the Constitution that would preserve its legitimacy on the grounds of the rights-based theory of human rights central to its claims to be the supreme law of the land.

Both Taney's originalism[53] and Stephen Douglas's majoritarian interpretation of popular sovereignty[54] were, from this perspective, equally illegitimate attempts to evade the interpretive responsibilities of making sense of the supremacy of the Constitution in terms of its protection of the human rights of all persons subject to political power. Taney's use of history and Douglas's majoritarianism substituted positivistic amoral facts or procedures for the deliberative rights-based normative judgments that could alone preserve the legitimacy of the Constitution as supreme law, namely, its principled protection of human rights to the fullest extent feasible. In light of the text and background of the Reconstruction Amendments, it would be, a fortiori, illegitimate today to make sense of these amendments in a comparably evasive positivistic way—by appeal to the concrete intentions of the founders (Bork)[55] or some picture of majoritarian democracy unconcerned with basic human rights (Ely).[56]

We mock our history and our traditions when we thus studiously unlearn everything that our history and traditions, properly interpreted, teach us. In contrast, we do interpretive justice to the role of the Reconstruction Amendments in the larger narrative integrity of American constitutionalism if and only if we ensure that the interpretation of the Constitution, in order to be supreme law, is based today on our best deliberative normative judgments about the principled protection of human rights in our circumstances. On this view, the enduring meaning of the

---

53. Taney argues in *Dred Scott*:

No one, we presume, supposes that any change in public opinion or feeling, in relation to this unfortunate race, in the civilized nations of Europe or in this country, should induce the court to give to the words of the Constitution a more liberal construction in their favor than they were intended to bear when the instrument was framed and adopted.

Scott v. Sandford, 60 U.S. (19 How.) 393, 426 (1857). In fact, as Justice Curtis points out in his dissent, Taney gets even his alleged originalist history of Founders' concrete intentions wrong. *See id.* at 572-74 (Curtis, J., dissenting).

54. Popular sovereignty, irrespective of constitutional or natural rights, allowed states to decide whether they would or would not have slavery. As one commentator observed, "Douglas looked upon popular sovereignty as essentially pragmatic and expedient." ROBERT W. JOHANNSEN, STEPHEN A. DOUGLAS 240 (1973).

55. *See* ROBERT BORK, THE TEMPTING OF AMERICA: THE POLITICAL SEDUCTION OF THE LAW 251-59 (1990). For criticism, see David A.J. Richards, *Originalism Without Foundations*, 65 N.Y.U. L. REV. 1373, 1376-77 (1990) (book review).

56. *See* JOHN HART ELY, DEMOCRACY AND DISTRUST: A THEORY OF JUDICIAL REVIEW 4-7 (1980).

Reconstruction Amendments is that each generation of Americans must strive by its own best lights to constitute itself on the basis of the most inclusively reasonable understanding of universal human rights in its circumstances, not on the basis of indefensible conceptions of national identity, like Taney's white supremacy, that rest on the degradation of the dignity of the human person. It is in light of such critical reflection on the meaning of human rights in contemporary circumstances that *Brown v. Board of Education* [57] was interpretively correct. It is for the same reason that the contemporary interpretation of the Reconstruction Amendments must strive deliberatively to articulate and protect a similarly inclusive progressive conception of human rights in light of the best arguments of public reason elaborated in our circumstances as a matter of principle.[58]

The interpretive attitude that radical antislavery had taken to the Constitution was, as we have seen, insistent on the primacy of rights-based political theory in constitutional interpretation, disowning history and straining text in order to give maximum expression to the fullest possible protection of human rights. We, however, need neither disown history nor strain text to interpret the Reconstruction Amendments consistent with the requirements of rights-based political theory, for both the history and text of the Reconstruction Amendments make the best sense only when understood in that way. Indeed, the enduring moral legacy of radical antislavery to American constitutionalism is that its once implausible interpretive attitude to the Constitution of 1787 has been rendered, by virtue of the Reconstruction Amendments, the only plausible attitude to the Constitution, as thus amended.

Rights-based egalitarian political theory must therefore play a central role in the interpretation of the requirements of the Reconstruction Amendments in contemporary circumstances. Such interpretive responsibilities require us to take seriously what our rights are and how they are to be understood and elaborated today on terms of principle.[59] The abolitionists give us a model of the forms of political and constitutional theory that such responsibilities require us to generate in our circumstances.

Four features of abolitionist thought and practice are, in this connection, notable. First, the abolitionists were the most principled and

---

57. 347 U.S. 483 (1954).

58. For example, the protection of women and homosexuals from conceptions of national identity is based on the abridgement of their basic human rights. For further development of this approach, see generally DAVID A.J. RICHARDS, TOLERATION AND THE CONSTITUTION (1986) [hereinafter RICHARDS, TOLERATION AND THE CONSTITUTION]; *see also* RICHARDS, *supra* note 34, at 252-72; Conscience and the Constitution, *supra* note 50.

59. *See* RICHARDS, TOLERATION AND THE CONSTITUTION, *supra* note 58.

morally independent advocates of the inalienable rights of conscience and free speech in the antebellum period against the hostile tyranny of majoritarian antebellum complacency so notably anatomized by de Tocqueville.[60] Second, their principled commitment to the inalienable right to conscience and free speech enabled the abolitionists to elaborate and extend the argument for toleration to identify critically new modes of unjust sectarian oppression of basic rights that could not be reasonably justified on the terms of public justification that were politically and constitutionally required. The abolitionist criticism of both slavery and racism rested on the remarkable moral and intellectual independence with which they made and pressed this argument.[61] Third, the forms of political and constitutional theory generated by the abolitionists critically tested conventionally popular moral and constitutional views against the most demanding standards of more abstract moral, political and constitutional argument. Consistent with the argument for toleration, they critically debunked what they found to be, on critical examination, polemical sectarian arguments for deprivation of human rights whose political force crucially depended on the viciously circular failure to allow any fair testing of the empirical and normative claims that allegedly justified the deprivation of basic rights, for example, slavery or racist subjugation. Finally, abolitionist argument, while often meeting and surpassing the highest intellectual and moral standards of the age, was not largely generated by mainstream politicians, judges or academics, but by remarkably courageous moral, political and constitutional activists whose concern was not with winning votes or securing judicial or academic tenure, but with confronting the American public mind and conscience with its failures of intellect, of morality and of civic republican fidelity to its revolutionary constitutionalism.[62] The abolitionists show us that the best theory and practice work in tandem stimulating one another to a more impartial realization of both the thought and practice of a political and constitutional community based on the normative demands of a principled commitment to basic human rights for all persons subject to its political power.

---

60. *See* 1 ALEXIS DE TOCQUEVILLE, DEMOCRACY IN AMERICA 264-80 (Phillips Bradley ed., 1945) (1835).

61. For two notable examples of arguments along these lines, see William E. Channing, *Slavery, reprinted in* THE WORKS OF WILLIAM E. CHANNING 688-743 (Burt Franklin ed., 1970) (1839); CHILD, *supra* note 45, at 42.

62. For some important recent general studies, see MERTON L. DILLON, THE ABOLITIONISTS: THE GROWTH OF A DISSENTING MINORITY (1974); LOUIS FILLER, THE CRUSADE AGAINST SLAVERY (1960); JAMES B. STEWART, HOLY WARRIORS: THE ABOLITIONISTS AND AMERICAN SLAVERY (1976); RONALD G. WALTERS, THE ANTISLAVERY APPEAL: AMERICAN ABOLITIONISM AFTER 1830 (1978).

V. Conclusion

The forms of interpretive argument, forged by the abolitionists, were precisely the same forms that have critically tested and transformed the interpretation of the Reconstruction Amendments often in service of the demands of activist civil rights advocates who in the twentieth century have played a role quite analogous to that of the abolitionists in the nineteenth century. The abolitionist argument of Frederick Douglass was very much, both in thought and practice, the tradition self-consciously carried forward by a civil rights advocate like Martin Luther King.[63] Our task surely is by our own lights to be intellectually and morally worthy of such a tradition or rather to embody in our thought and practice the standards of moral, political and constitutional independence and courage that will generate in our own terms and circumstances arguments of human rights adequate to identify and to challenge our corruptions, our decadent constitutionalism—whether the originalism of Bork or the majoritarianism of Ely. Abolitionist political and constitutional theory reminds us of how central to the American constitutional tradition that perennial challenge is, and also of our conservative responsibilities.

63. For the writings of Frederick Douglass, see 5 THE LIFE AND WRITINGS OF FREDERICK DOUGLASS (Philip S. Foner ed., 1975); for commentary, see WILLIAM S. MCFEELY, FREDERICK DOUGLASS (1991); FREDERICK DOUGLASS: NEW LITERARY AND HISTORICAL ESSAYS (Eric J. Sundquist ed., 1990). For the writings of Martin Luther King, Jr., see A TESTAMENT OF HOPE: THE ESSENTIAL WRITINGS OF MARTIN LUTHER KING, JR. (James M. Washington ed., 1986); for commentary, see TAYLOR BRANCH, PARTING THE WATERS: AMERICA IN THE KING YEARS 1954-63 (1990).

Acknowledgments

Alvis, John. "The Slavery Provisions of the U.S. Constitution: Means for Emancipation." *Political Science Reviewer* 17 (1987): 241–65. Reprinted with the permission of the Intercollegiate Studies Institute.

Lynd, Staughton. "The Compromise of 1787." *Political Science Quarterly* 81 (1966): 225–50. Reprinted with the permission of the author and The Academy of Political Science.

Zilversmit, Arthur. "Quok Walker, Mumbet, and the Abolition of Slavery in Massachusetts." *William and Mary Quarterly* 25 (1968): 614–24. Originally appeared in the *William and Mary Quarterly*.

Barnett, Randy E. "Was Slavery Unconstitutional Before the Thirteenth Amendment?: Lysander Spooner's Theory of Interpretation." *Pacific Law Journal* 28 (1997): 977–1014. Copyright 1997 by the University of the Pacific, McGeorge School of Law. Reprinted by permission.

Ernst, Daniel R. "Legal Positivism, Abolitionist Litigation, and the New Jersey Slave Case of 1845." *Law and History Review* 4 (1986): 337–65. Reprinted with the permission of the University of Illinois Press.

Wiecek, William M. "Slavery and Abolition Before the United States Supreme Court, 1820–1860." *Journal of American History* 65 (1978): 34–59. Reprinted with the permission of the *Journal of American History*.

Williams, Sandra Boyd. "The Indiana Supreme Court and the Struggle Against Slavery." *Indiana Law Review* 30 (1997): 305–17. Reprinted with the permission of Indiana University School of Law.

Finkelman, Paul. "The Kidnapping of John Davis and the Adoption of the Fugitive Slave Law of 1793." *Journal of Southern History* 56 (1990): 397–422. Copyright 1990 by the Southern Historical Association. Reprinted by permission of the Managing Editor.

Finkelman, Paul. "*Prigg* v. *Pennsylvania* and Northern State Courts: Anti-Slavery Use of a Pro-Slavery Decision." *Civil War History* 25 (1979): 5–35. Reprinted with the permission of Kent State University Press.

Finkelman, Paul. "State Constitutional Protections of Liberty and the Antebellum New Jersey Supreme Court: Chief Justice Hornblower and the Fugitive Slave Law." *Rutgers Law Journal* 23 (1992): 753–87. Reprinted with the permission of *Rutgers Law Journal*.

Gara, Larry. "The Fugitive Slave Law: A Double Paradox." *Civil War History* 10 (1964): 229–40. Reprinted with the permission of Kent State University Press.

Parrish, Jenni. "The *Booth* Cases: Final Step to the Civil War." *Willamette Law Review* 29 (1993): 237–78. Reprinted with the permission of the *Willamette Law Review*.

Rosenberg, Norman L. "Personal Liberty Laws and Sectional Crisis: 1850–1861." *Civil War History* 17 (1971): 25–44. Reprinted with the permission of Kent State University Press.

Silverman, Jason H. "Kentucky, Canada, and Extradition: The Jesse Happy Case." *Filson Club Historical Quarterly* 54 (1980): 50–60. Reprinted with the permission of the Filson Club, Inc.

McPherson, James M. "Abolitionists and the Civil Rights Act of 1875." *Journal of American History* 52 (1965): 493–510. Reprinted with the permission of the *Journal of American History*.

Richards, David A.J. "Abolitionist Political and Constitutional Theory and the Reconstruction Amendments." *Loyola of Los Angeles Law Review* 25 (1992): 1187–1205. Reprinted with the permission of Loyola of Los Angeles Law School.